AT

LONDON, NEW YORK, MELBOURNE,
MUNICH, AND DELHI

LONDON, NEW YORK, MELBOURNE,
MUNICH, AND DELHI

FOR THE FOURTH EDITION
Cartographic Manager David Roberts
Senior Cartographic Editor Simon Mumford
Cartographers Paul Eames, Encompass Graphics Limited
Designers Nimbus Design **Editors** Ben Hoare, Margaret Parrish, Cambridge International Reference on Current Affairs (CIRCA)
3D Globes Planetary Visions Ltd., London

Systems Co-ordinator Philip Rowles **Production** Imogen Boase

Art Director Bryn Walls **Publisher** Jonathan Metcalf
Associate Publisher Liz Wheeler

FOR PREVIOUS EDITIONS
Cartographic Director Andrew Heritage
Cartography Roger Bullen, Rob Stokes, Iorwerth Watkins
Project Editor Sam Atkinson **Art Editor** Karen Gregory

First published in Great Britain in 2001 by
Dorling Kindersley Limited, 80 Strand, London WC2R 0RL
A Penguin Company
Fourth Edition 2010
Previously published as the Ultimate Pocket Book of the World Atlas & Factfile

A CIP catalogue record for this book is available from the British Library

ISBN: 978-1-4053-5039-6

Printed and bound in Singapore by Star Standard

Key to map symbols

ELEVATION

- 6000m / 19,686ft
- 4000m / 13,124ft
- 2000m / 6562ft
- 1000m / 3281ft
- 500m / 1640ft
- 250m / 820ft
- 100m / 328ft
- 0
- Below sea level

▲ Mountain

• Depression

BORDERS

Full international

Disputed *de facto*

Territorial claim

Cease-fire line

Undefined

State/Province

DRAINAGE FEATURES

River

Seasonal river

Canal

Lake

Seasonal lake

SETTLEMENTS

● Capital city

◎ Major town

○ Minor town

● Major port

COMMUNICATIONS

Major road

Rail

International airport

◆ Insight; facts, figures, and amazing information from around the world

Atlas contents

North & Central America 16–17

South America 38–39

Africa 50–51

Europe 62–63

Atlas contents

See overleaf for contents

Factfile contents

Factfile contents

The Political World

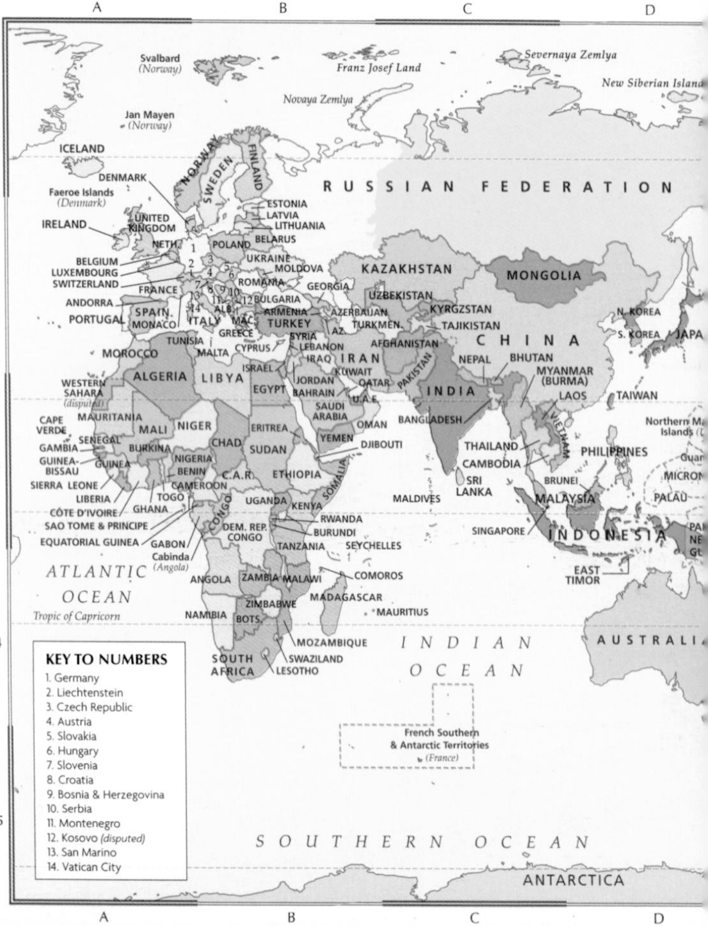
A
B
C
D
1
2
3
4
5
Svalbard (Norway)
Franz Josef Land
Severnaya Zemlya
New Siberian Islands
Novaya Zemlya
Jan Mayen (Norway)
ICELAND
NORWAY
SWEDEN
FINLAND
DENMARK
Faeroe Islands (Denmark)
RUSSIAN FEDERATION
ESTONIA
LATVIA
LITHUANIA
IRELAND
UNITED KINGDOM
NETH.
BELARUS
POLAND
UKRAINE
MOLDOVA
BELGIUM
LUXEMBOURG
SWITZERLAND
FRANCE
ROMANIA
GEORGIA
KAZAKHSTAN
MONGOLIA
UZBEKISTAN
ANDORRA
PORTUGAL
SPAIN
MONACO
ITALY
ALB.
MAC.
BULGARIA
ARMENIA
AZERBAIJAN
KYRGZSTAN
TURKMEN.
TAJIKISTAN
N. KOREA
S. KOREA
JAPAN
TURKEY
AZ.
GREECE
SYRIA
CHINA
TUNISIA
MALTA
CYPRUS
LEBANON
AFGHANISTAN
MOROCCO
IRAQ
IRAN
NEPAL
BHUTAN
ALGERIA
LIBYA
ISRAEL
JORDAN
KUWAIT
PAKISTAN
MYANMAR (BURMA)
WESTERN SAHARA (disputed)
EGYPT
BAHRAIN
QATAR
INDIA
LAOS
TAIWAN
U.A.E.
SAUDI ARABIA
CAPE VERDE
MAURITANIA
MALI
NIGER
ERITREA
OMAN
BANGLADESH
VIETNAM
Northern Mariana Islands
SENEGAL
GAMBIA
GUINEA-BISSAU
GUINEA
BURKINA
CHAD
SUDAN
YEMEN
DJIBOUTI
THAILAND
PHILIPPINES
Guam
NIGERIA
BENIN
C.A.R.
ETHIOPIA
SOMALIA
CAMBODIA
MICRONESIA
SIERRA LEONE
CAMEROON
SRI LANKA
BRUNEI
LIBERIA
TOGO
UGANDA
KENYA
MALDIVES
MALAYSIA
PALAU
CÔTE D'IVOIRE
GHANA
CONGO
RWANDA
SAO TOME & PRINCIPE
DEM. REP. CONGO
BURUNDI
SINGAPORE
INDONESIA
EQUATORIAL GUINEA
GABON
TANZANIA
SEYCHELLES
Cabinda (Angola)
ATLANTIC OCEAN
ANGOLA
ZAMBIA
MALAWI
COMOROS
EAST TIMOR
ZIMBABWE
MADAGASCAR
Tropic of Capricorn
NAMIBIA
BOTS.
MAURITIUS
MOZAMBIQUE
INDIAN OCEAN
AUSTRALIA
SOUTH AFRICA
SWAZILAND
LESOTHO
French Southern & Antarctic Territories (France)
SOUTHERN OCEAN
ANTARCTICA
KEY TO NUMBERS
1. Germany
2. Liechtenstein
3. Czech Republic
4. Austria
5. Slovakia
6. Hungary
7. Slovenia
8. Croatia
9. Bosnia & Herzegovina
10. Serbia
11. Montenegro
12. Kosovo (disputed)
13. San Marino
14. Vatican City

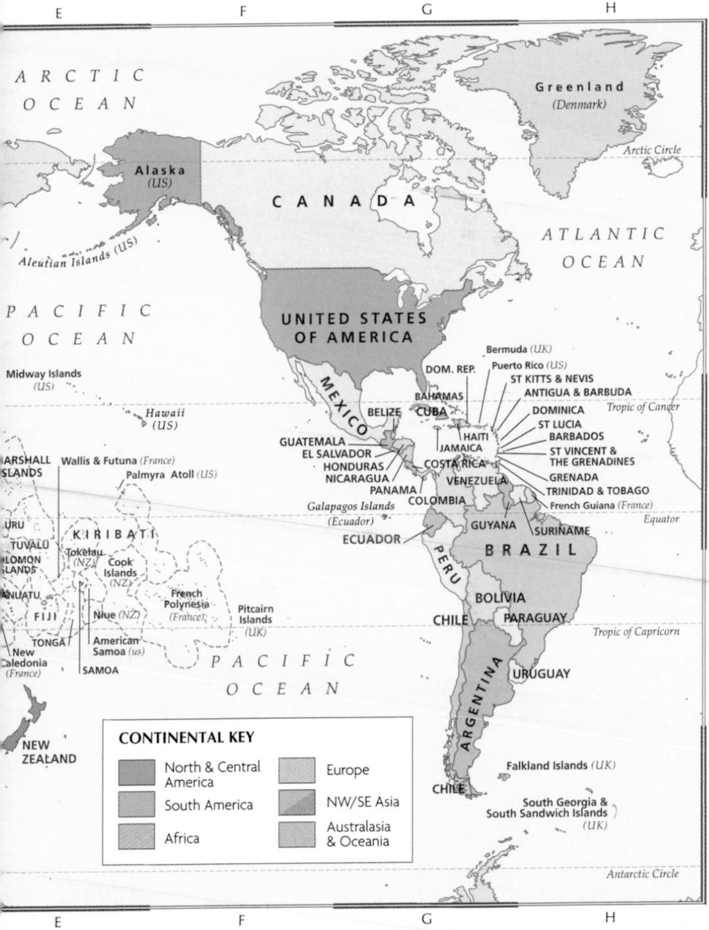
E
F
G
H
1
2
3
4
5
ARCTIC OCEAN
Greenland
(Denmark)
Arctic Circle
Alaska
(US)
CANADA
ATLANTIC OCEAN
Aleutian Islands (US)
PACIFIC OCEAN
UNITED STATES OF AMERICA
Bermuda (UK)
Puerto Rico (US)
DOM. REP.
ST KITTS & NEVIS
ANTIGUA & BARBUDA
Midway Islands
(US)
MEXICO
BAHAMAS
Tropic of Cancer
Hawaii
(US)
BELIZE
CUBA
DOMINICA
ST LUCIA
HAITI
BARBADOS
GUATEMALA
JAMAICA
ST VINCENT & THE GRENADINES
EL SALVADOR
MARSHALL ISLANDS
Wallis & Futuna (France)
HONDURAS
COSTA RICA
Palmyra Atoll (US)
NICARAGUA
VENEZUELA
GRENADA
PANAMA
TRINIDAD & TOBAGO
COLOMBIA
Galapagos Islands
(Ecuador)
French Guiana (France)
Equator
GUYANA
SURINAME
NAURU
KIRIBATI
ECUADOR
TUVALU
Tokelau
(NZ)
SOLOMON ISLANDS
Cook Islands
(NZ)
BRAZIL
PERU
VANUATU
French Polynesia
(France)
BOLIVIA
FIJI
Niue (NZ)
Pitcairn Islands
(UK)
CHILE
PARAGUAY
TONGA
American Samoa (us)
Tropic of Capricorn
New Caledonia
(France)
SAMOA
PACIFIC OCEAN
URUGUAY
ARGENTINA
NEW ZEALAND
CONTINENTAL KEY
North & Central America
South America
Africa
Europe
NW/SE Asia
Australasia & Oceania
Falkland Islands (UK)
CHILE
South Georgia & South Sandwich Islands
(UK)
Antarctic Circle
E
F
G
H

The Physical World

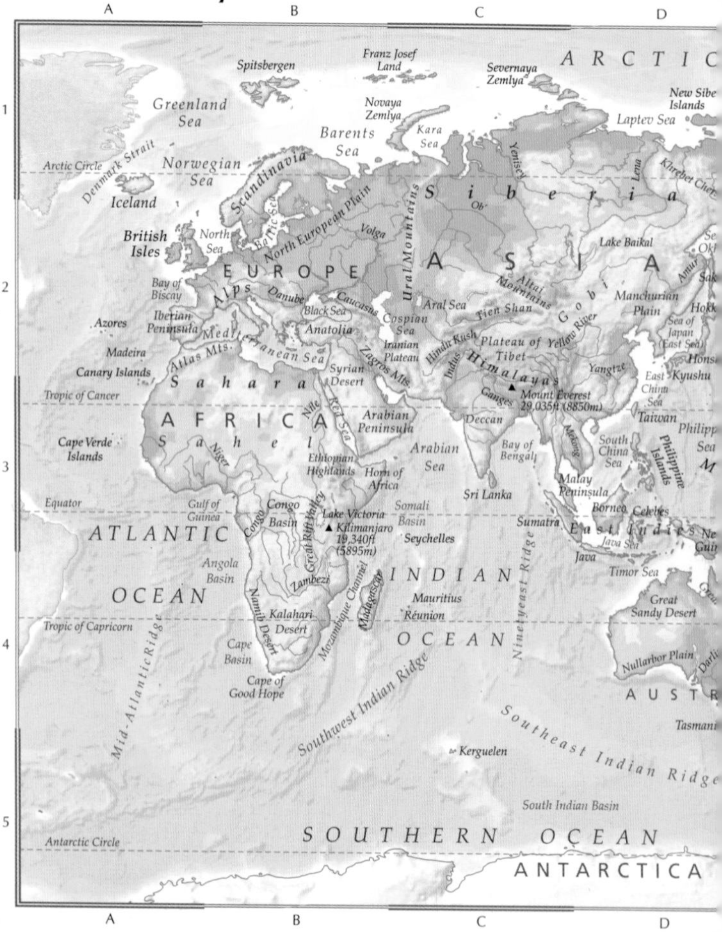
A
B
C
D
1
2
3
4
5
ARCTIC
Spitsbergen
Franz Josef Land
Severnaya Zemlya
New Sibe Islands
Greenland Sea
Novaya Zemlya
Barents Sea
Kara Sea
Laptev Sea
Arctic Circle
Denmark Strait
Norwegian Sea
Scandinavia
Yenisey
Lena
Khrebet Cher
Iceland
Siberia
Ob'
British Isles
North Sea
Baltic Sea
North European Plain
Volga
Ural Mountains
Lake Baikal
EUROPE
ASIA
Amur
Bay of Biscay
Alps
Danube
Caucasus
Altai Mountains
Gobi
Manchurian Plain
Azores
Iberian Peninsula
Black Sea
Aral Sea
Tien Shan
Sea of Japan (East Sea)
Anatolia
Caspian Sea
Yellow River
Mediterranean Sea
Iranian Plateau
Hindu Kush
Plateau of Tibet
Madeira
Atlas Mts.
Zagros Mts.
Indus
Himalayas
Kyushu
Canary Islands
Sahara
Syrian Desert
Yangtze
East China Sea
Tropic of Cancer
Nile
Ganges
Mount Everest 29,035ft (8850m)
AFRICA
Red Sea
Arabian Peninsula
Deccan
Taiwan
Cape Verde Islands
Sahel
Niger
Arabian Sea
Bay of Bengal
Mekong
South China Sea
Philippine Islands
Ethiopian Highlands
Horn of Africa
Malay Peninsula
Sri Lanka
Equator
Gulf of Guinea
Congo
Congo Basin
Great Rift Valley
Lake Victoria
Kilimanjaro 19,340ft (5895m)
Somali Basin
Sumatra
Borneo
Celebes
ATLANTIC
Seychelles
East Indies
Java Sea
Java
Angola Basin
Zambezi
Mozambique Channel
Madagascar
INDIAN
Ninetyeast Ridge
Timor Sea
OCEAN
Namib Desert
Mauritius
Réunion
Great Sandy Desert
Tropic of Capricorn
Kalahari Desert
OCEAN
Cape Basin
Mid-Atlantic Ridge
Nullarbor Plain
Cape of Good Hope
Southwest Indian Ridge
AUSTR
Southeast Indian Ridge
Kerguelen
South Indian Basin
SOUTHERN OCEAN
Antarctic Circle
ANTARCTICA
A
B
C
D

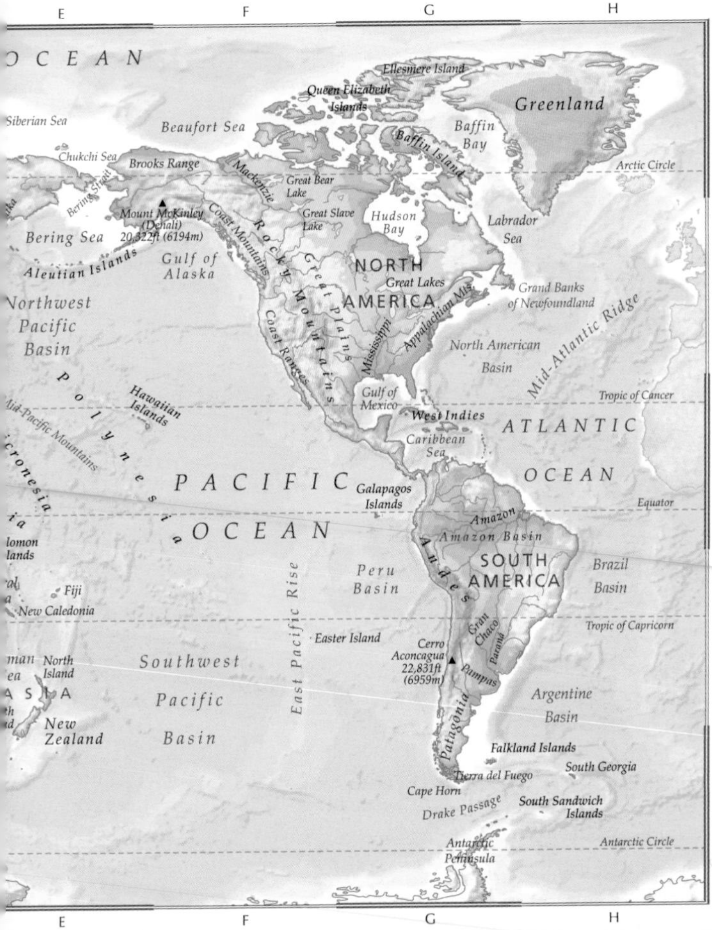
E
F
G
H
OCEAN
Siberian Sea
Beaufort Sea
Chukchi Sea
Brooks Range
Bering Strait
Mount McKinley (Denali) 20,322ft (6194m)
Bering Sea
Aleutian Islands
Gulf of Alaska
Coast Mountains
Mackenzie
Rocky Mountains
Queen Elizabeth Islands
Ellesmere Island
Greenland
Baffin Island
Baffin Bay
Arctic Circle
Great Bear Lake
Great Slave Lake
Hudson Bay
Labrador Sea
NORTH AMERICA
Great Lakes
Great Plains
Grand Banks of Newfoundland
Appalachian Mts
Mississippi
Coast Ranges
Northwest Pacific Basin
North American Basin
Mid-Atlantic Ridge
Hawaiian Islands
Polynesia
Mid-Pacific Mountains
Micronesia
Gulf of Mexico
West Indies
Tropic of Cancer
ATLANTIC OCEAN
Caribbean Sea
PACIFIC OCEAN
Galapagos Islands
Equator
Amazon
Amazon Basin
Andes
SOUTH AMERICA
Brazil Basin
Peru Basin
East Pacific Rise
Solomon Islands
Fiji
New Caledonia
Tropic of Capricorn
Easter Island
Cerro Aconcagua 22,831ft (6959m)
Gran Chaco
Paraná
Pampas
Patagonia
North Island
Tasman Sea
ASIA
New Zealand
Southwest Pacific Basin
Argentine Basin
Falkland Islands
South Georgia
Tierra del Fuego
Cape Horn
Drake Passage
South Sandwich Islands
Antarctic Peninsula
Antarctic Circle
1
2
3
4
5

Time Zones

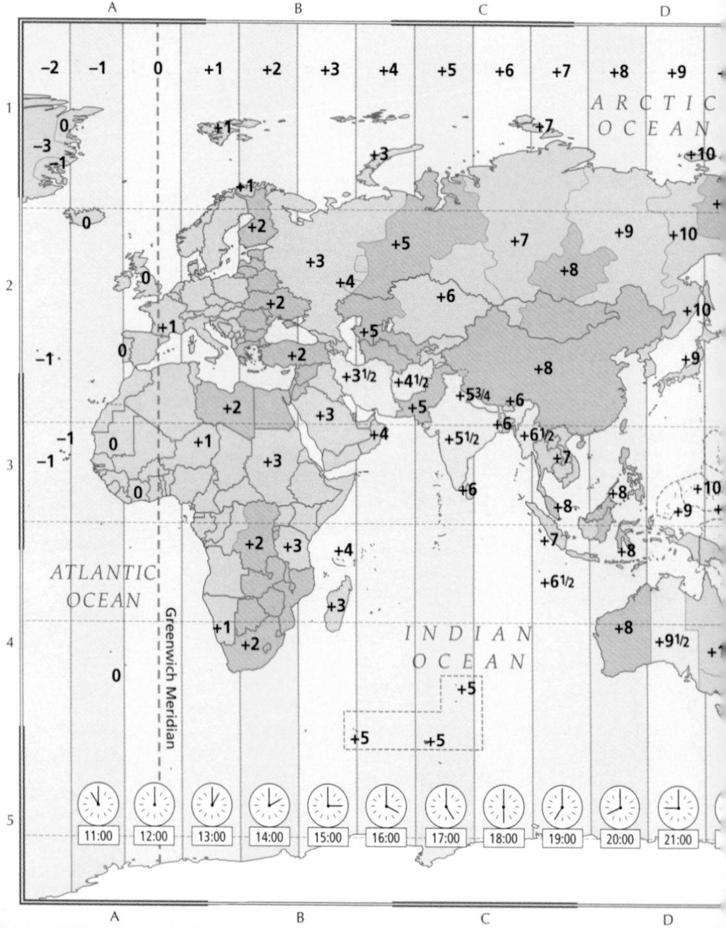
A
B
C
D
1
2
3
4
5
−2
−1
0
+1
+2
+3
+4
+5
+6
+7
+8
+9
ARCTIC OCEAN
ATLANTIC OCEAN
INDIAN OCEAN
Greenwich Meridian
+3½
+4½
+5¾
+5½
+6½
+9½
11:00
12:00
13:00
14:00
15:00
16:00
17:00
18:00
19:00
20:00
21:00

E
F
G
H
1
2
3
4
5
International Dateline
–11
–10
–9
–8
–7
–6
–5
–4
–3
–2
+12
–10
–9
–8
–7
–6
–5
–4
–3½
0
–3
–1
–4
PACIFIC OCEAN
ATLANTIC OCEAN
–11
–10
–10
–5
–4
–4½
+12
+13
+14
–9½
–5
–4
–3
–10
–10
+13
–8
–6
+11½
10½
+12
+12¾
–4
–3
PACIFIC OCEAN
–3
–4
–2
Equator
–3
24:00
01:00
02:00
03:00
04:00
05:00
06:00
07:00
08:00
09:00
10:00

The world's regions

North & Central America

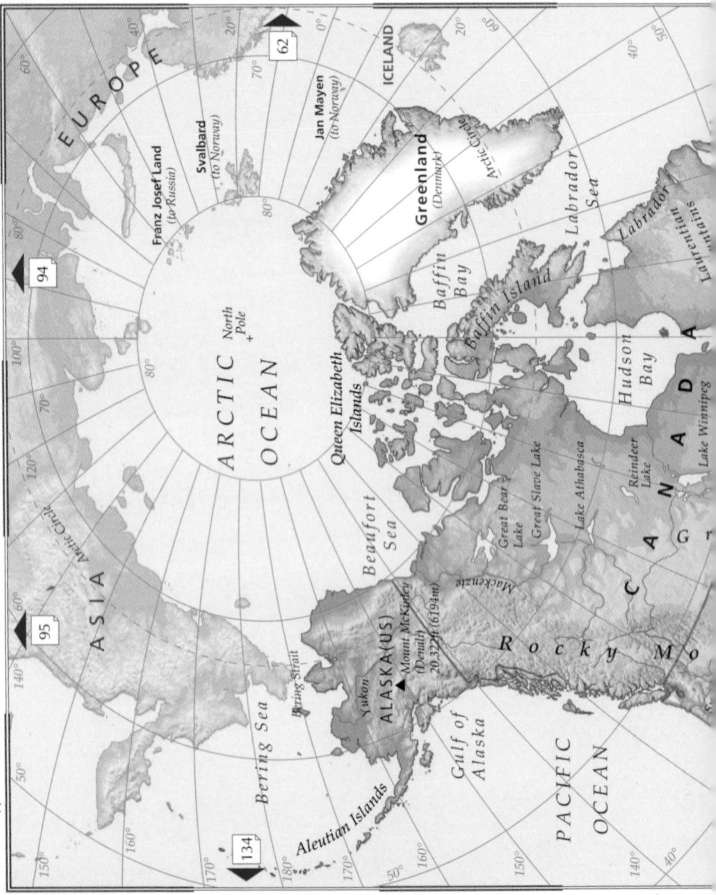
ARCTIC OCEAN
North Pole
EUROPE
ASIA
Franz Josef Land (to Russia)
Svalbard (to Norway)
Jan Mayen (to Norway)
ICELAND
Greenland (Denmark)
Arctic Circle
Labrador Sea
Labrador
Laurentian Mountains
Baffin Bay
Baffin Island
Hudson Bay
Queen Elizabeth Islands
Beaufort Sea
CANADA
Reindeer Lake
Lake Winnipeg
Lake Athabasca
Great Slave Lake
Great Bear Lake
Mackenzie
Rocky Mo
ALASKA (US)
Mount McKinley (Denali) 20,322ft (6194m)
Yukon
Bering Strait
Bering Sea
Aleutian Islands
Gulf of Alaska
PACIFIC OCEAN
94
95
62
134

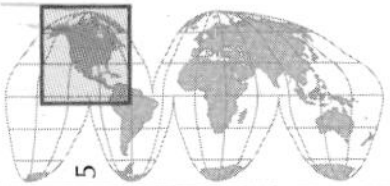

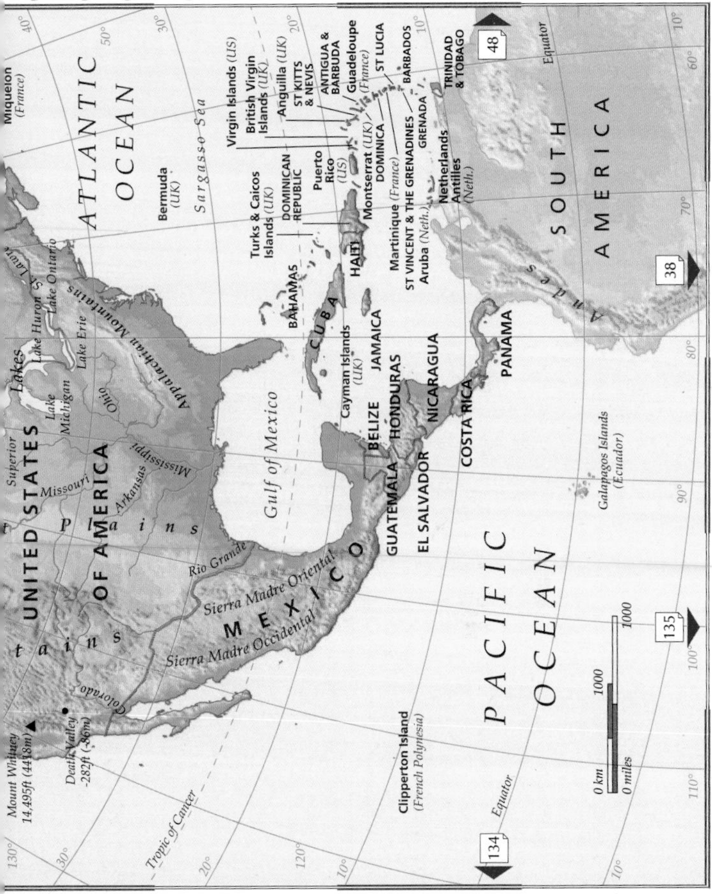
ATLANTIC OCEAN
PACIFIC OCEAN
UNITED STATES OF AMERICA
MEXICO
SOUTH AMERICA
Gulf of Mexico
Sargasso Sea
Bermuda (UK)
Miquelon (France)
Great Lakes
Lake Superior
Lake Michigan
Lake Huron
Lake Erie
Lake Ontario
St Lawrence
Appalachian Mountains
Great Plains
Missouri
Mississippi
Ohio
Arkansas
Rio Grande
Colorado
Sierra Madre Oriental
Sierra Madre Occidental
Mount Whitney 14,495ft (4418m)
Death Valley -282ft (-86m)
Tropic of Cancer
Equator
Andes
BAHAMAS
Turks & Caicos Islands (UK)
CUBA
Cayman Islands (UK)
JAMAICA
HAITI
DOMINICAN REPUBLIC
Puerto Rico (US)
Virgin Islands (US)
British Virgin Islands (UK)
Anguilla (UK)
ST KITTS & NEVIS
ANTIGUA & BARBUDA
Guadeloupe (France)
Montserrat (UK)
DOMINICA
Martinique (France)
ST LUCIA
ST VINCENT & THE GRENADINES
BARBADOS
GRENADA
TRINIDAD & TOBAGO
Aruba (Neth.)
Netherlands Antilles (Neth.)
BELIZE
GUATEMALA
HONDURAS
EL SALVADOR
NICARAGUA
COSTA RICA
PANAMA
Galapagos Islands (Ecuador)
Clipperton Island (French Polynesia)
0 km 1000
0 miles 1000
48
38
135
134
A
B
C
D
E
5
6
7
8

Western Canada & Alaska

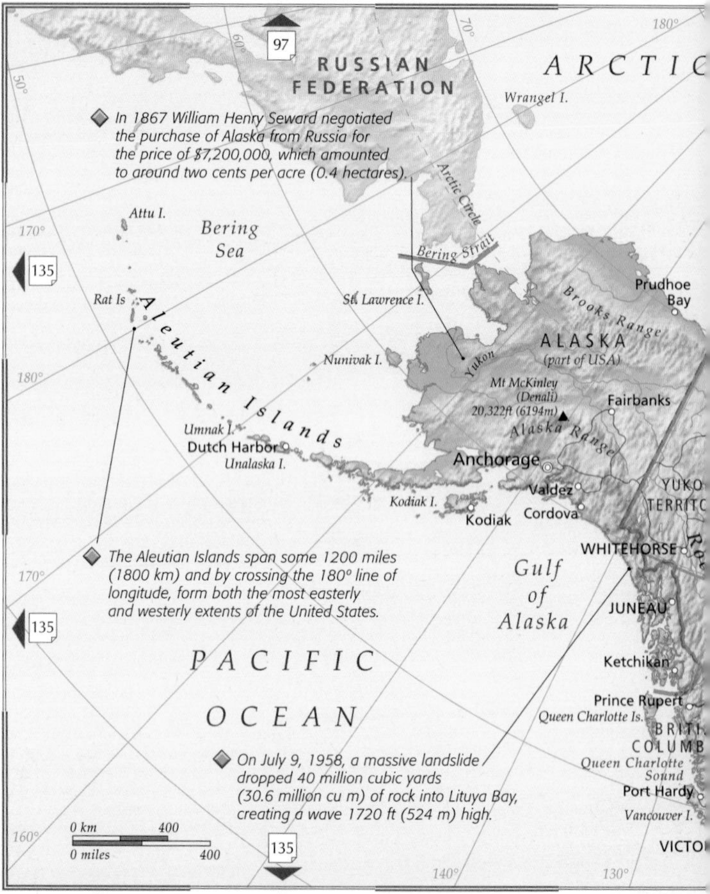
A
B
C
D
1
2
3
4
5
97
135
135
135
RUSSIAN FEDERATION
ARCTIC
Wrangel I.
Arctic Circle
Bering Strait
Attu I.
Bering Sea
Rat Is
Aleutian Islands
St. Lawrence I.
Nunivak I.
Brooks Range
Prudhoe Bay
ALASKA
(part of USA)
Yukon
Mt McKinley
(Denali)
20,322ft (6194m)
Fairbanks
Alaska Range
Umnak I.
Dutch Harbor
Unalaska I.
Anchorage
Valdez
Cordova
Kodiak I.
Kodiak
YUKON TERRITORY
WHITEHORSE
Gulf of Alaska
JUNEAU
Ketchikan
PACIFIC OCEAN
Prince Rupert
Queen Charlotte Is.
BRITISH COLUMBIA
Queen Charlotte Sound
Port Hardy
Vancouver I.
VICTORIA
0 km 400
0 miles 400
50°
60°
70°
180°
170°
180°
170°
160°
140°
130°

In 1867 William Henry Seward negotiated the purchase of Alaska from Russia for the price of $7,200,000, which amounted to around two cents per acre (0.4 hectares).

The Aleutian Islands span some 1200 miles (1800 km) and by crossing the 180° line of longitude, form both the most easterly and westerly extents of the United States.

On July 9, 1958, a massive landslide dropped 40 million cubic yards (30.6 million cu m) of rock into Lituya Bay, creating a wave 1720 ft (524 m) high.

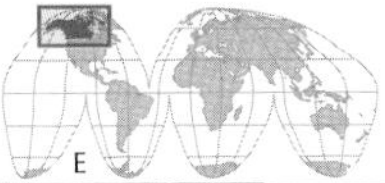

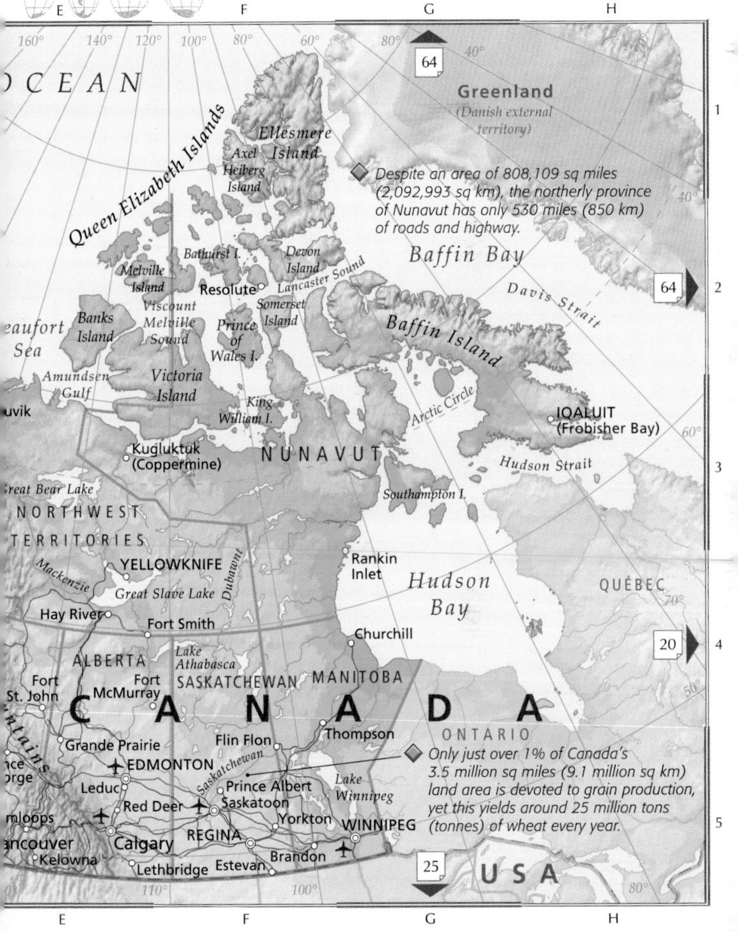
E
F
G
H
1
2
3
4
5
160°
140°
120°
100°
80°
60°
80°
40°
40°
60°
70°
50°
80°
110°
100°
64
64
20
25
OCEAN
Greenland
(Danish external territory)
Ellesmere Island
Axel Heiberg Island
Queen Elizabeth Islands
Despite an area of 808,109 sq miles (2,092,993 sq km), the northerly province of Nunavut has only 530 miles (850 km) of roads and highway.
Baffin Bay
Bathurst I.
Devon Island
Melville Island
Resolute
Lancaster Sound
Davis Strait
Somerset Island
Viscount Melville Sound
Banks Island
Prince of Wales I.
Beaufort Sea
Baffin Island
Amundsen Gulf
Victoria Island
King William I.
Arctic Circle
IQALUIT (Frobisher Bay)
Kugluktuk (Coppermine)
NUNAVUT
Hudson Strait
Great Bear Lake
Southampton I.
NORTHWEST TERRITORIES
Rankin Inlet
Mackenzie
YELLOWKNIFE
Dubawnt
Hudson Bay
QUÉBEC
Great Slave Lake
Hay River
Fort Smith
Churchill
ALBERTA
Lake Athabasca
Fort St. John
Fort McMurray
SASKATCHEWAN
MANITOBA
CANADA
Thompson
ONTARIO
Grande Prairie
Flin Flon
EDMONTON
Saskatchewan
Only just over 1% of Canada's 3.5 million sq miles (9.1 million sq km) land area is devoted to grain production, yet this yields around 25 million tons (tonnes) of wheat every year.
Leduc
Prince Albert
Lake Winnipeg
Red Deer
Saskatoon
Yorkton
WINNIPEG
REGINA
Calgary
Kelowna
Brandon
Lethbridge
Estevan
USA

Eastern Canada

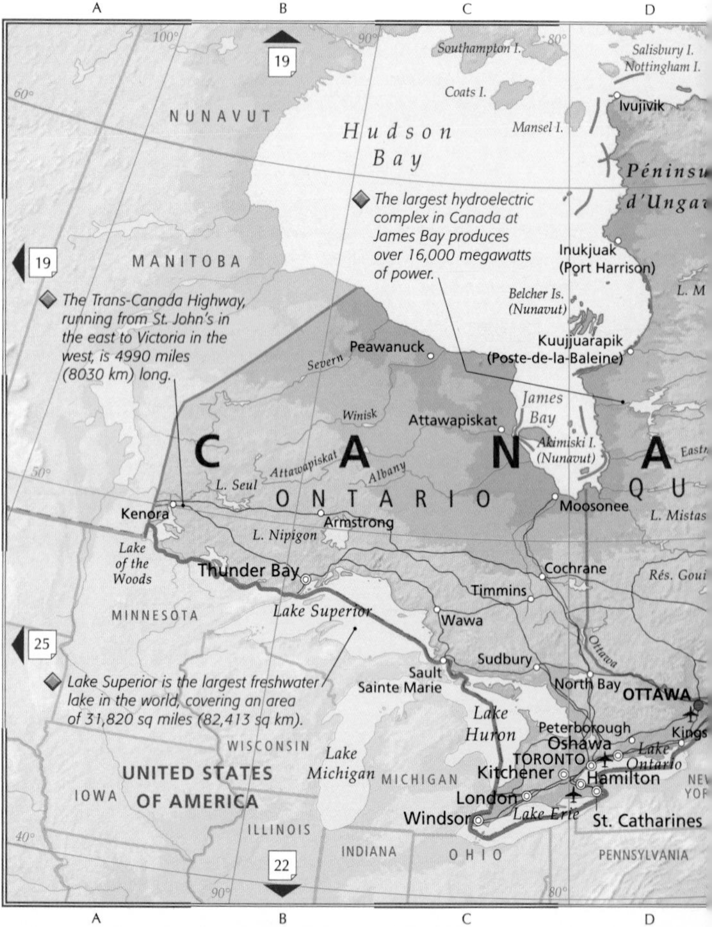
A
B
C
D
1
2
3
4
5
19
25
22
100°
90°
80°
60°
50°
40°
Southampton I.
Salisbury I.
Nottingham I.
Coats I.
Ivujivik
NUNAVUT
Hudson Bay
Mansel I.
Péninsu
d'Unga
The largest hydroelectric complex in Canada at James Bay produces over 16,000 megawatts of power.
Inukjuak (Port Harrison)
MANITOBA
The Trans-Canada Highway, running from St. John's in the east to Victoria in the west, is 4990 miles (8030 km) long.
Belcher Is. (Nunavut)
L. M
Kuujjuarapik (Poste-de-la-Baleine)
Peawanuck
Severn
James Bay
Winisk
Attawapiskat
C A N A
Akimiski I. (Nunavut)
East
Attawapiskat
Albany
L. Seul
ONTARIO
Moosonee
QU
Kenora
Armstrong
L. Mistas
L. Nipigon
Lake of the Woods
Thunder Bay
Cochrane
Rés. Goui
Timmins
MINNESOTA
Lake Superior
Wawa
Ottawa
Sudbury
Sault Sainte Marie
North Bay
OTTAWA
Lake Superior is the largest freshwater lake in the world, covering an area of 31,820 sq miles (82,413 sq km).
Lake Huron
Peterborough
Kings
WISCONSIN
Oshawa
Lake Ontario
TORONTO
UNITED STATES OF AMERICA
Lake Michigan
MICHIGAN
Kitchener
Hamilton
NEW YOR
IOWA
London
Lake Erie
Windsor
St. Catharines
ILLINOIS
INDIANA
OHIO
PENNSYLVANIA

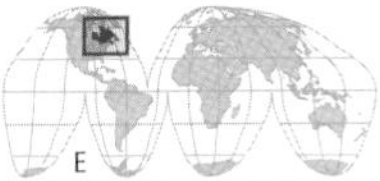

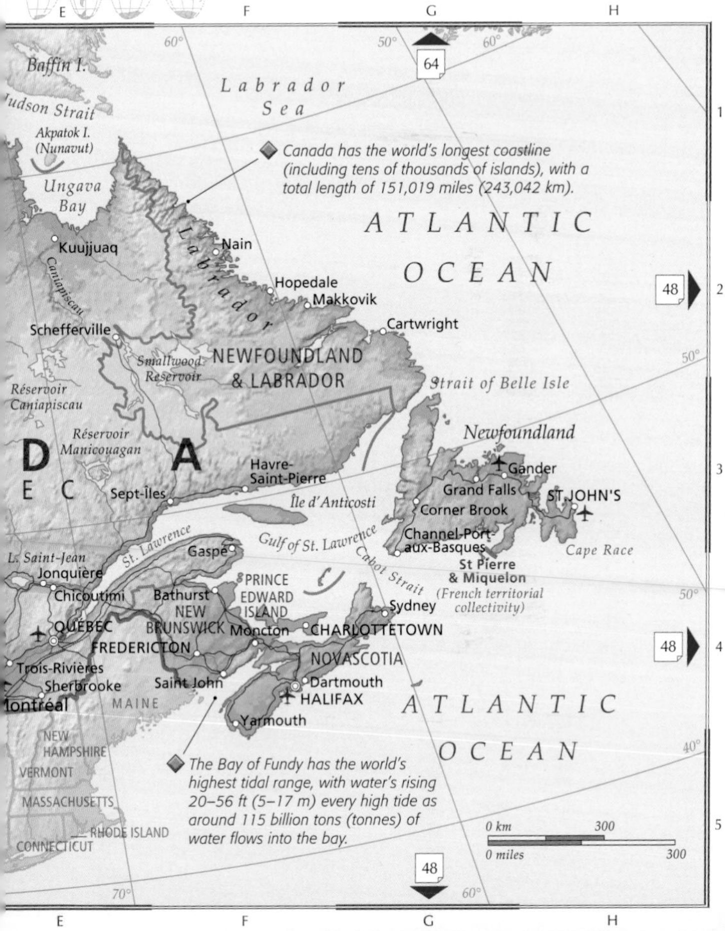
E
F
G
H
1
2
3
4
5
60°
50°
60°
64
48
48
48
50°
50°
40°
70°
60°
Baffin I.
Hudson Strait
Akpatok I.
(Nunavut)
Ungava
Bay
Labrador
Sea
Canada has the world's longest coastline (including tens of thousands of islands), with a total length of 151,019 miles (243,042 km).
ATLANTIC
OCEAN
Kuujjuaq
Caniapiscau
Labrador
Nain
Hopedale
Makkovik
Cartwright
Schefferville
Smallwood
Reservoir
NEWFOUNDLAND
& LABRADOR
Strait of Belle Isle
Réservoir
Caniapiscau
Réservoir
Manicouagan
Newfoundland
D
A
E
C
Havre-
Saint-Pierre
Gander
Grand Falls
ST.JOHN'S
Sept-Îles
Île d'Anticosti
Corner Brook
Channel-Port-
aux-Basques
Cape Race
St. Lawrence
Gulf of St. Lawrence
Cabot Strait
Gaspé
L. Saint-Jean
Jonquière
Chicoutimi
St Pierre
& Miquelon
(French territorial
collectivity)
PRINCE
EDWARD
ISLAND
Bathurst
NEW
BRUNSWICK
Sydney
QUÉBEC
Moncton
CHARLOTTETOWN
FREDERICTON
NOVA SCOTIA
Trois-Rivières
Sherbrooke
Saint John
Dartmouth
Montréal
MAINE
HALIFAX
ATLANTIC
Yarmouth
NEW
HAMPSHIRE
OCEAN
VERMONT
MASSACHUSETTS
The Bay of Fundy has the world's highest tidal range, with water's rising 20–56 ft (5–17 m) every high tide as around 115 billion tons (tonnes) of water flows into the bay.
RHODE ISLAND
CONNECTICUT
0 km
300
0 miles
300

USA: The Northeast

A
B
C
D
20
25
25
30
MINNESOTA
Lake Superior
ONTARIO
Superior
Ironwood
Marquette
Sault Ste Marie
Iron Mountain
Ladysmith
Cheboygan
Lake Huron
WISCONSIN
MICHIGAN
Eau Claire
Mississippi
Green Bay
Traverse City
La Crosse
Oshkosh
Lake Michigan
Bay City
IOWA
MADISON
Milwaukee
Grand Rapids
Saginaw
Flint
LANSING
Waukegan
Rockford
Detroit
Ann Arbor
Chicago
Lake Erie
Aurora
South Bend
Toledo
Joliet
Rock Island
Gary
Youngstown
Galesburg
Fort Wayne
Akron
Peoria
Mansfield
Canton
ILLINOIS
INDIANA
Champaign
Muncie
OHIO
Wheeling
SPRINGFIELD
Decatur
INDIANAPOLIS
COLUMBUS
Dayton
Effingham
Terre Haute
Cincinnati
Bloomington
Wabash
Ohio
East St Louis
Huntington
Mt. Vernon
Louisville
CHARLESTON
MISSOURI
Evansville
FRANKFORT
WEST VIRGINIA
Carbondale
Lexington
Owensboro
Richmond
KENTUCKY
Paducah
Hopkinsville
Bowling Green
London
ARKANSAS

The Chicago River originally flowed into Lake Michigan, but was reversed in 1900 by the completion of a canal.

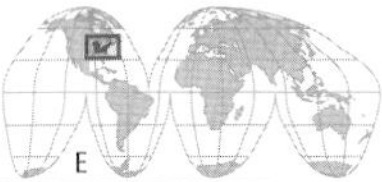

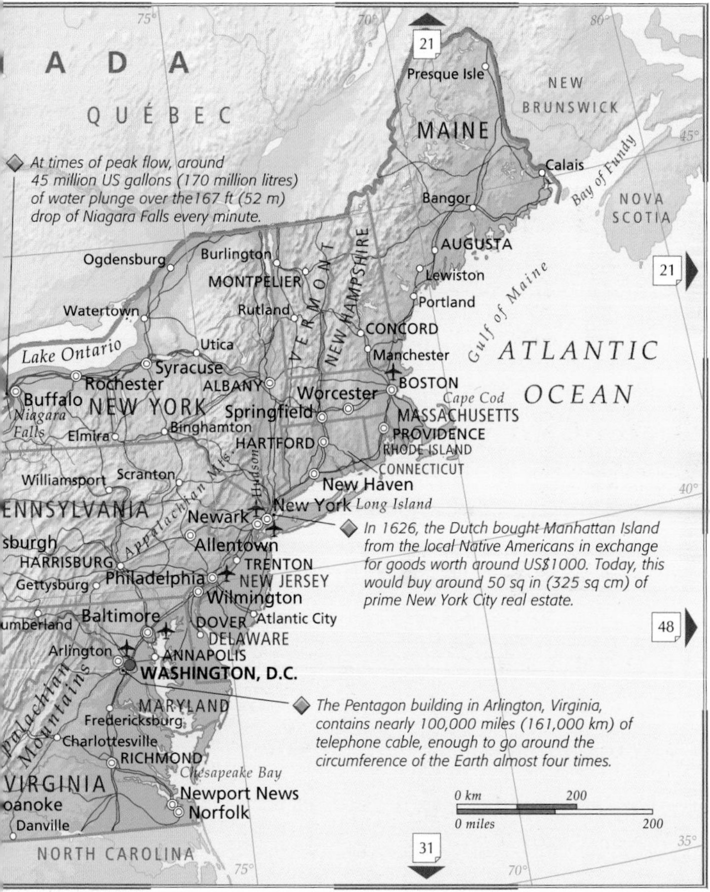
E
F
G
H
1
2
3
4
5
21
48
31
CANADA
QUÉBEC
NEW BRUNSWICK
NOVA SCOTIA
MAINE
Presque Isle
Calais
Bay of Fundy
Bangor
AUGUSTA
Lewiston
Portland
Gulf of Maine
At times of peak flow, around 45 million US gallons (170 million litres) of water plunge over the167 ft (52 m) drop of Niagara Falls every minute.
Ogdensburg
Burlington
MONTPELIER
VERMONT
NEW HAMPSHIRE
Watertown
Rutland
CONCORD
Manchester
ATLANTIC OCEAN
Lake Ontario
Utica
Syracuse
Rochester
ALBANY
BOSTON
Buffalo
NEW YORK
Niagara Falls
Worcester
Cape Cod
Springfield
MASSACHUSETTS
Elmira
Binghamton
PROVIDENCE
HARTFORD
RHODE ISLAND
CONNECTICUT
Williamsport
Scranton
New Haven
Appalachian Mts.
Hudson
New York
Long Island
PENNSYLVANIA
Newark
In 1626, the Dutch bought Manhattan Island from the local Native Americans in exchange for goods worth around US$1000. Today, this would buy around 50 sq in (325 sq cm) of prime New York City real estate.
Pittsburgh
Allentown
HARRISBURG
TRENTON
Gettysburg
Philadelphia
NEW JERSEY
Wilmington
Cumberland
Baltimore
DOVER
Atlantic City
DELAWARE
Arlington
ANNAPOLIS
WASHINGTON, D.C.
Appalachian Mountains
MARYLAND
The Pentagon building in Arlington, Virginia, contains nearly 100,000 miles (161,000 km) of telephone cable, enough to go around the circumference of the Earth almost four times.
Fredericksburg
Charlottesville
RICHMOND
Chesapeake Bay
VIRGINIA
Newport News
Roanoke
Norfolk
Danville
0 km 200
0 miles 200
NORTH CAROLINA
75°
70°
80°
45°
40°
35°

USA: Central States

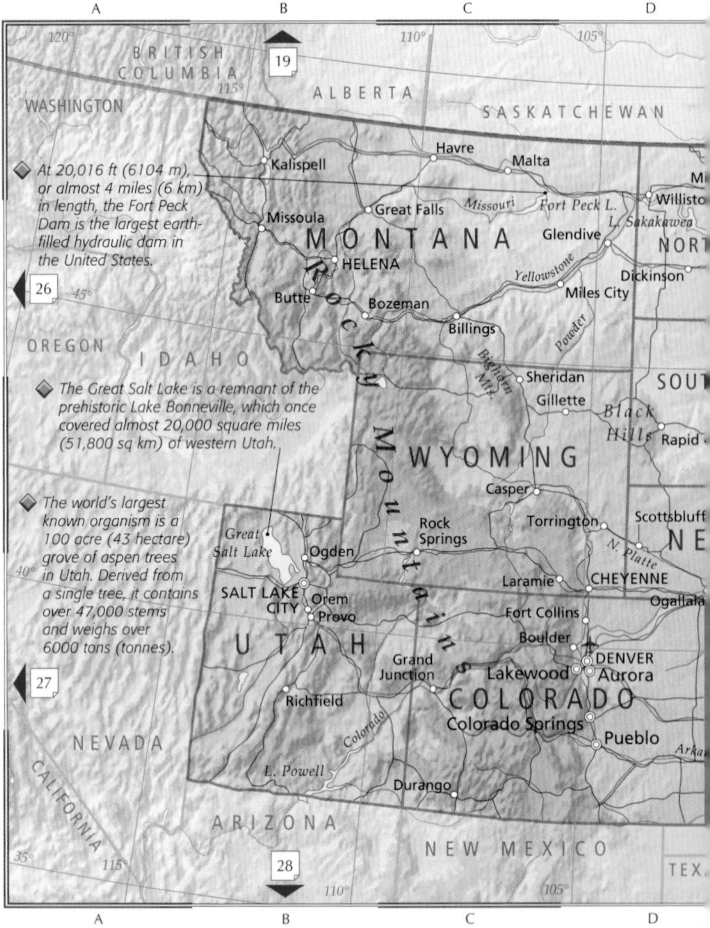
At 20,016 ft (6104 m), or almost 4 miles (6 km) in length, the Fort Peck Dam is the largest earth-filled hydraulic dam in the United States.
The Great Salt Lake is a remnant of the prehistoric Lake Bonneville, which once covered almost 20,000 square miles (51,800 sq km) of western Utah.
The world's largest known organism is a 100 acre (43 hectare) grove of aspen trees in Utah. Derived from a single tree, it contains over 47,000 stems and weighs over 6000 tons (tonnes).
A
B
C
D
1
2
3
4
5
19
26
27
28
120°
115°
110°
105°
45°
40°
35°
BRITISH COLUMBIA
ALBERTA
SASKATCHEWAN
WASHINGTON
OREGON
IDAHO
MONTANA
WYOMING
UTAH
COLORADO
NEVADA
CALIFORNIA
ARIZONA
NEW MEXICO
TEX
NORT
SOUT
NE
Rocky Mountains
Kalispell
Havre
Malta
Missoula
Great Falls
Missouri
Fort Peck L.
L. Sakakawea
Willisto
Glendive
HELENA
Yellowstone
Dickinson
Butte
Bozeman
Miles City
Billings
Powder
Bighorn Mts.
Sheridan
Gillette
Black Hills
Rapid
Casper
Great Salt Lake
Ogden
Rock Springs
Torrington
Scottsbluff
N. Platte
SALT LAKE CITY
Orem
Provo
Laramie
CHEYENNE
Ogallala
Fort Collins
Boulder
DENVER
Lakewood
Aurora
Grand Junction
Richfield
Colorado Springs
Pueblo
Colorado
Arka
L. Powell
Durango

E
F
G
H
95°
90°
50°
85°
20
CANADA
MANITOBA
Lake of the Woods
ONTARIO
1
MINNESOTA
Lake Superior
Grand Forks
Virginia
DAKOTA
Moorhead
Duluth
22
Fargo
BISMARCK
Brainerd
Access to the St. Lawrence Seaway via the Great Lakes makes Duluth the most westerly Atlantic port in the US, some 1100 miles (1770 km) from the Atlantic ocean.
45°
2
Aberdeen
St Cloud
SAINT PAUL
Minneapolis
MICHIGAN
DAKOTA
Watertown
WISCONSIN
PIERRE
Rochester
Lake Michigan
Mitchell
Sioux Falls
Mason City
Missouri
3
Dubuque
Sioux City
IOWA
Cedar Rapids
OHIO
NEBRASKA
ILLINOIS
INDIANA
DES MOINES
Davenport
Columbus
40°
North Platte
Council Bluffs
Omaha
Burlington
The deadliest tornado in US history struck Missouri on March 18, 1925. Leaving a continuous 219 mile (352 km) track, the tornado crossed three states and killed 695 people.
Platte
LINCOLN
Hastings
Kirksville
4
Mississippi
St Joseph
Independence
Kansas City
Missouri
Goodland
Hays
Kansas City
22
Saint Louis
TOPEKA
KANSAS
JEFFERSON CITY
MISSOURI
KENTUCKY
Pratt
Dodge City
Wichita
Springfield
Arkansas
Ozark Plateau
TENNESSEE
85°
5
0 km
200
35°
OKLAHOMA
ARKANSAS
30
0 miles
200
95°
E
F
G
H

NORTH AMERICA
USA: The West

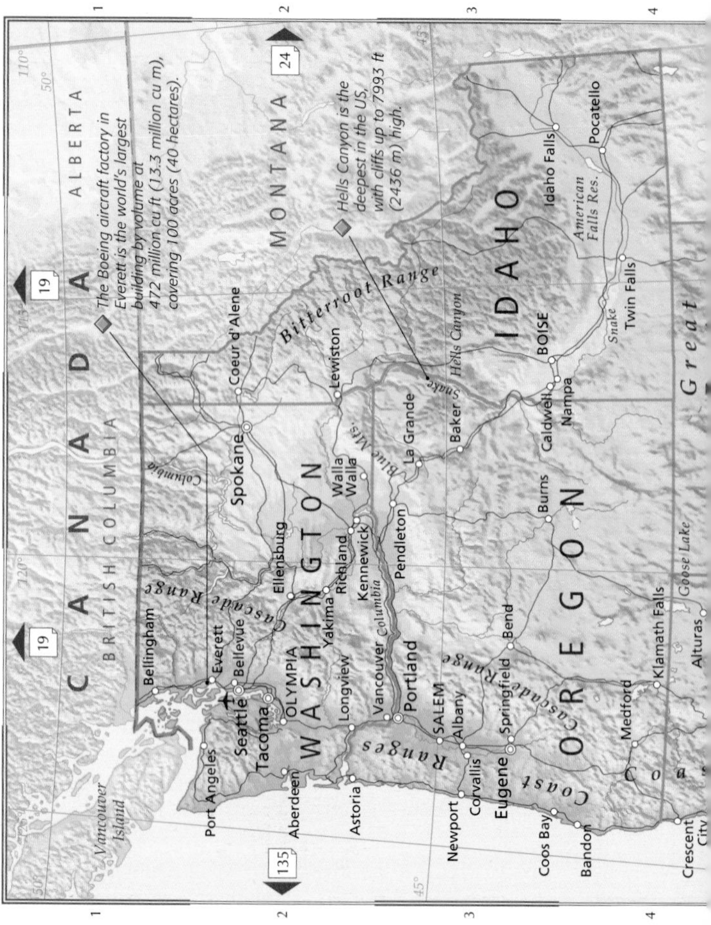
The Boeing aircraft factory in Everett is the world's largest building by volume at 472 million cu ft (13.3 million cu m), covering 100 acres (40 hectares).
Hells Canyon is the deepest in the US, with cliffs up to 7993 ft (2436 m) high.
CANADA
ALBERTA
BRITISH COLUMBIA
MONTANA
WASHINGTON
IDAHO
OREGON
Vancouver Island
Cascade Range
Bitterroot Range
Blue Mts.
Coast Ranges
Hells Canyon
Snake
Columbia
American Falls Res.
Goose Lake
Bellingham
Everett
Bellevue
Seattle
Tacoma
OLYMPIA
Port Angeles
Aberdeen
Astoria
Longview
Vancouver
Portland
SALEM
Albany
Corvallis
Newport
Eugene
Springfield
Coos Bay
Bandon
Crescent City
Medford
Klamath Falls
Alturas
Bend
Burns
Yakima
Ellensburg
Richland
Kennewick
Pendleton
Walla Walla
Spokane
Coeur d'Alene
Lewiston
La Grande
Baker
Caldwell
Nampa
BOISE
Twin Falls
Idaho Falls
Pocatello
Great
19
24
135

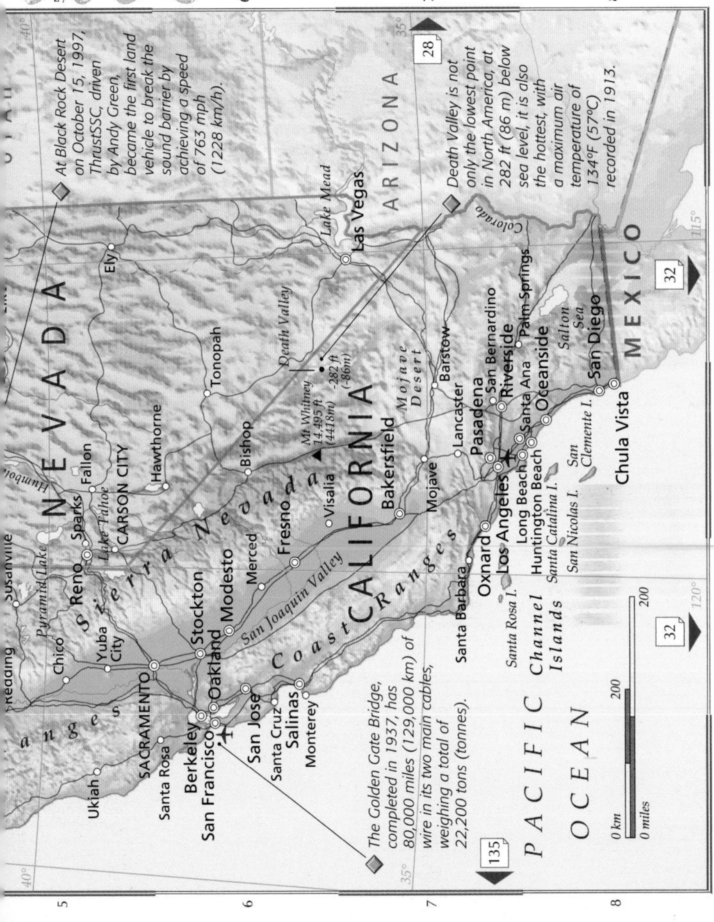
At Black Rock Desert on October 15, 1997, ThrustSSC, driven by Andy Green, became the first land vehicle to break the sound barrier by achieving a speed of 763 mph (1228 km/h).
Death Valley is not only the lowest point in North America, at 282 ft (86 m) below sea level, it is also the hottest, with a maximum air temperature of 134°F (57°C) recorded in 1913.
The Golden Gate Bridge, completed in 1937, has 80,000 miles (129,000 km) of wire in its two main cables, weighing a total of 22,200 tons (tonnes).
NEVADA
CALIFORNIA
ARIZONA
MEXICO
PACIFIC OCEAN
Sierra Nevada
Coast Ranges
San Joaquin Valley
Mojave Desert
Death Valley
Mt Whitney 14,495 ft (4418m)
-282 ft (-86m)
Lake Mead
Lake Tahoe
Pyramid Lake
Salton Sea
Colorado
Channel Islands
Santa Rosa I.
Santa Catalina I.
San Nicolas I.
San Clemente I.
Reno
Sparks
Fallon
CARSON CITY
Hawthorne
Tonopah
Ely
Las Vegas
Bishop
Chico
Yuba City
SACRAMENTO
Ukiah
Santa Rosa
Berkeley
San Francisco
Oakland
Stockton
Modesto
Merced
Fresno
Visalia
Bakersfield
San Jose
Santa Cruz
Salinas
Monterey
Santa Barbara
Oxnard
Los Angeles
Long Beach
Huntington Beach
Pasadena
Lancaster
Mojave
Barstow
San Bernardino
Riverside
Santa Ana
Oceanside
Palm Springs
San Diego
Chula Vista
0 km 200
0 miles 200
28
32
135
40°
35°
120°
115°
A B C D E
5 6 7 8

USA: The Southwest

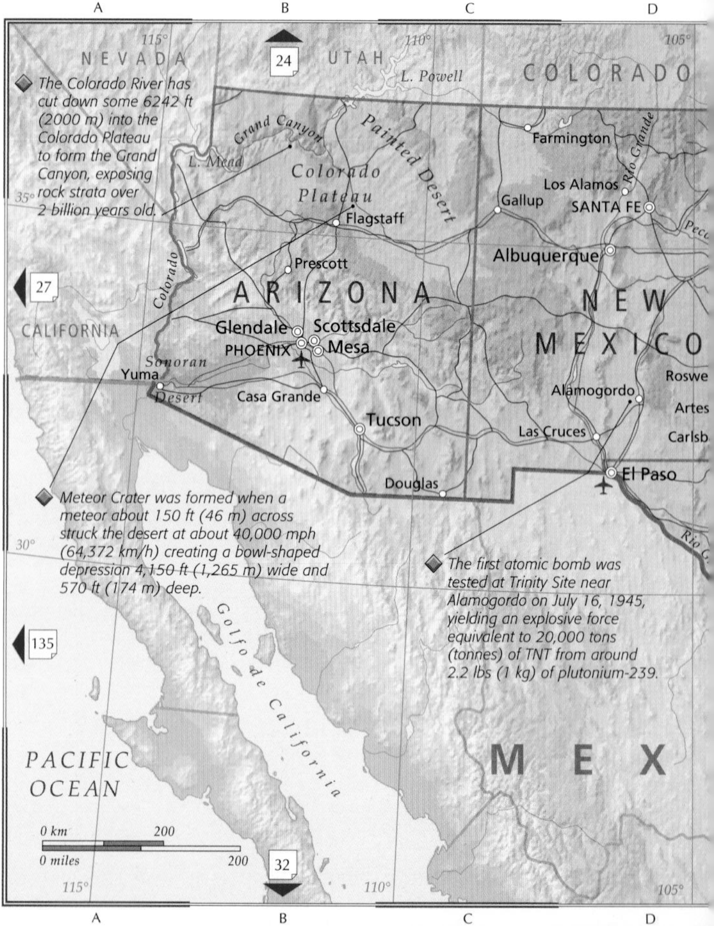
A
B
C
D
1
2
3
4
5
115°
110°
105°
35°
30°
NEVADA
UTAH
COLORADO
24
L. Powell
The Colorado River has cut down some 6242 ft (2000 m) into the Colorado Plateau to form the Grand Canyon, exposing rock strata over 2 billion years old.
Grand Canyon
Painted Desert
L. Mead
Colorado Plateau
Farmington
Rio Grande
Los Alamos
Gallup
SANTA FE
Flagstaff
Albuquerque
Prescott
27
Colorado
ARIZONA
NEW MEXICO
CALIFORNIA
Glendale
Scottsdale
PHOENIX
Mesa
Sonoran Desert
Yuma
Casa Grande
Roswe
Alamogordo
Artes
Tucson
Las Cruces
Carlsb
El Paso
Douglas
Meteor Crater was formed when a meteor about 150 ft (46 m) across struck the desert at about 40,000 mph (64,372 km/h) creating a bowl-shaped depression 4,150 ft (1,265 m) wide and 570 ft (174 m) deep.
The first atomic bomb was tested at Trinity Site near Alamogordo on July 16, 1945, yielding an explosive force equivalent to 20,000 tons (tonnes) of TNT from around 2.2 lbs (1 kg) of plutonium-239.
Golfo de California
135
MEX
PACIFIC OCEAN
0 km 200
0 miles 200
32

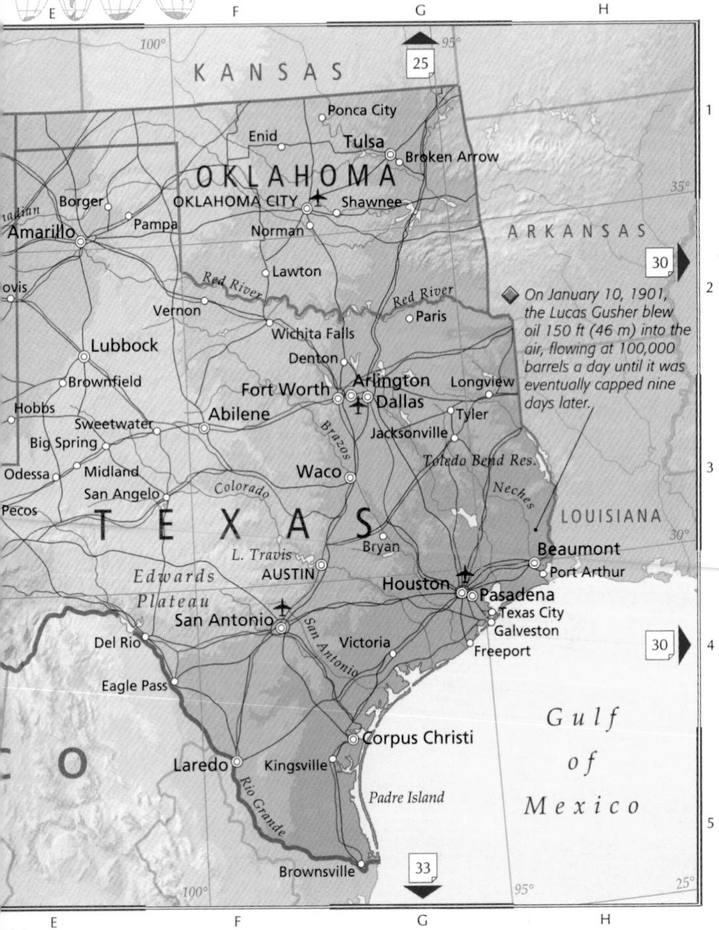
E
F
G
H
1
2
3
4
5
100°
95°
35°
30°
25°
25
30
30
33
KANSAS
OKLAHOMA
ARKANSAS
TEXAS
LOUISIANA
Ponca City
Enid
Tulsa
Broken Arrow
OKLAHOMA CITY
Shawnee
Borger
Pampa
Amarillo
Norman
Lawton
Red River
Red River
Vernon
Paris
Wichita Falls
Lubbock
Denton
Brownfield
Fort Worth
Arlington
Longview
Dallas
Hobbs
Abilene
Tyler
Sweetwater
Big Spring
Jacksonville
Brazos
Odessa
Midland
Waco
Toledo Bend Res.
San Angelo
Colorado
Neches
Pecos
Bryan
Beaumont
Port Arthur
L. Travis
AUSTIN
Edwards
Plateau
Houston
Pasadena
Texas City
Galveston
San Antonio
San Antonio
Del Rio
Victoria
Freeport
Eagle Pass
Corpus Christi
Laredo
Kingsville
Rio Grande
Padre Island
Brownsville
Gulf of Mexico
O
On January 10, 1901, the Lucas Gusher blew oil 150 ft (46 m) into the air, flowing at 100,000 barrels a day until it was eventually capped nine days later.

USA: The Southeast

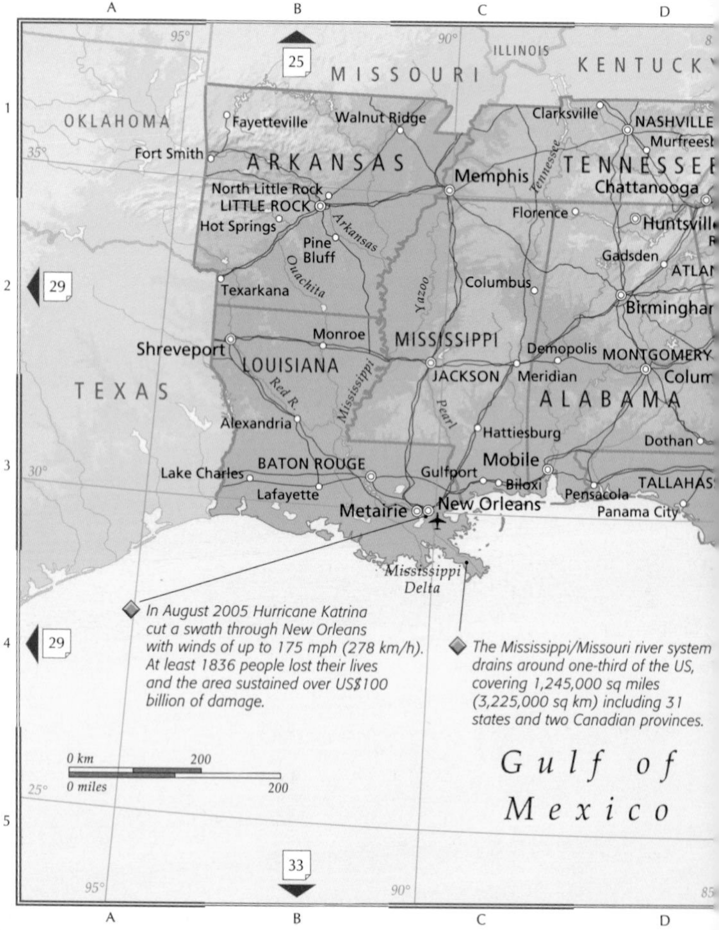
A
B
C
D
1
2
3
4
5
95°
90°
85°
35°
30°
25°
25
29
29
33
MISSOURI
ILLINOIS
KENTUCKY
OKLAHOMA
ARKANSAS
TENNESSEE
MISSISSIPPI
LOUISIANA
TEXAS
ALABAMA
Fayetteville
Walnut Ridge
Fort Smith
North Little Rock
LITTLE ROCK
Hot Springs
Pine Bluff
Texarkana
Memphis
Clarksville
NASHVILLE
Chattanooga
Florence
Huntsville
Gadsden
Columbus
Birmingham
Shreveport
Monroe
JACKSON
Meridian
Demopolis
MONTGOMERY
Alexandria
Hattiesburg
Dothan
Mobile
Lake Charles
BATON ROUGE
Lafayette
Gulfport
Biloxi
Pensacola
TALLAHASSEE
Panama City
Metairie
New Orleans
Arkansas
Ouachita
Yazoo
Tennessee
Red R.
Mississippi
Pearl
Mississippi Delta
In August 2005 Hurricane Katrina cut a swath through New Orleans with winds of up to 175 mph (278 km/h). At least 1836 people lost their lives and the area sustained over US$100 billion of damage.
The Mississippi/Missouri river system drains around one-third of the US, covering 1,245,000 sq miles (3,225,000 sq km) including 31 states and two Canadian provinces.
0 km
200
0 miles
200
Gulf of Mexico

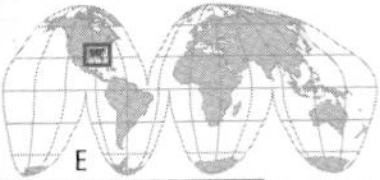

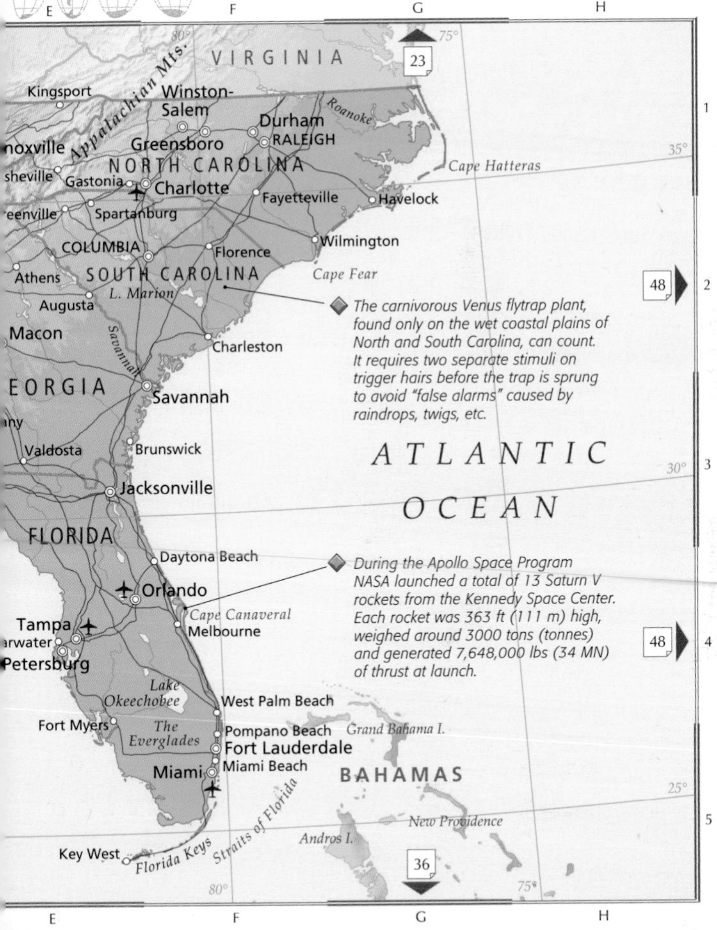
E
F
G
H
1
2
3
4
5
80°
75°
35°
30°
25°
VIRGINIA
23
Appalachian Mts.
Kingsport
Winston-Salem
Roanoke
Durham
RALEIGH
noxville
Greensboro
NORTH CAROLINA
Cape Hatteras
sheville
Gastonia
Charlotte
Fayetteville
Havelock
eenville
Spartanburg
COLUMBIA
Wilmington
Florence
Athens
SOUTH CAROLINA
Cape Fear
L. Marion
48
Augusta
The carnivorous Venus flytrap plant, found only on the wet coastal plains of North and South Carolina, can count. It requires two separate stimuli on trigger hairs before the trap is sprung to avoid "false alarms" caused by raindrops, twigs, etc.
Macon
Savannah
Charleston
EORGIA
Savannah
any
Valdosta
Brunswick
ATLANTIC
Jacksonville
OCEAN
FLORIDA
Daytona Beach
During the Apollo Space Program NASA launched a total of 13 Saturn V rockets from the Kennedy Space Center. Each rocket was 363 ft (111 m) high, weighed around 3000 tons (tonnes) and generated 7,648,000 lbs (34 MN) of thrust at launch.
Orlando
Cape Canaveral
Tampa
Melbourne
arwater
48
Petersburg
Lake Okeechobee
West Palm Beach
Fort Myers
The Everglades
Pompano Beach
Grand Bahama I.
Fort Lauderdale
Miami Beach
Miami
BAHAMAS
Straits of Florida
New Providence
Andros I.
Key West
Florida Keys
36

Mexico

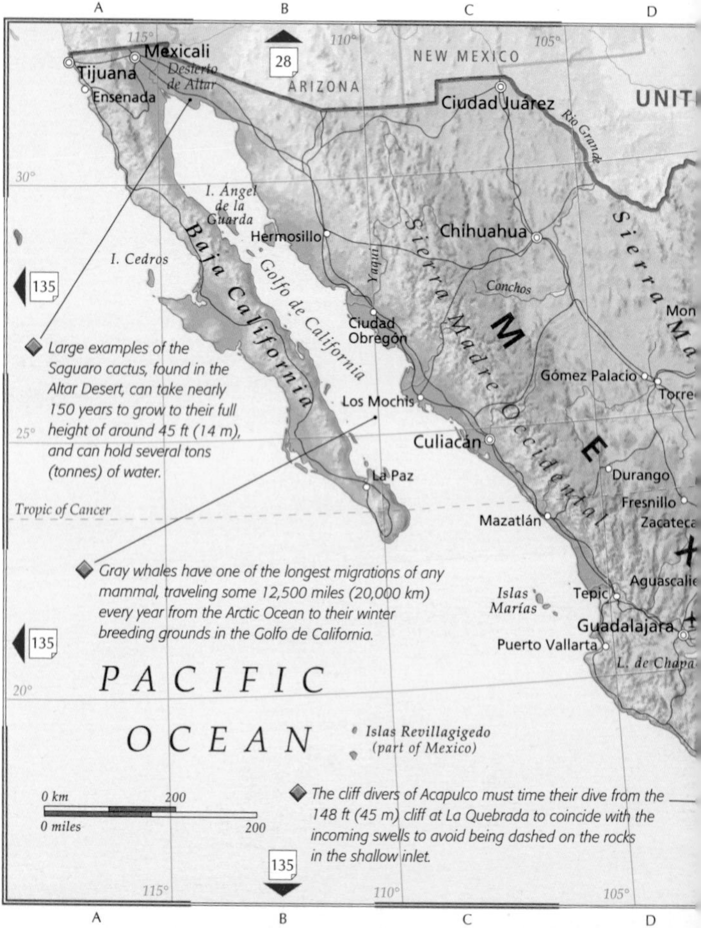
A
B
C
D
1
2
3
4
5
115°
110°
105°
30°
25°
20°
28
135
135
135
Mexicali
Tijuana
Ensenada
Desierto de Altar
ARIZONA
NEW MEXICO
Ciudad Juárez
UNIT
Rio Grande
I. Ángel de la Guarda
Hermosillo
Chihuahua
Sierra Madre Occidental
Sierra Ma
I. Cedros
Baja California
Golfo de California
Yaqui
Conchos
Ciudad Obregón
M
E
Mon
Gómez Palacio
Torre
Los Mochis
Culiacán
La Paz
Durango
Fresnillo
Zacateca
Mazatlán
Tropic of Cancer
Islas Marías
Tepic
Aguascali
Guadalajara
Puerto Vallarta
L. de Chapa
PACIFIC OCEAN
Islas Revillagigedo (part of Mexico)
0 km
200
0 miles
200
Large examples of the Saguaro cactus, found in the Altar Desert, can take nearly 150 years to grow to their full height of around 45 ft (14 m), and can hold several tons (tonnes) of water.
Gray whales have one of the longest migrations of any mammal, traveling some 12,500 miles (20,000 km) every year from the Arctic Ocean to their winter breeding grounds in the Golfo de California.
The cliff divers of Acapulco must time their dive from the 148 ft (45 m) cliff at La Quebrada to coincide with the incoming swells to avoid being dashed on the rocks in the shallow inlet.

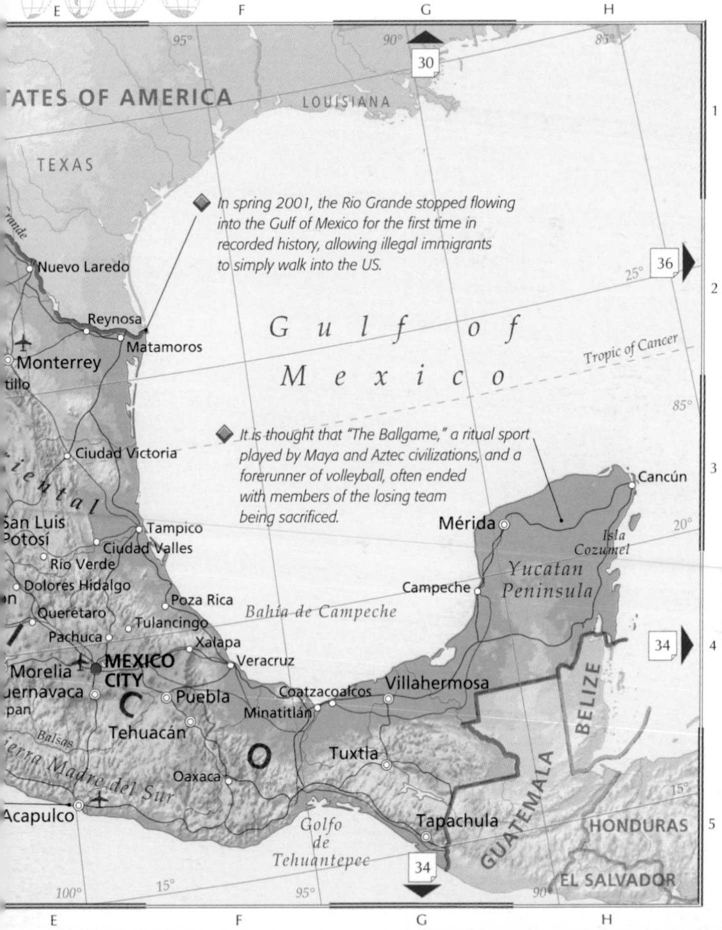
E
F
G
H
1
2
3
4
5
95°
90°
85°
30
TATES OF AMERICA
LOUISIANA
TEXAS
Grande
In spring 2001, the Rio Grande stopped flowing into the Gulf of Mexico for the first time in recorded history, allowing illegal immigrants to simply walk into the US.
36
25°
Nuevo Laredo
Reynosa
Matamoros
Monterrey
tillo
Gulf of Mexico
Tropic of Cancer
85°
It is thought that "The Ballgame," a ritual sport played by Maya and Aztec civilizations, and a forerunner of volleyball, often ended with members of the losing team being sacrificed.
Ciudad Victoria
iental
Cancún
San Luis Potosí
Tampico
Mérida
20°
Ciudad Valles
Isla Cozumel
Río Verde
Yucatan Peninsula
Dolores Hidalgo
Campeche
on
Poza Rica
Querétaro
Bahía de Campeche
Tulancingo
Pachuca
Xalapa
34
MEXICO CITY
Morelia
Veracruz
Cuernavaca
Villahermosa
Coatzacoalcos
Puebla
Minatitlán
BELIZE
Balsas
Tehuacán
Tuxtla
Sierra Madre del Sur
Oaxaca
GUATEMALA
15°
Acapulco
Golfo de Tehuantepec
Tapachula
HONDURAS
34
EL SALVADOR
100°
15°
95°
90°

Central America

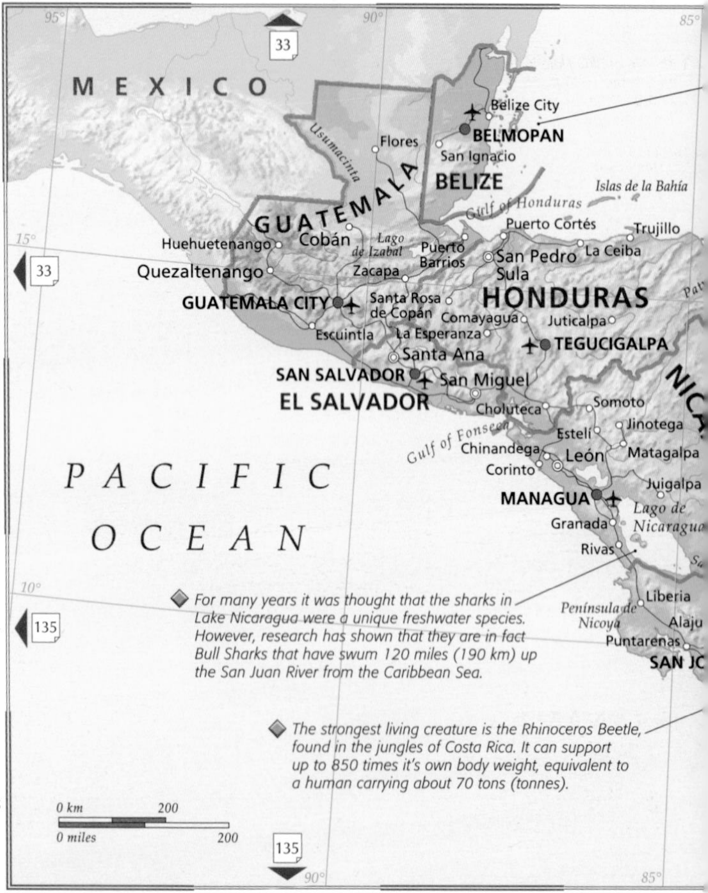
A
B
C
D
1
2
3
4
5
95°
90°
85°
15°
10°
33
135
MEXICO
Usumacinta
Flores
Belize City
BELMOPAN
San Ignacio
BELIZE
Islas de la Bahía
Gulf of Honduras
GUATEMALA
Huehuetenango
Cobán
Lago de Izabal
Puerto Barrios
Puerto Cortés
Trujillo
La Ceiba
San Pedro Sula
Quezaltenango
Zacapa
GUATEMALA CITY
Santa Rosa de Copán
HONDURAS
Comayagua
Juticalpa
Escuintla
La Esperanza
TEGUCIGALPA
Santa Ana
SAN SALVADOR
San Miguel
EL SALVADOR
Choluteca
Somoto
Jinotega
Estelí
Gulf of Fonseca
Chinandega
León
Matagalpa
Corinto
Juigalpa
MANAGUA
Granada
Lago de Nicaragua
Rivas
PACIFIC OCEAN
Liberia
Península de Nicoya
Puntarenas
0 km
200
0 miles
200

For many years it was thought that the sharks in Lake Nicaragua were a unique freshwater species. However, research has shown that they are in fact Bull Sharks that have swum 120 miles (190 km) up the San Juan River from the Caribbean Sea.

The strongest living creature is the Rhinoceros Beetle, found in the jungles of Costa Rica. It can support up to 850 times it's own body weight, equivalent to a human carrying about 70 tons (tonnes).

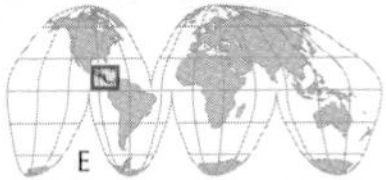

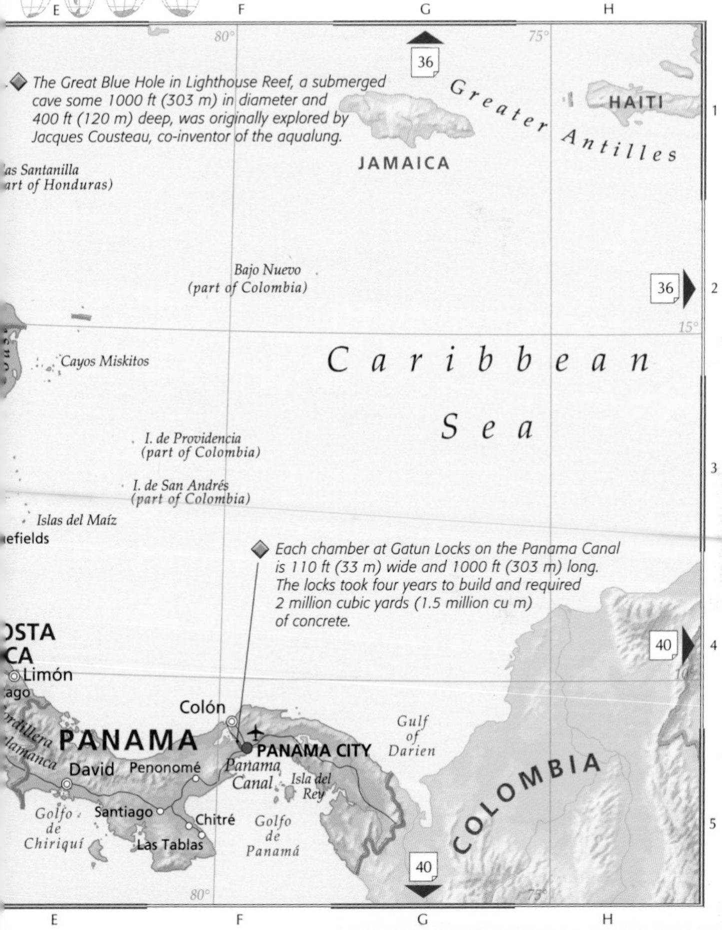
E
F
G
H
80°
75°
36
The Great Blue Hole in Lighthouse Reef, a submerged cave some 1000 ft (303 m) in diameter and 400 ft (120 m) deep, was originally explored by Jacques Cousteau, co-inventor of the aqualung.
Greater Antilles
HAITI
JAMAICA
1
as Santanilla
art of Honduras)
Bajo Nuevo
(part of Colombia)
36
2
15°
Cayos Miskitos
Caribbean
Sea
I. de Providencia
(part of Colombia)
3
I. de San Andrés
(part of Colombia)
Islas del Maíz
efields
Each chamber at Gatun Locks on the Panama Canal is 110 ft (33 m) wide and 1000 ft (303 m) long. The locks took four years to build and required 2 million cubic yards (1.5 million cu m) of concrete.
OSTA
CA
Limón
ago
40
4
Colón
PANAMA
PANAMA CITY
Gulf
of
Darien
David
Penonomé
Panama
Canal
Isla del
Rey
COLOMBIA
Santiago
Chitré
Golfo
de
Chiriquí
Las Tablas
Golfo
de
Panamá
5
40
80°
75°
E
F
G
H

The Caribbean

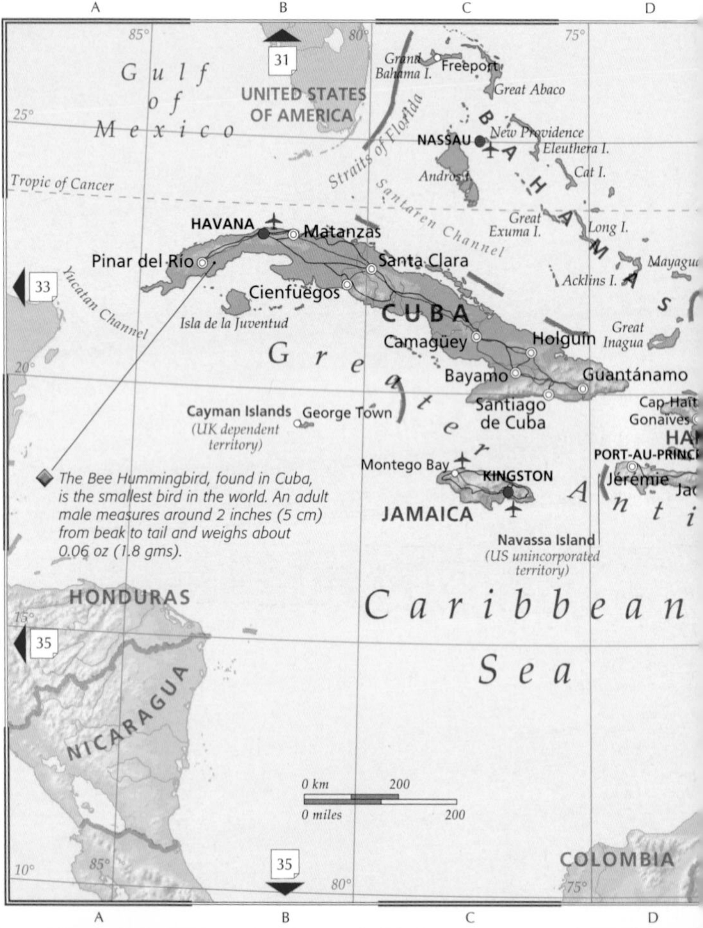

A
B
C
D
1
2
3
4
5
85°
80°
75°
25°
20°
15°
10°
31
33
35
Gulf of Mexico
UNITED STATES OF AMERICA
Grand Bahama I.
Freeport
Great Abaco
Straits of Florida
NASSAU
New Providence
Eleuthera I.
Andros I.
Cat I.
BAHAMAS
Tropic of Cancer
Santaren Channel
Great Exuma I.
Long I.
HAVANA
Matanzas
Pinar del Río
Santa Clara
Acklins I.
Mayaguana
Cienfuegos
Yucatan Channel
CUBA
Isla de la Juventud
Great Inagua
Camagüey
Holguín
Greater Antilles
Bayamo
Guantánamo
Cayman Islands
(UK dependent territory)
George Town
Santiago de Cuba
Gonaïves
Montego Bay
KINGSTON
PORT-AU-PRINCE
Jérémie
The Bee Hummingbird, found in Cuba, is the smallest bird in the world. An adult male measures around 2 inches (5 cm) from beak to tail and weighs about 0.06 oz (1.8 gms).
JAMAICA
Navassa Island
(US unincorporated territory)
HONDURAS
Caribbean Sea
NICARAGUA
0 km
200
0 miles
200
COLOMBIA

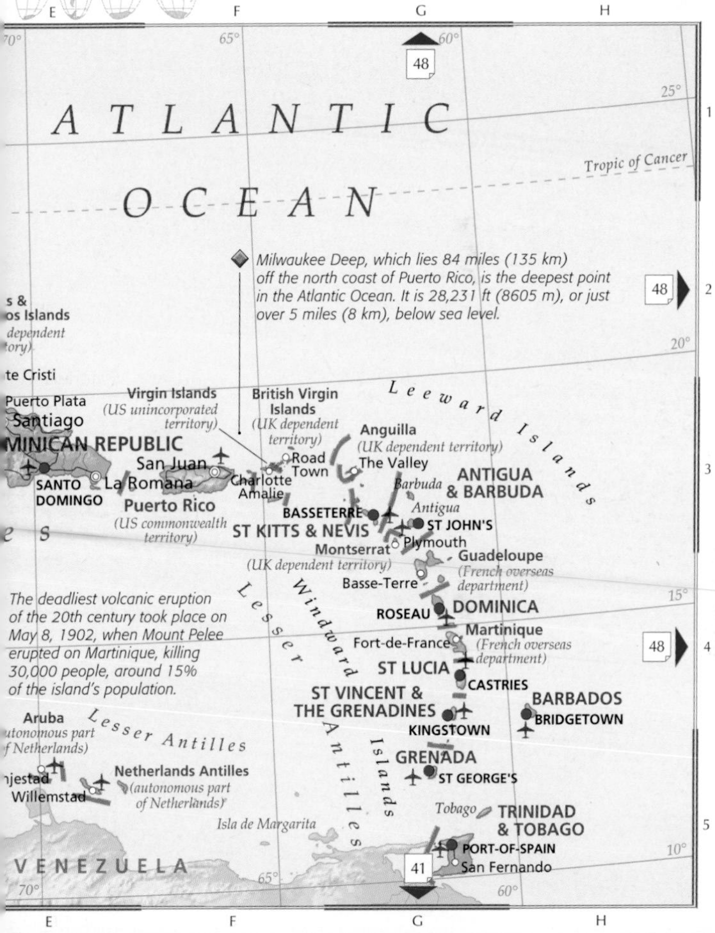
E
F
G
H
70°
65°
60°
25°
20°
15°
10°
1
2
3
4
5
48
41
A T L A N T I C
O C E A N
Tropic of Cancer
Milwaukee Deep, which lies 84 miles (135 km) off the north coast of Puerto Rico, is the deepest point in the Atlantic Ocean. It is 28,231 ft (8605 m), or just over 5 miles (8 km), below sea level.
s &
os Islands
dependent
tory)
te Cristi
Puerto Plata
Santiago
MINICAN REPUBLIC
SANTO DOMINGO
La Romana
San Juan
Puerto Rico
(US commonwealth territory)
Virgin Islands
(US unincorporated territory)
British Virgin Islands
(UK dependent territory)
Road Town
Charlotte Amalie
Anguilla
(UK dependent territory)
The Valley
Leeward Islands
ANTIGUA & BARBUDA
Barbuda
Antigua
ST JOHN'S
BASSETERRE
ST KITTS & NEVIS
Plymouth
Montserrat
(UK dependent territory)
Guadeloupe
(French overseas department)
Basse-Terre
ROSEAU
DOMINICA
Martinique
(French overseas department)
Fort-de-France
ST LUCIA
CASTRIES
ST VINCENT & THE GRENADINES
KINGSTOWN
BARBADOS
BRIDGETOWN
GRENADA
ST GEORGE'S
Tobago
TRINIDAD & TOBAGO
PORT-OF-SPAIN
San Fernando
Lesser Antilles
Windward Islands
The deadliest volcanic eruption of the 20th century took place on May 8, 1902, when Mount Pelee erupted on Martinique, killing 30,000 people, around 15% of the island's population.
Aruba
utonomous part
f Netherlands)
Lesser Antilles
njestad
Willemstad
Netherlands Antilles
(autonomous part of Netherlands)
Isla de Margarita
VENEZUELA

South America

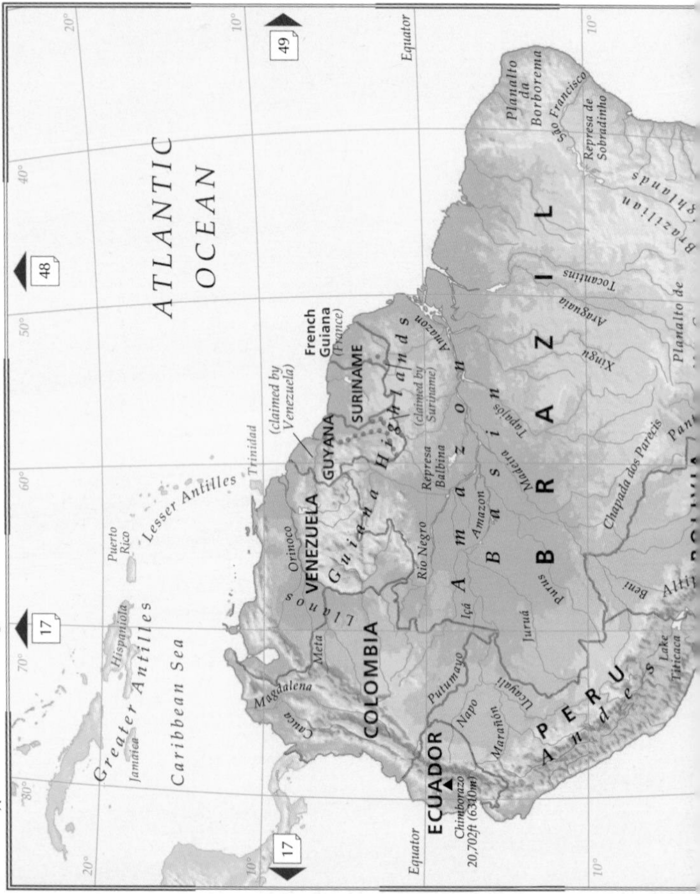
ATLANTIC OCEAN
Caribbean Sea
Greater Antilles
Lesser Antilles
Jamaica
Hispaniola
Puerto Rico
Trinidad
VENEZUELA
COLOMBIA
GUYANA
SURINAME
French Guiana (France)
(claimed by Venezuela)
(claimed by Suriname)
ECUADOR
PERU
BRAZIL
BOLIVIA
Guiana Highlands
Llanos
Amazon Basin
Andes
Brazilian Highlands
Planalto da Borborema
Planalto de
Chapada dos Parecis
Altiplano
Chimborazo 20,702ft (6310m)
Lake Titicaca
Represa Balbina
Represa de Sobradinho
Orinoco
Magdalena
Cauca
Meta
Putumayo
Napo
Marañón
Ucayali
Içá
Juruá
Purus
Rio Negro
Amazon
Madeira
Tapajós
Xingu
Araguaia
Tocantins
São Francisco
Beni
Equator
17
48
49

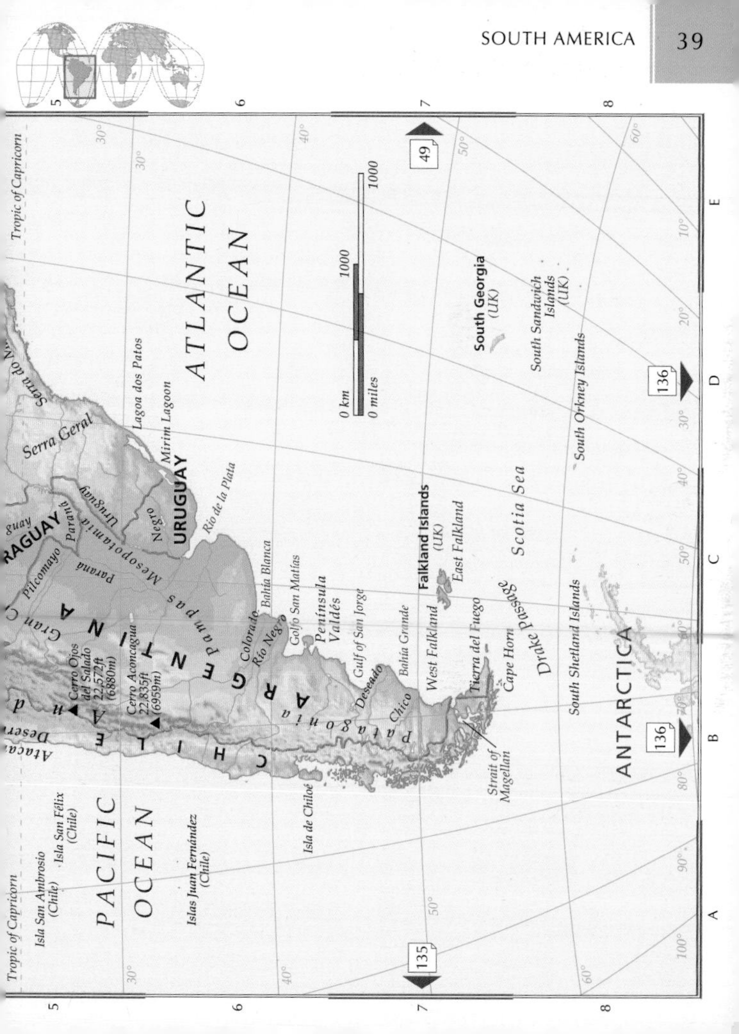
Tropic of Capricorn
ATLANTIC
OCEAN
PACIFIC
OCEAN
Serra Geral
Lagoa dos Patos
Mirim Lagoon
URUGUAY
Negro
Uruguay
Paraná
Mesopotamia
Pilcomayo
Río de la Plata
Pampas
Cerro Ojos del Salado 22,572ft (6880m)
Cerro Aconcagua 22,835ft (6959m)
ARGENTINA
CHILE
Colorado
Río Negro
Bahía Blanca
Golfo San Matías
Península Valdés
Gulf of San Jorge
Deseado
Bahía Grande
Chico
Patagonia
Isla de Chiloé
Strait of Magellan
Tierra del Fuego
Cape Horn
Drake Passage
West Falkland
East Falkland
Falkland Islands (UK)
Scotia Sea
South Georgia (UK)
South Sandwich Islands (UK)
South Orkney Islands
South Shetland Islands
ANTARCTICA
Isla San Ambrosio (Chile)
Isla San Félix (Chile)
Islas Juan Fernández (Chile)
0 km
1000
0 miles
1000
49
135
136
136

Northern South America

Caribbean Sea
PANAMA
PACIFIC OCEAN
COLOMBIA
ECUADOR
PERU
VEN
Andes
Gulf of Venezuela
Lago de Maracaibo
Golfo de Guayaquil
0° Equator
Santa Marta
Ríohacha
Maicao
Coro
CARAC
Barranquilla
Cartagena
Valledupar
Maracaibo
Cabimas
Maracay
Ciudad Ojeda
Barquisimeto
Valencia
Sincelejo
Montería
Valera
Acarigua
Mérida
Guanare
San Jua
de los Morr
Cúcuta
San Cristóbal
Barinas
San Fernand
Bucaramanga
Barrancaberneja
Arauca
Bello
Medellín
Itagüí
Quibdó
Tunja
Yopal
Puerto Carreño
Manizales
Pereira
Armenia
BOGOTÁ
Ibagué
Buenaventura
Villavicencio
Cali
Popayán
Neiva
San José
del Guaviare
Florencia
Pasto
Mocoa
Esmeraldas
Tulcán
Ibarra
QUITO
Mitú
Santo Domingo
de los Colorados
Manta
Ambato
Portoviejo
Riobamba
Guayaquil
Milagro
Cuenca
Machala
Loja
Cauca
Magdalena
Guanare
Arauca
Apure
Meta
Guaviare
Aguarico
Caquetá
Putumayo
Nestling between snow capped peaks, at 9350 ft (2850 m) Quito is the second highest capital in the world.
The first cof
seedlings we
brought to
Colombia in
1804 by Jes
missionaries
today, Color
produces ov
700,000 tor
(tonnes) of
coffee bean
every year.
36
35
135
42
A
B
C
D
1
2
3
4
5
80°
75°
70°
10°
5°

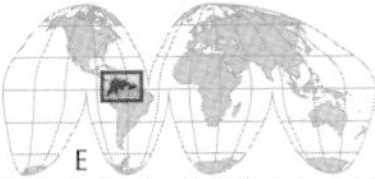

E
F
G
H
1
2
3
4
5
65°
60°
55°
10°
5°
0°
37
49
43
43
ntilles
GRENADA
Isla de Margarita
Carúpano
Cumaná
TRINIDAD & TOBAGO
ATLANTIC OCEAN
Barcelona
Maturín
Tucupita
The Serpent's Mouth
El Tigre
Orinoco
Ciudad Guayana
udad Bolívar
Embalse de Guri
UELA
The Guiana Shield is one of the Earth's oldest surfaces, formed around 2 billion years ago.
(claimed by Venezuela)
Cuyuni
GEORGETOWN
New Amsterdam
Nieuw Amsterdam
St.-Laurent-du-Maroni
Bartica
Rockstone
Linden
PARAMARIBO
Sinnamary
Kourou
Salto Ángel
Caura
Caroní
Paragua
GUYANA
W.J. van Blommesteinmeer
CAYENNE
Guiana Highlands
SURINAME
French Guiana
(French overseas department)
Essequibo
Courantyne
Marowijne
Acarai Mts.
(claimed by Suriname)
Angel Falls (Salto Ángel) plunge a total of 3212 ft (979 m) to form the world's highest waterfall.
(claimed by Suriname)
The European Space Agency launch facility at Kourou takes advantage of the Earth's spin near the equator to gain 10 percent more payload than an equivalent launch at Cape Canaveral in the US.
Equator
Amazon Basin
BRAZIL
2.47 acres (one hectare) of Amazon rain forest can contain more than 750 types of trees and 1500 plant species, amounting to around 900 tons (tonnes) of living plant material.
0 km 200
0 miles 200

Peru, Bolivia & North Brazil

A
B
C
D
1
2
3
4
5
80°
70°
60°
40
135
135
46
0 km
400
0 miles
400
VENEZUELA
COLOMBIA
Guiana Highlands
Boa Vista
Rio Negro
Equator
ECUADOR
Putumayo
Napo
Amazon
Manaus
Iquitos
Juruá
Madeira
Marañón
Moyobamba
Amazon Basin
Piura
Tarapoto
Ucayali
PERU
Andes
Chiclayo
BRA
Purus
Saña
Trujillo
Pucallpa
Porto Velho
Chimbote
Huaraz
Rio Branco
Huánuco
Madre de Dios
Riberalta
Huacho
La Oroya
Puerto Maldonado
Guaporé
Callao
LIMA
Huancayo
Beni
PACIFIC OCEAN
Ayacucho
Pisco
Cusco
Trinidad
Ica
Nazca
Puno
BOLIVIA
LA PAZ
Arequipa
Lake Titicaca
Cochabamba
Montero
Santa Cruz
Tacna
Oruro
Lago Poopó
SUCRE
Puerto Su
Potosí
Uyuni
Tupiza
Tarija
CHILE
PARAGUAY
ARGENTINA
10°
20°

Lake Titicaca is the largest lake in South America at 3220 sq miles (8340 sq km). With an altitude of 12,500 ft (3810 m) it is also the world's highest navigable lake.

BOLIVIA'S TWO CAPITALS	
La Paz -	legislative and administrative capital
Sucre -	legal capital

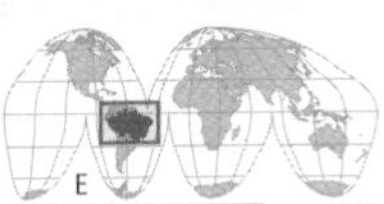

E
F
G
H
1
2
3
4
5
50°
40°
10°
20°
30°
48
49
49
44
SURINAME
French Guiana
(French overseas department)
The Amazon River is 4049 miles (6516 km) long, with an average flow of 7.7 million cubic feet (219,000 cu m) of water entering the Atlantic Ocean every second.
Macapá
Ilha Caviana de Fora
ATLANTIC
OCEAN
Equator
Ilha de Marajó
Belém
Amazon
Santarém
São Luís
Paranaíba
San Fernando de Noronha (part of Brazil)
Fortaleza
Represa de Tucuruí
Xingu
Imperatriz
Teresina
Mossoró
Natal
Carolina
Z I L
Campina Grande
João Pessoa
Juàzeiro do Norte
Recife
Tocantins
Araguaia
Pires
São Francisco
Represa de Sobradinho
Juàzeiro
Maceió
Aracaju
Taguatinga
Feira de Santana
ato Grosso
Salvador
Brazilian Highlands
Cuiabá
Itabuna
Anápolis
BRASÍLIA
Vitória da Conquista
Goiânia
Montes Claros
Governador Valadares
Uberlândia
Uberaba
Belo Horizonte
Divinópolis
mpo ande
Ribeirão Preto
Vitória
Paraná
Campos
Marília
Nova Iguaçu
Juiz de Fora
Campinas
Londrina
Sorocaba
Taubaté
Rio de Janeiro
São Paulo
Tropic of Capricorn

Paraguay, Uruguay & South Brazil

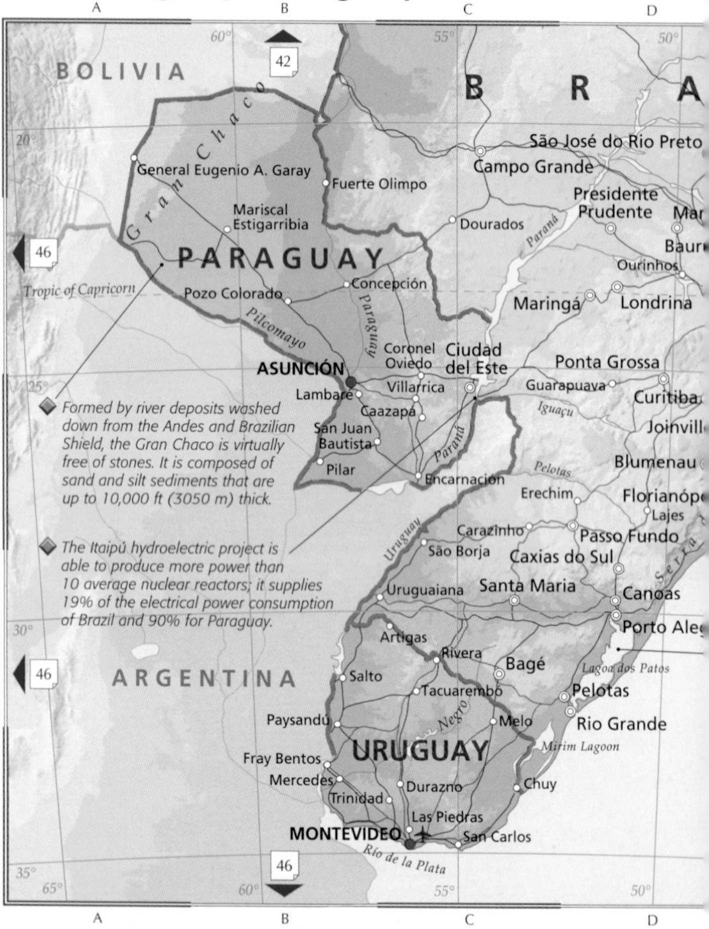
A
B
C
D
1
2
3
4
5
60°
55°
50°
20°
25°
30°
35°
65°
42
46
BOLIVIA
BRA
Gran Chaco
General Eugenio A. Garay
Fuerte Olimpo
Mariscal Estigarribia
PARAGUAY
Tropic of Capricorn
Pozo Colorado
Concepción
Pilcomayo
Paraguay
Coronel Oviedo
Ciudad del Este
ASUNCIÓN
Lambaré
Villarrica
Caazapá
San Juan Bautista
Pilar
Paraná
Encarnación
São José do Rio Preto
Campo Grande
Presidente Prudente
Dourados
Paraná
Ourinhos
Maringá
Londrina
Ponta Grossa
Guarapuava
Curitiba
Iguaçu
Joinvill
Blumenau
Pelotas
Erechim
Florianóp
Lajes
Carazinho
Passo Fundo
São Borja
Caxias do Sul
Uruguay
Serra
Uruguaiana
Santa Maria
Canoas
Porto Ale
Artigas
Rivera
Bagé
Lagoa dos Patos
Salto
Pelotas
Tacuarembó
Rio Grande
Paysandú
Negro
Melo
Mirim Lagoon
URUGUAY
Fray Bentos
Mercedes
Chuy
Durazno
Trinidad
Las Piedras
MONTEVIDEO
San Carlos
Río de la Plata
ARGENTINA
Formed by river deposits washed down from the Andes and Brazilian Shield, the Gran Chaco is virtually free of stones. It is composed of sand and silt sediments that are up to 10,000 ft (3050 m) thick.
The Itaipú hydroelectric project is able to produce more power than 10 average nuclear reactors; it supplies 19% of the electrical power consumption of Brazil and 90% for Paraguay.

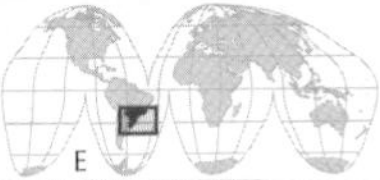

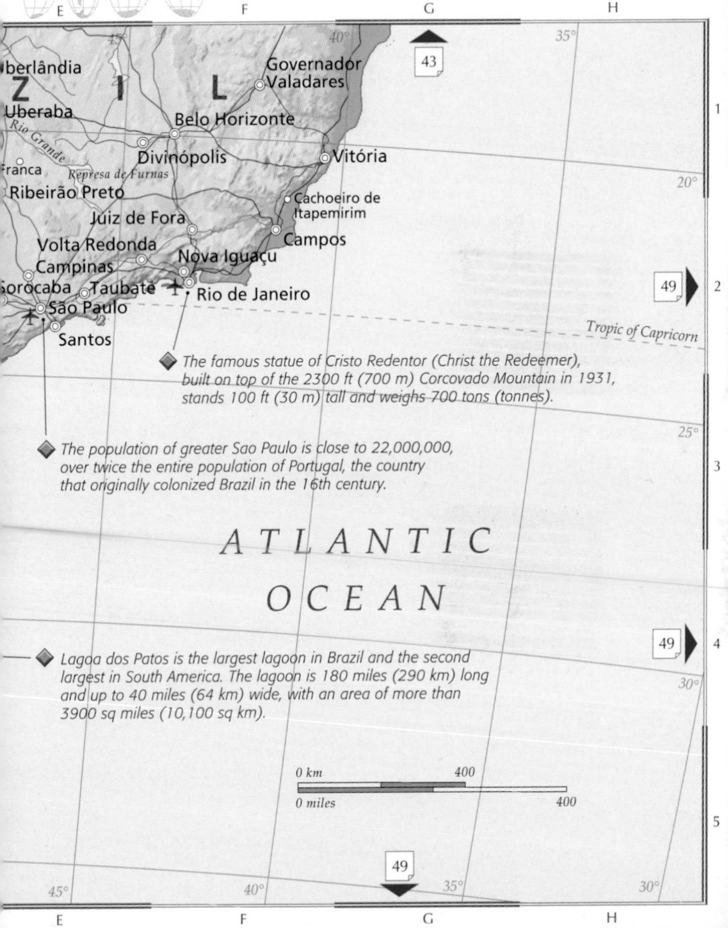
E
F
G
H
43
49
49
49
1
2
3
4
5
45°
40°
35°
30°
20°
25°
30°
berlândia
Z I L
Governador Valadares
Uberaba
Rio Grande
Belo Horizonte
Divinópolis
Vitória
Franca
Represa de Furnas
Ribeirão Preto
Cachoeiro de Itapemirim
Juiz de Fora
Campos
Volta Redonda
Nova Iguaçu
Campinas
Sorocaba
Taubaté
Rio de Janeiro
São Paulo
Santos
Tropic of Capricorn
The famous statue of Cristo Redentor (Christ the Redeemer), built on top of the 2300 ft (700 m) Corcovado Mountain in 1931, stands 100 ft (30 m) tall and weighs 700 tons (tonnes).
The population of greater Sao Paulo is close to 22,000,000, over twice the entire population of Portugal, the country that originally colonized Brazil in the 16th century.
ATLANTIC OCEAN
Lagoa dos Patos is the largest lagoon in Brazil and the second largest in South America. The lagoon is 180 miles (290 km) long and up to 40 miles (64 km) wide, with an area of more than 3900 sq miles (10,100 sq km).
0 km
400
0 miles
400

Southern South America

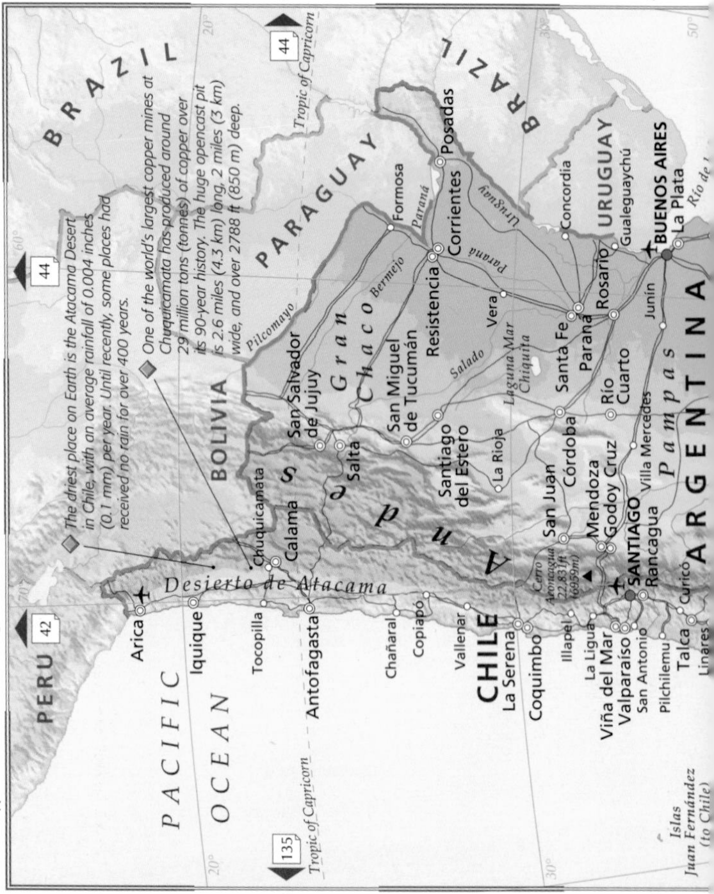

The driest place on Earth is the Atacama Desert in Chile, with an average rainfall of 0.004 inches (0.1 mm) per year. Until recently, some places had received no rain for over 400 years.
One of the world's largest copper mines at Chuquicamata has produced around 29 million tons (tonnes) of copper over its 90-year history. The huge opencast pit is 2.6 miles (4.3 km) long, 2 miles (3 km) wide, and over 2788 ft (850 m) deep.
BRAZIL
PERU
BOLIVIA
PARAGUAY
URUGUAY
CHILE
ARGENTINA
PACIFIC OCEAN
Tropic of Capricorn
Desierto de Atacama
Andes
Gran Chaco
Pampas
Arica
Iquique
Tocopilla
Antofagasta
Chañaral
Copiapó
Vallenar
La Serena
Coquimbo
Illapel
La Ligua
Viña del Mar
Valparaíso
San Antonio
Pilchilemu
Talca
Linares
Curicó
Rancagua
SANTIAGO
Chuquicamata
Calama
San Salvador de Jujuy
Salta
San Miguel de Tucumán
Santiago del Estero
La Rioja
San Juan
Mendoza
Godoy Cruz
Córdoba
Río Cuarto
Villa Mercedes
Santa Fe
Paraná
Rosario
Junín
BUENOS AIRES
La Plata
Gualeguaychú
Concordia
Corrientes
Resistencia
Formosa
Posadas
Vera
Laguna Mar Chiquita
Salado
Bermejo
Pilcomayo
Paraná
Uruguay
Río de
Cerro Aconcagua 22,831ft (6959m)
Islas Juan Fernández (to Chile)
42
44
44
135

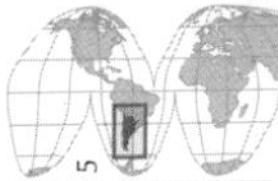

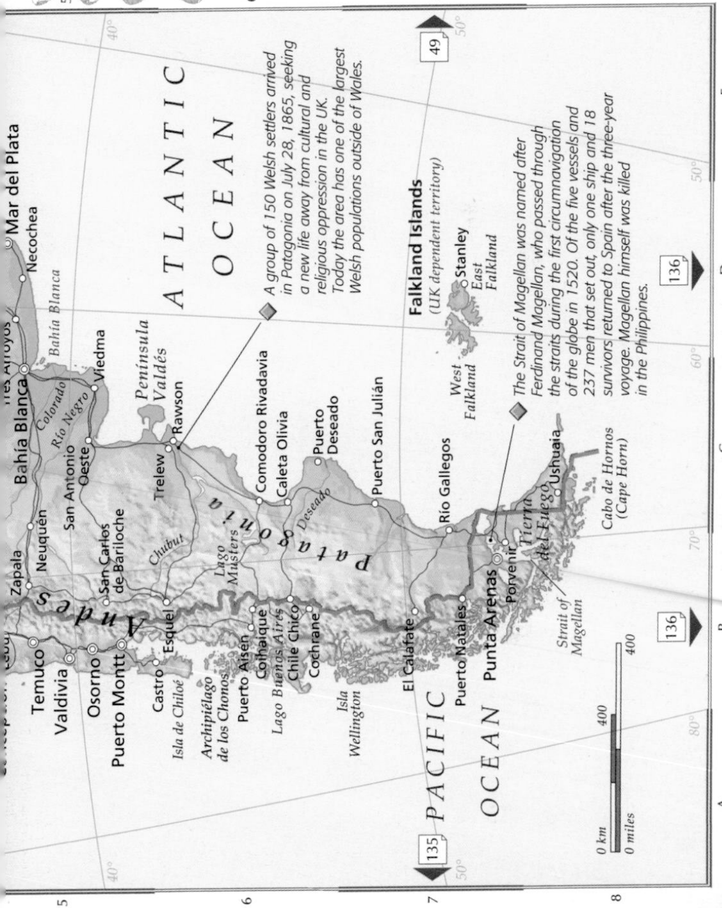

ATLANTIC OCEAN
PACIFIC OCEAN
Mar del Plata
Necochea
Bahía Blanca
Bahía Blanca
Viedma
Colorado
Río Negro
San Antonio Oeste
Península Valdés
Rawson
Trelew
Neuquén
Zapala
Temuco
Valdivia
Osorno
Puerto Montt
San Carlos de Bariloche
Andes
Chubut
Esquel
Castro
Isla de Chiloé
Archipiélago de los Chonos
Puerto Aisén
Coihaique
Lago Musters
Patagonia
Comodoro Rivadavia
Caleta Olivia
Puerto Deseado
Deseado
Lago Buenos Aires
Chile Chico
Cochrane
Isla Wellington
Puerto San Julián
El Calafate
Río Gallegos
Puerto Natales
Punta Arenas
Porvenir
Tierra del Fuego
Strait of Magellan
Ushuaia
Cabo de Hornos (Cape Horn)
Falkland Islands
(UK dependent territory)
Stanley
East Falkland
West Falkland
A group of 150 Welsh settlers arrived in Patagonia on July 28, 1865, seeking a new life away from cultural and religious oppression in the UK. Today the area has one of the largest Welsh populations outside of Wales.
The Strait of Magellan was named after Ferdinand Magellan, who passed through the straits during the first circumnavigation of the globe in 1520. Of the five vessels and 237 men that set out, only one ship and 18 survivors returned to Spain after the three-year voyage. Magellan himself was killed in the Philippines.
0 km 400
0 miles 400
135
136
136
49

The Atlantic Ocean

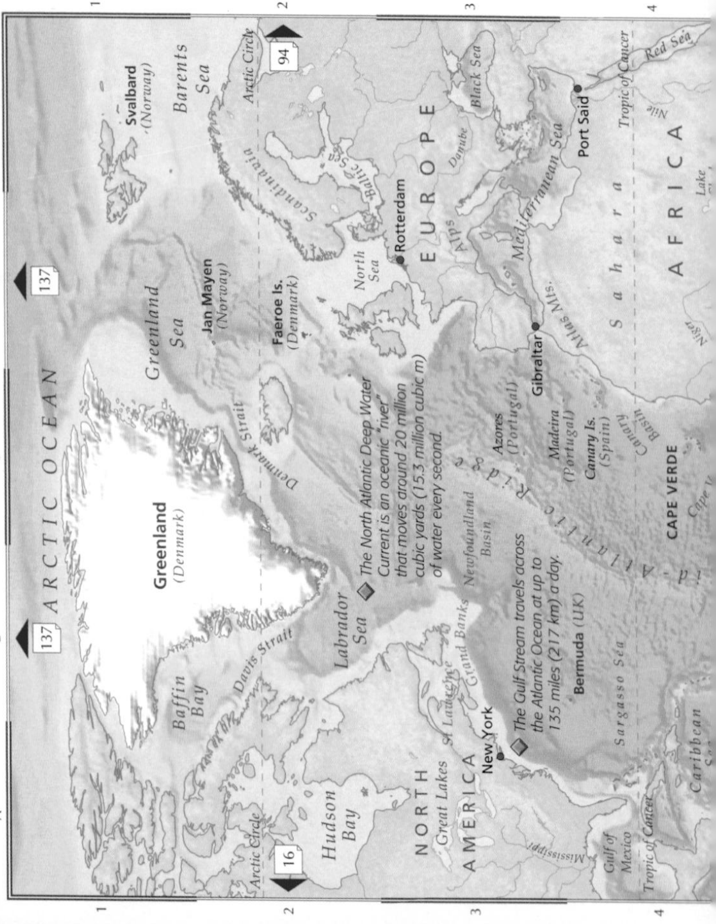
ARCTIC OCEAN
Greenland (Denmark)
Baffin Bay
Davis Strait
Labrador Sea
Hudson Bay
Arctic Circle
NORTH AMERICA
Great Lakes
St Lawrence
New York
Grand Banks
Newfoundland Basin
Mississippi
Gulf of Mexico
Tropic of Cancer
Sargasso Sea
Bermuda (UK)
Caribbean
Greenland Sea
Jan Mayen (Norway)
Svalbard (Norway)
Barents Sea
Faeroe Is. (Denmark)
Denmark Strait
Scandinavia
Baltic Sea
North Sea
Rotterdam
EUROPE
Alps
Danube
Black Sea
Mediterranean Sea
Port Said
Red Sea
Nile
Gibraltar
Atlas Mts.
Sahara
AFRICA
Niger
Azores (Portugal)
Madeira (Portugal)
Canary Is. (Spain)
Canary Basin
CAPE VERDE
Atlantic Ridge
The North Atlantic Deep Water Current is an oceanic "river" that moves around 20 million cubic yards (15.3 million cubic m) of water every second.
The Gulf Stream travels across the Atlantic Ocean at up to 135 miles (217 km) a day.
137
137
94
16
A
B
C
D
E
1
2
3
4

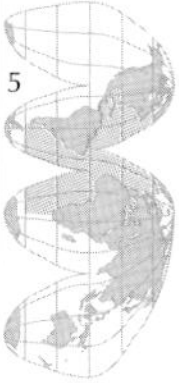

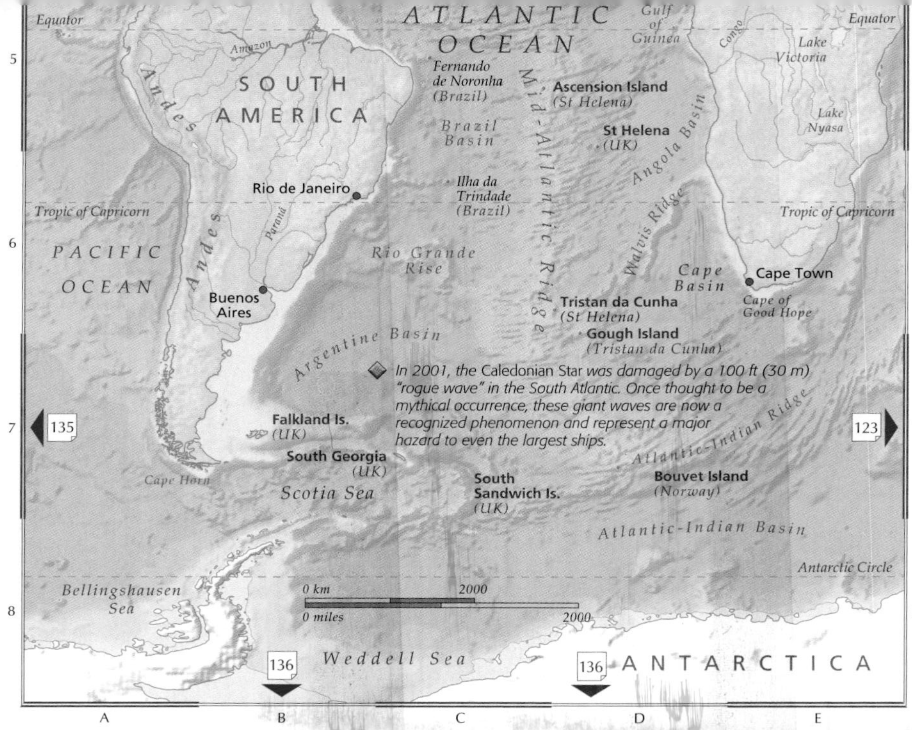
ATLANTIC OCEAN
Gulf of Guinea
Equator
Amazon
Andes
SOUTH AMERICA
Fernando de Noronha (Brazil)
Mid-Atlantic Ridge
Ascension Island (St Helena)
Brazil Basin
St Helena (UK)
Angola Basin
Congo
Lake Victoria
Lake Nyasa
Rio de Janeiro
Ilha da Trindade (Brazil)
Walvis Ridge
Tropic of Capricorn
Paraná
PACIFIC OCEAN
Rio Grande Rise
Cape Basin
Cape Town
Cape of Good Hope
Buenos Aires
Tristan da Cunha (St Helena)
Gough Island (Tristan da Cunha)
Argentine Basin
In 2001, the Caledonian Star was damaged by a 100 ft (30 m) "rogue wave" in the South Atlantic. Once thought to be a mythical occurrence, these giant waves are now a recognized phenomenon and represent a major hazard to even the largest ships.
Atlantic-Indian Ridge
Falkland Is. (UK)
South Georgia (UK)
Cape Horn
Scotia Sea
South Sandwich Is. (UK)
Bouvet Island (Norway)
Atlantic-Indian Basin
Antarctic Circle
Bellingshausen Sea
0 km 2000
0 miles 2000
Weddell Sea
ANTARCTICA
135
123
136
136
5
6
7
8
A
B
C
D
E

Africa

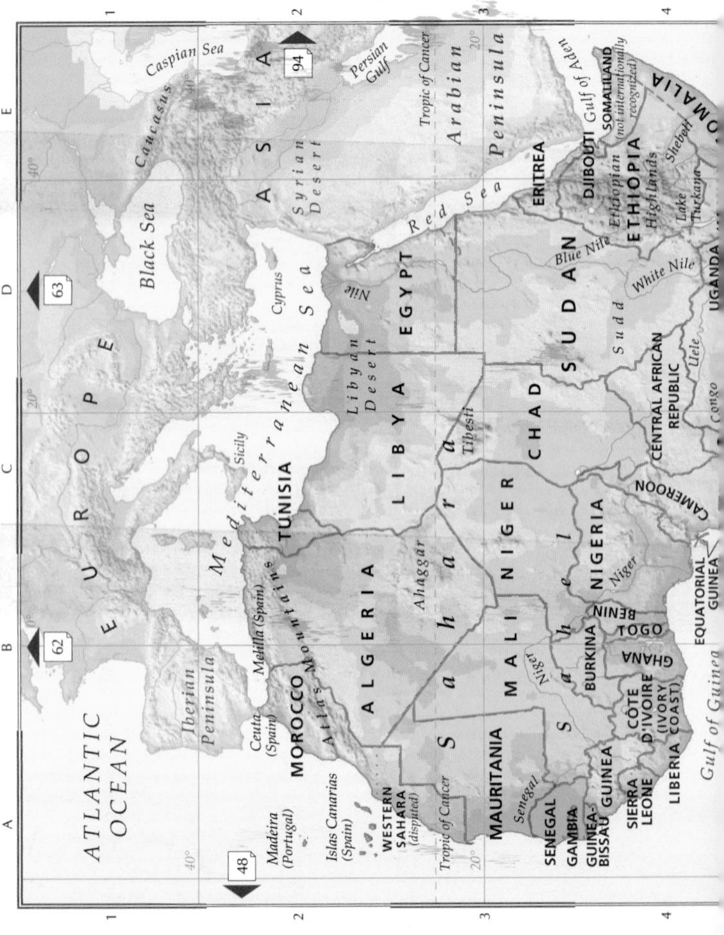

ATLANTIC OCEAN
E U R O P E
A S I A
Caspian Sea
Caucasus
Black Sea
Persian Gulf
Syrian Desert
Arabian Peninsula
Tropic of Cancer
Red Sea
Gulf of Aden
Iberian Peninsula
Mediterranean Sea
Sicily
Cyprus
Madeira (Portugal)
Islas Canarias (Spain)
Ceuta (Spain)
Melilla (Spain)
Atlas Mountains
MOROCCO
ALGERIA
TUNISIA
LIBYA
EGYPT
Libyan Desert
Nile
Ahaggar
Tibesti
Sahara
Sahel
WESTERN SAHARA (disputed)
MAURITANIA
MALI
NIGER
CHAD
SUDAN
ERITREA
DJIBOUTI
SOMALILAND (not internationally recognized)
SOMALIA
ETHIOPIA
Ethiopian Highlands
Blue Nile
White Nile
Sudd
Lake Turkana
Shebeli
UGANDA
CENTRAL AFRICAN REPUBLIC
Uele
Congo
CAMEROON
NIGERIA
Niger
BENIN
TOGO
GHANA
BURKINA
CÔTE D'IVOIRE (IVORY COAST)
LIBERIA
SIERRA LEONE
GUINEA
GUINEA-BISSAU
GAMBIA
SENEGAL
Senegal
EQUATORIAL GUINEA
Gulf of Guinea
62
63
94
48

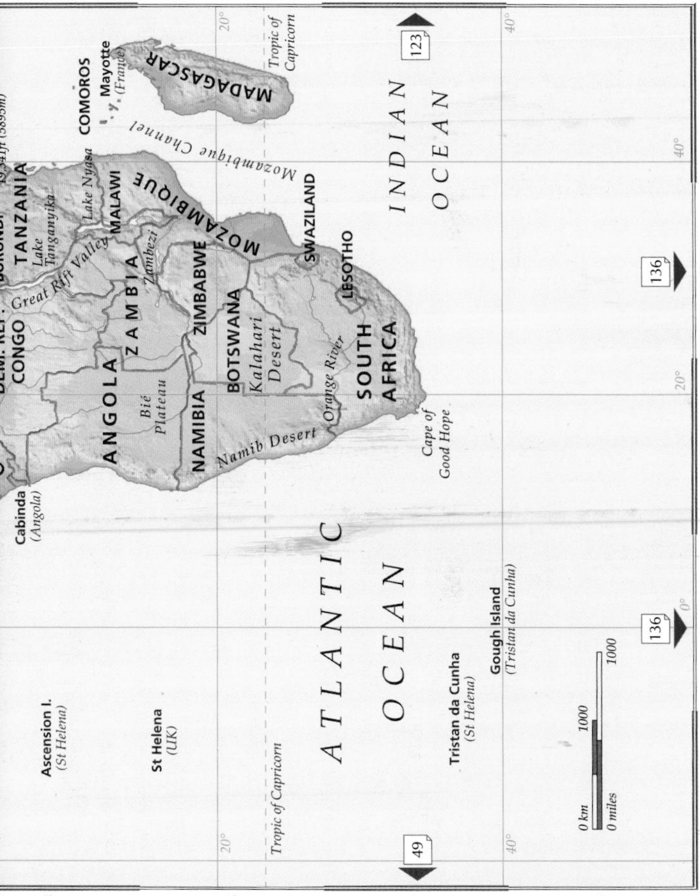
DEM. REP. CONGO
BURUNDI
TANZANIA
19,341ft (5895m)
Lake Tanganyika
Lake Nyasa
MALAWI
Great Rift Valley
ANGOLA
ZAMBIA
Zambezi
Bié Plateau
COMOROS
Mayotte (France)
MADAGASCAR
Mozambique Channel
MOZAMBIQUE
ZIMBABWE
NAMIBIA
BOTSWANA
Kalahari Desert
SWAZILAND
LESOTHO
Namib Desert
Orange River
SOUTH AFRICA
Cape of Good Hope
Cabinda (Angola)
Ascension I. (St Helena)
St Helena (UK)
Tristan da Cunha (St Helena)
Gough Island (Tristan da Cunha)
Tropic of Capricorn
ATLANTIC OCEAN
INDIAN OCEAN
0 km
1000
0 miles
1000
49
123
136
136
20°
40°
0°
A
B
C
D
E
5
6
7
8

Northwest Africa

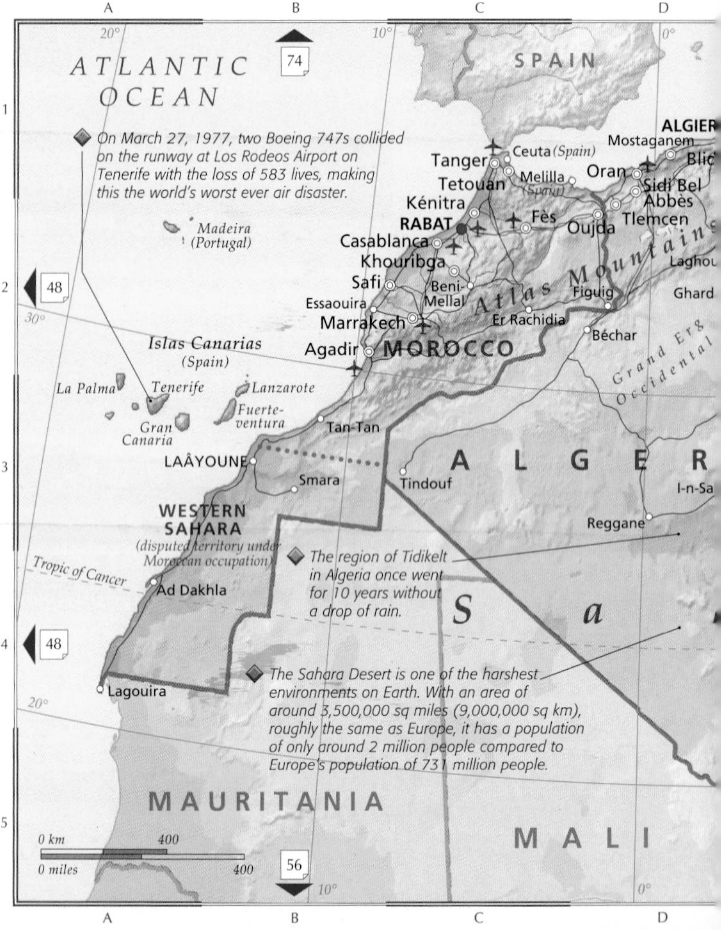
ATLANTIC OCEAN
On March 27, 1977, two Boeing 747s collided on the runway at Los Rodeos Airport on Tenerife with the loss of 583 lives, making this the world's worst ever air disaster.
Madeira (Portugal)
Islas Canarias (Spain)
La Palma
Tenerife
Lanzarote
Fuerteventura
Gran Canaria
SPAIN
ALGIERS
Mostaganem
Blida
Ceuta (Spain)
Tanger
Tetouan
Melilla (Spain)
Oran
Sidi Bel Abbès
Kénitra
RABAT
Fès
Oujda
Tlemcen
Casablanca
Khouribga
Safi
Beni-Mellal
Essaouira
Marrakech
Agadir
Atlas Mountains
Figuig
Er Rachidia
Béchar
Laghouat
Ghardaïa
MOROCCO
Grand Erg Occidental
Tan-Tan
LAÂYOUNE
Smara
Tindouf
ALGERIA
I-n-Salah
Reggane
WESTERN SAHARA (disputed territory under Moroccan occupation)
Tropic of Cancer
Ad Dakhla
Lagouira
The region of Tidikelt in Algeria once went for 10 years without a drop of rain.
Sahara
The Sahara Desert is one of the harshest environments on Earth. With an area of around 3,500,000 sq miles (9,000,000 sq km), roughly the same as Europe, it has a population of only around 2 million people compared to Europe's population of 731 million people.
MAURITANIA
MALI
0 km 400
0 miles 400
74
48
48
56
20° 10° 0°
30° 20°
A B C D
1 2 3 4 5

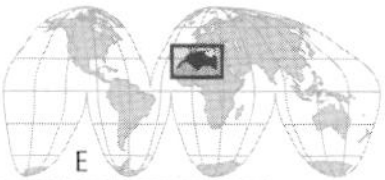

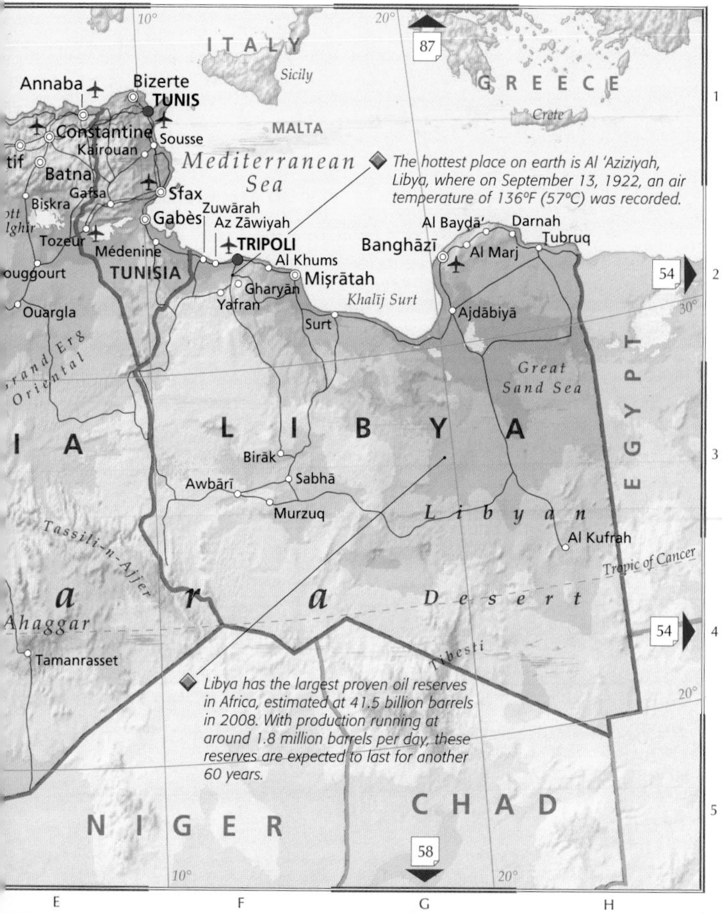
E
F
G
H
10°
20°
87
ITALY
Sicily
GREECE
Crete
MALTA
Annaba
Bizerte
TUNIS
Constantine
Sousse
Kairouan
Batna
Gafsa
Sfax
Biskra
Gabès
Zuwārah
Az Zāwiyah
Tozeur
Médenine
TRIPOLI
TUNISIA
Al Khums
Miṣrātah
Gharyān
Yafran
Ouargla
Mediterranean Sea
The hottest place on earth is Al 'Aziziyah, Libya, where on September 13, 1922, an air temperature of 136°F (57°C) was recorded.
Al Baydā'
Darnah
Tubruq
Banghāzī
Al Marj
54
Khalīj Surt
Surt
Ajdābiyā
30°
Great Sand Sea
Grand Erg Oriental
LIBYA
EGYPT
Birāk
Sabhā
Awbārī
Murzuq
Libyan Desert
Al Kufrah
Tropic of Cancer
Tassili-n-Ajjer
Ahaggar
Tamanrasset
Tibesti
54
Libya has the largest proven oil reserves in Africa, estimated at 41.5 billion barrels in 2008. With production running at around 1.8 million barrels per day, these reserves are expected to last for another 60 years.
20°
NIGER
CHAD
58
10°
20°
1
2
3
4
5

Northeast Africa

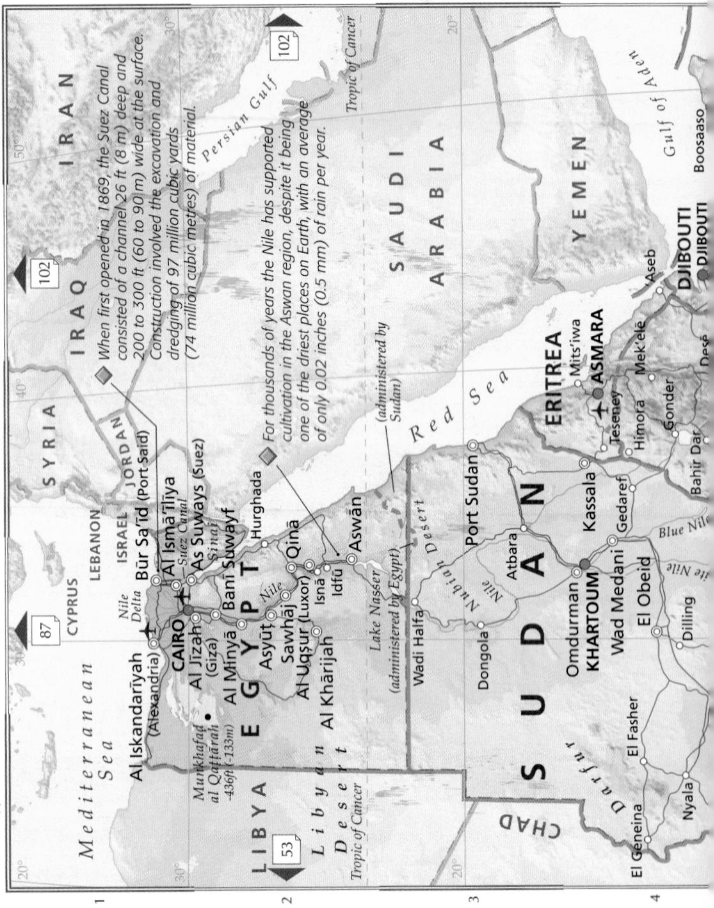

When first opened in 1869, the Suez Canal consisted of a channel 26 ft (8 m) deep and 200 to 300 ft (60 to 90 m) wide at the surface. Construction involved the excavation and dredging of 97 million cubic yards (74 million cubic metres) of material.
For thousands of years the Nile has supported cultivation in the Aswan region, despite it being one of the driest places on Earth, with an average of only 0.02 inches (0.5 mm) of rain per year.
Mediterranean Sea
CYPRUS
LEBANON
ISRAEL
SYRIA
JORDAN
IRAQ
IRAN
Persian Gulf
SAUDI ARABIA
YEMEN
Gulf of Aden
ERITREA
DJIBOUTI
LIBYA
EGYPT
SUDAN
CHAD
Red Sea
Libyan Desert
Nubian Desert
Darfur
Nile Delta
Sinai
Suez Canal
Nile
Blue Nile
Lake Nasser
(administered by Egypt)
(administered by Sudan)
Tropic of Cancer
Munkhafad al Qaţţārah -436ft (-133m)
Al Iskandarīyah (Alexandria)
CAIRO
Al Jīzah (Giza)
Bür Sa'īd (Port Said)
Al Ismā'īlīya
As Suways (Suez)
Banī Suwayf
Al Minyā
Asyūţ
Sawhāj
Qinā
Al Uqşur (Luxor)
Isnā
Idfū
Aswān
Hurghada
Al Khārijah
Wadi Halfa
Dongola
Atbara
Port Sudan
Kassala
Omdurman
KHARTOUM
Wad Medani
Gedaref
El Obeid
Dilling
El Fasher
Nyala
El Geneina
ASMARA
Mits'iwa
Teseney
Himora
Gonder
Bahir Dar
Mek'elē
Aseb
Boosaaso
87
102
53

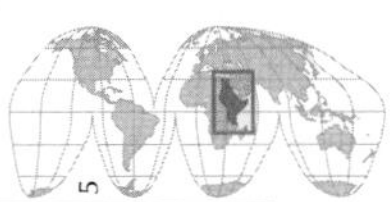

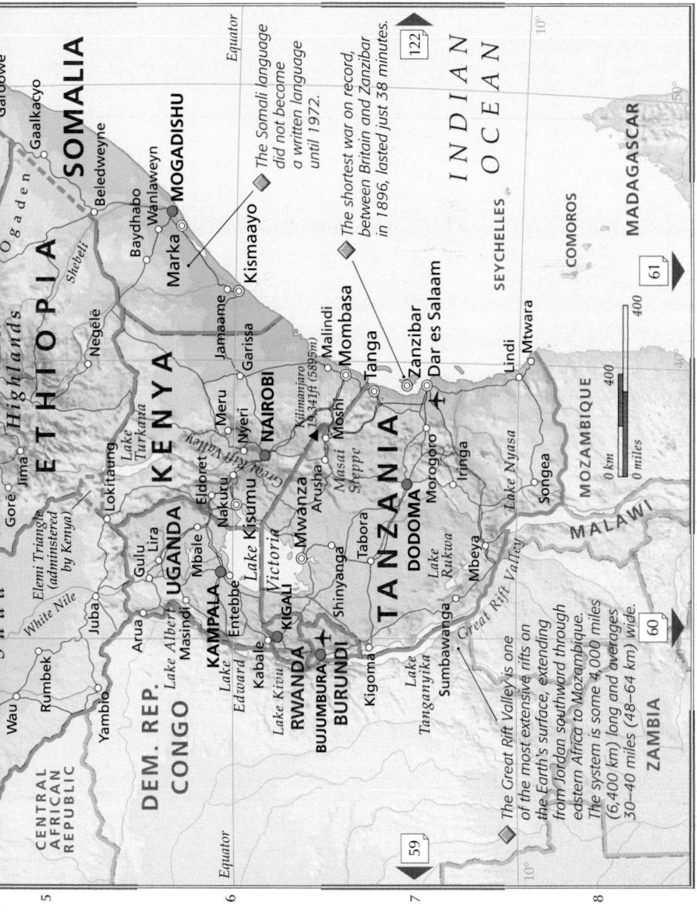
The Somali language did not become a written language until 1972.
The shortest war on record, between Britain and Zanzibar in 1896, lasted just 38 minutes.
The Great Rift Valley is one of the most extensive rifts on the Earth's surface, extending from Jordan southward through eastern Africa to Mozambique. The system is some 4,000 miles (6,400 km) long and averages 30–40 miles (48–64 km) wide.
CENTRAL AFRICAN REPUBLIC
DEM. REP. CONGO
ETHIOPIA
SOMALIA
KENYA
UGANDA
TANZANIA
RWANDA
BURUNDI
MOZAMBIQUE
MALAWI
ZAMBIA
MADAGASCAR
COMOROS
SEYCHELLES
INDIAN OCEAN
Ogaden
Highlands
Elemi Triangle (adminstered by Kenya)
MOGADISHU
NAIROBI
KAMPALA
KIGALI
BUJUMBURA
DODOMA
Garoowe
Gaalkacyo
Beledweyne
Wanlaweyn
Baydhabo
Marka
Kismaayo
Jamaame
Shebeli
Negēlē
Jīma
Gorē
Lokitaung
Lake Turkana
Meru
Nyeri
Garissa
Malindi
Mombasa
Tanga
Zanzibar
Dar es Salaam
Kilimanjaro 19,341ft (5895m)
Moshi
Arusha
Masai Steppe
Great Rift Valley
Eldoret
Nakuru
Kisumu
Lake Victoria
Mwanza
Shinyanga
Tabora
Morogoro
Iringa
Lake Nyasa
Songea
Lindi
Mtwara
Mbeya
Lake Rukwa
Sumbawanga
Lake Tanganyika
Kigoma
Lake Kivu
Lake Edward
Kabale
Lake Albert
Masindi
Entebbe
Mbale
Gulu
Lira
Arua
Juba
White Nile
Rumbek
Wau
Yambio
Equator
122
61
60
59
0 km 400
0 miles 400
A B C D E
5 6 7 8

West Africa

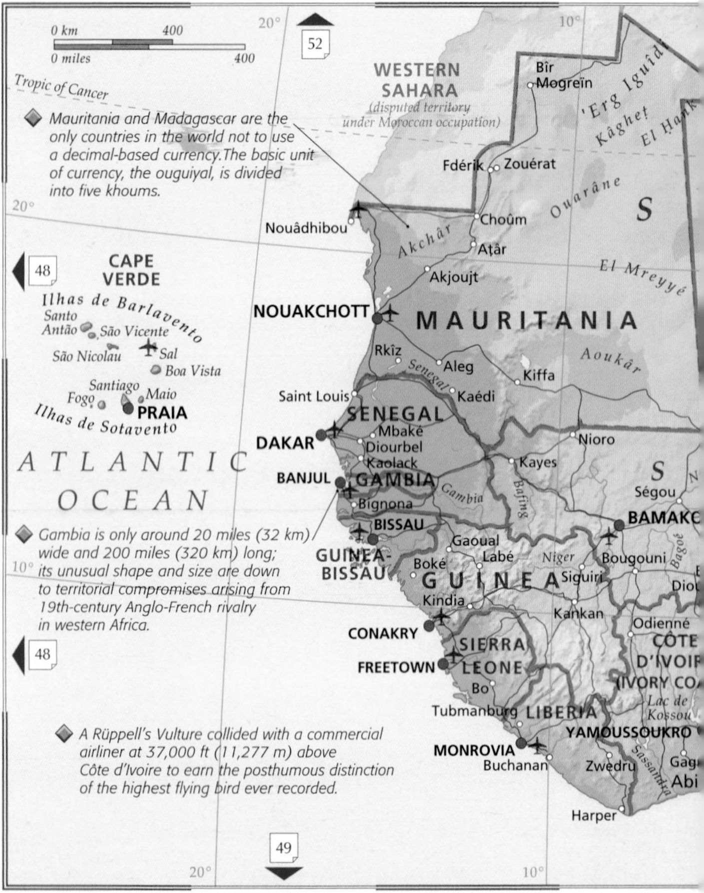
0 km 400
0 miles 400
Tropic of Cancer
52
48
48
49
WESTERN SAHARA
(disputed territory under Moroccan occupation)
Bîr Mogreïn
'Erg Iguîdi
Kâgheț
El Hank
Fdérik
Zouérat
Ouarâne
Choûm
Nouâdhibou
Akchâr
Ațâr
Akjoujt
El Mreyyé
CAPE VERDE
Ilhas de Barlavento
Santo Antão
São Vicente
São Nicolau
Sal
Boa Vista
Santiago
Maio
Fogo
PRAIA
Ilhas de Sotavento
NOUAKCHOTT
MAURITANIA
Rkîz
Senegal
Aleg
Kiffa
Aoukâr
Saint Louis
Kaédi
SENEGAL
DAKAR
Mbaké
Diourbel
Kaolack
Nioro
Kayes
ATLANTIC OCEAN
BANJUL
GAMBIA
Gambia
Bafing
Ségou
BAMAKO
Bignona
BISSAU
Gaoual
GUINEA-BISSAU
Labé
Niger
Bougouni
Boké
GUINEA
Siguiri
Kindia
Kankan
Odienné
CONAKRY
SIERRA LEONE
FREETOWN
Bo
Tubmanburg
LIBERIA
YAMOUSSOUKRO
MONROVIA
Buchanan
Zwedru
Sassandra
Harper
Lac de Kossou

◆ Mauritania and Madagascar are the only countries in the world not to use a decimal-based currency. The basic unit of currency, the ouguiyal, is divided into five khoums.

◆ Gambia is only around 20 miles (32 km) wide and 200 miles (320 km) long; its unusual shape and size are down to territorial compromises arising from 19th-century Anglo-French rivalry in western Africa.

◆ A Rüppell's Vulture collided with a commercial airliner at 37,000 ft (11,277 m) above Côte d'Ivoire to earn the posthumous distinction of the highest flying bird ever recorded.

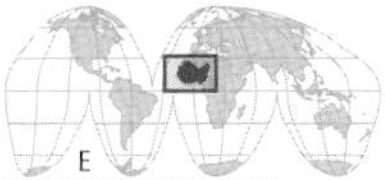

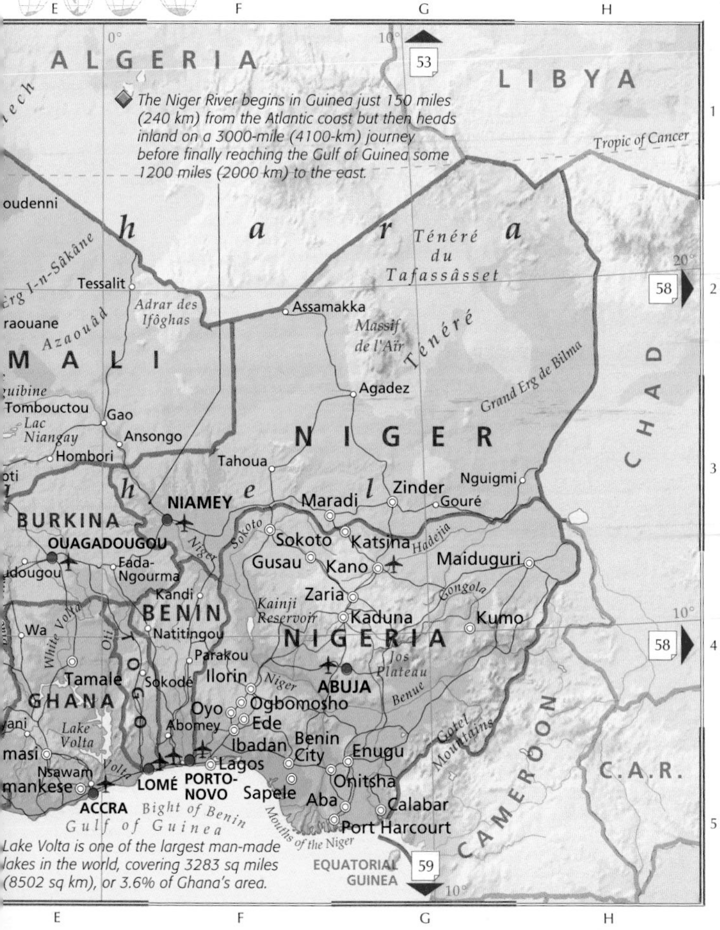
E
F
G
H
1
2
3
4
5
0°
10°
20°
ALGERIA
LIBYA
The Niger River begins in Guinea just 150 miles (240 km) from the Atlantic coast but then heads inland on a 3000-mile (4100-km) journey before finally reaching the Gulf of Guinea some 1200 miles (2000 km) to the east.
Tropic of Cancer
53
58
58
59
oudenni
h
a
r
a
Ténéré du Tafassâsset
Erg I-n-Sâkâne
Tessalit
Adrar des Ifôghas
Assamakka
raouane
Azaouâd
Massif de l'Aïr
Ténéré
MALI
Agadez
Grand Erg de Bilma
Tombouctou
Gao
Lac Niangay
Ansongo
NIGER
CHAD
Hombori
Tahoua
h
e
l
Zinder
Nguigmi
Maradi
Gouré
NIAMEY
BURKINA
Sokoto
Katsina
Hadejia
OUAGADOUGOU
Niger
Sokoto
Gusau
Kano
Maiduguri
Fada-Ngourma
Kandi
Zaria
Gongola
Kainji Reservoir
BENIN
Kaduna
Kumo
Wa
White Volta
Natitingou
NIGERIA
Oti
TOGO
Parakou
Jos Plateau
Tamale
Sokodé
Ilorin
Niger
ABUJA
GHANA
Ogbomosho
Benue
Oyo
Ede
Abomey
Lake Volta
Ibadan
Benin City
Gotel Mountains
CAMEROON
Enugu
Lagos
C.A.R.
Volta
Nsawam
LOMÉ
PORTO-NOVO
Onitsha
Sapele
ACCRA
Aba
Calabar
Bight of Benin
Mouths of the Niger
Gulf of Guinea
Port Harcourt
Lake Volta is one of the largest man-made lakes in the world, covering 3283 sq miles (8502 sq km), or 3.6% of Ghana's area.
EQUATORIAL GUINEA

Central Africa

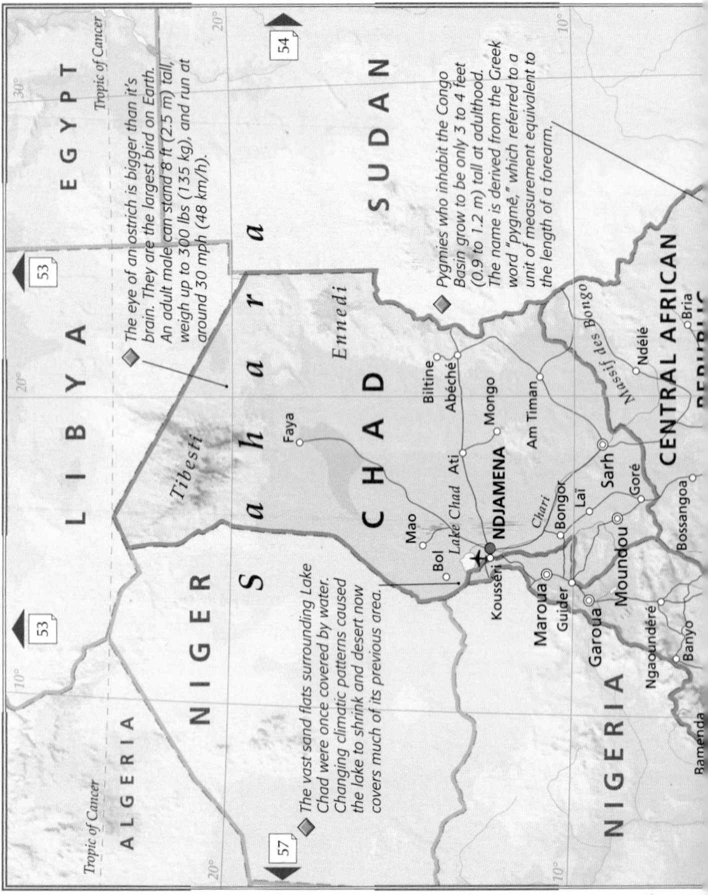

LIBYA
EGYPT
SUDAN
CHAD
NIGER
ALGERIA
NIGERIA
CENTRAL AFRICAN
Sahara
Tibesti
Ennedi
Tropic of Cancer
Massif des Bongo
Lake Chad
Chari
NDJAMENA
Faya
Mao
Bol
Ati
Biltine
Abéché
Mongo
Am Timan
Kousséri
Bongor
Laï
Sarh
Goré
Moundou
Maroua
Guider
Garoua
Ngaoundéré
Banyo
Bamenda
Bossangoa
Ndélé
Bria
53
54
57
The eye of an ostrich is bigger than it's brain. They are the largest bird on Earth. An adult male can stand 8 ft (2.5 m) tall, weigh up to 300 lbs (135 kg), and run at around 30 mph (48 km/h).
Pygmies who inhabit the Congo Basin grow to be only 3 to 4 feet (0.9 to 1.2 m) tall at adulthood. The name is derived from the Greek word "pygmē," which referred to a unit of measurement equivalent to the length of a forearm.
The vast sand flats surrounding Lake Chad were once covered by water. Changing climatic patterns caused the lake to shrink and desert now covers much of its previous area.

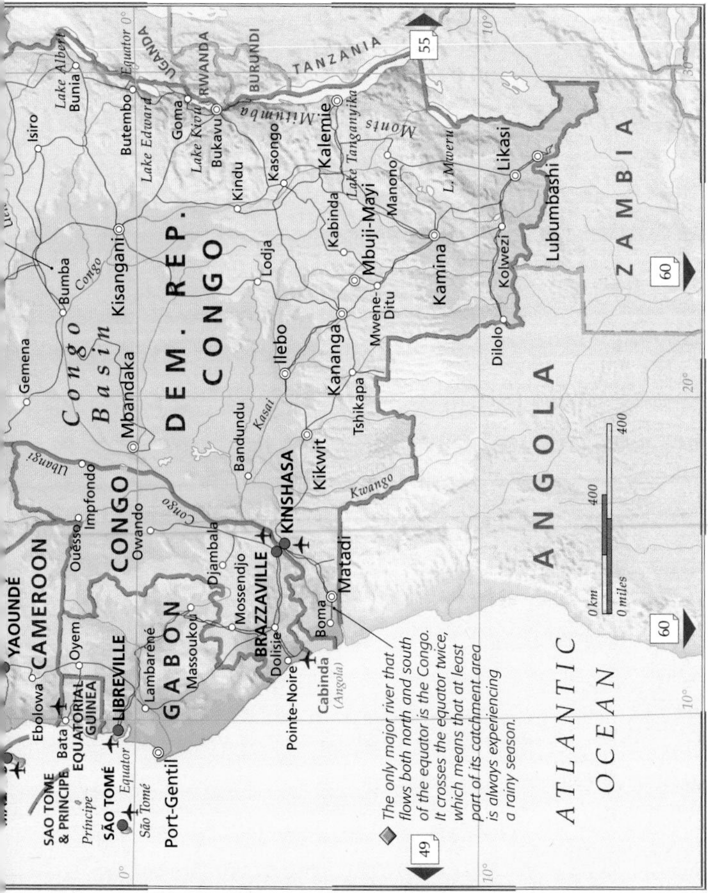
DEM. REP. CONGO
CONGO
GABON
CAMEROON
EQUATORIAL GUINEA
SAO TOME & PRINCIPE
ANGOLA
ZAMBIA
TANZANIA
UGANDA
RWANDA
BURUNDI
ATLANTIC OCEAN
KINSHASA
BRAZZAVILLE
LIBREVILLE
YAOUNDÉ
SÃO TOMÉ
Congo Basin
Príncipe
São Tomé
Equator
Port-Gentil
Lambaréné
Bata
Ebolowa
Oyem
Ouésso
Impfondo
Owando
Djambala
Mossendjo
Massoukou
Dolisie
Pointe-Noire
Cabinda (Angola)
Boma
Matadi
Kikwit
Bandundu
Mbandaka
Gemena
Bumba
Kisangani
Isiro
Bunia
Butembo
Goma
Bukavu
Kindu
Kasongo
Kalemie
Kabinda
Mbuji-Mayi
Manono
Lodja
Ilebo
Kananga
Tshikapa
Mwene-Ditu
Kamina
Dilolo
Kolwezi
Likasi
Lubumbashi
Lake Albert
Lake Edward
Lake Kivu
Lake Tanganyika
L. Mweru
Mitumba Monts
Ubangi
Congo
Kasai
Kwango
0 km 400
0 miles 400
10°
20°
30°
0°
49
55
60
A
B
C
D
E
5
6
7
8

The only major river that flows both north and south of the equator is the Congo. It crosses the equator twice, which means that at least part of its catchment area is always experiencing a rainy season.

Southern Africa

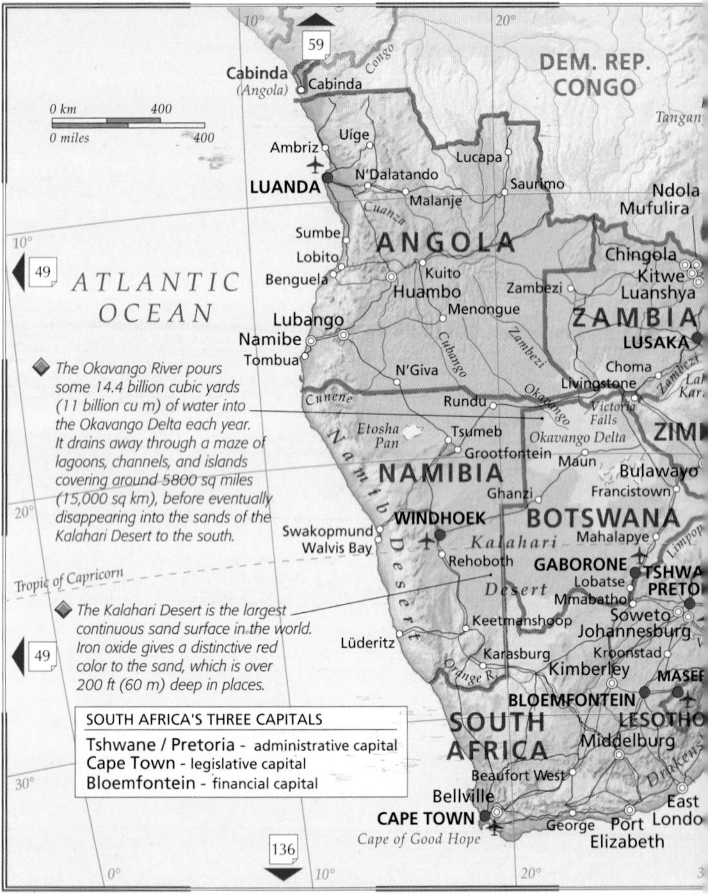
A B C D
1 2 3 4 5
59
49
49
136
0 km 400
0 miles 400
10° 20° 30° 0°
Tropic of Capricorn
ATLANTIC OCEAN
Cabinda (Angola)
Cabinda
DEM. REP. CONGO
Congo
ANGOLA
Ambriz
Uíge
LUANDA
N'Dalatando
Malanje
Lucapa
Saurimo
Cuanza
Sumbe
Lobito
Benguela
Huambo
Kuito
Menongue
Lubango
Namibe
Tombua
N'Giva
Cubango
Zambezi
Cunene
Rundu
Okavango
Etosha Pan
Tsumeb
Grootfontein
NAMIBIA
Namib Desert
WINDHOEK
Swakopmund
Walvis Bay
Rehoboth
Kalahari Desert
Keetmanshoop
Lüderitz
Karasburg
Orange R.
ZAMBIA
Ndola
Mufulira
Chingola
Kitwe
Luanshya
LUSAKA
Choma
Livingstone
Victoria Falls
Okavango Delta
Maun
Ghanzi
BOTSWANA
Francistown
Bulawayo
Mahalapye
Limpopo
GABORONE
Lobatse
Mmabatho
TSHWA PRETO
Soweto
Johannesburg
Kroonstad
Kimberley
MASEF
BLOEMFONTEIN
LESOTHO
SOUTH AFRICA
Middelburg
Drakens
Beaufort West
Bellville
CAPE TOWN
Cape of Good Hope
George
Port Elizabeth
East Londo
Tangan
ZIM

The Okavango River pours some 14.4 billion cubic yards (11 billion cu m) of water into the Okavango Delta each year. It drains away through a maze of lagoons, channels, and islands covering around 5800 sq miles (15,000 sq km), before eventually disappearing into the sands of the Kalahari Desert to the south.

The Kalahari Desert is the largest continuous sand surface in the world. Iron oxide gives a distinctive red color to the sand, which is over 200 ft (60 m) deep in places.

SOUTH AFRICA'S THREE CAPITALS

Tshwane / Pretoria - administrative capital
Cape Town - legislative capital
Bloemfontein - financial capital

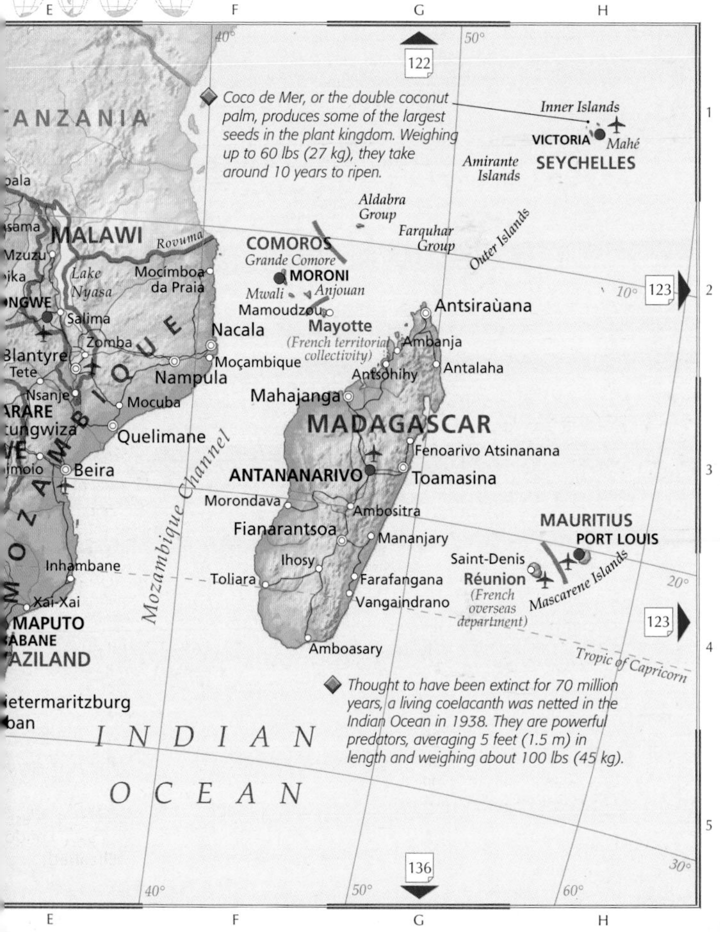

E
F
G
H
40°
50°
60°
10°
20°
30°
122
123
136
1
2
3
4
5
Coco de Mer, or the double coconut palm, produces some of the largest seeds in the plant kingdom. Weighing up to 60 lbs (27 kg), they take around 10 years to ripen.
Inner Islands
VICTORIA
Mahé
Amirante Islands
SEYCHELLES
TANZANIA
Aldabra Group
Farquhar Group
Outer Islands
MALAWI
Rovuma
COMOROS
Grande Comore
MORONI
Mwali
Anjouan
Mamoudzou
Mayotte
(French territorial collectivity)
Mzuzu
Lake Nyasa
Mocímboa da Praia
Salima
Zomba
Blantyre
Tete
Nacala
Moçambique
Nampula
MOZAMBIQUE
Antsiraùana
Ambanja
Antalaha
Antsohihy
Mahajanga
MADAGASCAR
Nsanje
Mocuba
Quelimane
Beira
Mozambique Channel
Fenoarivo Atsinanana
ANTANANARIVO
Toamasina
Morondava
Ambositra
Fianarantsoa
Mananjary
MAURITIUS
PORT LOUIS
Saint-Denis
Réunion
(French overseas department)
Mascarene Islands
Ihosy
Inhambane
Toliara
Farafangana
Vangaindrano
Xai-Xai
MAPUTO
AZILAND
Amboasary
Tropic of Capricorn
Thought to have been extinct for 70 million years, a living coelacanth was netted in the Indian Ocean in 1938. They are powerful predators, averaging 5 feet (1.5 m) in length and weighing about 100 lbs (45 kg).
INDIAN OCEAN

Europe

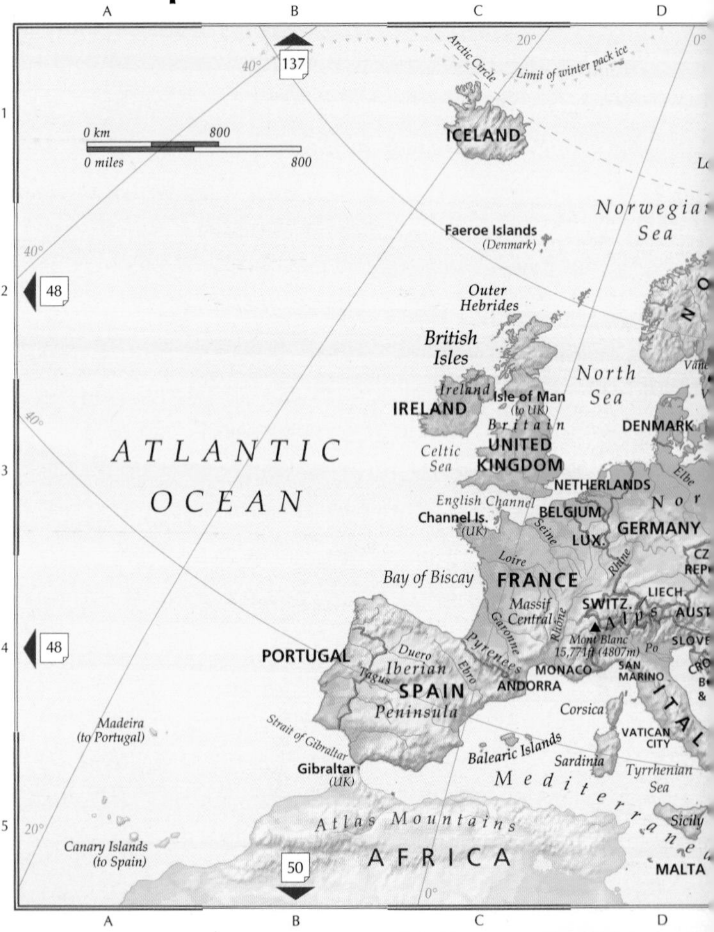
A
B
C
D
1
2
3
4
5
137
48
48
50
20°
0°
40°
Arctic Circle
Limit of winter pack ice
0 km
800
0 miles
800
ICELAND
Norwegian
Sea
Faeroe Islands
(Denmark)
Outer
Hebrides
British
Isles
North
Sea
Ireland
Isle of Man
(to UK)
IRELAND
Britain
DENMARK
ATLANTIC
OCEAN
Celtic
Sea
UNITED
KINGDOM
NETHERLANDS
Elbe
English Channel
Channel Is.
(UK)
BELGIUM
Seine
LUX.
GERMANY
Loire
Rhine
Bay of Biscay
FRANCE
LIECH.
SWITZ.
Massif
Central
Alps
AUST
Garonne
Rhône
Mont Blanc
15,771ft (4807m)
Po
SLOVE
PORTUGAL
Duero
Pyrenees
SAN
MARINO
Iberian
Ebro
MONACO
Tagus
SPAIN
ANDORRA
Peninsula
Corsica
ITAL
Madeira
(to Portugal)
Strait of Gibraltar
VATICAN
CITY
Balearic Islands
Gibraltar
(UK)
Sardinia
Tyrrhenian
Sea
Mediterranean
Atlas Mountains
Sicily
Canary Islands
(to Spain)
AFRICA
MALTA

E
F
G
H
1
2
3
4
5
20°
40°
60°
80°
137
94
94
94
Barents Sea
North Cape
Ostrov Kolguyev
Kola Peninsula
White Sea
FINLAND
Bothnia
Arctic Circle
Ural Mountains
Northern Dvina
Lake Onega
Lake Ladoga
RUSSIAN FEDERATION
ESTONIA
LATVIA
LITHUANIA
European Plain
Central Russian Upland
Volga Uplands
Volga
Ural
BELARUS
Pripet Marshes
Bug
UKRAINE
Dnieper Lowlands
Dnieper
Don
Dniester
Carpathian Mts.
MOLDOVA
Aral Sea
Caspian Sea
Sea of Azov
Crimea
Caucasus
El'brus 18,510ft (5642m)
Black Sea
ROMANIA
Danube
BULGARIA
Balkan Mts.
TURKEY
Aegean Sea
GREECE
Peloponnese
Crete
Anatolia
Cyprus
ASIA

The North Atlantic

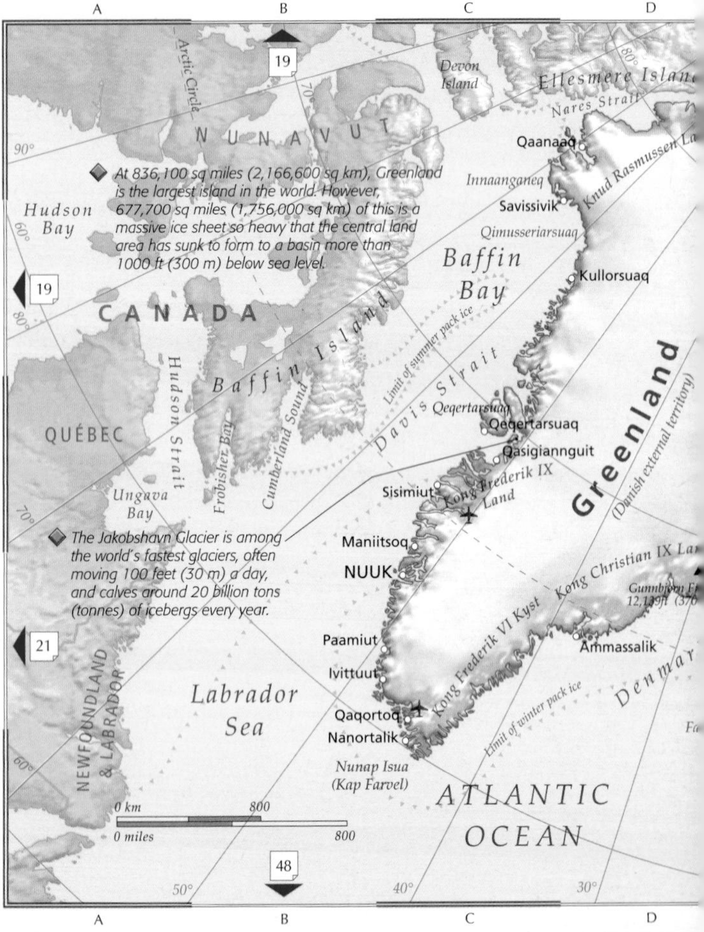
At 836,100 sq miles (2,166,600 sq km), Greenland is the largest island in the world. However, 677,700 sq miles (1,756,000 sq km) of this is a massive ice sheet so heavy that the central land area has sunk to form to a basin more than 1000 ft (300 m) below sea level.
The Jakobshavn Glacier is among the world's fastest glaciers, often moving 100 feet (30 m) a day, and calves around 20 billion tons (tonnes) of icebergs every year.
NUNAVUT
CANADA
QUÉBEC
NEWFOUNDLAND & LABRADOR
Hudson Bay
Hudson Strait
Ungava Bay
Baffin Island
Frobisher Bay
Cumberland Sound
Devon Island
Ellesmere Island
Nares Strait
Qaanaaq
Innaanganeq
Savissivik
Knud Rasmussen Land
Qimusseriarsuaq
Baffin Bay
Kullorsuaq
Limit of summer pack ice
Davis Strait
Qeqertarsuaq
Qasigiannguit
Kong Frederik IX Land
Sisimiut
Maniitsoq
NUUK
Paamiut
Ivittuut
Qaqortoq
Nanortalik
Nunap Isua (Kap Farvel)
Greenland
(Danish external territory)
Kong Christian IX Land
Kong Frederik VI Kyst
Ammassalik
Limit of winter pack ice
Labrador Sea
ATLANTIC OCEAN
Arctic Circle
0 km 800
0 miles 800
19
21
48
90°
80°
70°
60°
50°
40°
30°
A B C D
1 2 3 4 5

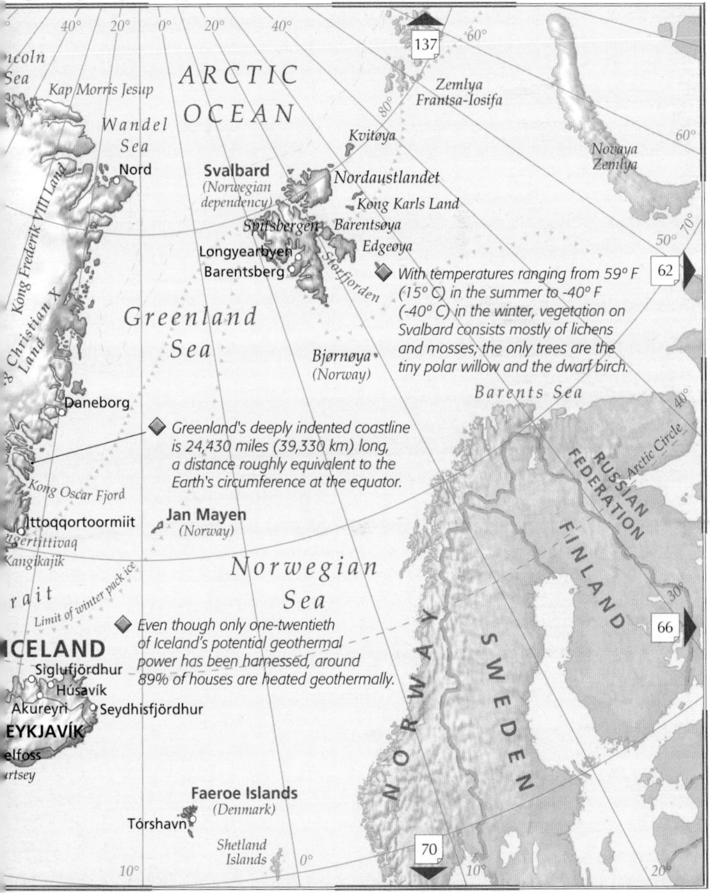
ARCTIC OCEAN
Kap Morris Jesup
Wandel Sea
Nord
Svalbard
(Norwegian dependency)
Zemlya Frantsa-Iosifa
Kvitøya
Nordaustlandet
Kong Karls Land
Spitsbergen
Barentsøya
Edgeøya
Longyearbyen
Barentsberg
Storfjorden
Novaya Zemlya
Kong Frederik VIII Land
Christian X Land
Greenland Sea
Bjørnøya
(Norway)
With temperatures ranging from 59° F (15° C) in the summer to -40° F (-40° C) in the winter, vegetation on Svalbard consists mostly of lichens and mosses; the only trees are the tiny polar willow and the dwarf birch.
Barents Sea
Daneborg
Greenland's deeply indented coastline is 24,430 miles (39,330 km) long, a distance roughly equivalent to the Earth's circumference at the equator.
Kong Oscar Fjord
Ittoqqortoormiit
Jan Mayen
(Norway)
Kangikajik
Limit of winter pack ice
Norwegian Sea
Even though only one-twentieth of Iceland's potential geothermal power has been harnessed, around 89% of houses are heated geothermally.
ICELAND
Siglufjördhur
Húsavík
Akureyri
Seydhisfjördhur
Faeroe Islands
(Denmark)
Tórshavn
Shetland Islands
RUSSIAN FEDERATION
Arctic Circle
FINLAND
NORWAY
SWEDEN
137
62
66
70

Scandinavia & Finland

ARCTIC OCEAN
The North Cape Current warms the northern coasts of Norway, Finland, and Russia's Kola Peninsula with water temperatures of 39–54° F (4–12° C), allowing this area of the Barents Sea to remain free of pack ice throughout the winter.
The sun is continuously visible from late May to late July in Tromsø because of its position well north of the Arctic Circle.
Scandinavia is still recovering from the last ice age, when the land was depressed 2000 ft (600 m) by the weight of the ice. Today, the Earth's crust is "rebounding" at the rate of 0.3 inches (9 mm) a year in the Gulf of Bothnia.
Barents Sea
Norwegian Sea
RUSSIAN FEDERATION
Arctic Circle
FINLAND
Lapland
Nordkapp (North Cape)
Vardø
Kirkenes
Hammerfest
Tromsø
Harstad
Narvik
Vesterålen
Lofoten
Bodø
Mo i Rana
Steinkjer
Trondheimsfjorden
Kiruna
Gällivare
Luleå
Piteå
Skellefteå
Kokkola
Tornio
Kemi
Oulu
Rovaniemi
Kemijärvi
Sodankylä
Kuusamo
Kajaani
Oulujoki
Oulujärvi
Kemijoki
Ounasjoki
Tornionjoki
Muonioälv
Deatnu
Ångermanälven
0 km 200
0 miles 200
137
137
92
65

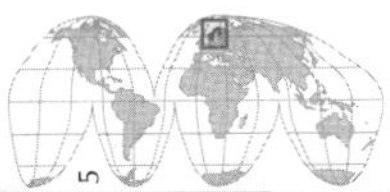

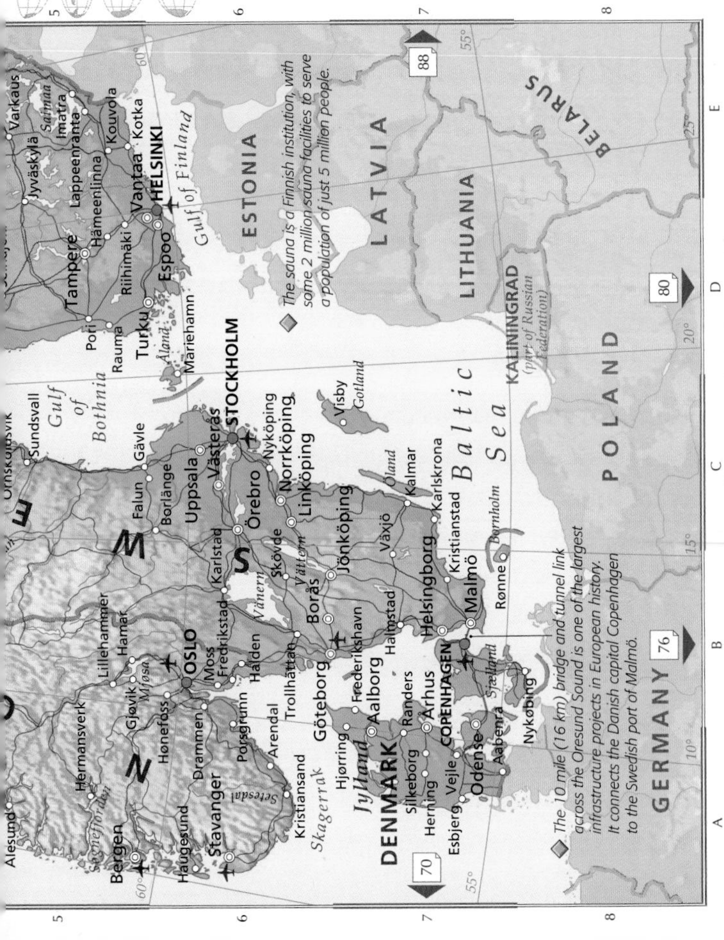

The sauna is a Finnish institution, with some 2 million sauna facilities to serve a population of just 5 million people.
The 10 mile (16 km) bridge and tunnel link across the Oresund Sound is one of the largest infrastructure projects in European history. It connects the Danish capital Copenhagen to the Swedish port of Malmö.
ESTONIA
LATVIA
LITHUANIA
BELARUS
KALININGRAD
(part of Russian Federation)
POLAND
GERMANY
DENMARK
Gulf of Bothnia
Gulf of Finland
Baltic Sea
Skagerrak
HELSINKI
STOCKHOLM
OSLO
COPENHAGEN
Tampere
Turku
Espoo
Vantaa
Göteborg
Malmö
Uppsala
Västerås
Örebro
Linköping
Norrköping
Jönköping
Helsingborg
Aalborg
Århus
Odense
Bergen
Stavanger
Gotland
Öland
Bornholm
Åland
Jylland
Sjælland
70
76
80
88

The Low Countries

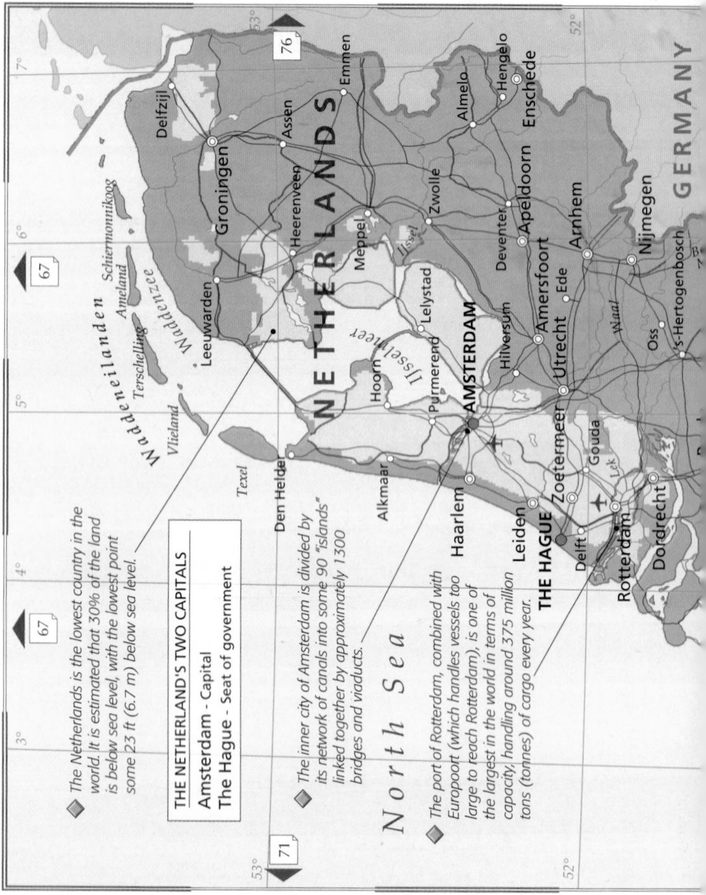
The Netherlands is the lowest country in the world. It is estimated that 30% of the land is below sea level, with the lowest point some 23 ft (6.7 m) below sea level.
THE NETHERLAND'S TWO CAPITALS
Amsterdam - Capital
The Hague - Seat of government
The inner city of Amsterdam is divided by its network of canals into some 90 "islands" linked together by approximately 1300 bridges and viaducts.
The port of Rotterdam, combined with Europoort (which handles vessels too large to reach Rotterdam), is one of the largest in the world in terms of capacity, handling around 375 million tons (tonnes) of cargo every year.
North Sea
Waddeneilanden
Waddenzee
Texel
Vlieland
Terschelling
Ameland
Schiermonnikoog
NETHERLANDS
GERMANY
IJsselmeer
IJssel
Waal
Lek
Den Helder
Alkmaar
Haarlem
Leiden
THE HAGUE
Delft
Rotterdam
Dordrecht
Zoetermeer
Gouda
AMSTERDAM
Purmerend
Hoorn
Lelystad
Hilversum
Utrecht
Amersfoort
Ede
Oss
's-Hertogenbosch
Nijmegen
Arnhem
Apeldoorn
Deventer
Zwolle
Meppel
Heerenveen
Leeuwarden
Groningen
Delfzijl
Assen
Emmen
Almelo
Hengelo
Enschede
67
71
76

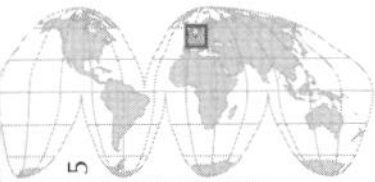

Belgium and the Netherlands have an underground boundary that differs from the surface boundary shown on maps. In 1950, the two countries agreed to move the underground boundary so as not to divide coal mines between the two countries.
On August 23, 1914, three weeks after Britain entered World War I, the 70,000 strong British Expeditionary Force encountered the advancing German army for the first time at the battle of Mons.
Echternach is the home of the only religious dancing procession remaining in the Western world. Every year since the 15th century, thousands of pilgrims have marched down the streets of the town performing a ritual dance involving specific movements, music, and prayers.
GERMANY
BELGIUM
FRANCE
LUXEMBOURG
Ardennes
Flanders
BRUSSELS
LUXEMBOURG
Oostende
Brugge
Gent
Antwerpen
Sint-Niklaas
Mechelen
Aalst
Roeselare
Ieper
Kortrijk
Mouscron
Tournai
La Louvière
Mons
Charleroi
Dinant
Namur
Leuven
Tienen
Hasselt
Genk
Maastricht
Heerlen
Liège
Seraing
Verviers
Bastogne
Arlon
Diekirch
Esch-sur-Alzette
Scheldt
Sambre
Meuse
Ourthe
Sûre
Our
Moselle
77
72
0 km
50
0 miles
50

The British Isles

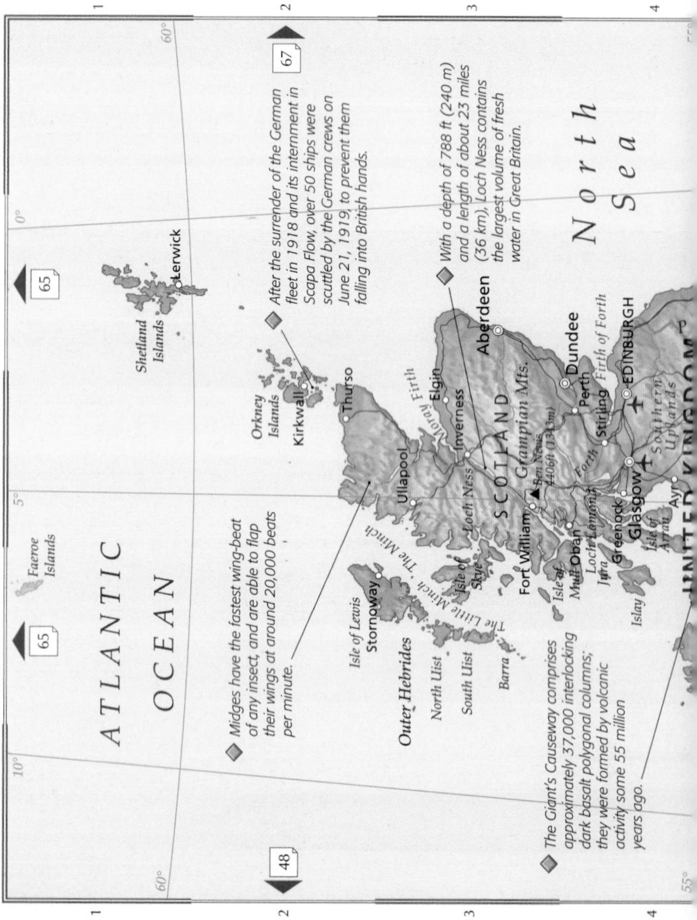

ATLANTIC OCEAN
North Sea
Faeroe Islands
Shetland Islands
Lerwick
Orkney Islands
Kirkwall
Thurso
Moray Firth
Elgin
Inverness
Aberdeen
SCOTLAND
Grampian Mts.
Ben Nevis 4406ft (1343m)
Dundee
Perth
Firth of Forth
EDINBURGH
Stirling
Forth
Southern Uplands
Glasgow
Greenock
Ayr
Isle of Arran
Loch Lomond
Jura
Islay
Isle of Mull
Oban
Fort William
Loch Ness
Isle of Skye
Ullapool
The Minch
The Little Minch
Isle of Lewis
Stornoway
Outer Hebrides
North Uist
South Uist
Barra
UNITED KINGDOM
65
67
48
Midges have the fastest wing-beat of any insect, and are able to flap their wings at around 20,000 beats per minute.
After the surrender of the German fleet in 1918 and its internment in Scapa Flow, over 50 ships were scuttled by the German crews on June 21, 1919, to prevent them falling into British hands.
With a depth of 788 ft (240 m) and a length of about 23 miles (36 km), Loch Ness contains the largest volume of fresh water in Great Britain.
The Giant's Causeway comprises approximately 37,000 interlocking dark basalt polygonal columns; they were formed by volcanic activity some 55 million years ago.

IRELAND
DUBLIN
Sligo
Athlone
Galway
Ennis
Limerick
Tralee
Killarney
Cork
Waterford
Wexford
Dundalk
Newry
Lough Ree
Lough Derg
Lough Corrib
Shannon
Barrow
Blackwater
Liffey
Wicklow Mts.
Bantry Bay
Irish Sea
Douglas
Anglesey
Holyhead
Bangor
Snowdonia
Cardigan Bay
Aberystwyth
Fishguard
Milford Haven
WALES
Swansea
CARDIFF
Newport
Brecon Beacons
ENGLAND
LONDON
York
Leeds
Bradford
Kingston upon Hull
Grimsby
Lancaster
Blackpool
Preston
Bolton
Manchester
Liverpool
Chester
Sheffield
Lincoln
Stoke-on-Trent
Derby
Nottingham
Leicester
Shrewsbury
Birmingham
Coventry
Worcester
Stratford-upon-Avon
Gloucester
Severn
Oxford
Thames
Swindon
Bristol
Bath
Reading
Peterborough
Cambridge
Norwich
Ipswich
Colchester
Southend-on-Sea
Canterbury
Dover
Channel Tunnel
The Wash
The Fens
Salisbury
Southampton
Portsmouth
Brighton
Bournemouth
Isle of Wight
Taunton
Barnstaple
Exmoor
Exeter
Dartmoor
Plymouth
Penzance
Land's End
Isles of Scilly
English Channel
Channel Islands (UK crown dependency)
Guernsey
St. Peter Port
Jersey
St. Helier
FRANCE
ATLANTIC OCEAN
Every year over 1.8 billion pints (0.561 litres) of Guinness® Irish stout are consumed in over 100 countries around the world.
The River Severn has the second highest tidal range in the world, as much as 50 ft (15 m), often giving rise to a tidal bore. In September 1996, one such wave carried a surfer for 5.7 miles (9 km).
0 km 100
0 miles 100
48
68
72
74
A B C D E
5 6 7 8
50°
0°
5°
10°

France, Andorra & Monaco

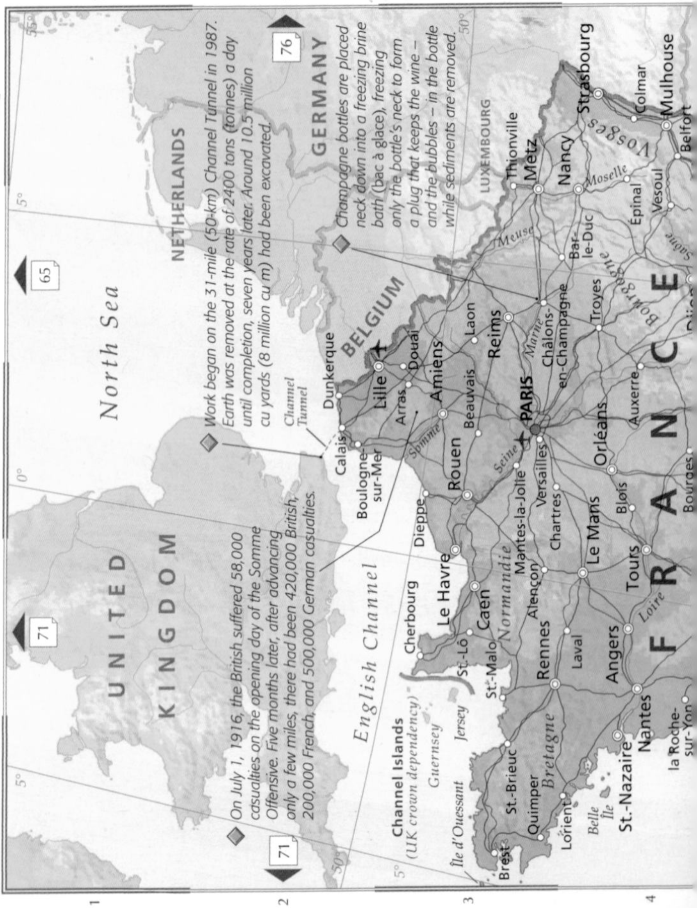

North Sea
English Channel
UNITED KINGDOM
NETHERLANDS
GERMANY
BELGIUM
LUXEMBOURG
FRANCE
Channel Islands
(UK crown dependency)
Guernsey
Jersey
Île d'Ouessant
Belle Île
Normandie
Bretagne
Bourgogne
Vosges
Channel Tunnel
Seine
Somme
Marne
Meuse
Moselle
Loire
Saône
PARIS
Dunkerque
Calais
Boulogne-sur-Mer
Lille
Douai
Arras
Amiens
Laon
Reims
Beauvais
Rouen
Dieppe
Le Havre
Cherbourg
Caen
St.-Lô
St.-Malo
Brest
Quimper
Lorient
St.-Brieuc
Rennes
Laval
Alençon
Le Mans
Chartres
Versailles
Mantes-la-Jolie
Châlons-en-Champagne
Troyes
Auxerre
Orléans
Blois
Tours
Angers
Nantes
St.-Nazaire
la Roche-sur-Yon
Bourges
Dijon
Bar-le-Duc
Thionville
Metz
Nancy
Épinal
Vesoul
Strasbourg
Colmar
Mulhouse
Belfort
On July 1, 1916, the British suffered 58,000 casualties on the opening day of the Somme Offensive. Five months later, after advancing only a few miles, there had been 420,000 British, 200,000 French, and 500,000 German casualties.
Work began on the 31-mile (50-km) Channel Tunnel in 1987. Earth was removed at the rate of 2400 tons (tonnes) a day until completion, seven years later. Around 10.5 million cu yards (8 million cu m) had been excavated.
Champagne bottles are placed neck down into a freezing brine bath (bac à glace), freezing only the bottle's neck to form a plug that keeps the wine – and the bubbles – in the bottle while sediments are removed.
71
65
76
A
B
C
D
E
1
2
3
4

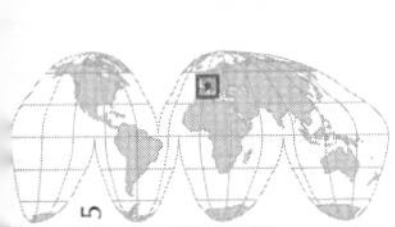

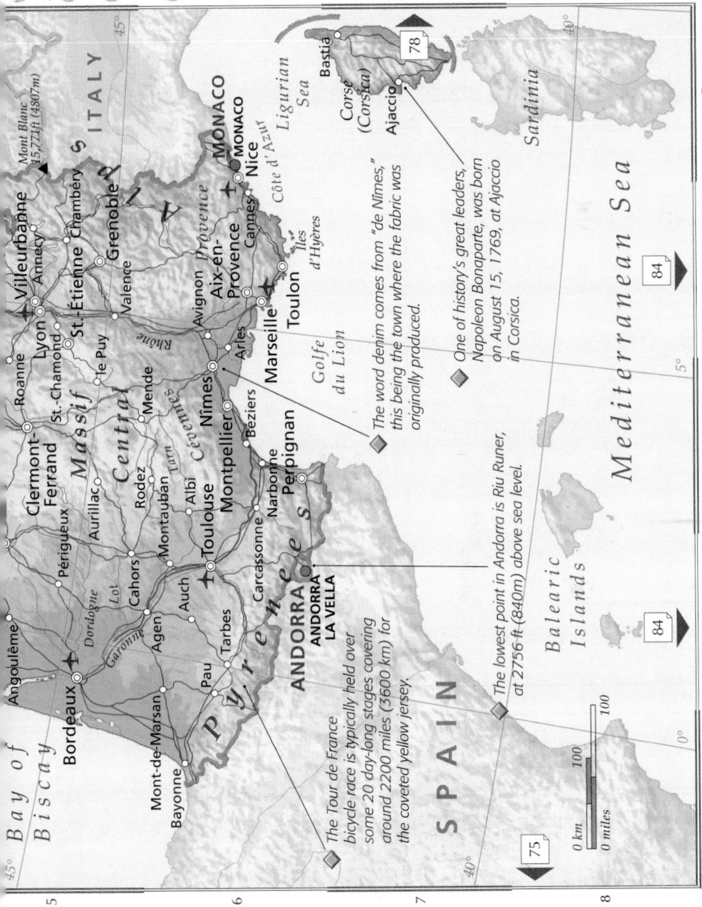
The Tour de France bicycle race is typically held over some 20 day-long stages covering around 2200 miles (3600 km) for the coveted yellow jersey.
The lowest point in Andorra is Riu Runer, at 2756 ft (840m) above sea level.
The word denim comes from "de Nîmes," this being the town where the fabric was originally produced.
One of history's great leaders, Napoleon Bonaparte, was born on August 15, 1769, at Ajaccio in Corsica.
Bay of Biscay
Bordeaux
Angoulême
Périgueux
Clermont-Ferrand
Roanne
Lyon
Villeurbanne
Annecy
Chambéry
Mont Blanc 15,771ft (4807m)
Grenoble
St.-Étienne
St.-Chamond
Valence
Le Puy
Massif Central
Aurillac
Rodez
Mende
Cahors
Montauban
Albi
Toulouse
Auch
Agen
Tarbes
Pau
Mont-de-Marsan
Bayonne
Dordogne
Lot
Garonne
Tarn
Cévennes
Rhône
Avignon
Nîmes
Montpellier
Béziers
Narbonne
Carcassonne
Perpignan
Arles
Marseille
Aix-en-Provence
Toulon
Cannes
Nice
Provence
Alps
ITALY
MONACO
Côte d'Azur
Îles d'Hyères
Ligurian Sea
Bastia
Corse (Corsica)
Ajaccio
Sardinia
Golfe du Lion
Mediterranean Sea
Balearic Islands
Pyrenees
ANDORRA
ANDORRA LA VELLA
SPAIN
0 km 100
0 miles 100
75
78
84
84

Spain & Portugal

A B C D
1 2 3 4 5
71
48
48
52
10°
5°
40°
35°
0 km 100
0 miles 100
ATLANTIC
OCEAN
Port has been produced in the Duoro Valley under strict regulation since the 1750s. Brandy is added to the grape juice to fortify and strengthen the wine.
Portugal is one of the world's largest producers of cork and has regulations protecting cork trees dating back to 1320.
Gibraltar was seized by a combined Anglo-Dutch fleet under Admiral Rooke in 1704. British sovereignty was then formalized in 1713 by the Treaty of Utrecht, and Gibraltar eventually became a British colony in 1830.
Ferrol
A Coruña (La Coruña)
Galicia
Santiago de Compostela
Lugo
Avilés
Gijon (Xixó
Oviedo
Cordillera Cantábrica
León
Miño
Pontevedra
Vigo
Ourense (Orense)
Minho
Emb. de Ricobayo
Pale
Viana do Castelo
Chaves
Braga
Bragança
Valladoli
Póvoa de Varzim
Guimarães
Duero
Matosinhos
Zamora
Porto
Vila Real
Vila Nova de Gaia
Douro
Aveiro
Viseu
Salamanca
Coimbra
Covilhã
Sistema Cent
Figueira da Foz
PORTUGAL
Plasencia
Castelo Branco
Tagus
Tagus
Caldas da Rainha
Cáceres
Santarém
Portalegre
Sintra
Cascais
Mérida
Guadiana
LISBON
Badajoz
Setúbal
Alcácer do Sal
Sierra Morena
Beja
Sines
Córdoba
Guadiana
Guadalquivir
Algarve
Sevilla
Huelva
Andalucí
Lagos
Faro
Olhão
Cabo de São Vicente
Anteque
Málag
El Puerto de Santa María
Cádiz
Algeciras
Gibra (UK)
Ceuta (Spain)
MOROCCO
A B C D

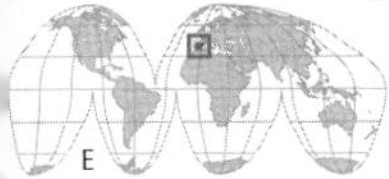

E
F
G
H
0°
5°
73
FRANCE
Bilbao
Donostia-San Sebastián
Pyrenees
Golfe du Lion
Pamplona (Iruña)
ANDORRA
Figueres
Logroño
Huesca
Girona (Gerona)
Ebro
Cataluña
Costa Brava
Soria
Lleida
Terrassa
Mataró
Zaragoza
Sabadell
Barcelona
78
Sistema Ibérico
Reus
L'Hospitalet de Llobregat
Tarragona
Work continues on the Sagrada Família, Gaudí's unfinished cathedral. Begun in 1882, the masterpiece is still without a roof.
Tortosa
Teruel
40°
Cuenca
Menorca
Júcar
Castellón de la Plana
Palma
Mallorca
País Valenciano
Valencia
Albacete
Gandía
Ibiza
Islas Baleares
(Balearic Islands)
Elda
Formentera
Benidorm
Segura
Cieza
Alicante (Alacant)
Elche (Elx)
Seat of many great civilizations throughout history, the name Mediterranean translates as "sea between the lands."
Murcia
Costa Blanca
79
Lorca
Cartagena
Mediterranean Sea
Almería
Costa del Sol
ALGERIA
52
1
2
3
4
5

Germany & The Alpine States

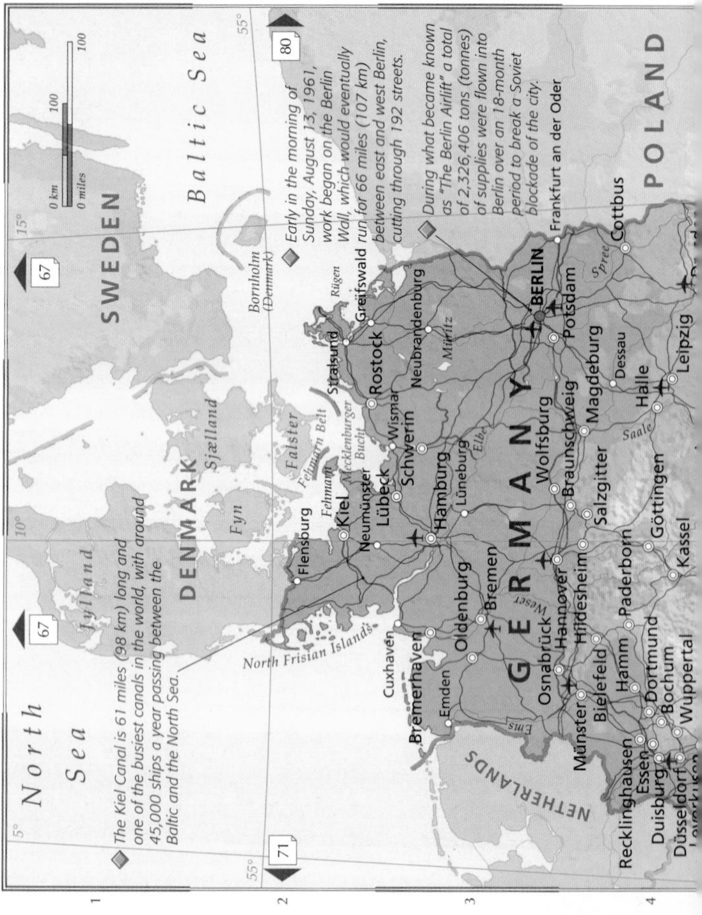

The Kiel Canal is 61 miles (98 km) long and one of the busiest canals in the world, with around 45,000 ships a year passing between the Baltic and the North Sea.
Early in the morning of Sunday, August 13, 1961, work began on the Berlin Wall, which would eventually run for 66 miles (107 km) between east and west Berlin, cutting through 192 streets.
During what became known as "The Berlin Airlift" a total of 2,326,406 tons (tonnes) of supplies were flown into Berlin over an 18-month period to break a Soviet blockade of the city.
67
67
71
80
0 km
100
0 miles
100
North Sea
Baltic Sea
SWEDEN
DENMARK
GERMANY
POLAND
NETHERLANDS
Jylland
Sjælland
Fyn
Falster
Fehmarn
Fehmarn Belt
Mecklenburger Bucht
Bornholm (Denmark)
Rügen
North Frisian Islands
Müritz
Elbe
Weser
Ems
Spree
Saale
Flensburg
Kiel
Neumünster
Lübeck
Rostock
Stralsund
Greifswald
Wismar
Schwerin
Neubrandenburg
Hamburg
Lüneburg
Cuxhaven
Bremerhaven
Emden
Oldenburg
Bremen
Wolfsburg
Braunschweig
Magdeburg
Dessau
Halle
Leipzig
BERLIN
Potsdam
Frankfurt an der Oder
Cottbus
Hannover
Hildesheim
Salzgitter
Göttingen
Kassel
Paderborn
Osnabrück
Bielefeld
Münster
Hamm
Dortmund
Bochum
Wuppertal
Recklinghausen
Essen
Duisburg
Düsseldorf
5°
10°
15°
55°
A
B
C
D
E
1
2
3
4

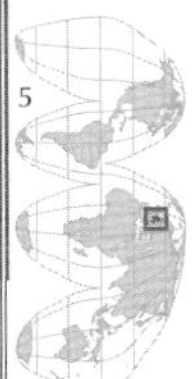

Frankfurt am Main
Wiesbaden
Mainz
Offenbach
Würzburg
Darmstadt
Erlangen
Mannheim
Kaiserslautern
Saarbrücken
Heidelberg
Nürnberg
Karlsruhe
Heilbronn
Pforzheim
Regensburg
Stuttgart
Ingolstadt
Reutlingen
Landshut
Ulm
Augsburg
München
Freiburg im Breisgau
Schaffhausen
Basel
Delémont
Zürich
Bregenz
Biel
Zug
LIECHTENSTEIN
VADUZ
Innsbruck
BERN
Luzern
Chur
Lac de Neuchâtel
Yverdon
Lausanne
SWITZERLAND
Thuner See
Berner Alpen
Lake Geneva
Sion
Brig
Genève
Monthey
Matterhorn 14,692ft (4478m)
Locarno
Lugano
Lake Maggiore
CZECH REPUBLIC
BELGIUM
LUX.
FRANCE
Mosel
Rhine
Neckar
Schwarzwald
Schwäbische Alb
Fränkische Alb
Bohemian Forest
Danube
Lake Constance
Bavarian Alps
Inn
Tirol
Hohe Tauern
Alps
Braunau am Inn
Linz
Wels
Salzburg
Hellejn
Krems an der Donau
Hollabrunn
VIENNA
Sankt Pölten
Barden
Eisenstadt
Wiener Neustadt
Neusiedler See
Enns
Kapfenberg
AUSTRIA
Judenburg
Graz
Mur
HUNGARY
Lienz
Villach
Klagenfurt
Maribor
Celje
Sava
Kranj
LJUBLJANA
SLOVENIA
Koper
Gulf of Venice
ITALY
CROATIA
50°
45°
10°
15°
73
78
78
81
A
B
C
D
E
5
6
7
8

At 528 ft (161 m) high and containing 768 steps, the spire of Ulm Cathedral is the tallest in the world.

Born in Salzburg on January 27, 1756, Wolfgang Amadeus Mozart was already writing music by the age of five, and at eleven he produced his first opera.

When it is completed in 2017, the Gotthard Base Tunnel will run for 35.5 miles (57 km) beneath the Lepontine Alps to become the longest tunnel in the world.

The acrylic glass roof over the Olympic stadium in München (Munich) measures 914,940 sq ft (85,000 sq m), making it the biggest structure of its kind in the world.

Italy

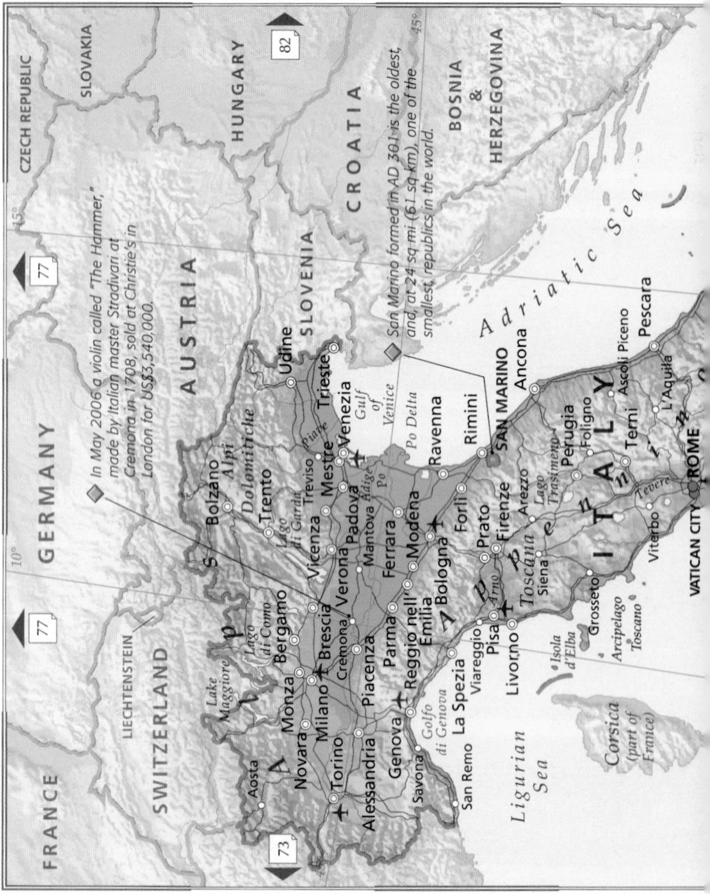
In May 2006 a violin called "The Hammer," made by Italian master Stradivari at Cremona in 1708, sold at Christie's in London for US$3,540,000.
San Marino formed in AD 301 is the oldest, and, at 24 sq mi (61 sq km), one of the smallest republics in the world.
FRANCE
SWITZERLAND
LIECHTENSTEIN
GERMANY
AUSTRIA
CZECH REPUBLIC
SLOVAKIA
HUNGARY
SLOVENIA
CROATIA
BOSNIA & HERZEGOVINA
ITALY
SAN MARINO
VATICAN CITY
ROME
Adriatic Sea
Ligurian Sea
Gulf of Venice
Golfo di Genova
Corsica (part of France)
Isola d'Elba
Arcipelago Toscano
Po Delta
Alpi Dolomitiche
Lake Maggiore
Lago di Como
Lago di Garda
Lago Trasimeno
Toscana
Po
Adige
Piave
Arno
Tevere
Aosta
Torino
Novara
Milano
Monza
Bergamo
Brescia
Cremona
Piacenza
Alessandria
Genova
Savona
San Remo
La Spezia
Viareggio
Pisa
Livorno
Parma
Reggio nell'Emilia
Modena
Bologna
Ferrara
Mantova
Verona
Vicenza
Padova
Trento
Bolzano
Treviso
Mestre
Venezia
Udine
Trieste
Ravenna
Forlì
Rimini
Prato
Firenze
Arezzo
Siena
Grosseto
Perugia
Foligno
Terni
Viterbo
Ancona
Ascoli Piceno
L'Aquila
Pescara
77
73
82
10°
15°
45°
A
B
C
D
E
1
2
3
4

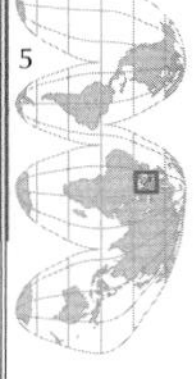

Algnero
Nuoro
Sardegna
(Sardinia)
Oristano
Iglesias
Cagliari
The medical school at Salerno is the oldest in Europe, established during the 11th and 12th centuries.
Napoli
Torre del Greco
Isola di Capri
Salerno
Golfo di Salerno
Potenza
Ofanto
Bari
Altamura
Taranto
Brindisi
Lecce
Gallipoli
Golfo di Taranto
Strait of Otranto
Tyrrhenian Sea
Mediterranean Sea
Isola d'Ustica
Isole Eolie
Isola Stromboli
Isola Lipari
Isola Vulcano
Cosenza
Calabria
Crotone
Catanzaro
Ionian Sea
Trapani
Isole Egadi
Marsala
Palermo
Cefalù
Messina
Sicilia
(Sicily)
Caltanissetta
Agrigento
Salso
Catania
Siracusa
Ragusa
Reggio di Calabria
Stretto di Messina
Strait of Sicily
Isola di Pantelleria
TUNISIA
Malta Channel
Gozo
VALLETTA
MALTA
Isole Pelagie
Mt. Etna began some 300,000 years ago as a submarine volcano and has since grown to a cone with a base 30 miles (48 km) wide and 10,922 ft (3329 m) high.
The George cross that appears on the Maltese flag was awarded to the islanders by King George VI of Britain for their heroism during World War II.
0 km 100
0 miles 100
40°
35°
10°
15°
83
53
53
53
A
B
C
D
E
5
6
7
8

Central Europe

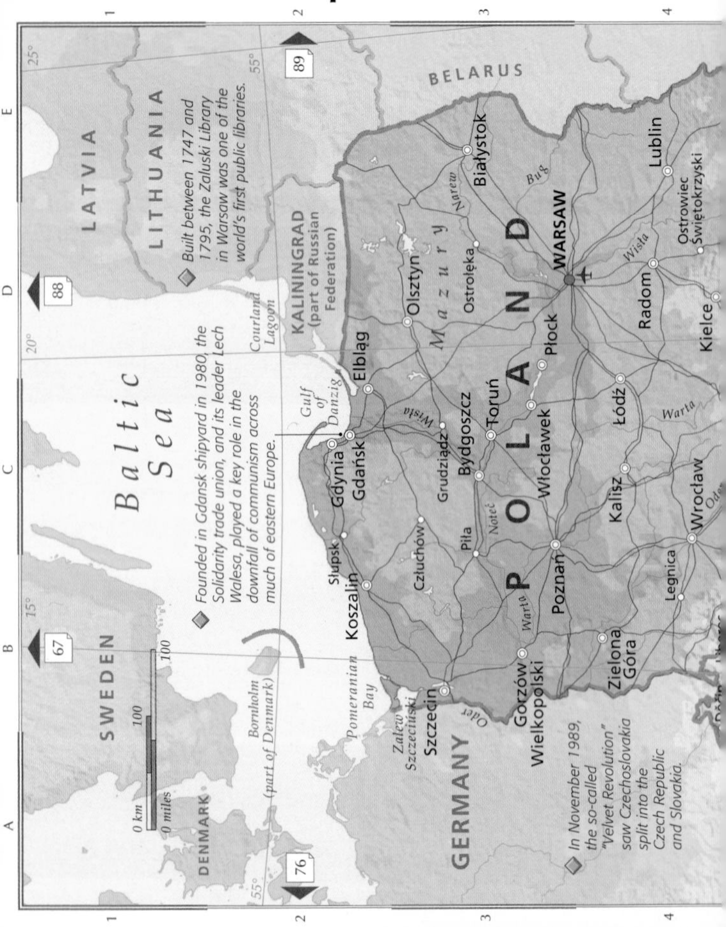
Baltic Sea
SWEDEN
DENMARK
LATVIA
LITHUANIA
BELARUS
KALININGRAD (part of Russian Federation)
GERMANY
POLAND
Bornholm (part of Denmark)
Pomeranian Bay
Zalew Szczeciński
Gulf of Danzig
Courland Lagoon
Mazury
0 km 100
0 miles 100
Built between 1747 and 1795, the Zaluski Library in Warsaw was one of the world's first public libraries.
Founded in Gdansk shipyard in 1980, the Solidarity trade union, and its leader Lech Walesa, played a key role in the downfall of communism across much of eastern Europe.
In November 1989, the so-called "Velvet Revolution" saw Czechoslovakia split into the Czech Republic and Slovakia.
WARSAW
Białystok
Lublin
Ostrowiec Świętokrzyski
Radom
Kielce
Ostrołęka
Olsztyn
Płock
Elbląg
Gdańsk
Gdynia
Słupsk
Koszalin
Człuchów
Grudziądz
Bydgoszcz
Toruń
Włocławek
Łódź
Kalisz
Piła
Poznań
Wrocław
Legnica
Zielona Góra
Gorzów Wielkopolski
Szczecin
Wisła
Narew
Bug
Warta
Noteć
Oder
67
76
88
89
55°
20°
15°
25°

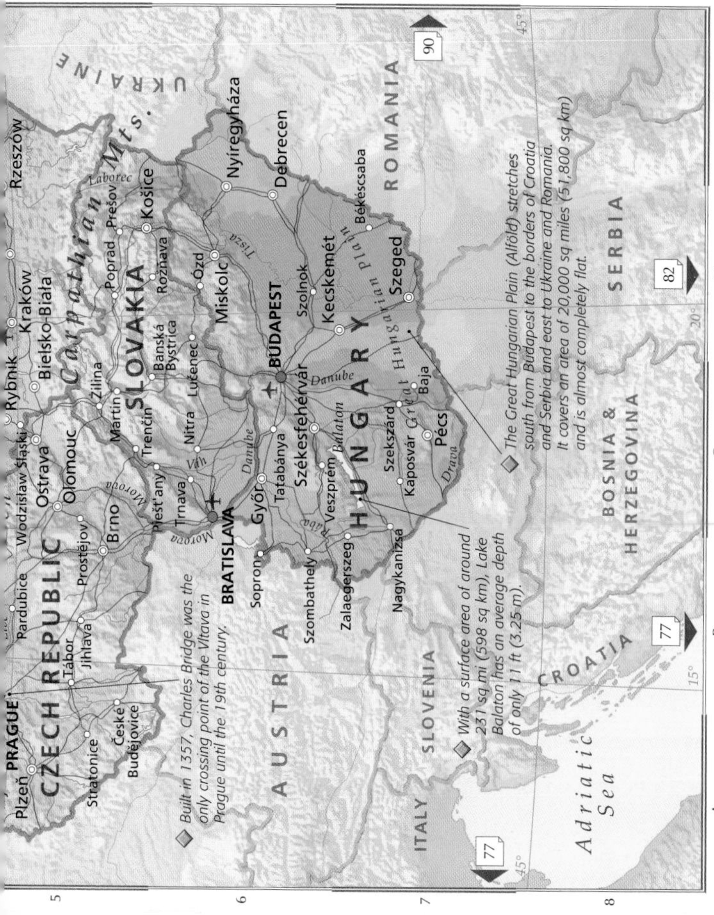
Built in 1357, Charles Bridge was the only crossing point of the Vltava in Prague until the 19th century.
With a surface area of around 231 sq mi (598 sq km), Lake Balaton has an average depth of only 11 ft (3.25 m).
The Great Hungarian Plain (Alföld) stretches south from Budapest to the borders of Croatia and Serbia and east to Ukraine and Romania. It covers an area of 20,000 sq miles (51,800 sq km) and is almost completely flat.
CZECH REPUBLIC
SLOVAKIA
HUNGARY
AUSTRIA
UKRAINE
ROMANIA
SERBIA
BOSNIA & HERZEGOVINA
CROATIA
SLOVENIA
ITALY
Adriatic Sea
Carpathian Mts.
Great Hungarian Plain
PRAGUE
BRATISLAVA
BUDAPEST
Plzeň
Stratonice
České Budějovice
Tábor
Jihlava
Pardubice
Prostějov
Brno
Olomouc
Ostrava
Wodzisław Śląski
Rybnik
Bielsko-Biała
Kraków
Rzeszów
Žilina
Martin
Trenčín
Piešťany
Trnava
Nitra
Banská Bystrica
Lučenec
Poprad
Prešov
Košice
Rožnava
Ózd
Miskolc
Nyíregyháza
Debrecen
Szolnok
Kecskemét
Békéscsaba
Szeged
Sopron
Győr
Tatabánya
Székesfehérvár
Veszprém
Szombathely
Zalaegerszeg
Nagykanizsa
Kaposvár
Szekszárd
Pécs
Baja
Danube
Tisza
Váh
Morava
Rába
Balaton
Drava
Laborec
90
82
77
77
15°
20°
45°
45°
A
B
C
D
E
5
6
7
8

Southeast Europe

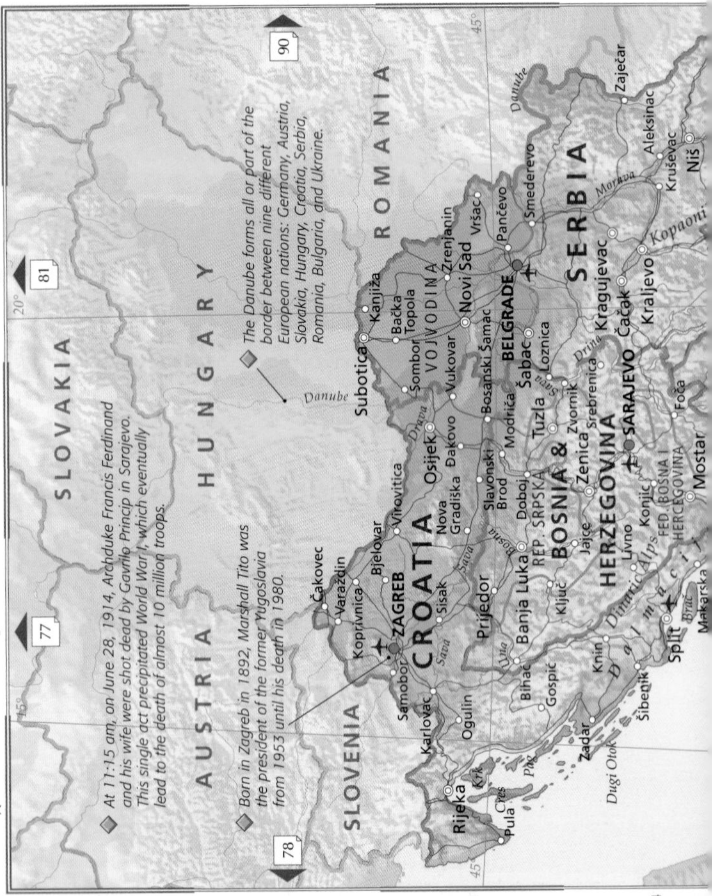
At 11:15 am, on June 28, 1914, Archduke Francis Ferdinand and his wife were shot dead by Gavrilo Princip in Sarajevo. This single act precipitated World War I, which eventually lead to the death of almost 10 million troops.
Born in Zagreb in 1892, Marshall Tito was the president of the former Yugoslavia from 1953 until his death in 1980.
The Danube forms all or part of the border between nine different European nations: Germany, Austria, Slovakia, Hungary, Croatia, Serbia, Romania, Bulgaria, and Ukraine.
SLOVAKIA
AUSTRIA
HUNGARY
ROMANIA
SLOVENIA
CROATIA
SERBIA
VOJVODINA
BOSNIA & HERZEGOVINA
REP. SRPSKA
FED. BOSNA I HERCEGOVINA
ZAGREB
BELGRADE
SARAJEVO
Danube
Drava
Sava
Bosna
Una
Drina
Morava
Dinaric Alps
Dalmacija
Kopaoni
Rijeka
Pula
Cres
Krk
Pag
Dugi Otok
Brač
Karlovac
Ogulin
Samobor
Koprivnica
Varaždin
Čakovec
Bjelovar
Virovitica
Sisak
Nova Gradiška
Osijek
Đakovo
Slavonski Brod
Vukovar
Subotica
Sombor
Bačka Topola
Kanjiža
Novi Sad
Zrenjanin
Vršac
Pančevo
Smederevo
Bosanski Šamac
Modriča
Doboj
Tuzla
Zvornik
Srebrenica
Šabac
Loznica
Prijedor
Banja Luka
Bihać
Gospić
Ključ
Jajce
Zenica
Livno
Konjic
Mostar
Foča
Knin
Šibenik
Zadar
Split
Makarska
Kragujevac
Čačak
Kraljevo
Kruševac
Aleksinac
Niš
Zaječar
77
78
81
90
20°
45°

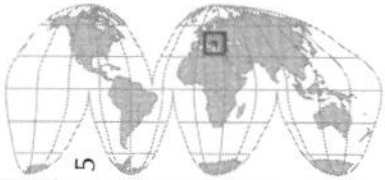

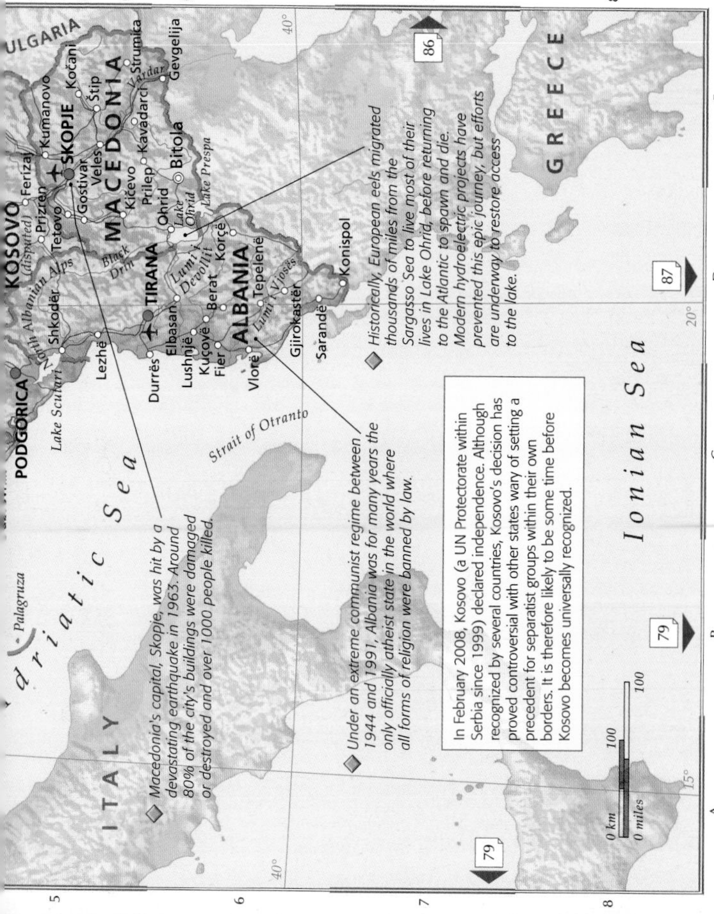
KOSOVO
(disputed)
BULGARIA
MACEDONIA
ALBANIA
GREECE
ITALY
Adriatic Sea
Ionian Sea
Strait of Otranto
Lake Scutari
North Albanian Alps
Black Drin
Lumi i Devollit
Lumi i Vjosës
Lake Ohrid
Lake Prespa
Vardar
Palagruza
PODGORICA
TIRANA
SKOPJE
Shkodër
Lezhë
Durrës
Elbasan
Lushnjë
Kuçovë
Fier
Berat
Vlorë
Tepelenë
Gjirokastër
Sarandë
Konispol
Korçë
Prizren
Ferizaj
Tetovo
Gostivar
Kičevo
Ohrid
Bitola
Prilep
Veles
Kumanovo
Kočani
Štip
Kavadarci
Strumica
Gevgelija
Macedonia's capital, Skopje, was hit by a devastating earthquake in 1963. Around 80% of the city's buildings were damaged or destroyed and over 1000 people killed.
Under an extreme communist regime between 1944 and 1991, Albania was for many years the only officially atheist state in the world where all forms of religion were banned by law.
Historically, European eels migrated thousands of miles from the Sargasso Sea to live most of their lives in Lake Ohrid, before returning to the Atlantic to spawn and die. Modern hydroelectric projects have prevented this epic journey, but efforts are underway to restore access to the lake.
In February 2008, Kosovo (a UN Protectorate within Serbia since 1999) declared independence. Although recognized by several countries, Kosovo's decision has proved controversial with other states wary of setting a precedent for separatist groups within their own borders. It is therefore likely to be some time before Kosovo becomes universally recognized.
0 km 100
0 miles 100
40°
20°
15°
79
86
87
A
B
C
D
E
5
6
7
8

The Mediterranean

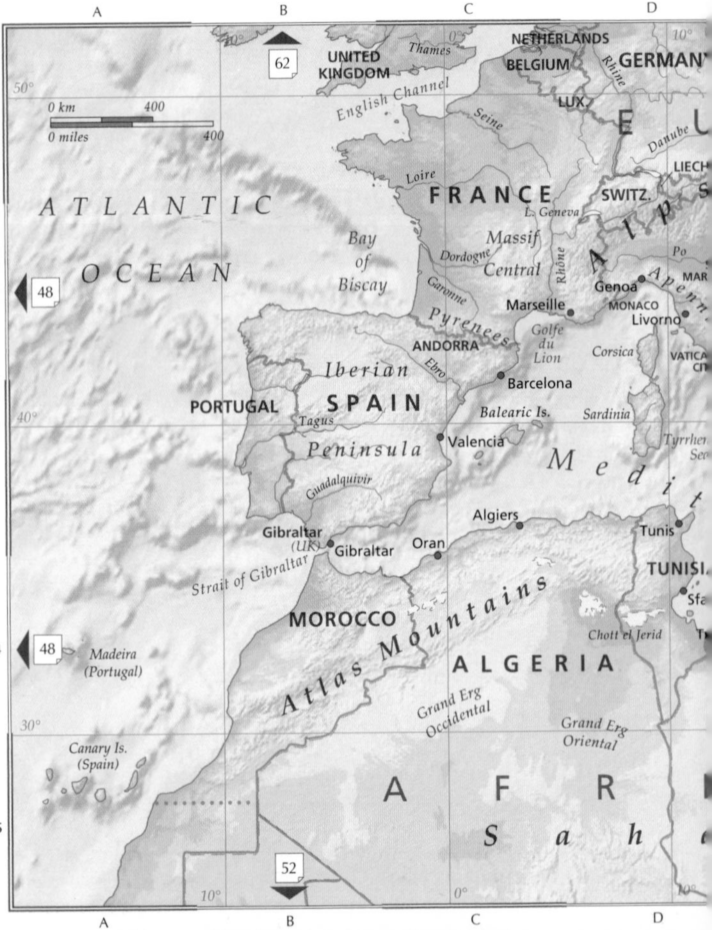
A
B
C
D
1
2
3
4
5
0 km 400
0 miles 400
62
48
48
52
50°
40°
30°
10°
0°
UNITED KINGDOM
Thames
English Channel
NETHERLANDS
BELGIUM
LUX.
GERMAN
Rhine
Seine
Danube
LIECH
SWITZ.
FRANCE
Loire
L. Geneva
Massif Central
Dordogne
Garonne
Rhône
Alp
Po
Apenn
Genoa
MONACO
Livorno
Marseille
Golfe du Lion
Corsica
VATICA CI
ATLANTIC OCEAN
Bay of Biscay
Pyrenees
ANDORRA
Ebro
Iberian Peninsula
SPAIN
PORTUGAL
Tagus
Guadalquivir
Barcelona
Balearic Is.
Sardinia
Tyrrhen Sea
Valencia
Med
Algiers
Tunis
TUNISI
Sfa
Gibraltar (UK)
Gibraltar
Oran
Strait of Gibraltar
MOROCCO
Atlas Mountains
ALGERIA
Chott el Jerid
Madeira (Portugal)
Grand Erg Occidental
Grand Erg Oriental
Canary Is. (Spain)
AFR
Sah

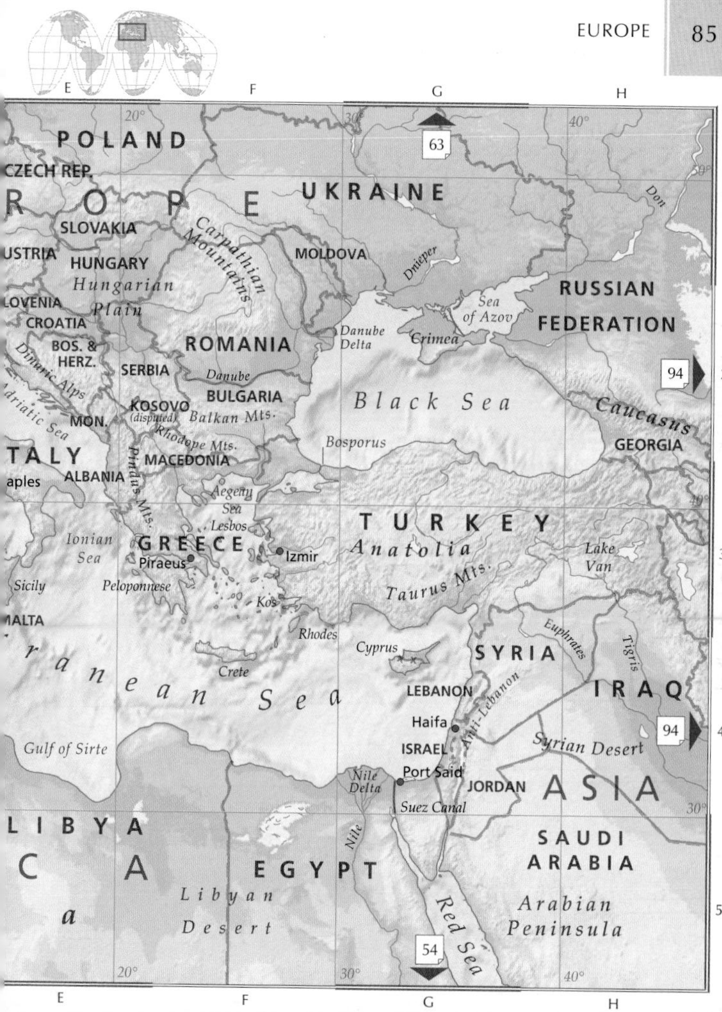
E
F
G
H
20°
30°
40°
63
POLAND
CZECH REP.
R O P E
UKRAINE
Don
SLOVAKIA
Carpathian Mountains
USTRIA
HUNGARY
Hungarian Plain
MOLDOVA
Dnieper
RUSSIAN FEDERATION
LOVENIA
CROATIA
Sea of Azov
Danube Delta
Crimea
BOS. & HERZ.
ROMANIA
Dinaric Alps
SERBIA
Danube
94
BULGARIA
Black Sea
Adriatic Sea
KOSOVO (disputed)
Balkan Mts.
Caucasus
MON.
Rhodope Mts.
Bosporus
GEORGIA
TALY
Pindus Mts.
MACEDONIA
aples
ALBANIA
Aegean Sea
Lesbos
TURKEY
Ionian Sea
GREECE
Izmir
Anatolia
Lake Van
Piraeus
Taurus Mts.
Sicily
Peloponnese
Kos
MALTA
Rhodes
Cyprus
Euphrates
Tigris
SYRIA
Crete
r a n e a n Sea
LEBANON
Anti-Lebanon
IRAQ
Haifa
94
Gulf of Sirte
ISRAEL
Syrian Desert
Nile Delta
Port Said
JORDAN
ASIA
Suez Canal
LIBYA
Nile
SAUDI ARABIA
C A
EGYPT
Libyan Desert
Red Sea
Arabian Peninsula
a
54
1
2
3
4
5

Bulgaria & Greece

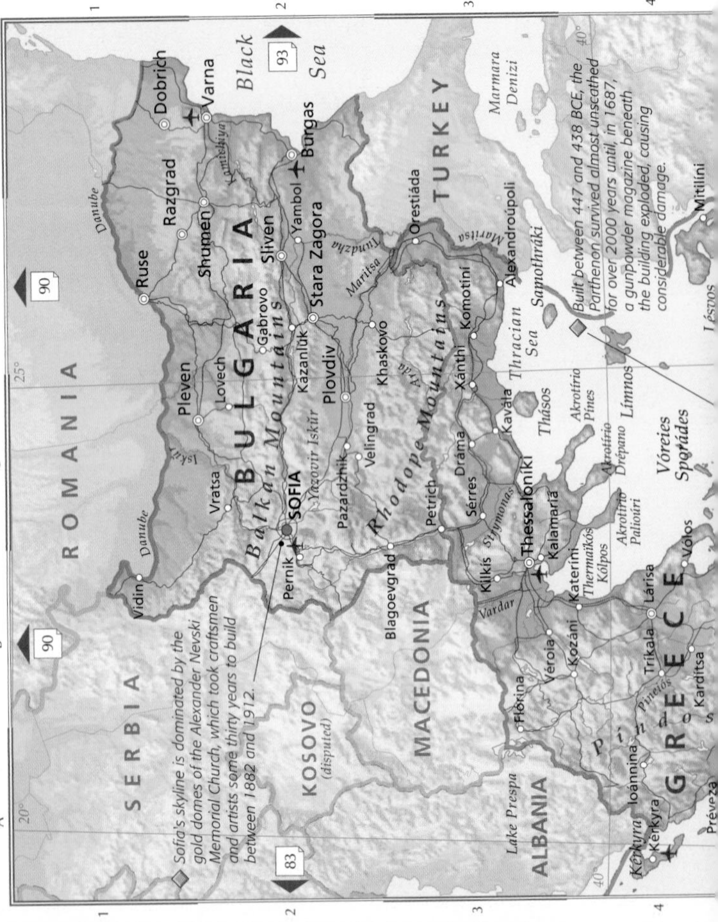
Sofia's skyline is dominated by the gold domes of the Alexander Nevski Memorial Church, which took craftsmen and artists some thirty years to build between 1882 and 1912.
Built between 447 and 438 BCE, the Parthenon survived almost unscathed for over 2000 years until, in 1687, a gunpowder magazine beneath the building exploded, causing considerable damage.
ROMANIA
SERBIA
KOSOVO
(disputed)
MACEDONIA
ALBANIA
BULGARIA
TURKEY
GREECE
Black Sea
Marmara Denizi
Thracian Sea
Balkan Mountains
Rhodope Mountains
Pindos
Danube
Iskŭr
Yazovir Iskŭr
Kamchiya
Tundzha
Maritsa
Arda
Strymonas
Vardar
Pineiós
SOFIA
Vidin
Vratsa
Pleven
Lovech
Ruse
Razgrad
Shumen
Dobrich
Varna
Burgas
Yambol
Sliven
Stara Zagora
Gabrovo
Kazanlŭk
Plovdiv
Pazardzhik
Velingrad
Khaskovo
Pernik
Blagoevgrad
Petrich
Orestiáda
Alexandroúpoli
Komotiní
Xánthi
Kavála
Dráma
Sérres
Kilkís
Thessaloníki
Kalamariá
Kateríni
Véroia
Kozáni
Flórina
Lárisa
Tríkala
Kardítsa
Vólos
Ioánnina
Kérkyra
Préveza
Mitilíni
Lake Prespa
Thermaïkós Kólpos
Akrotírio Palioúri
Akrotírio Drépano
Akrotírio Pínes
Thásos
Samothráki
Límnos
Lésvos
Vóreies Sporádes
20°
25°
40°
A
B
C
D
E
1
2
3
4
90
93
83

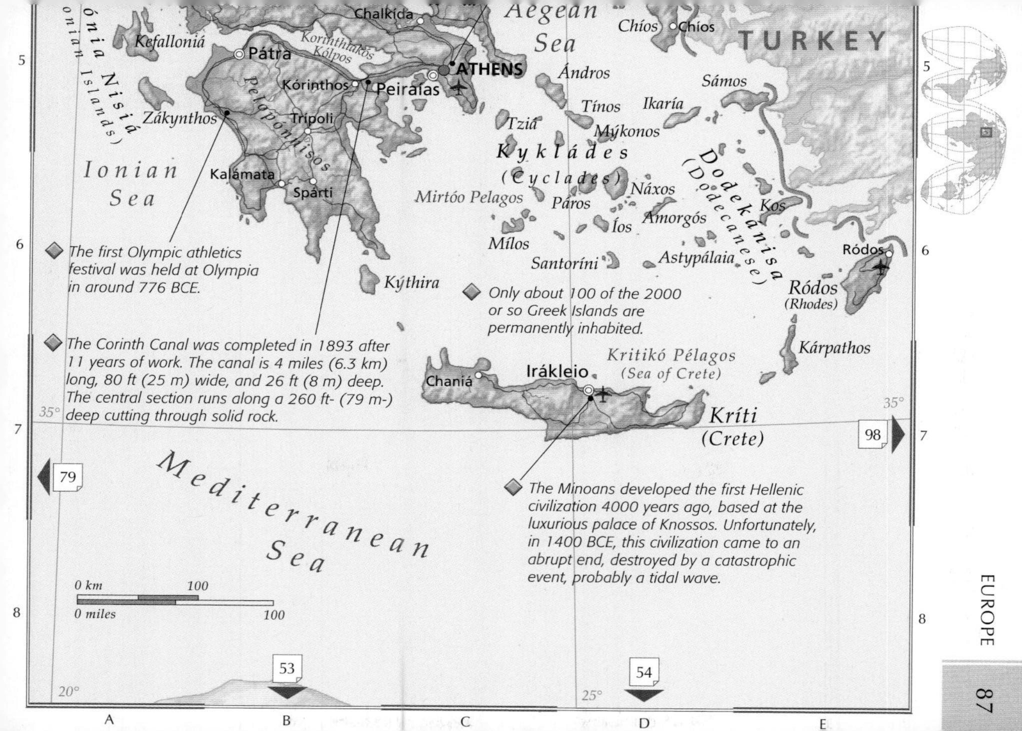
Aegean Sea
TURKEY
Chalkída
Chíos
Kefalloniá
Pátra
Korinthiakós Kólpos
ATHENS
Peiraías
Kórinthos
Ándros
Sámos
Tínos
Ikaría
Mýkonos
Tziá
Zákynthos
Tripoli
Pelopónnisos
Ionía Nisiá (Ionian Islands)
Kykládes (Cyclades)
Dodekánisa (Dodecanese)
Ionian Sea
Kalámata
Spárti
Mirtóo Pelagos
Páros
Náxos
Kos
Amorgós
Íos
Mílos
Santoríni
Astypálaia
Ródos
Ródos (Rhodes)
Kýthira
Kárpathos
Kritikó Pélagos (Sea of Crete)
Chaniá
Irákleio
Kríti (Crete)
Mediterranean Sea
The first Olympic athletics festival was held at Olympia in around 776 BCE.
The Corinth Canal was completed in 1893 after 11 years of work. The canal is 4 miles (6.3 km) long, 80 ft (25 m) wide, and 26 ft (8 m) deep. The central section runs along a 260 ft- (79 m-) deep cutting through solid rock.
Only about 100 of the 2000 or so Greek Islands are permanently inhabited.
The Minoans developed the first Hellenic civilization 4000 years ago, based at the luxurious palace of Knossos. Unfortunately, in 1400 BCE, this civilization came to an abrupt end, destroyed by a catastrophic event, probably a tidal wave.
0 km 100
0 miles 100
35°
20°
25°
79
98
53
54
A
B
C
D
E
5
6
7
8

The Baltic States & Belarus

SWEDEN
FINLAND
ESTONIA
LATVIA
LITHUANIA
RUSSIA
KALININGRAD (part of Russian Federation)
Gulf of Bothnia
Gulf of Finland
Gulf of Riga
Baltic Sea
Gotland
Hiiumaa
Saaremaa
Vormsi
Narva Bay
Lake Peipus
Lake Pskov
Burtnieku Ezers
Western Dvina
Venta
Neman
Narva
Courland Lagoon
TALLINN
RIGA
Loksa
Rakvere
Kohtla-Järve
Narva
Tapa
Paide
Tartu
Võru
Valga
Viljandi
Pärnu
Paldiski
Haapsalu
Virtsu
Kuressaare
Kolka
Talsi
Ventspils
Kuldīga
Saldus
Dobele
Jelgava
Liepāja
Valmiera
Cēsis
Ogre
Madona
Jēkabpils
Rēzekne
Daugavpils
Biržai
Panevėžys
Utena
Šiauliai
Radviliškis
Mažeikiai
Telšiai
Kelmė
Tauragė
Jurbarkas
Plungė
Šilutė
Kretinga
Klaipėda
Gusev
Kaliningrad
Rich oil shale deposits in northern Estonia are quarried, crushed, and heated to produce almost 7000 barrels of oil a day.
Low salinity and the shallow coastal waters cause pack ice to accumulate at the head of the Gulf of Bothnia and off Finland during most winters; occasionally the ice becomes banked up in pressure ridges that are almost 50 ft (15 m) high.
67
67
67
92
60°
25°
20°
30°
55°
A
B
C
D
E
1
2
3
4

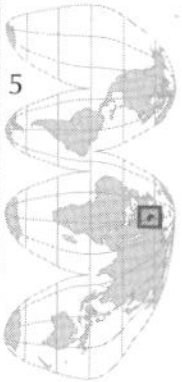

POLAND
VILNIUS
Druskininkai
Hrodna
Neman
Vawkavysk
Slonim
Brest
Kobryn
Pinsk
Luninyets
Pripet
Pripet Marshes
Hlybokaye
Lyepyel'
Western Dvina
Vitsyebsk
Maladzyechna
Barysaw
Orsha
MINSK
Zhodzina
BELARUS
Horki
Mahilyow
Baranavichy
Byerazino
Slutsk
Salihorsk
Babruysk
Krychaw
Ptsich
Zhlobin
Svyetlahorsk
Rechytsa
Homyel'
Mazyr
Kalinkavichy
Dnieper
Kyyivs'ke Vdskh
EDERATION
UKRAINE
55°
50°
25°
30°
0 km
100
0 miles
100
80
90
91
5
6
7
8
A
B
C
D
E

Formed in 1945 from the northern half of German East Prussia, and ceded to Russia under the Potsdam agreement, Kaliningrad oblast became a true enclave, completely separated from the rest of Russia, when Lithuania and Belarus achieved their independence in 1991.

Covering an area of approximately 34,000 sq miles (88,000 sq km), Pripet Marshes are the largest area of marshland in Europe.

Following the breakup of the Soviet Union, the Commonwealth of Independent States was established on December 8, 1991, by a treaty signed at Minsk, with the intent of coordinating the foreign policies of the newly independent former Soviet republics.

Ukraine, Moldova & Romania

A
B
C
D
1
2
3
4
5
20°
25°
50°
45°
81
82
86
POLAND
BELARUS
SLOVAKIA
HUNGARY
SERBIA
BULGARIA
ROMANIA
MOLDOVA
U K R
Pripet
Pripet Marshes
Kovel'
Luts'k
Korosten'
Bug
Rivne
Zhytomyr
L'viv
Ternopil'
Khmel'-nyts'kyy
Vinnytsya
Ivano-Frankivs'k
Uzhhorod
Kam"yanets'-Podil's'kyy
Dniester
Carpathian Mountains
Chernivtsi
Satu Mare
Ribnița
Bălți
Botoșani
Baia Mare
Suceava
Oradea
Dej
Dubăsari
Chișinău
Transylvania
Piatra-Neamț
Cluj-Napoca
Iași
Tiraspol
Arad
Târgu Mureș
Bacău
Tighina (Bendery)
Alba Iulia
Sighisoara
Timișoara
Siret
Basarabeasca
Deva
Sibiu
Reșița
Carpații Meridionali
Focșani
Brașov
Galați
Reni
Râmnicu Vâlcea
Buzău
Târgoviște
Brăila
Tulcea
Pitești
Ploiești
Drobeta-Turnu Severin
BUCHAREST
Craiova
Danube
Constanța
Corabia
Olt
Giurgiu
Eforie Sud
Mangalia
On April 25, 1986, engineers accidentally initiated an uncontrolled chain reaction in the number 4 reactor of the Chornobyl' nuclear power plant. The resulting explosion released 8 tons (tonnes) of radioactive material in the world's worst-ever nuclear accident.
Vlad Dracula or Vlad the Impaler was the real-life prince upon whom Bram Stoker based his famous Count Dracula. Dracula was born in Transylvania in 1431 in the town of Sighisoara.

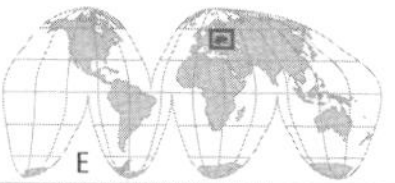

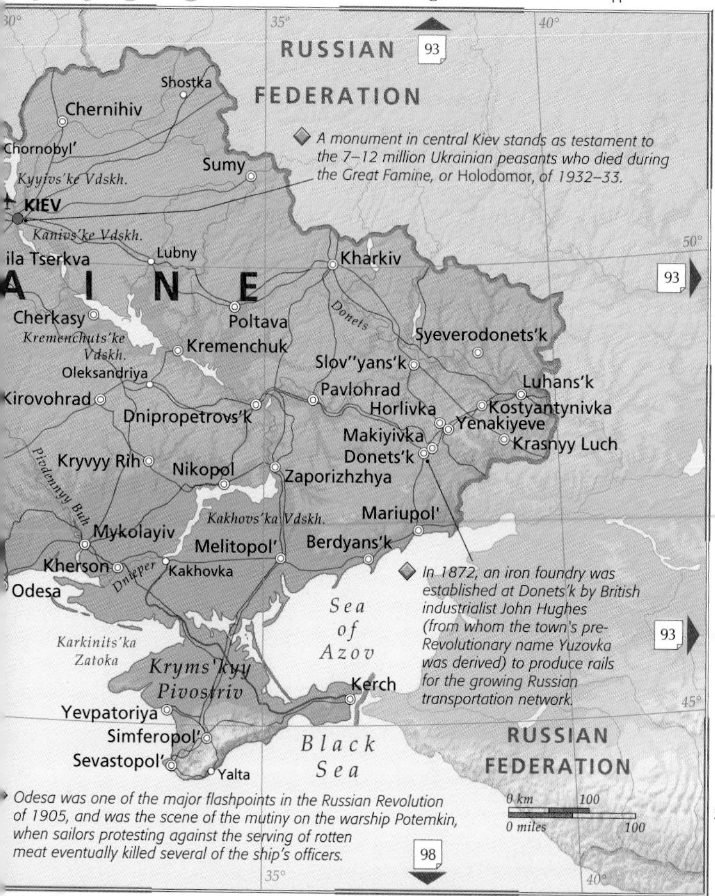

E
F
G
H
RUSSIAN FEDERATION
93
A monument in central Kiev stands as testament to the 7–12 million Ukrainian peasants who died during the Great Famine, or Holodomor, of 1932–33.
Shostka
Chernihiv
Chornobyl'
Sumy
Kyyivs'ke Vdskh.
KIEV
Kanivs'ke Vdskh.
ila Tserkva
Lubny
Kharkiv
AINE
Poltava
Cherkasy
Kremenchuts'ke Vdskh.
Kremenchuk
Donets
Syeverodonets'k
Slov''yans'k
Oleksandriya
Luhans'k
Pavlohrad
Kirovohrad
Horlivka
Kostyantynivka
Dnipropetrovs'k
Yenakiyeve
Makiyivka
Krasnyy Luch
Donets'k
Kryvyy Rih
Nikopol
Pivdennyy Buh
Zaporizhzhya
Kakhovs'ka Vdskh.
Mariupol'
Mykolayiv
Melitopol'
Berdyans'k
Kherson
Dnieper
Kakhovka
Odesa
In 1872, an iron foundry was established at Donets'k by British industrialist John Hughes (from whom the town's pre-Revolutionary name Yuzovka was derived) to produce rails for the growing Russian transportation network.
Sea of Azov
Karkinits'ka Zatoka
Kryms'kyy Pivostriv
Kerch
Yevpatoriya
Simferopol'
Black Sea
Sevastopol'
Yalta
RUSSIAN FEDERATION
Odesa was one of the major flashpoints in the Russian Revolution of 1905, and was the scene of the mutiny on the warship Potemkin, when sailors protesting against the serving of rotten meat eventually killed several of the ship's officers.
0 km 100
0 miles 100
98
30°
35°
40°
50°
45°
1
2
3
4
5

European Russia

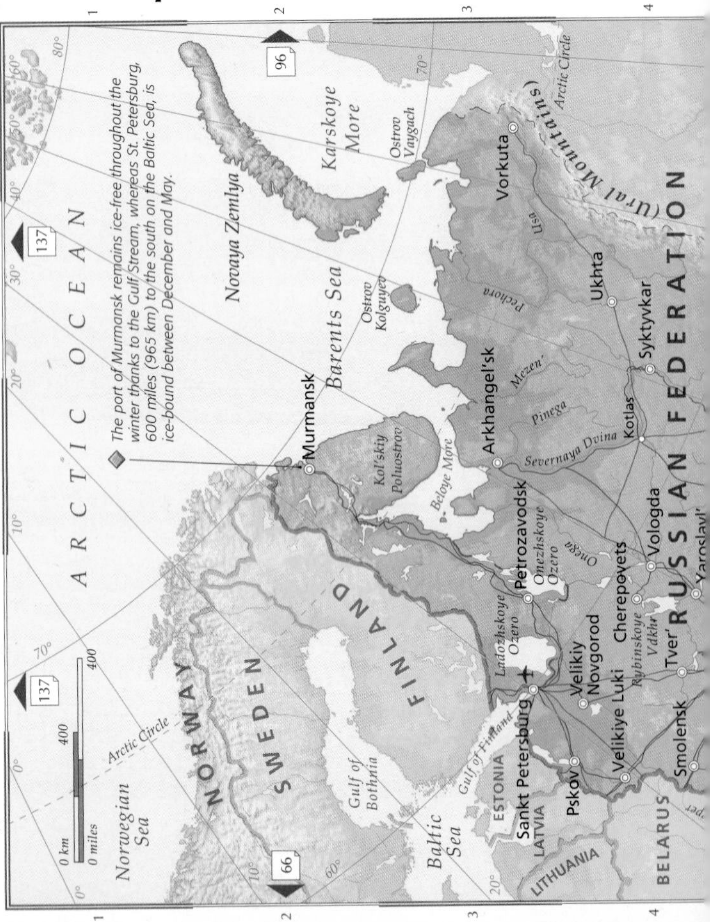
ARCTIC OCEAN
The port of Murmansk remains ice-free throughout the winter thanks to the Gulf Stream, whereas St. Petersburg, 600 miles (965 km) to the south on the Baltic Sea, is ice-bound between December and May.
Novaya Zemlya
Karskoye More
Ostrov Vaygach
Barents Sea
Ostrov Kolguyev
Murmansk
Kol'skiy Poluostrov
Beloye More
Arkhangel'sk
Mezen'
Pinega
Severnaya Dvina
Kotlas
Pechora
Usa
Vorkuta
Ukhta
Syktyvkar
(Ural Mountains)
Arctic Circle
RUSSIAN FEDERATION
Petrozavodsk
Onezhskoye Ozero
Onega
Vologda
Cherepovets
Yaroslavl'
Rybinskoye Vdkhr.
Ladozhskoye Ozero
Velikiy Novgorod
Tver'
Sankt Peterburg
Velikiye Luki
Smolensk
Pskov
Gulf of Finland
ESTONIA
LATVIA
LITHUANIA
BELARUS
FINLAND
SWEDEN
NORWAY
Gulf of Bothnia
Baltic Sea
Norwegian Sea
0 km 400
0 miles 400
137
96
66

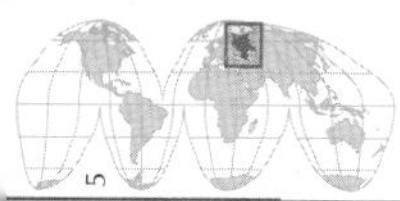

The Ural Mountains form the traditional boundary between Europe and Asia, extending some 1550 miles (2500 km). They were formed over 280 million years ago as the East European and Siberian plates moved together.
From August 1942 to February 1943, German armies laid siege to Volgograd, formerly known as Stalingrad. The Germans themselves were eventually surrounded and lost almost 250,000 men.
Caviar is the processed eggs, or roe, of sturgeon that live in the Caspian Sea and Volga River. Overfishing and poaching in recent years have seen the price of the finest caviar rise to around US$5000 for 2.2 lbs (1 kg).
Running from the Black Sea to the Caspian Sea, the Caucasus Mountains include Mt El'brus, which at 18,510 ft (5642 m) is the highest point in Europe, and still uplifting at the rate of 0.4 inches (1 cm) every year.
Ural'skiye Go
Perm'
Izhevsk
Naberezhnyye Chelny
Ufa
Orenburg
Orsk
Cheboksary
Vyatka
Kazan'
Volga
Ul'yanovsk
Tol'yatti
Samara
Balakovo
Saransk
Penza
Ryazan'
Tambov
Saratov
Mikhaylovka
Volgograd
Voronezh
Orël
Belgorod
Don
Donets
Rostov-na-Donu
Krasnodar
Stavropol'
Cherkessk
Elista
Kuma
Astrakhan'
Nal'chik
Vladikavkaz
Groznyy
Makhachkala
El'brus 18,510ft (5642m)
Caucasus
Sochi
Black Sea
Sea of Azov
Caspian Sea
Aral Sea
UKRAINE
KAZAKHSTAN
UZBEKISTAN
TURKMENISTAN
GEORGIA
ARMENIA
AZERBAIJAN
AZ.
TURKEY
IRAN
IRAQ
96
104
99
99
50°
60°
70°
40°
A
B
C
D
E
5
6
7
8

North & West Asia

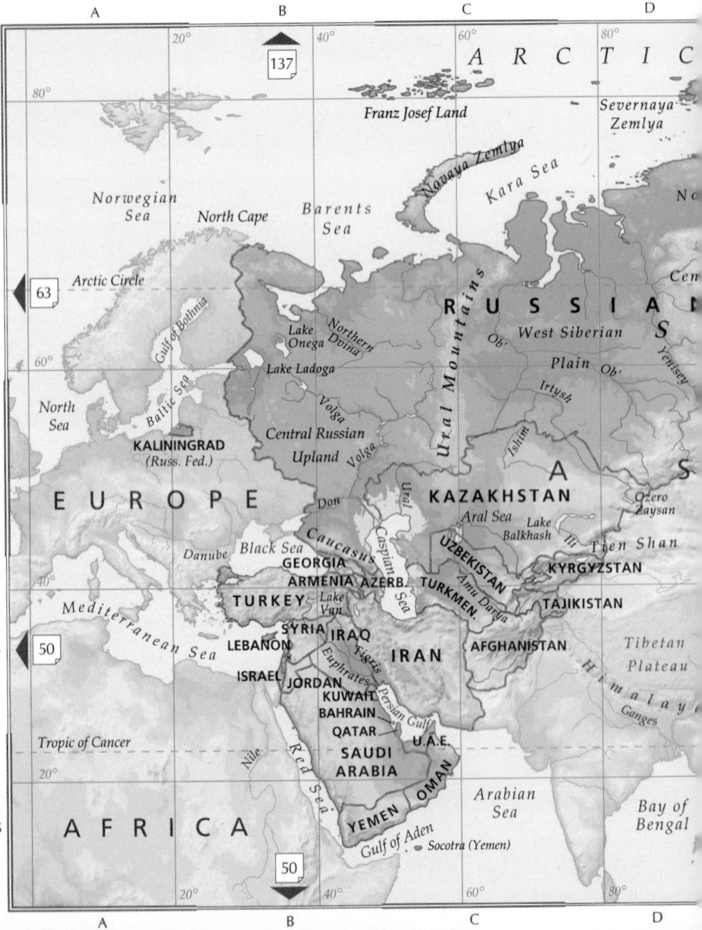
A
B
C
D
1
2
3
4
5
20°
40°
60°
80°
137
63
50
50
A R C T I C
Franz Josef Land
Severnaya Zemlya
Novaya Zemlya
Kara Sea
Norwegian Sea
North Cape
Barents Sea
Arctic Circle
Gulf of Bothnia
Lake Onega
Northern Dvina
Lake Ladoga
Baltic Sea
North Sea
KALININGRAD
(Russ. Fed.)
Volga
Central Russian Upland
Ural Mountains
RUSSIA
West Siberian Plain
Ob'
Irtysh
Yenisey
Ishim
EUROPE
Don
Ural
KAZAKHSTAN
Aral Sea
Lake Balkhash
Ili
Ozero Zaysan
Tien Shan
Danube
Black Sea
Caucasus
GEORGIA
ARMENIA
AZERB.
Caspian Sea
UZBEKISTAN
TURKMEN.
Amu Darya
KYRGYZSTAN
TAJIKISTAN
TURKEY
Lake Van
Mediterranean Sea
SYRIA
LEBANON
IRAQ
ISRAEL
JORDAN
Euphrates
Tigris
IRAN
AFGHANISTAN
Tibetan Plateau
Himalaya
Ganges
KUWAIT
BAHRAIN
QATAR
Persian Gulf
U.A.E.
Tropic of Cancer
Nile
Red Sea
SAUDI ARABIA
OMAN
YEMEN
Arabian Sea
Bay of Bengal
AFRICA
Gulf of Aden
Socotra (Yemen)

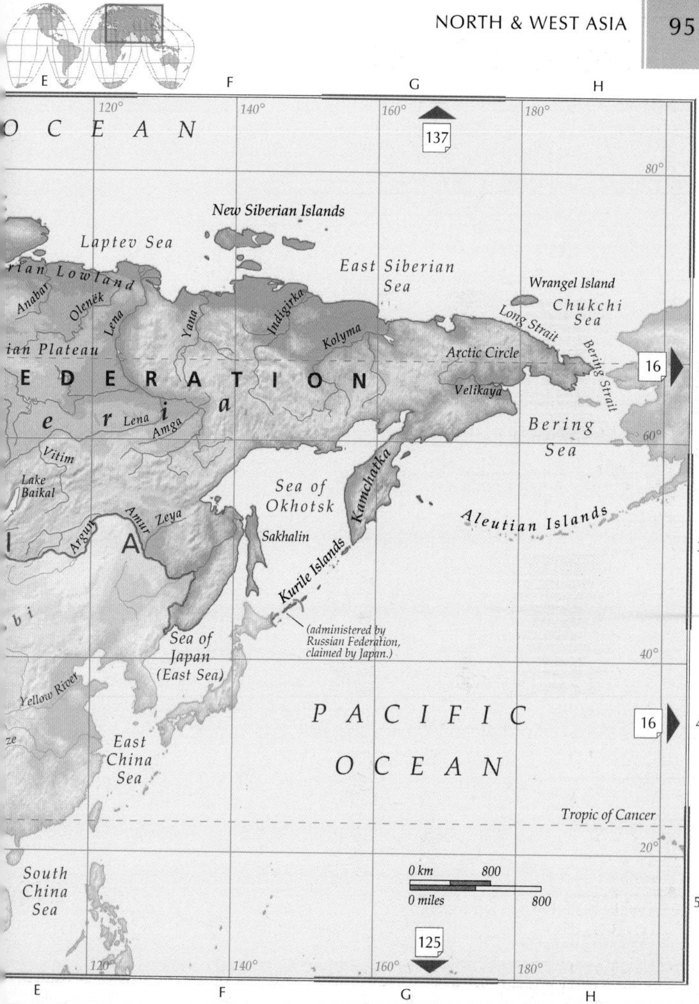
E
F
G
H
120°
140°
160°
180°
137
OCEAN
80°
1
New Siberian Islands
Laptev Sea
East Siberian Sea
rian Lowland
Anabar
Olenëk
Lena
Yana
Indigirka
Kolyma
Wrangel Island
Chukchi Sea
Long Strait
Bering Strait
ian Plateau
Arctic Circle
16
2
EDERATION
Velikaya
e r i a
Lena
Amga
Bering Sea
60°
Vitim
Lake Baikal
Sea of Okhotsk
Kamchatka
Amur
Zeya
Argun
Aleutian Islands
A
Sakhalin
3
Kurile Islands
bi
(administered by Russian Federation, claimed by Japan.)
Sea of Japan (East Sea)
40°
Yellow River
PACIFIC OCEAN
16
4
East China Sea
Tropic of Cancer
20°
South China Sea
0 km 800
0 miles 800
5
125
120°
140°
160°
180°
E
F
G
H

Russia & Kazakhstan

A
B
C
D
1
2
3
4
5
NORWAY
66
Arctic Circle
ARCTIC
DENMARK
GERMANY
SWEDEN
Barents Sea
Zemlya Frantsa-Iosifa
KALININGRAD
(part of Russian Federation)
FINLAND
Murmansk
POLAND
EST.
LAT.
LITH.
Novaya Zemlya
Karskoye Mo
Pskov
Sankt-Petersburg
91
Velikiy Novgorod
Arkhangel'sk
BELARUS
UKRAINE
Cherepovets
MOSCOW
Vologda
Vorkuta
MOLDOVA
Bryansk
Yaroslavl'
Nor
Tula
Syktyvkar
Salekhard
Ryazan'
Nizhniy Novgorod
Kirov
Ob'
Voronezh
Zapadno-Sibirskaya Ravnina
Rostov-na-Donu
Kazan'
Perm'
Izhevsk
Serov
R U
Volgograd
Samara
Ufa
Yekaterinburg
Nizhnevart
Sochi
Volga
Ural'sk
Ural'skiye Gory
Stavropol'
Chelyabinsk
F E D
GEORGIA
Nal'chik
Ural
Orenburg
Kostanay
Astrakhan'
Petropavlovsk
Krasnoya
Groznyy
Orsk
Rudnyy
Omsk
ARM.
Makhachkala
Kokshetau
Novosibirsk
To
102
Aktau
KAZAKHSTAN
ASTANA
Pavlodar
Keme
AZ.
Caspian Sea
Aral Sea
Barnaul
Karaganda
Novokuzn
Zhezkazgan
Semipalatinsk
TURKMENISTAN
UZBEKISTAN
Kyzylorda
Balkhash
Ust'-Kamenog
Ozero Balkhash
Shymkent
Taraz
Taldykorgan
IRAN
Almaty
KYRGYZSTAN
CHINA
104
A
B
C
D

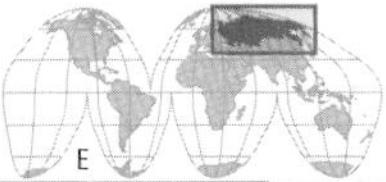

E
F
G
H
1
2
3
4
5
OCEAN
18
Ostrov Vrangelya
Vostochno-Sibirskoye More
Arctic Circle
Pevek
Anadyr'
Ambarchik
Bering Sea
Novosibirskiye Ostrova
More Laptevykh
Ozero Taymyr
Tiksi
134
Ossora
Ust'-Kamchatsks
Poluostov Kamchatka
Olenëk
Lena
Verkhoyanskiy Khrebet
Magadan
Petropavlovsk -Kamchatskiy
Okhotsk
Yakutsk
Sea of Okhotsk
Suntar
Siberia)
ATION
Sakhalin
Kuril'skiye Ostrova
Komsomol'sk-na-Amure
Skovorodno
Bratsk
Ozero Baykal
Blagoveshchensk
Yuzhhno-Sakhalinsk
Khabarovsk
Irkutsk
Chita
Amur
Ulan-Ude
CHINA
JAPAN
Vladivostok
MONGOLIA
0 km 500
0 miles 500
110
100°
110°
120°
130°
140°
160°
180°
80°
70°
60°
50°
40°

The Trans-Siberian Railroad, completed in 1916, runs 5578 miles (9297 km) between Moscow and Vladivostok. Crossing eight time zones, the journey takes six days.

Turkey & the Caucasus

A
B
C
D
1
2
3
4
5
25°
30°
35°
40°
91
86
87
54
ROMANIA
BULGARIA
Black Sea
An average of 50,000 commercial ships pass through the Bosporus a year, along with thousands of ferries and smaller passenger boats. The strait is three times busier than the Suez Canal and four times as busy as the Panama Canal.
Sinop
Edirne
Kırklareli
GREECE
Tekirdağ
Bosporus
İstanbul
Zonguldak
Küre Dağları
Kastamonu
Samsun
Çanakkale Boğazi (Dardanelles)
Marmara Denizi
İzmit
Adapazarı
Karabük
Canik Dağları
Bursa
Çanakkale
Çankırı
Kizil Irmak
Çorum
ANKARA
Tok
Balıkesir
Eskişehir
Kırıkkale
Sivas
Ayvalik
Kütahya
Lésvos
A n a t o l i a
T U R
Manisa
Afyon
Chíos
İzmir
Uşak
Tuz Gölü
Nevşehir
Kayseri
Sámos
Aydin
Niğde
Denizli
İsparta
Konya
Kahramanmara
Muğla
Ereğli
Bodrum
Antalya
Toros Dağları
Adana
Osmaniye
Dalaman
Mersin
Tarsus
Gaziar
İskenderun
Ródos
Antalya Körfezi
Megísti
Antak
Kárpathos
Kríti
TURKISH REPUBLIC OF NORTHERN CYPRUS
(recognized only by Turkey)
Girne (Kyrenia)
NICOSIA
Gazimağusa (Famagusta)
Larnaca
Paphos
Limassol
Mediterranean Sea
CYPRUS
LEBANON

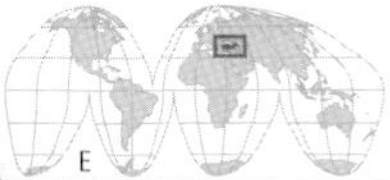

E
F
G
H
40°
45°
50°
RUSSIAN FEDERATION
93
The Spitak earthquake struck Armenia in 1988, killing at least 25,000 people and devastating the country's infrastructure.
1
Caucasus
Caspian Sea
Gagra
Sokhumi
Och'amch'ire
Enguri
K'ut'aisi
P'ot'i
GEORGIA
T'BILISI
Rust'avi
Bat'umi
Quba
Hopa
Kura
104
2
Sumqayıt
Mingäçevir
Vanadzor
Gäncä
BAKU
abzon
Rize
Gyumri
ARMENIA
AZERBAIJAN
40°
Karadeniz Dağları
Kars
Sevana Lich
Nagorno-Karabakh
YEREVAN
Aras
Xankändi
Erzurum
Erzincan
Büyükağri Daği (Mount Ararat) 16,853ft (5137m)
Aras
Naxçıvan
AZERBAIJAN
Länkäran
Y
Van Gölü
3
Muş
Elazig
Van
Azerbaijan has substantial oil reserves located in and around the Caspian Sea. They were some of the earliest oilfields in the world to be exploited.
Güney Dogu Toroslar
Tigris
alatya
Siirt
yarbakır
Batman
Kurdistan
diyaman
Mardin
IRAN
Şanliurfa
102
4
The salty water of Lake Van inhibits all animal life except the Pearl Mullet, a small fish that has adapted to the harsh conditions.
35°
Atatürk Dam, one of the largest dams in the world, was completed in 1990. The reservoir behind the dam covers an area of 315 sq miles (816 sq km) and often requires interruptions in the flow of the Euphrates River to maintain water levels.
0 km
200
0 miles
200
SYRIA
IRAQ
5
102
50°
40°
45°
E
F
G
H

The Near East

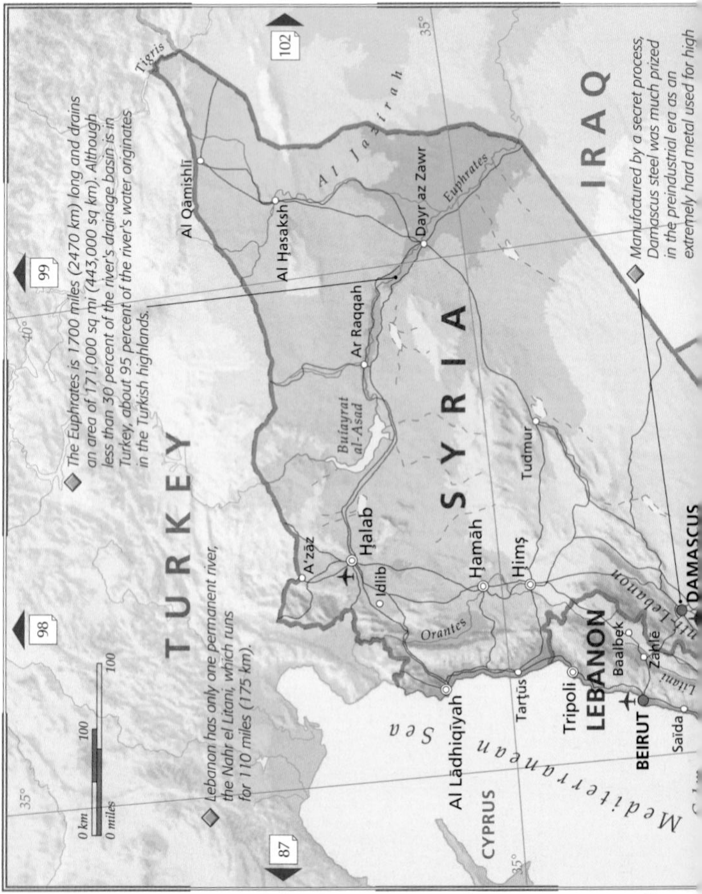
The Euphrates is 1700 miles (2470 km) long and drains an area of 171,000 sq mi (443,000 sq km). Although less than 30 percent of the river's drainage basin is in Turkey, about 95 percent of the river's water originates in the Turkish highlands.
Lebanon has only one permanent river, the Nahr el Litani, which runs for 110 miles (175 km).
Manufactured by a secret process, Damascus steel was much prized in the preindustrial era as an extremely hard metal used for high
TURKEY
SYRIA
IRAQ
LEBANON
CYPRUS
Mediterranean Sea
Al Jazīrah
Tigris
Euphrates
Orantes
Litani
Buḩayrat al-Asad
Al Qāmishlī
Al Ḩasaksh
Dayr az Zawr
Ar Raqqah
Tudmur
A'zāz
Ḩalab
Idlib
Ḩamāh
Ḩimş
Al Lādhiqīyah
Ţarţūs
Tripoli
Baalbek
Zahlé
BEIRUT
Saïda
DAMASCUS
0 km 100
0 miles 100
98
99
102
87

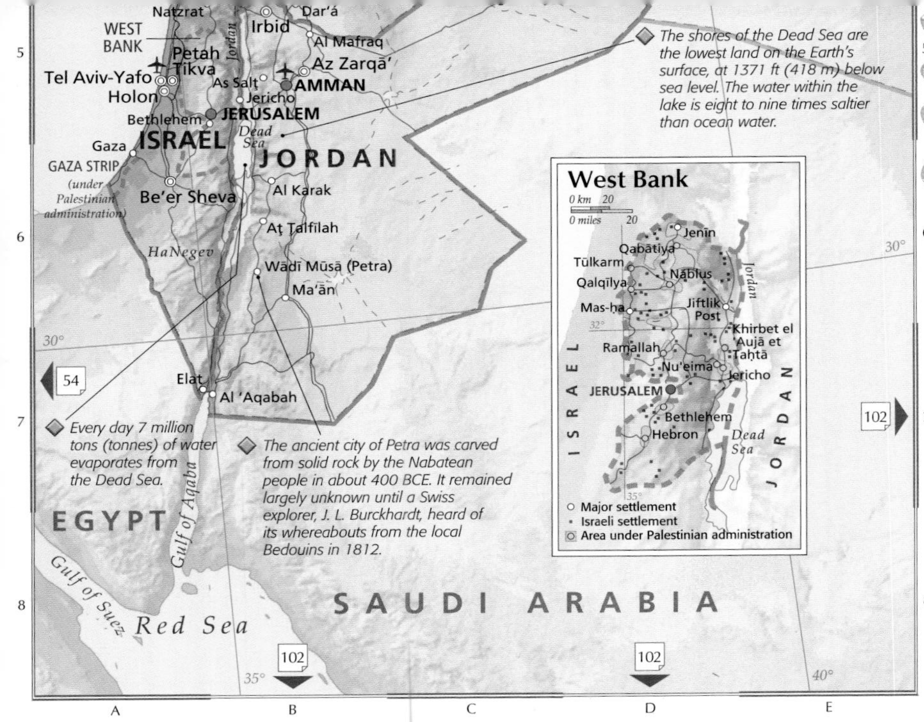
Natzrat
Dar'á
Irbid
WEST BANK
Jordan
Al Mafraq
Petah Tikva
Az Zarqā'
Tel Aviv-Yafo
As Salt
AMMAN
Holon
Jericho
Bethlehem
JERUSALEM
Dead Sea
Gaza
ISRAEL
JORDAN
GAZA STRIP
(under Palestinian administration)
Be'er Sheva
Al Karak
Aṭ Ṭafīlah
HaNegev
Wādī Mūsā (Petra)
Ma'ān
30°
54
Elat
Al 'Aqabah
Every day 7 million tons (tonnes) of water evaporates from the Dead Sea.
The ancient city of Petra was carved from solid rock by the Nabatean people in about 400 BCE. It remained largely unknown until a Swiss explorer, J. L. Burckhardt, heard of its whereabouts from the local Bedouins in 1812.
EGYPT
Gulf of Aqaba
Gulf of Suez
Red Sea
SAUDI ARABIA
102
35°
102
40°
The shores of the Dead Sea are the lowest land on the Earth's surface, at 1371 ft (418 m) below sea level. The water within the lake is eight to nine times saltier than ocean water.
West Bank
0 km 20
0 miles 20
Jenīn
Qabāṭiya
Ṭūlkarm
Nāblus
Qalqīlya
Jordan
Jiftlik Post
Mas-ḥa
32°
Khirbet el 'Aujā et Taḥtā
Ramallah
Nu'eima
Jericho
ISRAEL
JERUSALEM
Bethlehem
Hebron
Dead Sea
JORDAN
35°
Major settlement
Israeli settlement
Area under Palestinian administration
30°
102
5
6
7
8
A
B
C
D
E

The Middle East

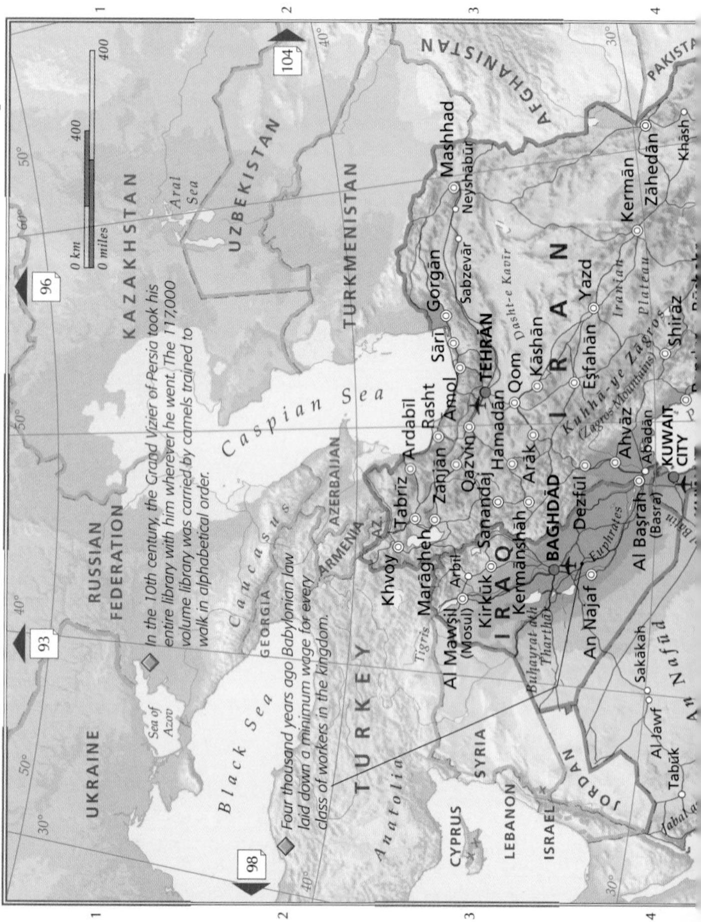

RUSSIAN FEDERATION
UKRAINE
KAZAKHSTAN
UZBEKISTAN
TURKMENISTAN
AFGHANISTAN
PAKISTAN
GEORGIA
ARMENIA
AZERBAIJAN
AZ.
TURKEY
SYRIA
LEBANON
ISRAEL
CYPRUS
JORDAN
IRAQ
IRAN
KUWAIT CITY
Sea of Azov
Black Sea
Caspian Sea
Aral Sea
Caucasus
Anatolia
Tigris
Euphrates
Buhayrat ath Tharthār
Dasht-e Kavir
Iranian Plateau
Kuhhā-ye Zāgros (Zagros Mountains)
An Nafūd
Jabal
In the 10th century, the Grand Vizier of Persia took his entire library with him wherever he went. The 117,000 volume library was carried by camels trained to walk in alphabetical order.
Four thousand years ago Babylonian law laid down a minimum wage for every class of workers in the kingdom.
0 km 400
0 miles 400
Mashhad
Neyshābūr
Sabzevār
Gorgān
Sārī
Āmol
TEHRĀN
Rasht
Ardabīl
Tabrīz
Zanjān
Qazvīn
Hamadān
Qom
Kāshān
Eşfahān
Yazd
Kermān
Zāhedān
Khāsh
Shīrāz
Arāk
Sanandaj
Kermānshāh
Khvoy
Marāgheh
Arbīl
Kirkūk
Al Mawşil (Mosul)
BAGHDĀD
Dezfūl
Ahvāz
Ābādān
Al Başrah (Basra)
An Najaf
Sakākah
Al Jawf
Tabūk
93
96
98
104

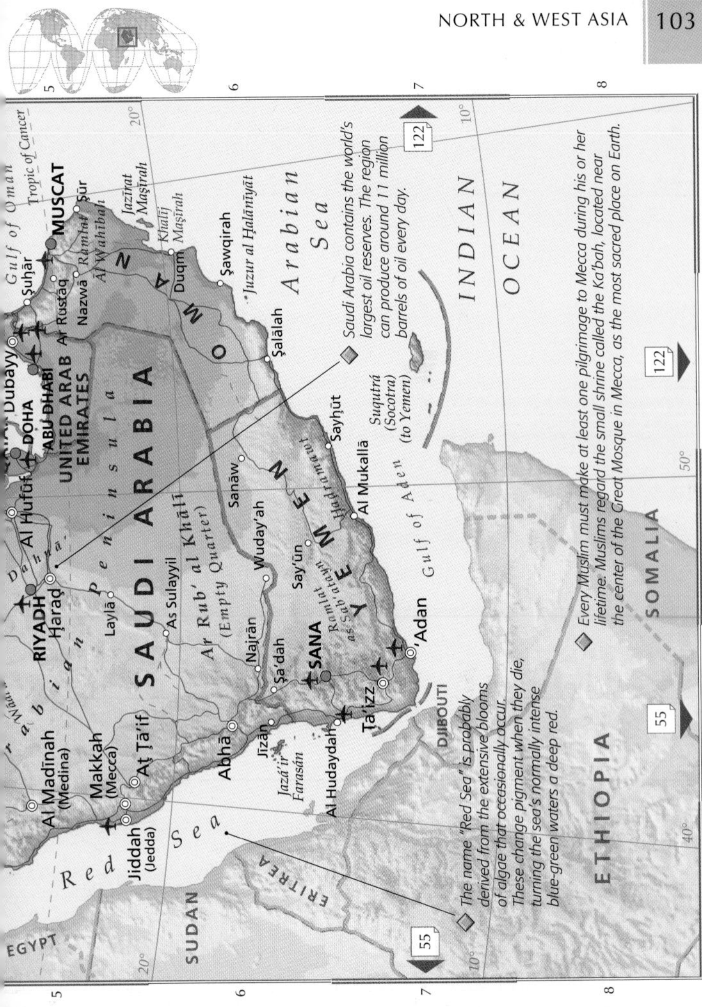
SAUDI ARABIA
YEMEN
OMAN
UNITED ARAB EMIRATES
ABU DHABI
DOHA
Dubayy
RIYADH
SANA
MUSCAT
Al Madinah (Medina)
Makkah (Mecca)
Jiddah (Jedda)
Aṭ Ṭā'if
Abhā
Jīzān
Jazā'ir Farasān
Al Hudaydah
Ta'izz
'Adan
Ṣa'dah
Najrān
As Sulayyil
Laylā
Ḥaraḍ
Al Hufūf
Wuday'ah
Say'ūn
Sanāw
Al Mukallā
Sayḥūt
Ṣalālah
Ṣawqirah
Duqm
Nazwá
Ar Rustāq
Ṣuḥār
Ṣūr
Ar Rub' al Khālī (Empty Quarter)
Ramlat as Sab'atayn
Ḥaḍramawt
Ad Dahnā
Arabian Peninsula
Ramlat Āl Wahībah
Jazīrat Maṣīrah
Khalīj Maṣīrah
Juzur al Ḥalānīyāt
Suquṭrá (Socotra) (to Yemen)
Gulf of Oman
Tropic of Cancer
Arabian Sea
INDIAN OCEAN
Gulf of Aden
Red Sea
EGYPT
SUDAN
ERITREA
ETHIOPIA
DJIBOUTI
SOMALIA
20°
10°
40°
50°
55
122
A
B
C
D
E
5
6
7
8
Saudi Arabia contains the world's largest oil reserves. The region can produce around 11 million barrels of oil every day.
Every Muslim must make at least one pilgrimage to Mecca during his or her lifetime. Muslims regard the small shrine called the Ka'bah, located near the center of the Great Mosque in Mecca, as the most sacred place on Earth.
The name "Red Sea" is probably derived from the extensive blooms of algae that occasionally occur. These change pigment when they die, turning the sea's normally intense blue-green waters a deep red.

Central Asia

A
B
C
D
1
2
3
4
5
96
99
102
KAZAKHSTAN
Aral Sea
Ustyurt Plateau
Turan Lowland
Since 1960, the Aral Sea has shrunk by 90 percent, becoming extremely saline and consequently losing all but one of its once-abundant fish species.
Nukus
Köneürgenç
UZBEKISTAN
Daşoguz
Urganch
To'rtko'l
Uchquduq
Zarafs
Aydark
Türkmenbaşy
Hazar
Balkanabat
Bereket
Caspian Sea
TURKMENISTAN
Garagum
Serdar
Seýdi
Buxoro
Nav
Samar
Qarshi
Baharly
Gökdepe
Türkmenabat
Abadan
AŞGABAT
Sayat
Amu Darya
Garagum Kanaly
Mary
Bayramaly
Kaka
Atamyrat
Tejen
Murgap
Aqcha
Sheberghān
Mazār-e Sh
The desert of Kara Kum (Garagum) occupies over 70 percent of Turkmenistan, severely limiting human settlement across much of the country.
Bālā Morghāb
Meyman
Serhetabat
Daryā-ye Morghā
IRAN
Harīrūd
Herāt
The Kara Kum (Garagum) Canal, the world's longest irrigation canal, stretches some 850 miles (1375 km) and is known as the "River of Life," since it irrigates large areas of arid land.
AFGHANISTAN
Farāh
Gereshk
Zaranj
Dasht-e-Mārgow
Kandahār
Daryā-ye Helmand
0 km 200
0 miles 200
50°
60°
40°
30°

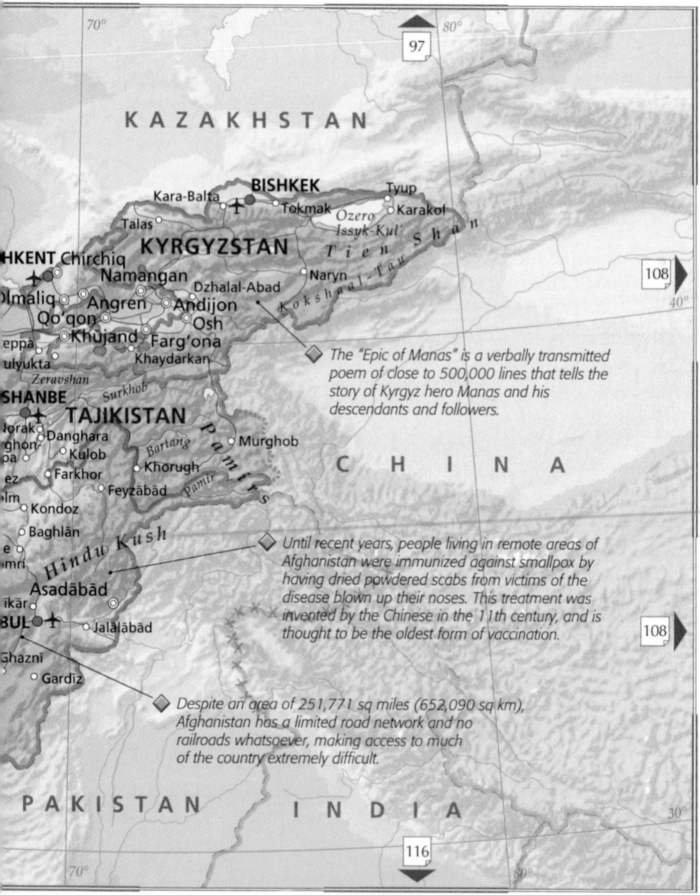
E
F
G
H
1
2
3
4
5
70°
80°
40°
30°
97
108
108
116
KAZAKHSTAN
BISHKEK
Kara-Balta
Tyup
Tokmak
Karakol
Ozero Issyk-Kul'
Talas
KYRGYZSTAN
Tien Shan
HKENT
Chirchiq
Namangan
Naryn
Kokshaal-Tau
Dzhalal-Abad
Olmaliq
Angren
Andijon
Qo'qon
Osh
Khujand
Farg'ona
eppa
Khaydarkan
ulyukta
Zeravshan
Surkhob
SHANBE
TAJIKISTAN
Pamirs
Norak
Danghara
Murghob
ghon
Bartang
Kulob
Khorugh
Farkhor
Pamir
Feyzābād
Kondoz
Baghlān
Hindu Kush
Asadābād
BUL
Jalālābād
Ghaznī
Gardīz
CHINA
PAKISTAN
INDIA
The "Epic of Manas" is a verbally transmitted poem of close to 500,000 lines that tells the story of Kyrgyz hero Manas and his descendants and followers.
Until recent years, people living in remote areas of Afghanistan were immunized against smallpox by having dried powdered scabs from victims of the disease blown up their noses. This treatment was invented by the Chinese in the 11th century, and is thought to be the oldest form of vaccination.
Despite an area of 251,771 sq miles (652,090 sq km), Afghanistan has a limited road network and no railroads whatsoever, making access to much of the country extremely difficult.

South & East Asia

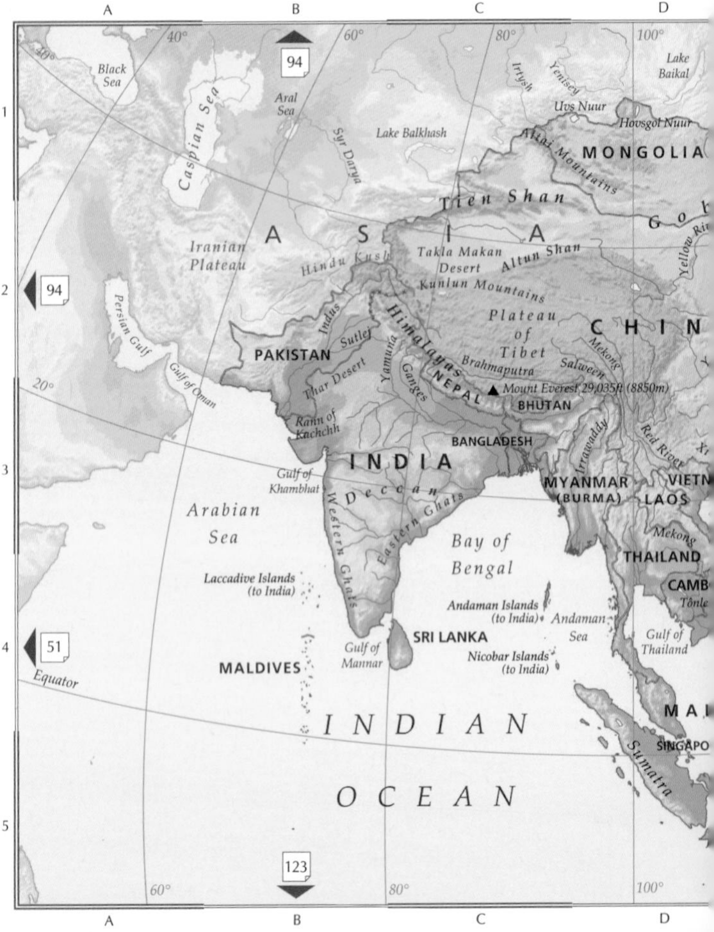
Black Sea
Caspian Sea
Aral Sea
Syr Darya
Lake Balkhash
Irtysh
Yenisey
Uvs Nuur
Lake Baikal
Hovsgol Nuur
Altai Mountains
MONGOLIA
Tien Shan
A S I A
Iranian Plateau
Hindu Kush
Takla Makan Desert
Altun Shan
Kunlun Mountains
Plateau of Tibet
Persian Gulf
Gulf of Oman
Indus
Sutlej
PAKISTAN
Thar Desert
Himalayas
Yamuna
Ganges
NEPAL
Brahmaputra
Mount Everest 29,035ft (8850m)
BHUTAN
Salween
Mekong
Rann of Kachchh
BANGLADESH
INDIA
Irrawaddy
Red River
Gulf of Khambhat
Deccan
Western Ghats
Eastern Ghats
MYANMAR (BURMA)
LAOS
Arabian Sea
Bay of Bengal
Mekong
THAILAND
Laccadive Islands (to India)
Andaman Islands (to India)
Andaman Sea
Gulf of Mannar
SRI LANKA
Gulf of Thailand
MALDIVES
Nicobar Islands (to India)
Equator
INDIAN OCEAN
SINGAPO
Sumatra
94
51
123
A B C D
1 2 3 4 5
40°
60°
80°
100°
20°

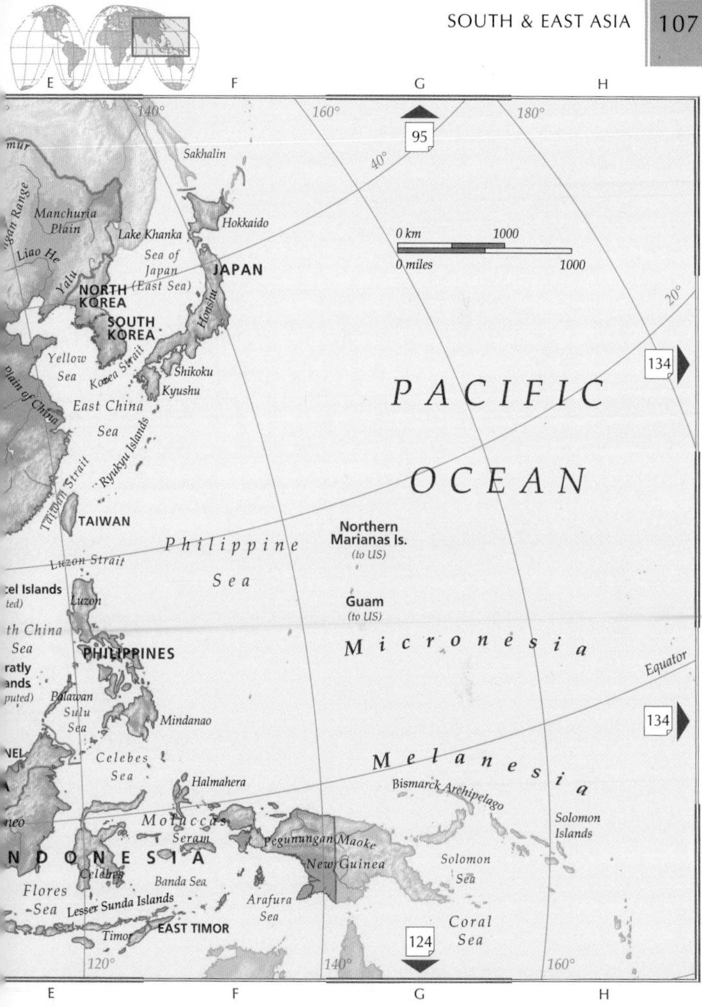
E
F
G
H
140°
160°
180°
95
Sakhalin
40°
Hokkaido
Manchuria Plain
Lake Khanka
Liao He
Sea of Japan (East Sea)
JAPAN
Yalu
NORTH KOREA
SOUTH KOREA
Honshu
0 km 1000
0 miles 1000
20°
Yellow Sea
Korea Strait
Shikoku
Kyushu
134
PACIFIC
OCEAN
East China Sea
Ryukyu Islands
Taiwan Strait
TAIWAN
Northern Marianas Is. (to US)
Philippine Sea
Luzon Strait
Luzon
Guam (to US)
PHILIPPINES
Micronesia
Equator
Palawan
Sulu Sea
Mindanao
134
Celebes Sea
Melanesia
Halmahera
Bismarck Archipelago
Moluccas
Seram
Solomon Islands
Pegunungan Maoke
New Guinea
Solomon Sea
Celebes
Banda Sea
Flores Sea
Lesser Sunda Islands
Arafura Sea
Coral Sea
Timor
EAST TIMOR
124
120°
140°
160°
1
2
3
4
5

Western China & Mongolia

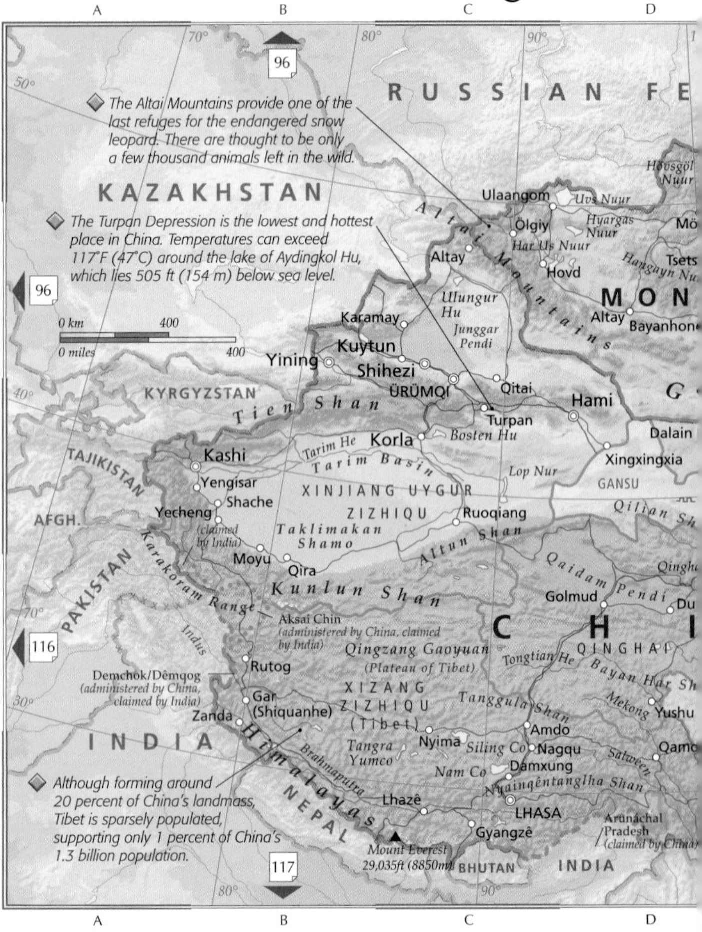
A
B
C
D
1
2
3
4
5
70°
80°
90°
50°
40°
30°
96
116
117
RUSSIAN FE
The Altai Mountains provide one of the last refuges for the endangered snow leopard. There are thought to be only a few thousand animals left in the wild.
KAZAKHSTAN
The Turpan Depression is the lowest and hottest place in China. Temperatures can exceed 117°F (47°C) around the lake of Aydingkol Hu, which lies 505 ft (154 m) below sea level.
0 km
400
0 miles
400
Hövsgöl Nuur
Ulaangom
Uvs Nuur
Ölgiy
Hyargas Nuur
Har Us Nuur
Hovd
Altay
Altai Mountains
Hangayn Nu
Tsets
MON
Altay
Bayanhon
Ulungur Hu
Junggar Pendi
Karamay
Kuytun
Yining
Shihezi
ÜRÜMQI
Qitai
Turpan
Hami
G
KYRGYZSTAN
Tien Shan
Bosten Hu
Korla
Dalain
Xingxingxia
TAJIKISTAN
Kashi
Tarim He
Tarim Basin
Lop Nur
GANSU
Yengisar
XINJIANG UYGUR
Shache
ZIZHIQU
Ruoqiang
Qilian Sh
AFGH.
Yecheng
(claimed by India)
Taklimakan Shamo
Altun Shan
Moyu
Qira
Qaidam Pendi
Qingh
Karakoram Range
Kunlun Shan
Golmud
Du
PAKISTAN
Aksai Chin
(administered by China, claimed by India)
C
H
I
Indus
Qingzang Gaoyuan
(Plateau of Tibet)
Tongtian He
QINGHAI
Bayan Har Sh
Rutog
Demchok/Dêmqog
(administered by China, claimed by India)
XIZANG
ZIZHIQU
(Tibet)
Gar
(Shiquanhe)
Tanggula Shan
Mekong
Yushu
Zanda
Amdo
INDIA
Himalayas
Brahmaputra
Tangra Yumco
Nyima
Siling Co
Nagqu
Salween
Qamd
Nam Co
Damxung
Nyainqêntanglha Shan
Although forming around 20 percent of China's landmass, Tibet is sparsely populated, supporting only 1 percent of China's 1.3 billion population.
NEPAL
Lhazê
LHASA
Arunachal Pradesh
(claimed by China)
Gyangzê
Mount Everest
29,035ft (8850m)
BHUTAN
INDIA

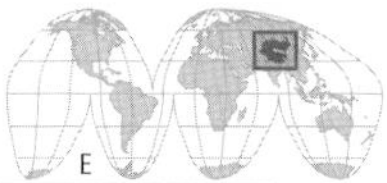

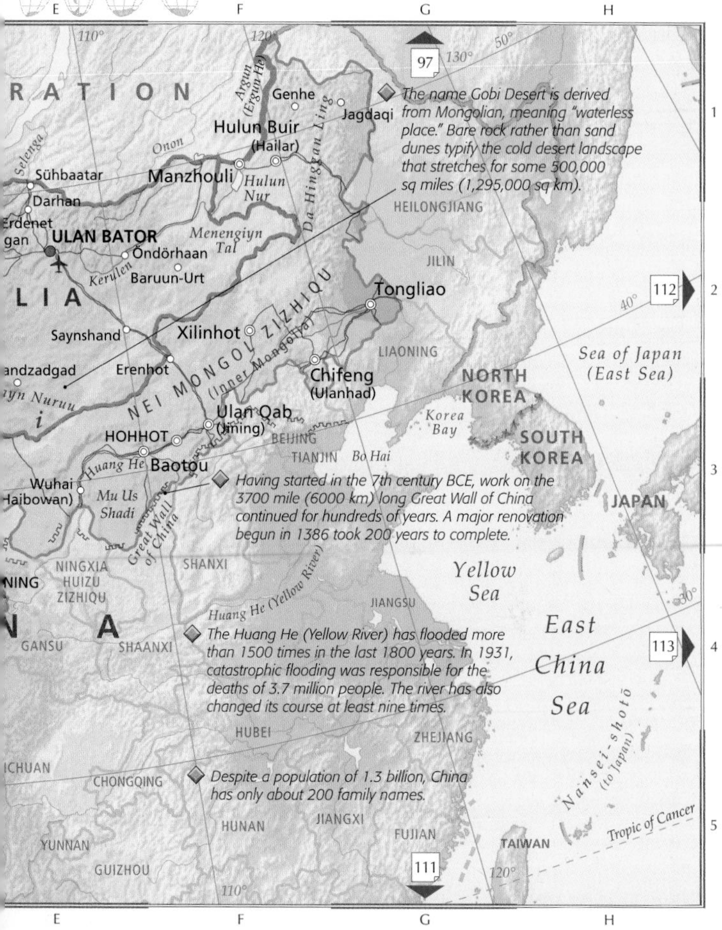
E
F
G
H
1
2
3
4
5
110°
120°
130°
50°
40°
30°
120°
110°
97
112
113
111
RATION
LIA
Argun (Ergun He)
Genhe
Jagdaqi
Hulun Buir (Hailar)
Da Hinggan Ling
Selenga
Onon
Sühbaatar
Manzhouli
Hulun Nur
Darhan
Erdenet
gan
ULAN BATOR
Menengiyn Tal
Öndörhaan
Kerulen
Baruun-Urt
HEILONGJIANG
JILIN
Tongliao
NEI MONGOL ZIZHIQU (Inner Mongolia)
Saynshand
Xilinhot
LIAONING
Sea of Japan (East Sea)
andzadgad
Erenhot
Chifeng (Ulanhad)
NORTH KOREA
Korea Bay
Ulan Qab (Jining)
HOHHOT
BEIJING
TIANJIN
Bo Hai
SOUTH KOREA
Huang He
Baotou
Wuhai
Haibowan)
Mu Us Shadi
Great Wall of China
JAPAN
NINGXIA HUIZU ZIZHIQU
NING
SHANXI
Yellow Sea
Huang He (Yellow River)
JIANGSU
A
GANSU
SHAANXI
East China Sea
HUBEI
ZHEJIANG
Nansei-shotō (to Japan)
ICHUAN
CHONGQING
HUNAN
JIANGXI
FUJIAN
TAIWAN
Tropic of Cancer
YUNNAN
GUIZHOU
The name Gobi Desert is derived from Mongolian, meaning "waterless place." Bare rock rather than sand dunes typify the cold desert landscape that stretches for some 500,000 sq miles (1,295,000 sq km).
Having started in the 7th century BCE, work on the 3700 mile (6000 km) long Great Wall of China continued for hundreds of years. A major renovation begun in 1386 took 200 years to complete.
The Huang He (Yellow River) has flooded more than 1500 times in the last 1800 years. In 1931, catastrophic flooding was responsible for the deaths of 3.7 million people. The river has also changed its course at least nine times.
Despite a population of 1.3 billion, China has only about 200 family names.

Eastern China & Korea

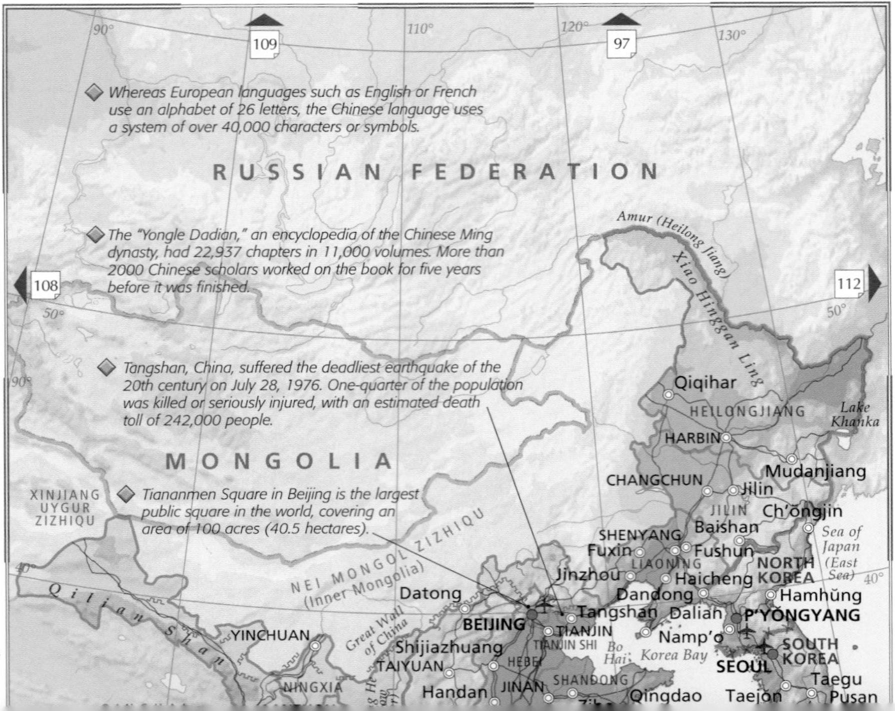

RUSSIAN FEDERATION
MONGOLIA
NEI MONGOL ZIZHIQU (Inner Mongolia)
XINJIANG UYGUR ZIZHIQU
HEILONGJIANG
JILIN
LIAONING
HEBEI
SHANDONG
TIANJIN SHI
NINGXIA
NORTH KOREA
SOUTH KOREA
Amur (Heilong Jiang)
Xiao Hinggan Ling
Qilian Shan
Lake Khanka
Sea of Japan (East Sea)
Korea Bay
Bo Hai
Great Wall of China
Qiqihar
HARBIN
Mudanjiang
CHANGCHUN
Jilin
Ch'ŏngjin
Baishan
SHENYANG
Fushun
Fuxin
Haicheng
Jinzhou
Dandong
Hamhŭng
P'YŎNGYANG
Namp'o
SEOUL
Taegu
Taejŏn
Pusan
Dalian
Tangshan
TIANJIN
BEIJING
Qingdao
JINAN
Shijiazhuang
Handan
Datong
TAIYUAN
YINCHUAN

◆ Whereas European languages such as English or French use an alphabet of 26 letters, the Chinese language uses a system of over 40,000 characters or symbols.

◆ The "Yongle Dadian," an encyclopedia of the Chinese Ming dynasty, had 22,937 chapters in 11,000 volumes. More than 2000 Chinese scholars worked on the book for five years before it was finished.

◆ Tangshan, China, suffered the deadliest earthquake of the 20th century on July 28, 1976. One-quarter of the population was killed or seriously injured, with an estimated death toll of 242,000 people.

◆ Tiananmen Square in Beijing is the largest public square in the world, covering an area of 100 acres (40.5 hectares).

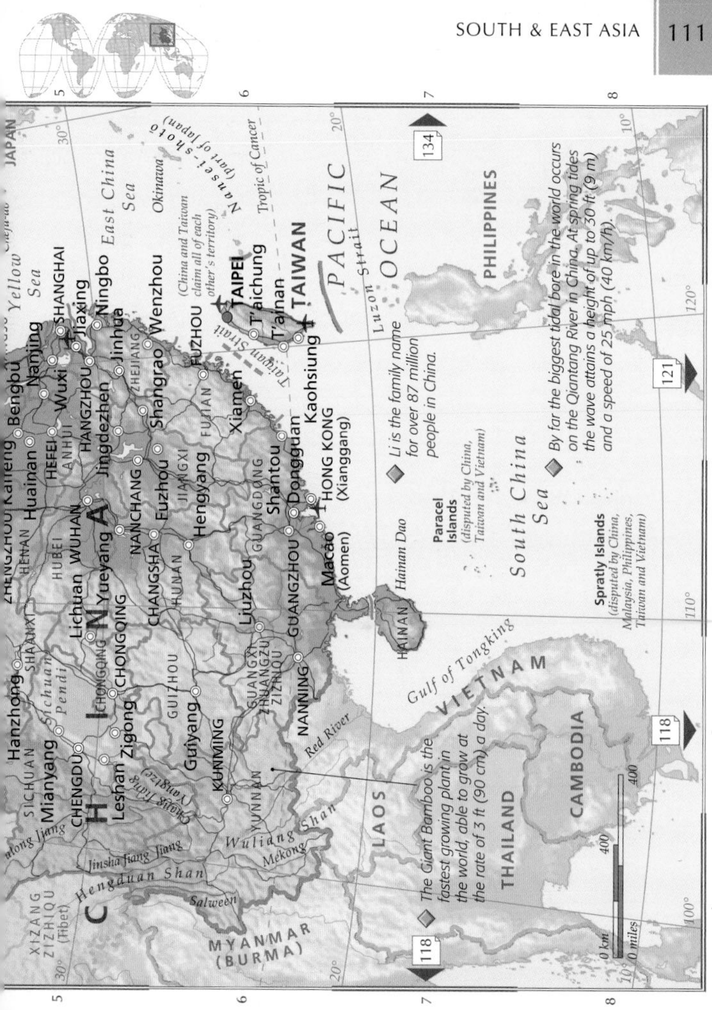
The Giant Bamboo is the fastest growing plant in the world, able to grow at the rate of 3 ft (90 cm) a day.
Li is the family name for over 87 million people in China.
By far the biggest tidal bore in the world occurs on the Qiantang River in China. At spring tides the wave attains a height of up to 30 ft (9 m) and a speed of 25 mph (40 km/h).
CHINA
JAPAN
Yellow Sea
East China Sea
Okinawa
Nansei-shoto (part of Japan)
(China and Taiwan claim all of each other's territory)
Tropic of Cancer
PACIFIC OCEAN
Luzon Strait
Taiwan Strait
TAIWAN
TAIPEI
T'aichung
T'ainan
Kaohsiung
PHILIPPINES
South China Sea
Paracel Islands (disputed by China, Taiwan and Vietnam)
Spratly Islands (disputed by China, Malaysia, Philippines, Taiwan and Vietnam)
Hainan Dao
HAINAN
Gulf of Tongking
VIETNAM
LAOS
THAILAND
CAMBODIA
MYANMAR (BURMA)
XIZANG ZIZHIQU (Tibet)
Hengduan Shan
Salween
Mekong
Wuliang Shan
Red River
Jinsha Jiang
Chang Jiang (Yangtze)
Sichuan Pendi
SICHUAN
YUNNAN
GUIZHOU
GUANGXI ZHUANGZU ZIZHIQU
GUANGDONG
HUNAN
HUBEI
HENAN
SHAANXI
ANHUI
JIANGXI
FUJIAN
ZHEJIANG
CHONGQING
Hanzhong
Mianyang
CHENGDU
Leshan
Zigong
CHONGQING
Lichuan
Guiyang
KUNMING
NANNING
Liuzhou
GUANGZHOU
Macao (Aomen)
HONG KONG (Xianggang)
Dongguan
Shantou
Xiamen
FUZHOU
Hengyang
CHANGSHA
Yueyang
WUHAN
NANCHANG
Fuzhou
Shangrao
Jingdezhen
HANGZHOU
HEFEI
Huainan
Bengbu
Nanjing
Wuxi
Jiaxing
SHANGHAI
Ningbo
Jinhua
Wenzhou
ZHENGZHOU
Kaifeng
0 km 400
0 miles 400
118
121
134

Japan

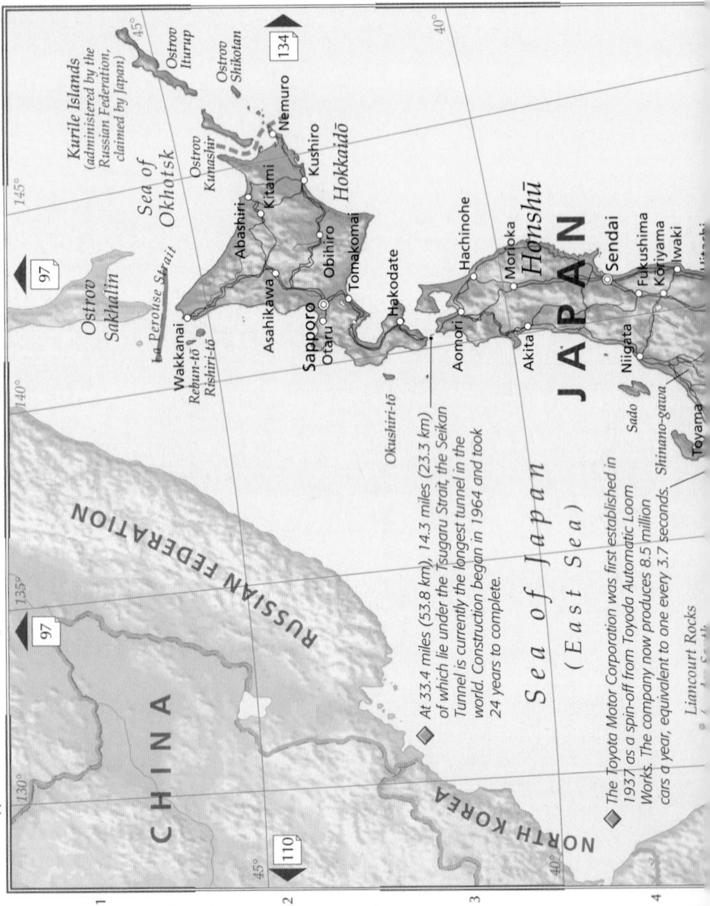
Kurile Islands
(administered by the Russian Federation, claimed by Japan)
Ostrov Iturup
Ostrov Shikotan
Ostrov Kunashir
Sea of Okhotsk
Nemuro
Kushiro
Hokkaidō
Kitami
Abashiri
Obihiro
Tomakomai
Asahikawa
Sapporo
Otaru
Hakodate
Wakkanai
Rebun-tō
Rishiri-tō
La Perouse Strait
Ostrov Sakhalin
Okushiri-tō
Aomori
Hachinohe
Morioka
Akita
Honshū
Sendai
Fukushima
Koriyama
Iwaki
Niigata
Sado
Shinano-gawa
Toyama
JAPAN
Sea of Japan
(East Sea)
Liancourt Rocks
RUSSIAN FEDERATION
CHINA
NORTH KOREA
97
134
110
45°
40°
130°
135°
140°
145°
A
B
C
D
E
1
2
3
4

At 33.4 miles (53.8 km), 14.3 miles (23.3 km) of which lie under the Tsugaru Strait, the Seikan Tunnel is currently the longest tunnel in the world. Construction began in 1964 and took 24 years to complete.

The Toyota Motor Corporation was first established in 1937 as a spin-off from Toyoda Automatic Loom Works. The company now produces 8.5 million cars a year, equivalent to one every 3.7 seconds.

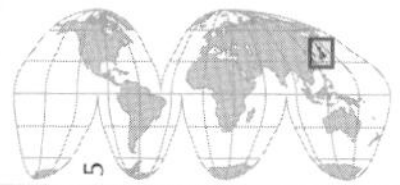

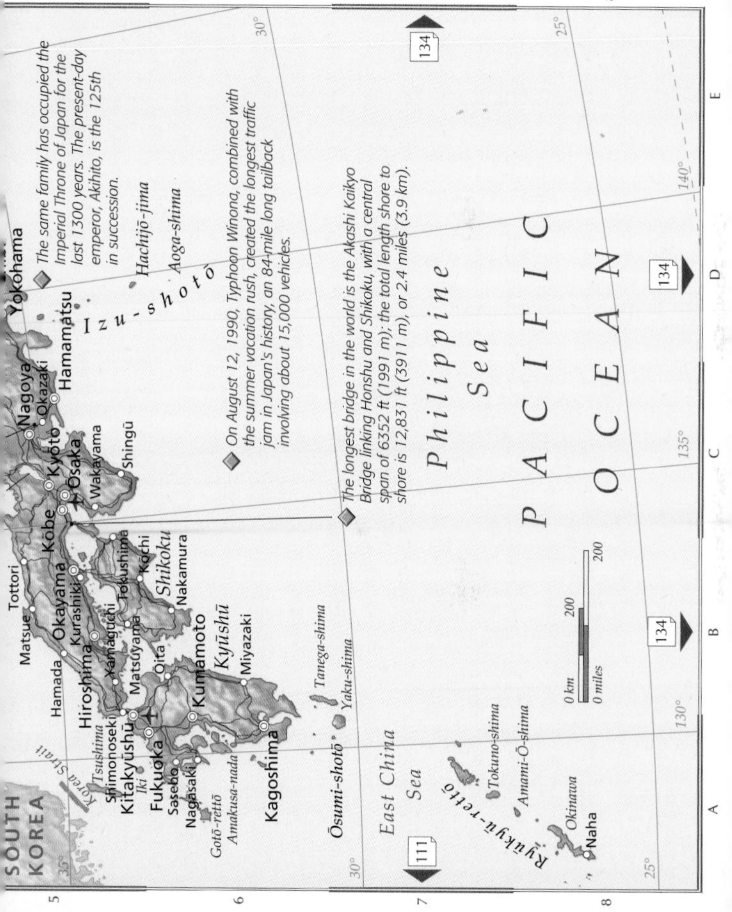
SOUTH KOREA
Korea Strait
Tsushima
Iki
Gotō-rettō
Amakusa-nada
Shimonoseki
Kitakyūshū
Fukuoka
Sasebo
Nagasaki
Kagoshima
Hamada
Hiroshima
Matsue
Tottori
Okayama
Kurashiki
Yamaguchi
Matsuyama
Ōita
Kumamoto
Kyūshū
Miyazaki
Tokushima
Kōchi
Shikoku
Nakamura
Kōbe
Kyōto
Ōsaka
Wakayama
Shingū
Nagoya
Okazaki
Hamamatsu
Yokohama
Izu-shotō
Hachijō-jima
Aoga-shima
Tanega-shima
Yaku-shima
Ōsumi-shotō
East China Sea
Tokuno-shima
Amami-Ō-shima
Ryukyu-rettō
Okinawa
Naha
Philippine Sea
PACIFIC OCEAN
The same family has occupied the Imperial Throne of Japan for the last 1300 years. The present-day emperor, Akihito, is the 125th in succession.
On August 12, 1990, Typhoon Winona, combined with the summer vacation rush, created the longest traffic jam in Japan's history, an 84-mile long tailback involving about 15,000 vehicles.
The longest bridge in the world is the Akashi Kaikyo Bridge linking Honshu and Shikoku, with a central span of 6352 ft (1991 m); the total length shore to shore is 12,831 ft (3911 m), or 2.4 miles (3.9 km).
0 km 200
0 miles 200
35°
30°
25°
130°
135°
140°
111
134
A
B
C
D
E
5
6
7
8

Southern India & Sri Lanka

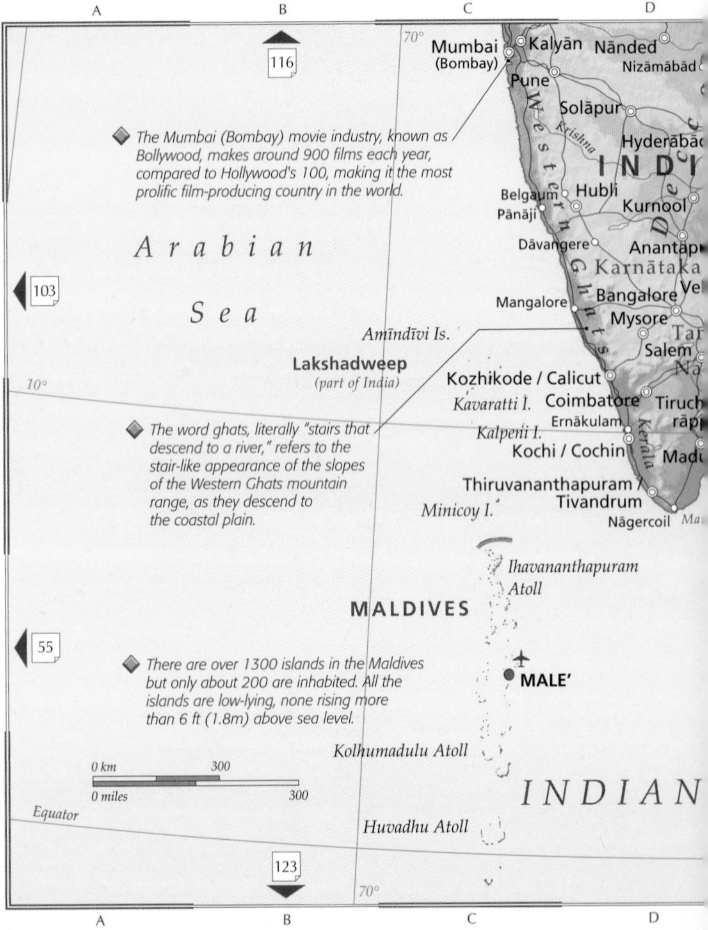
A
B
C
D
1
2
3
4
5
116
103
55
123
70°
10°
Mumbai
(Bombay)
Kalyān
Nānded
Nizāmābād
Pune
Solāpur
Hyderābād
Krishna
Western Ghats
Belgaum
Hubli
Pānāji
Kurnool
Dāvangere
Anantapur
Karnātaka
Bangalore
Mangalore
Mysore
Salem
Kozhikode / Calicut
Coimbatore
Ernākulam
Kerala
Kochi / Cochin
Madurai
Thiruvananthapuram / Tivandrum
Nāgercoil
Arabian Sea
Amīndīvi Is.
Lakshadweep
(part of India)
Kavaratti I.
Kalpeni I.
Minicoy I.
Ihavananthapuram Atoll
MALDIVES
MALE'
Kolhumadulu Atoll
Huvadhu Atoll
INDIAN
Equator
0 km
300
0 miles
300
The Mumbai (Bombay) movie industry, known as Bollywood, makes around 900 films each year, compared to Hollywood's 100, making it the most prolific film-producing country in the world.
The word ghats, literally "stairs that descend to a river," refers to the stair-like appearance of the slopes of the Western Ghats mountain range, as they descend to the coastal plain.
There are over 1300 islands in the Maldives but only about 200 are inhabited. All the islands are low-lying, none rising more than 6 ft (1.8m) above sea level.

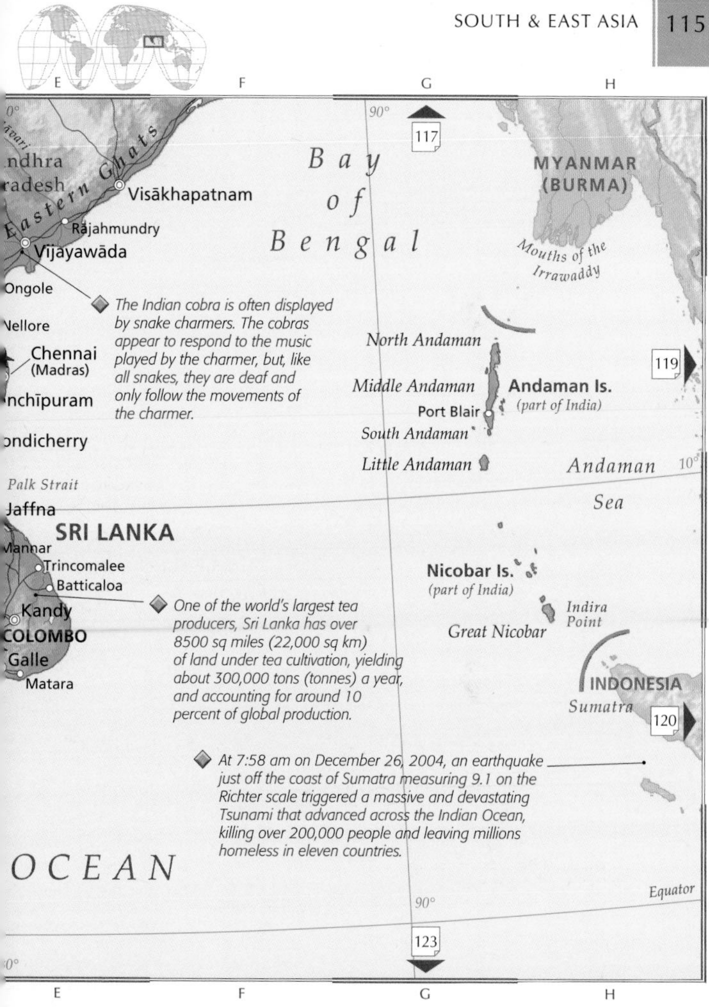
E
F
G
H
90°
117
Bay of Bengal
MYANMAR (BURMA)
Mouths of the Irrawaddy
Eastern Ghats
ndhra radesh
Visākhapatnam
Rājahmundry
Vijayawāda
Ongole
Nellore
Chennai (Madras)
nchīpuram
ondicherry
Palk Strait
Jaffna
SRI LANKA
Mannar
Trincomalee
Batticaloa
Kandy
COLOMBO
Galle
Matara
North Andaman
Middle Andaman
Andaman Is. (part of India)
Port Blair
South Andaman
Little Andaman
Andaman Sea
10°
119
Nicobar Is. (part of India)
Great Nicobar
Indira Point
INDONESIA
Sumatra
120
OCEAN
Equator
123
1
2
3
4
5
The Indian cobra is often displayed by snake charmers. The cobras appear to respond to the music played by the charmer, but, like all snakes, they are deaf and only follow the movements of the charmer.
One of the world's largest tea producers, Sri Lanka has over 8500 sq miles (22,000 sq km) of land under tea cultivation, yielding about 300,000 tons (tonnes) a year, and accounting for around 10 percent of global production.
At 7:58 am on December 26, 2004, an earthquake just off the coast of Sumatra measuring 9.1 on the Richter scale triggered a massive and devastating Tsunami that advanced across the Indian Ocean, killing over 200,000 people and leaving millions homeless in eleven countries.

North India & Pakistan

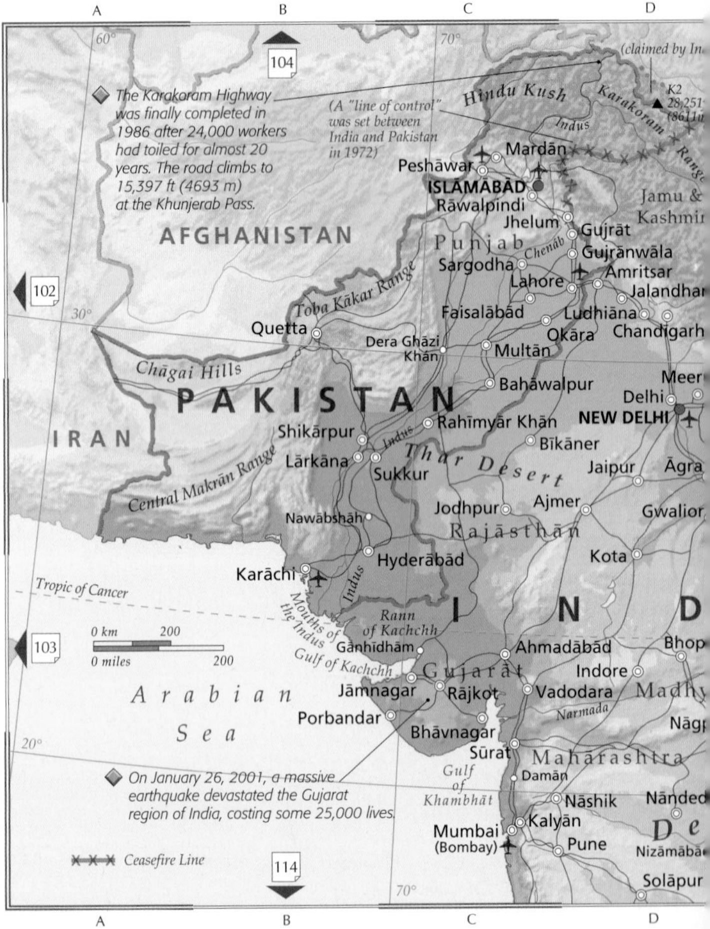

A
B
C
D
1
2
3
4
5
60°
70°
30°
20°
104
102
103
114
The Karakoram Highway was finally completed in 1986 after 24,000 workers had toiled for almost 20 years. The road climbs to 15,397 ft (4693 m) at the Khunjerab Pass.
(A "line of control" was set between India and Pakistan in 1972)
(claimed by In
K2
Hindu Kush
Karakoram Range
Indus
Jamu & Kashmir
AFGHANISTAN
Mardān
Peshāwar
ISLĀMĀBĀD
Rāwalpindi
Jhelum
Gujrāt
Gujrānwāla
Punjab
Chenāb
Sargodha
Amritsar
Lahore
Jalandhar
Toba Kākar Range
Faisalābād
Ludhiāna
Chandigarh
Quetta
Okāra
Dera Ghāzi Khān
Multān
Chāgai Hills
Bahāwalpur
Meer
PAKISTAN
Delhi
NEW DELHI
IRAN
Shikārpur
Rahīmyār Khān
Bīkāner
Lārkāna
Sukkur
Thar Desert
Jaipur
Āgra
Central Makrān Range
Jodhpur
Ajmer
Gwalior
Nawābshāh
Rajāsthān
Hyderābād
Kota
Karāchi
Tropic of Cancer
Indus
Mouths of the Indus
Rann of Kachchh
I N D
0 km 200
0 miles 200
Gānhīdhām
Ahmadābād
Bhop
Gulf of Kachchh
Gujarāt
Indore
Jāmnagar
Rājkot
Vadodara
Madhy
Arabian Sea
Porbandar
Narmada
Nāgp
Bhāvnagar
Sūrat
Mahārashtra
Gulf of Khambhāt
Damān
On January 26, 2001, a massive earthquake devastated the Gujarat region of India, costing some 25,000 lives.
Nāshik
Nānded
Kalyān
Mumbai (Bombay)
Pune
Nizāmābā
Solāpur
Ceasefire Line

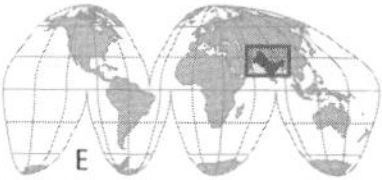

E
F
G
H
80°
90°
108
XINJIANGUYGUR ZIZHIQU
The northern ranges of the Himalayas contain the highest mountains in the world, with average heights of more than 23,000 ft (7000 m) and many peaks higher than 26,000 ft (8000m).
1
sai Chin
ninstered by China,
med by India)
CHINA
QINGHAI
mchok/Dêmqog
ministered by China,
imed by India)
Cherrapunji, 4872 ft (1484 m) above sea level, has an average annual rainfall of 450 inches (1143 cm), although most of this falls during the monsoon – the winter is a virtual drought. The highest-ever seasonal rainfall was 904 inches (2298 cm).
XIZANG ZIZHIQU
(Tibet)
108
2
The Kingdom of Bhutan is the only country in the world to measure the happiness of its citizens.
Himalayas
Arunachal Pradesh
(claimed by China)
30°
NEPAL
Mount Everest
29,035ft (8850m)
areilly
THIMPHU
KATHMANDU
BHUTAN
Uttar Pradesh
Gangtok
3
Guwāhāti
Lucknow
Birātnagar
Dispur
Kohīma
Kānpur
Saidpur
Brahmaputra
Vārānasi
Patna
Ganges
Jamālpur
Sylhet
Imphāl
Allahābād
Bihār
BANGLADESH
Gaya
Rājshāhi
Tropic of Cancer
IA
Dhanbād
West Bengal
DHAKA
Comilla
Rānchi
Jabalpur
Kolkata
(Calcutta)
Khulna
Chittagong
118
4
radesh
MYANMAR
(BURMA)
Raipur
Mouths of the Ganges
Mahānadī
20°
Orissa
Cuttack
Bay of Bengal
The heaviest hailstones on record, weighing about 2.25 lbs (1 kg), are reported to have killed 92 people in the Gopalganj area of Bangladesh on April 14, 1986.
Eastern Ghats
5
Varangal
Visákhapatnam
115
90°
E
F
G
H

Mainland Southeast Asia

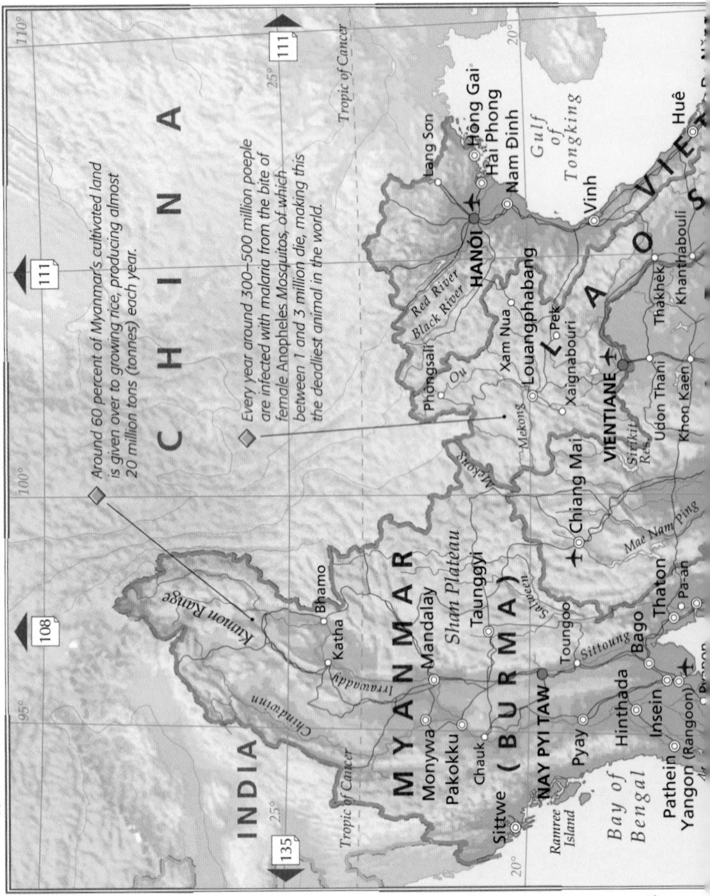
Around 60 percent of Myanmar's cultivated land is given over to growing rice, producing almost 20 million tons (tonnes) each year.
Every year around 300–500 million poeple are infected with malaria from the bite of female Anopheles Mosquitos, of which between 1 and 3 million die, making this the deadliest animal in the world.
CHINA
INDIA
MYANMAR (BURMA)
LAOS
VIET
111
108
135
Tropic of Cancer
Kumon Range
Bhamo
Katha
Irrawaddy
Chindwin
Mandalay
Shan Plateau
Taunggyi
Salween
Monywa
Pakokku
Chauk
NAY PYI TAW
Toungoo
Sittoung
Bago
Thaton
Pa-an
Pyay
Hinthada
Insein
Pathein
Yangon (Rangoon)
Sittwe
Ramree Island
Bay of Bengal
Chiang Mai
Mae Nam Ping
Mekong
Phongsali
Ou
Louangphabang
Xaignabouri
Pek
Xam Nua
Red River
Black River
HANOI
Lang Son
Hong Gai
Hai Phong
Nam Dinh
Gulf of Tongking
Vinh
Huê
VIENTIANE
Sirikit Res.
Udon Thani
Khon Kaen
Thakhek
Khanthabouli
95°
100°
110°
25°
20°

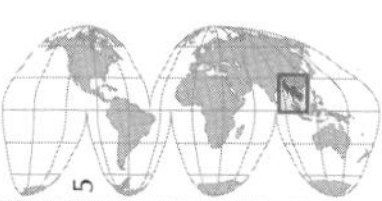

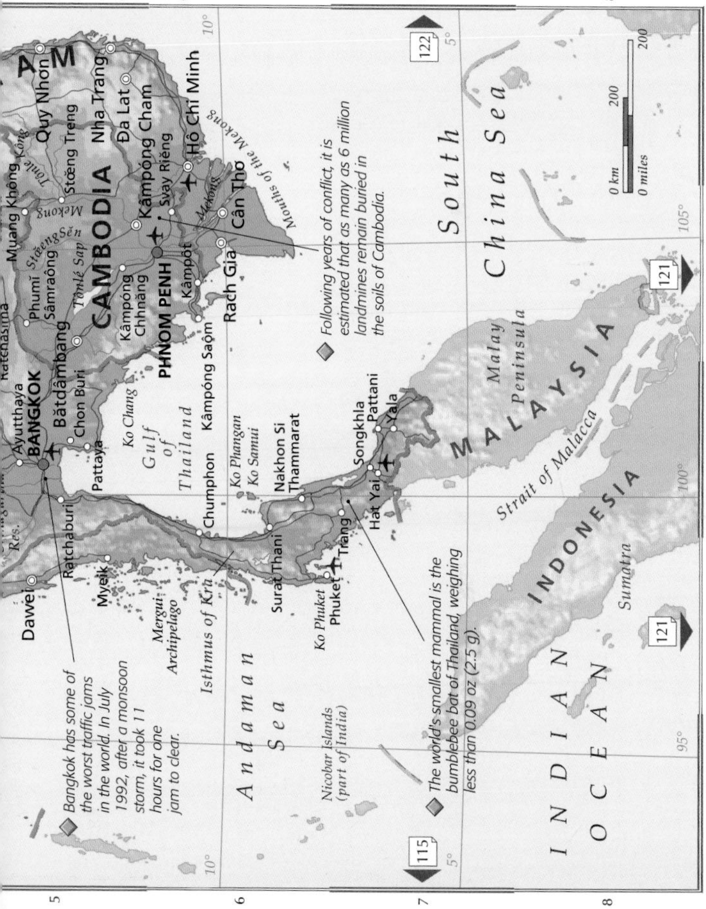
Bangkok has some of the worst traffic jams in the world. In July 1992, after a monsoon storm, it took 11 hours for one jam to clear.
The world's smallest mammal is the bumblebee bat of Thailand, weighing less than 0.09 oz (2.5 g).
Following years of conflict, it is estimated that as many as 6 million landmines remain buried in the soils of Cambodia.
Dawei
Ratchaburi
Myeik
Mergui Archipelago
Isthmus of Kra
Andaman Sea
Nicobar Islands (part of India)
Ko Phuket
Phuket
Surat Thani
Trang
Hat Yai
Chumphon
Ko Phangan
Ko Samui
Nakhon Si Thammarat
Songkhla
Pattani
Yala
Ayutthaya
BANGKOK
Pattaya
Chon Buri
Bătdâmbâng
Ko Chang
Gulf of Thailand
Kâmpóng Saôm
PHNOM PENH
Kâmpóng Chhnăng
Phumĭ Sâmraông
Tônlé Sap
CAMBODIA
Kâmpôt
Rach Gia
Cân Thơ
Svay Riĕng
Kâmpóng Cham
Hô Chi Minh
Mouths of the Mekong
Mekong
Muang Khong
Stœ̆ng Trêng
Quy Nhon
Nha Trang
Đa Lat
South China Sea
Malay Peninsula
MALAYSIA
Strait of Malacca
INDONESIA
Sumatra
INDIAN OCEAN
Res.
0 km 200
0 miles 200
95°
100°
105°
10°
5°
115
121
122
A
B
C
D
E
5
6
7
8

Maritime Southeast Asia

MALAYSIA'S TWO CAPITALS
Kuala Lumpur - Capital
Putrajaya - Administrative capital
The Rafflesia plant has the largest single flow
in the world. The bloom, 3 ft (90 cm) in
diameter, attracts insects by imitating
the foul smell of rotting flesh.
In August 1883, a devastating volcanic
eruption destroyed most of the island of
Krakatau and triggered a tsunami that
claimed around 35,000 lives.
0 km 400
0 miles 400
119
122
122
123
MYANMAR (BURMA)
THAILAND
LAOS
VIETNAM
CAMBODIA
MALAYSIA
BRUNEI
INDIAN OCEAN
Gulf of Tongking
Paracel Islands (disputed by China, Taiwan, and Vietnam)
Spratly Islands (disputed by China, Malaysia, Philippines, Taiwan, and Vietnam)
Andaman Sea
Gulf of Thailand
Nicobar Islands (to India)
Isthmus of Kra
Strait of Malacca
George Town
Kota Bharu
Kuala Terengganu
Kota Kinabalu
BANDAR SERI BEGAWAN
Bandaaceh
Taiping
Ipoh
Kuantan
Medan
Klang
KUALA LUMPUR
Pematangsiantar
Pulau Simeulue
Danau Toba
PUTRAJAYA
Sibolga
Johor Bahru
Sibu
Sarawak
Pegunungan Muller
Kuching
Pulau Nias
SINGAPORE
Equator
Sumatera (Sumatra)
Pekanbaru
Pontianak
Kapuas
Borneo
Padang
Pegunungan Barisan
Batang Hari
Selat Karimata
Pulau Siberut
Kepulauan Mentawai
Jambi
Bangka
Kalimantan
Palembang
Banjarmasin
Pulau Belitung
Bengkulu
Java Sea
Tegal
Bandar Lampung
JAKARTA
Pekalongan
Selat Sunda
Semarang
Kudus
Bogor
Sukabumi
Bandung
Jawa (Java)
Cilacap
Magelang
Yogyakarta
Surakarta
Madiun
Kediri
Malang
Denpasar
90°
100°
110°
10°

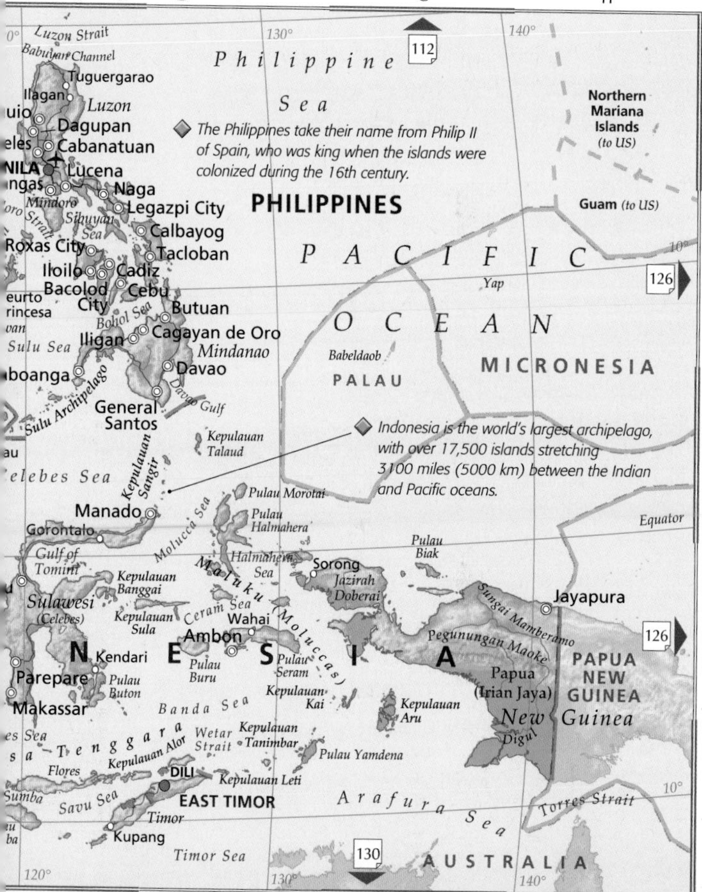
Luzon Strait
Babuyan Channel
Philippine Sea
Tuguergarao
Ilagan
Luzon
Dagupan
Cabanatuan
Lucena
Naga
Mindoro
Legazpi City
Sibuyan Sea
Calbayog
Roxas City
Tacloban
Iloilo
Cadiz
Bacolod City
Cebu
Butuan
Bohol Sea
Cagayan de Oro
Mindanao
Iligan
Sulu Sea
Davao
Davao Gulf
Sulu Archipelago
General Santos
The Philippines take their name from Philip II of Spain, who was king when the islands were colonized during the 16th century.
PHILIPPINES
PACIFIC OCEAN
Northern Mariana Islands (to US)
Guam (to US)
Yap
Babeldaob
PALAU
MICRONESIA
Indonesia is the world's largest archipelago, with over 17,500 islands stretching 3100 miles (5000 km) between the Indian and Pacific oceans.
Kepulauan Talaud
Kepulauan Sangir
Celebes Sea
Manado
Pulau Morotai
Pulau Halmahera
Molucca Sea
Gorontalo
Gulf of Tomini
Halmahera Sea
Sorong
Jazirah Doberai
Pulau Biak
Equator
Kepulauan Banggai
Maluku (Moluccas)
Sulawesi (Celebes)
Kepulauan Sula
Ceram Sea
Wahai
Jayapura
Sungai Mamberamo
Pegunungan Maoke
Ambon
Kendari
Pulau Buru
Pulau Seram
Parepare
Pulau Buton
Makassar
Kepulauan Kai
Banda Sea
Kepulauan Aru
Papua (Irian Jaya)
PAPUA NEW GUINEA
New Guinea
Digul
Tenggara
Wetar Strait
Kepulauan Tanimbar
Kepulauan Alor
Pulau Yamdena
Flores
DILI
Kepulauan Leti
Sumba
Savu Sea
EAST TIMOR
Arafura Sea
Torres Strait
Timor
Kupang
Timor Sea
AUSTRALIA
130°
140°
120°
10°
E
F
G
H
1
2
3
4
5

112
126
126
130

The Indian Ocean

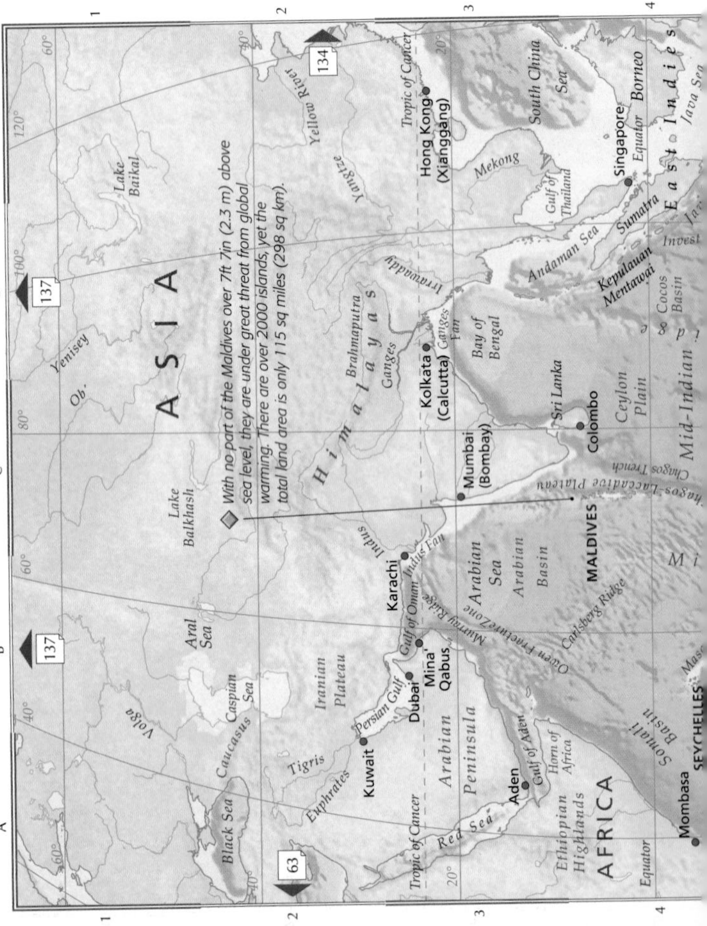
ASIA
AFRICA
With no part of the Maldives over 7ft 7in (2.3 m) above sea level, they are under great threat from global warming. There are over 2000 islands, yet the total land area is only 115 sq miles (298 sq km).
137
137
134
63
Lake Baikal
Yenisey
Ob'
Lake Balkhash
Aral Sea
Caspian Sea
Volga
Caucasus
Black Sea
Tigris
Euphrates
Iranian Plateau
Kuwait
Persian Gulf
Dubai
Mina' Qabus
Gulf of Oman
Karachi
Indus
Indus Fan
Himalayas
Brahmaputra
Ganges
Ganges Fan
Kolkata (Calcutta)
Mumbai (Bombay)
Irrawaddy
Yangtze
Yellow River
Hong Kong (Xianggang)
Tropic of Cancer
Mekong
Gulf of Thailand
South China Sea
Singapore
Equator
Borneo
Sumatra
Andaman Sea
Kepulauan Mentawai
Java Sea
East Indies
Bay of Bengal
Sri Lanka
Colombo
Ceylon Plain
Cocos Basin
Mid-Indian
Chagos Trench
Chagos-Laccadive Plateau
MALDIVES
Arabian Sea
Arabian Basin
Carlsberg Ridge
Owen Fracture Zone
Murray Ridge
Arabian Peninsula
Red Sea
Aden
Gulf of Aden
Horn of Africa
Ethiopian Highlands
Somali Basin
SEYCHELLES
Mombasa
Tropic of Cancer
Equator
A
B
C
D
E
1
2
3
4
20°
40°
60°
80°
100°
120°

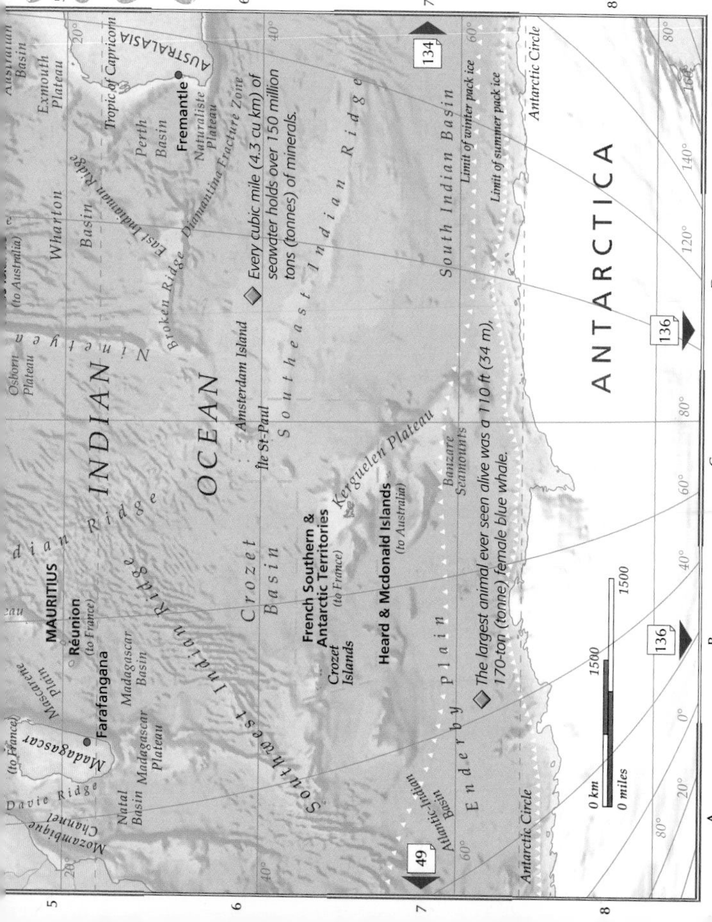
INDIAN OCEAN
ANTARCTICA
AUSTRALASIA
MAURITIUS
Réunion (to France)
Madagascar
Farafangana
Fremantle
Mozambique Channel
Davie Ridge
Natal Basin
Madagascar Basin
Madagascar Plateau
Madagascar Ridge
Mascarene Plain
Southwest Indian Ridge
Crozet Basin
Crozet Islands
French Southern & Antarctic Territories (to France)
Heard & Mcdonald Islands (to Australia)
Kerguelen Plateau
Banzare Seamounts
Atlantic-Indian Basin
Enderby Plain
Île St-Paul
Amsterdam Island
Southeast Indian Ridge
South Indian Basin
Ninetyeast Ridge
Osborn Plateau
Wharton Basin
Broken Ridge
East Indiaman Ridge
Diamantina Fracture Zone
Naturaliste Plateau
Perth Basin
Exmouth Plateau
Tropic of Capricorn
Antarctic Circle
Limit of winter pack ice
Limit of summer pack ice
Every cubic mile (4.3 cu km) of seawater holds over 150 million tons (tonnes) of minerals.
The largest animal ever seen alive was a 110 ft (34 m), 170-ton (tonne) female blue whale.
0 km 1500
0 miles 1500
49
134
136
136

Australasia & Oceania

A
B
C
D
1
2
3
4
5
107
107
123
136
120°
140°
160°
20°
20°
100°
40°
140°
160°
Northern Mariana Islands (to US)
Saipan
Guam (to US)
Micronesia
Wake Island (to US)
MARSHALL ISLANDS
Ratak Chain
Ralik Chain
Philippine Sea
Philippines
Sulu Sea
Celebes Sea
Borneo
Equator
Celebes
Banda Sea
Timor
Flores
Timor Sea
Arafura Sea
Yap
Babeldaob
PALAU
MICRONESIA
Caroline Islands
Chuuk Islands
Pohnpei
Kosrae
Melanesia
Nauru
NAURU
Banaba
KIRIBATI
Tungaru (Gilbert Isla
Bismarck Archipelago
Bismarck Sea
New Britain
Mount Wilhelm 14,793ft (4509m)
New Guinea
Solomon Sea
PAPUA NEW GUINEA
Solomon Islands
SOLOMON ISLANDS
Guadalcanal
Santa Cruz Islands
TUV
Torres Strait
Coral Sea
Coral Sea Islands (to Australia)
VANUATU
Espiritu Santo
Malekula
Efate
Vanu
Vi
Lev
New Caledonia (to France)
New Caledonia
Gulf of Carpentaria
Arnhem Land
Cape York Peninsula
Great Barrier Reef
Ashmore & Cartier Islands (to Australia)
INDIAN OCEAN
AUSTRALIA
Great Dividing Range
Great Sandy Desert
Macdonnell Ranges
Simpson Desert
Uluru (Ayers Rock)
Gibson Desert
L. Eyre North
Grey Range
Darling
Great Victoria Desert
L. Torrens
Tropic of Capricorn
Nullarbor Plain
Great Australian Bight
Murray
Mount Kosciuszko 7310ft (2228m)
Kangaroo Island
Bass Strait
Tasman Sea
Tasmania
Cape Leeuwin
Norfolk Islar (to Australia)
Lord Howe Island (to Australia)
North Island
NEW ZEALAND
South Island
Aoraki (Mt Cook) 12,283ft (3744m)
Auckland Islands (to New Zealand)
Anti Is

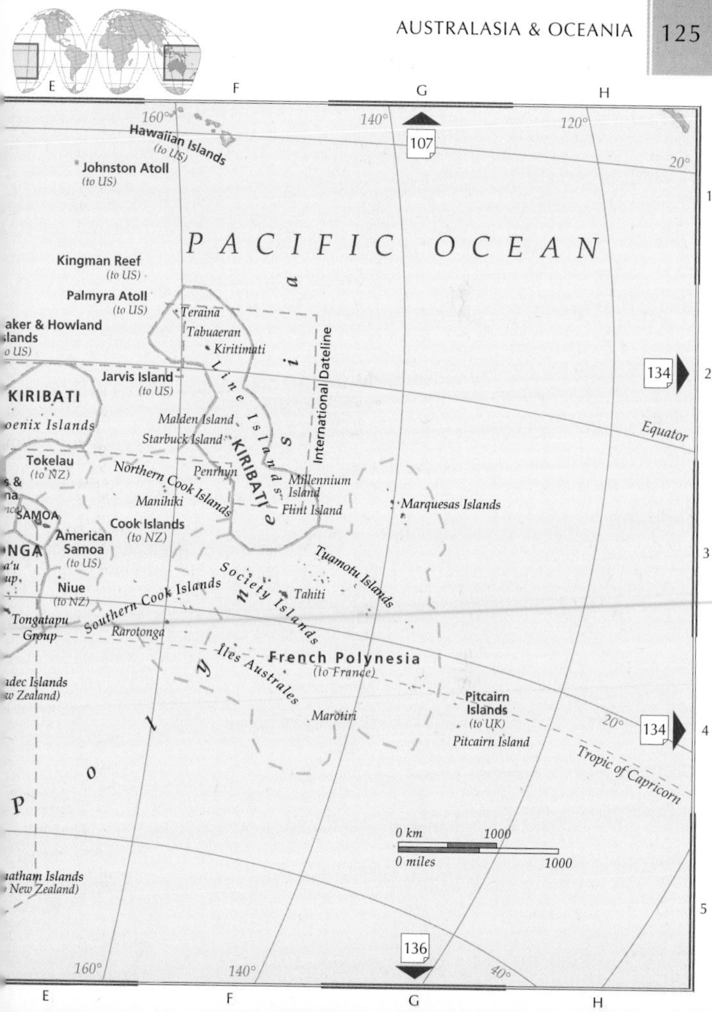
E
F
G
H
160°
140°
120°
20°
107
Hawaiian Islands
(to US)
Johnston Atoll
(to US)
PACIFIC OCEAN
Kingman Reef
(to US)
Palmyra Atoll
(to US)
Teraina
Tabuaeran
Kiritimati
aker & Howland
lands
o US)
International Dateline
Jarvis Island
(to US)
KIRIBATI
oenix Islands
Line Islands
Malden Island
Starbuck Island
KIRIBATI
134
2
Equator
Tokelau
(to NZ)
Northern Cook Islands
Penrhyn
Millennium Island
Flint Island
Marquesas Islands
Manihiki
SAMOA
Cook Islands
(to NZ)
American Samoa
(to US)
NGA
Tuamotu Islands
Society Islands
Tahiti
Niue
(to NZ)
Southern Cook Islands
Tongatapu Group
Rarotonga
Îles Australes
French Polynesia
(to France)
adec Islands
w Zealand)
Marotiri
Pitcairn Islands
(to UK)
Pitcairn Island
134
Tropic of Capricorn
Polynesia
0 km
1000
0 miles
1000
atham Islands
New Zealand)
136
40°
1
3
4
5

The Southwest Pacific

134
121
128
131
Guam
(US unincorporated territory)
HAGÅTÑA
Yap
Marianas Trench
Micronesia
MARSHALL ISLANDS
Ratak
Ralik Chain
Majuro
Caroline Islands
Chuuk Is.
Pohnpei
PALIKIR
MELEKEOK
PALAU
MICRONESIA
Kosrae
The Pitohui bird has a poison on its feathers and skin similar to the poison arrow tree frog, making it the only known example of a poisonous bird.
NAURU
0° Equator
PAPUA NEW GUINEA
Bismarck Archipelago
New Ireland
INDONESIA
Melanesia
Mt Wilhelm 14,793ft (4509m)
Madang
Bougainville I.
New Guinea
Lae
New Britain
New Georgia Islands
PORT MORESBY
Solomon Sea
HONIARA
Santa Cruz Islands
Arafura Sea
Torres Strait
SOLOMON ISLANDS
Gulf of Carpentaria
Coral Sea
Banks Is.
VANUATU
Found only in the rainforest of New Guinea, Queen Alexandra's Birdwing, with a wingspan of 11 inches (280 mm), is the largest butterfly in the world.
Coral Sea Islands
(Australian external territory)
New Caledonia
(French overseas territory)
PORT VILA
Great Barrier Reef
AUSTRALIA
NOUMÉA
Îles Loyauté
Tropic of Capricorn
130°
140°
150°
160°
170°
10°
20°
A
B
C
D
1
2
3
4
5

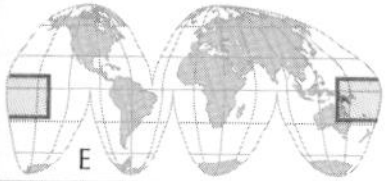

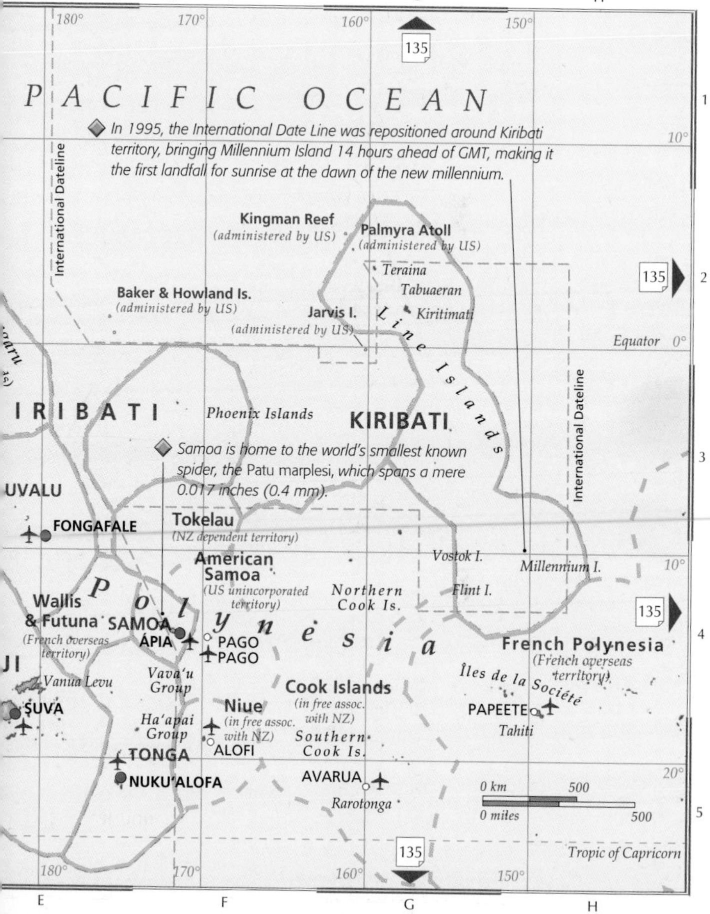
E
F
G
H
180°
170°
160°
150°
135
PACIFIC OCEAN
In 1995, the International Date Line was repositioned around Kiribati territory, bringing Millennium Island 14 hours ahead of GMT, making it the first landfall for sunrise at the dawn of the new millennium.
International Dateline
Kingman Reef
(administered by US)
Palmyra Atoll
(administered by US)
Teraina
Tabuaeran
Kiritimati
Baker & Howland Is.
(administered by US)
Jarvis I.
(administered by US)
Line Islands
Equator 0°
10°
IRIBATI
Phoenix Islands
KIRIBATI
Samoa is home to the world's smallest known spider, the Patu marplesi, which spans a mere 0.017 inches (0.4 mm).
UVALU
FONGAFALE
Tokelau
(NZ dependent territory)
American Samoa
(US unincorporated territory)
Vostok I.
Millennium I.
Flint I.
Northern Cook Is.
Polynesia
Wallis & Futuna
(French overseas territory)
SAMOA
ÁPIA
PAGO PAGO
French Polynesia
(French overseas territory)
Îles de la Société
JI
Vanua Levu
Vava'u Group
Cook Islands
(in free assoc. with NZ)
SUVA
Niue
(in free assoc. with NZ)
PAPEETE
Tahiti
Ha'apai Group
ALOFI
Southern Cook Is.
TONGA
AVARUA
NUKU'ALOFA
Rarotonga
20°
0 km
500
0 miles
500
Tropic of Capricorn
1
2
3
4
5

Western Australia

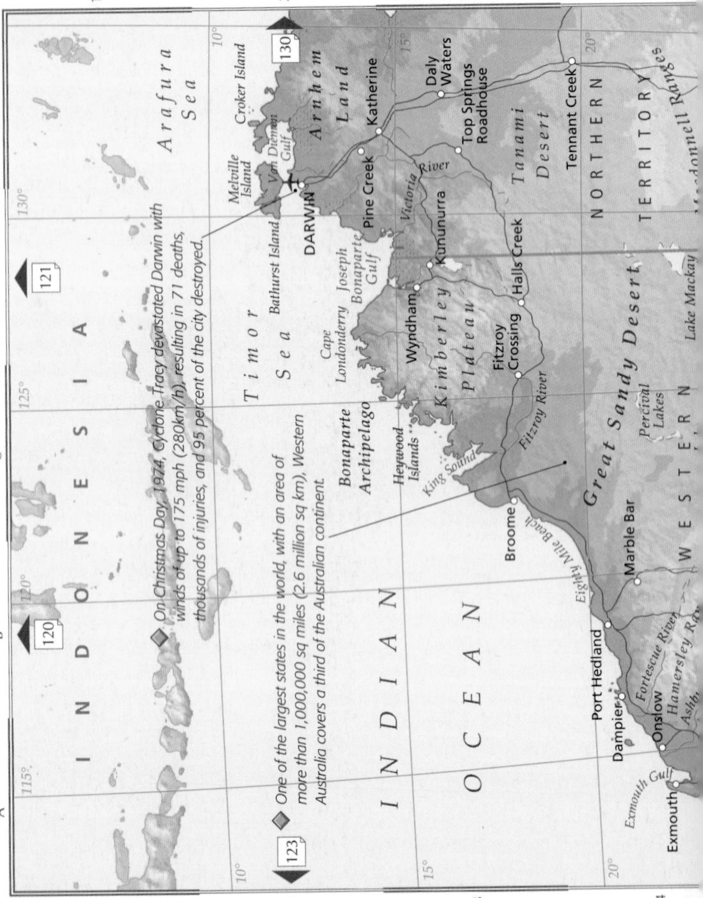
On Christmas Day, 1974, Cyclone Tracy devastated Darwin with winds of up to 175 mph (280km/h), resulting in 71 deaths, thousands of injuries, and 95 percent of the city destroyed.
One of the largest states in the world, with an area of more than 1,000,000 sq miles (2.6 million sq km), Western Australia covers a third of the Australian continent.
I N D O N E S I A
Arafura Sea
Timor Sea
INDIAN OCEAN
Croker Island
Melville Island
Van Diemen Gulf
Bathurst Island
DARWIN
Arnhem Land
Katherine
Daly Waters
Top Springs Roadhouse
Pine Creek
Victoria River
Kununurra
Joseph Bonaparte Gulf
Cape Londonderry
Bonaparte Archipelago
Wyndham
Kimberley Plateau
Halls Creek
Fitzroy Crossing
Fitzroy River
Heywood Islands
King Sound
Broome
Eighty Mile Beach
Tanami Desert
Tennant Creek
NORTHERN TERRITORY
Great Sandy Desert
Percival Lakes
Lake Mackay
WESTERN
Marble Bar
Port Hedland
Dampier
Onslow
Fortescue River
Hamersley Range
Exmouth Gulf
Exmouth
120
121
123
130

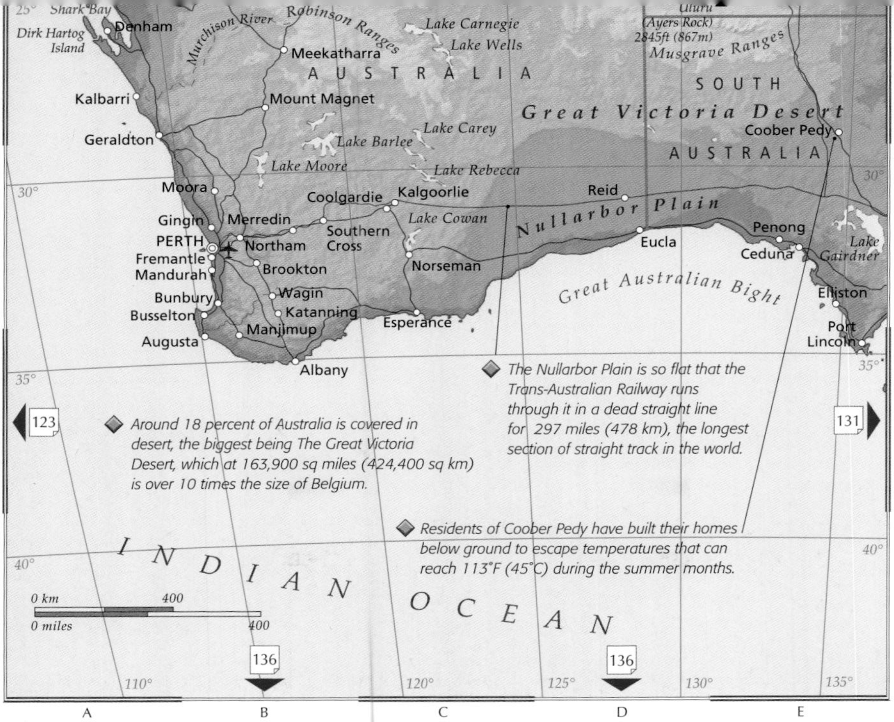
Shark Bay
Dirk Hartog Island
Denham
Murchison River
Robinson Ranges
Meekatharra
Lake Carnegie
Lake Wells
Uluru (Ayers Rock) 2845ft (867m)
Musgrave Ranges
AUSTRALIA
SOUTH AUSTRALIA
Kalbarri
Mount Magnet
Great Victoria Desert
Geraldton
Lake Carey
Lake Barlee
Lake Moore
Lake Rebecca
Coober Pedy
Moora
Coolgardie
Kalgoorlie
Reid
Nullarbor Plain
Gingin
Merredin
Lake Cowan
PERTH
Northam
Southern Cross
Fremantle
Mandurah
Brookton
Norseman
Eucla
Penong
Ceduna
Lake Gairdner
Bunbury
Wagin
Busselton
Katanning
Manjimup
Augusta
Albany
Esperance
Great Australian Bight
Elliston
Port Lincoln
INDIAN OCEAN
0 km 400
0 miles 400
25° 30° 35° 40°
110° 120° 125° 130° 135°
A B C D E
5 6 7 8
123 131 136 136

The Nullarbor Plain is so flat that the Trans-Australian Railway runs through it in a dead straight line for 297 miles (478 km), the longest section of straight track in the world.

Around 18 percent of Australia is covered in desert, the biggest being The Great Victoria Desert, which at 163,900 sq miles (424,400 sq km) is over 10 times the size of Belgium.

Residents of Coober Pedy have built their homes below ground to escape temperatures that can reach 113°F (45°C) during the summer months.

Eastern Australia

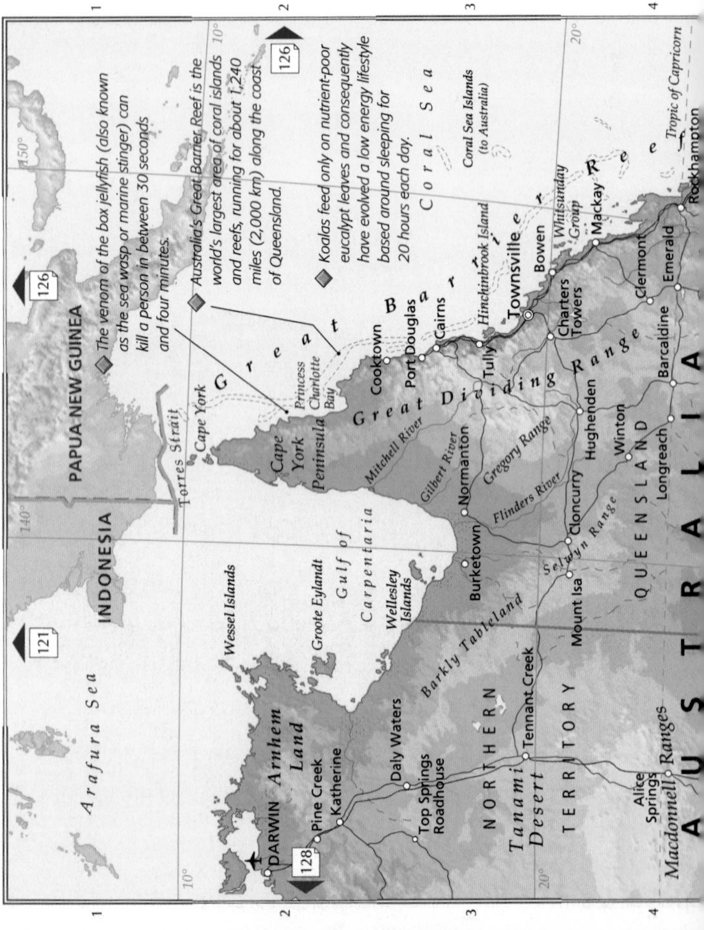
The venom of the box jellyfish (also known as the sea wasp or marine stinger) can kill a person in between 30 seconds and four minutes.
Australia's Great Barrier Reef is the world's largest area of coral islands and reefs, running for about 1,240 miles (2,000 km) along the coast of Queensland.
Koalas feed only on nutrient-poor eucalypt leaves and consequently have evolved a low energy lifestyle based around sleeping for 20 hours each day.
126
121
128
PAPUA NEW GUINEA
INDONESIA
Arafura Sea
Torres Strait
Cape York
Cape York Peninsula
Princess Charlotte Bay
Great Barrier Reef
Coral Sea
Coral Sea Islands (to Australia)
Wessel Islands
Groote Eylandt
Gulf of Carpentaria
Wellesley Islands
Arnhem Land
DARWIN
Pine Creek
Katherine
Daly Waters
Top Springs Roadhouse
Barkly Tableland
NORTHERN TERRITORY
Tanami Desert
Tennant Creek
Alice Springs
Macdonnell Ranges
AUSTRALIA
QUEENSLAND
Mitchell River
Gilbert River
Flinders River
Gregory Range
Selwyn Range
Great Dividing Range
Normanton
Burketown
Mount Isa
Cloncurry
Hughenden
Winton
Longreach
Barcaldine
Emerald
Clermont
Charters Towers
Cooktown
Port Douglas
Cairns
Tully
Hinchinbrook Island
Townsville
Bowen
Whitsunday Group
Mackay
Rockhampton
Tropic of Capricorn
10°
20°
140°
150°
A
B
C
D
E
1
2
3
4

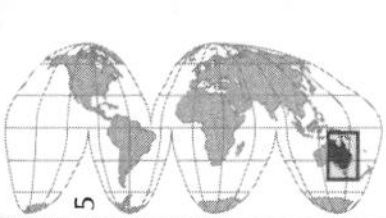

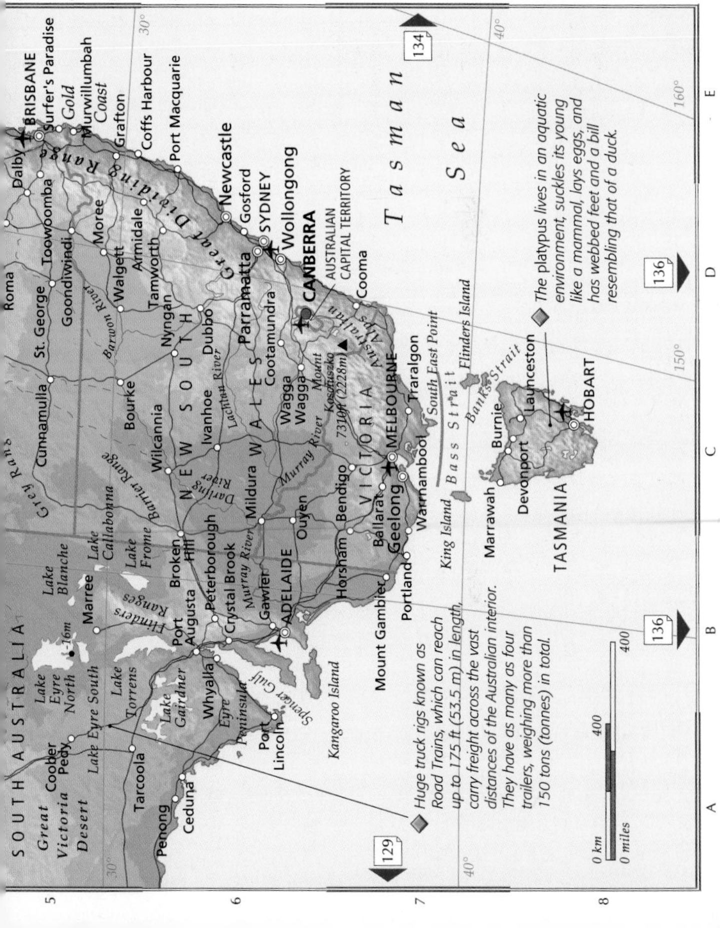
SOUTH AUSTRALIA
NEW SOUTH WALES
VICTORIA
TASMANIA
AUSTRALIAN CAPITAL TERRITORY
Tasman Sea
Bass Strait
Banks Strait
Spencer Gulf
Great Victoria Desert
Great Dividing Range
Grey Range
Barrier Range
Flinders Ranges
Australian Alps
Gold Coast
Lake Eyre North
Lake Eyre South
Lake Blanche
Lake Callabonna
Lake Frome
Lake Torrens
Lake Gairdner
Eyre Peninsula
Kangaroo Island
King Island
Flinders Island
South East Point
Murray River
Darling River
Lachlan River
Barwon River
Mount Kosciuszko 7310ft (2228m)
-16m
BRISBANE
SYDNEY
CANBERRA
MELBOURNE
ADELAIDE
HOBART
Surfer's Paradise
Murwillumbah
Grafton
Coffs Harbour
Port Macquarie
Newcastle
Gosford
Wollongong
Parramatta
Dalby
Toowoomba
Moree
Armidale
Tamworth
Roma
St. George
Goondiwindi
Walgett
Nyngan
Dubbo
Cunnamulla
Bourke
Wilcannia
Ivanhoe
Cootamundra
Wagga Wagga
Cooma
Traralgon
Mildura
Bendigo
Ballarat
Geelong
Warrnambool
Portland
Horsham
Ouyen
Mount Gambier
Gawler
Crystal Brook
Peterborough
Broken Hill
Port Augusta
Whyalla
Port Lincoln
Marree
Coober Pedy
Tarcoola
Ceduna
Penong
Marrawah
Devonport
Burnie
Launceston
129
134
136
136
30°
40°
150°
160°
0 km 400
0 miles 400
A B C D E
5 6 7 8

Huge truck rigs known as Road Trains, which can reach up to 175 ft (53.5 m) in length, carry freight across the vast distances of the Australian interior. They have as many as four trailers, weighing more than 150 tons (tonnes) in total.

The platypus lives in an aquatic environment, suckles its young like a mammal, lays eggs, and has webbed feet and a bill resembling that of a duck.

New Zealand

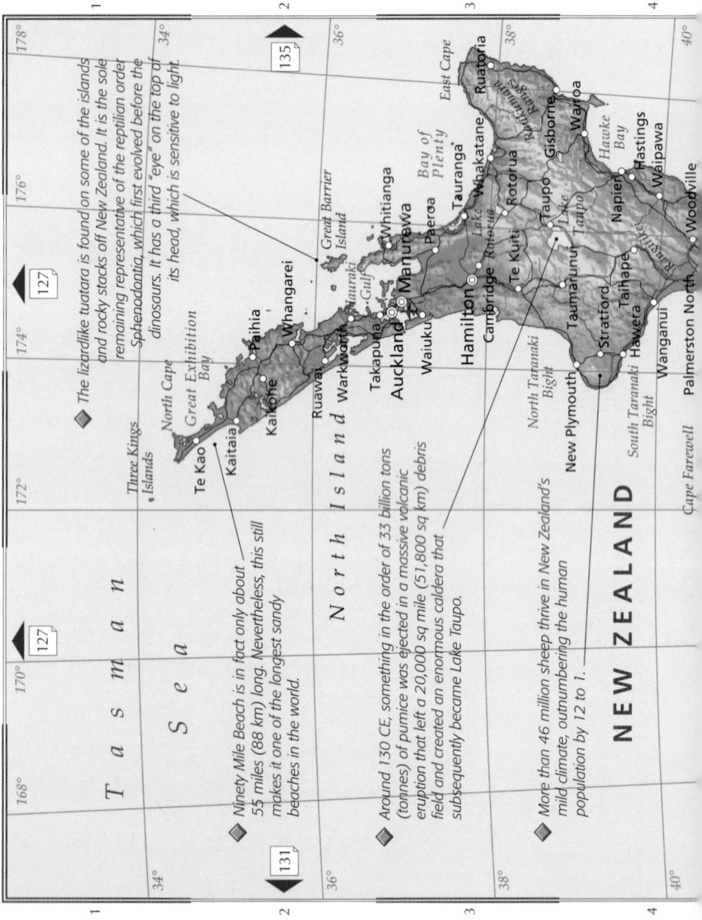
The lizardlike tuatara is found on some of the islands and rocky stacks off New Zealand. It is the sole remaining representative of the reptilian order Sphenodontia, which first evolved before the dinosaurs. It has a third "eye" on the top of its head, which is sensitive to light.
Ninety Mile Beach is in fact only about 55 miles (88 km) long. Nevertheless, this still makes it one of the longest sandy beaches in the world.
Around 130 CE, something in the order of 33 billion tons (tonnes) of pumice was ejected in a massive volcanic eruption that left a 20,000 sq mile (51,800 sq km) debris field and created an enormous caldera that subsequently became Lake Taupo.
More than 46 million sheep thrive in New Zealand's mild climate, outnumbering the human population by 12 to 1.
Tasman Sea
North Island
NEW ZEALAND
Three Kings Islands
North Cape
Great Exhibition Bay
Te Kao
Kaitaia
Kaikohe
Paihia
Whangarei
Ruawai
Warkworth
Great Barrier Island
Hauraki Gulf
Takapuna
Auckland
Manurewa
Waiuku
Whitianga
Paeroa
Bay of Plenty
Tauranga
Whakatane
East Cape
Ruatoria
Gisborne
Wairoa
Hawke Bay
Napier
Hastings
Waipawa
Woodville
Hamilton
Cambridge
Lake Rotorua
Rotorua
Te Kuiti
Taupo
Lake Taupo
Taumarunui
Taihape
North Taranaki Bight
New Plymouth
Stratford
Hawera
Wanganui
South Taranaki Bight
Palmerston North
Cape Farewell
127
135
131

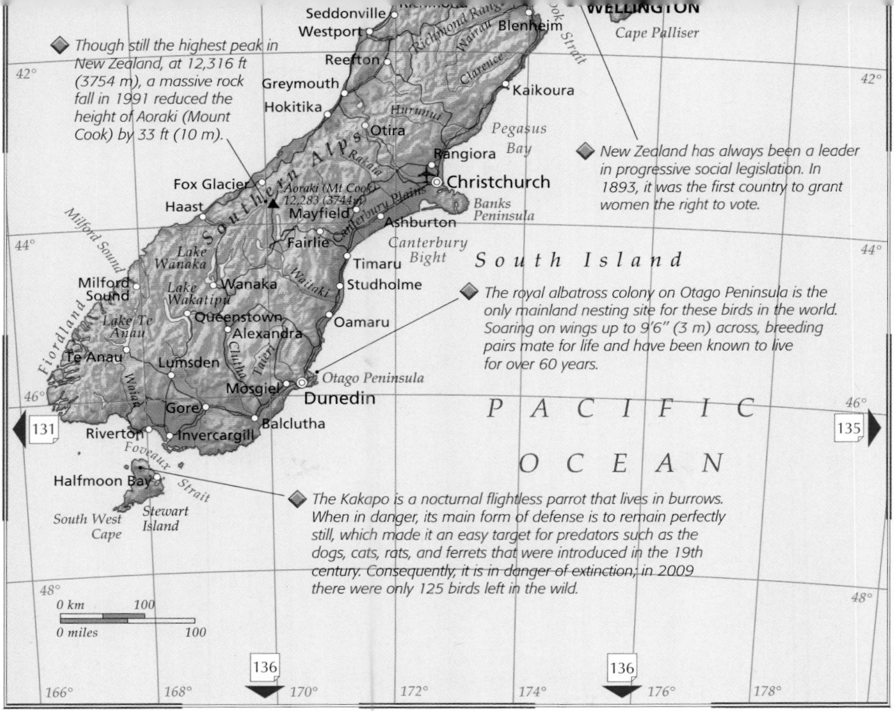
Though still the highest peak in New Zealand, at 12,316 ft (3754 m), a massive rock fall in 1991 reduced the height of Aoraki (Mount Cook) by 33 ft (10 m).
New Zealand has always been a leader in progressive social legislation. In 1893, it was the first country to grant women the right to vote.
The royal albatross colony on Otago Peninsula is the only mainland nesting site for these birds in the world. Soaring on wings up to 9′6″ (3 m) across, breeding pairs mate for life and have been known to live for over 60 years.
The Kakapo is a nocturnal flightless parrot that lives in burrows. When in danger, its main form of defense is to remain perfectly still, which made it an easy target for predators such as the dogs, cats, rats, and ferrets that were introduced in the 19th century. Consequently, it is in danger of extinction; in 2009 there were only 125 birds left in the wild.
Seddonville
Westport
Blenheim
Cape Palliser
Reefton
Greymouth
Hokitika
Kaikoura
Otira
Pegasus Bay
Rangiora
Christchurch
Banks Peninsula
Southern Alps
Aoraki (Mt Cook) 12,283 (3744m)
Fox Glacier
Haast
Mayfield
Ashburton
Canterbury Plains
Fairlie
Canterbury Bight
Timaru
South Island
Milford Sound
Lake Wanaka
Wanaka
Lake Wakatipu
Studholme
Queenstown
Alexandra
Oamaru
Lake Te Anau
Fiordland
Te Anau
Lumsden
Otago Peninsula
Mosgiel
Dunedin
Gore
Balclutha
Riverton
Invercargill
PACIFIC OCEAN
Foveaux Strait
Halfmoon Bay
South West Cape
Stewart Island
0 km 100
0 miles 100
131
135
136
136
42°
44°
46°
48°
166°
168°
170°
172°
174°
176°
178°
A
B
C
D
E
5
6
7
8

The Pacific Ocean

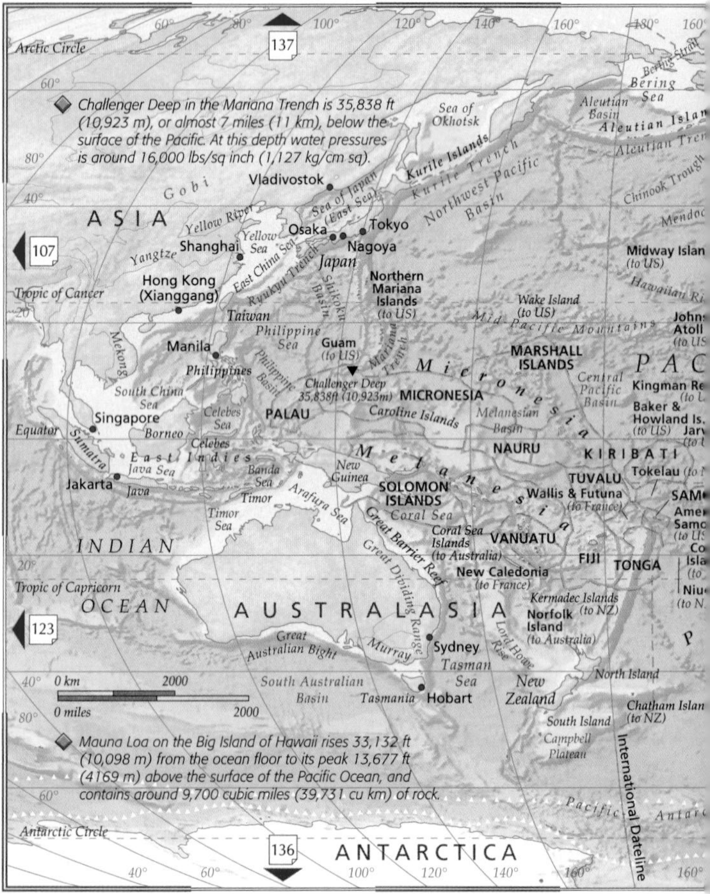
A
B
C
D
1
2
3
4
5
137
107
123
136
Arctic Circle
Bering Strait
Bering Sea
Aleutian Basin
Aleutian Islands
Aleutian Trench
Sea of Okhotsk
Kurile Islands
Kurile Trench
Northwest Pacific Basin
Chinook Trough
Gobi
Vladivostok
Sea of Japan (East Sea)
ASIA
Yellow River
Yellow Sea
Osaka
Tokyo
Nagoya
Japan
Shanghai
Yangtze
East China Sea
Ryukyu Trench
Shikoku Basin
Hong Kong (Xianggang)
Tropic of Cancer
Taiwan
Midway Islands (to US)
Hawaiian Ridge
Northern Mariana Islands (to US)
Wake Island (to US)
Mid-Pacific Mountains
Johnston Atoll (to US)
Philippine Sea
Manila
Mekong
Philippines
Guam (to US)
Mariana Trench
MARSHALL ISLANDS
Philippine Basin
Challenger Deep 35,838ft (10,923m)
Micronesia
MICRONESIA
South China Sea
Central Pacific Basin
Kingman Reef
Baker & Howland Is. (to US)
Singapore
Celebes Sea
PALAU
Caroline Islands
Melanesian Basin
Equator
Borneo
Sumatra
Celebes
East Indies
NAURU
KIRIBATI
Tokelau
Java Sea
Banda Sea
New Guinea
Melanesia
Jakarta
Java
Timor
Arafura Sea
SOLOMON ISLANDS
TUVALU
Wallis & Futuna (to France)
Timor Sea
Coral Sea
Great Barrier Reef
Coral Sea Islands (to Australia)
VANUATU
INDIAN
FIJI
TONGA
Great Dividing Range
New Caledonia (to France)
Tropic of Capricorn
OCEAN
Kermadec Islands (to NZ)
AUSTRALASIA
Norfolk Island (to Australia)
Lord Howe Rise
Great Australian Bight
Murray
Sydney
Tasman Sea
North Island
South Australian Basin
Tasmania
Hobart
New Zealand
Chatham Islands (to NZ)
South Island
Campbell Plateau
International Dateline
0 km
2000
0 miles
2000
Antarctic Circle
ANTARCTICA
60°
80°
100°
120°
140°
160°
180°
40°
20°

Challenger Deep in the Mariana Trench is 35,838 ft (10,923 m), or almost 7 miles (11 km), below the surface of the Pacific. At this depth water pressures is around 16,000 lbs/sq inch (1,127 kg/cm sq).

Mauna Loa on the Big Island of Hawaii rises 33,132 ft (10,098 m) from the ocean floor to its peak 13,677 ft (4169 m) above the surface of the Pacific Ocean, and contains around 9,700 cubic miles (39,731 cu km) of rock.

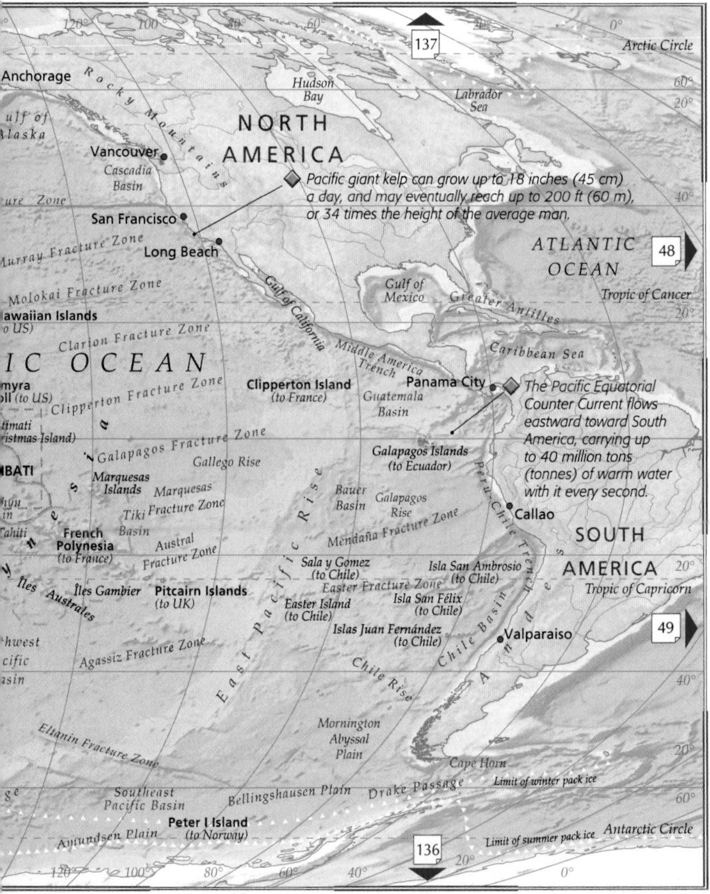
E
F
G
H
1
2
3
4
5
137
48
49
136
Arctic Circle
Antarctic Circle
Tropic of Cancer
Tropic of Capricorn
Anchorage
Rocky Mountains
Hudson Bay
Labrador Sea
NORTH AMERICA
Vancouver
Cascadia Basin
San Francisco
Long Beach
Murray Fracture Zone
Molokai Fracture Zone
Hawaiian Islands
Clarion Fracture Zone
Gulf of California
Gulf of Mexico
Greater Antilles
Caribbean Sea
ATLANTIC OCEAN
Middle America Trench
Clipperton Island
(to France)
Panama City
Guatemala Basin
Clipperton Fracture Zone
Galapagos Fracture Zone
Gallego Rise
Galapagos Islands
(to Ecuador)
Marquesas Islands
Marquesas Fracture Zone
Tiki Basin
French Polynesia
(to France)
Austral Fracture Zone
Bauer Basin
Galapagos Rise
Mendaña Fracture Zone
Peru-Chile Trench
Callao
SOUTH AMERICA
Sala y Gomez
(to Chile)
Easter Fracture Zone
Isla San Ambrosio
(to Chile)
Isla San Félix
(to Chile)
Îles Gambier
Pitcairn Islands
(to UK)
Îles Australes
Easter Island
(to Chile)
Islas Juan Fernández
(to Chile)
Chile Basin
Valparaiso
Andes
East Pacific Rise
Chile Rise
Agassiz Fracture Zone
Eltanin Fracture Zone
Mornington Abyssal Plain
Cape Horn
Limit of winter pack ice
Drake Passage
Bellingshausen Plain
Southeast Pacific Basin
Peter I Island
(to Norway)
Amundsen Plain
Limit of summer pack ice
PACIFIC OCEAN

Pacific giant kelp can grow up to 18 inches (45 cm) a day, and may eventually reach up to 200 ft (60 m), or 34 times the height of the average man.

The Pacific Equatorial Counter Current flows eastward toward South America, carrying up to 40 million tons (tonnes) of warm water with it every second.

Antarctica

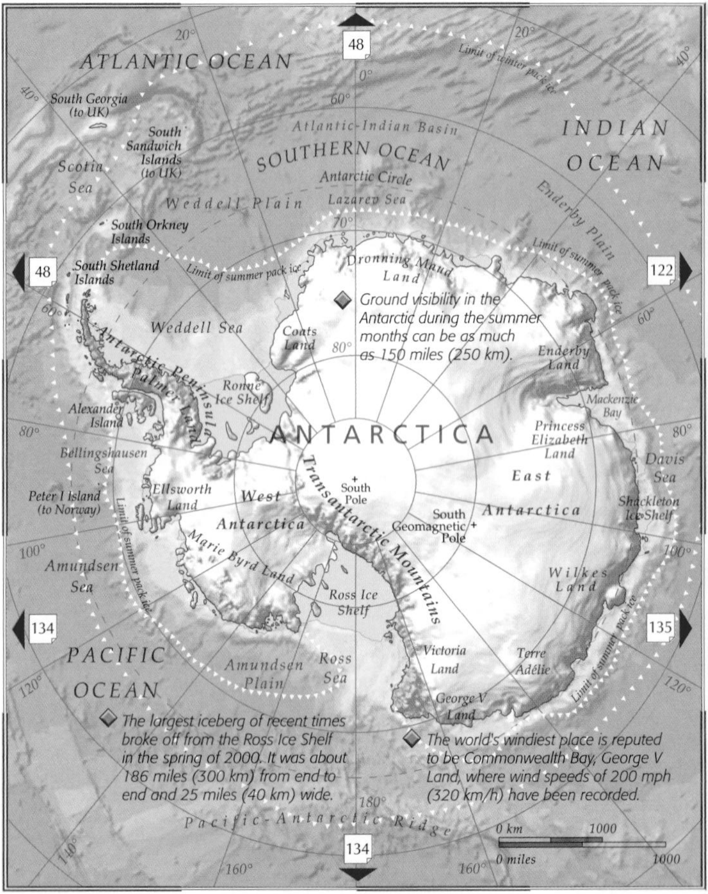
A
B
C
D
1
2
3
4
5
ATLANTIC OCEAN
48
0°
20°
40°
60°
Limit of winter pack ice
South Georgia (to UK)
South Sandwich Islands (to UK)
Atlantic-Indian Basin
INDIAN OCEAN
Scotia Sea
SOUTHERN OCEAN
Antarctic Circle
Weddell Plain
Lazarev Sea
Enderby Plain
South Orkney Islands
70°
Limit of summer pack ice
South Shetland Islands
Dronning Maud Land
122
Ground visibility in the Antarctic during the summer months can be as much as 150 miles (250 km).
Weddell Sea
Coats Land
80°
Enderby Land
Antarctic Peninsula
Palmer Land
Ronne Ice Shelf
Mackenzie Bay
Alexander Island
Princess Elizabeth Land
ANTARCTICA
Bellingshausen Sea
Davis Sea
East
South Pole
Transantarctic Mountains
Peter I Island (to Norway)
Ellsworth Land
West
Antarctica
South Geomagnetic Pole
Antarctica
Shackleton Ice Shelf
100°
Amundsen Sea
Marie Byrd Land
Wilkes Land
Ross Ice Shelf
134
135
PACIFIC OCEAN
Amundsen Plain
Ross Sea
Victoria Land
Terre Adélie
120°
George V Land
The largest iceberg of recent times broke off from the Ross Ice Shelf in the spring of 2000. It was about 186 miles (300 km) from end to end and 25 miles (40 km) wide.
The world's windiest place is reputed to be Commonwealth Bay, George V Land, where wind speeds of 200 mph (320 km/h) have been recorded.
180°
Pacific-Antarctic Ridge
140°
160°
0 km
1000
0 miles
1000

Arctic

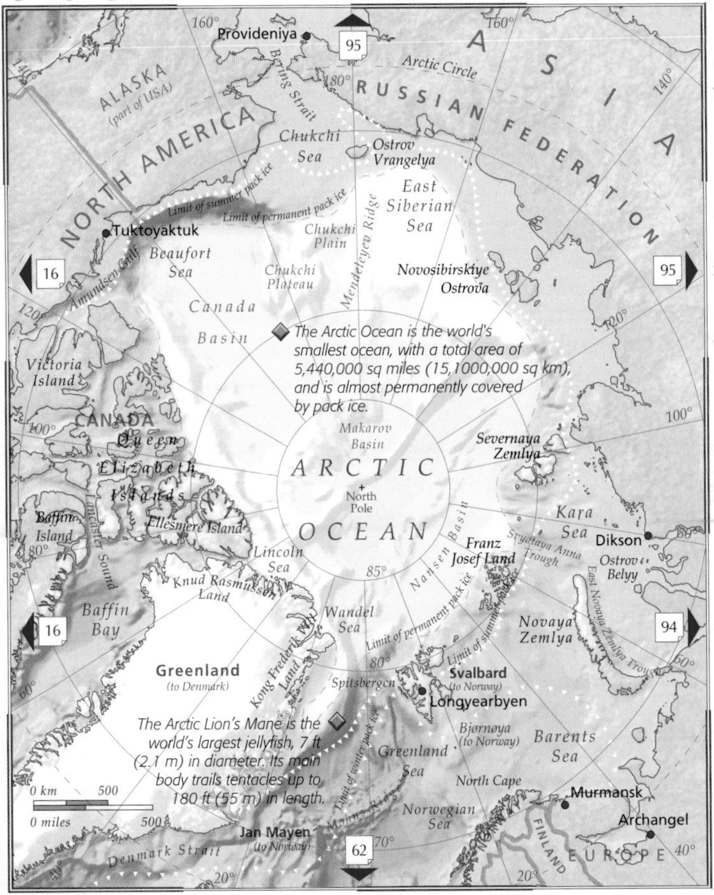
E
F
G
H
1
2
3
4
5
Providenya
95
Bering Strait
Arctic Circle
A S I A
ALASKA
(part of USA)
NORTH AMERICA
RUSSIAN FEDERATION
Chukchi Sea
Ostrov Vrangelya
East Siberian Sea
Limit of summer pack ice
Limit of permanent pack ice
Chukchi Plain
Mendeleyev Ridge
Tuktoyaktuk
Beaufort Sea
Amundsen Gulf
16
Chukchi Plateau
Novosibirskiye Ostrova
Canada Basin
The Arctic Ocean is the world's smallest ocean, with a total area of 5,440,000 sq miles (15,1000,000 sq km), and is almost permanently covered by pack ice.
Victoria Island
CANADA
Queen Elizabeth Islands
Makarov Basin
Severnaya Zemlya
ARCTIC OCEAN
North Pole
Baffin Island
Ellesmere Island
Lancaster Sound
Kara Sea
Dikson
Nansen Basin
Franz Josef Land
Svyataya Anna Trough
Ostrov Belyy
East Novaya Zemlya Trough
Lincoln Sea
85°
Knud Rasmussen Land
Baffin Bay
Wandel Sea
Kong Frederik VIII Land
Novaya Zemlya
94
Greenland
(to Denmark)
80°
Spitsbergen
Svalbard
(to Norway)
Longyearbyen
Bjørnøya
(to Norway)
Barents Sea
The Arctic Lion's Mane is the world's largest jellyfish, 7 ft (2.1 m) in diameter. Its main body trails tentacles up to 180 ft (55 m) in length.
Limit of winter pack ice
Greenland Sea
North Cape
Murmansk
0 km 500
0 miles 500
Norwegian Sea
Jan Mayen
(to Norway)
Archangel
FINLAND
EUROPE
Denmark Strait
62
70°
20°
40°
60°
100°
120°
140°
160°
180°

The world factfiles

North & Central America

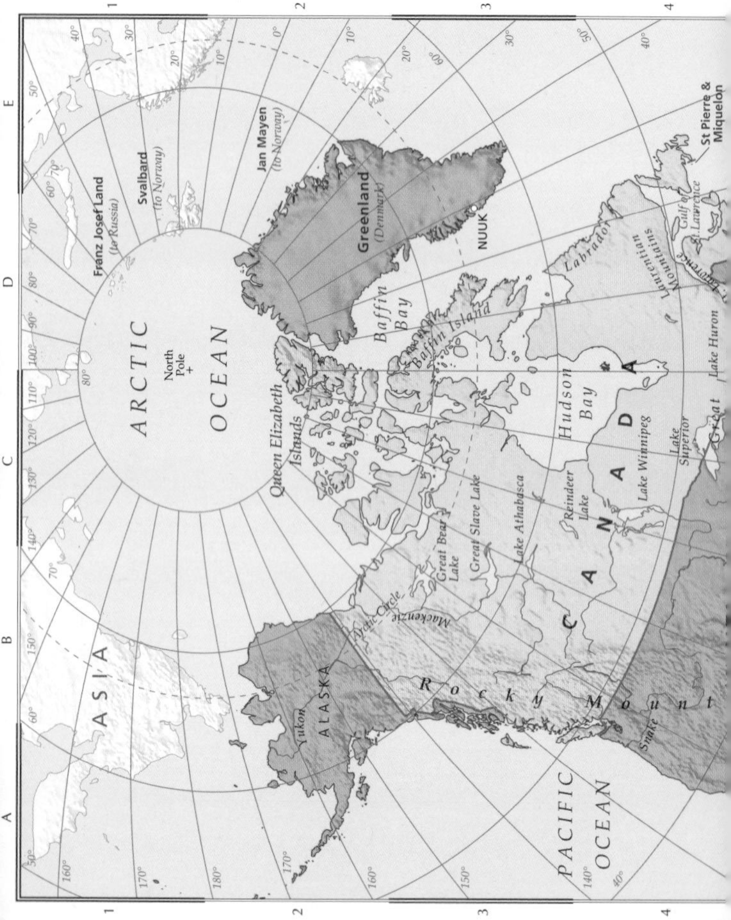
ARCTIC
OCEAN
North Pole
Franz Josef Land
(to Russia)
Svalbard
(to Norway)
Jan Mayen
(to Norway)
Greenland
(Denmark)
NUUK
Baffin Bay
Baffin Island
Queen Elizabeth Islands
Labrador
Laurentian Mountains
Gulf of St Lawrence
St Pierre & Miquelon
Hudson Bay
CANADA
Lake Winnipeg
Lake Superior
Lake Huron
Great
Reindeer Lake
Lake Athabasca
Great Slave Lake
Great Bear Lake
Arctic Circle
Mackenzie
Rocky Mount
ALASKA
Yukon
ASIA
PACIFIC
OCEAN
Snake

OF AMERICA
ATLANTIC
OCEAN
WASHINGTON, D.C.
Ohio
Arkansas
Mississippi
Appalachian Mountains
Bermuda
(UK)
Sargasso Sea
Tropic of Cancer
Sierra Madre Occidental
Rio Grande
MEXICO
Gulf of Mexico
Virgin Islands (US)
Turks & Caicos
Islands (UK)
British Virgin
Islands (UK)
NASSAU
BAHAMAS
DOMINICAN
REPUBLIC
Anguilla (UK)
ST KITTS & NEVIS
HAVANA
CUBA
Puerto
Rico (US)
ANTIGUA &
BARBUDA
MEXICO CITY
Cayman
Islands (UK)
HAITI
SANTO
DOMINGO
Guadeloupe
(France)
PORT-AU-PRINCE
BELMOPAN
Montserrat (UK)
DOMINICA
GUATEMALA
BELIZE
JAMAICA
KINGSTON
Martinique (France)
ST LUCIA
Clipperton Island
(French Polynesia)
GUATEMALA CITY
HONDURAS
ST VINCENT & THE GRENADINES
BARBADOS
SAN SALVADOR
TEGUCIGALPA
EL SALVADOR
Aruba (Neth.)
GRENADA
TRINIDAD
& TOBAGO
MANAGUA
NICARAGUA
Netherlands
Antilles
(Neth.)
COSTA RICA
SAN JOSÉ
PANAMA CITY
PANAMA
Andes
Equator
SOUTH
AMERICA
0
1000 km
0
1000 miles
30°
50°
20°
120°
10°
110°
100°
90°
80°
70°
60°
5
6
7
8
A
B
C
D
E

POLITICAL FACTFILE

TOTAL AREA:
8,116,571 sq miles
(21,021,940 sq km)

TOTAL NUMBER OF COUNTRIES:
23

TOTAL POPULATION:
536.1 million

LARGEST CITY WITH POPULATION:
Mexico City, Mexico 22.9 million

COUNTRY WITH HIGHEST POPULATION DENSITY:
Barbados 1542 people per sq mile
(595 people per sq km)

LARGEST COUNTRY:
Canada 3,855,171 sq miles
(9,984,670 sq km)

SMALLEST COUNTRY:
St. Kitts & Nevis 101 sq miles
(261 sq km)

South America

ATLANTIC OCEAN
Caribbean Sea
VENEZUELA
CARACAS
GUYANA
GEORGETOWN
SURINAME
PARAMARIBO
CAYENNE
French Guiana (France)
COLOMBIA
BOGOTÁ
ECUADOR
QUITO
PERU
LIMA
BOLIVIA
LA PAZ
SUCRE
BRAZIL
BRASÍLIA
Amazon Basin
Guiana Highlands
Andes
Isthmus of Panama
Equator
Orinoco
Meta
Guaviare
Magdalena
Cauca
Caquetá
Putumayo
Napo
Marañón
Rio Negro
Amazon
Juruá
Purus
Madeira
Madre de Dios
Beni
Lake Titicaca
Xingu
Araguaia
Tocantins
São Francisco
Represa de Sobradinho
A
B
C
D
E
1
2
3
4
80°
60°
40°
20°

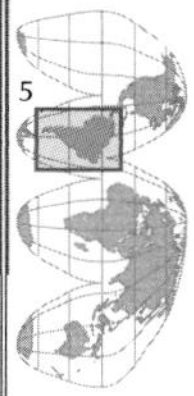

Ambrosio
(Chile)
(Chile)
Islas Juan Fernandez
(Chile)
SANTIAGO
CHILE
Andes
ARGENTINA
Paraná
Uruguay
URUGUAY
BUENOS AIRES
MONTEVIDEO
Lagoa dos Patos
PACIFIC
OCEAN
Colorado
Río Negro
Isla de Chiloé
Patagonia
ATLANTIC
OCEAN
Falkland Islands
(UK)
Strait of
Magellan
Tierra del Fuego
Cape Horn
South Georgia
(UK)
0
500 km
0
500 miles
40°
20°
60°
80°
100°
0°
A
B
C
D
E
5
6
7
8

POLITICAL FACTFILE

TOTAL AREA:
6,731,428 sq miles
(17,434,410 sq km)

TOTAL NUMBER OF COUNTRIES:
12

TOTAL POPULATION:
388.9 million

LARGEST CITY WITH POPULATION:
São Paulo, Brazil 21 million

COUNTRY WITH HIGHEST POPULATION DENSITY:
Ecuador 127 people per sq mile
(49 people per sq km)

LARGEST COUNTRY:
Brazil 3,286,470 sq miles
(8,511,965 sq km)

SMALLEST COUNTRY:
Suriname 63,039 sq miles
(163,270 sq km)

Africa

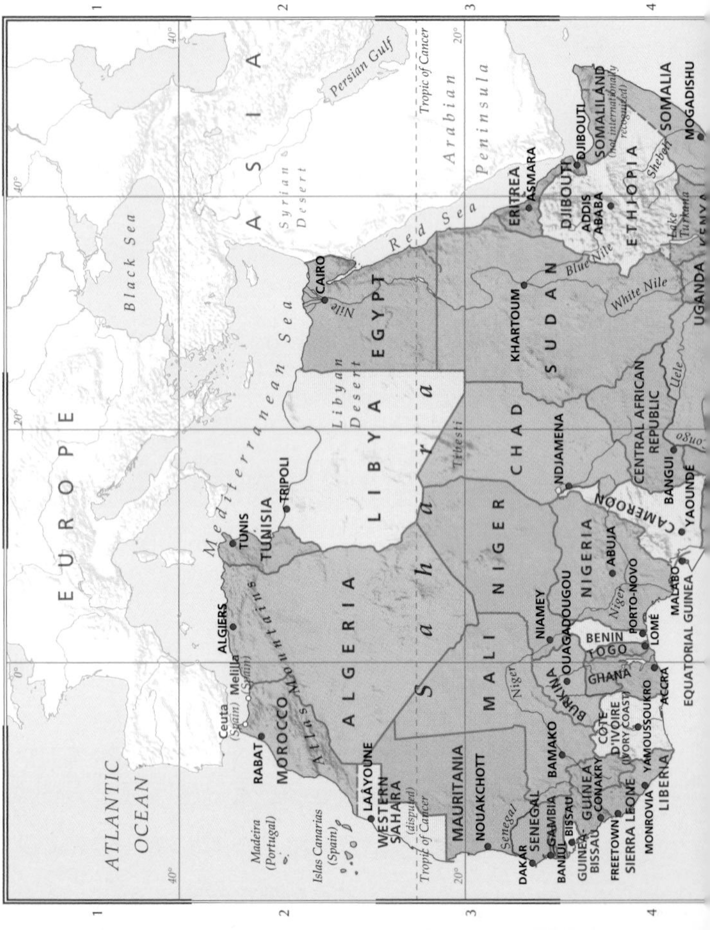

ATLANTIC OCEAN
EUROPE
ASIA
Black Sea
Persian Gulf
Mediterranean Sea
Red Sea
Syrian Desert
Arabian Peninsula
Libyan Desert
Sahara
Tibesti
Atlas Mountains
Tropic of Cancer
Madeira (Portugal)
Islas Canarias (Spain)
Ceuta (Spain)
Melilla (Spain)
MOROCCO
RABAT
ALGERIA
ALGIERS
TUNISIA
TUNIS
LIBYA
TRIPOLI
EGYPT
CAIRO
Nile
WESTERN SAHARA (disputed)
LAÂYOUNE
MAURITANIA
NOUAKCHOTT
MALI
BAMAKO
NIGER
NIAMEY
CHAD
NDJAMENA
SUDAN
KHARTOUM
Blue Nile
White Nile
ERITREA
ASMARA
DJIBOUTI
ETHIOPIA
ADDIS ABABA
SOMALILAND (not internationally recognized)
SOMALIA
MOGADISHU
Shebeli
Lake Turkana
UGANDA
CENTRAL AFRICAN REPUBLIC
BANGUI
Uele
Ubangi
CAMEROON
YAOUNDÉ
MALABO
EQUATORIAL GUINEA
NIGERIA
ABUJA
Niger
BENIN
PORTO-NOVO
TOGO
LOMÉ
GHANA
ACCRA
BURKINA
OUAGADOUGOU
CÔTE D'IVOIRE (IVORY COAST)
YAMOUSSOUKRO
LIBERIA
MONROVIA
SIERRA LEONE
FREETOWN
GUINEA
CONAKRY
GUINEA-BISSAU
BISSAU
GAMBIA
BANJUL
SENEGAL
DAKAR
Senegal

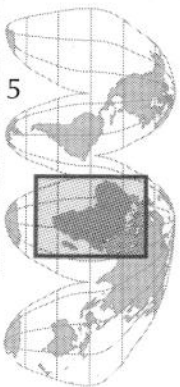

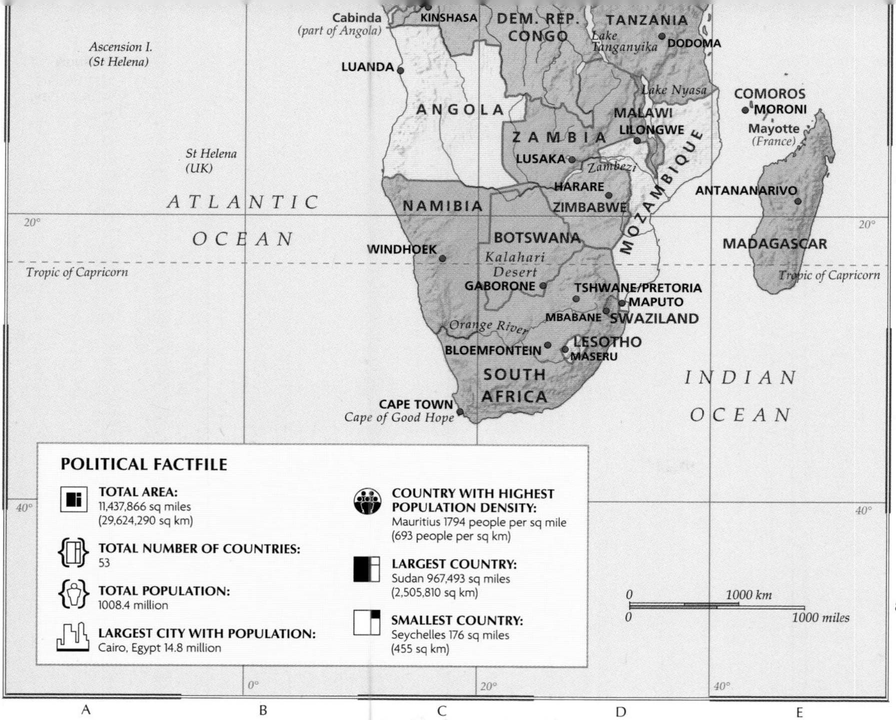
Cabinda
(part of Angola)
KINSHASA
DEM. REP. CONGO
TANZANIA
Lake Tanganyika
DODOMA
Ascension I.
(St Helena)
LUANDA
Lake Nyasa
COMOROS
MORONI
Mayotte
(France)
ANGOLA
MALAWI
LILONGWE
ZAMBIA
LUSAKA
Zambezi
St Helena
(UK)
MOZAMBIQUE
HARARE
ANTANANARIVO
ATLANTIC OCEAN
NAMIBIA
ZIMBABWE
BOTSWANA
MADAGASCAR
WINDHOEK
Kalahari Desert
Tropic of Capricorn
Tropic of Capricorn
GABORONE
TSHWANE/PRETORIA
MAPUTO
MBABANE
SWAZILAND
Orange River
LESOTHO
BLOEMFONTEIN
MASERU
SOUTH AFRICA
INDIAN OCEAN
CAPE TOWN
Cape of Good Hope
20°
40°
0°
20°
40°
0
1000 km
0
1000 miles
5
6
7
8
A
B
C
D
E

POLITICAL FACTFILE

TOTAL AREA:
11,437,866 sq miles
(29,624,290 sq km)

TOTAL NUMBER OF COUNTRIES:
53

TOTAL POPULATION:
1008.4 million

LARGEST CITY WITH POPULATION:
Cairo, Egypt 14.8 million

COUNTRY WITH HIGHEST POPULATION DENSITY:
Mauritius 1794 people per sq mile
(693 people per sq km)

LARGEST COUNTRY:
Sudan 967,493 sq miles
(2,505,810 sq km)

SMALLEST COUNTRY:
Seychelles 176 sq miles
(455 sq km)

Europe

POLITICAL FACTFILE

TOTAL AREA:
3,739,678 sq miles
(9,685,756 sq km)

TOTAL NUMBER OF COUNTRIES:
46

TOTAL POPULATION:
717.8 million

LARGEST CITY WITH POPULATION:
Moscow, European Russia 13.5 million

COUNTRY WITH HIGHEST POPULATION DENSITY:
Monaco 42,667 people per sq mile
(16,410 people per sq km)

LARGEST COUNTRY:
European Russia 1,527,341 sq miles
(3,955,818 sq km)

SMALLEST COUNTRY:
Vatican City, Italy 0.17 sq miles
(0.44 sq km)

A
B
C
D
1
2
3
4
5
REYKJAVÍK
ICELAND
Arctic Circle
Norwegian Sea
Faeroe Islands
(Denmark)
Shetland Islands
Outer Hebrides
Orkney Islands
British Isles
North Sea
OSLO
IRELAND
DUBLIN
UNITED KINGDOM
DENMARK
COPENHAGEN
AMSTERDAM
NETH.
Elbe
LONDON
THE HAGUE
BERLIN
Channel Is.
(UK)
BELGIUM
BRUSSELS
GERMANY
LUXEMBOURG
LUXEMBOURG
PARIS
Loire
Bay of Biscay
FRANCE
Rhine
CZECH REP
LIECH.
BERN
SWITZERLAND
ATLANTIC OCEAN
PORTUGAL
Garonne
Ebro
MONACO
LJUBLJANA
LISBON
Tagus
MADRID
ANDORRA
SAN MARINO
SPAIN
Corsica
VATICAN CITY
ROME
Madeira
(Portugal)
Guadalquivir
Gibraltar
(UK)
Balearic Islands
Sardinia
Ceuta
(Spain)
Melilla
(Spain)
Mediterranean
Canary Islands
(Spain)
Sicily
AFRICA
VALLETTA
MALTA
40°
20°
70°
0°
50°
60°
30°

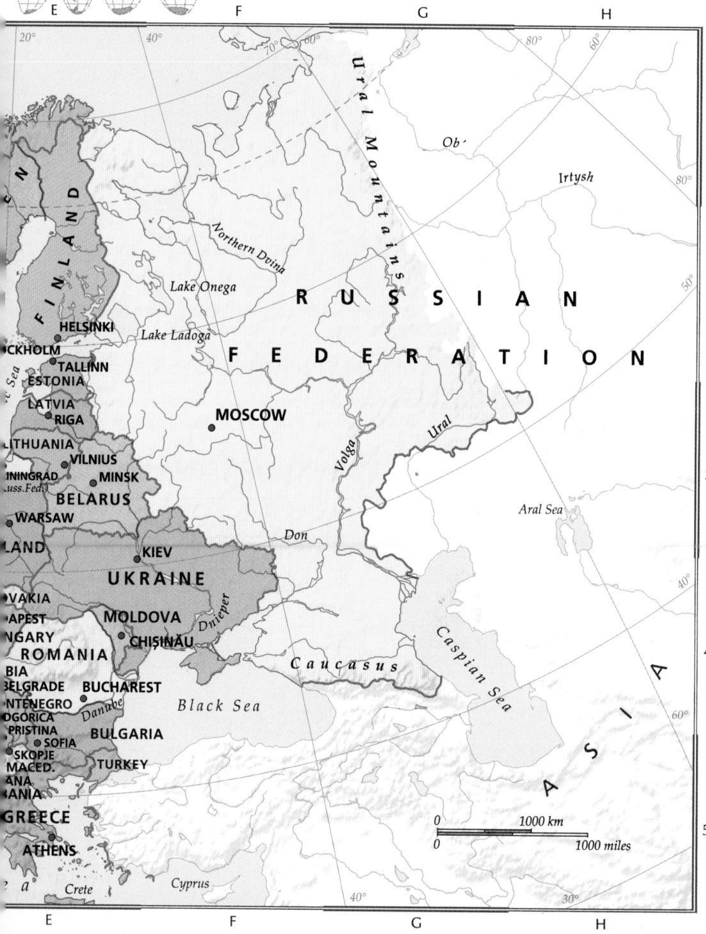
E
F
G
H
1
2
3
4
5
Ural Mountains
Ob'
Irtysh
Northern Dvina
Lake Onega
Lake Ladoga
RUSSIAN FEDERATION
FINLAND
HELSINKI
CKHOLM
TALLINN
ESTONIA
LATVIA
RIGA
LITHUANIA
VILNIUS
INGRAD
MINSK
BELARUS
WARSAW
LAND
MOSCOW
Volga
Ural
Aral Sea
Don
KIEV
UKRAINE
Dnieper
MOLDOVA
CHIŞINĂU
VAKIA
APEST
NGARY
ROMANIA
BIA
ELGRADE
BUCHAREST
NTENEGRO
DGORICA
PRISTINA
Danube
BULGARIA
SOFIA
SKOPJE
MACED.
ANA
ANIA
TURKEY
GREECE
ATHENS
Crete
Cyprus
Black Sea
Caucasus
Caspian Sea
ASIA
1000 km
1000 miles

Asia

A
B
C
D
1
2
3
4
5
ARCTIC OCEAN
Franz Josef Land
Severnaya Zemlya
Kara Sea
Laptev Sea
RUSSIAN FEDERATION
EUROPE
Ob
Yenisey
Irtysh
Lake Baikal
Black Sea
ASTANA
KAZAKHSTAN
ULAN BATOR
MONGOLIA
ANKARA
TURKEY
GEORGIA
TBILISI
ARMENIA
AZERBAIJAN
CYPRUS
NICOSIA
YEREVAN
BAKU
UZBEKISTAN
BEIRUT
SYRIA
TURKMENISTAN
BISHKEK
LEBANON
DAMASCUS
AŞGABAT
KYRGYZSTAN
JERUSALEM
AMMAN
TEHRĀN
TASHKENT
ISRAEL
JORDAN
BAGHDAD
DUSHANBE
TAJIKISTAN
IRAQ
IRAN
KABUL
CHINA
KUWAIT
KUWAIT
AFGHANISTAN
ISLAMABAD
MANAMA
BAHRAIN
QATAR
PAKISTAN
NEW DELHI
RIYADH
DOHA
NEPAL
THIMPHU
SAUDI ARABIA
ABU DHABI
Indus
KATHMANDU
BHUTAN
U.A.E.
Ganges
BANGLADESH
MUSCAT
DHAKA
Red Sea
AFRICA
SANA
OMAN
INDIA
MYANMAR (BURMA)
YEMEN
Arabian Sea
NAY PYI TAW
Socotra (Yemen)
Bay of Bengal
BANGKOK
THAILAND
VIENTIANE
Laccadive Islands (India)
Andaman & Nicobar Islands (India)
COLOMBO
MALE'
SRI LANKA
MALDIVES
KUALA LUMPUR
PUTRAJAYA
SINGAPORE
INDIAN OCEAN
Tropic of Cancer
Equator
0°
20°
40°
60°
80°
100°
140°

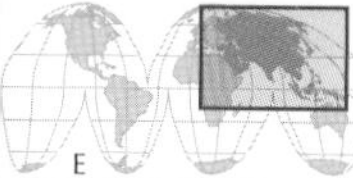

POLITICAL FACTFILE

TOTAL AREA:
17,006,354 sq miles
(44,046,472 sq km)

TOTAL NUMBER OF COUNTRIES:
49

TOTAL POPULATION:
4148.4 million

LARGEST CITY WITH POPULATION:
Tokyo, Japan 33.8 million

COUNTRY WITH HIGHEST POPULATION DENSITY:
Singapore 20,072 people per sq mile
(7765 people per sq km)

LARGEST COUNTRY:
Asiatic Russia 5,065,394 sq miles
(13,119,382 sq km)

SMALLEST COUNTRY:
Maldives 116 sq miles
(300 sq km)

E
F
G
H
1
2
3
4
5
Sea of Okhotsk
Kurile Islands
NORTH KOREA
JAPAN
TOKYO
SEOUL
SOUTH KOREA
Ryukyu Islands
TAIPEI
TAIWAN
PACIFIC OCEAN
Tropic of Cancer
Equator
MANILA
PHILIPPINES
BANDAR SERI BEGAWAN
DILI
EAST TIMOR
AUSTRALASIA & OCEANIA
0 1000 km
0 1000 miles
60°
160°
40°
140°
180°
20°
120°

Australasia & Oceania

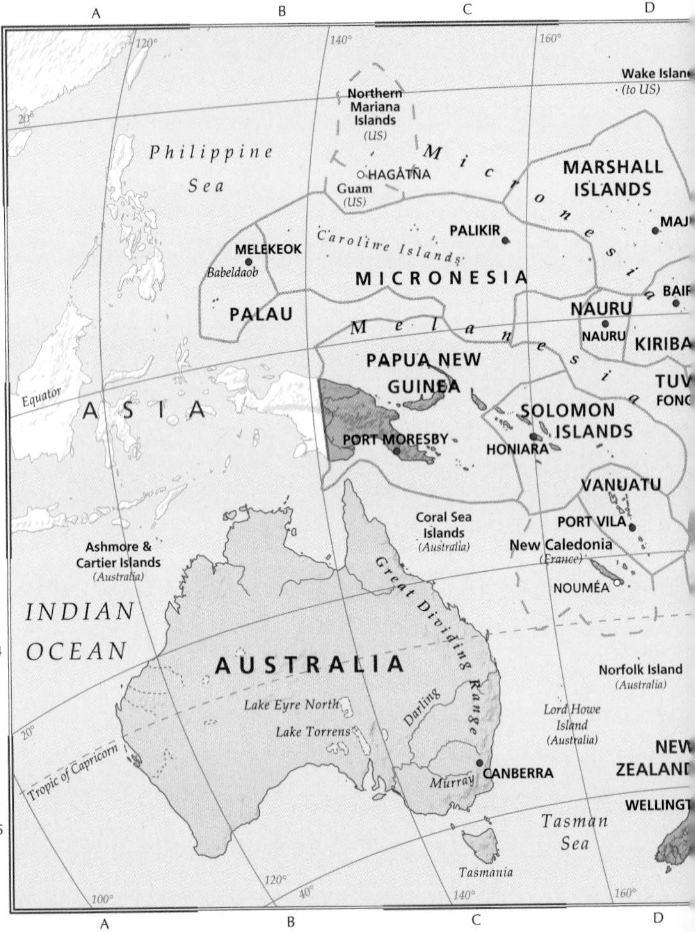
A
B
C
D
1
2
3
4
5
120°
140°
160°
20°
Northern Mariana Islands (US)
Wake Island (to US)
Philippine Sea
Micronesia
HAGÅTÑA
Guam (US)
MARSHALL ISLANDS
MAJ
PALIKIR
Caroline Islands
MELEKEOK
Babeldaob
MICRONESIA
BAIR
PALAU
NAURU
NAURU
KIRIBA
Melanesia
PAPUA NEW GUINEA
TUV
FONG
Equator
ASIA
SOLOMON ISLANDS
PORT MORESBY
HONIARA
VANUATU
Coral Sea Islands (Australia)
PORT VILA
Ashmore & Cartier Islands (Australia)
New Caledonia (France)
Great Dividing Range
NOUMÉA
INDIAN OCEAN
AUSTRALIA
Norfolk Island (Australia)
Lake Eyre North
Darling
Lord Howe Island (Australia)
Lake Torrens
NEW ZEALAND
Tropic of Capricorn
Murray
CANBERRA
WELLINGT
Tasman Sea
Tasmania
120°
40°
100°
140°
160°
A
B
C
D

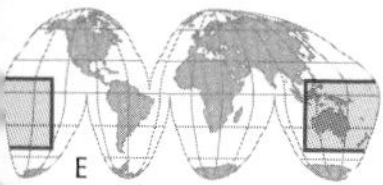

POLITICAL FACTFILE

TOTAL AREA:
3,244,632 sq miles (8,403,608 sq km)

TOTAL NUMBER OF COUNTRIES:
14

TOTAL POPULATION:
34.5 million

LARGEST CITY WITH POPULATION:
Sydney, Australia 4.4 million

COUNTRY WITH HIGHEST POPULATION DENSITY:
Nauru 1210 people per sq mile (467 people per sq km)

LARGEST COUNTRY:
Australia 2,967,893 sq miles (7,686,850 sq km)

SMALLEST COUNTRY:
Nauru 8.1 sq miles (21 sq km)

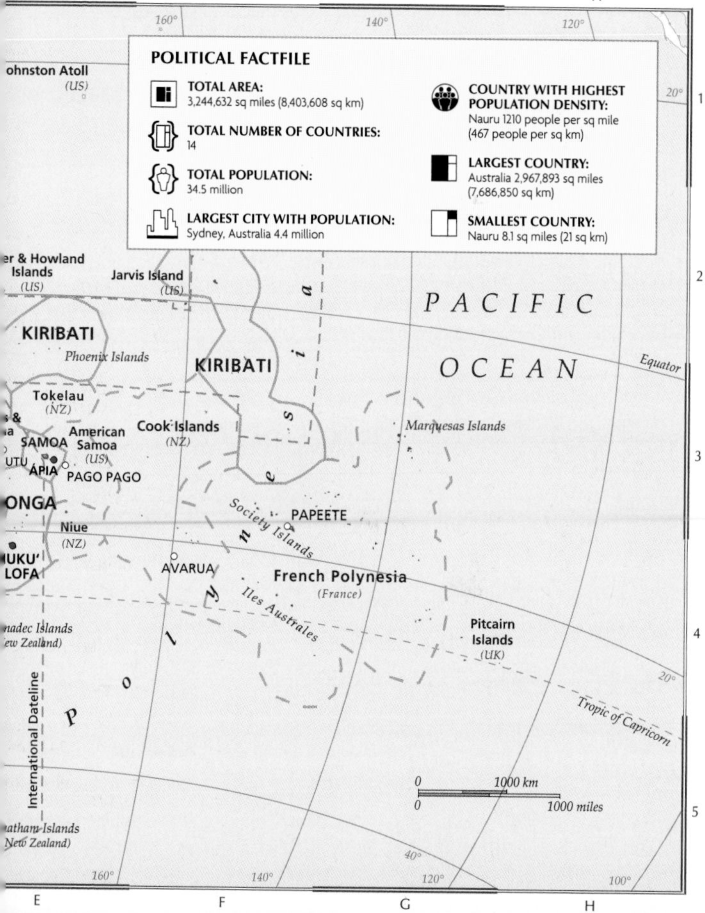
E
F
G
H
160°
140°
120°
20°
1
2
3
4
5
ohnston Atoll
(US)
er & Howland Islands
(US)
Jarvis Island
(US)
KIRIBATI
Phoenix Islands
KIRIBATI
PACIFIC
OCEAN
Equator
Tokelau
(NZ)
SAMOA
American Samoa
(US)
UTU
APIA
PAGO PAGO
Cook Islands
(NZ)
Marquesas Islands
ONGA
Niue
(NZ)
Society Islands
PAPEETE
UKU' LOFA
AVARUA
French Polynesia
(France)
Iles Australes
Pitcairn Islands
(UK)
nadec Islands
ew Zealand)
International Dateline
Tropic of Capricorn
P o l y n e s i a
0
1000 km
0
1000 miles
athan Islands
New Zealand)
40°
100°

Key to factfile maps

FOREWORD

This factfile is intended as a guide to a world that is continually changing as political fashions and personalities come and go. Nevertheless, all the material in these factfiles has been researched from the most up-to-date and authoritative sources to give an incisive portrait of the geographical, social, and economic characteristics that make each country unique.

KEY TO MAP SYMBOLS

ELEVATION

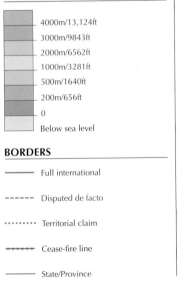

- 4000m/13,124ft
- 3000m/9843ft
- 2000m/6562ft
- 1000m/3281ft
- 500m/1640ft
- 200m/656ft
- 0
- Below sea level

BORDERS

- Full international
- Disputed de facto
- Territorial claim
- Cease-fire line
- State/Province

DRAINAGE FEATURES

- River
- Seasonal river
- Canal
- Lake
- Seasonal lake

SYMBOLS

- ● Capital city
- ○ Major town
- International airport
- ▲ Mountain

The asterisk in the Factfile denotes the country's official language(s)

Date of formation denotes the date of political origin or independence; the second date (if any) identifies when its current borders were established

The area figure denotes total land area

Afghanistan

About 75% of this landlocked Asian country is inaccessible. The Islamist *Taliban*, ousted in 2001, continue to fight a guerrilla war against Afghan and NATO-led forces.

GEOGRAPHY

Predominantly mountainous. ighest range is the Hindu Kush. 1ountains are bordered by fertile plains. esert plateau in the south.

CLIMATE

Harsh continental. Hot, dry ummers. Cold winters with heavy now, especially in the Hindu Kush.

PEOPLE & SOCIETY

Mujahideen factions fought first gainst Soviet invaders (from 1979), nd then against each other (after 1989), efore the *Taliban* won control in 1996. nder their strict Islamist regime omen were denied all rights and thnic tensions were exacerbated. he US assisted anti-*Taliban* forces in 001 as part of its "war on terrorism." new democratic government truggles to maintain control as surgency continues.

THE ECONOMY

Mainly agricultural, severely disrupted by war. Illicit opium trade is big cash earner. Natural gas pipeline planned from the Caspian Sea to Pakistan.

INSIGHT: *The UN estimates that it could take 100 years to remove the 10 million landmines laid since 1979*

70°
TAJIKISTAN
CHINA
65°
UZBEK.
TURKMENISTAN
Mazār-e Sharīf
Feyzābād
Kondoz
Baghlān
Meymaneh
Hindu Kush
35°
Chārīkār
Herāt
KABUL
Jalālābād
Khyber Pass
Ghaznī
PAKISTAN
Gereshk
Kandahār
IRAN
30°
0 100 km
0 100 miles
3000m/9843ft
2000m/6562ft
1000m/3281ft
500m/1640ft
200m/656ft

FACTFILE

OFFICIAL NAME: Islamic State of Afghanistan
DATE OF FORMATION: 1919
CAPITAL: Kabul
POPULATION: 28.1 million
TOTAL AREA: 250,000 sq. miles (647,500 sq. km)
DENSITY: 112 people per sq. mile
LANGUAGES: Pashtu*, Dari*, Tajik, other
RELIGIONS: Sunni Muslim 84%, Shi'a Muslim 15%, other 1%
ETHNIC MIX: Pashtun 38%, Tajik 25%, Hazara 19%, Uzbek, Turkmen, other 18%
GOVERNMENT: Presidential system
CURRENCY: Afghani = 100 puls

Albania

Lying at the southeastern end of the Adriatic Sea, Albania was the last east European country to liberalize its economy. The regional strife of the 1990s has left a difficult legacy

GEOGRAPHY

Narrow coastal plain. Interior is mostly hills and mountains. Forest and scrub cover over 40% of the land.

CLIMATE

Mediterranean coastal climate, with warm summers and cool winters. Mountains receive heavy rains or snows in winter.

PEOPLE & SOCIETY

The pace of economic reform remains a major issue. EU membership, applied for in 2009, is a distant prospect. Mosques and churches have reopened in what was once the world's only officially atheist state. The Greek minority in the south suffers much discrimination.

INSIGHT: *The Albanians' name for their country, Shqipërisë, means "Land of the Eagles"*

THE ECONOMY

Oil and natural gas reserves have potential to offset rudimentary infrastructure and lack of foreign investment. Organized crime problem.

Sea Level
MONTENEGRO
Lake Scutari
KOSOVO
Shkodër
Kukës
42°
Adriatic Sea
MACEDONIA
Durrës
TIRANA
Elbasan
Lake Ohrid
41°
Lushnjë
Lake Prespa
Fier
Berat
Vlorë
Korçë
40°
Delvinë
Ionian Sea
GREECE
20°
0 50 km
0 50 miles

FACTFILE

OFFICIAL NAME: Republic of Albania
DATE OF FORMATION: 1912
CAPITAL: Tirana
POPULATION: 3.16 million
TOTAL AREA: 11,100 sq. miles (28,748 sq. km)
DENSITY: 298 people per sq. mile
LANGUAGES: Albanian*, Greek
RELIGIONS: Sunni Muslim 70%, Orthodox Christian 20%, Roman Catholic 10%
ETHNIC MIX: Albanian 93%, Greek 5%, other 2%
GOVERNMENT: Parliamentary system
CURRENCY: Lek = 100 qindarka (qintars)

Algeria

Africa's second-largest country, Algeria won independence from France in 1962. Today, national reconciliation is key to recovery from a conflict launched by Islamic extremists in 1992.

GEOGRAPHY

85% of the country lies within the ahara Desert. Fertile coastal region with lains and hills rises from the southeast ɔ the Atlas Mountains.

CLIMATE

Coastal areas are warm and emperate, with most rainfall during the iild winters. The south is very hot, with egligible rainfall.

PEOPLE & SOCIETY

Algerians are predominantly rab, under 30 years of age, and ·ban. Most indigenous Berbers ɔnsider the mountainous Kabylia ·gion in the northeast to be their ɔmeland. They have been granted ·eater ethnic rights in recent years. ıe Sahara sustains just 500,000 people, ıainly oil workers and Tuareg nomads ith goat and camel herds, who move etween the irrigated oases.

THE ECONOMY

Oil and natural gas exports. Political turmoil has led to exodus of skilled foreign labor. Limited agriculture.

INSIGHT: *The world's highest dunes are located in the deserts of east central Algeria*

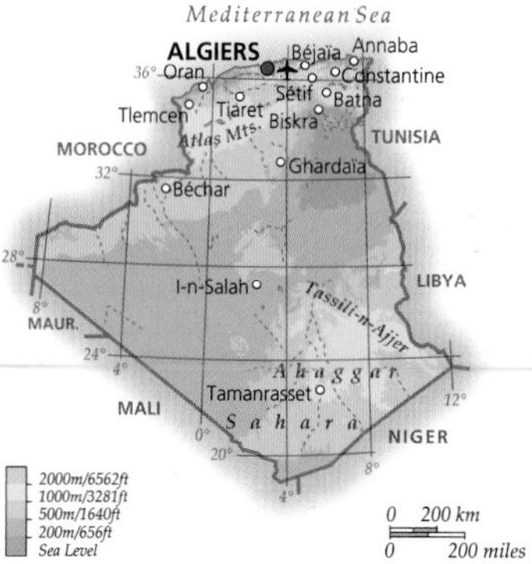
Mediterranean Sea
ALGIERS
Béjaïa
Annaba
Oran
Constantine
Sétif
Batna
Tlemcen
Tiaret
Biskra
Atlas Mts.
MOROCCO
TUNISIA
Ghardaïa
Béchar
I-n-Salah
Tassili-n-Ajjer
LIBYA
MAUR.
Ahaggar
Tamanrasset
MALI
Sahara
NIGER
36°
32°
28°
24°
20°
12°
8°
4°
0°
2000m/6562ft
1000m/3281ft
500m/1640ft
200m/656ft
Sea Level
0 200 km
0 200 miles

FACTFILE

OFFICIAL NAME: People's Democratic Republic of Algeria
DATE OF FORMATION: 1962
CAPITAL: Algiers
POPULATION: 34.9 million
TOTAL AREA: 919,590 sq. miles (2,381,740 sq. km)
DENSITY: 38 people per sq. mile
LANGUAGES: Arabic*, Tamazight, French
RELIGIONS: Sunni Muslim 99%, Christian and Jewish 1%
ETHNIC MIX: Arab 75%, Berber 24%, European and Jewish 1%
GOVERNMENT: Presidential system
CURRENCY: Algerian dinar = 100 centimes

Andorra

A tiny landlocked principality, Andorra lies high in the eastern Pyrenees between France and Spain. It held its first full elections in 1993. Tourism is the main source of income.

GEOGRAPHY

High mountains, with six deep, glaciated valleys that drain into the Valira River as it flows into Spain.

CLIMATE

Cool, wet springs followed by dry, warm summers. Mountain snows linger until March.

PEOPLE & SOCIETY

Immigration is strictly monitored and restricted by quota to French and Spanish nationals seeking employment in Andorra. Low taxes attract wealthy expatriates. A referendum in 1993 ended 715 years of semifeudal status, but Andorran society remains conservative.

INSIGHT: *Andorra's coprincipality status dates from the 13th century. The "princes" are the president of France and the bishop of Urgel in Spain.*

THE ECONOMY

Tourism and duty-free sales dominate the economy. Banking secrecy laws and low consumer taxes promote investment and commerce. France and Spain effectively decide economic polic[y]. Dependence on imported food and raw materials.

FRANCE
SPAIN
Pyrenees
Arinsal
Soldeu
Canillo
Ordino
Encamp
Port d'Enval
Escaldes
ANDORRA LA VELLA
Valira
Sant Julià de Lòria
42°35'
42°30'
1°25'
1°30'
1°35'
1°40'
0 5 km
0 5 miles

FACTFILE

OFFICIAL NAME: Principality of Andorra
DATE OF FORMATION: 1278
CAPITAL: Andorra la Vella
POPULATION: 82,200
TOTAL AREA: 181 sq. miles (468 sq. km)
DENSITY: 457 people per sq. mile
LANGUAGES: Spanish, Catalan*, French, Portuguese
RELIGIONS: Roman Catholic 94%, other 6%
ETHNIC MIX: Spanish 46%, Andorran 28%, other 18%, French 8%
GOVERNMENT: Parliamentary system
CURRENCY: Euro = 100 cents

Angola

Located in southwest Africa, Angola suffered a civil war following independence from Portugal in 1975, until a 2002 peace deal. Hundreds of thousands of people died.

GEOGRAPHY

Most of the land is hilly and grass-covered. Desert in the south. Mountains in the center and north.

CLIMATE

Varies from temperate to tropical. Rainfall decreases north to south. Coast is cooler and dry.

PEOPLE & SOCIETY

Civil war pitched the ruling Kimbundu-dominated MPLA against UNITA, representing the Ovimbundu. Multiparty elections in 1991–1992, after the MPLA had abandoned Marxism, failed to stall the war for long. Power-sharing from 2002 ended when the MPLA won the 2008 election; a presidential poll has yet to be held.

INSIGHT: *Angola has the greatest number of amputees (caused by landmines) in the world*

THE ECONOMY

Potentially one of Africa's richest countries, but long civil war hampered economic development. Oil and diamonds are exported.

CONGO
CABINDA
(part of Angola)
Congo
DEM. REP. CONGO
M'Banza Congo
Uíge
LUANDA
Malanje
Lucapa
Saurimo
ATLANTIC OCEAN
Cuanza
Luena
Zambezi
Lobito
Benguela
Huambo
Planalto do Bié
Lubango
Menongue
ZAMBIA
Namibe
Cunene
NAMIBIA
BOTSWANA
12°
16°
20°
24°
4°
8°
2000m/6562ft
1000m/3281ft
500m/1640ft
200m/656ft
Sea Level
0 200 km
0 200 miles

FACTFILE

OFFICIAL NAME: Republic of Angola
DATE OF FORMATION: 1975
CAPITAL: Luanda
POPULATION: 18.5 million
TOTAL AREA: 481,351 sq. miles (1,246,700 sq. km)
DENSITY: 38 people per sq. mile
LANGUAGES: Portuguese*, Umbundu, Kimbundu, Kikongo
RELIGIONS: Roman Catholic 50%, other 30%, Protestant 20%
ETHNIC MIX: Ovimbundu 37%, other 25%, Kimbundu 25%, Bakongo 13%
GOVERNMENT: Presidential system
CURRENCY: Readjusted kwanza = 100 lwei

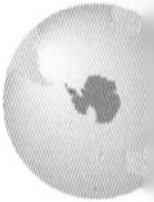

Antarctica

The circumpolar continent of Antarctica is almost entirely covered by ice, some up to 1.2 miles (2 km) thick. It also contains 90% of the Earth's freshwater reserves.

GEOGRAPHY

The bulk of Antarctica's ice is contained in the Greater Antarctic Ice Sheet – a huge dome that rises steeply from the coast and flattens to a plateau in the interior.

CLIMATE

Powerful winds create a storm belt around the continent, which brings cloud, fog, and blizzards. Winter temperatures can fall to –112°F (–80°C).

PEOPLE & SOCIETY

No indigenous population. Scientists and logistical staff work at the 40 permanent, and as many as 100 temporary, research stations. A few Chilean settler families live on King George Island. Tourism is mostly by cruise ship to the Antarctic Peninsula. Annual tourist numbers have reached nearly 50,000.

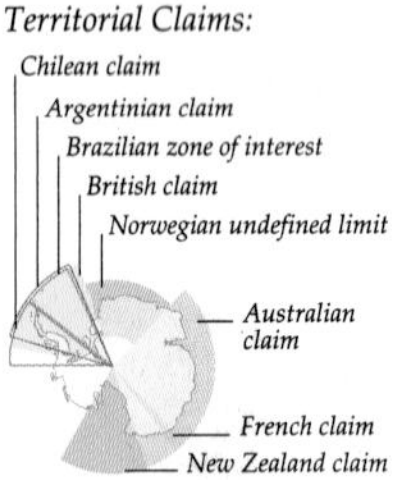
Territorial Claims:
Chilean claim
Argentinian claim
Brazilian zone of interest
British claim
Norwegian undefined limit
Australian claim
French claim
New Zealand claim

The Antarctic Treaty of 1959 holds all territorial claims in abeyance in the interest of international cooperation

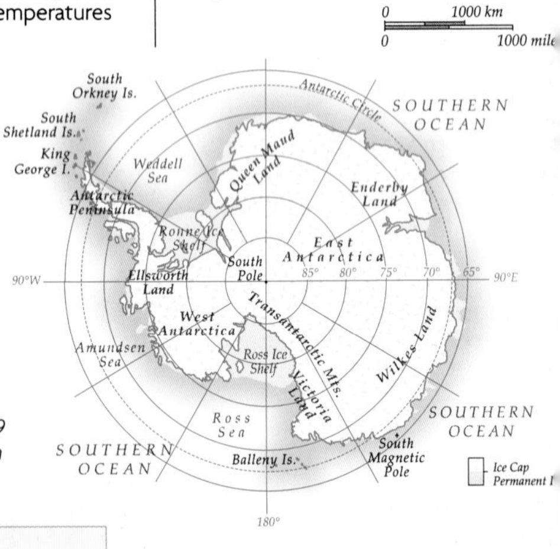
0 1000 km
0 1000 mile
South Orkney Is.
South Shetland Is.
King George I.
Antarctic Peninsula
Weddell Sea
Queen Maud Land
Antarctic Circle
SOUTHERN OCEAN
Enderby Land
Ronne Ice Shelf
East Antarctica
South Pole
Ellsworth Land
90°W
90°E
85°
80°
75°
70°
65°
West Antarctica
Transantarctic Mts.
Amundsen Sea
Ross Ice Shelf
Wilkes Land
Victoria Land
Ross Sea
SOUTHERN OCEAN
SOUTHERN OCEAN
Balleny Is.
South Magnetic Pole
Ice Cap
Permanent I
180°

FACTFILE

DATE OF FORMATION: 1961

TOTAL AREA: 5,405,000 sq. miles (14,000,000 sq. km)

◆ **INSIGHT:** *If the ice sheets of Antarctica were to melt, the world's oceans would rise by as much as 200–210 ft (60–65 m)*

Antigua & Barbuda

A former colony of Spain, France, and the UK, Antigua and Barbuda lies at the outer edge of the Leeward Islands group in the Caribbean, and includes the uninhabited islet of Redonda.

GEOGRAPHY

Mainly low-lying limestone and oral islands with some higher volcanic reas. Antigua's coast is indented with ays and harbors.

CLIMATE

Tropical, moderated by trade winds nd sea breezes. Humidity and rainfall are ow for the region.

PEOPLE & SOCIETY

Population almost entirely of frican origin, with small communities of uropeans and South Asians. Women's tatus has risen as a result of greater ccess to education. Wealth disparities re small. The Bird family dominated olitics from 1960, but lost power to the nited Progressive Party (UPP) from 2004.

INSIGHT: *In 1865, Redonda was "claimed" by an eccentric Englishman as kingdom for his son*

THE ECONOMY

Tourism is the main source of revenue and the biggest provider of jobs. Financial services and Internet gambling are expanding. High debt.

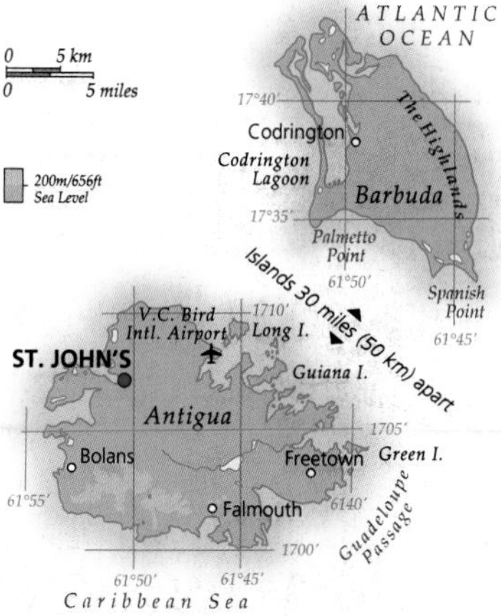
ATLANTIC OCEAN
0 5 km
0 5 miles
200m/656ft
Sea Level
17°40'
Codrington
Codrington Lagoon
The Highlands
Barbuda
17°35'
Palmetto Point
61°50'
Islands 30 miles (50 km) apart
Spanish Point
61°45'
17°10'
V.C. Bird Intl. Airport
Long I.
ST. JOHN'S
Guiana I.
Antigua
17°05'
Bolans
Freetown
Green I.
61°55'
Falmouth
61°40'
Guadeloupe Passage
17°00'
61°50'
61°45'
Caribbean Sea

FACTFILE

OFFICIAL NAME: Antigua and Barbuda
DATE OF FORMATION: 1981
CAPITAL: St. John's
POPULATION: 82,800
TOTAL AREA: 170 sq. miles (442 sq. km)
DENSITY: 487 people per sq. mile
LANGUAGES: English*, English patois
RELIGIONS: Anglican 45%, other Protestant 42%, Roman Catholic 10%, other 2%, Rastafarian 1%
ETHNIC MIX: Black African 95%, other 5%
GOVERNMENT: Parliamentary system
CURRENCY: E. Caribbean $ = 100 cents

Argentina

Argentina occupies most of southern South America. After 30 years of intermittent military rule, democracy returnec in 1983. Economy has slowed since its recovery from 2001 crash

GEOGRAPHY

The Andes form a natural border with Chile in the west. East are the heavily wooded plains (Gran Chaco) and treeless but fertile Pampas plains. Bleak and arid Patagonia in the south.

CLIMATE

The Andes are semiarid in the north and snowy in the south. Pampas have a mild climate with summer rains.

PEOPLE & SOCIETY

People are largely of European descent; over one-third are of Italian origin. Indigenous peoples are now in a minority, living mainly in Andean regions or in the Gran Chaco. The middle classes were worst hit by the economic meltdown of 2001–2002.

INSIGHT: *The Tango originated in the poorer quarters of Buenos Aires at the end of the 19th century*

THE ECONOMY

Agricultural exports restored growth from 2003, but bad drought in 2008 coincided with global downturn.

BOLIVIA
60° PARAGUAY
50°
Salta
San Miguel de Tucumán
Gran Chaco
Salado
Posadas
Corrientes
BRAZIL
CHILE
30°
Santa Fe
Paraná
URUGUAY
San Juan
Córdoba
Rosario
BUENOS AIRES
Mendoza
La Plata
Pampas
Santa Rosa
Mar del Plata
Bahía Blanca
Bahía Blanca
Neuquén
Negro
40°
Viedma
ATLANTIC OCEAN
Patagonia
Golfo San Jorge
Falkland Islands (to UK)
Bahía Grande
50°
Río Gallegos
Strait of Magellan
Tierra del Fuego
0 400 km
0 400 miles
4000m/1312
3000m/9843f
2000m/6562f
1000m/3281f
200m/656ft
Sea Level

FACTFILE

OFFICIAL NAME: Republic of Argentina
DATE OF FORMATION: 1816
CAPITAL: Buenos Aires
POPULATION: 40.3 million
TOTAL AREA: 1,068,296 sq. miles (2,766,890 sq. km)
DENSITY: 38 people per sq. mile
LANGUAGES: Spanish*, Italian, Amerindian languages
RELIGIONS: Roman Catholic 90%, other 6%, Protestant 2%, Jewish 2%
ETHNIC MIX: Indo-European 83%, Mestizo 14%, Jewish 2%, Amerindian 1%
GOVERNMENT: Presidential system
CURRENCY: Argentine peso = 100 centavos

Armenia

The smallest of the former USSR's republics, Armenia lies landlocked in the Lesser Caucasus Mountains. After 1988, a confrontation with Azerbaijan dominated national life.

GEOGRAPHY

Rugged and mountainous, with expanses of semidesert and a large lake in the east: Sevana Lich.

CLIMATE

Continental climate, with little rainfall in the lowlands. The winters are often bitterly cold.

PEOPLE & SOCIETY

Christianity is the dominant religion, but minority groups are well integrated. War with Azerbaijan over the enclave of Nagorno Karabakh forced 350,000 Armenians living in Azerbaijan to return home, many to live in poverty. There are close and important ties to the seven-million-strong Armenian diaspora.

INSIGHT: *In the 4th century, Armenia became the first country to adopt Christianity as its state religion*

THE ECONOMY

Overseas remittances and agriculture each account for a sixth of GDP. Main products are wine, tobacco, potatoes, and fruit. Well-developed machine-building and manufacturing – includes textiles and bottling of mineral water.

3000m/9843ft
2000m/6562ft
1000m/3281ft
500m/1640ft
44°
GEORGIA
Alaverdi
Vanadzor
Gyumri
Sevan
AZERBAIJAN
46°
TURKEY
Hrazdan
Ashtarak
Sevana Lich
Vagharshapat
Armavir
YEREVAN
40°
Ararat
Aras
Lesser Caucasus
AZERBAIJAN
Kapan
Aras
IRAN
0 50 km
0 50 miles

FACTFILE

OFFICIAL NAME: Republic of Armenia
DATE OF FORMATION: 1991
CAPITAL: Yerevan
POPULATION: 3.08 million
TOTAL AREA: 11,506 sq. miles (29,800 sq. km)
DENSITY: 268 people per sq. mile
LANGUAGES: Armenian*, Azeri, Russian
RELIGIONS: Armenian Apostolic Church (Orthodox) 88%, Armenian Catholic Church 6%, other 6%
ETHNIC MIX: Armenian 98%, Yezidi 1%, other 1%
GOVERNMENT: Parliamentary system
CURRENCY: Dram = 100 luma

Australia

An island continent in its own right, Australia is the world's sixth-largest country. European settlement began over 200 years ago. Most Australians now live in cities along the coast

GEOGRAPHY

Located between the Indian and Pacific oceans, Australia has a variety of landscapes, including tropical rainforests, the arid plateaus, ridges, and vast deserts of the "red center," the lowlands and river systems draining into Lake Eyre, rolling tracts of pastoral land, and magnificent beaches around much of the coastline. In the far east are the mountains of the Great Dividing Range. Famous natural features include Uluru (Ayers Rock) and the Great Barrier Reef.

CLIMATE

The west and south are semi-arid with hot summers. The arid interior can reach 120°F (50°C) in the central desert areas. The north is hot throughout the year, and humid during the summer monsoon. East, southeast, and southwest coastal areas are temperate.

PEOPLE & SOCIETY

The first settlers arrived in Australia at least 100,000 years ago. Today, the Aborigines make up around 2% of the population. European colonization began in 1788, and was dominated by British and Irish immigrants, some of whom were convicts. White-only immigration drives brought many Europeans to Australia, but since the 1960s multi-culturalism has been encouraged and most new settlers are Asian; Cantonese has overtaken Italian as the second most widely spoken language. Wealth disparities are small, but Aborigines, the exception in an otherwise integrated society, are marginalized: their average life expectancy is around 11 years less than other Australians. The new Labor government from 2007 has overturned right-wing policies on illegal immigration and has signed up to limiting greenhouse gas emissions.

FACTFILE

OFFICIAL NAME: Commonwealth of Australia
DATE OF FORMATION: 1901
CAPITAL: Canberra
POPULATION: 21.3 million
TOTAL AREA: 2,967,893 sq. miles (7,686,850 sq. km)
DENSITY: 7 people per sq. mile
LANGUAGES: English*, Cantonese, other
RELIGIONS: Various Protestant 38%, other 36%, Roman Catholic 26%
ETHNIC MIX: European 90%, Asian 7%, Aboriginal 2%, other 1%
GOVERNMENT: Parliamentary system
CURRENCY: Australian dollar = 100 cents

THE ECONOMY

Efficient mining and agriculture: particular success in viticulture. Large resource base: coal, iron ore, bauxite, and most other minerals. Protectionism abandoned to open up Australian markets. Concentration on trade with Asia: China's expanding demand for minerals spurred a return to strong economic growth after the 1997 Asian financial crisis. China now rivals Japan as Australia's major trading partner. Upward trend in Asian visitor arrivals has strengthened tourism.

INSIGHT: *Sydney has the world's largest suburban area, a conurbation so vast that the city is twice as large as Beijing and six times the size of Rome*

Arafura Sea
Timor Sea
Darwin
Arnhem Land
Gulf of Carpentaria
Bamaga
Cape York
Great Barrier Reef
PACIFIC OCEAN
Coral Sea
INDIAN OCEAN
Kimberley Plateau
NORTHERN TERRITORY
Cairns
Great Dividing Range
Townsville
Port Hedland
Great Sandy Desert
Lake Disappointment
Lake Mackay
Hamersley Range
Gibson Desert
Macdonnell Ranges
Alice Springs
Mount Isa
Mackay
Rockhampton
QUEENSLAND
Bundaberg
Uluru (Ayers Rock) (867m)
Simpson Desert
Fraser I.
Carnarvon
WESTERN AUSTRALIA
Lake Carnegie
Meekatharra
Gympie
Brisbane
Toowoomba
Ipswich
Gold Coast
Surfers Paradise
Great Victoria Desert
Lake Eyre
SOUTH AUSTRALIA
raldton
Kalgoorlie
Nullarbor Plain
Flinders Ranges
Darling
Grafton
Coffs Harbour
NEW SOUTH WALES
Broken Hill
Port Augusta
Whyalla
Port Pirie
Perth
Fremantle
ockingham
Bunbury
Darling Range
e Leeuwin
Esperance
Port Lincoln
Elizabeth
Adelaide
Newcastle
Sydney
Wagga Wagga
Wollongong
Murray
Albury
CANBERRA
AUSTRALIAN CAPITAL TERRITORY
Albany
Kangaroo I.
Bendigo
VICTORIA
Australian Alps
Great Australian Bight
Melbourne
Geelong
Tasman Sea
Bass Strait
Burnie
TASMANIA
Launceston
Hobart
South East Cape
10°
20°
30°
40°
120°
130°
140°
150°
1000m/3281ft
500m/1640ft
200m/656ft
Sea Level
Below Sea Level
0 400 km
0 400 miles

Austria

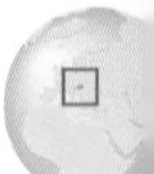

Bordering eight countries in the heart of Europe, Austria was created in 1918 after the collapse of the Habsburg Empire. Neutral after World War II, it joined the EU in 1995.

GEOGRAPHY

Mainly mountainous. Alps and foothills cover the west and south. Lowlands in the east are part of the Danube River basin.

CLIMATE

Temperate continental climate. The western Alpine regions have colder winters and more rainfall.

PEOPLE & SOCIETY

Though Austrians speak German, they like to stress their distinctive identity in relation to Germany. Vienna is a major cultural center. Minorities are few; there are some ethnic Croats, Slovenes, and Hungarians, plus refugees from conflict in former Yugoslavia. Though strongly Roman Catholic, Austrian society is less conservative than some southern German *Länder*. Class divisions remain strong.

THE ECONOMY

Large manufacturing base, despite lack of energy resources. The skilled labor force is key to high-tech exports. Eurozone membership since 2002 has boosted investment.

INSIGHT: *Many of the world's great composers were Austrian, including Mozart, Haydn, Schubert, and Strauss*

3000m/9843ft
2000m/6562ft
1000m/3281ft
500m/1640ft
200m/656ft
Sea Level
CZECH REP.
14°
16°
Linz
Danube
VIENNA
Wels
12°
48°
Steyr
Sankt Pölten
Salzburg
Wiener Neustadt
10°
GERMANY
Bad Ischl
Dornbirn
Leoben
HUNG.
LIECH.
Innsbruck
Graz
Wolfsberg
SWITZ.
ITALY
Villach
Klagenfurt
SLOVENIA
0 50 km
0 50 miles

FACTFILE

OFFICIAL NAME: Republic of Austria
DATE OF FORMATION: 1918
CAPITAL: Vienna
POPULATION: 8.36 million
TOTAL AREA: 32,378 sq. miles (83,858 sq. km)
DENSITY: 262 people per sq. mile
LANGUAGES: German*, Croatian, Slovenian, Hungarian (Magyar)
RELIGIONS: Roman Catholic 78%, nonreligious 9%, other 8%, Protestant 5%
ETHNIC MIX: Austrian 93%, Croat, Slovene, and Hungarian 6%, other 1%
GOVERNMENT: Parliamentary system
CURRENCY: Euro = 100 cents

Azerbaijan

Situated on the western coast of the Caspian Sea, it was the first Soviet republic to declare independence in 1991. Territorial disputes with Armenia have dominated politics since.

GEOGRAPHY

Caucasus Mountains in west, ncluding Naxçivan exclave south of rmenia. Flat, low-lying terrain on the oast of the Caspian Sea.

CLIMATE

Low rainfall. Continental, with itter winters, inland. Subtropical in oastal regions.

PEOPLE & SOCIETY

Azeris, a Muslim people with thnic links to Turks, form a large najority. Thousands of Armenians, ussians, and Jews have left since ndependence. Influx of half a million zeri refugees fleeing war with Armenia ver the disputed enclave of Nagorno arabakh. Armenians there operate with le facto independence. The status of vomen deteriorated after the fall of ommunism but they are slowly egaining their position.

THE ECONOMY

Oil and natural gas exports drive economic growth. Pipeline to Ceyhan, Turkey, has opened up European market. Severe pollution in Baku.

INSIGHT: *The fire-worshipping Zoroastrian faith originated in Azerbaijan in the 6th century BCE*

RUSS. FED.
GEORGIA
ARMENIA
IRAN
Caspian Sea
Caucasus
Lesser Caucasus
Kura
Aras
Nagorno-Karabakh
Quba
Şäki
Gäncä
Mingäçevir
Sumqayıt
BAKU
Äli-Bayramlı
Xankändi
Naxçivan
Länkäran
42°
40°
46°
48°
50°
4000m/13124ft
3000m/9843ft
2000m/6562ft
1000m/3281ft
500m/1640ft
200m/656ft
Sea Level
Below Sea Level
0 100 km
0 100 miles

FACTFILE

OFFICIAL NAME: Republic of Azerbaijan
DATE OF FORMATION: 1991
CAPITAL: Baku
POPULATION: 8.83 million
TOTAL AREA: 33,436 sq. miles (86,600 sq. km)
DENSITY: 264 people per sq. mile
LANGUAGES: Azeri*, Russian
RELIGIONS: Shi'a Muslim 68%, Sunni Muslim 26%, Russian Orthodox 3%, Armenian Orthodox 2%, other 1%
ETHNIC MIX: Azeri 91%, other 3%, Lazs 2%, Russian 2%, Armenian 2%
GOVERNMENT: Presidential system
CURRENCY: New manat = 100 gopik

Bahamas

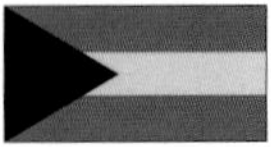

Located off the Florida coast in the western Atlantic, the Bahamas comprises an archipelago of some 700 islands and 2400 cays, only around 30 of which are inhabited.

GEOGRAPHY

Long, mainly flat coral formations with a few low hills. Some islands have pine forests, lagoons, and mangrove swamps.

CLIMATE

Subtropical. Hot summers and mild winters. Heavy rainfall, especially in summer. Hurricanes can strike in July–December.

PEOPLE & SOCIETY

Over 60% of the population live on New Providence. Tourism employs over 40% of the labor force. There are marked wealth disparities, from urban professionals in the banking sector to traditional fishermen on outlying islands and illegal Haitian and Cuban immigrants. More women are now entering the professions. Government priorities are tackling narcotics trafficking and money laundering.

THE ECONOMY

Major tourist destination, especially for US visitors. Financial services: banking and insurance.

INSIGHT: *The country's extensive merchant fleet consists mainly of "flag-of-convenience" vessels registered by foreign owners*

Straits of Florida
Grand Bahama I.
Freeport
Great Abaco
Berry Is.
New Providence
Eleuthera I.
Nicholls Town
NASSAU
ATLANTIC OCEAN
Andros I.
Andros Town
Exuma Sound
Cat I.
San Salvador
Exuma Cays
Rum Cay
Long I.
Crooked I.
Mayaguana
Acklins I.
Caicos Passage
Great Inagua
26°
24°
22°
78°
76°
74°
200m/656
Sea Level
0 100 km
0 100 miles

FACTFILE

OFFICIAL NAME: Commonwealth of the Bahamas
DATE OF FORMATION: 1973
CAPITAL: Nassau
POPULATION: 341,700
TOTAL AREA: 5382 sq. miles (13,940 sq. km)
DENSITY: 88 people per sq. mile
LANGUAGES: English*, English Creole, French Creole
RELIGIONS: Baptist 32%, other 29%, Anglican 20%, Roman Catholic 19%
ETHNIC MIX: Black African 85%, other 15%
GOVERNMENT: Parliamentary system
CURRENCY: Bahamian dollar = 100 cents

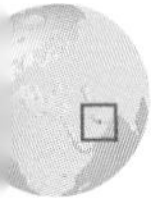

Bahrain

Bahrain is an archipelago of 49 islands between the Qatar peninsula and the Saudi Arabian mainland. Only three of the islands are inhabited. It was the first Gulf emirate to export oil.

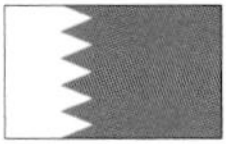

GEOGRAPHY

All islands are low-lying. The argest, Bahrain Island, is mainly sandy plains and salt marshes.

CLIMATE

Summers are hot and humid. Winters are mild. Low rainfall.

PEOPLE & SOCIETY

The key social division is between the Shi'a majority and Sunni minority. Sunnis hold the best obs in bureaucracy and business while Shi'as tend to do menial work. The al-Khalifa family has ruled since 1783, but transformed Bahrain into a constitutional monarchy, with imited democracy, in 2002. Bahrain s socially liberal.

INSIGHT: *The 16 Hawar Islands were awarded to Bahrain in 2001 after a engthy dispute with Qatar*

THE ECONOMY

Main exports are refined petroleum and aluminum products. As oil reserves run out, natural gas is of increasing importance. Major Middle East offshore banking center, hit by global banking crisis in 2008–2009.

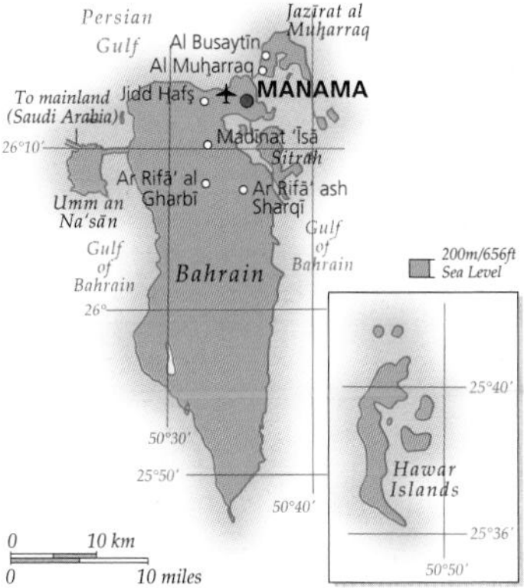
Persian Gulf
Jazīrat al Muḩarraq
Al Busaytīn
Al Muḩarraq
MANAMA
To mainland (Saudi Arabia)
Jidd Ḩafş
Madīnat 'Īsā
Sitrah
26°10'
Ar Rifā' al Gharbī
Ar Rifā' ash Sharqī
Umm an Na'sān
Gulf of Bahrain
Bahrain
Gulf of Bahrain
200m/656ft
Sea Level
26°
50°30'
25°50'
50°40'
25°40'
Hawar Islands
25°36'
50°50'
0 10 km
0 10 miles

FACTFILE

OFFICIAL NAME: Kingdom of Bahrain
DATE OF FORMATION: 1971
CAPITAL: Manama
POPULATION: 791,500
TOTAL AREA: 239 sq. miles (620 sq. km)
DENSITY: 2899 people per sq. mile
LANGUAGES: Arabic*
RELIGIONS: Muslim (mainly Shi'a) 99%, other 1%
ETHNIC MIX: Bahraini 70%, Iranian, Indian, and Pakistani 24%, other 6%
GOVERNMENT: Mixed monarchical-parliamentary system
CURRENCY: Bahraini dinar = 1000 fils

Bangladesh

Bangladesh lies at the north end of the Bay of Bengal and frequently suffers devastating flood, cyclones, and famine. It seceded from Pakistan in 1971.

GEOGRAPHY

Mostly flat alluvial plains and deltas of the Brahmaputra and Ganges rivers. Southeast coasts are fringed with mangrove forests.

CLIMATE

Hot and humid. During the monsoon, water levels can rise 20 ft (6 m) above sea level.

PEOPLE & SOCIETY

After a period of military rule, Bangladesh returned to democracy in 1991; political instability has continued, however, and corruption is a major problem. Half of the population live in poverty, but living standards are improving. Women are prominent in politics, but their rights are neglected.

INSIGHT: *Torrential monsoon rains flood two-thirds of the country every year*

THE ECONOMY

Agriculture is vulnerable to unpredictable climate. Bangladesh accounts for 90% of world jute fiber exports. Poor infrastructure deters investment. Growing textile industry.

500m/1640ft
200m/656ft
Sea Level
88°
90°
92°
26°
24°
22°
Rangpur
Saidpur
Dinajpur
Brahmaputra
INDIA
Sylhet
Jamalpur
Mymensingh
Rajshahi
Shirajganj Ghat
Brahmanbaria
Pabna
Ganges (Padma)
DHAKA
INDIA
Comilla
Haringhat
Jessore
Khulna
Barisal
Mouths of the Ganges
Chittagong
Bay of Bengal
MYANMAR (BURMA)
0
100 km
0
100 miles

FACTFILE

OFFICIAL NAME: People's Republic of Bangladesh
DATE OF FORMATION: 1971
CAPITAL: Dhaka
POPULATION: 162 million
TOTAL AREA: 55,598 sq. miles (144,000 sq. km)
DENSITY: 3138 people per sq. mile
LANGUAGES: Bengali*, Urdu, Chakma, Marma, Garo, Khasi, Santhali, Tripuri, Mro
RELIGIONS: Muslim (mainly Sunni) 87%, Hindu 12%, other 1%
ETHNIC MIX: Bengali 98%, other 2%
GOVERNMENT: Parliamentary system
CURRENCY: Taka = 100 poisha

Barbados

Barbados is the most easterly of the Caribbean islands. Once solely inhabited by the native Arawak, Barbados was first colonized by British settlers in the 1620s.

GEOGRAPHY

Encircled by coral reefs. Fertile and predominantly flat, with a few gentle hills to the north.

CLIMATE

Moderate tropical climate. Sunnier and drier than its more mountainous neighbors.

PEOPLE & SOCIETY

Some latent tension between white community, which controls politics and much of the economy, and majority black population, but violence is rare. Increasing social mobility has enabled black Barbadians to enter the professions. Despite political stability, and good welfare and education services, pockets of abject poverty remain.

INSIGHT: *Barbados retains a strong British influence and is referred to by its neighbors as "Little England"*

THE ECONOMY

Well-developed tourism sector based on climate and accessibility. Financial services, offshore banking, and information processing are key industries. Sugar production has dwindled. High cost of living.

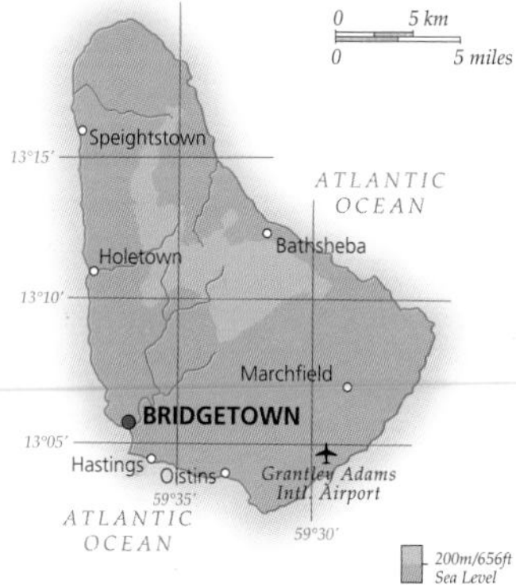
0 5 km
0 5 miles
Speightstown
13°15'
ATLANTIC OCEAN
Bathsheba
Holetown
13°10'
Marchfield
BRIDGETOWN
13°05'
Hastings
Oistins
Grantley Adams Intl. Airport
59°35'
ATLANTIC OCEAN
59°30'
200m/656ft
Sea Level

FACTFILE

OFFICIAL NAME: Barbados
DATE OF FORMATION: 1966
CAPITAL: Bridgetown
POPULATION: 255,900
TOTAL AREA: 166 sq. miles (430 sq. km)
DENSITY: 1542 people per sq. mile
LANGUAGES: Bajan (Barbadian English), English*
RELIGIONS: Anglican 40%, other 24%, nonreligious 17%, Pentecostal 8%, Methodist 7%, Roman Catholic 4%
ETHNIC MIX: Black African 92%, other 8%
GOVERNMENT: Parliamentary system
CURRENCY: Barbados dollar = 100 cents

Belarus

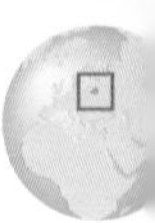

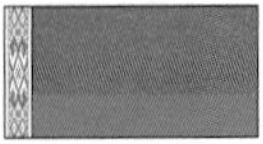

Literally "White Russia," Belarus lies landlocked in eastern Europe. It reluctantly became independent when the USSR broke up in 1991. It has few resources other than agriculture

GEOGRAPHY

Mainly plains and low hills. The Dnieper and Dvina rivers drain the eastern lowlands. Vast Pripet Marshes in the southwest.

CLIMATE

Extreme continental climate. Winters are long, sub-freezing, but mainly dry; summers are hot.

PEOPLE & SOCIETY

Only 2% of people are non-Slav, so ethnic tension is minimal. Russian culture dominates. Belarus was the slowest ex-Soviet state to implement political reform; President Lukashenka has been labeled as Europe's last dictator. Enthusiasm for a merger with Russia has waned. Wealth is held by a small ex-Communist elite. Fallout from the 1986 Chernobyl nuclear disaster in Ukraine still seriously affects health and the environment.

THE ECONOMY

Low unemployment. Industry outmoded and mainly state-owned. Depends on Russia for energy and raw materials: tensions over natural gas prices

INSIGHT: *The number of cancer and leukemia cases soared after the 1986 Chernobyl disaster*

LATVIA
56°
200m/656ft
Sea Level
Western Dvina
Vitsyebsk
RUSS. FED.
LITHUANIA
Orsha
54°
Barysaw
Lida
MINSK
Mahilyow
POLAND
Hrodna
Slutsk
Babruysk
Baranavichy
Dnieper
Homyel'
Brest
Pinsk
Pripet Marshes
Rechytsa
Mazyr
52°
32°
26°
UKRAINE
UKRAINE
24°
28°
30°
0
100 km
0
100 miles

FACTFILE

OFFICIAL NAME: Republic of Belarus
DATE OF FORMATION: 1991
CAPITAL: Minsk
POPULATION: 9.63 million
TOTAL AREA: 80,154 sq. miles (207,600 sq. km)
DENSITY: 120 people per sq. mile
LANGUAGES: Belarussian*, Russian*
RELIGIONS: Orthodox Christian 60%, other (including Muslim, Jewish, and Protestant) 32%, Roman Catholic 8%
ETHNIC MIX: Belarussian 81%, Russian 11%, Polish 4%, Ukrainian 2%, other 2%
GOVERNMENT: Presidential system
CURRENCY: Belarussian rouble = 100 kopeks

Belgium

Belgium lies in northwestern Europe. Its history has been marked by tensions between the majority Dutch-speaking (Flemish) and minority French-speaking (Walloon) communities.

GEOGRAPHY

Low-lying coastal plain covers two-thirds of the country. Land becomes hilly and forested in the southeast (Ardennes) region.

CLIMATE

Maritime climate with Gulf Stream influences. Temperatures are mild, with heavy cloud cover and rain. More rainfall and weather fluctuations at the coast.

PEOPLE & SOCIETY

Since 1970, Flemish regions have become more prosperous than those of the minority Walloons, overturning traditional roles and increasing friction. Belgium moved to a federal system from 1980 in order to contain tensions, but recent fractious politics have raised doubts over the union's survival. Brussels hosts key European Union institutions.

THE ECONOMY

Variety of industrial exports, including steel, glassware, cut diamonds, and textiles. Very high levels of public debt. Bureaucracy larger than European average.

INSIGHT: *The Ardennes region, in the southeast of the country, is famous for its forests, lakes, and cuisine*

North Sea
NETHERLANDS
Oostende
Brugge
Antwerpen
Gent
Mechelen
Kortrijk
Aalst
Leuven
BRUSSELS
Meuse
51°
Tournai
Liège
3°
La Louvière
GER.
Mons
Namur
Charleroi
FRANCE
4°
Ardennes
50°
LUX.
5°
6°
500m/1640ft
200m/656ft
Sea Level
0 40 km
0 40 miles

FACTFILE

OFFICIAL NAME: Kingdom of Belgium
DATE OF FORMATION: 1830
CAPITAL: Brussels
POPULATION: 10.6 million
TOTAL AREA: 11,780 sq. miles (30,510 sq. km)
DENSITY: 840 people per sq. mile
LANGUAGES: Dutch*, French*, German*
RELIGIONS: Roman Catholic 88%, other 10%, Muslim 2%
ETHNIC MIX: Flemish 58%, Walloon 33%, other 6%, Italian 2%, Moroccan 1%
GOVERNMENT: Parliamentary system
CURRENCY: Euro = 100 cents

Belize

Belize lies on the eastern shore of the Yucatan Peninsula. Formerly called British Honduras, Belize was the last Central American country to gain its independence, in 1981.

GEOGRAPHY

Almost half the land area is forested. Low mountains in southeast. Flat swampy coastal plains.

CLIMATE

Tropical. Very hot and humid, with May–December rainy season.

PEOPLE & SOCIETY

English-speaking black Creoles are outnumbered by Spanish speakers, including native *mestizos* and immigrants from neighboring states. The Creoles have traditionally dominated society, but high levels of emigration to the US have weakened their influence. The Afro-Carib *garifuna* have their own language. Corruption, and trafficking of people and narcotics, are major problems.

INSIGHT: *Belize's barrier reef is the second-largest in the world*

THE ECONOMY

Tourism, agriculture, and offshore banking. Oil extraction began in 2005. Sugar, textiles, lobsters, and shrimp are exported. Serious hurricane damage is a recurring problem.

0 50 km
0 50 miles
88°
Corozal
Louisville
Hondo
MEXICO
Orange Walk
18°
Maskall
New River
Crooked Tree
Belize City
Belize
BELMOPAN
Reef
San Ignacio
17°
Dangriga
GUATEMALA
Mts
Maya
Barrier
Monkey River Town
San Antonio
Punta Gorda
16°
Caribbean Sea
Sarstoon
89°
1000m/3281ft
500m/1640ft
200m/656ft
Sea Level

FACTFILE

OFFICIAL NAME: Belize
DATE OF FORMATION: 1981
CAPITAL: Belmopan
POPULATION: 306,800
TOTAL AREA: 8867 sq. miles (22,966 sq. km)
DENSITY: 35 people per sq. mile
LANGUAGES: English Creole, Spanish, English*, Mayan, Garifuna (Carib)
RELIGIONS: Roman Catholic 62%, other 20%, Anglican 12%, Methodist 6%
ETHNIC MIX: Mestizo 49%, Creole 25%, Maya 11%, other 9%, Garifuna 6%
GOVERNMENT: Parliamentary system
CURRENCY: Belizean dollar = 100 cents

Benin

Benin stretches north from the west African coast. In 1990, Benin became one of the pioneers of African democratization, ending 17 years of one-party Marxist-Leninist rule.

GEOGRAPHY

Sandy coastal region. Numerous lagoons lie just behind the shoreline. Forested plateaus inland. Mountains in the northwest.

CLIMATE

Hot and humid in the south. Two rainy seasons. Hot, dusty *harmattan* winds blow during the December–February dry season.

PEOPLE & SOCIETY

There are 42 different ethnic groups. The southern Fon have tended to dominate politics. Other major groups are the Adja and Yoruba. The northern Fulani follow a nomadic lifestyle. North–south tension is mainly due to the south being more developed. French culture, centered on Cotonou, is highly prized. Substantial differences in wealth reflect a strongly hierarchical society.

THE ECONOMY

Strong agricultural sector: cash crops include cotton, oil palm, and cashew nuts. Large-scale smuggling is a serious problem. France is the main aid donor.

INSIGHT: *Voodoo is thought to have originated in Benin, and was taken to Haiti by slaves*

2°
4°
12°
10°
8°
NIGER
Niger
BURKINA
Malanville
Kandi
Natitingou
Ndali
Djougou
Parakou
TOGO
NIGERIA
Savè
Ouémé
Lokossa
PORTO-NOVO
Ouidah
Cotonou
ATLANTIC OCEAN

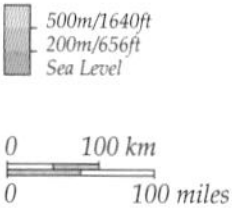
500m/1640ft
200m/656ft
Sea Level
0 100 km
0 100 miles

FACTFILE

OFFICIAL NAME: Republic of Benin
DATE OF FORMATION: 1960
CAPITAL: Porto-Novo
POPULATION: 8.94 million
TOTAL AREA: 43,483 sq. miles (112,620 sq. km)
DENSITY: 209 people per sq. mile
LANGUAGES: Fon, Bariba, Yoruba, Adja, Houeda, Somba, French*
RELIGIONS: 50%, Muslim 30%, Christian 20%
ETHNIC MIX: Fon 41%, other 21%, Adja 16%, Yoruba 12%, Bariba 10%
GOVERNMENT: Presidential system
CURRENCY: CFA franc = 100 centimes

Bhutan

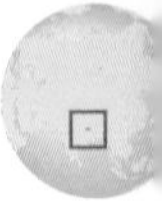

Perched in the eastern Himalayas between India and China lies the landlocked Kingdom of Bhutan. It is largely closed to the outside world to protect its culture; TV was banned until 1999.

GEOGRAPHY

Low, tropical southern strip rising through fertile central valleys to high Himalayas in the north. Around 70% of the land is forested.

CLIMATE

South is tropical, north is alpine, cold, and harsh. Central valleys warmer in east than west.

PEOPLE & SOCIETY

The king was absolute monarch until 1998, and the first democratic elections were held a decade later. Most people are devoutly Buddhist and originate from Tibet. The Hindu Nepalese settled in the south. Bhutan has 20 languages. In 1988, Dzongkha (a Tibetan dialect native to just 16% of the people) was made the official language. The Nepalese community regard this as "cultural imperialism," causing considerable ethnic tensions.

THE ECONOMY

Reliant on India for trade. Most people farm their own plots of land and herd cattle and yaks. Steep land unsuited for cultivation. Development of cash crops for Asian markets.

INSIGHT: *In 2004 Bhutan became the first country in the world to ban smoking and the sale of tobacco*

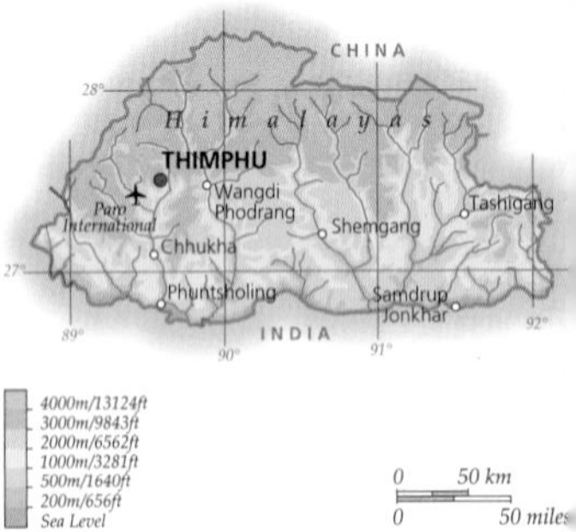
CHINA
Himalayas
THIMPHU
Paro International
Wangdi Phodrang
Shemgang
Tashigang
Chhukha
Phuntsholing
Samdrup Jonkhar
INDIA
28°
27°
89°
90°
91°
92°
4000m/13124ft
3000m/9843ft
2000m/6562ft
1000m/3281ft
500m/1640ft
200m/656ft
Sea Level
0 50 km
0 50 miles

FACTFILE

OFFICIAL NAME: Kingdom of Bhutan
DATE OF FORMATION: 1656
CAPITAL: Thimphu
POPULATION: 697,300
TOTAL AREA: 18,147 sq. miles (47,000 sq. km)
DENSITY: 38 people per sq. mile
LANGUAGES: Dzongkha*, Nepali
RELIGIONS: Mahayana Buddhist 70%, Hindu 24%, other 6%
ETHNIC MIX: Bhute 50%, other 25%, Nepalese 25%
GOVERNMENT: Mixed monarchical–parliamentary system
CURRENCY: Ngultrum = 100 chetrum

Bolivia

Landlocked high in central South America, Bolivia is one of the region's poorest countries. La Paz is the world's highest capital city: 13,385 feet (3631 m) above sea level.

GEOGRAPHY

A high windswept plateau, the *altiplano*, lies between two Andean mountain ranges. Semiarid grasslands to the east; dense tropical forests to the north.

CLIMATE

Altiplano has extreme tropical climate, with night-frost in winter. North and east are hot and humid.

PEOPLE & SOCIETY

The indigenous majority faces widespread discrimination. Wealthy Spanish-descended families have traditionally controlled the economy. Amerindian Evo Morales, president from 2005, pledged to cut poverty, legalize coca, and redistribute land.

INSIGHT: *Between 1825 and 1982 Bolivia averaged more than one armed coup a year*

THE ECONOMY

Gold, silver, zinc, tin, oil, natural gas: all vulnerable to world price fluctuations. Social issues and nationalization of natural gas sector deter investors. Major coca producer. Lack of manufacturing. Rich eastern provinces want autonomy.

3000m/9843ft
2000m/6562ft
1000m/3281ft
500m/1640ft
200m/656ft
Sea Level
68°
64°
60°
12°
16°
20°
Guayaramerín
Riberalta
PERU
Beni
Guaporé
Trinidad
Lake Titicaca
BRAZIL
LA PAZ
Montero
Cochabamba
Santa Cruz
Oruro
SUCRE
Puerto Suárez
Altiplano
Gran Chaco
Potosí
CHILE
Tupiza
Tarija
PARAGUAY
ARGENTINA
0 200 km
0 200 miles

FACTFILE

OFFICIAL NAME: Republic of Bolivia
DATE OF FORMATION: 1825
CAPITAL: La Paz (administrative); Sucre (judicial)
POPULATION: 9.86 million
TOTAL AREA: 424,162 sq. miles (1,098,580 sq. km)
DENSITY: 24 people per sq. mile
LANGUAGES: Aymara*, Quechua*, Spanish*
RELIGIONS: Roman Catholic 93%, other 7%
ETHNIC MIX: Quechua 37%, Aymara 32%, mixed 13%, European 10%, other 8%
GOVERNMENT: Presidential system
CURRENCY: Boliviano = 100 centavos

Bosnia & Herzegovina

Perched in the highlands of southeast Europe, Bosnia and Herzegovina was the focus of the bitter ethnic conflict which accompanied the early 1990s dissolution of the Yugoslav state.

GEOGRAPHY

Hills and mountains, with narrow river valleys. Lowlands in the north. Mainly deciduous forest covers about half of the total area.

CLIMATE

Continental. Hot summers and cold, often snowy winters.

PEOPLE & SOCIETY

Despite sharing the same origin and spoken language, Bosnians have been divided by history between Orthodox Serbs, Catholic Croats, and Muslim Bosniaks. Ethnic cleansing was practiced by all sides in the civil war, displacing about 60% of the population. Hopes for EU integration will require further ethnic reconciliation.

INSIGHT: *The murder of Archduke Ferdinand of Austria in Sarajevo in 1914 triggered the First World War*

THE ECONOMY

Potential to recover status as a thriving market economy with a strong manufacturing base, but still struggles with resettling refugees and the legacy of war. Little investment.

CROATIA
Sava
Prijedor
Modriča
REPUBLICA SRPSKA
Bihać
Banja Luka
Doboj
Tuzla
SERBI
Dinaric Alps
Bosna
Zvornik
Drina
Travnik
Zenica
Srebrenica
Bugojno
44°
16°
FEDERACIJA BOSNA I HERCEGOVINA
SARAJEVO
CROATIA
Mostar
MONTENEGI
2000m/6562ft
1000m/3281ft
500m/1640ft
200m/656ft
Sea Level
18°
0
50 km
0
50 miles

FACTFILE

OFFICIAL NAME: Bosnia and Herzegovina
DATE OF FORMATION: 1992
CAPITAL: Sarajevo
POPULATION: 3.77 million
TOTAL AREA: 19,741 sq. miles (51,129 sq. km)
DENSITY: 191 people per sq. mile
LANGUAGES: Bosnian*, Serbian*, Croatian*
RELIGIONS: Muslim 40%, Orthodox Christian 31%, Catholic 15%, other 14%
ETHNIC MIX: Bosniak 44%, Serb 31%, Croat 17%, other 8%
GOVERNMENT: Parliamentary system
CURRENCY: Marka = 100 pfeninga

Botswana

Landlocked in the heart of southern Africa, Botswana boasts the world's largest inland river delta. Diamonds provide potential wealth, but the country is crippled by HIV/AIDS.

GEOGRAPHY

Lies on vast plateau, high above sea level. Hills in the east. Kalahari Desert in center and southwest. Swamps and salt pans elsewhere and in Okavango Basin.

CLIMATE

Dry and prone to drought. Summer wet season, April–October. Winters are warm, with cold nights.

PEOPLE & SOCIETY

The nomadic San bushmen, the first inhabitants, are marginalized. One in four adults are living with HIV/AIDS: only Swaziland is worse affected. Life expectancy is around 50 years. Diamond revenue has widened wealth inequalities.

INSIGHT: *Water, Botswana's most precious resource, is honored in the name of the currency – pula*

THE ECONOMY

Overreliance on diamonds: vulnerable to world price fluctuations. Beef is exported to Europe. Tourism aimed at wealthy wildlife enthusiasts. AIDS is devastating the population.

1000m/3281ft
500m/1640ft
ZAMBIA
Kwando
Kasane
Okavango
Delta
NAMIBIA
ZIMBABWE
Maun
20°
Makgadikgadi
Francistown
Ghanzi
Selebi Phikwe
Serowe
Kalahari
Desert
Mahalapye
Limpopo
24°
28°
GABORONE
Mochudi
Kanye
Lobatse
SOUTH
AFRICA
24°
20°
0
200 km
0
200 miles

FACTFILE

OFFICIAL NAME: Republic of Botswana
DATE OF FORMATION: 1966
CAPITAL: Gaborone
POPULATION: 1.95 million
TOTAL AREA: 231,803 sq. miles (600,370 sq. km)
DENSITY: 9 people per sq. mile
LANGUAGES: Setswana, English*, Shona, San, Khoikhoi, isiNdebele
RELIGIONS: Traditional beliefs 50%, Christian (mainly Protestant) 30%, other (including Muslim) 20%
ETHNIC MIX: Tswana 98%, other 2%
GOVERNMENT: Presidential system
CURRENCY: Pula = 100 thebe

Brazil

Covering almost half of South America, Brazil is the site of the world's largest and ecologically most important rainforest. The country has immense natural and economic resources.

GEOGRAPHY

Rainforest grows around the massive Amazon River and its delta, covering almost half of Brazil's total land area. Apart from the basin of the River Plate to the south, the rest of the country consists of highlands. The mountainous east is part-forested and part-desert. The coastal plain in the southeast has swampy areas. The Atlantic coastline is 1240 miles (2000 km) long.

CLIMATE

Brazil's share of the Amazon Basin has a model tropical equatorial climate, with high temperatures and rainfall all year round. The Brazilian plateau has far greater seasonal variation. The dry northeast suffers frequent droughts, though coastal regions are occasionally flooded by bouts of torrential rain. The south has hot summers and cool winters.

PEOPLE & SOCIETY

Diverse population includes Amerindians, black people of African descent, European immigrants, and those of mixed race. Amerindians suffer prejudice from most other groups. Shanty towns in the cities attract poor migrants from the northeast. Urban crime, violent land disputes, and unchecked development in Amazonia tarnish Brazil's image as a modern nation. Catholicism and the family unit remain strong.

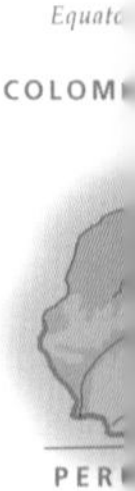

THE ECONOMY

Dominant regional economy. Huge potential for growth based on abundant natural resources. A leading exporter of coffee, sugar, and orange juice. Social tension threatens stability. Infrastructure needs investment.

FACTFILE

OFFICIAL NAME: Federative Rep. of Brazil
DATE OF FORMATION: 1822
CAPITAL: Brasília
POPULATION: 194 million
TOTAL AREA: 3,286,470 sq. miles (8,511,965 sq. km)
DENSITY: 59 people per sq. mile
LANGUAGES: Portuguese*, German, Italian, Spanish, Polish, Japanese, other
RELIGIONS: Roman Catholic 74%, Protestant 15%, atheist 7%, other 4%
ETHNIC MIX: White 54%, Mixed race 38%, Black 6%, other 2%
GOVERNMENT: Presidential system
CURRENCY: Real = 100 centavos

INSIGHT: *Since 1900, a third of Brazil's indigenous Amerindian groups have become extinct due to disease, starvation, or the forceful taking of land by miners, loggers, and settlers*

VENEZUELA
French Guiana (France)
SURINAME
GUYANA
ATLANTIC OCEAN
Boa Vista
Branco
Guiana Highlands
Macapá
Rio Negro
Equator
Ilha de Marajó
Belém
Amazon
Amazon Basin
Manaus
Santarém
São Luís
Madeira
Tapajós
Tocantins
Parnaíba
Fortaleza
Imperatriz
Teresina
San Fernando de Noronha
Purus
Iriri
Xingu
Natal
Porto Velho
Rio Branco
Aripuanã
São Manuel
Tocantins
Juazeiro do Norte
João Pessoa
Campina Grande
Olinda
Recife
Represa de Sobradinho
Juruena
Maceió
Chapada dos Parecis
Guaporé
Planalto de Mato Grosso
Taguatinga
10°
Aracaju
São Francisco
Feira de Santana
BOLIVIA
Araguaia
Salvador
Cuiabá
Brazilian Highlands
Itabuna
BRASÍLIA
Vitória da Conquista
Goiânia
Montes Claros
60°
Pantanal
Paraguay
Uberlândia
Governador Valadares
Uberaba
Campo Grande
Belo Horizonte
Bauru
Ribeirão Preto
Vitória
20°
PARAGUAY
Nova Iguaçu
Campos
Londrina
Campinas
Duque de Caxias
São Paulo
Rio de Janeiro
Paraná
Santos
Curitiba
40°
Joinville
Florianópolis
ARGENTINA
ATLANTIC OCEAN
2000m/6562ft
1000m/3281ft
500m/1640ft
200m/656ft
Sea Level
Caxias do Sul
Porto Alegre
30°
Lagoa dos Patos
Pelotas
50°
URUGUAY
Rio Grande
Mirim Lagoon
0 500 km
0 500 miles

Brunei

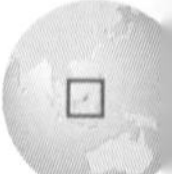

Lying on the northern coast of the island of Borneo, Brunei is surrounded and divided in two by the Malaysian state of Sarawak. It has been independent since 1984.

GEOGRAPHY

Mostly dense lowland rainforest and mangrove swamps, with some mountains in the southeast.

CLIMATE

Tropical. Six-month rainy season with very high humidity.

PEOPLE & SOCIETY

Malays benefit from positive discrimination. Many in the Chinese community are stateless. Since a failed rebellion in 1962, Brunei has been ruled by decree of the sultan. In 1990, "Malay Muslim Monarchy" was introduced, promoting Islamic values as state ideology. Women, less restricted than in some Muslim states, usually wear headscarves but not the veil.

INSIGHT: *The sultan spent US$350 million building the world's largest palace at Bandar Seri Begawan*

THE ECONOMY

Oil and natural gas production has brought one of the world's highest standards of living. Massive overseas investments. Major consumer of high-tech hi-fi, video equipment, and Western designer clothes.

1000m/3281ft
500m/1640ft
200m/656ft
Sea Level
South China Sea
Pekan Muara
5°
Kampong Bunut
BANDAR SERI BEGAWAN
Tutong
Bangar
Pekan Seria
Kuala Belait
Kampong Bukit Sawat
Kampong Batang Duri
4°30'
115°
Kampong Tanajor
Kampong Sukang
Kampong Teraja
MALAYSIA
Borneo
114°30'
0 20 km
0 20 miles

FACTFILE

OFFICIAL NAME: Sultanate of Brunei
DATE OF FORMATION: 1984
CAPITAL: Bandar Seri Begawan
POPULATION: 399,700
TOTAL AREA: 2228 sq. miles (5770 sq. km)
DENSITY: 196 people per sq. mile
LANGUAGES: Malay*, English, Chinese
RELIGIONS: Muslim (mainly Sunni) 66%, Buddhist 14%, other 10%, Christian 10%
ETHNIC MIX: Malay 67%, Chinese 16%, other 11%, indigenous 6%
GOVERNMENT: Monarchy
CURRENCY: Brunei dollar = 100 cents

Bulgaria

Located in southeastern Europe, Bulgaria was under communist rule from 1947 to 1989. Political and economic reform since then enabled it to join the EU in 2007.

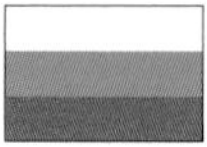

GEOGRAPHY

Mountains run east–west across center and along southern border. Danube plain in north, Thracian plain in southeast. Black Sea to the east.

CLIMATE

Warm summers and snowy winters, especially in mountains. East winds bring seasonal extremes.

PEOPLE & SOCIETY

The communists tried forcibly to suppress cultural identities, leading to a large exodus of Bulgarian Turks in 1989. Later privatization programs left many Turks landless, prompting further emigration. Roma suffer discrimination at all levels of society. Women have equal rights in theory, but society remains patriarchal. EU accession included caveats demanding further action against organized crime, human trafficking, and corruption.

THE ECONOMY

Good agricultural production, including grapes, for well-developed wine industry, and tobacco. Expertise in software development. Industry and infrastructure are outdated.

INSIGHT: *Archaeologists have found evidence of wine-making in Bulgaria dating back over 5000 years*

ROMANIA
44°
Danube
Ruse
Dobrich
Pleven
Vratsa
Shumen
Varna
SERBIA
Veliko Tŭrnovo
Balkan Mountains
SOFIA
Sliven
Burgas
Pernik
Kazanlŭk
Stara Zagora
Yambol
Black Sea
Pazardzhik
Plovdiv
42°
MAC.
Khaskovo
TURKEY
28°
24°
GREECE
26°
0 50 km
0 50 miles
2000m/6562ft
1000m/3281ft
500m/1640ft
200m/656ft
Sea Level

FACTFILE

OFFICIAL NAME: Republic of Bulgaria
DATE OF FORMATION: 1908
CAPITAL: Sofia
POPULATION: 7.54 million
TOTAL AREA: 42,822 sq. miles (110,910 sq. km)
DENSITY: 177 people per sq. mile
LANGUAGES: Bulgarian*, Turkish, Romani
RELIGIONS: Orthodox Christian 83%, Muslim 12%, other 4%, Catholic 1%
ETHNIC MIX: Bulgarian 84%, Turkish 9%, Roma 5%, other 2%
GOVERNMENT: Parliamentary system
CURRENCY: Lev = 100 stotinki

Burkina

The west African state of Burkina was known as Upper Volta until 1984. It became a multiparty state in 1991, though former military ruler Blaise Compaoré remains in power.

GEOGRAPHY

The Sahara covers the north of the country. The south is largely savanna. The three main rivers are the Black, White, and Red Voltas.

CLIMATE

Tropical. Dry, cool weather November–February. Erratic rain March–April, mostly in southeast.

PEOPLE & SOCIETY

No single ethnic group is dominant, but the Mossi, from around Ouagadougou, have always played an important part in government. The people from the west are much more ethnically mixed. Extreme poverty has led to a strong sense of egalitarianism. Most women are still denied access to education, though their absence from public life belies their real power and social influence.

THE ECONOMY

Cotton is the major cash crop, but the encroaching Sahara Desert is restricting agriculture. Beneficiary of foreign debt cancellation plans.

INSIGHT: *Droughts and poor soils mean that many Burkinabes seek work southward in Ghana and Côte d'Ivoire*

500m/1640ft
200m/656ft
Sea Level
MALI
NIGER
Ouahigouya
Kaya
Koudougou
OUAGADOUGOU
Fada-Ngourma
12°
Black Volta
White Volta
Red Volta
Tenkodogo
Bobo-Dioulasso
Léo
BENIN
Banfora
Black Volta
GHANA
TOGO
0°
CÔTE D'IVOIRE (IVORY COAST)
4°
0 100 km
0 100 miles

FACTFILE

OFFICIAL NAME: Burkina Faso
DATE OF FORMATION: 1960
CAPITAL: Ouagadougou
POPULATION: 15.8 million
TOTAL AREA: 105,869 sq. miles (274,200 sq. km)
DENSITY: 149 people per sq. mile
LANGUAGES: Mossi, Fulani, French*, Tuareg, Dyula, Songhai
RELIGIONS: Muslim 55%, Traditional beliefs 35%, Roman Catholic 9%, other Christian 1%
ETHNIC MIX: Other 52%, Mossi 48%
GOVERNMENT: Presidential system
CURRENCY: CFA franc = 100 centimes

Burundi

Small, densely populated and landlocked, Burundi lies just south of the equator, on the Nile–Congo watershed in central Africa. Its people have the world's lowest per capita income.

GEOGRAPHY

Hilly with high plateaus in center and savanna in the east. Great Rift Valley on western side.

CLIMATE

Temperate, with high humidity. Heavy and frequent rainfall, mostly October–May. Highlands have frost.

PEOPLE & SOCIETY

Burundi has been riven by ethnic conflict between majority Hutu and the Tutsi, who controlled the army – with repeated large-scale massacres: hundreds of thousands of people have died since 1993. The constitution now guarantees an ethnic balance in the government and army. Twa pygmies were not involved in the conflict.

INSIGHT: *Burundi's fertility rate is one of the highest in Africa. On average, women have seven children*

THE ECONOMY

Overwhelmingly agricultural economy, mostly subsistence. Small quantities of gold and tungsten. Potential of oil in Lake Tanganyika. Little prospect of lasting stability.

RWANDA
Kirundo
Ngozi
Muyinga
Kayanza
3°
Bubanza
Cankuzo
Karuzi
BUJUMBURA
Ruyigi
Gitega
DEM.REP.
CONGO
TANZANIA
Bururi
Rutana
4°
Lake
Tanganyika
29°
Makamba
Nyanza-Lac
30°
0
50 km
0
50 miles
2000m/6562ft
1000m/3281ft
500m/1640ft

FACTFILE

OFFICIAL NAME: Republic of Burundi
DATE OF FORMATION: 1962
CAPITAL: Bujumbura
POPULATION: 8.3 million
TOTAL AREA: 10,745 sq. miles (27,830 sq. km)
DENSITY: 838 people per sq. mile
LANGUAGES: Kirundi*, French*, Kiswahili
RELIGIONS: Christian (mainly Roman Catholic) 60%, traditional beliefs 39%, Muslim 1%
ETHNIC MIX: Hutu 85%, Tutsi 14%, Twa 1%
GOVERNMENT: Presidential system
CURRENCY: Burundi franc = 100 centimes

Cambodia

Located on the Indochinese peninsula in southeast Asia, Cambodia has emerged from genocide, civil war, and invasion from Vietnam. Tourists are returning. Rice is the principal crop.

GEOGRAPHY

Mostly low-lying basin. Tônlé Sap (Great Lake) drains into the Mekong River. Forested mountains and plateau east of the Mekong.

CLIMATE

Tropical. High temperatures throughout the year. Heavy rainfall during May–October monsoon.

PEOPLE & SOCIETY

Devastated by US bombing, then by the Khmer Rouge regime, whose extreme Marxist program killed over a million between 1975 and 1979, Cambodia then endured further civil conflict and Vietnamese occupation. The effects are still felt, reflected in the high rates of orphans, widows, and land-mine victims. A fragile stability has lasted since elections in 1993. King Norodom Sihanouk, a key figure in politics, abdicated in 2004.

THE ECONOMY

Economy is heavily aid-reliant, still recovering from civil war. Exports rubber and timber. Self-sufficient in rice. Garment industry is growing. Land disputes and corruption issues.

INSIGHT: *Cambodia has many impressive temples, dating from when the country was the center of the Khmer Empire*

THAILAND
LAOS
Phumĭ Sâmraông
Virôchey
Choâm Khsant
Sisŏphŏn
Phumĭ Kâmpóng Trâbék
Bătdâmbâng
Tônlé Sap
Mekong
Poŭthĭsăt
Kâmpóng Chhnăng
Krâchéh
Kâmpóng Cham
Krŏng Kaôh Kŏng
PHNOM PENH
Prey Vêng
Gulf of Thailand
Kâmpóng Saôm
VIETNAM
14°
12°
104°
106°
1000m/3281ft
500m/1640ft
200m/656ft
Sea Level
0 100 km
0 100 miles

FACTFILE

OFFICIAL NAME: Kingdom of Cambodia
DATE OF FORMATION: 1953
CAPITAL: Phnom Penh
POPULATION: 14.8 million
TOTAL AREA: 69,900 sq. miles (181,040 sq. km)
DENSITY: 217 people per sq. mile
LANGUAGES: Khmer*, French, Chinese, Vietnamese, Cham
RELIGIONS: Buddhist 93%, Muslim 6%, Christian 1%
ETHNIC MIX: Khmer 90%, other 5%, Vietnamese 4%, Chinese 1%
GOVERNMENT: Parliamentary system
CURRENCY: Riel = 100 sen

Cameroon

Situated in the corner of the Gulf of Guinea, Cameroon was effectively a one-party state for 30 years. Multiparty elections, since 1992, regularly return that same party to power.

GEOGRAPHY

Over half the land is forested: equatorial rainforest in north, evergreen forest and wooded savanna in south. Mountains in the west.

CLIMATE

South is equatorial, with plentiful rainfall, declining inland. Far north is beset by drought.

PEOPLE & SOCIETY

Around 230 ethnic groups; no single group is dominant. The Bamileke is the largest, though it has never held political power. North–south tensions are diminished by the ethnic diversity. There is more rivalry between majority French- and minority English-speakers.

INSIGHT: *Cameroon's name derives from the Portuguese word* camarões, *after the shrimp fished by the early European explorers*

THE ECONOMY

Oil reserves. Very diversified agricultural economy – timber, cocoa, bananas, coffee. Fuel smuggling from Nigeria undermines refinery profits. Corruption. Port for Chad and CAR.

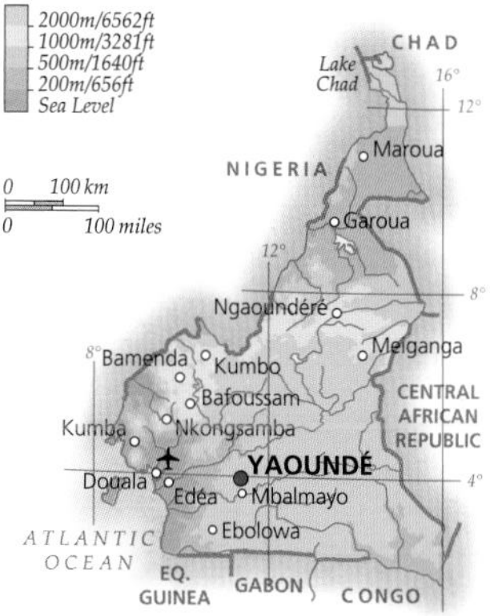
2000m/6562ft
1000m/3281ft
500m/1640ft
200m/656ft
Sea Level
0 100 km
0 100 miles
CHAD
Lake Chad
16°
12°
Maroua
NIGERIA
Garoua
12°
8°
Ngaoundéré
8°
Bamenda
Kumbo
Meiganga
Bafoussam
CENTRAL AFRICAN REPUBLIC
Kumba
Nkongsamba
YAOUNDÉ
4°
Douala
Edéa
Mbalmayo
Ebolowa
ATLANTIC OCEAN
EQ. GUINEA
GABON
CONGO

FACTFILE

OFFICIAL NAME: Republic of Cameroon
DATE OF FORMATION: 1960
CAPITAL: Yaoundé
POPULATION: 19.5 million
TOTAL AREA: 183,567 sq. miles (475,400 sq. km)
DENSITY: 109 people per sq. mile
LANGUAGES: Bamileke, Fang, Fulani, French*, English*
RELIGIONS: Catholic 35%, traditional beliefs 25%, Muslim 22%, Protestant 18%
ETHNIC MIX: Highlanders 31%, other 39%, equatorial Bantu 19%, Kirdi 11%
GOVERNMENT: Presidential system
CURRENCY: CFA franc = 100 centimes

Canada

Canada extends from the Arctic to its US border along the 49th parallel. Unified under British rule from 1763, its development and expansion attracted large-scale immigration.

GEOGRAPHY

The world's second-largest country, stretching north to Cape Colombia on Ellesmere Island, south to Lake Erie, and across five time zones from the Pacific seaboard to Newfoundland. Arctic tundra and islands in the far north give way southward to forests, interspersed with lakes and rivers, and then the vast Canadian Shield, which covers over half the area of Canada. Rocky Mountains in west, beyond which are the Coast Mountains, islands, and fjords. Fertile lowlands in the east.

CLIMATE

Ranges from polar and subpolar in the north, to continental in the south. Winters in the interior are colder and longer than on the coast, with temperatures well below freezing and deep snow; summers are hotter. Pacific coast has the mildest winters.

PEOPLE & SOCIETY

Two-thirds of the population live in the Great Lakes–St. Lawrence lowlands, fostering some shared cultural values with the neighboring US. Important differences, however, include wider welfare provision and Commonwealth membership. The French-speaking Québécois wish to preserve their culture and language from further Anglicization, and demand to be recognized as a "distinct society." The government welcomes ethnic diversity among immigrants, promoting a policy that encourages each group to maintain its own culture. Land claims made by the indigenous peoples are bein redressed. Nunavut, an Inuit-governed territory that covers nearly a quarter of Canada's land area, was created from a portion of the Northwest Territories in 1999. Women are well represented at most levels of business and government.

FACTFILE

OFFICIAL NAME: Canada
DATE OF FORMATION: 1867
CAPITAL: Ottawa
POPULATION: 33.6 million
TOTAL AREA: 3,855,171 sq. miles (9,984,670 sq. km)
DENSITY: 9 people per sq. mile
LANGUAGES: English*, French*, other
RELIGIONS: Roman Catholic 44%, Protestant 29%, other 27%
ETHNIC ORIGIN: British, French, and other European 87%, Asian 9%, Amerindian, Métis, and Inuit 4%
GOVERNMENT: Parliamentary system
CURRENCY: Canadian dollar = 100 cents

THE ECONOMY

Wide-ranging resources, providing exports, cheap energy, and raw materials for manufacturing, underpin a high standard of living, with smaller wealth disparities than in the US. Prices for primary exports fluctuate, but the high oil price has encouraged development of Alberta's vast oil fields. Manufactured exports have flourished under growing global competition, especially since the creation of the NAFTA free trade area, but reliance on the US market makes the Canadian economy vulnerable to US slowdowns. Unemployment rose during the 2009 recession.

INSIGHT: *The Magnetic North Pole, where the dipping needle of a compass stands still, migrates across northern Canada*

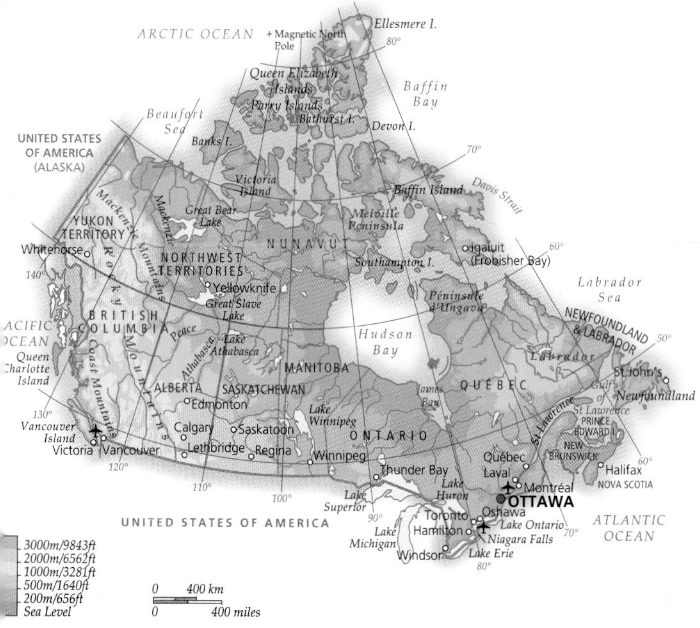
ARCTIC OCEAN
+Magnetic North Pole
Ellesmere I.
80°
Queen Elizabeth Islands
Parry Islands
Bathurst I.
Baffin Bay
Devon I.
Beaufort Sea
Banks I.
UNITED STATES OF AMERICA (ALASKA)
70°
Victoria Island
Baffin Island
Davis Strait
Mackenzie
Mackenzie Mountains
Great Bear Lake
Melville Peninsula
YUKON TERRITORY
NUNAVUT
Whitehorse
Iqaluit (Frobisher Bay)
60°
NORTHWEST TERRITORIES
Southampton I.
140°
Yellowknife
Labrador Sea
Great Slave Lake
Péninsule d'Ungava
BRITISH COLUMBIA
Rocky Mountains
PACIFIC OCEAN
Peace
NEWFOUNDLAND & LABRADOR
50°
Lake Athabasca
Athabasca
Hudson Bay
Queen Charlotte Island
Labrador
MANITOBA
St John's
Coast Mountains
ALBERTA
SASKATCHEWAN
James Bay
QUEBEC
Gulf of St Lawrence
Newfoundland
Edmonton
St Lawrence
130°
Lake Winnipeg
PRINCE EDWARD I.
Vancouver Island
Calgary
Saskatoon
ONTARIO
NEW BRUNSWICK
Victoria
Vancouver
Lethbridge
Regina
Winnipeg
Québec
60°
Laval
Halifax
120°
Thunder Bay
NOVA SCOTIA
Lake Huron
Montréal
110°
100°
Lake Superior
OTTAWA
Toronto
Oshawa
ATLANTIC OCEAN
UNITED STATES OF AMERICA
90°
Lake Michigan
Hamilton
Lake Ontario
70°
Niagara Falls
Windsor
Lake Erie
80°
3000m/9843ft
2000m/6562ft
1000m/3281ft
500m/1640ft
200m/656ft
Sea Level
0 400 km
0 400 miles

Cape Verde

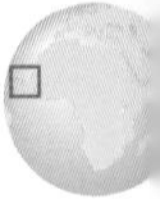

Off the west coast of Africa, in the Atlantic Ocean, lies the group of islands that make up Cape Verde, a Portuguese colony until it gained independence in 1975.

GEOGRAPHY

Ten main islands and eight smaller islets, all of volcanic origin. Mostly mountainous, with steep cliffs and rocky headlands.

CLIMATE

Warm, and very dry. Subject to droughts that can sometimes last for years at a time.

PEOPLE & SOCIETY

Most people are of mixed Portuguese–African origin; the rest are descendants of African slaves or more recent immigrants. Creolization of the culture negates ethnic tensions. Almost half of the population live on Santiago. Around 700,000 Cape Verdeans live abroad, mostly in the US.

INSIGHT: *Poor soils and lack of surface water mean that Cape Verde is dependent on food aid*

THE ECONOMY

Most people are subsistence farmers. Clothing is the main export. No natural resources. Mid-Atlantic location ensures work maintaining ships and planes.

0
50 km
0
50 miles
2000m/6562ft
1000m/3281ft
500m/1640ft
200m/656ft
Sea Level
Santo Antão
17°
Mindelo
São Vicente
Santa Luzia
Sal
São Nicolau
25°
Sal Rei
Boa Vista
Ilhas de Barlavento
16°
ATLANTIC
OCEAN
Ilhas de Sotavento
Maio
Tarrafil
15°
Brava
São Filipe
PRAIA
Fogo
Santiago (São Tiago)
23°
24°

FACTFILE

OFFICIAL NAME: Republic of Cape Verde
DATE OF FORMATION: 1975
CAPITAL: Praia
POPULATION: 505,600
TOTAL AREA: 1557 sq. miles (4033 sq. km)
DENSITY: 325 people per sq. mile
LANGUAGES: Creole, Portuguese*
RELIGIONS: Roman Catholic 97%, other 2%, Protestant 1%
ETHNIC MIX: Mestiço 60%, African 30%, other 10%
GOVERNMENT: Mixed presidential-parliamentary system
CURRENCY: C.V. escudo = 100 centavos

Central African Republic

The Central African Republic (CAR) is a landlocked country lying between the basins of the Chad and Congo Rivers. Politics has suffered frequent interruption by military coups.

GEOGRAPHY

Comprises a low plateau, covered by scrub or savanna. North is arid. Equatorial rainforests in the south. The Ubangi River forms the border with the Democratic Republic of the Congo.

CLIMATE

The south is equatorial; the north is hot and dry. Rain occurs all year round, with heaviest falls between July and October.

PEOPLE & SOCIETY

The Baya and Banda are the largest ethnic groups, but the lingua franca is Sango, a trading creole spoken by the minorities in the south who have traditionally provided most political leaders. Less than 2% of the population live in the north. Recent rebellions by northern groups have displaced thousands of people.

THE ECONOMY

Dominated by subsistence farming. Exports include diamonds, cotton, timber, and coffee. Aid needed to support refugees. Instability and poor infrastructure hinder progress.

INSIGHT: *"Emperor" Bokassa's eccentric rule from 1965 to 1979 was followed by military dictatorship until democracy was restored in 1993*

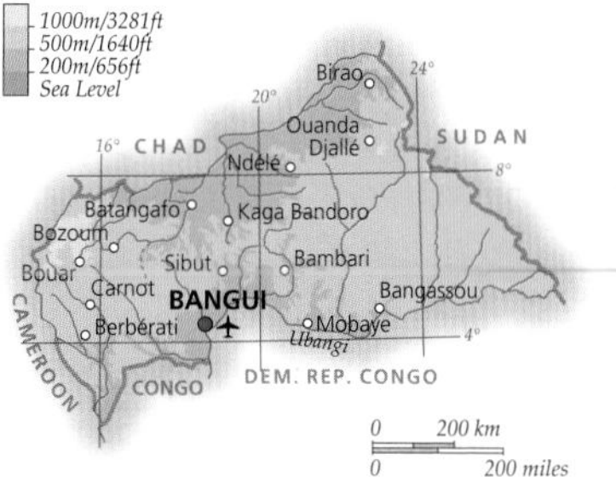
1000m/3281ft
500m/1640ft
200m/656ft
Sea Level
Birao
24°
20°
Ouanda Djallé
SUDAN
16°
CHAD
Ndélé
8°
Batangafo
Kaga Bandoro
Bozoum
Sibut
Bambari
Bouar
Carnot
BANGUI
Bangassou
Berbérati
Mobaye
Ubangi
4°
CAMEROON
CONGO
DEM. REP. CONGO
0 200 km
0 200 miles

FACTFILE

OFFICIAL NAME: Central African Republic
DATE OF FORMATION: 1960
CAPITAL: Bangui
POPULATION: 4.42 million
TOTAL AREA: 240,534 sq. miles (622,984 sq. km)
DENSITY: 18 people per sq. mile
LANGUAGES: Sango, Banda, Gbaya, French*
RELIGIONS: Traditional beliefs 60%, Christian 35%, Muslim 5%
ETHNIC MIX: Baya 34%, Banda 27%, Mandjia 21%, Sara 10%, other 8%
GOVERNMENT: Presidential system
CURRENCY: CFA franc = 100 centimes

Chad

Landlocked in north-central Africa, Chad has had a turbulent history since independence from France in 1960. Intermittent periods of civil war followed a military coup in 1975.

GEOGRAPHY

Mostly plateaus sloping west-ward to Lake Chad. Northern third is Sahara. Tibesti Mountains in north rise to 10,826 ft (3300 m).

CLIMATE

Three distinct zones: desert in north, semiarid region in center, and tropics in south.

PEOPLE & SOCIETY

Half the population live in the southern fifth of Chad. The northern third has only 100,000 people, mainly Muslim Toubou nomads. Democracy was restored in 1996 by ex-coup leader Idriss Déby. Instability has continued, first with tension between Muslims and southern Christians and, more recently, with rebellions in the east.

INSIGHT: *Lake Chad is slowly drying up – it is now estimated to be just 10% of the size it was in 1970*

THE ECONOMY

The discovery of oil, and the opening of a pipeline to the coast via Cameroon, are transforming Chad's economy, though the new wealth is unlikely to reach most people.

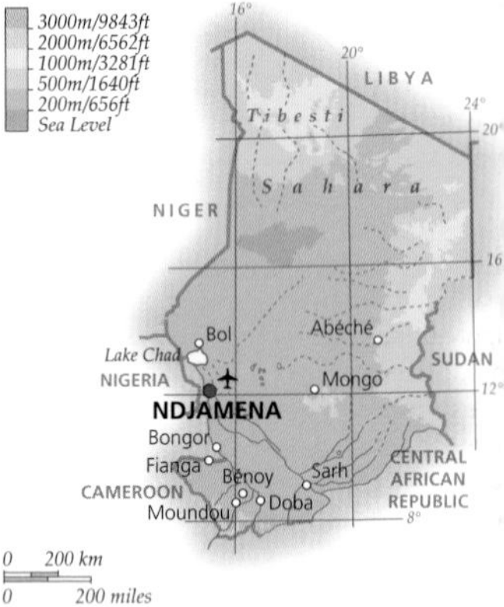
3000m/9843ft
2000m/6562ft
1000m/3281ft
500m/1640ft
200m/656ft
Sea Level
16°
20°
24°
20°
16
12°
8°
LIBYA
Tibesti
Sahara
NIGER
Bol
Abéché
Lake Chad
NIGERIA
Mongo
SUDAN
NDJAMENA
Bongor
Fianga
Bénoy
Sarh
CENTRAL AFRICAN REPUBLIC
CAMEROON
Moundou
Doba
0 200 km
0 200 miles

FACTFILE

OFFICIAL NAME: Republic of Chad
DATE OF FORMATION: 1960
CAPITAL: Ndjamena
POPULATION: 11.2 million
TOTAL AREA: 495,752 sq. miles (1,284,000 sq. km)
DENSITY: 23 people per sq. mile
LANGUAGES: French*, Sara, Arabic*, Maba
RELIGIONS: Muslim 55%, traditional beliefs 35%, Christian 10%
ETHNIC MIX: Other 30%, Sara 28%, Mayo-Kebbi 12%, Arab 12%, Ouaddai 9%, Kanem-Bornou 9%
GOVERNMENT: Presidential system
CURRENCY: CFA franc = 100 centimes

Chile

Chile extends in a ribbon down the west coast of South America. It returned to elected civilian rule in 1989 after a referendum forced out military dictator General Pinochet.

GEOGRAPHY

Fertile valleys in the center etween the coast and the Andes. ıtacama Desert in north. Deep-sea hannels, lakes, and fjords in south.

CLIMATE

Arid in the north. Hot, dry ummers and mild winters in the center. ligher Andean peaks have glaciers and ear-round snow. Very wet and stormy ı the south.

PEOPLE & SOCIETY

Most people are of mixed panish–Amerindian descent, and are ighly urbanized. Almost a third of ıe population live in Santiago, many ı large slums. There are three main ıdigenous groups, including the .apa Nui of Easter Island. General inochet's dictatorship was brutally epressive, but the business and ıiddle classes prospered.

THE ECONOMY

World's biggest copper producer. Growth in foreign investment due to political stability. Exports include wine, fishmeal, fruits, and salmon.

INSIGHT: *Chile's Atacama Desert is the driest place on Earth*

70°
PERU
BOLIVIA
Arica
20°
Iquique
Atacama Desert
Antofagasta
Andes
PACIFIC OCEAN
30°
Viña del Mar
SANTIAGO
Valparaíso
Rancagua
Talcahuano
Talca
Concepción
Chillán
Temuco
Valdivia
40°
Puerto Montt
Isla de Chiloé
Andes
ARGENTINA
50°
Punta Arenas
Strait of Magellan
Cape Horn

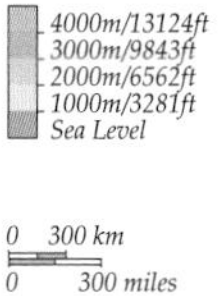
4000m/13124ft
3000m/9843ft
2000m/6562ft
1000m/3281ft
Sea Level
0 300 km
0 300 miles

FACTFILE

OFFICIAL NAME: Republic of Chile
DATE OF FORMATION: 1818
CAPITAL: Santiago
POPULATION: 17 million
TOTAL AREA: 292,258 sq. miles (756,950 sq. km)
DENSITY: 59 people per sq. mile
LANGUAGES: Spanish*, Amerindian languages
RELIGIONS: Roman Catholic 80%, other and nonreligious 20%
ETHNIC MIX: Mixed and European 90%, other Amerindian 9%, Mapuche 1%
GOVERNMENT: Presidential system
CURRENCY: Chilean peso = 100 centavos

China

Covering a vast area of eastern Asia, China is bordered by 14 countries. A one-party Communist state since 1949, it has recently become a dominant force in global manufacturing.

GEOGRAPHY

A land of huge physical diversity, China has a long Pacific coastline to the east. Two-thirds of the country is uplands. The southwestern mountains include Tibet, the world's highest plateau; in the northwest, the Tien Shan Mountains separate the arid Tarim and Dzungarian basins. The rolling hills and plains of the low-lying east are home to two-thirds of the population.

CLIMATE

China is divided into two main climatic regions. The north and west are semiarid or arid, with extreme temperature variations. The south and east are warmer and more humid, with year-round rainfall. Winter temperatures vary with latitude, but are warmest on the subtropical southeast coast. Summer temperatures are more uniform, rising above 70°F (21°C).

PEOPLE & SOCIETY

Most people are Han Chinese. The rest of the population belong to one of 55 minority nationalities, or recognized ethnic groups. Many of these groups have a disproportionate political significance as they live in strategic border areas. A policy of resettling Han Chinese in remote regions is deeply resented and has led to uprisings in Xinjiang and Tibet. The government has relaxed the one-child family policy, particularly for minorities, after some small groups were brought close to extinction. Chinese society is patriarchal in practice, and generations tend to live together. However, economic change is breaking down the social controls of t Mao Zedong era. Divorce and unemployment are rising; materialism has replaced the puritanism of the past. A resurgence of religious belief has occurred in recent years.

FACTFILE

OFFICIAL NAME: People's Rep. of China
DATE OF FORMATION: 960
CAPITAL: Beijing
POPULATION: 1.35 billion
TOTAL AREA: 3,705,386 sq. miles (9,596,960 sq. km)
DENSITY: 374 people per sq. mile
LANGUAGES: Mandarin*, other
RELIGIONS: Nonreligious 59%, traditional beliefs 20%, other 13%, Buddhist 6%, Muslim 2%
ETHNIC MIX: Han 92%, other 4%, Hui 1%, Miao 1%, Manchu 1%, Zhuang 1%
GOVERNMENT: One-party state
CURRENCY: Yuan = 10 jiao = 100 fen

THE ECONOMY

China has shifted from a centrally lanned to a market-oriented economy; beralization has gone furthest in the outh where the emerging business lass is based. The Tenth Five-Year lan (2001–2005) emphasized rapid levelopment; the Eleventh Plan aims to educe wealth disparities. Exports led ustained GDP growth from 2003; China as become the world's third-largest economy. Faced with a global downturn from 2008, Chinese stimulus packages have boosted domestic spending. The buying power of China's huge market for raw materials and consumer goods could drive global recovery.

INSIGHT: *China has the world's oldest continuous civilization. Its recorded history began 4000 years ago, with the Shang dynasty*

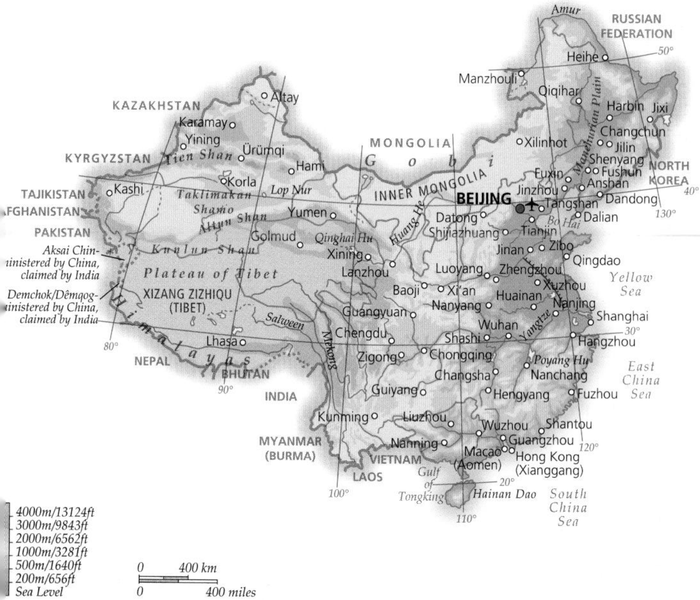
Amur
RUSSIAN FEDERATION
50°
Heihe
Manzhouli
Qiqihar
Manchurian Plain
Harbin
Jixi
Changchun
Jilin
Shenyang
Fushun
Anshan
NORTH KOREA
40°
Dandong
130°
Dalian
Xilinhot
Euxin
Jinzhou
Tangshan
BEIJING
Bo Hai
Tianjin
Zibo
Qingdao
Yellow Sea
KAZAKHSTAN
Altay
Karamay
Yining
Tien Shan
Ürümqi
KYRGYZSTAN
Hami
MONGOLIA
Gobi
INNER MONGOLIA
TAJIKISTAN
Kashi
Korla
Taklimakan Shamo
Lop Nur
FGHANISTAN
Altun Shan
Yumen
Datong
Shijiazhuang
PAKISTAN
Golmud
Qinghai Hu
Huang He
Jinan
Aksai Chin
inistered by China, claimed by India
Kunlun Shan
Xining
Plateau of Tibet
Lanzhou
Luoyang
Zhengzhou
Xuzhou
Demchok/Dêmqog
inistered by China, claimed by India
XIZANG ZIZHIQU (TIBET)
Baoji
Xi'an
Huainan
Nanyang
Nanjing
Shanghai
Guangyuan
Salween
Wuhan
Yangtze
30°
Hangzhou
Lhasa
Mekong
Chengdu
Shashi
80°
NEPAL
Himalayas
Zigong
Chongqing
Poyang Hu
Nanchang
East China Sea
BHUTAN
Changsha
90°
INDIA
Guiyang
Hengyang
Fuzhou
Kunming
Liuzhou
Wuzhou
Shantou
MYANMAR (BURMA)
Nanning
Guangzhou
120°
VIETNAM
Macao (Aomen)
Hong Kong (Xianggang)
LAOS
Gulf of Tongking
20°
100°
Hainan Dao
South China Sea
110°
4000m/13124ft
3000m/9843ft
2000m/6562ft
1000m/3281ft
500m/1640ft
200m/656ft
Sea Level
0 400 km
0 400 miles

Colombia

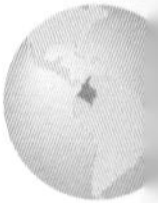

Lying in northwest South America, Colombia has coastlines on both the Caribbean and the Pacific. It is primarily noted for its coffee, emeralds, gold, and cocaine trafficking.

GEOGRAPHY

The densely forested and almost uninhabited east is separated from the western coastal plains by the Andes, which divide into three ranges *(cordilleras)* with intervening valleys.

CLIMATE

Coastal plains are hot and wet. The highlands are much cooler. The equatorial east has two wet seasons.

PEOPLE & SOCIETY

Most Colombians are of mixed blood. Blacks and Amerindians have the least political representation. Civil conflict over four and a half decades has displaced millions of people, and left over 200,000 dead. The fighting is deeply entwined with the narcotics trade. Violent crime is common.

INSIGHT: *Over 50% of the world's cocaine is produced in Colombia*

THE ECONOMY

Healthy and diversified export sector – includes coffee and coal. Considerable growth potential, but drugs-related violence and corruption deter foreign investors.

Caribbean Sea
12°
Santa Marta
Barranquilla
Valledupar
Cartagena
Sincelejo
Montería
PANAMA
8°
Cúcuta
VENEZUELA
Bucaramanga
Medellín
Manizales
Armenia
BOGOTÁ
Villavicencio
Meta
Orinoco
PACIFIC OCEAN
4°
Cali
Neiva
Popayán
Pasto
Negro
68°
Equator
ECUADOR
Caquetá
BRAZIL
Putumayo
76°
PERU
72°
3000m/9843ft
2000m/6562ft
1000m/3281ft
500m/1640ft
Sea Level
0 200 km
0 200 miles

FACTFILE

OFFICIAL NAME: Republic of Colombia
DATE OF FORMATION: 1819
CAPITAL: Bogotá
POPULATION: 45.7 million
TOTAL AREA: 439,733 sq. miles (1,138,910 sq. km)
DENSITY: 114 people per sq. mile
LANGUAGES: Spanish*, Wayuu, Páez, other Amerindian languages
RELIGIONS: Catholic 95%, other 5%
ETHNIC MIX: Mestizo 58%, White 20%, European-African 14%, African 4%, African-Amerindian 3%, other 1%
GOVERNMENT: Presidential system
CURRENCY: Col. peso = 100 centavos

Comoros

Off the east African coast, between Mozambique and Madagascar, lies the archipelago republic of the Comoros, comprising three main islands and a number of smaller islets.

GEOGRAPHY

Main islands are of volcanic origin nd are heavily forested. The remainder re coral atolls.

CLIMATE

Hot and humid all year round, specially on the coasts. November to lay is hottest and wettest period.

PEOPLE & SOCIETY

The Comoros has absorbed a iversity of people over the years, ncluding Africans, Arabs, Polynesians, nd Persians. There have also been ortuguese, Dutch, French, and Indian nmigrants. Ethnic discord is rare, but egional tensions between islands are narked. The country is politically nstable and there have been frequent oups. A fragile new federal system has een in place since 2002. Wealth is oncentrated within a political and usiness elite.

THE ECONOMY

One of the world's poorest countries. Subsistence-level farming. Vanilla and cloves are main cash crops. Lack of basic infrastructure.

INSIGHT: *The Comoros is the world's largest producer of ylang-ylang – an extract from tree blossom used in manufacturing perfumes*

Grande Comore
(Njazidja)
1000m/3281ft
500m/1640ft
200m/656ft
Sea Level
12°30'
Koimbani
MORONI
Foumbouni
Dembéni
INDIAN OCEAN
12°
43°30'
Mohéli
(Mwali)
Mozambique
Channel
Fomboni
Ouani
Moutsamudou
Moya
Anjouan
(Nzwani)
0 20 km
0 20 miles
11°30'
44°
44°30'

FACTFILE

OFFICIAL NAME: Union of the Comoros
DATE OF FORMATION: 1975
CAPITAL: Moroni
POPULATION: 676,000
TOTAL AREA: 838 sq. miles (2170 sq. km)
DENSITY: 785 people per sq. mile
LANGUAGES: Arabic*, Comoran*, French*
RELIGIONS: Muslim (mainly Sunni) 98%, Roman Catholic 1%, other 1%
ETHNIC MIX: Comoran 97%, other 3%
GOVERNMENT: Presidential system
CURRENCY: Comoros franc = 100 centimes

Congo

Astride the equator in west-central Africa, this former French colony emerged from 20 years of Marxist-Leninist rule in 1990. Democracy was soon overshadowed by years of violence.

GEOGRAPHY

Mostly forest- or savanna-covered plateaus, drained by the Ubangi and Congo river systems. Narrow coastal plain is lined with sand dunes and lagoons.

CLIMATE

Hot, tropical. Temperatures rarely fall below 86°F (30°C). Two wet and two dry seasons. Rainfall is heaviest south of the equator.

PEOPLE & SOCIETY

One of the most tribally conscious and heavily urbanized countries in Africa, with most people living in the Brazzaville–Pointe-Noire region. Main tensions are between the Bakongo in the north and the Mbochi in the south. Relative peace was secured in 1999, and "ninja" rebels in the Pool region, around Brazzaville, signed a peace deal in 2003.

THE ECONOMY

Oil provides over 95% of export revenue. Timber is extracted. Foreign debt high. Substantial industrial base around Brazzaville and Pointe-Noire.

INSIGHT: *In 1970, Congo became the first African country to declare itself a communist state*

0 200 km
0 200 miles
500m/1640ft
200m/656ft
Sea Level
C. A. R.
CAMEROON
Ouésso
Sangha
Ubangi
Equator
Owando
GABON
Congo
Djambala
Mossendjo
DEM. REP. CONGO
Loudima
Nkayi
4°
BRAZZAVILLE
ATLANTIC OCEAN
Kinkala
Pointe-Noire
ANGOLA
(Cabinda)
12°
16°

FACTFILE

OFFICIAL NAME: Republic of the Congo
DATE OF FORMATION: 1960
CAPITAL: Brazzaville
POPULATION: 3.68 million
TOTAL AREA: 132,046 sq. miles (342,000 sq. km)
DENSITY: 28 people per sq. mile
LANGUAGES: Kongo, Teke, Lingala, French*
RELIGIONS: Traditional 50%, Catholic 25%, Protestant 23%, Muslim 2%
ETHNIC MIX: Bakongo 51%, Teke 17%, other 16%, Mbochi 11%, Mbédé 5%
GOVERNMENT: Presidential system
CURRENCY: CFA franc = 100 centimes

Congo, (DRC)

Lying in east-central Africa, the Democratic Republic of the Congo (DRC) is one of Africa's largest countries, and the scene of one of its worst regional wars.

GEOGRAPHY

Rainforested basin of Congo River occupies 60% of the land area. High mountain ranges and lakes stretch down the eastern border.

CLIMATE

Tropical and humid. Distinct wet and dry seasons south of the equator. The north is mainly wet.

PEOPLE & SOCIETY

There are 12 main ethnic groups and around 190 smaller ones. The indigenous forest pygmies, victimized in the war, are now a marginalized group. Civil war from 1996 drew neighboring countries into a bloody conflict. Tentative peace in 2003 was soon undermined by rebels in the east.

INSIGHT: *The DRC's rainforests comprise 6% of the world's, and 50% of Africa's, remaining woodlands*

THE ECONOMY

Rich resource base: minerals (copper, coltan, cobalt, diamonds) dominate export earnings. War and decades of corruption have caused economic collapse. Food aid is needed to ease humanitarian crisis.

20°
28°
CENTRAL AFRICAN REPUBLIC
SUDAN
Ubangi
Bumba
Isiro
Lake Albert
Equator
Mbandaka
Kisangani
UGANDA
CONGO
Congo
Congo Basin
Lualaba
Goma
RWANDA
12°
Bukavu
BURUNDI
ANGOLA (Cabinda)
KINSHASA
Ilebo
Kananga
Kalemie
TANZANIA
Matadi
Kikwit
Mbuji-Mayi
Lake Tanganyika
ATLANTIC OCEAN
8°
Kamina
ANGOLA
Kasai
Likasi
ZAMBIA
Lubumbashi
ZAMBIA
2000m/6562ft
1000m/3281ft
500m/1640ft
200m/656ft
Sea Level
0 200 km
0 200 miles

FACTFILE

OFFICIAL NAME: Democratic Republic of the Congo
DATE OF FORMATION: 1960
CAPITAL: Kinshasa
POPULATION: 66 million
TOTAL AREA: 905,563 sq. miles (2,345,410 sq. km)
DENSITY: 75 people per sq. mile
LANGUAGES: Kiswahili, Tshiluba, French*
RELIGIONS: Christian 70%, Kimbanguist 10%, traditional beliefs 10%, Muslim 10%
ETHNIC MIX: Other 55%, Mongo, Luba, Kongo, and Mangbetu-Azande 45%
GOVERNMENT: Presidential system
CURRENCY: Congolese franc = 100 centimes

Costa Rica

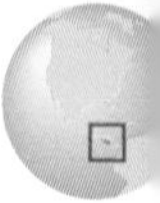

Costa Rica, Central America's most stable country, is rich in pristine scenery and exotic wildlife. Its neutrality in foreign affairs is long-standing, but it has strong ties with the US.

GEOGRAPHY

Coastal plains of swamp and savanna rise to a fertile central plateau, which leads to a mountain range with active volcanic peaks.

CLIMATE

Hot and humid in coastal regions. Temperate central uplands. High annual rainfall.

PEOPLE & SOCIETY

Most people are *mestizo*, of partly Spanish origin. There is a black, English-speaking minority and around 35,000 indigenous Amerindians. Plantation owners are the wealthiest group, while one in six people live in poverty. Nonetheless, living standards are high for the region, and education and healthcare provision is good.

INSIGHT: *Costa Rica's 1949 constitution bans a national army*

THE ECONOMY

Stability has attracted multinationals. The main exports are bananas, pineapples, coffee, and beef, but all are vulnerable to fluctuating world prices. History of high inflation. Pioneer of eco-tourism. Pledged to be carbon neutral by 2021.

0 50 km
0 50 miles
85°
84°
83°
11°
10°
9°
8°
NICARAGUA
San Juan
Caribbean Sea
Liberia
Cañas
Quesada
San Ramón
Heredia
Puntarenas
SAN JOSÉ
Turrialba
Limón
Cartago
San Isidro
Cordillera de Talamanca
PACIFIC OCEAN
PANAMA
Península de Osa
3000m/9843ft
2000m/6562ft
1000m/3281ft
500m/1640ft
200m/656ft
Sea Level

FACTFILE

OFFICIAL NAME: Republic of Costa Rica
DATE OF FORMATION: 1838
CAPITAL: San José
POPULATION: 4.58 million
TOTAL AREA: 19,730 sq. miles (51,100 sq. km)
DENSITY: 232 people per sq. mile
LANGUAGES: Spanish*, English Creole, Bribri, Cabecar
RELIGIONS: Roman Catholic 76%, other (including Protestant) 24%
ETHNIC MIX: Mestizo and European 96%, Black 2%, Chinese 1%, Amerindian 1%
GOVERNMENT: Presidential system
CURRENCY: C.R. colón = 100 céntimos

Côte d'Ivoire (Ivory Coast)

One of the larger nations along the coast of west Africa, Côte d'Ivoire is the world's biggest cocoa producer. An image of stability was rocked by civil war in 2002–2005.

GEOGRAPHY

Sandy coastal strip backed by a largely rainforested interior, and a savanna plateau in the north.

CLIMATE

High temperatures all year round. South has two wet seasons; north has one, with lower rainfall.

PEOPLE & SOCIETY

There are over 60 tribes; the largest is the Baoulé (an Akan group). Southern Christians harbor resentment against non-Ivorian Muslims in the north. Plantations employ millions of migrant workers (including children), though thousands fled back to Burkina during the civil war. Rebels joined a transitional government in 2007.

INSIGHT: *The Basilica of Our Lady of Peace in Yamoussoukro is the largest church in the world*

THE ECONOMY

Main crops are cocoa and coffee. Oil is now major export. Good infrastructure. Lack of professional training. Instability deters investment.

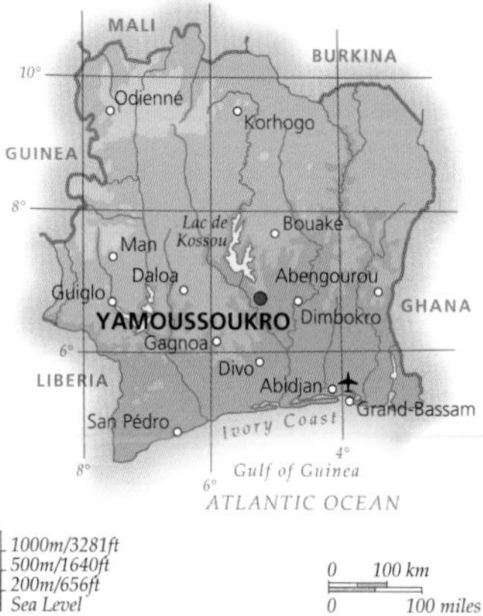
MALI
BURKINA
GUINEA
GHANA
LIBERIA
10°
8°
6°
4°
Odienné
Korhogo
Lac de Kossou
Bouaké
Man
Daloa
Abengourou
Guiglo
YAMOUSSOUKRO
Dimbokro
Gagnoa
Divo
Abidjan
Grand-Bassam
San Pédro
Ivory Coast
Gulf of Guinea
ATLANTIC OCEAN
1000m/3281ft
500m/1640ft
200m/656ft
Sea Level
0 100 km
0 100 miles

FACTFILE

OFFICIAL NAME: Republic of Côte d'Ivoire
DATE OF FORMATION: 1960
CAPITAL: Yamoussoukro
POPULATION: 21.1 million
TOTAL AREA: 124,502 sq. miles (322,460 sq. km)
DENSITY: 172 people per sq. mile
LANGUAGES: Akan, French*, Krou, other
RELIGIONS: Muslim 38%, Christian 31%, traditional beliefs 25%, other 6%
ETHNIC MIX: Akan 42%, Voltaïque 18%, Mandé du Nord 17%, Krou 11%, other 12%
GOVERNMENT: Transitional regime
CURRENCY: CFA franc = 100 centimes

Croatia

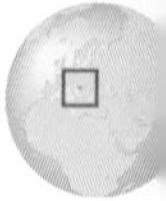

Though it was controlled by Hungary from medieval times and was a part of the Yugoslav state for much of the 20th century, Croatia has a very strong national identity.

GEOGRAPHY

Rocky, mountainous Adriatic coastline is dotted with islands. Interior is a mixture of wooded mountains and broad valleys.

CLIMATE

The interior has a temperate continental climate. Mediterranean climate along the Adriatic coast.

PEOPLE & SOCIETY

Croats are distinguished from Bosniaks and Serbs by their Roman Catholic faith and use of the Latin alphabet. Many Serbs fled Croatia during the early 1990s conflict that accompanied Yugoslavia's breakup. Minority rights and fighting organized crime are key issues in the quest for EU membership by 2011.

INSIGHT: *Croatia only regained control of Serb-occupied Eastern Slavonia, around Vukovar, in 1998*

THE ECONOMY

The war cost the economy an estimated $50 billion. Unemployment has been persistently high. Corruption deters foreign investment. Tourism is mainly on the Dalmatian coast.

0 50 km
0 50 miles
Varaždin
Čakovec
Koprivnica
HUNGARY
Drava
46°
SLOVENIA
Virovitica
ZAGREB
Karlovac
Osijek
Danube
SERBIA
Rijeka
Kupa
Slavonia
Sava
Vukovar
Istra
Slavonski Brod
Pula
BOSNIA & HERZEGOVINA
14°
Zadar
44°
Dalmatia
Dinaric Alps
Split
Adriatic Sea
16°
Dubrovnik
MON.
18°
1000m/3281ft
500m/1640ft
200m/656ft
Sea Level

FACTFILE

OFFICIAL NAME: Republic of Croatia
DATE OF FORMATION: 1991
CAPITAL: Zagreb
POPULATION: 4.42 million
TOTAL AREA: 21,831 sq. miles (56,542 sq. km)
DENSITY: 202 people per sq. mile
LANGUAGES: Croatian
RELIGIONS: Roman Catholic 88%, other 7%, Orthodox Christian 4%, Muslim 1%
ETHNIC MIX: Croat 90%, other 5%, Serb 5%
GOVERNMENT: Parliamentary system
CURRENCY: Kuna = 100 lipa

Cuba

A former Spanish colony, Cuba is the largest island in the Caribbean. It became the only communist country in the Americas after Fidel Castro seized power in 1959.

GEOGRAPHY

Mostly fertile plains and basins. Three mountainous areas. Forests of pine and mahogany cover one-quarter of the country.

CLIMATE

Subtropical. Hot all year round, and very hot in summer. Heaviest rainfall in the mountains. Hurricanes can strike in the fall.

PEOPLE & SOCIETY

The Castro regime has reduced formerly extreme wealth disparities, given education a high priority, and established an efficient health service. Political dissent, however, is not tolerated. A dramatic fall in living standards since the late 1980s has led thousands of Cubans to flee to the US, to seek asylum. About 70% of Cubans are of Spanish descent. There is little ethnic tension.

THE ECONOMY

Sugar industry now superseded by tourism and nickel. US trade embargo, since 1961. Shortages drive a black market. Parallel use of US dollar (1993–2004), and then convertible peso, has boosted investment but created a "dollarized" elite.

INSIGHT: *Fidel Castro had become the world's longest-serving non-hereditary ruler before handing power to his brother Raúl in 2006*

Straits of Florida
HAVANA
Marianao
Matanzas
ATLANTIC OCEAN
Pinar del Río
Cienfuegos
Santa Clara
22°
Ciego de Avila
Camagüey
84°
Archipiélago de los Canarreos
82°
80°
Holguín
Bayamo
Caribbean Sea
Guantánamo
20°
Santiago de Cuba
78°
76°
GUANTÁNAMO BAY
(to USA)
1000m/3281ft
500m/1640ft
200m/656ft
Sea Level
0 100 km
0 100 miles

FACTFILE

OFFICIAL NAME: Republic of Cuba
DATE OF FORMATION: 1902
CAPITAL: Havana
POPULATION: 11.2 million
TOTAL AREA: 42,803 sq. miles (110,860 sq. km)
DENSITY: 262 people per sq. mile
LANGUAGES: Spanish
RELIGIONS: Nonreligious 49%, Roman Catholic 40%, atheist 6%, other 4%, Protestant 1%
ETHNIC MIX: White 66%, European–African 22%, Black 12%
GOVERNMENT: One-party state
CURRENCY: Cuban peso = 100 centavos

Cyprus

Cyprus lies south of Turkey in the eastern Mediterranean. Since 1974, it has been partitioned between the Turkish-occupied north and the Greek-Cypriot south.

GEOGRAPHY

Mountains in the center-west give way to a fertile plain in the east, flanked by hills to the northeast.

CLIMATE

Mediterranean. Summers are hot and dry. Winters are mild, with snow in the mountains.

PEOPLE & SOCIETY

The Greek majority practice Orthodox Christianity. Since the 16th century, a minority community of Turkish Muslims has lived in the north of the island. In 1974 Turkish troops occupied the north and proclaimed the Turkish Republic of Northern Cyprus (TRNC), but it is recognized only by Turkey. Over 100,000 mainland Turks have settled there since. UN-led mediation failed to reunite the island ahead of EU accession in 2004, so the north was left out of membership.

THE ECONOMY

Financial services and tourism. Eurozone member with best economic performance and lowest unemployment in 2009 downturn. North suffers from lack of investment and lower wages.

INSIGHT: *The Green Line, which separates north from south, was opened for the first time in 2003*

Mediterranean Sea
Dipkarpaz (Rizokarpasor
Turkish Republic of Northern Cyprus (only recognized by Turkey)
Lapta (Lápithos)
Girne (Kerýneia)
Famagusta Bay
Güzelyurt (Mórfou)
Değirmenlik (Kythréa)
Gazimağusa (Famagusta)
NICOSIA
35°
Troodos Mts.
Lárnaka
Agia Nápa
Páfos
Sovereign Base Area (to UK)
34°
Lemesós (Limassol)
Akrotiri
33°
Cease-fire line
1000m/3281ft
500m/1640ft
200m/656ft
Sea Level
0 25 km
0 25 miles

FACTFILE

OFFICIAL NAME: Republic of Cyprus
DATE OF FORMATION: 1960
CAPITAL: Nicosia
POPULATION: 871,000
TOTAL AREA: 3571 sq. miles (9250 sq. km)
DENSITY: 244 people per sq. mile
LANGUAGES: Greek*, Turkish*
RELIGIONS: Orthodox Christian 78%, Muslim 18%, other 4%
ETHNIC MIX: Greek 81%, Turkish 11%, other 8%
GOVERNMENT: Presidential systems
CURRENCY: Euro = 100 cents (new Turkish lira in TRNC = 100 kurus)

Czech Republic

Once part of Czechoslovakia, a central European communist state in 1948–1989, the Czech Republic peacefully dissolved its union with Slovakia in 1993. It joined the EU in 2004.

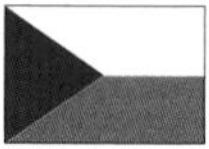

GEOGRAPHY

Landlocked in central Europe. Bohemia, the western territory, is a plateau surrounded by mountains. Moravia, in the east, is characterized by hills and lowlands.

CLIMATE

Cool, sometimes cold winters and warm summer months, which bring most of the annual rainfall.

PEOPLE & SOCIETY

Secular and urban society, with high divorce rates. Czechs make up the vast majority of the population, while the next largest group are Moravians. The 300,000 Slovaks left after partition are now permitted dual citizenship. Ethnic tensions are few, but there is widespread hostility toward the Roma minority. A new commercial elite is emerging alongside postcommunist entrepreneurs.

THE ECONOMY

Traditional heavy industries (machinery, iron, car-making) have been successfully privatized. Prague attracts tourists. Skilled workforce. Will join euro in 2013 at earliest.

INSIGHT: *Charles University in Prague was founded in the 13th century*

GERMANY
Liberec
Ústí nad Labem
Karlovy Vary
50°
Elbe
POLAND
Kladno
Hradec Králové
PRAGUE
Plzeň
Pardubice
Bohemia
Ostrava
Olomouc
Havířov
České Budějovice
Moravia
Zlín
Brno
14°
AUSTRIA
16°
SLOVAKIA
18°
1000m/3281ft
500m/1640ft
200m/656ft
Sea Level
0 50 km
0 50 miles

FACTFILE

OFFICIAL NAME: Czech Republic
DATE OF FORMATION: 1993
CAPITAL: Prague
POPULATION: 10.4 million
TOTAL AREA: 30,450 sq. miles (78,866 sq. km)
DENSITY: 341 people per sq. mile
LANGUAGES: Czech*, Slovak, Hungarian
RELIGIONS: Roman Catholic 39%, atheist 38%, other 18%, Protestant 3%, Hussite 2%
ETHNIC MIX: Czech 90%, other 4%, Moravian 4%, Slovak 2%
GOVERNMENT: Parliamentary system
CURRENCY: Czech koruna = 100 haleru

Denmark

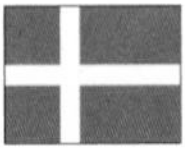

Denmark occupies the Jutland peninsula and over 400 islands in southern Scandinavia. Greenland and the Faeroe Islands are self-governing associated territories.

GEOGRAPHY

Fertile farmland covers two-thirds of the terrain, which is among the flattest in the world. About 100 islands are inhabited.

CLIMATE

Damp, temperate climate with mild summers and cold, wet winters. Rainfall is moderate.

PEOPLE & SOCIETY

Income distribution is the most even in the West: society is egalitarian with few tensions. Cultural clashes have arisen with immigrant minorities. Almost all women now work and Denmark is a world leader in childcare provision. Marriage is becoming less common, even for couples with children.

INSIGHT: *Denmark is Europe's oldest kingdom – the monarchy dates back to the 10th century*

THE ECONOMY

Natural gas and oil reserves. Skilled workforce key to high-tech industrial success. Pork, bacon, dairy products are exported. Opted not to join the euro, though its currency is pegged.

200m/656ft
Sea Level
Bornholm
15°
Rønne
55°
Skagerrak
Aalborg
Kattegat
Jylland
Viborg
Randers
Silkeborg
56°
Herning
Århus
Helsingør
Horsens
COPENHAGEN
Vejle
Roskilde
Esbjerg
Odense
Kolding
Fyn
Sjælland
North Sea
Svendborg
Næstved
Baltic Sea
Sønderborg
8°
GERMANY
Lolland
Nykøbing
Falster
10°
12°
0 50 km
0 50 miles

FACTFILE

OFFICIAL NAME: Kingdom of Denmark
DATE OF FORMATION: 950
CAPITAL: Copenhagen
POPULATION: 5.47 million
TOTAL AREA: 16,639 sq. miles (43,094 sq. km)
DENSITY: 334 people per sq. mile
LANGUAGES: Danish
RELIGIONS: Evangelical Lutheran 89%, other 10%, Roman Catholic 1%
ETHNIC MIX: Danish 96%, other (including Scandinavian and Turkish) 3%, Faeroese and Inuit 1%
GOVERNMENT: Parliamentary system
CURRENCY: Danish krone = 100 øre

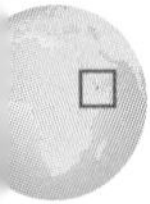

Djibouti

A city-state with a desert hinterland, Djibouti lies in northeast Africa on the Red Sea. Once known as the French Territory of the Afars and Issas, independence came in 1977.

GEOGRAPHY

Mainly low-lying desert and emidesert, with a volcanic mountain ange in the north.

CLIMATE

Almost no rain, though the nonsoon is very humid. The 109°F (45°C) ieat of summer is unbearable.

PEOPLE & SOCIETY

The main ethnic groups are he Issas in the south, and the iomadic Afars in the north. Tensions etween them developed into a uerrilla war in 1991–1994. Smaller ribal groups make up the rest of he population, and the rural peoples re mostly nomadic. Wealth is oncentrated in Djibouti city. rance exerts considerable influence n Djibouti, supporting it financially ind maintaining a naval base and military garrison.

THE ECONOMY

Djibouti's major assets are its ports in a key Red Sea location.

INSIGHT: *Chewing the leaves of the mildly narcotic qat shrub is an age-old social ritual in Djibouti*

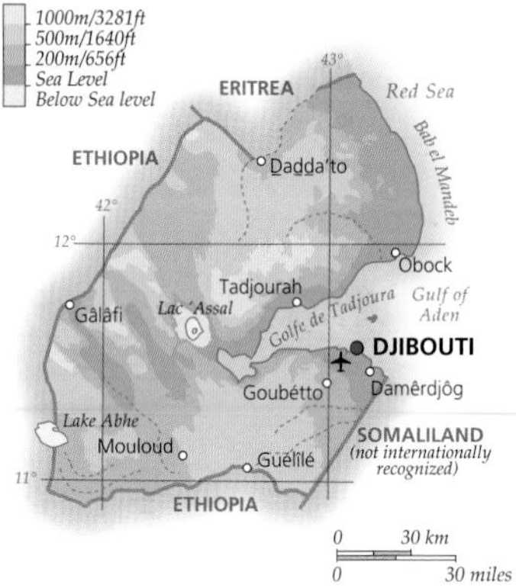
1000m/3281ft
500m/1640ft
200m/656ft
Sea Level
Below Sea level
ERITREA
Red Sea
Bab el Mandeb
ETHIOPIA
Dadda'to
43°
42°
12°
Obock
Tadjourah
Gulf of Aden
Lac 'Assal
Gâlâfi
Golfe de Tadjoura
DJIBOUTI
Goubétto
Damêrdjôg
Lake Abhe
Mouloud
Guélîlé
SOMALILAND
(not internationally recognized)
11°
ETHIOPIA
0
30 km
0
30 miles

FACTFILE

OFFICIAL NAME: Republic of Djibouti
DATE OF FORMATION: 1977
CAPITAL: Djibouti
POPULATION: 864,200
TOTAL AREA: 8494 sq. miles (22,000 sq. km)
DENSITY: 97 people per sq. mile
LANGUAGES: Somali, Afar, French*, Arabic*
RELIGIONS: Muslim (mainly Sunni) 94%, Christian 6%
ETHNIC MIX: Issa 60%, Afar 35%, other 5%
GOVERNMENT: Presidential system
CURRENCY: Djibouti franc = 100 centimes

Dominica

Dominica is renowned as the Caribbean island that resisted European colonization until the 18th century. It achieved independence from the UK in 1978.

GEOGRAPHY

Mountainous and densely forested. Volcanic activity has given the land very fertile soils, hot springs, geysers, and black sand beaches.

CLIMATE

Tropical, cooled by constant trade winds. Heavy annual rainfall. Tropical depressions and hurricanes are likely June–November.

PEOPLE & SOCIETY

The majority of Dominicans are descendants of African slaves brought over to work on banana plantations. The Carib Territory on the northeast of the island is home to the only surviving indigenous community in the Caribbean. Wealth disparities are not as marked as elsewhere in the region, but the alleviation of poverty has become a major plank of government policy.

THE ECONOMY

Based on bananas, but has lost preferential access to EU market. Some diversification: flowers, coffee, fruit. Agriculture vulnerable to hurricanes. Eco-tourism. Some offshore banking.

INSIGHT: *Dominica is known as "Nature Island," due to its spectacula flora and fauna*

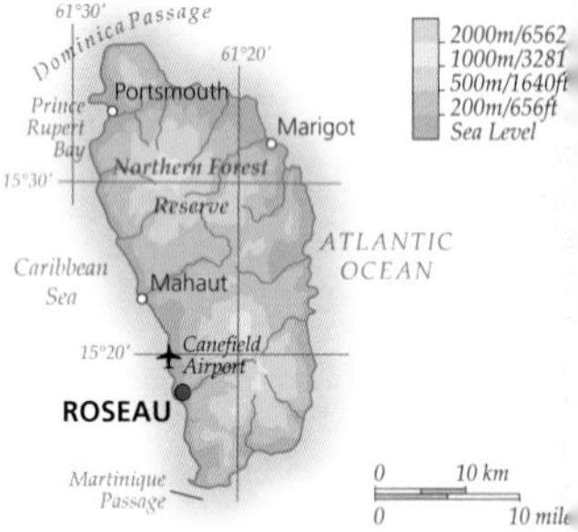
61°30'
Dominica Passage
61°20'
Portsmouth
Prince Rupert Bay
Marigot
15°30'
Northern Forest Reserve
ATLANTIC OCEAN
Caribbean Sea
Mahaut
15°20'
Canefield Airport
ROSEAU
Martinique Passage
2000m/6562
1000m/3281
500m/1640ft
200m/656ft
Sea Level
0
10 km
0
10 mile

FACTFILE

OFFICIAL NAME: Commonwealth of Dominica
DATE OF FORMATION: 1978
CAPITAL: Roseau
POPULATION: 70,400
TOTAL AREA: 291 sq. miles (754 sq. km)
DENSITY: 243 people per sq. mile
LANGUAGES: French Creole, English*
RELIGIONS: Roman Catholic 77%, Protestant 15%, other 8%
ETHNIC MIX: Black 87%, Mixed race 9%, Carib 3%, other 1%
GOVERNMENT: Parliamentary system
CURRENCY: East Caribbean dollar = 100 cents

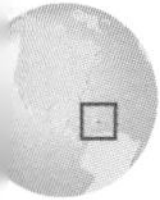

Dominican Republic

The Dominican Republic occupies the eastern two-thirds of the island of Hispaniola in the Caribbean. Spanish-speaking, it seeks closer ties to the anglophone West Indies.

GEOGRAPHY

Highlands and rainforested mountains – including the highest peak in the Caribbean, Pico Duarte – interspersed with fertile valleys. Extensive coastal plain in the east.

CLIMATE

Hot and humid close to sea level, cooler at altitude. Heavy rainfall, especially in the northeast.

PEOPLE & SOCIETY

White landowners – especially those descended from the original Spanish settlers – form the wealthy elite. Mixed-race majority controls commerce and forms the bulk of the professional middle classes. White and mixed-race women are entering the professions. Great disparities of wealth exist; the black and Haitian-immigrant populations occupy the bottom of the social ladder.

THE ECONOMY

Mining (nickel and gold), sugar, and textiles. Tourism, remittances, and exports all rely heavily on US market. Hidden economy based on trans-shipment of narcotics to the US.

INSIGHT: *Santo Domingo is the oldest city in the Americas. It was founded in 1496 by the brother of Christopher Columbus*

20°
Monte Cristi
Puerto Plata
Mao
Santiago
ATLANTIC OCEAN
Pico Duarte 10,417ft(3175m)
San Francisco de Macorís
HAITI
La Vega
19°
Cordillera Central
San Juan
SANTO DOMINGO
El Seibo
Lago Enriquillo
San Cristóbal
La Romana
San Pedro de Macorís
Barahona
70°
69°
18°
71°
Caribbean Sea
2000m/6562ft
1000m/3281ft
500m/1640ft
200m/656ft
Sea Level
0 50 km
0 50 miles

FACTFILE

OFFICIAL NAME: Dominican Republic
DATE OF FORMATION: 1865
CAPITAL: Santo Domingo
POPULATION: 10.1 million
TOTAL AREA: 18,679 sq. miles (48,380 sq. km)
DENSITY: 540 people per sq. mile
LANGUAGES: Spanish*, French Creole
RELIGIONS: Roman Catholic 92%, other and nonreligious 8%
ETHNIC MIX: Mixed race 75%, White 15%, Black 10%
GOVERNMENT: Presidential system
CURRENCY: Dominican Republic peso = 100 centavos

East Timor

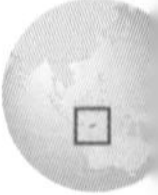

East Timor occupies the once Portuguese-owned eastern half of the island of Timor. Invaded by Indonesia in 1975, it became independent in 2002 following a long struggle.

GEOGRAPHY

A narrow coastal plain gives way to forested highlands. The mountain backbone rises to 9715 ft (2963 m).

CLIMATE

Tropical. Heavy rain in wet season (December–March), then dry and hot, particularly in the north.

PEOPLE & SOCIETY

The population is almost entirely Roman Catholic. The Timorese are a mix of Malay and Papuan peoples, and many indigenous Papuan tribes survive. There is an urban Chinese minority, and ethnic Indonesian settlers became numerous after annexation in 1975. Preindependence violence in 1999 was politically rather than ethnically motivated. Women do not have access to the professions and levels of domestic violence are notably high. Living standards are low.

THE ECONOMY

Widespread poverty. Violence in 1999 damaged infrastructure. Riots in 2006 undermined stability, further deterring foreign investment. Agreement with Australia on division of oil revenue from the Timor Sea.

INSIGHT: *Once dependent on sandalwood, the economy is being transformed by oil under the Timor Sea*

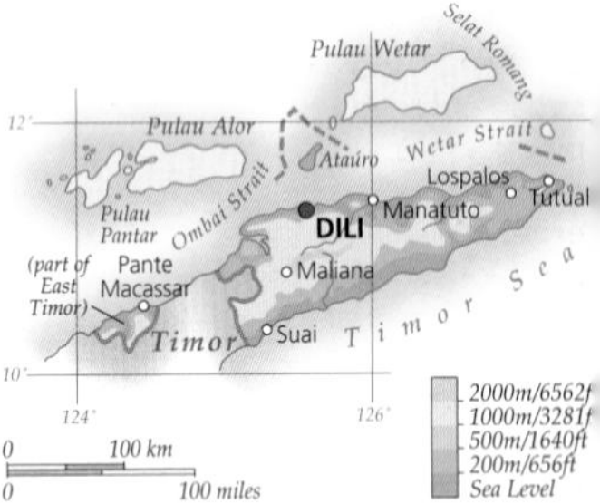

Selat Romang
Pulau Wetar
Pulau Alor
Wetar Strait
Atauro
Lospalos
Tutual
Manatuto
DILI
Pulau Pantar
Ombai Strait
(part of East Timor)
Pante Macassar
Maliana
Timor
Suai
Timor Sea
12°
10°
124°
126°
0
100 km
0
100 miles
2000m/6562ft
1000m/3281ft
500m/1640ft
200m/656ft
Sea Level

FACTFILE

OFFICIAL NAME: Democratic Republic of Timor-Leste

DATE OF FORMATION: 2002

CAPITAL: Dili

POPULATION: 1.13 million

TOTAL AREA: 5756 sq. miles (14,874 sq. km)

DENSITY: 201 people per sq. mile

LANGUAGES: Tetum*, Bahasa Indonesia, Portuguese*

RELIGIONS: Catholic 95%, other 5%

ETHNIC MIX: Malay/Papuan groups c. 85%, Indonesian c. 13%, Chinese 2%

GOVERNMENT: Parliamentary system

CURRENCY: US dollar = 100 cents

Ecuador

Once part of the Inca heartland, Ecuador lies on the western coast of South America. Its territory includes the fascinating Galápagos Islands, 610 miles (970 km) to the west.

GEOGRAPHY

Broad coastal plain, inter-Andean central highlands, dense jungle in upper Amazon basin.

CLIMATE

The climate is hot and moist on the coast, cool in the Andes, and hot equatorial in the Amazon basin.

PEOPLE & SOCIETY

Most people are of Amerindian–Spanish extraction (mestizo). Black communities exist on the coast. The strong and largely unified Amerindian movement leads the pressure for social reform; one in eight people live in extreme poverty. Recent left-wing policies have given greater rights to women, the poor, and Amerindians.

INSIGHT: *Darwin's study on the Galápagos Islands in 1856 played a major part in his theory of evolution*

THE ECONOMY

Oil provides half of export earnings. World's biggest banana exporter. US dollar offers stability, but less control. Defaulted on debt in 2008, prioritizing social spending.

0 100 km
0 100 miles
PACIFIC OCEAN
COLOMBIA
76°
Esmeraldas
San Miguel
Ibarra
Equator
QUITO
Napo
Santo Domingo de los Colorados
Manta
Portoviejo
Ambato
Riobamba
Milagro
Guayaquil
Gulf of Guayaquil
Cuenca
Machala
A n d e s
4°
Loja
PERU
80°
4000m/13124ft
3000m/9843ft
2000m/6562ft
1000m/3281ft
500m/1640ft
200m/656ft
Sea Level

FACTFILE

OFFICIAL NAME: Republic of Ecuador
DATE OF FORMATION: 1830
CAPITAL: Quito
POPULATION: 13.6 million
TOTAL AREA: 109,483 sq. miles (283,560 sq. km)
DENSITY: 127 people per sq. mile
LANGUAGES: Spanish*, Quechua, other Amerindian languages
RELIGIONS: Roman Catholic 93%; Protestant, Jewish, and other 7%
ETHNIC MIX: *Mestizo* 55%, Amerindian 25%, White 10%, Black 10%
GOVERNMENT: Presidential system
CURRENCY: US dollar = 100 cents

Egypt

Occupying the northeast corner of Africa, Egypt is divided by the highly fertile Nile Valley. Its essentially pro-Western, military-backed regime is being challenged by Islamic fundamentalists.

GEOGRAPHY

Fertile Nile Valley separates arid Libyan Desert from smaller semiarid eastern desert. Sinai peninsula has mountains in south.

CLIMATE

Summers are very hot, but winters are cooler. Rainfall is negligible, except on the coast.

PEOPLE & SOCIETY

Despite a long tradition of ethnic and religious tolerance, the rise of Islam has sparked clashes between Muslims and Copts (Coptic Christianity is one of the Church's earliest branches). Women play a full part in education and the economy, though this is threatened by Islamism. Rapidly growing population is a problem. Poverty is rife around Cairo.

INSIGHT: *In 450 BCE Herodotus visited the already-ancient pyramids*

THE ECONOMY

Oil and gas. Cotton. Tolls from the Suez Canal. Successful tourist industry, in spite of terrorist attacks. High birth-rate and rural poverty.

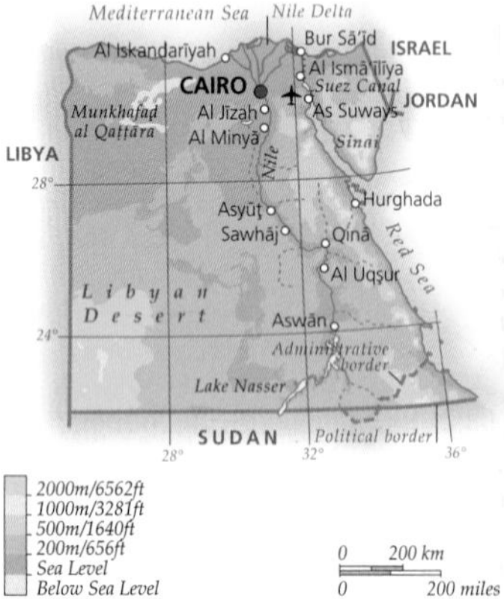
Mediterranean Sea
Nile Delta
Al Iskandarīyah
Bur Sa'īd
ISRAEL
Al Ismā'īlīya
Suez Canal
CAIRO
JORDAN
As Suways
Munkhafaḍ al Qaṭṭāra
Al Jīzah
Al Minyā
Sinai
LIBYA
Nile
28°
Hurghada
Asyūṭ
Sawhāj
Qinā
Red Sea
Al Uqṣur
Libyan Desert
Aswān
24°
Administrative border
Lake Nasser
SUDAN
Political border
28°
32°
36°
2000m/6562ft
1000m/3281ft
500m/1640ft
200m/656ft
Sea Level
Below Sea Level
0 200 km
0 200 miles

FACTFILE

OFFICIAL NAME: Arab Republic of Egypt
DATE OF FORMATION: 1936
CAPITAL: Cairo
POPULATION: 83 million
TOTAL AREA: 386,660 sq. miles (1,001,450 sq. km)
DENSITY: 216 people per sq. mile
LANGUAGES: Arabic*, French, English, Berber
RELIGIONS: Muslim (mainly Sunni) 94%, Coptic Christian and other 6%
ETHNIC MIX: Egyptian 99%, other (Nubian, Armenian, Greek, Berber) 1%
GOVERNMENT: Presidential system
CURRENCY: Egyptian pound = 100 piastres

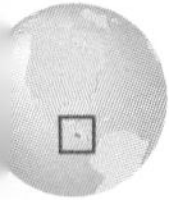

El Salvador

El Salvador is Central America's smallest and most densely populated country. Already struggling to recover from a civil war in the 1980s, it was badly struck by earthquakes in 2001.

GEOGRAPHY

El Salvador is a narrow coastal belt backed by two mountain ranges. There is a central plateau. The country is located within a seismic zone, and there are more than 20 volcanic peaks.

CLIMATE

Tropical coastal belt is very hot, with seasonal rains. Cooler, temperate climate in highlands.

PEOPLE & SOCIETY

Population is largely mestizo; ethnic tensions are few. The 1981–1991 civil war was fought between the US-backed right-wing government and left-wing FMLN guerrillas, over gross economic disparities, which still exist despite some reform. During the war, 75,000 people died, many of whom were unarmed civilians, and human rights abuses were widespread. The FMLN won the presidency in 2009.

THE ECONOMY

Coffee, sugar. Garment industry. Remittances from overseas. Frequent natural disasters damage infrastructure and homes and deepen country's reliance on aid. Five-year anti-poverty program for north from 2007.

INSIGHT: *Independent since 1841, El Salvador is named after Jesus Christ, "the savior" of Christians*

GUATEMALA
HONDURAS
Metapán
Santa Ana
Lempa
Chalatenango
Lempa
Ahuachapán
Embalse Cerrón Grande
Sensuntepeque
Sonsonate
SAN SALVADOR
San Vicente
Zacatecoluca
Lempa
San Miguel
La Unión
Usulután
PACIFIC OCEAN
89°
90°
14°
88°
13°
2000m/6562ft
1000m/3281ft
500m/1640ft
200m/656ft
Sea Level
0 25 km
0 25 miles

FACTFILE

OFFICIAL NAME: Republic of El Salvador
DATE OF FORMATION: 1841
CAPITAL: San Salvador
POPULATION: 6.16 million
TOTAL AREA: 8124 sq. miles (21,040 sq. km)
DENSITY: 770 people per sq. mile
LANGUAGES: Spanish
RELIGIONS: Roman Catholic 80%, Evangelical 18%, other 2%
ETHNIC MIX: *Mestizo* 94%, Amerindian 5%, White 1%
GOVERNMENT: Presidential system
CURRENCY: Salvadorean colón = 100 centavos; US dollar = 100 cents

Equatorial Guinea

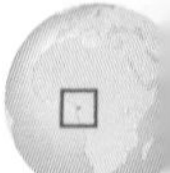

Comprising the mainland territory of Río Muni and five islands on the west coast of central Africa, Equatorial Guinea, despite its name, lies just north of the equator.

GEOGRAPHY

The islands are mountainous and volcanic. The mainland is lower, with mangrove swamps along the coast.

CLIMATE

The island of Bioko is extremely wet and humid. The mainland is only marginally drier and cooler.

PEOPLE & SOCIETY

Equatorial Guinea is the only Spanish-speaking country in Africa. Río Muni is sparsely populated and most people there are Fang, an ethnic group also found in Cameroon and northern Gabon. Bioko is populated by Bubi and a minority of Creoles known as Fernandinos. Tensions between the two territories have been reignited by the discovery of oil off Bioko. Wealth is concentrated in the ruling clan; oil revenue in the last decade has made little impact on most people.

THE ECONOMY

Oil and gas now account for 97% of exports; the government has promised to reinvest the new funds in development. Timber, cocoa, coffee.

INSIGHT: *In 2003, state radio declared President Obiang Nguema to be "like God in Heaven"*

2000m/6562ft
1000m/3281ft
500m/1640ft
200m/656ft
Sea Level
MALABO
3°30'N
Isla da Bioco
Bight of Biafra
9°
ATLANTIC OCEAN
CAMEROON
Micomeseng
2°
Gulf of Guinea
Bata
Niefang
Mongomo
Uolo
Mbini
Río Muni
Etembue
Cabo San Juan
Cogo
Nsoc
Isla de Corisco
GABON
10°
0
40 km
0
40 miles

FACTFILE

OFFICIAL NAME: Republic of Equatorial Guinea
DATE OF FORMATION: 1968
CAPITAL: Malabo
POPULATION: 676,300
TOTAL AREA: 10,830 sq. miles (28,051 sq. km)
DENSITY: 62 people per sq. mile
LANGUAGES: Spanish*, Fang, Bubi, French*
RELIGIONS: Roman Catholic 90%, other 10%
ETHNIC MIX: Fang 85%, other 11%, Bubi 4%
GOVERNMENT: Presidential system
CURRENCY: CFA franc = 100 centimes

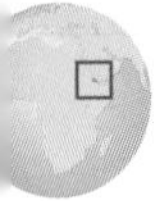

Eritrea

Lying along the southwest shore of the Red Sea, Eritrea won a long war for independence from Ethiopia in 1993. The two neighbors fought a bitter border war in 1998–2000.

GEOGRAPHY

Mostly consists of rugged mountains, bush, and the Danakil Desert, which falls below sea level.

CLIMATE

Warm in the mountains; desert areas are hot. Droughts from July onward are common.

PEOPLE & SOCIETY

Tigrinya-speakers, mainly Orthodox Christians, are the most numerous of nine main ethnic groups. A strong sense of nationhood has been forged by war. Women played a vital role in combat. Over 80% of people are subsistence farmers. Multiparty elections, expected since 1997, have been persistently postponed.

INSIGHT: *Eritrea is the only country to secede successfully in postcolonial Africa*

THE ECONOMY

Legacy of disruption and destruction from wars; resettlement of refugees. Susceptible to drought and famine: dependent on food aid. Most of the population live at subsistence level. Potential for extraction of gold, copper, and oil. Red Sea location: port at Massawa.

0 100 km
0 100 miles
SUDAN
Kerora
Red Sea
40°
Dahlak Archipelago
16°
Ak'ordat
Keren
Mits'iwa (Massawa)
Barentu
ASMARA
Teseney
Adi Ugri
ETHIOPIA
Suwa
Red Sea
Danakil
'Aseb
DJIBOUTI
2000m/6562ft
1000m/3281ft
500m/1640ft
200m/656ft
Sea Level
Below Sea Level

FACTFILE

OFFICIAL NAME: State of Eritrea
DATE OF FORMATION: 1993
CAPITAL: Asmara
POPULATION: 5.07 million
TOTAL AREA: 46,842 sq. miles (121,320 sq. km)
DENSITY: 112 people per sq. mile
LANGUAGES: Tigrinya*, English*, Tigre, Afar, Arabic*, Bilen, Kunama, other
RELIGIONS: Christian 45%, Muslim 45%, other 10%
ETHNIC MIX: Tigray 50%, Tigre 31%, other 9%, Saho 5%, Afar 5%
GOVERNMENT: Transitional regime
CURRENCY: Nakfa = 100 cents

Estonia

The smallest and most Western-oriented of the former Soviet-ruled Baltic states, Estonia is also the most developed, but its standard of living is well below the EU average.

GEOGRAPHY

Estonia's terrain is flat, boggy, and partly forested, with over 1500 islands. Lake Peipus forms much of the eastern border with Russia.

CLIMATE

Maritime, with some continental extremes. Harsh winters, with cool summers and damp springs.

PEOPLE & SOCIETY

Estonians are related ethnically and linguistically to the Finns. Friction between ethnic Estonians and the large Russian minority led to a reassertion of Estonian culture and language. Outright discrimination against the Russian language was only ended in 2000. Estonians are predominantly Lutheran. Families are small and divorce rates are high. Market reforms have increased prosperity; a few people have become very rich.

THE ECONOMY

Timber and oil shale. Currency pegged to euro: hopes to join in 2011. Good productivity. Strong growth accompanied EU accession, but first EU country to enter recession in 2008.

INSIGHT: *Estonia pioneered online voting in 2007, and plans voting by cell phone in 2011*

Gulf of Finland
26°
28°
Kohtla-Järve
TALLINN
Rakvere
Narv
Baltic Sea
Tapa
Haapsalu
59°
Paide
Lake Peipus
RUSS
FED
Hiiumaa
Saaremaa
Pärnu
Viljandi
Tartu
Võrtsjärv
Gulf of Riga
Lake Psko
58°
Valga
Võru
LATVIA
22°
24°
200m/656ft
Sea Level
0 50 km
0 50 miles

FACTFILE

OFFICIAL NAME: Republic of Estonia
DATE OF FORMATION: 1991
CAPITAL: Tallinn
POPULATION: 1.34 million
TOTAL AREA: 17,462 sq. miles (45,226 sq. km)
DENSITY: 77 people per sq. mile
LANGUAGES: Estonian*, Russian
RELIGIONS: Evangelical Lutheran 56%, Orthodox Christian 25%, other 19%
ETHNIC MIX: Estonian 68%, Russian 26%, other 4%, Ukrainian 2%
GOVERNMENT: Parliamentary system
CURRENCY: Kroon = 100 senti

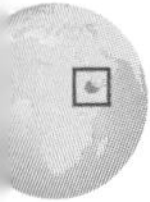

Ethiopia

The former empire of Ethiopia once dominated northeast Africa. A Marxist regime in 1974–1991, now a free-market democracy, it has suffered economic, civil, and natural crises.

GEOGRAPHY

Great Rift Valley divides nountainous northwest region from lesert lowlands in northeast and outheast. Ethiopian Plateau is drained nainly by the Blue Nile.

CLIMATE

Moderate, with summer rains. Highlands are warm, with night frost and snowfalls on the mountains.

PEOPLE & SOCIETY

76 Ethiopian nationalities speak 286 anguages. Oromo (or Gallas) are the argest group. Ethnic representation is a najor political issue. Orthodox Christianity has a very ancient history in Ethiopia. Former emperor Haile Selassie nspired Rastafarianism.

INSIGHT: *King Solomon and the Queen of Sheba are said to have founded the <ingdom of Abyssinia (Ethiopia) c. 1000 BCE*

THE ECONOMY

Overwhelmingly dependent on agriculture; coffee is main export crop. War-damaged infrastructure and periodic serious droughts and famines undermine growth. There is a heavy reliance on food aid. Landlocked since secession of Eritrea.

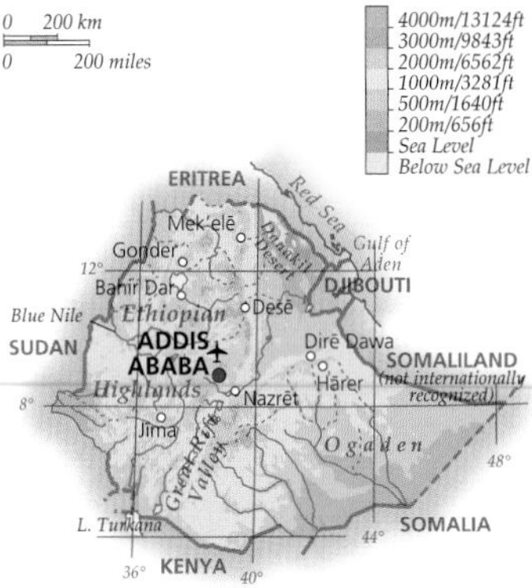
0 200 km
0 200 miles
4000m/13124ft
3000m/9843ft
2000m/6562ft
1000m/3281ft
500m/1640ft
200m/656ft
Sea Level
Below Sea Level
ERITREA
Red Sea
Mek'elē
Gonder
Danakil Desert
Gulf of Aden
DJIBOUTI
12°
Bahir Dar
Blue Nile
Ethiopian
Desē
SUDAN
ADDIS ABABA
Dirē Dawa
SOMALILAND
(not internationally recognized)
Hārer
Highlands
Nazrēt
8°
Jīma
Great Rift Valley
Ogaden
48°
L. Turkana
44°
SOMALIA
36°
KENYA
40°

FACTFILE

OFFICIAL NAME: Federal Democratic Republic of Ethiopia
DATE OF FORMATION: 1896
CAPITAL: Addis Ababa
POPULATION: 82.8 million
TOTAL AREA: 435,184 sq. miles (1,127,127 sq. km)
DENSITY: 193 people per sq. mile
LANGUAGES: Amharic*, Tigrinya, other
RELIGIONS: Orthodox Christian 40%, Muslim 40%, traditional 15%, other 5%
ETHNIC MIX: Oromo 32%, Amhara 30%, other 26%, Tigray 6%, Somali 6%
GOVERNMENT: Parliamentary system
CURRENCY: Ethiopian birr = 100 cents

Fiji

A volcanic archipelago in the South Pacific, with two large islands and 880 islets. Tensions between native Fijians and the Indian minority have sparked a succession of coups.

GEOGRAPHY

Main islands are mountainous, fringed by coral reefs. Remainder are limestone and coral formations.

CLIMATE

Tropical. High temperatures all year round. Cyclones are a hazard.

PEOPLE & SOCIETY

The British introduced workers from India in the late 19th century, and by 1946 their descendants outnumbered the indigenous Fijian population. Ethnic-Fijian nationalism is strong. Many Indo-Fijians left after the 1987 coup, restoring ethnic Fijians to a majority. In 2000, the first Indian-dominated government was ousted. The army led another coup in 2006. Women are lobbying for more rights.

INSIGHT: *Both Fijians and Indians practice fire-walking; Indians walk on hot embers, Fijians on heated stones*

THE ECONOMY

Tourism was main sector, though damaged by instability. Coups have also caused international isolation. All sectors struggling: sugar production, gold mining, textiles, timber, and commercial fishing.

1000m/3281ft
500m/1640ft
Sea Level
PACIFIC OCEAN
16°
Vanua Levu
Yasawa Group
Nabavatu
Labasa
Nabouwalu
Bligh Water
Taveuni
Koro
Rakiraki
Lautoka
Ovalau
Viti Levu
Koro Sea
Lakeba Passage
18°
Gau
SUVA
Sigatoka
Lau Group
Kadavu Passage
Moala
Kadavu
178°E
180°
PACIFIC OCEAN
0 100 km
0 100 miles

FACTFILE

OFFICIAL NAME: Republic of the Fiji Islands
DATE OF FORMATION: 1970
CAPITAL: Suva
POPULATION: 849,200
TOTAL AREA: 7054 sq. miles (18,270 sq. km)
DENSITY: 120 people per sq. mile
LANGUAGES: Fijian, English*, Hindi, Urdu, Tamil, Telugu
RELIGIONS: Hindu 38%, Methodist 37%, Catholic 9%, Muslim 8%, other 8%
ETHNIC MIX: Melanesian (Fijian) 51%, Indian 44%, other 5%
GOVERNMENT: Transitional regime
CURRENCY: Fiji dollar = 100 cents

Finland

Finland's language and national identity have been influenced by both its Scandinavian and Russian neighbors. Once aligned with the USSR, Finland is now a member of the EU.

GEOGRAPHY

South and center are flat, with low ills and many lakes. Uplands and low ıountains in the north. 60% of the ınd area is forested.

CLIMATE

Long, harsh winters with frequent ıowfalls. Short, warmer summers. ainfall is low, and decreases northward.

PEOPLE & SOCIETY

One in four of the population ves in the Greater Helsinki region. wedish-speakers live mainly in the land Islands in the southwest. The ámi (Lapps) lead a seminomadic xistence inside the Arctic Circle. Vomen make up 48% of the labor ɔrce, continuing a long tradition f equality between the sexes. amilies tend to be close-knit, hough marriage is becoming ɛss common.

THE ECONOMY

Strong engineering and electronics sectors: home of Nokia. Wood, pulp, and paper production.

INSIGHT: *Finland has Europe's largest inland waterway system*

500m/1640ft
200m/656ft
Sea Level
0 100 km
0 100 miles
70°
NORWAY
Inarijärvi
Lapland
SWEDEN
RUSS. FED.
Arctic Circle
Rovaniemi
65°
Oulu
Gulf of Bothnia
Vaasa
Kuopio
Joensuu
Jyväskylä
Haukivesi
Pori
Tampere
Saimaa
Lahti
Turku
30°
Åland
60°
Kotka
Espoo
HELSINKI
20°
Baltic Sea
25°

FACTFILE

OFFICIAL NAME: Republic of Finland

DATE OF FORMATION: 1917

CAPITAL: Helsinki

POPULATION: 5.33 million

TOTAL AREA: 130,127 sq. miles (337,030 sq. km)

DENSITY: 45 people per sq. mile

LANGUAGES: Finnish*, Swedish*, Sámi

RELIGIONS: Evangelical Lutheran 89%, other 9%, Orthodox Christian 1%, Roman Catholic 1%

ETHNIC MIX: Finnish 93%, other (including Sámi) 7%

GOVERNMENT: Parliamentary system

CURRENCY: Euro = 100 cents

France

Stretching across western Europe, from the English Channel (la Manche) to the Mediterranean Sea, France was Europe's first modern republic, and is still a leading industrial power.

GEOGRAPHY

Broad plain covers northern half of the country. Tall mountain ranges in the east and southwest, with a mountainous plateau in the center.

CLIMATE

Three main climates: temperate and damp northwest; continental east; and Mediterranean south.

PEOPLE & SOCIETY

Strong French national identity coexists with pronounced regional differences, including local languages. Immigration laws have been tightened since the 1970s, but ethnic minorities growing up in city suburbs feel increasingly alienated. New rules aim to bring more women into politics.

INSIGHT: *France is the most popular tourist destination in the world, with over 80 million visitors a year*

THE ECONOMY

Chemicals, electronics, heavy engineering, cars, and aircraft typify a strong and diversified export sector. World leader in cosmetics, perfumes, and quality wines. Modernized agriculture.

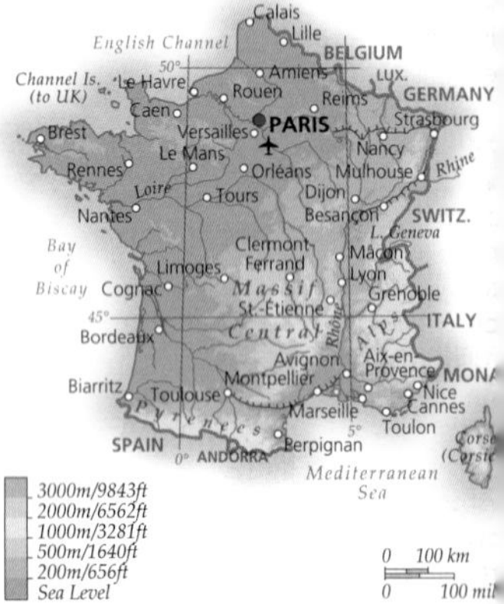

Calais
Lille
English Channel
BELGIUM
50°
Amiens
LUX.
Channel Is. (to UK)
Le Havre
Rouen
Reims
GERMANY
Caen
PARIS
Strasbourg
Brest
Versailles
Le Mans
Nancy
Rennes
Orléans
Mulhouse
Rhine
Loire
Tours
Dijon
Nantes
Besançon
SWITZ.
L. Geneva
Bay of Biscay
Clermont-Ferrand
Mâcon
Limoges
Lyon
Cognac
Massif Central
Grenoble
45°
St.-Étienne
ITALY
Bordeaux
Rhône
Alps
Avignon
Aix-en-Provence
Montpellier
Biarritz
Toulouse
Nice
Cannes
Pyrenees
Marseille
Toulon
5°
SPAIN
0°
ANDORRA
Perpignan
Mediterranean Sea
3000m/9843ft
2000m/6562ft
1000m/3281ft
500m/1640ft
200m/656ft
Sea Level
0 100 km
0 100 mi

FACTFILE

OFFICIAL NAME: French Republic
DATE OF FORMATION: 987
CAPITAL: Paris
POPULATION: 62.3 million
TOTAL AREA: 211,208 sq. miles (547,030 sq. km)
DENSITY: 294 people per sq. mile
LANGUAGES: French*, Provençal, other
RELIGIONS: Catholic 88%, Muslim 8%, Protestant 2%, Jewish 1%, Buddhist 1%
ETHNIC MIX: French 90%, North African 6%, German 2%, Breton 1%, other 1%
GOVERNMENT: Mixed presidential–parliamentary system
CURRENCY: Euro = 100 cents

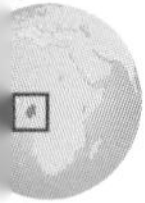

Gabon

Gabon is a former French colony straddling the equator on Africa's west coast. Independent since 1960, it returned to multiparty politics in 1990, after 22 years of one-party rule.

GEOGRAPHY

Low plateaus and mountains lie eyond the coastal strip. Two-thirds of he land is covered by rainforest.

CLIMATE

Hot and tropical, with little istinction between seasons. Cold enguela current cools the coast.

PEOPLE & SOCIETY

Some 40 different languages are poken. The Fang, who live mainly in the orth, are the largest ethnic group, but ave yet to gain control of the overnment. Oil wealth has led to the rowth of an affluent middle class, but ne in three people still lives in poverty. Menial jobs are done by immigrant orkers. Education follows the French ystem. With 85% of people living in owns, Gabon is one of Africa's most rbanized countries. The government is ncouraging population growth.

THE ECONOMY

Oil accounts for 80% of exports, but reserves are dwindling: not much post-oil planning. High debt problem. Tropical hardwoods and manganese.

INSIGHT: *Libreville was founded as a settlement for freed French slaves in 1849*

CAMEROON
EQUATORIAL GUINEA
Oyem
CONGO
Makokou
LIBREVILLE
Equator
Port-Gentil
Ogooué
Lambaréné
Koulamoutou
Moanda
Franceville
Mouila
Tchibanga
CONGO
ATLANTIC OCEAN
12°
0 100 km
0 100 miles
500m/1640ft
200m/656ft
Sea Level

FACTFILE

OFFICIAL NAME: Gabonese Republic
DATE OF FORMATION: 1960
CAPITAL: Libreville
POPULATION: 1.47 million
TOTAL AREA: 103,346 sq. miles (267,667 sq. km)
DENSITY: 15 people per sq. mile
LANGUAGES: Fang, French*, Punu, other
RELIGIONS: Christian (mainly Roman Catholic) 55%, traditional beliefs 40%, other 4%, Muslim 1%
ETHNIC MIX: Fang 26%, Shira-punu 24%, other 24%, foreign 15%, Nzabi-duma 11%
GOVERNMENT: Presidential system
CURRENCY: CFA franc = 100 centimes

Gambia

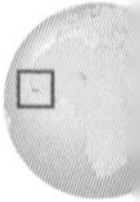

Gambia is a riverbank state on the west coast of Africa, almost entirely surrounded by Senegal. It was renowned for its stability until its government was overthrown in a coup in 1994.

GEOGRAPHY

Located on the narrow strip of land bordering the Gambia River. Long, sandy beaches are backed by mangrove swamps along the river. Savanna and tropical forests higher up.

CLIMATE

Subtropical, with wet, humid months July–October, and warm, dry season November–May.

PEOPLE & SOCIETY

Little tension between various ethnic groups. The largest group, the Mandinka, has traditionally held power. Islam is a strong social influence, though there is no official state religion. A small expatriate community from the UK lives on the coast. Seasonal migrants come from neighboring states to harvest groundnuts each year. Women are very active as traders.

THE ECONOMY

Around 70% of the labor force is involved in agriculture. Groundnuts are the principal crop. Fish stocks are declining. Eco-tourism is promoted, though most visitors come for the beaches. Banjul is one of west Africa's finest deepwater ports: significant re-export trade. Smuggling problems.

INSIGHT: *Overfishing in the waters off Gambia and Senegal, mainly by foreign vessels, is a growing problem*

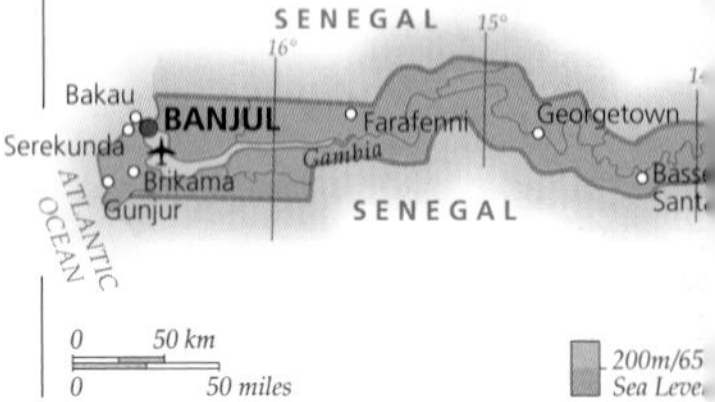
SENEGAL
15°
16°
Bakau
BANJUL
Farafenni
Georgetown
Serekunda
Gambia
Brikama
Gunjur
SENEGAL
ATLANTIC OCEAN
0 50 km
0 50 miles

FACTFILE

OFFICIAL NAME: Republic of the Gambia
DATE OF FORMATION: 1965
CAPITAL: Banjul
POPULATION: 1.71 million
TOTAL AREA: 4363 sq. miles (11,300 sq. km)
DENSITY: 442 people per sq. mile
LANGUAGES: Mandinka, Fulani, Wolof, Jola, Soninke, English*
RELIGIONS: Sunni Muslim 90%, Christian 9% traditional beliefs 1%
ETHNIC MIX: Mandinka 40%, Fulani 19%, Wolof 15%, Jola 11%, Serahuli 9%, other 6%
GOVERNMENT: Presidential system
CURRENCY: Dalasi = 100 butut

Georgia

Located on the eastern shore of the Black Sea, Georgia has been torn by civil war and ethnic disputes since achieving independence from the Soviet Union in 1991.

GEOGRAPHY

Kura Valley lies between Caucasus Mountains in the north and Lesser Caucasus range in south. Lowlands along the Black Sea coast.

CLIMATE

Subtropical along the coast, changing to continental extremes at high altitudes. Rainfall is moderate.

PEOPLE & SOCIETY

Paternalistic society, with strong family, cultural, and literary traditions. Georgia was converted to Christianity in 326 CE. Armenians in the south are the poorest group. Civil conflicts in the early 1990s against Abkhaz and Osset separatists displaced 300,000 people. Abkhazia and South Ossetia now effectively operate as separate states, backed up by Russian forces since the 2008 war. Russia opposes Georgian hopes of joining the EU and NATO.

THE ECONOMY

Transit revenues from pipelines taking oil to the West. Long-established and booming wine industry. Political instability. Fast pace of reforms in late 2000s, at cost of high unemployment.

INSIGHT: *Western Georgia was the land of the legendary Golden Fleece of Greek mythology*

40°
42°
44°
46°
42°
RUSSIAN FEDERATION
Caucasus
Sokhumi
Zugdidi
Black Sea
P'ot'i
K'ut'aisi
Samtredia
Ts'khinvali
Gori
T'elavi
Bat'umi
Kura
Akhalts'ikhe
TBILISI
Rust'avi
Lesser Caucasus
TURKEY
ARMENIA
AZERBAIJAN
3000m/9843ft
2000m/6562ft
1000m/3281ft
500m/1640ft
200m/656ft
Sea Level
0 100 km
0 100 miles

FACTFILE

OFFICIAL NAME: Georgia
DATE OF FORMATION: 1991
CAPITAL: Tbilisi
POPULATION: 4.26 million
TOTAL AREA: 26,911 sq. miles (69,700 sq. km)
DENSITY: 158 people per sq. mile
LANGUAGES: Georgian*, Russian, other
RELIGIONS: Georgian Orthodox 65%, Muslim 11%, Russian Orthodox 10%, Armenian Orthodox 8%, other 6%
ETHNIC MIX: Georgian 84%, Armenian 6%, Azeri 6%, Russian 2%, other 2%
GOVERNMENT: Presidential system
CURRENCY: Lari = 100 tetri

Germany

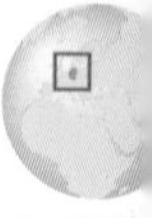

Europe's strongest industrial power and its most populous nation, Germany was divided after military defeat in 1945 into a free-market west and a communist east, but reunified in 1990

GEOGRAPHY

Central European coastal plains in the north, rising to rolling hills of central region and Alps in far south.

CLIMATE

Damp, temperate in northern and central regions. Continental extremes in mountainous south.

PEOPLE & SOCIETY

Regionalism is strong. The north is mainly Protestant, while the south is staunchly Roman Catholic. Social and economic differences still exist between east and west. Turks are the largest single ethnic minority; many came as guest workers in the 1950s–1970s. Immigration rules now favor skilled workers. Feminism is strong.

INSIGHT: *Germany's rivers and canals carry as much freight as its busy highways*

THE ECONOMY

Major exporter of electronics, heavy engineering, chemicals, and cars. Worst recession for 60 years in 2008–2009. Aging population.

DENMARK
Baltic Sea
Kiel
Rostock
North Sea
54°
Hamburg
Lübeck
POLAND
Bremen
Elbe
Oder
NETHER-LANDS
Hannover
BERLIN
Magdeburg
52°
Dortmund
Duisburg
Essen
Kassel
Leipzig
Düsseldorf
Köln
Erfurt
Dresden
Bonn
Chemnitz
BELGIUM
Rhine
Frankfurt am Main
14°
50°
CZECH REPUBLIC
LUX.
Mannheim
Nürnberg
6°
FRANCE
Stuttgart
Danube
Rhine
München
14°
48°
SWITZ.
Bavarian Alps
AUSTRIA
8°
10°
12°
2000m/6562ft
1000m/3281ft
500m/1640ft
200m/656ft
Sea Level
0
100 km
0
100 miles

FACTFILE

OFFICIAL NAME: Federal Republic of Germany

DATE OF FORMATION: 1871

CAPITAL: Berlin

POPULATION: 82.2 million

TOTAL AREA: 137,846 sq. miles (357,021 sq. km)

DENSITY: 609 people per sq. mile

LANGUAGES: German*, Turkish

RELIGIONS: Protestant 34%, Roman Catholic 33%, other 30%, Muslim 3%

ETHNIC MIX: German 92%, other 3%, other European 3%, Turkish 2%

GOVERNMENT: Parliamentary system

CURRENCY: Euro = 100 cents

Ghana

The heartland of the ancient Ashanti kingdom, Ghana in ʋest Africa was once known as the Gold Coast. It has experienced intermittent periods of military rule since independence in 1957.

GEOGRAPHY

Mostly low-lying. The west is overed by rainforest. One of the ʋorld's largest artificial lakes – Lake 'olta – was created by damming the Vhite Volta River.

CLIMATE

Tropical. There are two wet seasons ı the south, but the north is drier, and as just one.

PEOPLE & SOCIETY

Around 75 cultural-linguistic groups. 'he largest is the Akan, who include he Ashanti and Fanti peoples. outhern peoples are richer and more ırban than those of the north. There re few tribal tensions. Family ties are trong. Women play a major role in narket trading. The 2000 election saw Ghana's first peaceful handover of ower. Poverty levels have been ignificantly reduced.

THE ECONOMY

World's second-largest cocoa producer. Oil discovered in 2007: on stream in 2011. Hardwood trees such as maple and sapele. Gold mining.

INSIGHT: *Ghana was the first colony in west Africa to gain independence*

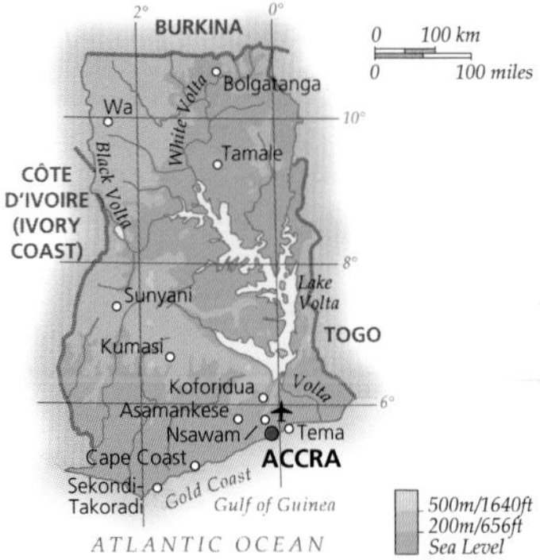

2°
0°
BURKINA
0 100 km
0 100 miles
Bolgatanga
Wa
White Volta
10°
Tamale
Black Volta
CÔTE D'IVOIRE (IVORY COAST)
8°
Lake Volta
Sunyani
TOGO
Kumasi
Koforidua
Volta
6°
Asamankese
Nsawam
Tema
ACCRA
Cape Coast
Sekondi-Takoradi
Gold Coast
Gulf of Guinea
ATLANTIC OCEAN
500m/1640ft
200m/656ft
Sea Level

FACTFILE

OFFICIAL NAME: Republic of Ghana

DATE OF FORMATION: 1957

CAPITAL: Accra

POPULATION: 23.8 million

TOTAL AREA: 92,100 sq. miles (238,540 sq. km)

DENSITY: 268 people per sq. mile

LANGUAGES: Twi, Fanti, Ewe, Ga, Adangbe, Gurma, Dagomba, English*

RELIGIONS: Christian 69%, Muslim 16%, traditional beliefs 9%, other 6%

ETHNIC MIX: Akan 49%, Mole-Dagbani 17%, Ewe 13%, other 13%, Ga 8%

GOVERNMENT: Presidential system

CURRENCY: Cedi = 100 pesewas

Greece

The Balkan state of Greece is bounded on three sides by the Mediterranean, Aegean, and Ionian seas. It has a strong seafaring tradition, with some of the world's richest shipowners.

GEOGRAPHY

Mountainous peninsula and over 2000 islands. Large plain along the mainland's Aegean coast.

CLIMATE

Mainly Mediterranean, with dry, hot summers. Alpine climate in northern mountain areas.

PEOPLE & SOCIETY

Postwar industrial development altered the dominance of agriculture and seafaring. The rural exodus to industrial cities has been stemmed but a third of the population now lives in Athens. Age-old culture and Greek Orthodox Church balance social mobility. Civil marriage and divorce became legal only in 1982.

INSIGHT: *The modern Olympics, first held in Athens in 1896, evolved from Olympia's ancient Greek games*

THE ECONOMY

One of Europe's leading tourist destinations. World's largest shipping fleet. Fruit, vegetables, olives. Large black economy. Public debt and budget deficit remain high.

BULGARIA
MACEDONIA
Dráma
Xánthi
TURKEY
Sérres
ALBANIA
Thessaloníki
Alexandroúpoli
Kateríni
Thracian Sea
40°
Ioánnina
Lárisa
Límnos
Kérkyra (Corfu)
Kérkyra
Vólos
Vóreies Sporádes
Lésvos
20°
Píndos
Lamía
Aegean Sea
Kefallonía
Pátra
Peiraías
ATHENS
Chíos
38°
Kórinthos
Sámos
Zákynthos
Pelopónnisos
Isthmós Korinthou
Ionian Sea
Náxos
Kalámata
Kos
22°
Sea of Crete
Ródos
36°
Mediterranean Sea
Chaniá
Irákleio
Kárpathos
24°
26°
Kríti (Crete)
2000m/6562ft
1000m/3281ft
500m/1640ft
200m/656ft
Sea Level
0 100 km
0 100 miles

FACTFILE

OFFICIAL NAME: Hellenic Republic

DATE OF FORMATION: 1829

CAPITAL: Athens

POPULATION: 11.2 million

TOTAL AREA: 50,942 sq. miles (131,940 sq. km)

DENSITY: 221 people per sq. mile

LANGUAGES: Greek*, Turkish, Macedonian, Albanian

RELIGIONS: Orthodox Christian 98%, Muslim 1%, other 1%

ETHNIC MIX: Greek 98%, other 2%

GOVERNMENT: Parliamentary system

CURRENCY: Euro = 100 cents

Grenada

The southernmost of the Windward Islands, Grenada made world headlines in 1983 when the US and Caribbean allies mounted an invasion to sever links with Castro's Cuba.

GEOGRAPHY

Volcanic in origin, with densely forested central mountains. Its territory also includes the islands of Carriacou and Petite Martinique.

CLIMATE

Tropical, tempered by trade winds. Hurricanes are a hazard in the July–November wet season.

PEOPLE & SOCIETY

Grenadians are mainly of African origin; their traditions remain strong, especially on Carriacou. Inter-ethnic marriage has reduced tensions between the groups. Extended families, often headed by women, are the norm. Wealth disparities are not marked, but levels of poverty are growing.

INSIGHT: *Known as "the spice island of the Caribbean," it is the world's second-largest nutmeg producer*

THE ECONOMY

Severe damage from Hurricane Ivan in 2004 to crops and 90% of buildings; reconstruction will take years. Nutmeg, cocoa, bananas, and mace. Smuggling is a serious problem.

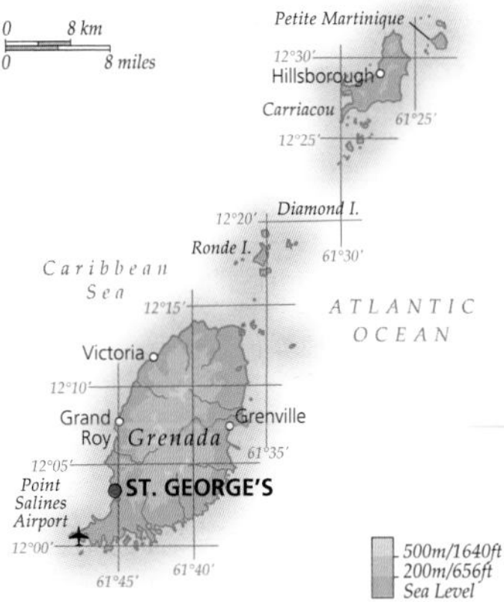
0 8 km
0 8 miles
Petite Martinique
12°30′
Hillsborough
Carriacou
61°25′
12°25′
Diamond I.
12°20′
Ronde I.
61°30′
Caribbean Sea
12°15′
ATLANTIC OCEAN
Victoria
12°10′
Grand Roy
Grenada
Grenville
61°35′
12°05′
Point Salines Airport
ST. GEORGE'S
12°00′
61°45′
61°40′
500m/1640ft
200m/656ft
Sea Level

FACTFILE

OFFICIAL NAME: Grenada
DATE OF FORMATION: 1974
CAPITAL: St. George's
POPULATION: 103,900
TOTAL AREA: 131 sq. miles (340 sq. km)
DENSITY: 793 people per sq. mile
LANGUAGES: English*, English Creole
RELIGIONS: Roman Catholic 68%, Anglican 17%, other 15%
ETHNIC MIX: Black African 82%, Mixed race 13%, East Indian 3%, other 2%
GOVERNMENT: Parliamentary system
CURRENCY: East Caribbean dollar = 100 cents

Guatemala

The largest and most populous nation on the Central American isthmus, Guatemala returned to civilian rule in 1986 after 32 years of violent and repressive military rule.

GEOGRAPHY

Narrow Pacific coastal plain. Central highlands with volcanoes. Short coast on the Caribbean Sea. Tropical rainforests in the north.

CLIMATE

Tropical: hot and humid in coastal regions and north. More temperate in central highlands.

PEOPLE & SOCIETY

Amerindians, concentrated in the highlands, form a majority. Power, wealth, and land are controlled by *ladinos* (Westernized Amerindians and *mestizos*). Catholicism is predominant, mixed with Amerindian beliefs. A third of the population lives on less than $2 a day. Literacy levels are low.

INSIGHT: *Guatemala, which means "land of trees," was the center of the ancient Mayan civilization*

THE ECONOMY

Coffee, sugar, and bananas are top exports. Tourism. Damage from natural disasters. Marked wealth inequalities inhibit domestic market.

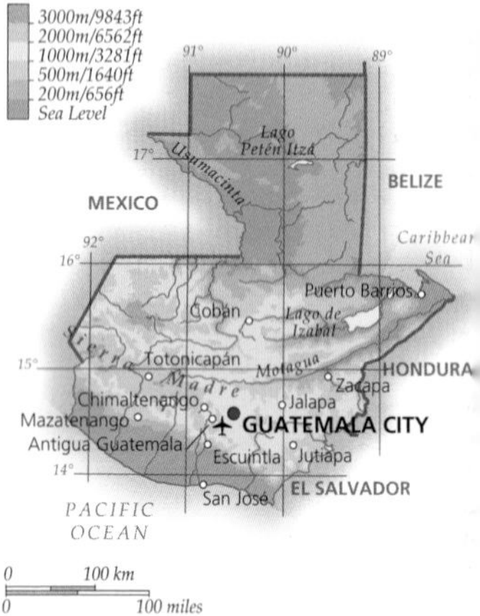
3000m/9843ft
2000m/6562ft
1000m/3281ft
500m/1640ft
200m/656ft
Sea Level
91°
90°
89°
17°
16°
15°
14°
92°
Usumacinta
Lago Petén Itzá
BELIZE
MEXICO
Caribbean Sea
Puerto Barrios
Cobán
Lago de Izabal
Sierra Madre
Totonicapán
Motagua
HONDURAS
Zacapa
Chimaltenango
Jalapa
Mazatenango
GUATEMALA CITY
Antigua Guatemala
Escuintla
Jutiapa
San José
EL SALVADOR
PACIFIC OCEAN
0
100 km
0
100 miles

FACTFILE

OFFICIAL NAME: Republic of Guatemala
DATE OF FORMATION: 1838
CAPITAL: Guatemala City
POPULATION: 14 million
TOTAL AREA: 42,042 sq. miles (108,890 sq. km)
DENSITY: 335 people per sq. mile
LANGUAGES: Quiché, Mam, Cakchiquel, Kekchí, Spanish*
RELIGIONS: Roman Catholic 65%, Protestant 33%, other 2%
ETHNIC MIX: Amerindian 60%, Mestizo 30%, other 10%
GOVERNMENT: Presidential system
CURRENCY: Quetzal = 100 centavos

Guinea

Located on the west coast of Africa, Guinea became the first French colony in Africa to gain independence, in 1958. The country was under military rule from 1984 to 1995.

GEOGRAPHY

Coastal plains and mangrove wamps in west rise to forested or avanna highlands in the south. emidesert in the north.

CLIMATE

Tropical, with a wet season April–)ctober. Conakry is especially rainy. łot, dry *harmattan* wind blows from ahara during dry season.

PEOPLE & SOCIETY

Peul and Malinké make up nost of the population, but rivalries etween them have allowed coastal eoples such as the Soussou to ominate politics. Daily life revolves round the extended family. Women cquired influence under Marxist party ule between 1958 and 1984, but the Auslim revival since then has reversed ne trend. Private enterprise has reated a business class.

THE ECONOMY

Substantial gold, diamond, and especially bauxite reserves. Cash crops: bananas, coffee, pineapples, palm oil. Poor infrastructure. Instability.

INSIGHT: *The colors of Guinea's flag represent the three words of the country's motto: work (red), justice (yellow), and solidarity (green)*

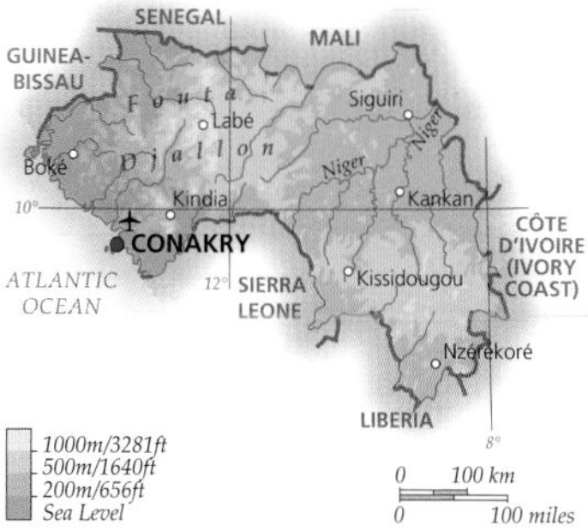
SENEGAL
MALI
GUINEA-BISSAU
Fouta Djallon
Labé
Siguiri
Niger
Boké
Kindia
Kankan
10°
CONAKRY
CÔTE D'IVOIRE (IVORY COAST)
ATLANTIC OCEAN
12°
SIERRA LEONE
Kissidougou
Nzérékoré
LIBERIA
8°
1000m/3281ft
500m/1640ft
200m/656ft
Sea Level
0 100 km
0 100 miles

FACTFILE

OFFICIAL NAME: Republic of Guinea
DATE OF FORMATION: 1958
CAPITAL: Conakry
POPULATION: 10.1 million
TOTAL AREA: 94,925 sq. miles (245,857 sq. km)
DENSITY: 106 people per sq. mile
LANGUAGES: Pulaar, Malinké, Soussou, French*
RELIGIONS: Muslim 65%, traditional beliefs 33%, Christian 2%
ETHNIC MIX: Peul 39%, Malinké 23%, other 21%, Soussou 11%, Kissi 6%
GOVERNMENT: Presidential system
CURRENCY: Guinea franc = 100 centimes

Guinea-Bissau

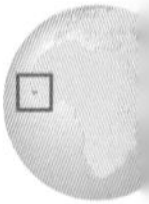

Known as Portuguese Guinea while a colony, Guinea-Bissau lies on Africa's west coast. Since 1994, its nascent democracy has been plagued by coups and rebellions.

GEOGRAPHY

Low-lying, apart from savanna highlands in northeast. Rainforests and swamps are found along coastal areas.

CLIMATE

Tropical, with wet season May-November and dry season December-April. Hot, dry *harmattan* desert wind blows during dry season.

PEOPLE & SOCIETY

The largest ethnic group is the Balante, who live in the south. Though only around 1% of the population, the mixed Portuguese–African *mestiços* dominate the top ranks of government and bureaucracy. Most people live and work on small family farms, grouped in self-contained villages. The bulk of the urban population live in Bissau, where they face economic hardship. Narcotics traffickers are taking advantage of the ongoing instability.

THE ECONOMY

Mostly subsistence farming. Lack o sufficiency in rice staple. Main cash crop is cashew nuts. Major cocaine transit route from South America to Europe. Offshore oil as yet untapped. Fisheries and timber potential.

INSIGHT: *In 1974, Guinea-Bissau became the first Portuguese colony to gain independence*

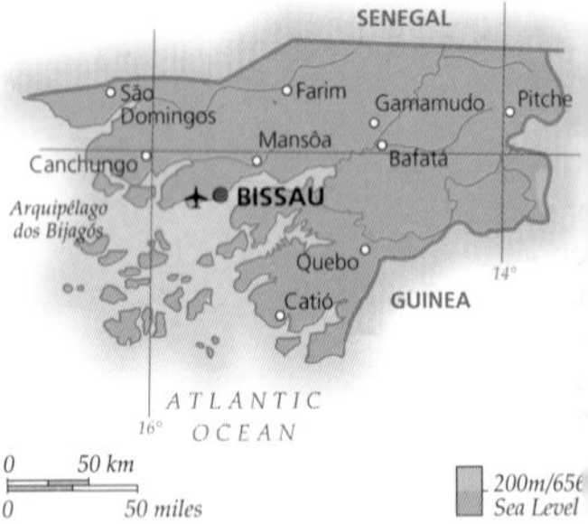
SENEGAL
São Domingos
Farim
Gamamudo
Pitche
Mansôa
Bafatá
Canchungo
BISSAU
Arquipélago dos Bijagós
Quebo
Catió
GUINEA
14°
ATLANTIC OCEAN
16°
0 50 km
0 50 miles
200m/656
Sea Level

FACTFILE

OFFICIAL NAME: Rep. of Guinea-Bissau
DATE OF FORMATION: 1974
CAPITAL: Bissau
POPULATION: 1.61 million
TOTAL AREA: 13,946 sq. miles (36,120 sq. km)
DENSITY: 148 people per sq. mile
LANGUAGES: Portuguese Creole, Balante, Fulani, Malinke, Portuguese*
RELIGIONS: Indigenous beliefs 52%, Muslim 40%, Christian 8%
ETHNIC MIX: Balante 30%, other 24%, Fulani 20%, Mandyako 14%, Mandinka 12%
GOVERNMENT: Presidential system
CURRENCY: CFA franc = 100 centimes

Guyana

On the northeast coast of South America, Guyana is the continent's only English-speaking country. Independent since 1966, it has close ties with the anglophone Caribbean.

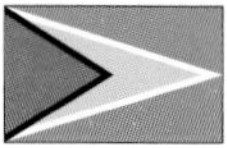

GEOGRAPHY

Mainly artificial coast, reclaimed by dikes and dams from swamps and tidal marshes. Forests cover 85% of the interior, rising to savanna uplands and mountains.

CLIMATE

Tropical. Coast cooled by sea breezes. Lowlands are hot, wet, and humid. Highlands are a little cooler.

PEOPLE & SOCIETY

Guyana is a complex multiracial society. Tension exists between the Afro-Guyanese, descended from slaves, and the Indo-Guyanese, descendants of laborers brought over after slavery was abolished. Politics is highly polarized around this split and has often spilled over into violence on the streets. Amerindian subsistence farmers are the poorest people in society and have little representation.

THE ECONOMY

Diverse exports: gold, sugar, fish, bauxite, rice, timber, diamonds. Debt relief granted. Narcotics transit zone.

INSIGHT: *Guyana means "land of many waters," reflecting its dense network of rivers*

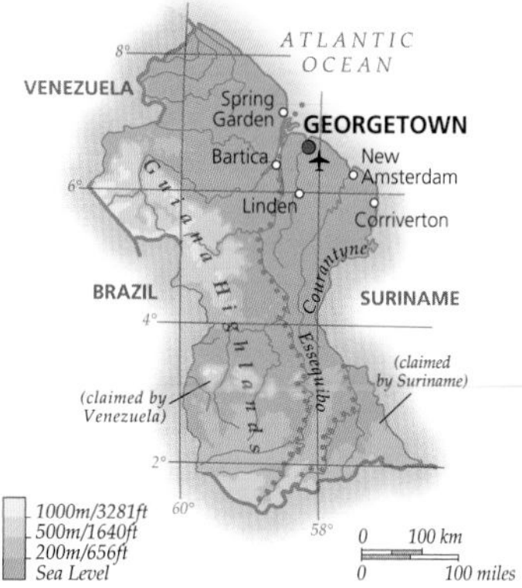
ATLANTIC OCEAN
8°
6°
4°
2°
60°
58°
VENEZUELA
BRAZIL
SURINAME
Spring Garden
GEORGETOWN
Bartica
New Amsterdam
Linden
Corriverton
Courantyne
Guiana Highlands
Essequibo
(claimed by Suriname)
(claimed by Venezuela)
1000m/3281ft
500m/1640ft
200m/656ft
Sea Level
0 100 km
0 100 miles

FACTFILE

OFFICIAL NAME: Cooperative Republic of Guyana
DATE OF FORMATION: 1966
CAPITAL: Georgetown
POPULATION: 762,500
TOTAL AREA: 83,000 sq. miles (214,970 sq. km)
DENSITY: 10 people per sq. mile
LANGUAGES: Creole, Hindi, English*
RELIGIONS: Christian 57%, Hindu 33%, Muslim 9%, other 1%
ETHNIC MIX: East Indian 43%, Black African 30%, other 18%, Amerindian 9%
GOVERNMENT: Presidential system
CURRENCY: Guyanese dollar = 100 cents

Haiti

Formerly a French colony, Haiti shares the Caribbean island of Hispaniola with the Dominican Republic. At independence in 1804, it became the world's first black republic.

GEOGRAPHY

Predominantly mountainous, with forests and fertile plains.

CLIMATE

Tropical, with rain throughout the year. Humid in coastal areas, much cooler in the mountains.

PEOPLE & SOCIETY

Most Haitians are of African descent. A few have European roots, primarily French. The rigid class structure maintains vast disparities of wealth. The majority of the population live in extreme poverty; Haiti is one of the poorest countries in the Americas. A combination of political oppression and a collapsing economy led thousands to seek asylum in the US or the Dominican Republic. Though most are Christians, many Haitians practice Voodoo, which was recognized as an official religion in 2003.

THE ECONOMY

In crisis due to instability, hurricane damage, and corruption. Profiteering from narcotics trade to US. Food shortages. 70% unemployment.

INSIGHT: *A slave rebellion headed by Toussaint Louverture in 1791 led to Haiti's independence*

Île de la Tortue
ATLANTIC OCEAN
20°
Port-de-Paix
Cap-Haïtien
Limbé
Fort-Liber
1000m/3281ft
500m/1640ft
200m/656ft
Sea Level
Massif du Nord
Gonaïves
Golfe de la Gonâve
Desdunes
Hinche
St-Marc
Petite-Rivière-de-l'Artibonite
19°
Île de la Gonâve
Jérémie
PORT-AU-PRINCE
Pétionville
Massif de La Hotte
Cayes
Jacmel
18°
Caribbean Sea
74°
72°
0 50 km
0 50 miles

FACTFILE

OFFICIAL NAME: Republic of Haiti
DATE OF FORMATION: 1804
CAPITAL: Port-au-Prince
POPULATION: 10 million
TOTAL AREA: 10,714 sq. miles (27,750 sq. km)
DENSITY: 943 people per sq. mile
LANGUAGES: French Creole*, French
RELIGIONS: Roman Catholic 80%, Protestant 16%, other 3%, nonreligious 1%; Voodoo is widely practiced
ETHNIC MIX: Black African 95%, Mixed race and European 5%
GOVERNMENT: Presidential system
CURRENCY: Gourde = 100 centimes

Honduras

Straddling the Central American isthmus, Honduras returned to democratic rule in 1984, after a period of military government. Hurricane Mitch devastated the country in 1998.

GEOGRAPHY

Narrow plains along both coasts, vith a mountainous interior, cut by river valleys. Tropical forests, swamps, and agoons in the east.

CLIMATE

Tropical coastal lowlands are hot and humid, with May–October rains. nterior is cooler and drier.

PEOPLE & SOCIETY

The majority of the population is *nestizo* (mixed race). An English-speaking *garífuna* (black) community and Miskito Amerindians struggle to preserve their ights to land along the remote Caribbean coast. Women's status remains ow. Hurricane Mitch impoverished 85% of the population. Wealth inequalities are large and poverty is at the root of social tension. The army ousted the president in 2009. Violent crime s a major issue.

THE ECONOMY

Garments, coffee, bananas, and shellfish are exported. Remittances account for a fifth of GDP. Debt relief from 2005. Mineral potential. High underemployment and corruption.

INSIGHT: *The Honduran currency is named after a Lenca Indian chief who was the main leader of resistance to the Spanish conquest in the 16th century*

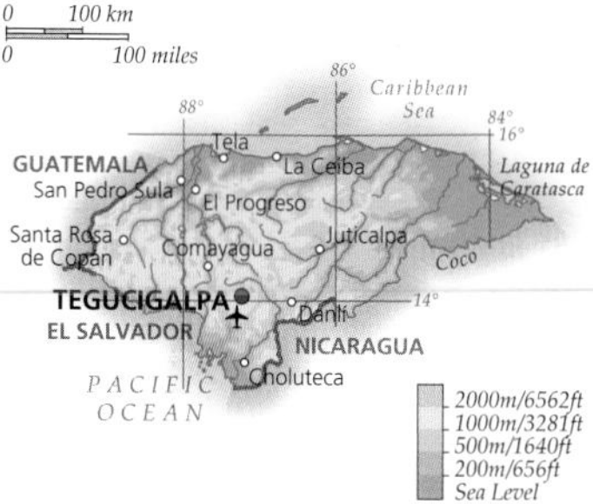
0 100 km
0 100 miles
86°
Caribbean Sea
88°
84°
16°
Tela
GUATEMALA
La Ceiba
Laguna de Caratasca
San Pedro Sula
El Progreso
Santa Rosa de Copán
Comayagua
Juticalpa
Coco
TEGUCIGALPA
14°
Danlí
EL SALVADOR
NICARAGUA
PACIFIC OCEAN
Choluteca
2000m/6562ft
1000m/3281ft
500m/1640ft
200m/656ft
Sea Level

FACTFILE

OFFICIAL NAME: Republic of Honduras
DATE OF FORMATION: 1838
CAPITAL: Tegucigalpa
POPULATION: 7.47 million
TOTAL AREA: 43,278 sq. miles (112,090 sq. km)
DENSITY: 173 people per sq. mile
LANGUAGES: Spanish*, Garífuna, English Creole
RELIGIONS: Roman Catholic 97%, Protestant 3%
ETHNIC MIX: Mestizo 90%, Black African 5%, Amerindian 4%, White 1%
GOVERNMENT: Transitional regime
CURRENCY: Lempira = 100 centavos

Hungary

Landlocked in central Europe, Hungary was one of the twin centers of the once-great Habsburg Empire. It lost two-thirds of its historical territory for supporting Germany in World War I.

GEOGRAPHY

Landlocked. Fertile plains in east and northwest; west and north are hilly. The Danube River cuts through the country and the capital.

CLIMATE

Continental, with wet springs, late but very hot summers, and cold, cloudy winters. The transition between seasons tends to be sudden.

PEOPLE & SOCIETY

Hungary's population shrank in the 1990s. Mostly ethnic Hungarian (Magyar), there are small minorities of Germans, Jews, and neighboring peoples. Roma face particular discrimination. The government is greatly concerned about the fate of ethnic Hungarians in Romania, Serbia, and Slovakia. Hungary joined the EU in 2004. Working hours are longer than in western Europe.

THE ECONOMY

Strong industrial base. Hard-hit in 2007–2008 "global downturn." Currency plummeted, $25 billion from IMF to avoid meltdown. Tough spending cuts needed to keep on path to join euro.

INSIGHT: *The Hungarian language is Asian in origin and is most closely related to Finnish*

SLOVAKIA
UKRAI
AUST.
SLOVENIA
CROATIA
SERBIA
ROMANIA
Miskolc
Nyíregyháza
Debrecen
Győr
Danube
Tatabánya
BUDAPEST
Szombathely
Szolnok
Székesfehérvár
Balaton
Kecskemét
Békéscsaba
Nagykanizsa
Danube
Szeged
Pécs
48°
46°
18°
20°
22°
0 50 km
0 50 miles
500m/1640
200m/656f
Sea Level

FACTFILE

OFFICIAL NAME: Republic of Hungary
DATE OF FORMATION: 1918
CAPITAL: Budapest
POPULATION: 9.99 million
TOTAL AREA: 35,919 sq. miles (93,030 sq. km)
DENSITY: 280 people per sq. mile
LANGUAGES: Hungarian*
RELIGIONS: Catholic 52%, Calvinist 16%, other 15%, nonreligious 14%, Lutheran 3%
ETHNIC MIX: Magyar 94%, other 5%, Roma 1%
GOVERNMENT: Parliamentary system
CURRENCY: Forint = 100 fillér

Iceland

Europe's westernmost country, Iceland's strategic ocean location straddles the Mid-Atlantic Ridge. Its spectacular landscape is largely uninhabited, aside from coastal towns.

GEOGRAPHY

Grassy coastal lowlands, with fjords n the north. Central plateau of cold lava desert, geothermal springs, and glaciers. Around 200 volcanoes, with numerous geysers and solfataras.

CLIMATE

Its location in the middle of the Gulf Stream moderates the climate. Mild winters and brief, cool summers.

PEOPLE & SOCIETY

Icelanders share a strong national identity, with few foreign residents. Their language has changed little in 700 years, in part due to the country's isolation. There is high social mobility, free health care, and low-cost heating (geothermal and hydropower). Iceland's recent banking collapse and near financial ruin has swung the long-running debate over EU membership in favor of joining.

THE ECONOMY

Once reliant on fish. Aluminum smelting. Tourism. Banks overexposed in 2007–2008 "global downturn." Nation bankrupt, króna depreciated 90%.

INSIGHT: *The word geyser is taken from Geysir (the "gusher") in southwest Iceland*

Denmark Strait
Arctic Circle
0 50 km
0 50 miles
Norwegian Sea
24°
Akureyri
Húsavík
Akranes
Keflavík
REYKJAVÍK
Hafnarfjördhur
Kópavogur
66°
Selfoss
Egilsstadhir
22°
Vestmannaeyjar
Vatnajökull
20°
14°
18°
16°
64°
ATLANTIC OCEAN
1000m/3281ft
500m/1640ft
200m/656ft
Sea Level
Ice Cap

FACTFILE

OFFICIAL NAME: Republic of Iceland
DATE OF FORMATION: 1944
CAPITAL: Reykjavík
POPULATION: 322,700
TOTAL AREA: 39,768 sq. miles (103,000 sq. km)
DENSITY: 8 people per sq. mile
LANGUAGES: Icelandic*
RELIGIONS: Evangelical Lutheran 93%, nonreligious 6%, other (mostly Christian) 1%
ETHNIC MIX: Icelandic 94%, other 5%, Danish 1%
GOVERNMENT: Parliamentary system
CURRENCY: Icelandic króna = 100 aurar

India

India is the world's second most populous country and largest democracy. Despite some success in reducing the birth rate, its population will probably overtake China's by 2035.

GEOGRAPHY

Separated from northern Asia by the Himalaya mountain range, India forms a subcontinent. As well as the Himalayas, there are two other main geographical regions, the Indo-Gangetic plain, which lies between the foothills of the Himalayas and the Vindhya Mountains, and the central-southern Deccan plateau. The Ghats are smaller mountain ranges located on the east and west coasts.

CLIMATE

Varies greatly according to latitude, altitude, and season. Most of India has three seasons: hot, wet, and cool. Summer temperatures in the north can reach 104°F (40°C). Monsoon rains normally break in June, petering out in September to October. In the cool season, the weather is mainly dry. The climate in the warmer south is less variable than in the north.

PEOPLE & SOCIETY

India's planners, overseeing an economic revolution, see its growing population rather than environmental constraints as the main brake on development. Nationwide awareness campaigns promote birth control but cultural and religious pressures encourage large families. Rural deprivation spurs urban migration, to live in sprawling slums. Almost 70% of people survive on less than $2 a day. The majority of Indians are Hindu. Various attempts to reform the Hindu caste system, which determines social standing and even marriage, have met with violent opposition. Severe tensions exist between Hindus and the Muslim minority, especially in Kashmir and Gujarat. Smaller ethnic groups exist in the northeast, and many struggle for greater autonomy. Over two million people are living with HIV/AIDS.

FACTFILE

OFFICIAL NAME: Republic of India
DATE OF FORMATION: 1947
CAPITAL: New Delhi
POPULATION: 1.2 billion
TOTAL AREA: 1,269,338 sq. miles (3,287,590 sq. km)
DENSITY: 1044 people per sq. mile
LANGUAGES: Hindi*, English*, Urdu, Bengali, Marathi, Telugu, Tamil, other
RELIGIONS: Hindu 81%, Muslim 13%, Christian 2%, Sikh 2%, other 2%
ETHNIC MIX: Indo-Aryan 72%, Dravidian 25%, Mongoloid and other 3%
GOVERNMENT: Parliamentary system
CURRENCY: Indian rupee = 100 paise

THE ECONOMY

One of Asia's fastest-growing economies. Protectionism has given way to free-market economics. Tea, gems, textiles exported. High-tech industries, outsourcing center. Success of "Bollywood" films. Cheap labor. Huge market, held back by poverty.

INSIGHT: *India's national animal, the tiger, was depicted as early as 4000 years ago by the Mohenjo-Daro civilization*

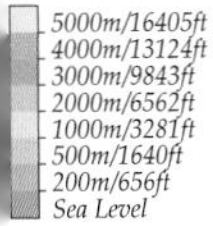
5000m/16405ft
4000m/13124ft
3000m/9843ft
2000m/6562ft
1000m/3281ft
500m/1640ft
200m/656ft
Sea Level

A 'line of control' was agreed between India and Pakistan in 1972
Aksai Chin - administered by China, claimed by India
Demchok/Dêmqog - administered by China, claimed by India
Much of Arunāchal Pradesh is claimed by China
CHINA
PAKISTAN
NEPAL
BHUTAN
BANGLADESH
MYANMAR (BURMA)
NEW DELHI
Srinagar
Jammu & Kashmir
Amritsar
Jalandhar
Ludhiāna
Chandīgarh
Meerut
Delhi
Bareilly
Āgra
Lucknow
Jaipur
Jodhpur
Kānpur
Gwalior
Kota
Vārānasi
Patna
Shiliguri
Imphāl
Assam
Brahmaputra
Ganges
Thar Desert
Dhanbād
Rānchi
Hāora
Kolkata (Calcutta)
Jamshedpur
Mouths of the Ganges
Rann of Kachchh
Gulf of Kachchh
Ahmadābād
Bhopāl
Indore
Jabalpur
Narmada
Jāmnagar
Rājkot
Vadodara
Nāgpur
Mahanadi
Cuttack
Sūrat
Gulf of Khambhāt
Kalyān
Nānded
Mumbai (Bombay)
Pune
Deccan
Godavari
Eastern Ghats
Western Ghats
Visākhapatnam
Bay of Bengal
Hyderābād
Arabian Sea
Solāpur
Krishna
Hubli
Panaji
Andaman Islands
North Andaman
Middle Andaman
South Andaman
Port Blair
Little Andaman
Chennai (Madras)
INDIAN OCEAN
Bangalore
Mysore
Salem
Lakshadweep (Laccadive Is.)
Coimbatore
Kochi/Cochin
Madurai
Nicobar Islands
Indira Point
Great Nicobar
Himalaya
Indus
35°
30°
25°
20°
15°
10°
70°
75°
80°
85°
90°
95°
0 200 km
0 200 miles

Indonesia

Formerly called the Dutch East Indies, Indonesia is the world's largest archipelago, with 18,108 islands scattered across 3000 miles (5000 km). It is the world's fourth most populous nation.

GEOGRAPHY

Indonesia is highly mountainous, with numerous tropical swamps. The land is covered with dense rainforest, especially on New Guinea, where it remains largely unexplored. There are more than 200 volcanoes, many of which are still active. Earthquakes, eruptions, and tsunamis are hazards. The islands of Java, Bali, Lombok, Sumatra, and Borneo were once joined together by dry land, which has since been submerged by rising sea levels. Coastal lowland development distinguishes some of the large islands.

CLIMATE

The climate is predominantly tropical monsoon. Variations relate mainly to differences in latitude and altitude; hilly areas are cooler overall. Rain falls throughout the year, often in thunderstorms, but there is a relatively dry season from June to September.

PEOPLE & SOCIETY

The basic Melanesian–Malay ethnic division disguises a diverse society. Bahasa Indonesia, the national language, coexists with at least 250 other spoken languages or dialects. Attempts by the Javanese

Strait of Malacca
Bandaaceh
100°
Langsa
Aceh
Medan
Kepulauan Natuna
Pematangsiantar
Pulau Nias
Pakanbaru
Singkawang
Padang
Sumatra
Kepulauan Mentawai
Pegunungan Barisan
Jambi
Bangka
Pangkalpinang
Palembang
Bengkulu
Bandar Lampung
INDIAN OCEAN
Bogor
Bandung

FACTFILE

OFFICIAL NAME: Republic of Indonesia
DATE OF FORMATION: 1949
CAPITAL: Jakarta
POPULATION: 230 million
TOTAL AREA: 741,096 sq. miles (1,919,440 sq. km)
DENSITY: 332 people per sq. mile
LANGUAGES: Javanese, Sundanese, Madurese, Bahasa Indonesia*, Dutch
RELIGIONS: Sunni Muslim 87%, Christian 9%, Hindu 2%, other 2%
ETHNIC MIX: Javanese 42%, other 31%, Sundanese 15%, coastal Malays 12%
GOVERNMENT: Presidential system
CURRENCY: Rupiah = 100 sen

political elite to suppress local cultures have been vigorously opposed, especially by the Aceh of northern Sumatra, and the Papuans. Religious and interethnic hostility is a problem, with clashes between Christians and Muslims in many areas, and discrimination against ethnic Chinese leading to mob attacks on their businesses. Gender equality is enshrined in law; women are active in public life.

THE ECONOMY

Varied resources, especially natural gas. Cheap and plentiful labor pool. Sizable state-owned sector, and state control of prices of basic goods. Large foreign debt rescheduled. Bureaucracy and corruption damage business confidence. Regional conflicts and terrorist attacks deter tourists and investors. Piracy is rife. The 2004 tsunami, which killed over 130,000 people, devastated northern Sumatra.

RUNEI
LAYSIA
Pegunungan Muller
120°
130°
140°
Celebes Sea
PACIFIC OCEAN
Leok
Manado
Ternate
Halmahera
Gorontalo
Equator
rneo
Samarinda
Balikpapan
Palu
Poso
Molucca Sea
Sorong
Manokwari
Sulawesi
Maluku (Moluccas)
Ceram Sea
Waflia
Fakfak
Maniwori
Jayapura
Kotabaru
Martapura
Kendari
Ambon
Pulau Seram
Parepare
Makassar
Pegunungan Maoke
Amamapare
Papua (Irian Jaya)
PAPUA NEW GUINEA
Java Sea
Banda Sea
Kepulauan Damar
Pulau Yamdenu
Kepulauan Aru
New Guinea
Probolinggo
Jember
Denpasar
Raba
Flores
Kepulauan Tanimbar
Bali
Endeh
EAST TIMOR
Arafura Sea
10°
Pulau Sumba
Kupang
Timor

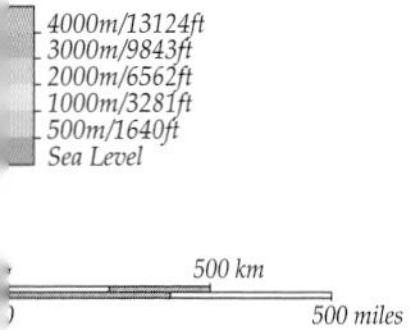
4000m/13124ft
3000m/9843ft
2000m/6562ft
1000m/3281ft
500m/1640ft
Sea Level
500 km
500 miles

INSIGHT: *Indonesia has a very youthful population: almost 30% of its people are under 15 years of age*

Iran

Since the 1979 Islamic fundamentalist revolution led by Ayatollah Khomeini, the Middle Eastern country of Iran has been the world's largest theocracy.

GEOGRAPHY

High desert plateau with large salt pans in the east. West and north are mountainous. Coastal land bordering Caspian Sea is rainy and forested.

CLIMATE

Desert climate. Hot summers, and bitterly cold winters. Area around the Caspian Sea is more temperate.

PEOPLE & SOCIETY

Many ethnic groups, including Persians, Azaris (ethnically related to Azeris), and Kurds. Militant Shi'a Islamism has dominated since the 1979 revolution. The mullahs' belief that adherence to religious values is more important than economic welfare has resulted in declining living standards. Female emancipation has been reversed. Student-backed demonstrations favoring greater liberalism have been suppressed.

THE ECONOMY

A leading oil producer: 80% of exports. Government restricts contact with the West, blocking acquisition of vital technology. High unemployment and inflation. Sizable black market.

INSIGHT: *More than a hundred offenses carry the death penalty*

40° AZERBAIJAN
TURKMENISTAN
TURKEY
Tabriz
Ardabīl
Caspian Sea
Orūmīyeh
Mashhad
TEHRĀN
35°
Qom
Kermānshāh
Arāk
Zagros Mountains
Iranian Plateau
AFGHANIST
45°
Eşfahān
IRAQ
Ahvāz
Khorramshahr
Kermān
30°
Ābādān
KUWAIT
Shīrāz
Zāhedān
PAKISTA
50°
Persian Gulf
Bandar-e 'Abbās
55°
60°
3000m/9843ft
2000m/6562ft
1000m/3281ft
500m/1640ft
200m/656ft
Sea Level
0 200 km
0 200 miles

FACTFILE

OFFICIAL NAME: Islamic Republic of Iran
DATE OF FORMATION: 1502
CAPITAL: Tehran
POPULATION: 74.2 million
TOTAL AREA: 636,293 sq. miles (1,648,000 sq. km)
DENSITY: 117 people per sq. mile
LANGUAGES: Farsi*, Azeri, Luri, Gilaki, Mazanderani, Kurdish, Turkmen, Arabic
RELIGIONS: Shi'a Muslim 93%, Sunni Muslim 6%, other 1%
ETHNIC MIX: Persian 50%, Azari 24%, other 10%, Kurd 8%, Lur and Bakhtiari 8%
GOVERNMENT: Islamic theocracy
CURRENCY: Iranian rial = 100 dinars

Iraq

Oil-rich Iraq is situated in the central Middle East. The last 50 years have been dominated by dictatorship, war, and civil strife. A US-led Coalition ousted Saddam Hussein in April 2003.

الله اكبر

GEOGRAPHY

Mainly desert. The Tigris and Euphrates rivers water fertile regions and create the southern marshland. Mountains along northeast border.

CLIMATE

Southern deserts have hot, dry summers and mild winters. North has dry summers, but winters can be harsh in the mountains. Rainfall is low.

PEOPLE & SOCIETY

Carved out of remnants of the Ottoman Empire, Iraq is home to Arab Muslims (mainly Shi'a, some Sunni), northern Kurds (who were persecuted under Saddam's regime), and smaller minorities. Since Saddam's removal, sectarian violence has overshadowed the new democratic state. Now that security is improving, Coalition forces are pulling out. After years of war and sanctions, poverty is widespread.

THE ECONOMY

Economy and infrastructure have been destroyed. Given stability and aid for reconstruction, hopes of recovery rest on massive oil reserves.

INSIGHT: *As Mesopotamia, Iraq was the site where the Sumerians established the world's first civilization*

0 100 km
0 100 miles
TURKEY
Al Mawşil
Arbīl
36°
As Sulaymānīyah
SYRIA
Kirkūk
Tigris
IRAN
40°
Euphrates
Buḩayrat ath Tharthār
Ba'qūbah
Ar Ramādī
BAGHDAD
Syrian Desert
JORDAN
Karbalā'
32°
Al 'Amārah
An Najaf
Euphrates
Tigris
SAUDI ARABIA
An Nāşirīyah
Al Başrah
30°
KUWAIT
44°
48°
3000m/9843ft
2000m/6562ft
1000m/3281ft
500m/1640ft
200m/656ft
Sea Level

FACTFILE

OFFICIAL NAME: Republic of Iraq
DATE OF FORMATION: 1932
CAPITAL: Baghdad
POPULATION: 30.7 million
TOTAL AREA: 168,753 sq. miles (437,072 sq. km)
DENSITY: 182 people per sq. mile
LANGUAGES: Arabic*, Kurdish, Turkic languages, Armenian, Assyrian
RELIGIONS: Shi'a Muslim 60%, Sunni Muslim 35%, other 5%
ETHNIC MIX: Arab 80%, Kurdish 15%, Turkmen 3%, other 2%
GOVERNMENT: Parliamentary system
CURRENCY: New Iraqi dinar = 1000 fils

Ireland

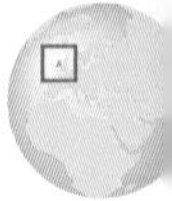

In the Atlantic Ocean off the west coast of Britain, the Irish Republic governs about 85% of the island of Ireland, with the remainder (Northern Ireland) being part of the UK.

GEOGRAPHY

Low mountain ranges along an irregular coastline surround an inland plain punctuated by lakes, undulating hills, and peat bogs.

CLIMATE

The Gulf Stream accounts for the mild and wet climate. Snow is rare, except in the mountains.

PEOPLE & SOCIETY

Though homogeneous in ethnicity and Roman Catholic by religion, society has undergone a major generational change, liberalizing birth control, divorce, abortion, and general attitudes. Traditionally an emigrant nation, there is now net immigration. The Good Friday peace agreement over Northern Ireland was reached in 1998.

INSIGHT: *About 40% of Irish people can speak Irish Gaelic*

THE ECONOMY

Strong growth until 2008, when housing bubble burst and banks faltered. Struggling to cut budget deficit. Skilled workforce. Efficient agriculture, food-processing, and electronics industries.

1000m/3281ft
500m/1640ft
200m/656ft
Sea Level
Donegal
Donegal Bay
UNITED KINGDOM (Northern Ireland)
Sligo
54°
Dundalk
Irish Sea
Westport
Mullingar
Athlone
Galway
DUBLIN
Dún Laoghaire
Shannon Airport
Shannon
Lough Derg
Wicklow Mts.
ATLANTIC OCEAN
Limerick
Kilkenny
Tipperary
Wexford
Tralee
Clonmel
Waterford
Killarney
52°
Cork
Celtic Sea
6°
8°
10°
0 50 km
0 50 miles

FACTFILE

OFFICIAL NAME: Ireland
DATE OF FORMATION: 1922
CAPITAL: Dublin
POPULATION: 4.52 million
TOTAL AREA: 27,135 sq. miles (70,280 sq. km)
DENSITY: 170 people per sq. mile
LANGUAGES: English*, Irish Gaelic*
RELIGIONS: Roman Catholic 88%, other and nonreligious 9%, Anglican 3%
ETHNIC MIX: Irish 99%, other 1%
GOVERNMENT: Parliamentary system
CURRENCY: Euro = 100 cents

Israel

Created as a new state in 1948, Israel lies on the eastern Mediterranean. The current phase of the Palestinian intifada (armed struggle) against Israeli occupation began in 2000.

GEOGRAPHY

Coastal plain. Desert in the south. In the east lie the Great Rift Valley and the Dead Sea – the lowest point on the Earth's land surface.

CLIMATE

Summers are hot and dry. Wet season, March–November, is mild.

PEOPLE & SOCIETY

Large numbers of Jews settled in Palestine before Israel was founded in 1948. After World War II, there was a massive increase in immigration. Sephardi Jews from the Middle East and Mediterranean are now in the majority, but Ashkenazi Jews from central Europe still dominate business and politics. Palestinians in Gaza and Jericho gained limited autonomy in 1994 but their desire, backed by most of the world, for a separate state has led to years of fierce violence.

THE ECONOMY

High-tech industries, modern infrastructure and educated workforce, but hampered by conflict and boycotts.

INSIGHT: *All Jews worldwide have the right to Israeli citizenship*

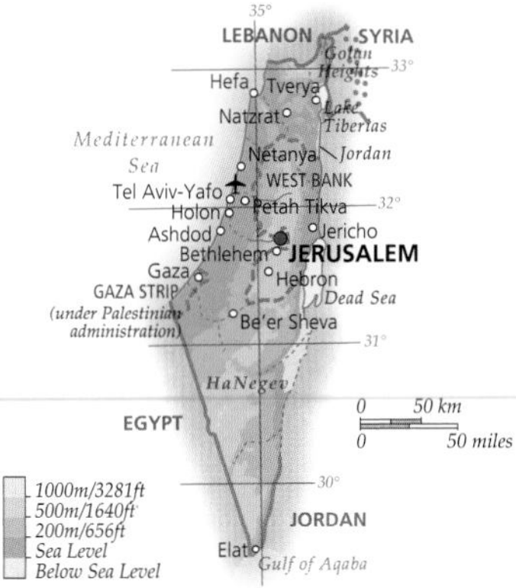
35°
LEBANON
SYRIA
Golan Heights
33°
Hefa
Tverya
Natzrat
Lake Tiberias
Mediterranean Sea
Netanya
Jordan
WEST BANK
Tel Aviv-Yafo
Holon
Petah Tikva
32°
Ashdod
Jericho
Bethlehem
JERUSALEM
Gaza
Hebron
GAZA STRIP
(under Palestinian administration)
Dead Sea
Be'er Sheva
31°
HaNegev
EGYPT
0 50 km
0 50 miles
30°
JORDAN
Elat
Gulf of Aqaba
1000m/3281ft
500m/1640ft
200m/656ft
Sea Level
Below Sea Level

FACTFILE

OFFICIAL NAME: State of Israel
DATE OF FORMATION: 1948
CAPITAL: Jerusalem (unrecognized by UN)
POPULATION: 7.17 million
TOTAL AREA: 8019 sq. miles (20,770 sq. km)
DENSITY: 913 people per sq. mile
LANGUAGES: Hebrew*, Arabic*, Yiddish, German, Russian, Polish, other
RELIGIONS: Jewish 76%, Muslim (mainly Sunni) 16%, other 6%, Christian 2%
ETHNIC MIX: Jewish 76%, other (mostly Arab) 24%
GOVERNMENT: Parliamentary system
CURRENCY: Shekel = 100 agorot

Italy

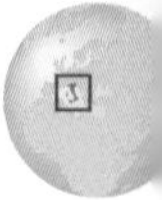

The Italian peninsula was home to the Roman Empire, one of the greatest ancient civilizations. The south has two famous volcanoes, Vesuvius and Etna.

GEOGRAPHY

The Appennines form the backbone of a rugged peninsula, extending from the Alps into the Mediterranean Sea. Alluvial plain in the north.

CLIMATE

Mediterranean in the south. Seasonal extremes in the mountains and on the northern alluvial plain.

PEOPLE & SOCIETY

Ethnically homogeneous, but with a gulf between the prosperous, industrial north and the poorer, agricultural south. Strong regional identities persist, especially on Sicily and Sardinia. Family ties remain strong, though the influence of the Roman Catholic Church has lessened.

INSIGHT: *Italy was a collection of dukedoms, monarchies, and city-states before unification in the 1860s*

THE ECONOMY

World leader in industrial and product design, fashion, textiles. Strong tourism and agriculture sectors. Large public sector debt.

3000m/9843ft
2000m/6562ft
1000m/3281ft
500m/1640ft
200m/656ft
Sea Level
SWITZERLAND
AUSTRIA
SLOVENIA
FRANCE
Bolzano
Milano
Verona
Trieste
Torino
Venezia
Parma
Golfo di Venezia
Genova
Bologna
Rimini
SAN MARINO
Pisa
Firenze
Ancona
Perugia
Adriatic Sea
ROME
VATICAN CITY
Bari
Sassari
Napoli
Taranto
Lecce
Salerno
Sardegna (Sardinia)
Tyrrhenian Sea
Ionian Sea
Cagliari
Cosenza
Messina
Mediterranean Sea
Palermo
Sicilia (Sicily)
Siracusa
45°
40°
15°
100 km
100 miles

FACTFILE

OFFICIAL NAME: Italian Republic
DATE OF FORMATION: 1861
CAPITAL: Rome
POPULATION: 59.9 million
TOTAL AREA: 116,305 sq. miles (301,230 sq. km)
DENSITY: 527 people per sq. mile
LANGUAGES: Italian*, German, French, Rhaeto-Romanic, Sardinian
RELIGIONS: Roman Catholic 85%, other and nonreligious 13%, Muslim 2%
ETHNIC MIX: Italian 94%, other 4%, Sardinian 2%
GOVERNMENT: Parliamentary system
CURRENCY: Euro = 100 cents

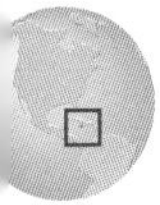

Jamaica

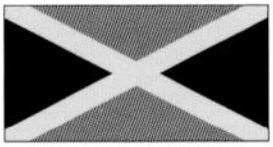

First colonized by the Spanish and then by the English, the Caribbean island of Jamaica achieved independence in 1962. It remains an influential force in Caribbean politics.

GEOGRAPHY

Mainly mountainous, with lush tropical vegetation. Inaccessible limestone area in the northwest. Low, irregular coastal plains are broken by hills and plateaus.

CLIMATE

Tropical. Hot and humid at sea level, with temperate mountain areas. Hurricanes are likely June–November.

PEOPLE & SOCIETY

Social tensions result from vast disparities in wealth, rather than race. Economic and political life is dominated by a few wealthy, long-established families. Many women hold senior positions in public life. Armed crime, much of it narcotics-related, is a problem. Large areas of Kingston, which have their own patois, are ruled by violent gangs. Jamaican music styles are influential worldwide.

THE ECONOMY

Major bauxite producer, though sector suffering from low world prices. Tourism and light industry. Sugar, bananas, coffee, and rum are exported. Debt burden dominates budget. High underemployment.

INSIGHT: *Jamaica's Rastafarians revere the late emperor of Ethiopia, Haile Selassie, as their spiritual leader, and see Africa as their spiritual home*

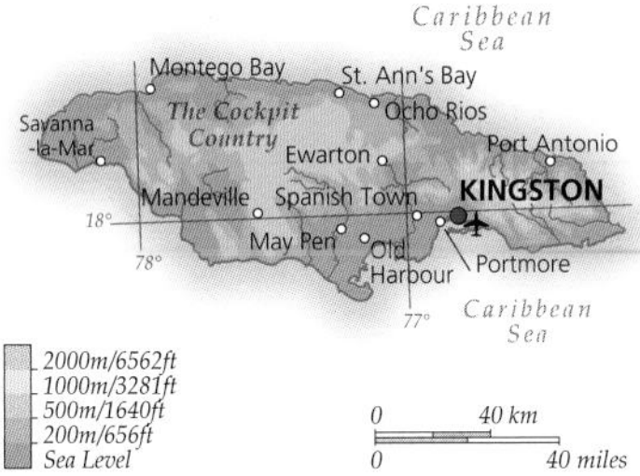
Caribbean Sea
Montego Bay
St. Ann's Bay
Ocho Rios
The Cockpit Country
Savanna -la-Mar
Ewarton
Port Antonio
Mandeville
Spanish Town
KINGSTON
18°
May Pen
Old Harbour
Portmore
78°
77°
Caribbean Sea
2000m/6562ft
1000m/3281ft
500m/1640ft
200m/656ft
Sea Level
0
40 km
0
40 miles

FACTFILE

OFFICIAL NAME: Jamaica
DATE OF FORMATION: 1962
CAPITAL: Kingston
POPULATION: 2.72 million
TOTAL AREA: 4243 sq. miles (10,990 sq. km)
DENSITY: 650 people per sq. mile
LANGUAGES: English Creole, English*
RELIGIONS: Protestant 55%, other and nonreligious 45%
ETHNIC MIX: Black African 92%, Mulatto 6%, European and Chinese 1%, East Indian 1%
GOVERNMENT: Parliamentary system
CURRENCY: Jamaican dollar = 100 cents

Japan

Japan is located off the east Asian coast and comprises four principal islands and over 3000 smaller ones. A powerful economy, it has an emperor as ceremonial head of state.

GEOGRAPHY

The terrain is predominantly mountainous, with fertile coastal plains; over two-thirds is woodland. There is no single continuous mountain range; the mountains divide into many small land blocks separated by lowlands and dissected by numerous river valleys. The islands lie on the Pacific "Ring of Fire," and earthquakes and volcanic eruptions are frequent. The Pacific coast is vunerable to *tsunamis*. There are numerous hot springs.

CLIMATE

Generally temperate–oceanic. Spring is warm and sunny, while summer is hot and humid, with high rainfall. In western Hokkaido and northwest Honshu, winters are very cold, with heavy snowfall. Freak storms and damaging floods in recent years have raised concern over global climate changes.

PEOPLE & SOCIETY

One of the most racially homogeneous societies in the world. A sense of order and social structure was founded on a strongly ingrained respect for elders and social superiors. In business, this underpinned the now much-diluted "lifetime employer" concept, where company allegiance determined social life as well as career. There is little tradition of generational rebellion, but the youth market is powerful and current fashions focus on teenagers. The education system is highly pressurized. Nongraduates have difficulty reaching management-level jobs, so competition for university places is intense. Long-term jobs for women are now the norm. One of the world's best healthcare systems and increased longevity have led to an aging population with one in five people already over 65. The cost of living is high, especially in Tokyo.

FACTFILE

OFFICIAL NAME: Japan
DATE OF FORMATION: 1590
CAPITAL: Tokyo
POPULATION: 127 million
TOTAL AREA: 145,882 sq. miles (377,835 sq. km)
DENSITY: 875 people per sq. mile
LANGUAGES: Japanese*, Korean, Chinese
RELIGIONS: Shinto and Buddhist 76%, Buddhist 16%, other (including Christian) 8%
ETHNIC MIX: Japanese 99%, other (mainly Korean) 1%
GOVERNMENT: Parliamentary system
CURRENCY: Yen = 100 sen

THE ECONOMY

World's second-largest economy. stablished market leader in high-tech lectronic goods and cars. Talent for leveloping ideas from abroad. Global pread of business – especially to EU, US. Once-revolutionary management and production methods. Long-term research nd development. Largest coal importer. Trade surplus causes international tension. Protectionism in domestic economy. Much-needed reform of financial sector has been obstructed by traditional economic power brokers. Significant id donor.

INSIGHT: *The Japanese are among the world's most avid newspaper readers, with daily sales exceeding 70 million copies*

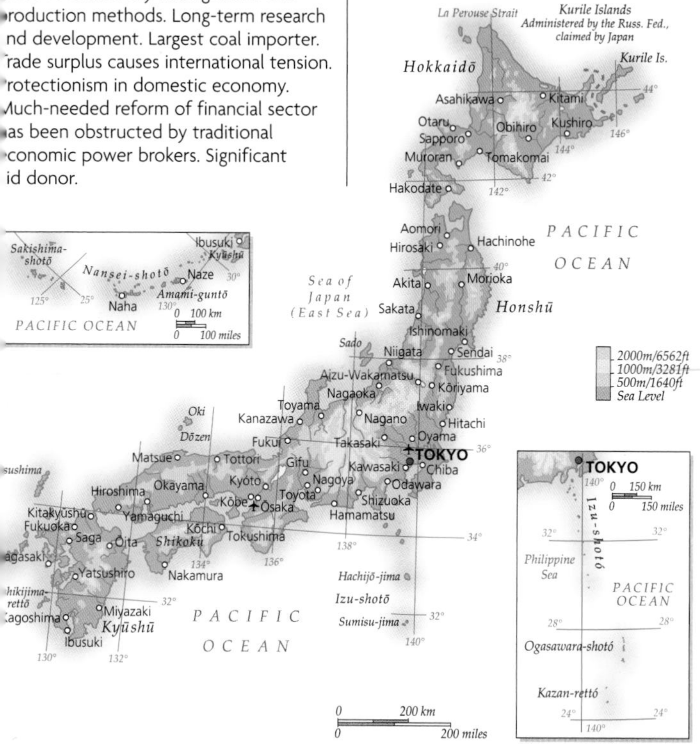

La Perouse Strait
Kurile Islands
Administered by the Russ. Fed., claimed by Japan
Kurile Is.
Hokkaidō
Asahikawa
Kitami
Otaru
Sapporo
Obihiro
Kushiro
Muroran
Tomakomai
Hakodate
Aomori
Hirosaki
Hachinohe
PACIFIC OCEAN
Akita
Morioka
Sea of Japan (East Sea)
Sakata
Honshū
Ishinomaki
Sado
Niigata
Sendai
Aizu-Wakamatsu
Fukushima
Nagaoka
Kōriyama
Toyama
Iwaki
Oki
Kanazawa
Nagano
Hitachi
Dōzen
Fukui
Takasaki
Oyama
Matsue
Tottori
Gifu
TOKYO
Kawasaki
Chiba
Hiroshima
Okayama
Kyōto
Nagoya
Odawara
Kōbe
Toyota
Ōsaka
Shizuoka
Kitakyūshū
Yamaguchi
Hamamatsu
Fukuoka
Kōchi
Tokushima
Saga
Ōita
Shikoku
Nakamura
Yatsushiro
Miyazaki
Kyūshū
Ibusuki
PACIFIC OCEAN
Hachijō-jima
Izu-shotō
Sumisu-jima
Sakishima-shotō
Nansei-shotō
Naze
Ibusuki
Kyūshū
Amami-guntō
Naha
0 100 km
0 100 miles
2000m/6562ft
1000m/3281ft
500m/1640ft
Sea Level
TOKYO
0 150 km
0 150 miles
Izu-shotō
Philippine Sea
PACIFIC OCEAN
Ogasawara-shotó
Kazan-rettó
0 200 km
0 200 miles

Jordan

The Kingdom of Jordan lies east of Israel, and borders the Palestinian West Bank. Its relations with its Arab neighbors are troubled by its relatively close ties to the US.

GEOGRAPHY

Mostly desert plateaus, with occasional salt pans. Lowest parts lie along the eastern shores of the Dead Sea and the Jordan River.

CLIMATE

Hot, dry summers. Cool, wet winters. Areas below sea level very hot in summer, and warm in winter.

PEOPLE & SOCIETY

Jordan is predominantly Muslim with a strong national identity, but its people have Bedouin roots. There is a Christian minority, while Palestinians who have emigrated from Israeli-occupied territory make up a third of the population. Jordan ceded its claim to the West Bank to the aspiring Palestinian state in 1988. The monarchy's power base lies among the rural tribes, which also provide the backbone of the military.

THE ECONOMY

Lack of water. Exports garments, potash, fertilizers, and phosphates. Tourism hit by regional instability.

INSIGHT: *The Nabataean ruins of the ancient city of Petra attract thousands of tourists every year*

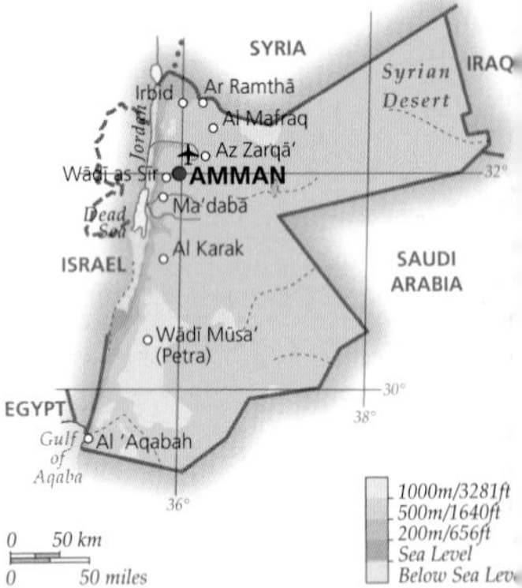
SYRIA
IRAQ
Syrian Desert
Irbid
Ar Ramthā
Al Mafraq
Jordan
Az Zarqā'
Wādī as Sīr
AMMAN
Ma'dabā
Dead Sea
ISRAEL
Al Karak
SAUDI ARABIA
Wādī Mūsā'
(Petra)
EGYPT
Gulf of Aqaba
Al 'Aqabah
32°
30°
38°
36°
0 50 km
0 50 miles
1000m/3281ft
500m/1640ft
200m/656ft
Sea Level
Below Sea Lev

FACTFILE

OFFICIAL NAME: Hashemite Kingdom of Jordan

DATE OF FORMATION: 1946

CAPITAL: Amman

POPULATION: 6.32 million

TOTAL AREA: 35,637 sq. miles (92,300 sq. km)

DENSITY: 184 people per sq. mile

LANGUAGES: Arabic

RELIGIONS: Muslim (mainly Sunni) 92%, other (mostly Christian) 8%

ETHNIC MIX: Arab 98%, Circassian 1%, Armenian 1%

GOVERNMENT: Monarchy

CURRENCY: Jordanian dinar = 1000 fils

Kazakhstan

Kazakhstan was the last of the former Soviet republics to declare independence. Foreign investment in he oil and natural gas sector is strengthening its regional power.

GEOGRAPHY

Mainly steppe. Volga Delta and :aspian Sea in the west. Central plateau. ıhospitable Altai Mountains in the east. emidesert in the south.

CLIMATE

Dry continental. Temperature ariations between desert south and orthern steppes are large. Winters are ıildest near the Caspian Sea.

PEOPLE & SOCIETY

Kazakhstan's ethnic diversity rose mainly from forced settlements ıere during Soviet times. Since ıdependence, the proportion of ethnic ussians has dropped. Many emigrated, vhile ethnic Kazakhs arrived from eighboring states. Very few Kazakhs ıaintain a traditional nomadic lifestyle, ut Islam and loyalty to clans remain trong. There are significant disparities f wealth.

THE ECONOMY

Vast mineral resources: natural gas, oil, bismuth, uranium, and cadmium. Oil pipelines to China and Black Sea. Many Western investors. Wheat exported. Sale of farmland only legal since 2003.

INSIGHT: *The Soviet-built Baykonyr space center is still an important launch site for international missions*

RUSS. FED.
RUSS. FED.
Kostanay
Rudnyy
Ural'sk
ASTANA
Irtysh
Kirghiz Steppe
Karaganda
Ust'-Kamenogorsk
Zhezkazgan
Ozero Balkhash
Caspian Sea
Baykonyr
Taldykorgan
Aktau
Syr Darya
Kyzylorda
Almaty
CHINA
Aral Sea
Taraz
UZBEK.
Shymkent
TURKMEN.
KYRGYZSTAN
3000m/9843ft
2000m/6562ft
1000m/3281ft
500m/1640ft
200m/656ft
Sea Level
Below Sea level
0 400 km
0 400 miles

FACTFILE

OFFICIAL NAME: Republic of Kazakhstan
DATE OF FORMATION: 1991
CAPITAL: Astana
POPULATION: 15.6 million
TOTAL AREA: 1,049,150 sq. miles (2,717,300 sq. km)
DENSITY: 15 people per sq. mile
LANGUAGES: Kazakh*, Russian, Ukrainian, Tatar, Uzbek, Uighur, other
RELIGIONS: Muslim (mainly Sunni) 47%, Orthodox Christian 44%, other 9%
ETHNIC MIX: Kazakh 57%, Russian 27%, other 10%, Ukrainian 3%, Uzbek 3%
GOVERNMENT: Presidential system
CURRENCY: Tenge = 100 tiyn

Kenya

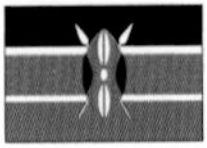

Kenya straddles the equator on Africa's east coast. After nearly 40 years in power, the KANU party was soundly defeated in elections in 2002. Corruption is a serious issue.

GEOGRAPHY

A central plateau is divided by the Great Rift Valley. North of the equator is mainly semidesert. To the east lies a fertile coastal belt.

CLIMATE

The coast and the Great Rift Valley are hot and humid. The plateau interior is temperate. The northeastern desert is hot and dry. Rain usually falls April–May and October–November.

PEOPLE & SOCIETY

70 ethnic groups share about 40 languages. Strong clan and family links in rural areas are being weakened by urban migration. Poverty, severe drought, and years of high population growth exacerbate ethnic tensions.

INSIGHT: *Kenya has more than 50 game reserves, national parks, and marine reservations*

THE ECONOMY

Tourism: image damaged by 2008 post-election violence. Flowers, tea, and coffee are cash crops. Needs food aid. Diversified manufacturing sector. Sizable informal economy.

SUDAN
Elemi Triangle
36°
ETHIOPIA
40°
4°
Lake Turkana
Great Rift Valley
Chalbi Desert
Marsabit
UGANDA
SOMALIA
Eldoret
Meru
Kisumu
Nakuru
Equator
Lake Victoria
Nyeri
Kericho
Thika
NAIROBI
Machakos
TANZANIA
Ungama Bay
Malindi
Mombasa
4°
INDIAN OCEAN
5000m/16405ft
4000m/13124ft
3000m/9843ft
2000m/6562ft
1000m/3281ft
500m/1640ft
200m/656ft
Sea Level
0 100 km
0 100 miles

FACTFILE

OFFICIAL NAME: Republic of Kenya
DATE OF FORMATION: 1963
CAPITAL: Nairobi
POPULATION: 39.8 million
TOTAL AREA: 224,961 sq. miles (582,650 sq. km)
DENSITY: 182 people per sq. mile
LANGUAGES: Kiswahili*, English*, other
RELIGIONS: Christian 60%, traditional beliefs 25%, other 9%, Muslim 6%
ETHNIC MIX: Other 42%, Kikuyu 20%, Luhya 14%, Luo 13%, Kalenjin 11%
GOVERNMENT: Mixed presidential–parliamentary system
CURRENCY: Kenya shilling = 100 cents

Kiribati

Situated in the mid-Pacific, the islands adopted the name Kiribati (pronounced "Keer-ee-bus," a corruption of their former name "Gilberts") upon independence from Britain in 1979.

GEOGRAPHY

Kiribati consists of three groups of tiny, very low-lying coral atolls scattered across 1,930,000 sq. miles (5 million sq. km) of ocean. Most of the 33 atolls have central lagoons.

CLIMATE

Central islands have a maritime equatorial climate. Those to north and south are tropical, with constant high temperatures. There is little rainfall.

PEOPLE & SOCIETY

Officially I-Kiribati, many local people still refer to themselves as Gilbertese. Almost all are Micronesian, apart from the inhabitants of the island of Banaba, who employed anthropologists to establish their racial distinction. Most people are poor subsistence farmers and many travel abroad to work. The islands are effectively ruled by traditional chiefs.

THE ECONOMY

Since exhaustion of Banaba's phosphate deposits in 1980, copra (dried coconut) and fish have become the main exports. Foreign aid and remittances are vital to compensate for Kiribati's isolation and lack of resources.

INSIGHT: *In 1981, the UK paid A$10 million to Banabans for the destruction of their island by mining*

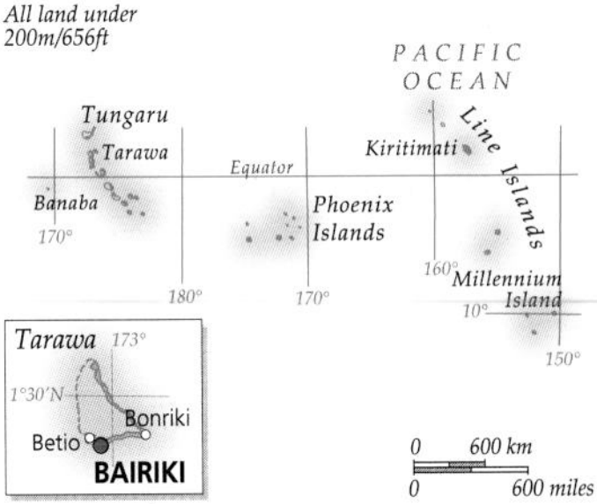
All land under 200m/656ft
PACIFIC OCEAN
Tungaru
Tarawa
Banaba
170°
Equator
180°
Phoenix Islands
170°
Kiritimati
Line Islands
160°
Millennium Island
10°
150°
Tarawa 173°
1°30′N
Bonriki
Betio
BAIRIKI
0 600 km
0 600 miles

FACTFILE

OFFICIAL NAME: Republic of Kiribati
DATE OF FORMATION: 1979
CAPITAL: Bairiki (Tarawa Atoll)
POPULATION: 99,000
TOTAL AREA: 277 sq. miles (717 sq. km)
DENSITY: 361 people per sq. mile
LANGUAGES: English*, Kiribati
RELIGIONS: Roman Catholic 53%, Kiribati Protestant Church 39%, other 8%
ETHNIC MIX: Micronesian 99%, other 1%
GOVERNMENT: Nonparty system
CURRENCY: Australian dollar = 100 cents

North Korea

Separated from the democratic South by the world's most heavily defended border, the Stalinist North Korean state has been isolated from the outside world since 1948.

GEOGRAPHY

Mostly mountainous, with fertile plains in the southwest.

CLIMATE

Continental. Warm summers and cold winters, especially in the north, where snow is common.

PEOPLE & SOCIETY

Life is heavily regulated. Cult of personality is more powerful than the state-controlled religions, which include Korea's own Chondogyo. Women are expected to work and to run the home. Children are looked after in state-run crèches. The Korean Worker's Party is the sole party. Its elite have a privileged lifestyle. Globally condemned for its nuclear weapons development, its grip on power perpetuates its pariah status.

INSIGHT: *Only the political elite are allowed phones and private cars*

THE ECONOMY

Minerals are only resource. Vital aid streams lost with global collapse of communism after 1989. Decades of economic mismanagement have led to chronic food shortages. Lack of fuel. Disproportionate defense budget.

2000m/6562ft
1000m/3281ft
500m/1640ft
200m/656ft
Sea Level
CHINA
RUSS FED
42°
Ch'ŏngjin
Kanggye
130°
Kimch'aek
Hŭich'ŏn
Sinŭiju
Hamhŭng
Iwŏn
40°
Hŭngnam
124°
Korea Bay
Wŏnsan
Sea of Japan (East Sea)
PYONGYANG
Namp'o
Haeju
SOUTH KOREA
38°
Kaesŏng
Yellow Sea
126°
128°
0 50 km
0 50 miles

FACTFILE

OFFICIAL NAME: Democratic People's Republic of Korea
DATE OF FORMATION: 1948
CAPITAL: Pyongyang
POPULATION: 23.9 million
TOTAL AREA: 46,540 sq. miles (120,540 sq. km)
DENSITY: 514 people per sq. mile
LANGUAGES: Korean*, Chinese
RELIGIONS: Government-controlled religions include Chondogyo, Buddhism, and Christianity
ETHNIC MIX: Korean 100%
GOVERNMENT: One-party state
CURRENCY: N. Korean won = 100 chon

South Korea

South Korea occupies the southern half of the Korean peninsula. Under US sponsorship, it was separated from the communist North in 1948 and is now a capitalist economy.

GEOGRAPHY

Over 80% is mountainous and two-hirds is forested. The flattest and most opulous parts lie along the west coast nd in the extreme south.

CLIMATE

There are four distinct seasons. Vinters are dry, and bitterly cold. ummers are hot and humid.

PEOPLE & SOCIETY

Inhabited for the last 2000 years by single ethnic group. The nuclear family s replacing traditional extended ouseholds. Since the 1953 armistice, the Coreas have remained technically at war. Reunification is the ultimate goal, but in 009 the South became less conciliatory nd the North retaliated by ending its offer of cooperation.

INSIGHT: *Half of all Koreans are named Kim, Lee, Park, or Choi*

THE ECONOMY

World's biggest shipbuilder. High-tech goods and cars: rising demand from China. Strong regional competition. Aging population.

0 50 km
0 50 miles
NORTH KOREA
128°
126°
Sea of Japan (East Sea)
38°
Kangnŭng
Tonghae
SEOUL
Inch'ŏn
Sŏngnam
Suwŏn
Yellow Sea
Taejŏn
36°
Kunsan
Taegu
Ulsan
Kwangju
Masan
Pusan
Korea Strait
Mokp'o
Yŏsu
34°
Cheju Strait
Cheju
Cheju-do
1000m/3281ft
500m/1640ft
200m/656ft
Sea Level

FACTFILE

OFFICIAL NAME: Republic of Korea
DATE OF FORMATION: 1948
CAPITAL: Seoul
POPULATION: 48.3 million
TOTAL AREA: 38,023 sq. miles (98,480 sq. km)
DENSITY: 1268 people per sq. mile
LANGUAGES: Korean*, Chinese
RELIGIONS: Mahayana Buddhist 47%, Protestant 38%, Roman Catholic 11%, Confucianist 3%, other 1%
ETHNIC MIX: Korean 100%
GOVERNMENT: Presidential system
CURRENCY: South Korean won = 100 chon

Kosovo

Once part of the former Yugoslav state, Kosovo seceded from Serbia in 2008. International recognition, mainly from Western countries, is strongly opposed by Serbia and Russia.

GEOGRAPHY

Landlocked and mountainous, with two plains in the east and west.

CLIMATE

Continental, with warm, sunny summers and cold, snowy winters.

PEOPLE & SOCIETY

The balance of Albanians to Serbs in Kosovo has changed dramatically over centuries, both groups suffering interethnic violence at various times. Attacks against Albanians in the late 1990s caused a million to flee. After NATO stepped in, many Serbs left: Albanians now form a 92% majority. Most Albanians are Muslim. Serbs dominate three northern provinces, which have threatened to secede.

INSIGHT: *The UN administered Kosovo in 1999–2008 after NATO intervention to stop Serb ethnic cleansing*

THE ECONOMY

One of the two poorest countries in Europe. Aid and remittances cover a large trade deficit. Organized crime: smuggling of fuel, cigarettes, and cemen Uncertain status deters foreign investors High unemployment. Use of euro has kept inflation low. Lignite deposits. Inefficient agriculture.

SERBIA
MONT.
ALBANIA
MACEDONIA
Mokra Gora
Mitrovicë
Peje
Vushtrri
Kamenicë
PRISTINA
Deçan
Klinë
Gjilan
Gjakovë
Ferizaj
Prizren
21°
20°
22°
43°
42°
1000m/3281ft
500m/1640ft
200m/656ft
0
50 km
0
50 miles

FACTFILE

OFFICIAL NAME: Republic of Kosovo
DATE OF FORMATION: 2008
CAPITAL: Pristina
POPULATION: 2.1 million
TOTAL AREA: 4212 sq. miles (10,908 sq. km)
DENSITY: 499 people per sq. mile
LANGUAGES: Albanian*, Serbian*, Bosniak, Gorani, Roma, Turkish
RELIGIONS: Muslim 92%, Roman Catholic 4%, Orthodox Christian 4%
ETHNIC MIX: Albanian 92%, Serb 4%, Bosniak and Gorani 2%, other 2%
GOVERNMENT: Parliamentary system
CURRENCY: Euro = 100 cents

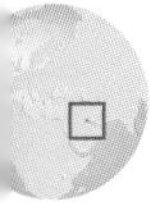

Kuwait

Kuwait lies at the northwest tip of the Gulf, dwarfed by its neighbors Iraq, Iran, and Saudi Arabia. It was a British protectorate until 1961, when full independence was granted.

GEOGRAPHY

Terrain is low-lying desert. The owest land is in the north. Cultivation is only possible along the coast.

CLIMATE

Summers are very hot and dry. Vinters are cooler, with some rain and occasional frost at night.

PEOPLE & SOCIETY

Oil-rich monarchy, ruled by the l-Sabah family. It is a conservative Sunni Muslim society, but women are relatively ree. Nonetheless, a 1999 decree giving vomen the vote was blocked for six ears in parliament by Islamic raditionalists. Immigrant workers, from other Arab states, India, and Pakistan, now outnumber native citizens. US-led orces rescued Kuwait after the 1990 raqi invasion, and later used it as a aunchpad for the 2003 invasion to oust Saddam Hussein.

THE ECONOMY

Oil and natural gas dominate the economy. Skilled workforce, raw materials, and food are imported. High standard of living. Financial services: stock market lost 40% of value in 2008.

INSIGHT: *During the 1991 Gulf War, Iraq deliberately set fire to 800 of Kuwait's 950 oil wells*

0 25 km
0 25 miles
IRAQ
30°
48°
Jazīrat Būbīyān
Jāl al-Liyāh
Shiqqat al Qalīb
Al Bahrah
Persian Gulf
KUWAIT CITY
Al Jahrā'
As Salimiyah
As Salmī
Qalib ash Shuyūkh
Al Fuhayhīl
Al Ahmadī
Aş Şubayhīyah
SAUDI ARABIA
Ash Shuqayq
Al Wafrā'
200m/656ft
Sea Level

FACTFILE

OFFICIAL NAME: State of Kuwait
DATE OF FORMATION: 1961
CAPITAL: Kuwait City
POPULATION: 2.99 million
TOTAL AREA: 6880 sq. miles (17,820 sq. km)
DENSITY: 434 people per sq. mile
LANGUAGES: Arabic*, English
RELIGIONS: Sunni Muslim 45%, Shi'a Muslim 40%, Christian, Hindu, and other 15%
ETHNIC MIX: Kuwaiti 45%, other Arab 35%, South Asian 9%, other 11%
GOVERNMENT: Monarchy
CURRENCY: Kuwaiti dinar = 1000 fils

Kyrgyzstan

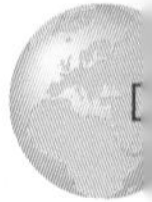

A small and mountainous landlocked state in central Asia, Kyrgyzstan is one of the least urbanized ex-Soviet republic and was slow to develop its own sense of cultural identity.

GEOGRAPHY

The mountainous spurs of the Tien Shan range contain glaciers, alpine meadows, forests, and narrow valleys. Semidesert in the west.

CLIMATE

Varies from permanent snow and cold deserts at high altitudes, to hot deserts in low regions.

PEOPLE & SOCIETY

Ethnic Kyrgyz have only been in the majority since the late 1980s – due to a high birth rate and the emigration of ethnic Russians. Wary of losing skills vital to the economy, the government has attempted to deter Russians from leaving; concessions include making Russian an official language. There are some tensions between Kyrgyz and Uzbeks, and a trend toward greater Islamization, particularly in the poorer south.

THE ECONOMY

Mainly still under state control; corruption issues. Agriculture employs half of the labor force. Cotton, wool, meat, and tobacco exports. Mercury, gold, and antimony are mined. Great potential for hydroelectric power.

INSIGHT: *Kyrgyz folklore is based around the 1000-year-old poem, Manas which takes a week to recite*

KAZAKHSTAN
76°
72°
BISHKEK
Tokmak
Ozero
Issyk-Kul'
Talas
Kara-Balta
Issyk-Kul'
Tien Shan
42°
Naryn
Dzhalal-Abad
UZBEKISTAN
Osh
CHINA
40°
Sulyukta
TAJIKISTAN
0 100 km
0 100 miles
3000m/9843ft
2000m/6562ft
1000m/3281ft
500m/1640ft

FACTFILE

OFFICIAL NAME: Kyrgyz Republic
DATE OF FORMATION: 1991
CAPITAL: Bishkek
POPULATION: 5.48 million
TOTAL AREA: 76,641 sq. miles (198,500 sq. km)
DENSITY: 72 people per sq. mile
LANGUAGES: Kyrgyz*, Russian*, other
RELIGIONS: Muslim (mainly Sunni) 70%, Orthodox Christian 30%
ETHNIC MIX: Kyrgyz 65%, Uzbek 14%, Russian 13%, other 6%, Dungan 1%, Ukrainian 1%
GOVERNMENT: Presidential system
CURRENCY: Som = 100 tyiyn

Laos

A French colony prior to 1953, Laos lies landlocked in southeast Asia. Heavily bombed during the Vietnam War, it fell in 1975 to communist insurgents, whose regime remains in power.

GEOGRAPHY

Largely forested mountains, ·oadening in the north to a plateau. ›wlands along the Mekong Valley.

CLIMATE

Monsoon rains September–May. ne rest of the year is hot and dry.

PEOPLE & SOCIETY

There are over 60 ethnic groups. ›wland Laotians (Lao Loum) live along ıe Mekong River and are rice farmers. pland and highland Laotians (Lao neung and Lao Soung) traditionally nploy environmentally damaging ash-and-burn farming, and grow egal cash crops (notably opium). overnment efforts to reform these ·actices are resisted.

INSIGHT: *Three small Laotian kingdoms were unified under ·ench control in 1899*

THE ECONOMY

One of world's least developed nations. Poor infrastructure. Gold, copper, electricity, timber, garments, and coffee are exported. Levels of foreign investment are rising.

0 100 km
0 100 miles
CHINA
22°
Phôngsali
MYANMAR (BURMA)
VIETNAM
Houayxay
Xam Nua
20°
Mekong
Louangphabang
Xaignabouli
Xiangkhoang
100°
THAILAND
Ban Naxon
Pakxan
VIENTIANE
18°
102°
Mekong
Thakhek
THAILAND
Khanthabouli
16°
Muang Khôngxédôn
Salavan
104°
Pakxé
14°
CAMBODIA
106°
2000m/6562ft
1000m/3281ft
500m/1640ft
200m/656ft
Sea Level

FACTFILE

OFFICIAL NAME: Lao People's Democratic Republic
DATE OF FORMATION: 1953
CAPITAL: Vientiane
POPULATION: 6.32 million
TOTAL AREA: 91,428 sq. miles (236,800 sq. km)
DENSITY: 71 people per sq. mile
LANGUAGES: Lao*, Mon-Khmer, other
RELIGIONS: Buddhist 85%, other (including animist) 15%
ETHNIC MIX: Lao Loum 66%, Lao Theung 30%, Lao Soung 2%, other 2%
GOVERNMENT: One-party state
CURRENCY: New kip = 100 at

Latvia

Latvia lies on the east coast of the Baltic Sea. Like its Baltic neighbors, it regained independence from Moscow in 1991, and joined the EU and NATO in 2004.

GEOGRAPHY

A flat coastal plain which is deeply indented by the Gulf of Riga. Poor drainage creates many bogs and swamps in the forested interior.

CLIMATE

Temperate, with warm summers and cold winters. There is steady rainfall throughout the year.

PEOPLE & SOCIETY

Latvians make up just over half of the population and are mostly Lutheran. They have been officially favored by the state since 1991 over the largely Orthodox Christian Russian minority. Latvian was declared the only official language in 2000 and has been used exclusively in schools since 2004. This discrimination has strained relations with neighboring Russia. Women enjoy full equality. The divorce rate is high.

THE ECONOMY

Services sector now accounts for over 70% of GDP. EU's fastest-growing economy in 2004–2006. High inflation has delayed prospect of joining euro. Global credit crunch brought Latvia to verge of bankruptcy in 2008: banks were bailed out and severe recession followed.

INSIGHT: *Ethnic Latvians are outnumbered by Russians in Riga*

Baltic Sea
ESTONIA
58°
Gulf of Riga
Valmiera
Ventspils
Cēsis
RIGA
Jūrmala
Western Dvina
Saldus
Dobele
Jelgava
Jēkabpils
Liepāja
56°
22°
24°
LITHUANIA
26°
Daugavpils
28°
BELARUS
200m/656ft
Sea Level
0 50 km
0 50 mi

FACTFILE

OFFICIAL NAME: Republic of Latvia
DATE OF FORMATION: 1991
CAPITAL: Riga
POPULATION: 2.25 million
TOTAL AREA: 24,938 sq. miles (64,589 sq. km)
DENSITY: 90 people per sq. mile
LANGUAGES: Latvian*, Russian
RELIGIONS: Lutheran 55%, Catholic 24%, other 12%, Orthodox Christian 9%
ETHNIC MIX: Latvian 59%, Russian 29%, Belarussian 4%, Ukrainian 3%, Polish 3%, other 2%
GOVERNMENT: Parliamentary system
CURRENCY: Lats = 100 santimi

Lebanon

Once a vibrant cultural hotspot, Lebanon suffered badly from years of civil war and occupation until a 1989 peace deal. Reconstruction was reversed by Israeli bombardment in 2006.

GEOGRAPHY

Behind a narrow Mediterranean oastal plain, two parallel mountain nges run the length of the country, eparated by the fertile Beqaa Valley.

CLIMATE

Winters are mild and summers are ot, with high coastal humidity. Snow alls on high ground in winter.

PEOPLE & SOCIETY

Politics has long been dominated y divisions between Sunni and Shi'a uslims and the traditional ruling aronite Christians. Power-sharing ended years of civil war in 1989. Syria acted s power broker until made to withdraw 2005. Israel attacked in 2006 in a otched bid to crush Iranian-backed ezbollah militants. A huge gulf exists etween the poor and a small, immensely ch elite. Lebanon hosts 420,000 alestinian refugees.

THE ECONOMY

Much infrastructure destroyed. Instability undermines Beirut's role as regional financial center. Wine and fruit production. High public debt.

INSIGHT: *The Cedar of Lebanon has been the nation's symbol for more than 2000 years*

Mediterranean
Sea
Tripoli
Zgharta
SYRIA
0 20 km
0 20 miles
Liban
Anti-Lebanon
Joûnié
Baalbek
34°
BEIRUT
Baabda
Zahlé
El Beqaa
SYRIA
Saïda
Nabatîyé
36°
Soûr
Golan
Heights
ISRAEL
33°
3000m/9843ft
2000m/6562ft
1000m/3281ft
500m/1640ft
200m/656ft
Sea Level

FACTFILE

OFFICIAL NAME: Republic of Lebanon
DATE OF FORMATION: 1941
CAPITAL: Beirut
POPULATION: 4.22 million
TOTAL AREA: 4015 sq. miles (10,400 sq. km)
DENSITY: 1069 people per sq. mile
LANGUAGES: Arabic*, French, Armenian, Assyrian
RELIGIONS: Muslim 70%, Christian 30%
ETHNIC MIX: Arab 94%, Armenian 4%, other 2%
GOVERNMENT: Parliamentary system
CURRENCY: Lebanese pound = 100 piastres

Lesotho

The landlocked Kingdom of Lesotho is entirely surrounded by – and economically dependent on – South Africa, which even sent in troops to restore calm after rioting in 1998.

GEOGRAPHY

A high mountainous plateau, cut by valleys and ravines. The Maluti Range runs through the center. The Drakensberg Range lies to the east.

CLIMATE

Temperate. Summers are hot with torrential rain storms. Snow is frequent in the mountains in winter.

PEOPLE & SOCIETY

The overwhelming majority of people are Sotho, though there are some South Asians, Europeans, and Chinese. A strong sense of national identity has tended to minimize ethnic tensions. Many men work as migrant laborers in South Africa, leaving women to run households.

INSIGHT: *Lesotho has one of the highest literacy rates in Africa – but one of the highest rates of HIV/AIDS too*

THE ECONOMY

Dependent on South Africa. Water and energy exported from new Highland Water Scheme. Subsistence farming. Garment exports struggle to compete. HIV/AIDS is depleting workforce.

Caledon
SOUTH AFRICA
29°
Hlotse
Teyateyaneng
MASERU
Mokhotlong
Maluti
Mantsonyane
Morija
Mafeteng
Drakensberg
30°
Orange River
Mohales Hoek
SOUTH AFRICA
29°
28°
3000m/9843ft
2000m/6562ft
1000m/3281ft
0 50 km
0 50 miles

FACTFILE

OFFICIAL NAME: Kingdom of Lesotho
DATE OF FORMATION: 1966
CAPITAL: Maseru
POPULATION: 2.07 million
TOTAL AREA: 11,720 sq. miles (30,355 sq. km)
DENSITY: 176 people per sq. mile
LANGUAGES: English*, Sesotho*, isiZulu
RELIGIONS: Christian 90%, traditional beliefs 10%
ETHNIC MIX: Sotho 97%, European and Asian 3%
GOVERNMENT: Parliamentary system
CURRENCY: Loti = 100 lisente

Liberia

Liberia, on Africa's Atlantic coast, was founded as a republic of freed slaves. A brutal coup in 1980 and years of civil war have left gang violence and looting widespread.

GEOGRAPHY

A coastline of beaches and ıangrove swamps rises to forested ateaus and highlands inland.

CLIMATE

High temperatures. There is only ne wet season, from May to October, xcept in the extreme southeast.

PEOPLE & SOCIETY

The key social distinction used to e between Americo-Liberians – escendants of freed slaves – and the ıdigenous tribal peoples. However, olitical assimilation and intermarriage ave eased tensions. Intertribal tension is ɔw a much more serious problem, ıeling the civil war which ravaged the ɔuntry from 1990 to 2003.

INSIGHT: *Liberia is named after the people liberated from slavery ʼho arrived from the US in the 1800s*

THE ECONOMY

War caused economic collapse. Rubber is key export. Bans now lifted on timber and diamond exports. Revenue from merchant shipping licenses. Debt burden. Income well below prewar levels. Vast iron ore reserves.

1000m/3281ft
500m/1640ft
200m/656ft
Sea Level
SIERRA LEONE
Voinjama
GUINEA
8°
Tubmanburg
Robertsport
Gbanga
CÔTE D'IVOIRE (IVORY COAST)
MONROVIA
Harbel
Zwedru
6°
Buchanan
ATLANTIC OCEAN
10°
Greenville
Harper
8°
0 50 km
0 50 miles

FACTFILE

OFFICIAL NAME: Republic of Liberia
DATE OF FORMATION: 1847
CAPITAL: Monrovia
POPULATION: 3.96 million
TOTAL AREA: 43,000 sq. miles (111,370 sq. km)
DENSITY: 106 people per sq. mile
LANGUAGES: Kpelle, Vai, Bassa, Kru, Grebo, Kissi, Gola, Loma, English*
RELIGIONS: Christian 68%, traditional beliefs 18%, Muslim 14%
ETHNIC MIX: Indigenous tribes (16 main groups) 95%, Americo-Liberians 5%
GOVERNMENT: Presidential system
CURRENCY: Liberian dollar = 100 cents

Libya

Situated on north Africa's Mediterranean coast, Libya was declared a revolutionary state in 1969 by Colonel Gaddafi, who promotes Islam, African unity, and a communal lifestyle.

GEOGRAPHY

Apart from the coastal strip and a mountain range in the south, Libya is desert or semidesert. Natural oases provide the agricultural land.

CLIMATE

Hot and arid. The coastal area has a temperate climate, with mild, wet winters and hot, dry summers.

PEOPLE & SOCIETY

Most Libyans are of Arab and Berber origin. Once a nation of nomads and livestock herders, it is almost 80% urban. Revolution wiped out private enterprise and the middle classes. Jews and European settlers were banished. Years of political marginalization and sanctions ended after Libya offered compensation for terrorist bombings. The voluntary ending of its Weapons of Mass Destruction (WMD) program was also welcomed by the West.

THE ECONOMY

Oil is key export. Dates, olives, and fruit grow in oases, but most food is imported. Corruption and mismanagement. High inflation.

INSIGHT: *90% of Libya is still desert, despite grand irrigation projects*

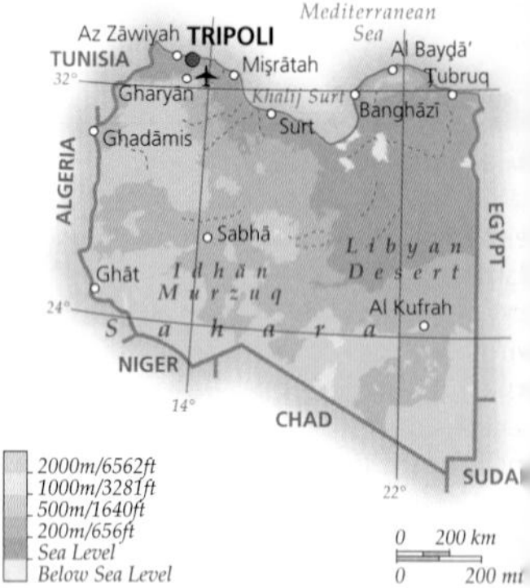
Mediterranean Sea
Az Zāwiyah
TRIPOLI
TUNISIA
Mişrātah
Al Bayḍā'
Tubruq
32°
Gharyān
Khalīj Surt
Banghāzī
Surt
Ghadāmis
ALGERIA
EGYPT
Sabhā
Libyan Desert
Ghāt
Idhān Murzuq
Al Kufrah
24°
Sahara
NIGER
14°
CHAD
SUDA
22°
2000m/6562ft
1000m/3281ft
500m/1640ft
200m/656ft
Sea Level
Below Sea Level
0 200 km
0 200 mi

FACTFILE

OFFICIAL NAME: Great Socialist People's Libyan Arab Jamahariyah
DATE OF FORMATION: 1951
CAPITAL: Tripoli
POPULATION: 6.42 million
TOTAL AREA: 679,358 sq. miles (1,759,540 sq. km)
DENSITY: 9 people per sq. mile
LANGUAGES: Arabic*, Tuareg
RELIGIONS: Muslim (mainly Sunni) 97%, other 3%
ETHNIC MIX: Arab and Berber 95%, other 5%
GOVERNMENT: One-party state
CURRENCY: Libyan dinar = 1000 dirhams

Liechtenstein

Perched in the Alps between Switzerland and Austria, he state of Liechtenstein became an independent principality of he Holy Roman Empire in 1719. It has close links with Switzerland.

GEOGRAPHY

The upper Rhine Valley covers the estern third of the country. The ountains and narrow valleys of the astern Alps make up the remainder.

CLIMATE

Warm, dry summers. Winters are ɔld, with heavy snow in the mountains om December to March.

PEOPLE & SOCIETY

Principality's role as a financial enter accounts for its many foreign esidents (a third of the population). alf of the workforce are cross-border ommuters. Living standards are high, vith few social tensions. Linked by a ustoms union since 1924, Switzerland andles Liechtenstein's foreign affairs nd defense issues.

INSIGHT: *Women in Liechtenstein obtained the vote only in 1984*

THE ECONOMY

Banking secrecy (now modified) and low taxes help attract foreign investment. Anti-money-laundering rules are recent. Diversified exports include precision instruments, dental products, and chemicals.

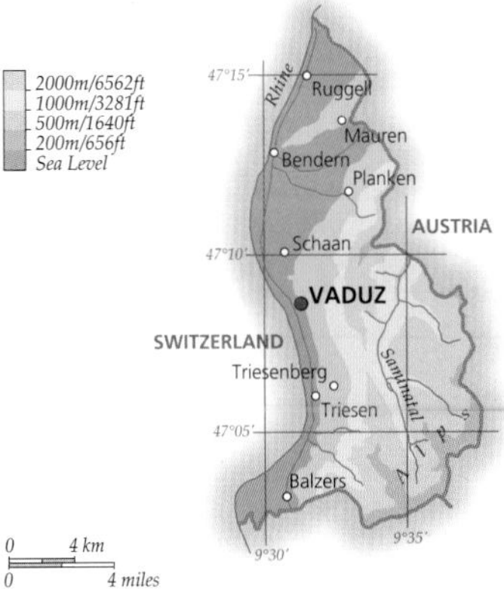
2000m/6562ft
1000m/3281ft
500m/1640ft
200m/656ft
Sea Level
47°15′
47°10′
47°05′
Rhine
Ruggell
Mauren
Bendern
Planken
AUSTRIA
Schaan
VADUZ
SWITZERLAND
Triesenberg
Triesen
Saminatal
Balzers
9°30′
9°35′
0 4 km
0 4 miles

FACTFILE

OFFICIAL NAME: Principality of Liechtenstein
DATE OF FORMATION: 1719
CAPITAL: Vaduz
POPULATION: 35,000
TOTAL AREA: 62 sq. miles (160 sq. km)
DENSITY: 565 people per sq. mile
LANGUAGES: German*, Italian, Alemannish dialect
RELIGIONS: Catholic 81%, other 19%
ETHNIC MIX: Liechtensteiner 66%, other 18%, Swiss 10%, Austrian 6%
GOVERNMENT: Parliamentary system
CURRENCY: Swiss franc = 100 centimes

Lithuania

Lying on the eastern coast of the Baltic Sea, Lithuania is the largest of the Baltic states. The first Soviet republic to declar independence from Moscow in 1991, it joined the EU in 2004.

GEOGRAPHY

Mostly flat with moors, bogs, and an intensively farmed central lowland. Numerous lakes and forested sandy ridges in the east.

CLIMATE

Coastal location moderates continental extremes. Cold winters, cool summers, and steady rainfall.

PEOPLE & SOCIETY

Homogeneous population, with Lithuanians forming a large majority. Only 4000 Jews, known as Litvaks, remain in Lithuania. Strong Roman Catholic tradition and historic links with Poland. There are better relations among ethnic groups than in other Baltic states and interethnic marriages are fairly common. However, ethnic Russians and Poles see a threat from "Lithuanianization." A large income gap has grown since independence.

THE ECONOMY

High-tech and heavy industries: engineering, shipbuilding, and food processing. Litas pegged to euro. High inflation has delayed euro's adoption. Recession in 2009 after strong growth.

INSIGHT: *The "amber coast" of Lithuania produces most of the world's amber – fossilized resin*

22°
24°
26°
56°
54°
LATVIA
Viekšniai
Telšiai
Šiauliai
Plungė
Panevėžys
Baltic Sea
Klaipėda
Skaudvilė
Ukmergė
Neman
Kaunas
RUSSIAN FEDERATION
VILNIUS
BELARU
Alytus
POLAND
Druskininkai
200m/656ft
Sea Level
0 50 km
0 50 mi

FACTFILE

OFFICIAL NAME: Republic of Lithuania
DATE OF FORMATION: 1991
CAPITAL: Vilnius
POPULATION: 3.29 million
TOTAL AREA: 25,174 sq. miles (65,200 sq. km)
DENSITY: 131 people per sq. mile
LANGUAGES: Lithuanian*, Russian
RELIGIONS: Roman Catholic 83%, other 12%, Protestant 5%
ETHNIC MIX: Lithuanian 85%, Polish 6%, Russian 5%, other 3%, Belarussian 1%
GOVERNMENT: Parliamentary system
CURRENCY: Litas = 100 centu

Luxembourg

Part of the plateau of the Ardennes in western Europe, Luxembourg is one of Europe's richest states. A tax haven and banking center, it is also home to key EU institutions.

GEOGRAPHY

Dense Ardennes forests in the orth, with a low, open plateau to the outh. Undulating terrain throughout.

CLIMATE

The climate is moist, with warm ummers and mild winters. Snow is ommon only in the Ardennes.

PEOPLE & SOCIETY

Ethnic tensions are rare, despite a rge proportion of foreigners (over a hird of residents). Integration has been traightforward; most are fellow western uropeans and Catholics, mainly from taly and Portugal. Low unemployment nd high salaries promote stability. ivorce rates are rising and marriage is ecoming less common.

INSIGHT: *Luxembourg's capital is home to around 2000 investment unds and over 150 banks*

THE ECONOMY

Traditional industries such as steelmaking have given way to the banking and service sectors. Low taxes and banking secrecy laws attract foreign investors.

500m/1640ft
200m/656ft
Sea Level
Clervaux
Ardennes
50°
GERMANY
Ettelbrück
Echternach
Mersch
Moselle
BELGIUM
LUXEMBOURG
Pétange
Differdange
49°30′
Esch-sur -Alzette
Dudelange
FRANCE
6°
6°30′
0 10 km
0 10 miles

FACTFILE

OFFICIAL NAME: Grand Duchy of Luxembourg

DATE OF FORMATION: 1867

CAPITAL: Luxembourg-Ville

POPULATION: 486,200

TOTAL AREA: 998 sq. miles (2586 sq. km)

DENSITY: 487 people per sq. mile

LANGUAGES: Luxembourgish*, German*, French*

RELIGIONS: Roman Catholic 97%, Jewish, Greek Orthodox, and Protestant 3%

ETHNIC MIX: Luxembourger 62%, foreign residents 38%

GOVERNMENT: Parliamentary system

CURRENCY: Euro = 100 cents

Macedonia

Landlocked Macedonia was hit hard by the sanctions placed on its northern trading partners in the mid-1990s, and by violent conflict with ethnic Albanians in 2001.

GEOGRAPHY

Mainly mountainous or hilly, with deep river basins in the center. Plains in the northeast and southwest.

CLIMATE

Continental climate with wet springs and dry autumns. Heavy snowfalls in northern mountains.

PEOPLE & SOCIETY

Slav Macedonians are mostly Orthodox Christians, with some Muslims. Officially, Muslim Albanians account for 25% of the population, but they claim to number a third. In 2001 Albanian militants fought a bitter war against the government. A peace deal promised greater equality. A major stumbling block to EU and NATO accession is Greece's objection to the name Macedonia, in order to prevent any possibility of claims to historic "Macedonian" lands in north Greece.

THE ECONOMY

Steel, minerals, clothing, shoes, and tobacco exported. Slow transition to market economy. Organized crime and large gray economy. Investment boosted by EU candidate status.

INSIGHT: *Ohrid is the deepest lake in Europe at 964 ft (294 m)*

0 50 km
0 50 miles
SERBIA
BULGARI
Kumanovo
Tetovo
SKOPJE
42°
Kočani
Veles
Štip
Gostivar
ALBANIA
Strumica
Vardar
Kičevo
Prilep
Ohrid
Bitola
Lake Ohrid
41°
Lake Prespa
22°
GREECE
1000m/3281
500m/1640ft
200m/656ft
Sea Level

FACTFILE

OFFICIAL NAME: Republic of Macedonia
DATE OF FORMATION: 1991
CAPITAL: Skopje
POPULATION: 2.04 million
TOTAL AREA: 9781 sq. miles (25,333 sq. km)
DENSITY: 206 people per sq. mile
LANGUAGES: Macedonian*, Albanian*
RELIGIONS: Orthodox Christian 59%, Muslim 26%, other 11%, Catholic 4%
ETHNIC MIX: Macedonian 64%, Albanian 25%, other 5%, Turkish 4%, Serb 2%
GOVERNMENT: Mixed presidential–parliamentary system
CURRENCY: Macedonian denar = 100 deni

Madagascar

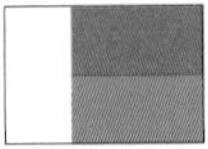

Lying off east Africa in the Indian Ocean, the former French colony of Madagascar is the world's fourth-largest island. Power struggles erupted onto the streets in 2002 and 2009.

GEOGRAPHY

More than two-thirds of the ountry forms a savanna-covered plateau, vhich drops in the east through ainforests to the coast.

CLIMATE

Tropical and often hit by cyclones. Aonsoons affect the east coast. The outhwest is much drier.

PEOPLE & SOCIETY

People are Malay-Indonesian 1 origin, intermixed with later migrants rom the African mainland. The main ethnic division is between the Merina of the central plateau and the poorer *côtier* (coastal) peoples. The Merina vere the country's historic rulers, and emain the social elite.

INSIGHT: *80% of Madagascar's plants and many of its animal species are found nowhere else*

THE ECONOMY

Most people are farmers. Cash crops are vanilla, coffee, and cloves. Garments and shrimp also exported. Political crises deter investors.

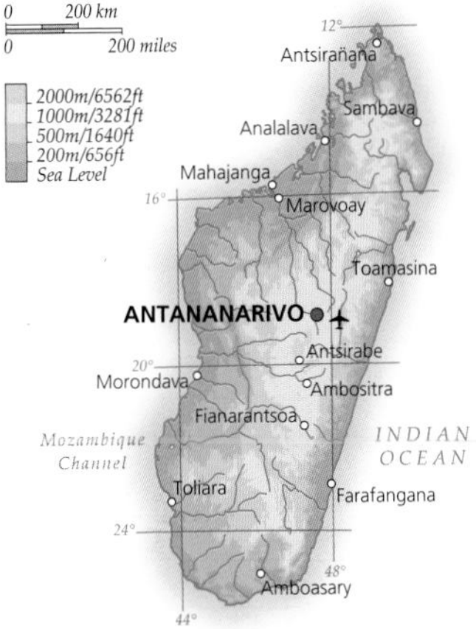
0 200 km
0 200 miles
2000m/6562ft
1000m/3281ft
500m/1640ft
200m/656ft
Sea Level
12°
16°
20°
24°
44°
48°
Antsirañana
Sambava
Analalava
Mahajanga
Marovoay
Toamasina
ANTANANARIVO
Antsirabe
Morondava
Ambositra
Fianarantsoa
Mozambique Channel
INDIAN OCEAN
Toliara
Farafangana
Amboasary

FACTFILE

OFFICIAL NAME: Republic of Madagascar
DATE OF FORMATION: 1960
CAPITAL: Antananarivo
POPULATION: 219.6 million
TOTAL AREA: 226,656 sq. miles (587,040 sq. km)
DENSITY: 87 people per sq. mile
LANGUAGES: Malagasy*, French*
RELIGIONS: Traditional beliefs 52%, Christian 41%, Muslim 7%
ETHNIC MIX: Other Malay 46%, Merina 26%, Betsimisaraka 15%, Betsileo 12%, other 1%
GOVERNMENT: Presidential system
CURRENCY: Ariary = 5 iraimbilanja

Malawi

A former colony of the UK, Malawi lies landlocked in southeast Africa, following the Great Rift Valley. Its name means "the land where the sun is reflected in the water like fire."

GEOGRAPHY

Lake Nyasa takes up one-fifth of the landscape. Highlands lie west of the lake. Much of the land is covered by forests and savanna.

CLIMATE

Mainly subtropical. The south is hot and humid. Highlands are cooler.

PEOPLE & SOCIETY

Most Malawians share a common Bantu origin. Ethnicity has not been exploited for political ends as has happened in neighboring states. Four out of five people live in poverty. The election in 1994 of a member of the Muslim minority as president signaled the failure of previous attempts to enforce Protestant dominance.

INSIGHT: *Lake Nyasa is 353 miles (568 km) in length and contains at least 500 species of fish*

THE ECONOMY

Mainly subsistence farming. Tobacco accounts for 60% of export earnings. Tea and sugar are grown. Drought and corruption are problems.

0 100 km
0 100 miles
34°
Karonga
10°
TANZANIA
Mzuzu
Euthini
12°
ZAMBIA
Chisumulti Likoma (to Malawi)
Great Rift Valley
Lake Nyasa
MOZAMBIQUE
LILONGWE
Salima
36°
14°
Dedza
Mangochi
MOZAMBIQUE
Zomba
Blantyre
16°
Nsanje
2000m/6562ft
1000m/3281ft
500m/1640ft
200m/656ft
Sea Level

FACTFILE

OFFICIAL NAME: Republic of Malawi
DATE OF FORMATION: 1964
CAPITAL: Lilongwe
POPULATION: 15.3 million
TOTAL AREA: 45,745 sq. miles (118,480 sq. km)
DENSITY: 420 people per sq. mile
LANGUAGES: Chewa, Lomwe, Yao, Ngoni, English*
RELIGIONS: Protestant 55%, Muslim 20%, Catholic 20%, traditional beliefs 5%
ETHNIC MIX: Bantu 99%, other 1%
GOVERNMENT: Presidential system
CURRENCY: Malawi kwacha = 100 tambala

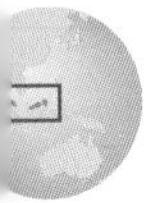

Malaysia

Malaysia stretches 1240 miles (2000 km) across southeast Asia from the Malay peninsula to Sabah in eastern Borneo. Federated in 1963, it included Singapore for two years.

GEOGRAPHY

The Malay Peninsula has central mountains, an eastern coastal belt, and fertile western plains. Swampy coastal plains rise to mountains on Borneo.

CLIMATE

Warm equatorial. Rainfall always heavy, but with distinct rainy seasons.

INSIGHT: *Malaysia is southeast Asia's major tourist destination, with over 20 million visitors a year*

PEOPLE & SOCIETY

The key distinction is between Malays (Bumiputras, literally "sons of the soil") and the Chinese, who traditionally controlled most economic activity. Since the 1970s, Malays have been favored for education and jobs, in order to address this imbalance.

THE ECONOMY

Successful industrial base include manufacturing and heavy industry. Tourism is a major earner. Leading producer of palm oil, tin, and tropical hardwoods.

THAILAND
Kangar
Kota Bharu
George Town
Kuala Terengganu
Taiping
Malay Peninsula
KUALA LUMPUR
PUTRAJAYA
Klang
Mersing
SINGAPORE
INDONESIA
South China Sea
Kepulauan Natuna
Natuna Sea
Kuching
Sri Aman
Sibu
Sarawak
Bintulu
Miri
BRUNEI
Kota Kinabalu
Kudat
Sandakan
Keningau
Sabah
Sulu Sea
Borneo
INDONESIA
INDONESIA
2000m/6562ft
1000m/3281ft
500m/1640ft
200m/656ft
Sea Level
0 100 km
0 100 miles
4°
2°
100°
102°
104°
106°
108°
110°
112°
114°
116°
118°

FACTFILE

OFFICIAL NAME: Federation of Malaysia

DATE OF FORMATION: 1963

CAPITAL: Kuala Lumpur and Putrajaya

POPULATION: 27.5 million

TOTAL AREA: 127,316 sq. miles (329,750 sq. km)

DENSITY: 217 people per sq. mile

LANGUAGES: Bahasa Malaysia*, Malay, Chinese, Tamil, English

RELIGIONS: Muslim 53%, Buddhist 19%, Chinese faiths 12%, other 9%, Christian 7%

ETHNIC MIX: Malay 50%, Chinese 25%, indigenous tribes 11%, other 14%

GOVERNMENT: Parliamentary system

CURRENCY: Ringgit = 100 sen

Maldives

Set in the Indian Ocean, southwest of Sri Lanka, the Maldives is an archipelago of 1191 small coral islands, or atolls. 200 are inhabited. The word atoll comes from the Dhivehi word "atolu.'

GEOGRAPHY

Consists of low-lying islands and coral atolls. The larger ones are covered in lush, tropical vegetation.

CLIMATE

Tropical. Rain falls throughout the year, but is heaviest June–November, during the monsoon. Violent storms occasionally hit the northern islands.

PEOPLE & SOCIETY

Maldivians, who are all Sunni Muslim, are descended from Sinhalese, Dravidian, Arab, and black ancestors. About 25% of the population live on Male'. Tourism has grown on separate resort islands away from residents. Politics has been controlled by a small group of influential families. However, a young elite pushed for reform: parties were legalized in 2005, and the presidential election in 2008 brought in a new regime.

THE ECONOMY

The fluctuating tourist industry is the economic mainstay. Fish, especially tuna, are the main export. Construction boom to repair 2004 tsunami damage.

INSIGHT:

The islands, which all lie below 4 ft (1.2 m), are threatened by rising sea levels, brought about by global warming and climatic changes

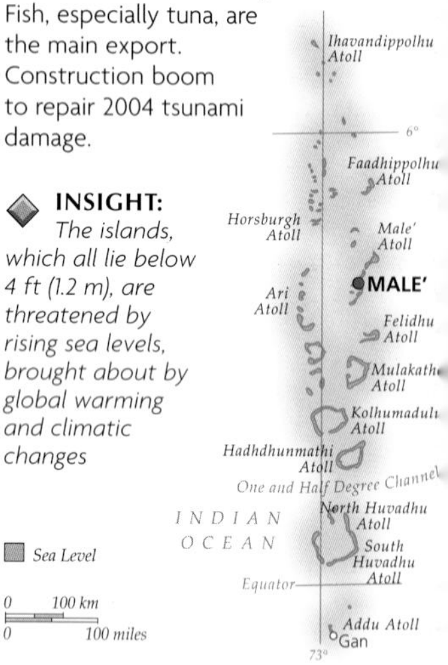
Ihavandippolhu Atoll
6°
Faadhippolhu Atoll
Horsburgh Atoll
Male' Atoll
MALE'
Ari Atoll
Felidhu Atoll
Mulakatholhu Atoll
Kolhumadulu Atoll
Hadhdhunmathi Atoll
One and Half Degree Channel
INDIAN OCEAN
North Huvadhu Atoll
South Huvadhu Atoll
Equator
Addu Atoll
Gan
73°
Sea Level
0 100 km
0 100 miles

FACTFILE

OFFICIAL NAME: Republic of Maldives

DATE OF FORMATION: 1965

CAPITAL: Male'

POPULATION: 309,400

TOTAL AREA: 116 sq. miles (300 sq. km)

DENSITY: 2667 people per sq. mile

LANGUAGES: Dhivehi* (Maldivian), Sinhala, Tamil, Arabic

RELIGIONS: Sunni Muslim 100%

ETHNIC MIX: All Maldivians are of Arab–Sinhalese–Malay descent

GOVERNMENT: Presidential system

CURRENCY: Rufiyaa = 100 laari

Mali

A former French colony, Mali is landlocked in the heart of west Africa. The 1991 coup ended the 23-year dictatorship of Moussa Traoré and ushered in multiparty elections from 1992.

GEOGRAPHY

The northern half of the country es in the Sahara. The inland delta of the Niger River flows through a grassy avanna region in the south.

CLIMATE

In the south, intensely hot, dry weather precedes the westerly rains. The north is almost rainless.

PEOPLE & SOCIETY

Most people live in the southern savanna region. The Bambara tribe are culturally and politically dominant. A few nomadic Fulani and Tuareg herders travel the northern plains. There is tension between the peoples of the south and Tuareg in the north. Malian women have ittle status.

INSIGHT: *Tombouctou (Timbuktu) was the center of the 14th-century Malinké trading empire*

THE ECONOMY

Widespread poverty. Most people are farmers, herders, or river fishermen. Less than 2% of land can be cultivated. High-quality cotton, gold, and livestock account for 80% of exports. Vulnerable to drought.

ALGERIA
MAURITANIA
Sahara
Adrar des Ifôghas
Niger
Tombouctou
Gao
NIGER
Mopti
Senegal
SENEGAL
Kayes
Ségou
BAMAKO
Koulikoro
BURKINA
Sikasso
GUINEA
CÔTE D'IVOIRE (IVORY COAST)
24°
20°
16°
12°
8°
4°
0°
0 200 km
0 200 miles
500m/1640ft
200m/656ft
Sea Level

FACTFILE

OFFICIAL NAME: Republic of Mali
DATE OF FORMATION: 1960
CAPITAL: Bamako
POPULATION: 13 million
TOTAL AREA: 478,764 sq. miles (1,240,000 sq. km)
DENSITY: 28 people per sq. mile
LANGUAGES: Bambara, Fulani, Senufo, Soninke, French*
RELIGIONS: Muslim 80%, traditional beliefs 18%, Christian 1%, other 1%
ETHNIC MIX: Bambara 32%, other 33%, Fulani 14%, Senufu 12%, Soninka 9%
GOVERNMENT: Presidential system
CURRENCY: CFA franc = 100 centimes

Malta

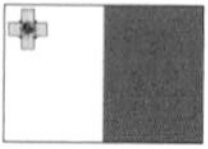

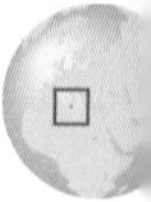

The densely populated Maltese archipelago lies between Africa and Europe. Controlled throughout its history by successive colonial powers, it gained independence from the UK in 1964.

GEOGRAPHY

The main island of Malta has low hills and a ragged coastline with numerous harbors, bays, sandy beaches, and rocky coves. The island of Gozo is more densely vegetated.

CLIMATE

Mediterranean climate. There are many hours of sunshine all year round, with very little rainfall.

PEOPLE & SOCIETY

Over the centuries, the Maltese have been subject to Arab, Sicilian, Spanish, French, and British influences. Today, the population is socially conservative and devoutly Roman Catholic – on a percentage basis, risen more so than virtually any other nation. Unemployment is high, particularly for women. Divorce is banned. Illegal migration from Africa has increased since Malta joined the EU in 2004.

THE ECONOMY

Tourism provides 30% of GDP. Joined eurozone in 2008. Developing offshore banking, high-tech industry. Semiconductors exported. Most goods have to be imported.

INSIGHT: *The Maltese language has Phoenician origins but features Arabic etymology and intonation*

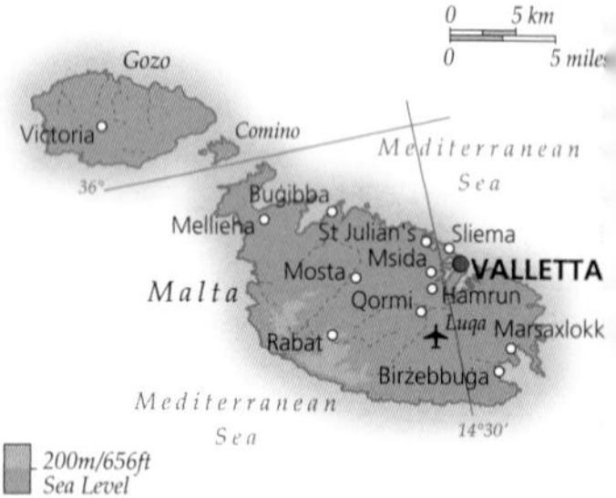
0 5 km
0 5 miles
Gozo
Victoria
Comino
Mediterranean Sea
36°
Bugibba
Mellieha
St Julian's
Sliema
Msida
VALLETTA
Mosta
Malta
Hamrun
Qormi
Luqa
Marsaxlokk
Rabat
Birzebbuga
Mediterranean Sea
14°30'
200m/656ft
Sea Level

FACTFILE

OFFICIAL NAME: Republic of Malta
DATE OF FORMATION: 1964
CAPITAL: Valletta
POPULATION: 408,700
TOTAL AREA: 122 sq. miles (316 sq. km)
DENSITY: 3296 people per sq. mile
LANGUAGES: Maltese*, English*
RELIGIONS: Roman Catholic 98%, other and nonreligious 2%
ETHNIC MIX: Maltese 96%, other 4%
GOVERNMENT: Parliamentary system
CURRENCY: Euro = 100 cents

Marshall Islands

Under US rule as part of the UN Trust Territory of the Pacific Islands until independence in 1986, the Marshall Islands comprises a group of 34 widely scattered atolls.

GEOGRAPHY

Narrow coral rings with sandy beaches enclosing lagoons. Those in the south have thicker vegetation. Kwajalein is the world's largest atoll.

CLIMATE

Tropical oceanic, cooled year round by northeast trade winds.

PEOPLE & SOCIETY

Majuro, the capital city and commercial center, is home to almost half the population. Tensions are high due to poor living conditions. Life on the outlying islands is still traditional, based around subsistence agriculture and fishing. Society is matrilineal, with land and titles handed down through the mother's clan.

INSIGHT: *In 1954, Bikini Atoll was the site for the testing of the largest US H-bomb – the 18–22 megaton Bravo*

THE ECONOMY

Almost totally dependent on US aid and the rent paid by the US for its missile base on Kwajalein Atoll. High unemployment. Revenue from licenses to fish in Marshallese waters for tuna. Copra and coconut oil are the only significant agricultural exports.

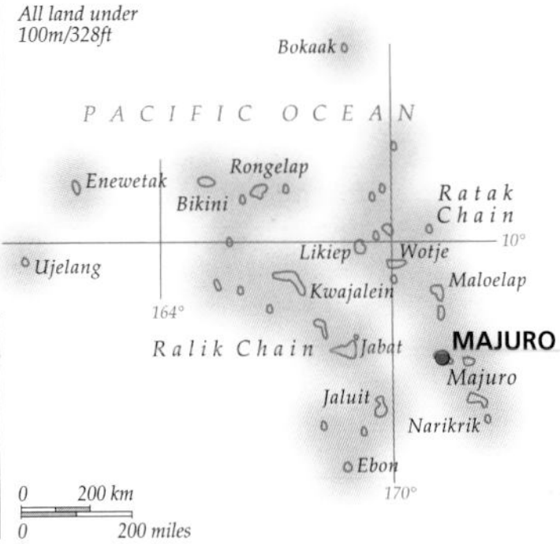
All land under 100m/328ft
Bokaak
PACIFIC OCEAN
Enewetak
Rongelap
Bikini
Ratak Chain
10°
Ujelang
Likiep
Wotje
Maloelap
Kwajalein
164°
Ralik Chain
Jabat
MAJURO
Majuro
Jaluit
Narikrik
Ebon
170°
0 200 km
0 200 miles

FACTFILE

OFFICIAL NAME: Republic of the Marshall Islands

DATE OF FORMATION: 1986

CAPITAL: Majuro

POPULATION: 54,100

TOTAL AREA: 70 sq. miles (181 sq. km)

DENSITY: 733 people per sq. mile

LANGUAGES: Marshallese*, English*, Japanese, German

RELIGIONS: Protestant 90%, Roman Catholic 8%, other 2%

ETHNIC MIX: Micronesian 97%, other 3%

GOVERNMENT: Presidential system

CURRENCY: US dollar = 100 cents

Mauritania

Two-thirds of Mauritania's territory is desert – the only productive land is that drained by the Senegal River. The country has taken a strongly Arab direction since 1964.

GEOGRAPHY

The Sahara, barren except for some scattered oases, covers the north. Savanna lands lie to the south.

CLIMATE

The climate is generally hot and dry, aggravated by the dusty *harmattan* wind. Summer rain in the south, virtually none in the north.

PEOPLE & SOCIETY

The majority Maures control political and economic life. Family solidarity among nomadic peoples is particularly strong. Ethnic tension centers on the oppression of the sizable black minority by Maures. Tens of thousands of blacks are estimated to be in illegal slavery.

INSIGHT: *Slavery officially became illegal in Mauritania in 1980, but de facto slavery still persists*

THE ECONOMY

Agriculture and herding. Iron, copper, and gold mining. World's largest gypsum deposits. Offshore oil from 2006. Rich fishing grounds.

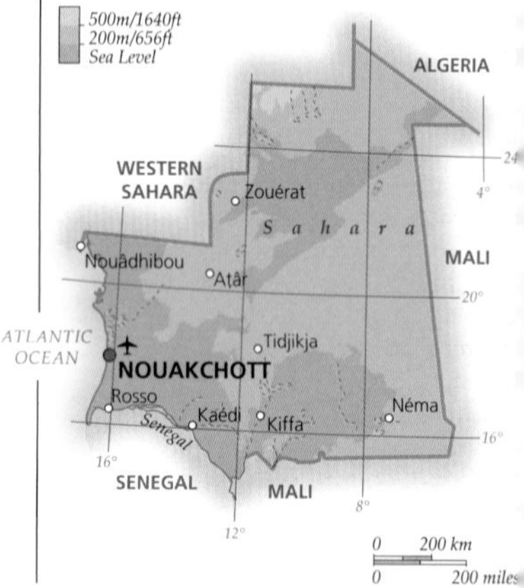

500m/1640ft
200m/656ft
Sea Level
ALGERIA
WESTERN SAHARA
Zouérat
S a h a r a
MALI
Nouâdhibou
Atâr
20°
ATLANTIC OCEAN
Tidjikja
NOUAKCHOTT
Rosso
Kaédi
Kiffa
Néma
Senegal
16°
SENEGAL
MALI
12°
8°
4°
0 200 km
0 200 miles

FACTFILE

OFFICIAL NAME: Islamic Republic of Mauritania

DATE OF FORMATION: 1960

CAPITAL: Nouakchott

POPULATION: 3.29 million

TOTAL AREA: 397,953 sq. miles (1,030,700 sq. km)

DENSITY: 8 people per sq. mile

LANGUAGES: Hassaniyah Arabic*, Wolof, French

RELIGIONS: Sunni Muslim 100%

ETHNIC MIX: Maure 81%, Wolof 7%, Tukolor 5%, other 4%, Soninka 3%

GOVERNMENT: Presidential system

CURRENCY: Ouguiya = 5 khoums

Mauritius

The islands that make up Mauritius lie in the Indian Ocean east of Madagascar. They have enjoyed considerable economic success following recent industrial diversification and expansion.

GEOGRAPHY

The volcanic main island of Mauritius is ringed by coral reefs, and rises from the coast to a fertile central plateau. The outer islands – Rodriguez, the Agalega Islands, and the Cargados Carajos Shoals – lie some 300 miles (500 km) to the north.

CLIMATE

Warm and humid. Tropical storms are frequent December–March, the hottest and wettest months.

PEOPLE & SOCIETY

Most people are descendants of laborers brought over from India in the 19th century. A small minority of French descent form the wealthiest group. Creoles (descendants of African slaves) complain of discrimination. Literacy is high. Health care is free. Criminal offenses are usually traffic-related; little crime on outer islands.

THE ECONOMY

Clothing manufacture, tourism, and sugar. Loss of preferential trade terms for sugar and textiles. Offshore financial center. New outsourcing and ICT industries. Most food is imported.

INSIGHT: *The islands form part of the Mascarene Archipelago – once a land bridge between Asia and Africa*

500m/1640ft
200m/656ft
Sea Level
Ile Plate
57°30′
Rodrigues
Port Mathurin
19°45′
63°25′
20°
Triolet
Grand Baie
Pamplemousses
PORT LOUIS
INDIAN
OCEAN
Curepipe
Mahébourg
Bel Ombre
Souillac
20°30′
0 10 km
0 10 miles

FACTFILE

OFFICIAL NAME: Republic of Mauritius
DATE OF FORMATION: 1968
CAPITAL: Port Louis
POPULATION: 1.29 million
TOTAL AREA: 718 sq. miles (1860 sq. km)
DENSITY: 1794 people per sq. mile
LANGUAGES: French Creole, Hindi, Urdu, Tamil, Chinese, English*, French
RELIGIONS: Hindu 52%, Catholic 26%, Muslim 17%, other 3%, Protestant 2%
ETHNIC MIX: Indo-Mauritian 68%, Creole 27%, other 5%
GOVERNMENT: Parliamentary system
CURRENCY: Mauritian rupee = 100 cents

Mexico

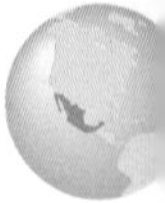

Mexico stretches from the US border southward into the ancient Aztec and Mayan heartlands. Independence from Spain came in 1836. One in five Mexicans lives in the sprawling capital.

GEOGRAPHY

Coastal plains along the Pacific and Atlantic seaboards rise to a high arid central plateau. To the east and west are the Sierra Madre mountain ranges. Limestone lowlands form the projecting Yucatan peninsula.

CLIMATE

The plateau and high mountains are warm for much of the year. Pacific coast is tropical: storms occur mostly March–December. Northwest is dry.

PEOPLE & SOCIETY

Most Mexicans are *mestizos* of Spanish–Amerindian descent. Rural Amerindians are largely segregated from Hispanic society and most live in poverty, though the state promotes their culture. The Zapatista movement backs indigenous rights. Few women in male-dominated politics and business. Narcotics-related violent crime is rising.

THE ECONOMY

One of the world's largest oil producers. Corn, fruit, vegetables, sugar are cash crops. NAFTA has boosted exports, but exposes farmers to subsidized US competition. Huge wealth disaprity. Swine flu crippled economy in 2009.

INSIGHT: *More people cross the US–Mexican border each year – illegally or legally – than any other border in the world*

UNITED STATES OF AMERICA
Tijuana
Ciudad Juárez
Chihuahua
Baja California
Sierra Madre Occidental
Sierra Madre Oriental
Rio Grande
Monterrey
Gulf of Mexico
San Luis Potosí
León
Guadalajara
MEXICO CITY
Puebla
Sierra Madre del Sur
Acapulco
PACIFIC OCEAN
BEL
GUAT.
30°
110°
20°
100°
90°
3000m/9843ft
2000m/6562ft
1000m/3281ft
500m/1640ft
200m/656ft
Sea Level
0 500 km
0 500 miles

FACTFILE

OFFICIAL NAME: United Mexican States
DATE OF FORMATION: 1836
CAPITAL: Mexico City
POPULATION: 110 million
TOTAL AREA: 761,602 sq. miles (1,972,550 sq. km
DENSITY: 149 people per sq. mile
LANGUAGES: Spanish*, Nahuatl, Mayan, Zapotec, Mixtec, Otomi, Totonac, other
RELIGIONS: Roman Catholic 88%, other 7%, Protestant 5%
ETHNIC MIX: *Mestizo* 60%, Amerindian 30%, European 9%, other 1%
GOVERNMENT: Presidential system
CURRENCY: Mexican peso = 100 centavos

Micronesia

The Federated States of Micronesia (FSM), situated in the western Pacific, comprise 607 islands and atolls grouped into four main island states: Pohnpei, Kosrae, Chuuk, and Yap.

GEOGRAPHY

Mixture of high volcanic islands with forested interiors, and low-lying coral atolls. Some of the islands have coastal mangrove swamps.

CLIMATE

Tropical, with high humidity. There is very heavy rainfall outside the January–March dry season.

INSIGHT: *Chuuk's lagoon contains the sunken wrecks of over 100 Japanese ships and 270 planes from World War II*

PEOPLE & SOCIETY

Micronesians are physically, culturally, and linguistically diverse. Melanesians live on Yap, Polynesians in Pohnpei. The supply of electricity and running water is limited. Society is based on matrilineal clans.

THE ECONOMY

Dependent on US aid. Fishing licenses are a key source of foreign revenue. Tourism, fishing, betel nuts, copra are economic mainstays. Trust fund created to reduce aid reliance.

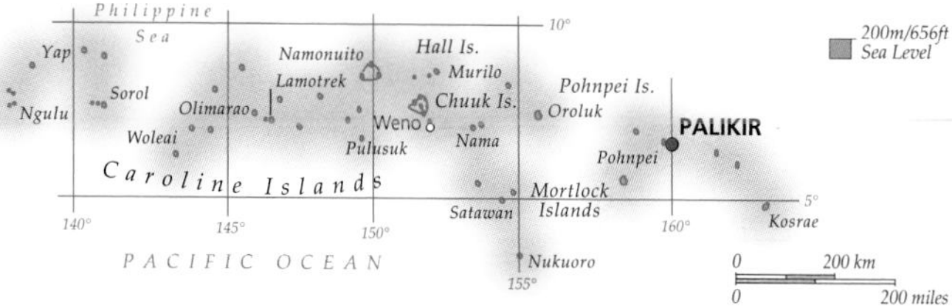
Philippine Sea
Yap
Ngulu
Sorol
Olimarao
Woleai
Namonuito
Lamotrek
Hall Is.
Murilo
Chuuk Is.
Weno
Pulusuk
Nama
Pohnpei Is.
Oroluk
PALIKIR
Pohnpei
Caroline Islands
Mortlock Islands
Satawan
Kosrae
Nukuoro
PACIFIC OCEAN
10°
5°
140°
145°
150°
155°
160°
200m/656ft
Sea Level
0 200 km
0 200 miles

FACTFILE

OFFICIAL NAME: Federated States of Micronesia
DATE OF FORMATION: 1986
CAPITAL: Palikir (Pohnpei Island)
POPULATION: 110,700
TOTAL AREA: 271 sq. miles (702 sq. km)
DENSITY: 408 people per sq. mile
LANGUAGES: Trukese, Pohnpeian, Kosraean, Yapese, English*
RELIGIONS: Roman Catholic 50%, Protestant 48%, other 2%
ETHNIC MIX: Chuukese 49%, Pohnpeian 24%, other 19%, Kosraean 6%, Asian 2%
GOVERNMENT: Nonparty system
CURRENCY: US dollar = 100 cents

Moldova

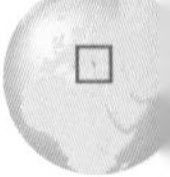

The most densely populated of the former Soviet republics, Moldova has strong ethnic, linguistic, and cultural links with Romania, but relations with Russia remain paramount.

GEOGRAPHY

Steppes and hilly plains are drained by the Dniester and Prut rivers.

CLIMATE

Warm summers and relatively mild winters. Moderate rainfall is evenly spread throughout the year.

PEOPLE & SOCIETY

A shared heritage with Romania defines national identity, though in 1994 Moldovans voted against possible reunification with Romania. Most of the population is engaged in intensive agriculture. Transnistria is a breakaway state along the east bank of the Dniester, home to a largely ethnic Slav population. The Gagauz, in the south, have accepted autonomy.

INSIGHT: *Vast underground wine vaults contain entire "streets" of bottles built into rock quarries*

THE ECONOMY

One of the two poorest countries in Europe. Mainly agricultural: produces wine, tobacco, fruit. Food processing and textiles. Depends on Russia for raw materials, fuel, exports. Instability.

UKRAINE
Dniester
Edinet
Rîşcani
Soroca
Floreşti
Rîbniţa
Bălţi
Prut
Dniester
Dubăsari Reservoir
Orhei
TRANSNISTRIA (disputed)
CHIŞINĂU
Tiraspol
ROMANIA
Tighina (Bendery)
Comrat
Cahul
48°
46°
28°
0 50 km
0 50 miles
200m/656ft
Sea Level

FACTFILE

OFFICIAL NAME: Republic of Moldova
DATE OF FORMATION: 1991
CAPITAL: Chisinau
POPULATION: 3.6 million
TOTAL AREA: 13,067 sq. miles (33,843 sq. km)
DENSITY: 277 people per sq. mile
LANGUAGES: Moldovan*, Ukrainian, Russian
RELIGIONS: Orthodox Christian 98%, Jewish 2%
ETHNIC MIX: Moldovan 64%, Ukrainian 14%, Russian 13%, Gagauz 4%, other 5%
GOVERNMENT: Parliamentary system
CURRENCY: Moldovan leu = 100 bani

Monaco

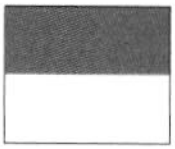

Monaco is a tiny principality on the Côte d'Azur. Its destiny changed radically when the casino was opened in 1863. Today, it promotes its image as an upmarket, glamorous destination.

GEOGRAPHY

A rocky promontory overlooking a narrow coastal strip that has been enlarged through land reclamation.

CLIMATE

Mediterranean. Summers are hot and dry; days with 12 hours of sunshine are not uncommon. Winters are mild and sunny.

PEOPLE & SOCIETY

Less than 20% of residents are Monégasques. Around a third are French, the rest Italian, American, British, Belgian, and many others. Nationals enjoy considerable privileges, including housing subsidies to protect them from Monaco's high property prices, and the right of first refusal before a job can be offered to a foreigner. Women have equal status, but only acquired the vote in 1962.

THE ECONOMY

Tourism, gambling, financial services. Banking secrecy laws and tax-haven conditions attract foreign investment. Close links and customs union with France (but not in EU). No resources: depends on imports.

INSIGHT: *High-profile social and sporting events attract large crowds each spring, including the Rose Ball, Tennis Open, and Grand Prix*

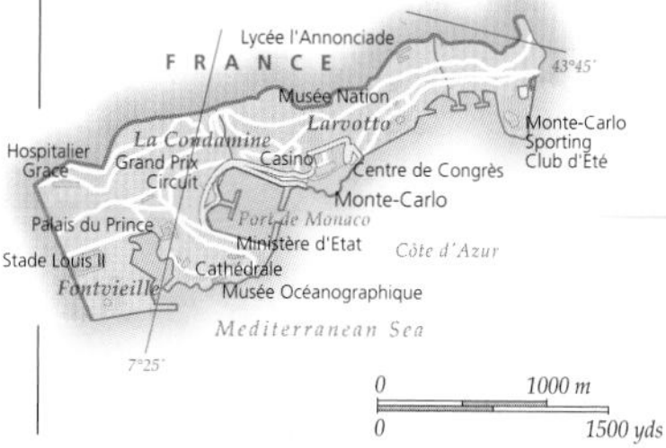
Lycée l'Annonciade
FRANCE
43°45'
Musée Nation
Larvotto
Monte-Carlo Sporting Club d'Été
Hospitalier Grace
La Condamine
Grand Prix Circuit
Casino
Centre de Congrès
Monte-Carlo
Palais du Prince
Port de Monaco
Ministère d'Etat
Côte d'Azur
Stade Louis II
Cathédrale
Fontvieille
Musée Océanographique
Mediterranean Sea
7°25'
0
1000 m
0
1500 yds

FACTFILE

OFFICIAL NAME: Principality of Monaco
DATE OF FORMATION: 1861
CAPITAL: Monaco-Ville
POPULATION: 32,000
TOTAL AREA: 0.75 sq. miles (1.95 sq. km)
DENSITY: 42,667 people per sq. mile
LANGUAGES: French*, Italian, Monégasque
RELIGIONS: Roman Catholic 89%, Protestant 6%, other 5%
ETHNIC MIX: French 32%, other 29%, Italian 20%, Monégasque 19%
GOVERNMENT: Mixed monarchical–parliamentary system
CURRENCY: Euro = 100 cents

Mongolia

Landlocked between Russia and China, Mongolia is a huge, isolated, and sparsely populated nation. Over two-thirds of the country is part of the Gobi Desert.

GEOGRAPHY

A mountainous steppe plateau in the north, with lakes in the north and west. The desert region of the Gobi dominates the south.

CLIMATE

Continental. Mild summers and long, dry, very cold winters, with heavy snowfall. Temperatures can drop as low as –22°F (–30°C).

PEOPLE & SOCIETY

Mongolia was unified by Genghis Khan in 1206 and was later absorbed into Manchu China. A majority of ethnic Mongolians live within China in Inner Mongolia. Tibetan Buddhism dominates. The traditional, nomadic way of life has been eroded as urban migration continues, spurred by ferocious winters, known as *zud*, which can devastate the rural economy.

THE ECONOMY

Rich deposits of oil, coal, copper, uranium, and other minerals remain largely untapped. Cashmere exports. Democracy, from 1990, brought a shift toward a market economy, but also rising poverty. State involvement in mining is an issue. Agriculture uses 40% of workforce, mainly as herders.

INSIGHT: *Horseracing, wrestling, and archery are the national sports*

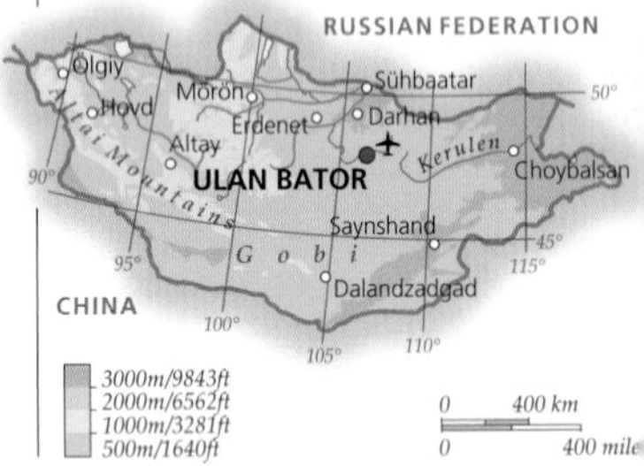
RUSSIAN FEDERATION
Ölgiy
Hovd
Mörön
Sühbaatar
Darhan
Erdenet
Altay
Altai Mountains
ULAN BATOR
Kerulen
Choybalsan
Saynshand
Gobi
Dalandzadgad
CHINA
50°
45°
90°
95°
100°
105°
110°
115°
3000m/9843ft
2000m/6562ft
1000m/3281ft
500m/1640ft
0 400 km
0 400 miles

FACTFILE

OFFICIAL NAME: Mongolia
DATE OF FORMATION: 1924
CAPITAL: Ulan Bator
POPULATION: 2.67 million
TOTAL AREA: 604,247 sq. miles (1,565,000 sq. km)
DENSITY: 4 people per sq. mile
LANGUAGES: Khalkha Mongolian*, other
RELIGIONS: Tibetan Buddhist 96%, Muslim 4%
ETHNIC MIX: Khalkh 82%, other 9%, Kazakh 4%, Dorvod 3%, Bayad 2%
GOVERNMENT: Mixed presidential–parliamentary system
CURRENCY: Tugrik (tögrög) = 100 möngö

Montenegro

Perched on the Adriatic coast, this tiny republic became a separate state in 2006, after 88 years of federation with its neighbors in various forms of the state of Yugoslavia.

GEOGRAPHY

A narrow coastal strip on the Adriatic. Fertile lowland plains around Lake Scutari. Mountainous interior with deep canyons.

CLIMATE

The lowlands have hot, dry summers and mild winters. Heavy snow in winter in the mountains.

PEOPLE & SOCIETY

Most Montenegrins are Orthodox Christians. They speak a language closely related to Serbian, using the same Cyrillic script. Muslim Albanians, who make up 80% of the population of the southern Ulcinj region, supported independence and are now asking for autonomy.

INSIGHT: *Dark forests once cloaked Montenegro's mountains; its name means "Black Mountain"*

THE ECONOMY

Tourism (along Adriatic) drives growth. Bauxite reserves, aluminum industry. Economy dominated by black market; cigarette smuggling is rife. Return of foreign aid and investment. The 2007 accord with the EU is the first step toward eventual accession.

BOSNIA & HERZEGOVINA
SERBIA
CRO.
ALBANIA
20°
43°
42°
Pljevlja
Bijelo Polje
Pivsko Jezero
Piva
Sinjavina
Tara
Berane
Hajla
Rožaje
Lim
Dinaric Alps
Nikšić
Herceg-Novi
Tivat
Cetinje
PODGORICA
Budva
Adriatic Sea
Lake Scutari
Bar
Ulcinj
0 20 km
0 20 miles
2000m/6562ft
1000m/3281ft
500m/1640ft
200m/656ft
Sea Level

FACTFILE

OFFICIAL NAME: Republic of Montenegro
DATE OF FORMATION: 2006
CAPITAL: Podgorica
POPULATION: 624,200
TOTAL AREA: 5332 sq. miles (13,812 sq. km)
DENSITY: 117 people per sq. mile
LANGUAGES: Montenegrin*, Serbian, Albanian
RELIGIONS: Orthodox Christian 74%, Muslim 18%, Catholic 4%, other 4%
ETHNIC MIX: Montenegrin 43%, Serb 32%, other 12%, Bosniak 8%, Albanian 5%
GOVERNMENT: Parliamentary system
CURRENCY: Euro = 100 cents

Morocco

Morocco is a former French colony in northwest Africa. Since 1975, it has occupied the territory of Western Sahara, the future of which is yet to be determined by UN-supervised referendum.

GEOGRAPHY

Fertile coastal plain is interrupted in the east by the Rif Mountains. Atlas Mountain ranges to the south. Beyond lies the outer fringe of the Sahara.

CLIMATE

Ranges from temperate and warm in the north, to semiarid in the south. Cooler in the mountains.

PEOPLE & SOCIETY

Around 30% of the population are descendants of original Berber inhabitants of north Africa, and live mainly in mountain villages. The Arab majority inhabits the lowlands. Morocco is unusual among Arab states in granting Jews religious freedom and civil rights. The king is spiritual leader and head of state. Islamists have gained influence in politics. Islamist militancy and the emergence of terrorist cells are of concern.

THE ECONOMY

Major exporter of phosphates. Investment in tourism and agriculture. Fishing. Relations with EU strained over illegal immigrants and cannabis trade.

INSIGHT: *Karueein University in Fès, founded in 859 CE, is the world's oldest existing educational institution*

Mediterranean Sea
ATLANTIC OCEAN
Tanger
Ceuta (to Spain)
Melilla (to Spain)
Tétouan
RABAT
Kénitra
Oujda
Fès
Mohammedia
Salé
Casablanca
34°
Khouribga
Safi
Marrakech
Atlas Mountains
Essaouira
Agadir
Ouarzazate
ALGERIA
Anti - Atlas
30°
4°
WESTERN SAHARA
(Occupied by Morocco)
8°
12°
0 100 km
0 100 miles
3000m/9843ft
2000m/6562ft
1000m/3281ft
500m/1640ft
200m/656ft
Sea Level

FACTFILE

OFFICIAL NAME: Kingdom of Morocco
DATE OF FORMATION: 1956
CAPITAL: Rabat
POPULATION: 32 million
TOTAL AREA: 172,316 sq. miles (446,300 sq. km)
DENSITY: 186 people per sq. mile
LANGUAGES: Arabic*, Tamazight, French
RELIGIONS: Muslim (mainly Sunni) 99%, other (mostly Christian) 1%
ETHNIC MIX: Arab 70%, Berber 29%, European 1%
GOVERNMENT: Mixed monarchical–parliamentary system
CURRENCY: Mor. dirham = 100 centimes

Mozambique

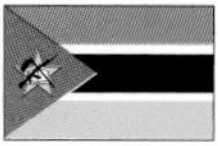

Mozambique lies on the southeast African coast. It was torn apart by a savage and devastating civil war between the Marxist government and a rebel faction between 1977 and 1992.

GEOGRAPHY

Largely a savanna-covered plateau. The coast is fringed by coral reefs and lagoons. The Zambezi River bisects the country.

CLIMATE

Tropical. Temperatures are hottest on the coast. Extremes of rainfall: drought and flood.

PEOPLE & SOCIETY

Tensions exist between north and south, rather than between ethnic groups. Life is centered on the extended family. Polygamy is fairly common. The country is struggling with the legacy of a war that killed around a million people, and the effects of frequent floods and droughts. Half the population lives in abject poverty.

INSIGHT: *Maputo's busy port serves Zimbabwe and South Africa*

THE ECONOMY

Extremely dependent on aid. Mineral potential. Cashew nuts, shrimp, cotton exported. Debt relief.

0 200 km
0 200 miles
TANZANIA
Rovuma
12°
Lake Nyasa
MALAWI
Lichinga
Pemba
Lúrio
Nacala
ZAMBIA
Lumbo
Lake Cahora Bassa
Nampula
16°
Tete
Zambezi
Quelimane
40°
ZIMBABWE
Beira
Mozambique Channel
20°
INDIAN OCEAN
Limpopo
Funhalouro
Inhambane
24°
SOUTH AFRICA
Xai-Xai
36°
MAPUTO
SWAZILAND
SOUTH AFRICA
32°
2000m/6562ft
1000m/3281ft
500m/1640ft
200m/656ft
Sea Level

FACTFILE

OFFICIAL NAME: Rep. of Mozambique
DATE OF FORMATION: 1975
CAPITAL: Maputo
POPULATION: 22.9 million
TOTAL AREA: 309,494 sq. miles (801,590 sq. km)
DENSITY: 76 people per sq. mile
LANGUAGES: Makua, Xitsonga, Sena, Lomwe, Portuguese*
RELIGIONS: Traditional beliefs 56%, Christian 30%, Muslim 14%
ETHNIC MIX: Makua Lomwe 47%, Tsonga 23%, Malawi 12%, Shona 11% other 7%
GOVERNMENT: Presidential system
CURRENCY: New metical = 100 centavos

Myanmar (Burma)

Forming the eastern shores of the Bay of Bengal and the Andaman Sea in southeast Asia, Myanmar suffers from isolation, political repression, and ethnic conflict.

GEOGRAPHY

The fertile Irrawaddy basin lies at the center. Mountains to the west, Shan plateau to the east. Tropical rainforest covers much of the land.

CLIMATE

Tropical. Hot summers, with high humidity, and warm winters.

PEOPLE & SOCIETY

The military, in power since 1962, rules Myanmar with little regard to human rights. Opposition is not tolerated. The National League for Democracy won elections in 1990, but was kept from power. Its leader, Aung San Suu Kyi, is frequently detained. Minority groups maintain low-level guerrilla activity against the state.

INSIGHT: *Myanmar is one of the world's biggest teak exporters, though reserves are diminishing rapidly*

THE ECONOMY

Corrupt, mismanaged, subject to sanctions – but gas, teak, and gems are exported. Illicit opium production has fallen. Rice shortages in 2008 after Cyclone Nargis. Prices are high on the black market.

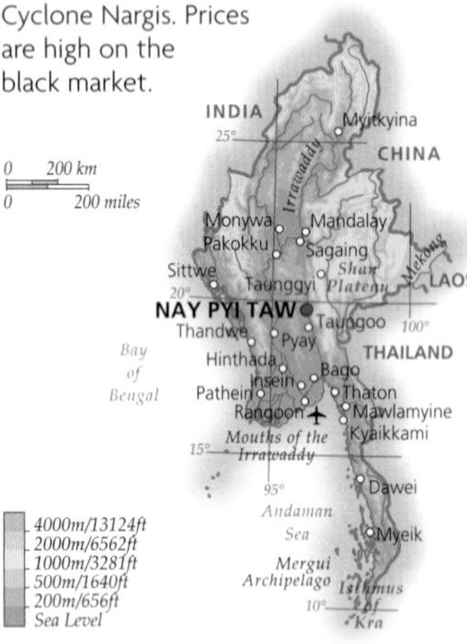
INDIA
CHINA
LAOS
THAILAND
Myitkyina
25°
Irrawaddy
0 200 km
0 200 miles
Monywa
Mandalay
Pakokku
Sagaing
Shan Plateau
Mekong
Sittwe
20°
Taunggyi
NAY PYI TAW
Taungoo
100°
Thandwe
Pyay
Bay of Bengal
Hinthada
Bago
Insein
Pathein
Thaton
Rangoon
Mawlamyine
Mouths of the Irrawaddy
Kyaikkami
15°
95°
Dawei
Andaman Sea
Myeik
Mergui Archipelago
Isthmus of Kra
10°
4000m/13124ft
2000m/6562ft
1000m/3281ft
500m/1640ft
200m/656ft
Sea Level

FACTFILE

OFFICIAL NAME: Union of Myanmar
DATE OF FORMATION: 1948
CAPITAL: Nay Pyi Taw
POPULATION: 50 million
TOTAL AREA: 261,969 sq. miles (678,500 sq. km)
DENSITY: 197 people per sq. mile
LANGUAGES: Burmese*, Shan, Karen, Rakhine, Chin, Yangbye, Kachin, Mon
RELIGIONS: Buddhist 87%, Christian 6%, Muslim 4%, other 2%, Hindu 1%
ETHNIC MIX: Burman 68%, other 13%, Shan 9%, Karen 6%, Rakhine 4%
GOVERNMENT: Military-based regime
CURRENCY: Kyat = 100 pyas

Namibia

Located in southwestern Africa, Namibia gained independence from South Africa in 1990, after 24 years of armed struggle. It regained the territory of Walvis Bay in 1994.

GEOGRAPHY

The Namib Desert stretches along the coastal strip. Inland, a ridge of mountains rises to 8000 ft (2500 m). The Kalahari Desert lies in the east.

CLIMATE

Almost rainless. The coast is usually shrouded in thick fog, unless the hot, dry *berg* wind is blowing.

PEOPLE & SOCIETY

The Ovambo, the main ethnic group, live mainly in the more populous north. Some 100,000 whites, many of German descent, are centered around Windhoek and still control the economy. The minority San and Khoi bushmen are among the oldest human communities in the world. The ban on homosexuality is contentious.

INSIGHT: *The Namib is the Earth's oldest, and one of its driest, deserts*

THE ECONOMY

Varied mineral resources, notably uranium and diamonds. Rich offshore fishing grounds. High unemployment. HIV/AIDS epidemic. One of Africa's most skewed distributions of wealth.

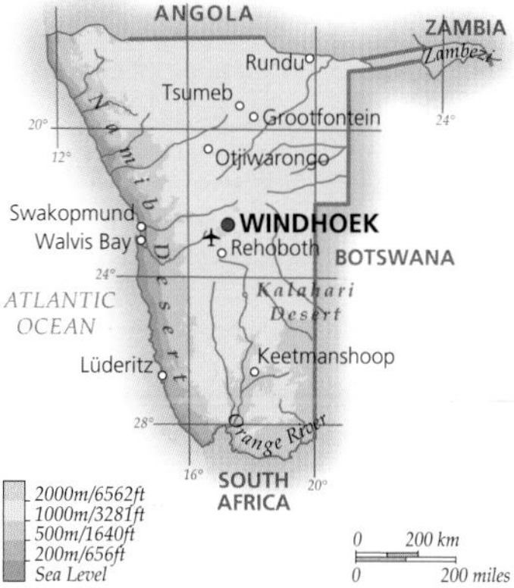
ANGOLA
ZAMBIA
Zambezi
Rundu
Tsumeb
Grootfontein
Otjiwarongo
Namib Desert
Swakopmund
Walvis Bay
WINDHOEK
Rehoboth
BOTSWANA
ATLANTIC OCEAN
Kalahari Desert
Keetmanshoop
Lüderitz
Orange River
SOUTH AFRICA
20°
12°
24°
24°
28°
16°
20°
2000m/6562ft
1000m/3281ft
500m/1640ft
200m/656ft
Sea Level
0 200 km
0 200 miles

FACTFILE

OFFICIAL NAME: Republic of Namibia
DATE OF FORMATION: 1990
CAPITAL: Windhoek
POPULATION: 2.17 million
TOTAL AREA: 318,694 sq. miles (825,418 sq. km)
DENSITY: 7 people per sq. mile
LANGUAGES: Ovambo, Kavango, English*, Bergdama, German, Afrikaans
RELIGIONS: Christian 90%, traditional beliefs 10%
ETHNIC MIX: Ovambo 50%, other 25%, Kavango 9%, Damara 8%, Herero 8%
GOVERNMENT: Presidential system
CURRENCY: Namibian dollar = 100 cents

Nauru

Nauru lies in the Pacific, northeast of Australia. Phosphate deposits gave its inhabitants huge temporary wealth but economic mismanagement has left them facing ruin.

GEOGRAPHY

A single low-lying coral atoll, with a fertile coastal belt. Coral cliffs encircle an elevated interior plateau.

CLIMATE

Equatorial, moderated by sea breezes. Occasional long droughts.

PEOPLE & SOCIETY

Native Nauruans are of mixed Micronesian and Polynesian origin. Most live in simple, traditional houses and spend their money on luxury cars and consumer goods. Welfare and education are free. A diet of imported processed foods has caused widespread obesity and diabetes. Mining was left to imported laborers, mainly from Kiribati, who lived in enclaves of male-only barracks and had few rights. Many young Nauruans leave to seek a better life in Australia or New Zealand.

THE ECONOMY

Phosphate revenues all but dried up. Sale of fishing rights sole resource. State trust fund invested badly overseas. Offshore banking facilities closed after international pressure.

INSIGHT: *Phosphate mining has left 80% of the island uninhabitable*

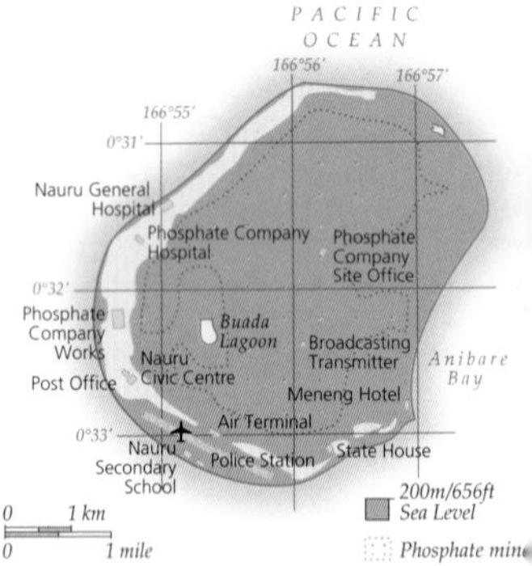
PACIFIC OCEAN
166°56′
166°57′
166°55′
0°31′
Nauru General Hospital
Phosphate Company Hospital
Phosphate Company Site Office
0°32′
Phosphate Company Works
Buada Lagoon
Broadcasting Transmitter
Anibare Bay
Nauru Civic Centre
Post Office
Meneng Hotel
Air Terminal
0°33′
Nauru Secondary School
Police Station
State House
200m/656ft
Sea Level
0 1 km
0 1 mile
Phosphate min

FACTFILE

OFFICIAL NAME: Republic of Nauru
DATE OF FORMATION: 1968
CAPITAL: None
POPULATION: 9800
TOTAL AREA: 8.1 sq. miles (21 sq. km)
DENSITY: 1210 people per sq. mile
LANGUAGES: Nauruan*, Kiribati, Chinese, Tuvaluan, English
RELIGIONS: Nauruan Congregational Church 60%, Catholic 35%, other 5%
ETHNIC MIX: Nauruan 62%, other Pacific islanders 27%, Asian 8%, European 3%
GOVERNMENT: Nonparty system
CURRENCY: Australian dollar = 100 cents

Nepal

Nepal, lying between India and China on the southern shoulder of the Himalayas, is one of the world's poorest countries. Its agricultural economy is heavily dependent on the monsoon.

GEOGRAPHY

Mainly mountainous. The area includes some of the highest mountains in the world, including Mount Everest. Flat, fertile river plains form the south.

CLIMATE

Warm monsoon season from July to October. The rest of the year is dry, sunny, and mild. Winter temperatures in the Himalayas average 14°F (–10°C).

PEOPLE & SOCIETY

Tensions are few between the diverse ethnic groups. Buddhist women, including Sherpas, face fewer social restrictions than Hindus. Trafficking of women and child labor are problems. Human rights violations rose during the 1999–2006 Maoist insurgency. The peace deal led to the abolition of the monarchy and Maoist victory in elections, but fractious coalitions mean instability continues.

THE ECONOMY

Agriculture employs 70% of people. Crops include rice and wheat. Tourism and investment affected by instability and Maoist insurgency. Reliant on aid. Hydropower potential.

INSIGHT: *Southern Nepal was the birthplace of Buddha (Prince Siddhartha Gautama) in 563 BCE*

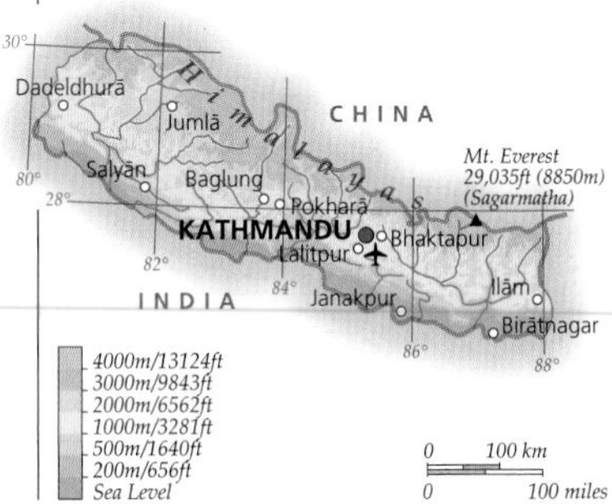
30°
Dadeldhurā
Jumlā
Himalayas
CHINA
Mt. Everest
29,035ft (8850m)
(Sagarmatha)
80°
Salyān
Baglung
28°
Pokharā
KATHMANDU
Bhaktapur
Lalitpur
82°
84°
INDIA
Janakpur
Ilām
Birātnagar
86°
88°
4000m/13124ft
3000m/9843ft
2000m/6562ft
1000m/3281ft
500m/1640ft
200m/656ft
Sea Level
0 100 km
0 100 miles

FACTFILE

OFFICIAL NAME: Federal Democratic Republic of Nepal
DATE OF FORMATION: 1769
CAPITAL: Kathmandu
POPULATION: 29.3 million
TOTAL AREA: 54,363 sq. miles (140,800 sq. km)
DENSITY: 555 people per sq. mile
LANGUAGES: Nepali*, Maithili, Bhojpuri
RELIGIONS: Hindu 90%, Buddhist 5%, Muslim 3%, other (incl. Christian) 2%
ETHNIC MIX: Other 57%, Chhetri 16%, Hill Brahman 13%, Tharu 7%, Magar 7%
GOVERNMENT: Transitional regime
CURRENCY: Nepalese rupee = 100 paisa

Netherlands

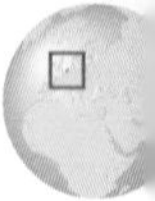

Astride the delta of five major rivers in northwest Europe, the Netherlands built its historic wealth on maritime trade. Rotterdam is Europe's largest port.

GEOGRAPHY

Mainly flat, with 27% of the land below sea level and protected by dunes, dikes, and canals. There are a few low hills in the south and east.

CLIMATE

Mild, rainy winters and cool summers. Gales from the North Sea are common in fall and winter.

PEOPLE & SOCIETY

The Dutch have a long history of welcoming immigrants from former colonies and refugees seeking asylum. However, lack of integration is now raising fears about the failing asylum system, immigrant crime, and militant Islam. Population is mostly urban and the density is high. The state does not try to impose a particular morality on its citizens. Laws concerning sexuality, narcotics-taking, and euthanasia are among the world's most liberal.

THE ECONOMY

Major trading hub. High-profile multinationals. Diverse industrial base: chemicals, machinery, electronics, and metals. Costly social welfare system.

INSIGHT: *In 2002, the Netherlands became the first country in the world to legalize euthanasia*

Sea Level
Below Sea Level
Waddeneilanden
Waddenzee
North Sea
IJsselmeer
Groningen
Leeuwarden
Haarlem
AMSTERDAM
'S-GRAVENHAGE
(THE HAGUE)
Leiden
Apeldoorn
Enschede
Utrecht
Delft
Neder Rijn
Arnhem
Rotterdam
Nijmegen
Maas
GERMANY
Breda
Tilburg
Eindhoven
BELGIUM
Maastricht
0 40 km
0 40 miles

FACTFILE

OFFICIAL NAME: Kingdom of the Netherlands
DATE OF FORMATION: 1648
CAPITAL: Amsterdam and The Hague
POPULATION: 16.6 million
TOTAL AREA: 16,033 sq. miles (41,526 sq. km)
DENSITY: 1267 people per sq. mile
LANGUAGES: Dutch*, Frisian
RELIGIONS: Roman Catholic 36%, other 34%, Protestant 27%, Muslim 3%
ETHNIC MIX: Dutch 82%, other 12%, Surinamese, Turkish, and Moroccan 6%
GOVERNMENT: Parliamentary system
CURRENCY: Euro = 100 cents

New Zealand

Lying in the South Pacific, 990 miles (1600 km) outheast of Australia, New Zealand comprises North and South Islands, separated by the Cook Strait, and many smaller islands.

GEOGRAPHY

North Island, noted for hot springs nd geysers, has the bulk of the opulation. South Island is mostly ountainous, with eastern lowlands.

CLIMATE

Generally temperate and damp. he far north is almost subtropical, hereas southern winters are cold.

PEOPLE & SOCIETY

Maoris were the first settlers, 200 years ago. Today's majority uropean population is descended ainly from British migrants who settled fter 1840. Maoris' living and education tandards are generally lower than verage. The government is continuing o negotiate the settlement of Maori nd claims.

INSIGHT: *New Zealand women were the first to get the vote (1893)*

THE ECONOMY

Tourism is the biggest foreign-exchange earner. Modern agricultural sector; world's top exporter of dairy products. Hi-tech manufacturing. Open economy. Strong trade links.

2000m/6562ft
1000m/3281ft
500m/1640ft
200m/656ft
Sea Level
North Island
36°
Auckland
Hamilton
Tauranga
Rotorua
New Plymouth
Hastings
40°
Palmerston North
Tasman Sea
Blenheim
WELLINGTON
Greymouth
176°
Cook Strait
South Island
Southern Alps
Christchurch
44°
Timaru
172°
Queenstown
PACIFIC OCEAN
Dunedin
Invercargill
Stewart Island
168°
0 200 km
0 200 miles

FACTFILE

OFFICIAL NAME: New Zealand
DATE OF FORMATION: 1947
CAPITAL: Wellington
POPULATION: 4.27 million
TOTAL AREA: 103,737 sq. miles (268,680 sq. km)
DENSITY: 41 people per sq. mile
LANGUAGES: English*, Maori*
RELIGIONS: Anglican 24%, other 22%, Presbyterian 18%, nonreligious 16%, Roman Catholic 15%, Methodist 5%
ETHNIC MIX: European 75%, Maori 15%, other 7%, Samoan 3%
GOVERNMENT: Parliamentary system
CURRENCY: New Zealand dollar = 100 cents

Nicaragua

Nicaragua lies at the heart of Central America. The Sandinista revolution of 1978 led to 11 years of civil war between the left-wing Sandinistas and the right-wing US-backed Contras

GEOGRAPHY

Extensive forested plains in the east. Central mountain region with many active volcanoes. The Pacific coastlands are dominated by lakes.

CLIMATE

Tropical. The lowlands are hot all year round. The mountains are cooler. Prone to occasional hurricanes.

PEOPLE & SOCIETY

Most of the population is mixed race, and there is a large white elite. The Caribbean regions are home to communities of Miskito Amerindians and blacks, who gained autonomy in 1987. The revolution improved the status of women, but these gains have been undone by rampant poverty.

INSIGHT: *Lake Nicaragua is the only freshwater lake in the world to contain marine animals*

THE ECONOMY

Textiles, coffee, meat, tobacco are main exports: affected by world price fluctuations. Remittances from abroad. Substantial debt relief has cut debt to 60% of GDP. Corruption.

1000m/3281ft
500m/1640ft
200m/656ft
Sea Level
Coco
HONDURAS
14°
Ocotal
Mosquito Coast
Caribb
Sea
Estelí
Matagalpa
Chinandega
Matiguas
León
MANAGUA
12°
Juigalpa
Bluefields
San Rafael del Sur
Granada
Rivas
Lago de Nicaragua
(Lake Nicaragua)
86°
COSTA RICA
San Juan
84°
0
100 km
0
100 miles

FACTFILE

OFFICIAL NAME: Republic of Nicaragua

DATE OF FORMATION: 1838

CAPITAL: Managua

POPULATION: 5.74 million

TOTAL AREA: 49,998 sq. miles (129,494 sq. km)

DENSITY: 125 people per sq. mile)

LANGUAGES: Spanish*, English Creole, Miskito

RELIGIONS: Roman Catholic 80%, Protestant Evangelical 17%, other 3%

ETHNIC MIX: Mestizo 69%, White 14%, Black 8%, Amerindian 5%, Zambo 4%

GOVERNMENT: Presidential system

CURRENCY: Córdoba oro = 100 centavos

Niger

Niger lies in west Africa, upstream from Nigeria on the Niger River. One of the world's poorest states, it was ruled by one-party or military regimes until multipartyism was allowed in 1992.

GEOGRAPHY

The north and northeast regions are part of the Sahara. The Aïr Mountains in the center rise high above the desert. Savanna lies to the south.

CLIMATE

High temperatures persist for most of the year at around 95°F (35°C). The north is virtually rainless.

PEOPLE & SOCIETY

Tuareg nomads in the north feel excluded from politics and the benefits of development of their area's uranium resources. An early 1990s rebellion was reignited in 2007. In the south, egalitarianism and a sense of community help to combat economic difficulties. Almost the entire urban population lives in slum conditions. Two-thirds of the population is under 25. Women have limited rights and restricted access to education.

THE ECONOMY

Vast uranium deposits. Frequent droughts and food shortages. Banditry. Expansion of Sahara. Oil potential.

INSIGHT: *The name Niger comes from the Tuareg word* n'eghirren, *which means "flowing water"*

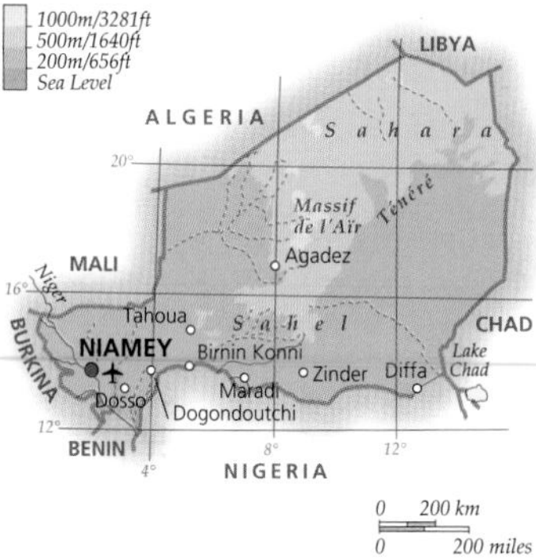
1000m/3281ft
500m/1640ft
200m/656ft
Sea Level
LIBYA
ALGERIA
Sahara
20°
Massif de l'Aïr
Ténéré
Agadez
MALI
16°
Niger
Tahoua
Sahel
CHAD
BURKINA
NIAMEY
Birnin Konni
Zinder
Diffa
Lake Chad
Dosso
Maradi
Dogondoutchi
12°
BENIN
4°
8°
12°
NIGERIA
0 200 km
0 200 miles

FACTFILE

OFFICIAL NAME: Republic of Niger
DATE OF FORMATION: 1960
CAPITAL: Niamey
POPULATION: 15.3 million
TOTAL AREA: 489,188 sq. miles (1,267,000 sq. km)
DENSITY: 31 people per sq. mile
LANGUAGES: Hausa, French*, other
RELIGIONS: Muslim 85%, traditional beliefs 14%, other (incl. Christian) 1%
ETHNIC MIX: Hausa 55%, Djerma and Songhai 21%, Peul 9%, Tuareg 9%, other 6%
GOVERNMENT: Presidential system
CURRENCY: CFA franc = 100 centimes

Nigeria

West Africa's biggest nation, Nigeria is a federation of 36 states and the capital, Abuja. Dominated by military governments since 1966, democracy returned in 1999.

GEOGRAPHY

Coastal area of beaches, swamps, and lagoons gives way to rainforest, and then to savanna on the high plateaus. Semidesert to the north.

CLIMATE

The south is hot, rainy and humid for most of the year. The arid north has one very humid wet season. The Jos Plateau and highlands are cooler.

PEOPLE & SOCIETY

Some 250 ethnic groups: tensions threaten national unity, with sporadic intercommunal violence. The northern states have introduced *sharia* (Islamic law) for their majority Muslim populations. Women have more economic independence in the south. In the Niger Delta, where 70% of people live on less than a dollar a day, militants are fighting for a share of the benefits of the region's oil wealth.

THE ECONOMY

Overdependent on oil, principal export since 1970s. Mismanagement and corruption. Foreign debt reduced.

INSIGHT: *Nigeria is Africa's most populous state – one in every seven Africans is Nigerian*

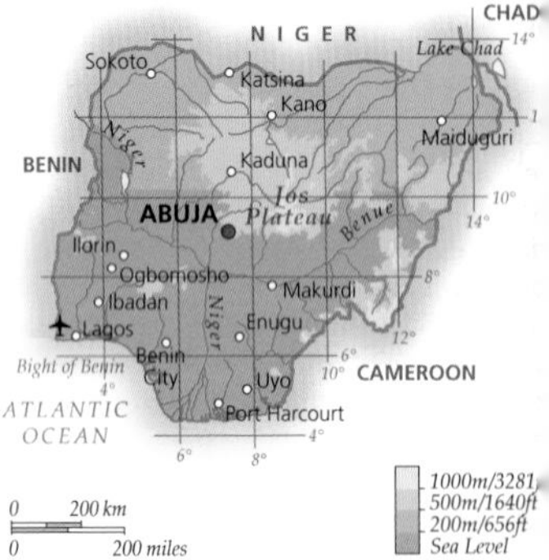

CHAD
NIGER
Lake Chad
Sokoto
Katsina
Kano
Maiduguri
Niger
BENIN
Kaduna
Jos Plateau
ABUJA
Benue
Ilorin
Ogbomosho
Makurdi
Ibadan
Lagos
Niger
Enugu
Benin City
Bight of Benin
CAMEROON
Uyo
ATLANTIC OCEAN
Port Harcourt
0 200 km
0 200 miles
1000m/3281ft
500m/1640ft
200m/656ft
Sea Level

FACTFILE

OFFICIAL NAME: Federal Republic of Nigeria
DATE OF FORMATION: 1960
CAPITAL: Abuja
POPULATION: 155 million
TOTAL AREA: 356,667 sq. miles (923,768 sq. km)
DENSITY: 440 people per sq. mile
LANGUAGES: Hausa, English*, Yoruba, Ibo
RELIGIONS: Muslim 50%, Christian 40%, traditional beliefs 10%
ETHNIC MIX: Hausa 21%, Yoruba 21%, Ibo 18%, Fulani 11%, other 29%
GOVERNMENT: Presidential system
CURRENCY: Naira = 100 kobo

Norway

The Kingdom of Norway traces the rugged western coast of Scandinavia. Settlements are largely restricted to southern and coastal areas. Vast oil and natural gas revenues bring prosperity.

GEOGRAPHY
The western coast is indented with numerous fjords and features tens of thousands of islands. Mountains and plateaus cover most of the country.

CLIMATE
Mild coastal climate. Inland, the weather is more extreme, with warmer summers and cold, snowy winters.

PEOPLE & SOCIETY
Fairly homogeneous; influx of refugees from 1990s Bosnian conflict. Strong family tradition despite high divorce rate. Fair-minded consensus promotes female equality, boosted by the generous childcare provision. Wealth is more evenly distributed than in most developed countries. Voted not to join EU in 1994.

INSIGHT: *Near Narvik, mainland Norway is only 4 miles (7 km) wide*

THE ECONOMY
Western Europe's top oil and natural gas producer: trust fund saves for post-oil future. Metal, chemical, and engineering industries. Generous aid donor. High cost of living.

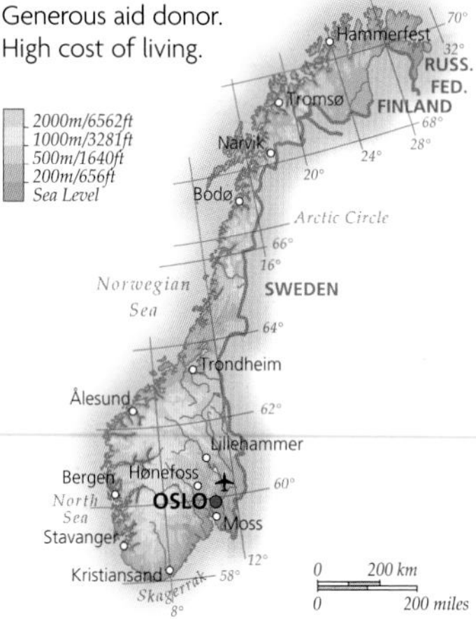
2000m/6562ft
1000m/3281ft
500m/1640ft
200m/656ft
Sea Level
Hammerfest
Tromsø
Narvik
Bodø
Arctic Circle
RUSS. FED.
FINLAND
SWEDEN
Norwegian Sea
Trondheim
Ålesund
Lillehammer
Bergen
Hønefoss
OSLO
North Sea
Moss
Stavanger
Kristiansand
Skagerrak
70°
32°
68°
28°
24°
20°
66°
16°
64°
62°
60°
12°
58°
8°
0 200 km
0 200 miles

FACTFILE

OFFICIAL NAME: Kingdom of Norway
DATE OF FORMATION: 1905
CAPITAL: Oslo
POPULATION: 4.81 million
TOTAL AREA: 125,181 sq. miles (324,220 sq. km)
DENSITY: 41 people per sq. mile
LANGUAGES: Norwegian* (Bokmål and Nynorsk), Sámi
RELIGIONS: Evangelical Lutheran 89%, other 10%, Roman Catholic 1%
ETHNIC MIX: Norwegian 93%, other 6%, Sámi 1%
GOVERNMENT: Parliamentary system
CURRENCY: Norwegian krone = 100 øre

Oman

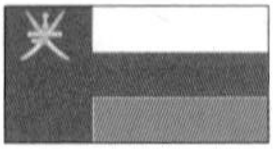

Oman occupies a strategic position on the Arabian Peninsula, at the entrance to the Persian Gulf. It is the least developed Gulf state, despite modest oil exports.

GEOGRAPHY

Mostly gravelly desert, with mountains in the north and south. Some narrow fertile coastal strips.

CLIMATE

Blistering heat in the west. Summer temperatures often climb above 113°F (45°C). Southern uplands receive rains June–September.

PEOPLE & SOCIETY

Urban drift has seen most Omanis move to northern towns. The majority are Ibadi Muslims who follow an appointed leader, the imam. Ibadism is not opposed to freedom for women, and a few women hold positions of authority. Baluchi from Pakistan are the largest group of foreign workers.

INSIGHT: *Until the late 1980s, Oman was closed to all but business or official visitors*

THE ECONOMY

Oil and natural gas account for almost all export revenue. Commercially extractable reserves are limited. Other exports include fish, animals, and dates. Foreigners work in all sectors.

2000m/6562ft
1000m/3281ft
500m/1640ft
200m/656ft
Sea Level
Strait of Hormuz
Al Khaşab
Musandam Peninsula
Gulf of Oman
UAE
Şuḩār
MUSCAT
24°
Al Qābil
Ar Rustāq
Bahlah
Şamad
Şūr
60°
Arabian Sea
SAUDI ARABIA
20°
Duqm
Ar Rub' al Khali
INDIAN OCEAN
Şawqirah
YEMEN
Şalālah
52°
56°
0 100 km
0 100 miles

FACTFILE

OFFICIAL NAME: Sultanate of Oman
DATE OF FORMATION: 1951
CAPITAL: Muscat
POPULATION: 2.85 million
TOTAL AREA: 82,031 sq. miles (212,460 sq. km)
DENSITY: 35 people per sq. mile
LANGUAGES: Arabic*, Baluchi, other
RELIGIONS: Ibadi Muslim 75%, other Muslim and Hindu 25%
ETHNIC MIX: Arab 88%, Baluchi 4%, Persian 3%, Indian and Pakistani 3%, African 2%
GOVERNMENT: Monarchy
CURRENCY: Omani rial = 1000 baisa

Pakistan

Once a part of British India, Pakistan was created in 1947 in response to demands for an independent Muslim state. In 1971, Bangladesh (former East Pakistan) became a separate state.

GEOGRAPHY

Indus floodplain across east and ɔuth. Hindu Kush mountains in north. emidesert plateau, mountains in west.

CLIMATE

Temperatures can soar to 122°F ɔ0°C) in south and west, and fall to –4°F -20°C) in the Hindu Kush.

PEOPLE & SOCIETY

Punjabis dominate government and ɪe army. Tensions with minority groups, xacerbated by the vast gap between ch and poor. Strong family ties ermeate politics and business. elations with India are tense over ashmir. Islamist taliban insurgency in ibal areas on Afghan border: in 2009, ghting displaced two million.

INSIGHT: *In 1988, Pakistan elected Benazir Bhutto as the first female prime ɪinister in the Muslim world*

THE ECONOMY

Major cotton and rice producer, but unpredictable weather conditions often affect crop. Textiles. Instability. Corruption. Aid to fight terrorism and for earthquake reconstruction.

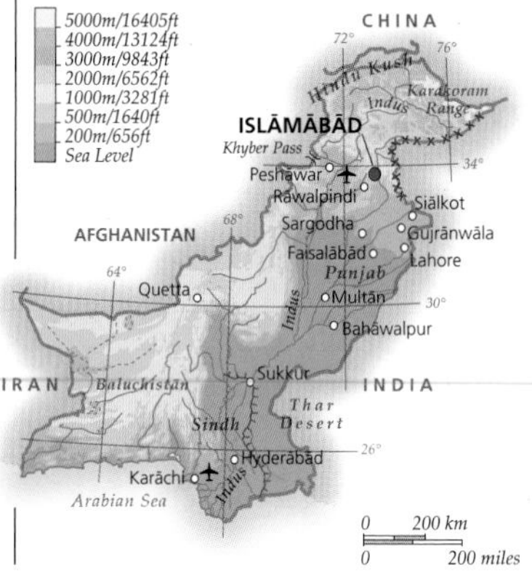
5000m/16405ft
4000m/13124ft
3000m/9843ft
2000m/6562ft
1000m/3281ft
500m/1640ft
200m/656ft
Sea Level
CHINA
72°
76°
Hindu Kush
Karakoram Range
Indus
ISLĀMĀBĀD
Khyber Pass
Peshāwar
Rawalpindi
34°
Siālkot
AFGHANISTAN
68°
Sargodha
Gujrānwāla
Faisalābād
Lahore
64°
Punjab
Quetta
Indus
Multān
30°
Bahāwalpur
IRAN
Baluchistān
Sukkur
INDIA
Thar Desert
Sindh
26°
Hyderābād
Karāchi
Indus
Arabian Sea
0 200 km
0 200 miles

FACTFILE

OFFICIAL NAME: Islamic Rep. of Pakistan
DATE OF FORMATION: 1947
CAPITAL: Islamabad
POPULATION: 181 million
TOTAL AREA: 310,401 sq. miles (803,940 sq. km)
DENSITY: 607 people per sq. mile
LANGUAGES: Punjabi, Sindhi, Pashtu, Urdu*, Baluchi, Brahui
RELIGIONS: Sunni Muslim 77%, Shi'a Muslim 20%, Hindu 2%, Christian 1%
ETHNIC MIX: Punjabi 56%, Pathan 15%, Sindhi 14%, other 8%, Mohajir 7%
GOVERNMENT: Presidential system
CURRENCY: Pakistani rupee = 100 paisa

Palau

The 300-island Palau archipelago (known locally as Belau) lies in the western Pacific Ocean. It achieved independenc in 1994, and is gradually reducing its aid dependence.

GEOGRAPHY

Terrain varies from thickly forested mountains to limestone and coral reefs. Babeldaob, the largest island, is volcanic, with many rivers and waterfalls.

CLIMATE

Hot and wet. Little variation in daily and seasonal temperatures. February–April is the dry season.

PEOPLE & SOCIETY

Native Palauans are a mix of the original Southeast Asian migrants and Pacific settlers. A modern influx from Asia has led to tension. 70% of the population lives on the island-city of Koror, prompting the construction of a new capital on Babeldaob. Native culture is preserved on outer islands despite strong influence from the US and Japan. Modekngei is a blend of Christianity and local beliefs.

THE ECONOMY

Tourism and fishing licenses are main earners. Coconuts, taro, and bananas. 15-year US aid plan to 2009.

INSIGHT: *Palau's reefs contain 1500 species of fish and 700 types of corc*

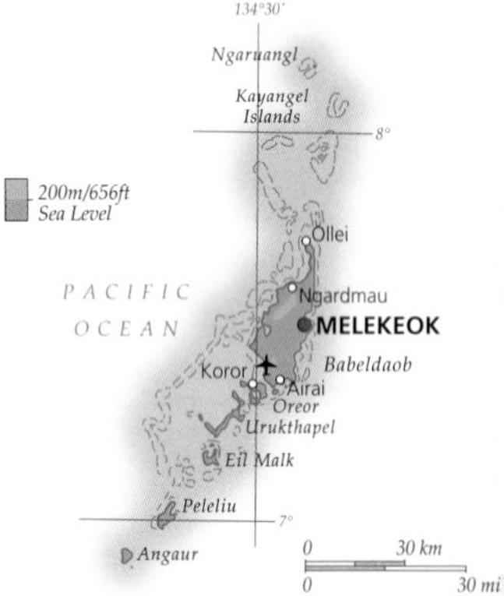
134°30'
Ngaruangl
Kayangel Islands
8°
200m/656ft
Sea Level
Ollei
PACIFIC OCEAN
Ngardmau
MELEKEOK
Babeldaob
Koror
Airai
Oreor
Urukthapel
Eil Malk
Peleliu
7°
Angaur
0 30 km
0 30 mi

FACTFILE

OFFICIAL NAME: Republic of Palau
DATE OF FORMATION: 1994
CAPITAL: Melekeok
POPULATION: 20,400
TOTAL AREA: 177 sq. miles (458 sq. km)
DENSITY: 104 people per sq. mile
LANGUAGES: Palauan*, English*, Japanese, Angaur, Tobi, Sonsorolese
RELIGIONS: Christian 66%, Modekngei 34%
ETHNIC MIX: Palauan 74%, Filipino 16%, other 6%, Chinese and other Asian 4%
GOVERNMENT: Nonparty system
CURRENCY: US dollar = 100 cents

Panama

Panama is the southernmost country in Central America. The colossal Panama Canal (which was under US control until 2000) links the Pacific and Atlantic oceans.

GEOGRAPHY

Lowlands along both coasts, with avanna-covered plains and rolling hills. Mountainous interior. Swamps and ainforests in the east.

CLIMATE

Hot and humid, with heavy rainfall n the May–December wet season. Cooler at high altitudes.

PEOPLE & SOCIETY

A multiethnic society, dominated by people of Spanish origin. Amerindians ive in remote areas. The Panama Canal and former US military bases (the last of which closed n 1999) have given society a cosmopolitan outlook, but Catholicism and the extended family remain strong. Crime is high; money-laundering, narcotics trafficking, and corruption are rife.

THE ECONOMY

Colón Free Trade Zone: world's second-largest. Income from the canal (expansion project underway) and merchant ships sailing under flag of Panama. Banana and shrimp exports.

INSIGHT: *The Panama Canal shortens the sea route between the east coast of the US and Japan by 3000 miles (4800 km)*

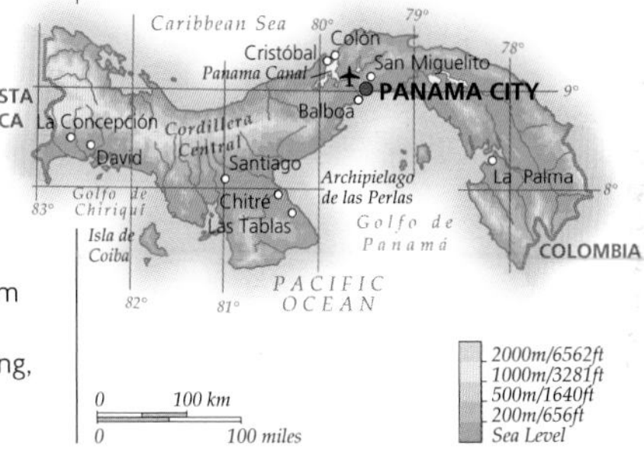
Caribbean Sea
80°
79°
78°
Colón
Cristóbal
San Miguelito
Panama Canal
PANAMA CITY
9°
COSTA RICA
La Concepción
Cordillera Central
Balboa
David
Santiago
Archipielago de las Perlas
La Palma
8°
Golfo de Chiriquí
83°
Chitré
Las Tablas
Golfo de Panamá
Isla de Coiba
COLOMBIA
PACIFIC OCEAN
82°
81°
0
100 km
0
100 miles
2000m/6562ft
1000m/3281ft
500m/1640ft
200m/656ft
Sea Level

FACTFILE

OFFICIAL NAME: Republic of Panama
DATE OF FORMATION: 1903
CAPITAL: Panama City
POPULATION: 3.45 million
TOTAL AREA: 30,193 sq. miles (78,200 sq. km)
DENSITY: 118 people per sq. mile
LANGUAGES: English Creole, Spanish*, Amerindian and Chibchan languages
RELIGIONS: Roman Catholic 86%, other 8%, Protestant 6%
ETHNIC MIX: *Mestizo* 60%, White 14%, Black 12%, Amerindian 8%, other 6%
GOVERNMENT: Presidential system
CURRENCY: Balboa = 100 centésimos

Papua New Guinea

A former Australian colony, Papua New Guinea (PNG) occupies the eastern section of the island of New Guinea and several other island groups. Much of the country is isolated.

GEOGRAPHY

Mountainous and forested mainland, with broad, swampy river valleys. 40 active volcanoes in the north. Around 600 outer islands.

CLIMATE

Hot and humid in lowlands, cooling toward highlands, where snow can fall on highest peaks.

PEOPLE & SOCIETY

Around 800 language groups and even more tribes. The main social distinction is between lowlanders, who have frequent contact with the outside world, and the very isolated, but increasingly threatened, highlanders. Great tensions exist between highland tribes, and vendettas can often last several generations. The island of Bougainville has been granted autonomy and promised an eventual referendum on independence.

THE ECONOMY

Minerals: significant quantities of gold, copper, oil, and natural gas. High government spending almost led to national bankruptcy in 2002.

INSIGHT: *PNG is home to the only known poisonous birds; contact with the feathers of some species of pitohui produces skin blisters*

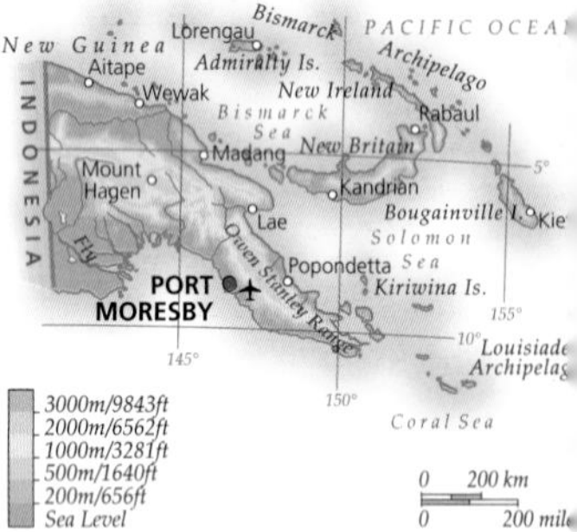
New Guinea
Lorengau
Bismarck Archipelago
PACIFIC OCEAN
Aitape
Admiralty Is.
Wewak
New Ireland
Bismarck Sea
Rabaul
INDONESIA
Madang
New Britain
Mount Hagen
Kandrian
Lae
Bougainville I.
Kieta
Solomon Sea
Fly
Owen Stanley Range
Popondetta
PORT MORESBY
Kiriwina Is.
5°
10°
145°
150°
155°
Louisiade Archipelago
Coral Sea
3000m/9843ft
2000m/6562ft
1000m/3281ft
500m/1640ft
200m/656ft
Sea Level
0 200 km
0 200 miles

FACTFILE

OFFICIAL NAME: Independent State of Papua New Guinea
DATE OF FORMATION: 1975
CAPITAL: Port Moresby
POPULATION: 6.73 million
TOTAL AREA: 178,703 sq. miles (462,840 sq. km)
DENSITY: 39 people per sq. mile
LANGUAGES: Pidgin English, Papuan, English*, Motu, c.800 native languages
RELIGIONS: Protestant 60%, Roman Catholic 37%, other 3%
ETHNIC MIX: Melanesian and mixed 100%
GOVERNMENT: Parliamentary system
CURRENCY: Kina = 100 toea

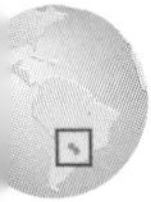

Paraguay

Landlocked in central South America, and once a Spanish colony, Paraguay's postindependence history has ncluded periods of military rule. Free elections were held in 1993.

GEOGRAPHY

The Paraguay River divides the hilly nd forested east from a flat alluvial lain, with marsh and semidesert scrub and in the west.

CLIMATE

Subtropical. The Gran Chaco is generally hotter and drier. All areas xperience floods and droughts.

PEOPLE & SOCIETY

Population mainly of mixed Spanish nd native Guaraní origin. Most people re bilingual, though in rural areas Guaraní s more widely used. Cattle ranchers opulate the Chaco, along with ommunities of the German-origin Mennonite Church. The army is olitically active.

INSIGHT: *The War of the Triple Alliance (1864–1870) killed almost 90% of Paraguay's male population*

THE ECONOMY

Agriculture: soybeans are the main export. Electricity exported from massive hydroelectric dams, including Itaipú (world's second-largest, jointly run with Brazil). Large informal economy. Corruption and smuggling.

BOLIVIA
60°
0 100 km
0 100 miles
20°
Paraguay
Gran Chaco
BRAZIL
Pedro Juan Caballero
Concepción
ARGENTINA
Represa de Itaipú
25°
ASUNCIÓN
Coronel Oviedo
Lambaré
Villarrica
Ciudad del Este
Pilar
Paraná
Encarnación
55°
1000m/3281ft
500m/1640ft
200m/656ft
Sea Level

FACTFILE

OFFICIAL NAME: Republic of Paraguay
DATE OF FORMATION: 1811
CAPITAL: Asunción
POPULATION: 6.35 million
TOTAL AREA: 157,046 sq. miles (406,750 sq. km)
DENSITY: 41 people per sq. mile
LANGUAGES: Guaraní*, Spanish*, German
RELIGIONS: Roman Catholic 96%, Protestant (including Mennonite) 4%
ETHNIC MIX: *Mestizo* 91%, other 7%, Amerindian 2%
GOVERNMENT: Presidential system
CURRENCY: Guaraní = 100 céntimos

Peru

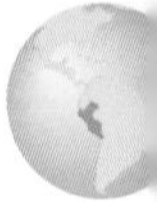

Once the heart of the Inca Empire, before the Spanish conquest in the 16th century, Peru lies on the Pacific coast of South America, just south of the equator.

GEOGRAPHY

Coastal plain rises to Andes Mountains. Uplands, dissected by fertile valleys, lie east of the Andes. Tropical forest in extreme east.

CLIMATE

Coast is mainly arid. Middle slopes of the Andes are temperate; higher peaks are snow-covered. East is hot, humid, and very wet.

PEOPLE & SOCIETY

Though most people are Amerindians or mixed-race *mestizos*, society is dominated by a small group of Spanish descendants. Amerindians, and the small black community, suffer discrimination in towns, but access to information and political power are growing; the first Amerindian president was elected in 2001–2006. Clashes with left-wing militants killed almost 70,000 people between 1980 and 2000.

THE ECONOMY

Abundant mineral resources: notably copper and gold. Rich Pacific fish stocks. Illegal cocaine producer.

INSIGHT: *Lake Titicaca is the world highest navigable lake*

Equator
COLOMBIA
ECUADOR
Putumayo
Amazon
Iquitos
Marañón
4°
Piura
Chiclayo
Ucayali
BRAZIL
8°
Trujillo
Chimbote
Pucallpa
Huánuco
80°
Andes
LIMA
Huancayo
12°
Callao
Cusco
PACIFIC
OCEAN
Ayacucho
Ica
Juliaca
Lake Titicaca
16°
Arequipa
76°
BOLIVIA
Tacna
72°
CHILE
4000m/13124ft
2000m/6562ft
500m/1640ft
Sea Level
0 200 km
0 200 miles

FACTFILE

OFFICIAL NAME: Republic of Peru
DATE OF FORMATION: 1824
CAPITAL: Lima
POPULATION: 29.2 million
TOTAL AREA: 496,223 sq. miles (1,285,200 sq. km)
DENSITY: 59 people per sq. mile
LANGUAGES: Spanish*, Quechua*, Aymara
RELIGIONS: Roman Catholic 95%, other 5%
ETHNIC MIX: Amerindian 50%, *Mestizo* 40%, White 7%, other 3%
GOVERNMENT: Presidential system
CURRENCY: New sol = 100 céntimos

Philippines

Lying in the western Pacific Ocean, the Philippines is the world's second-largest archipelago, with 7107 islands, of which 4600 are named but only around 1000 inhabited.

GEOGRAPHY

Larger islands are forested and nountainous. Over 20 active volcanoes. 'requent earthquakes.

CLIMATE

Tropical. Warm and humid all year ound. Typhoons occur in the rainy eason: June–October.

PEOPLE & SOCIETY

Over 100 ethnic groups, most of vhich are of Malay origin. The Catholic Church is a dominant cultural force; it opposes family-planning, despite high population growth. The Chinese minority as been established for 400 years. Vomen play a prominent part in society. High literacy levels. Islamist separatists and communist insurgents undermine stability.

INSIGHT: *Mass "People Power" demonstrations have brought down wo presidents, in 1986 and 2001*

THE ECONOMY

Coconuts, bananas, pineapples exported. Growing outsourcing center. Remittances from abroad. Corruption and poor infrastructure limit growth.

2000m/6562ft
1000m/3281ft
500m/1640ft
200m/656ft
Sea Level
20°
Babuyan Is.
PACIFIC OCEAN
Luzon
Philippine Sea
16°
Cabanatuan
Angeles
MANILA
Batangas
Legazpi City
South China Sea
Mindoro
12°
Calbayog
Samar
Panay
Iloilo
Bacolod City
Cebu
Palawan
Puerto Princesa
Butuan
Negros
Sulu Sea
Iligan
8°
Balabac Strait
Davao
116°
Zamboanga
General Santos
Sulu Archipelago
Mindanao
124°
4°
Celebes Sea
120°
0 200 km
0 200 miles

FACTFILE

OFFICIAL NAME: Rep. of the Philippines
DATE OF FORMATION: 1946
CAPITAL: Manila
POPULATION: 92 million
TOTAL AREA: 115,830 sq. miles (300,000 sq. km)
DENSITY: 799 people per sq. mile
LANGUAGES: Filipino*, Tagalog, Cebuano, Hiligaynon, other, including English*
RELIGIONS: Roman Catholic 83%, Protestant 9%, Muslim 5%, other 3%
ETHNIC MIX: Tagalog 28%, Cebuano 13%, Ilocano 9%, Hiligaynon 8%, other 42%
GOVERNMENT: Presidential system
CURRENCY: Philippine peso = 100 centavos

Poland

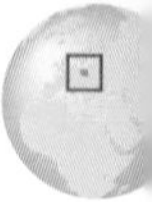

Located in the heart of Europe, Poland has undergone massive social, economic, and political change since the collapse of communism in 1989. It joined the EU in 2004.

GEOGRAPHY

Lowlands, part of the North European Plain, cover most of the country. The Tatra Mountains run along the southern border.

CLIMATE

Rainfall peaks during the hot summers. Cold winters with snow, especially in mountains.

PEOPLE & SOCIETY

Ethnic homogeneity masks a number of tensions. Secular liberals criticize the semiofficial status of the Roman Catholic Church, and emerging wealth disparities are resented by those not profiting from the free market. The German minority in the west is growing more assertive.

INSIGHT: *Wild wisent (European bison) live in the Bialowieza Forest straddling the Poland–Belarus border*

THE ECONOMY

Foreign investment reflects the country's large potential market. Rapid privatization. Heavy industries dominate, though services growing. Plans to join euro in 2012.

Baltic Sea
RUSSIAN FEDERATION
LITHUANIA
BELARUS
GERMANY
CZECH REP.
SLOVAKIA
UKRAINE
Gdynia
Gdańsk
Olsztyn
Szczecin
Bydgoszcz
Białystok
Oder
Włocławek
Poznań
WARSAW
Wisła
Zielona Góra
Łódź
Radom
Lublin
Wrocław
Częstochowa
Gliwice
Katowice
Rzeszów
Kraków
Tatra Mts.
14°
16°
18°
20°
22°
24°
54°
52°
50°
1000m/3281ft
500m/1640ft
200m/656ft
Sea Level
0 100 km
0 100 miles

FACTFILE

OFFICIAL NAME: Republic of Poland
DATE OF FORMATION: 1918
CAPITAL: Warsaw
POPULATION: 38.1 million
TOTAL AREA: 120,728 sq. miles (312,685 sq. km)
DENSITY: 324 people per sq. mile
LANGUAGES: Polish
RELIGIONS: Roman Catholic 93%, other and nonreligious 5%, Orthodox Christian 2%
ETHNIC MIX: Polish 97%, other 2%, Silesian 1%
GOVERNMENT: Parliamentary system
CURRENCY: Zloty = 100 groszy

Portugal

Portugal, with its long Atlantic coast, lies on the western side of the Iberian Peninsula, which it shares with Spain. It is the most westerly country on the European mainland.

GEOGRAPHY

The Tagus River bisects the country roughly east to west, dividing mountainous north from lower and more undulating south.

CLIMATE

North is cool and moist. South is warmer, with dry, mild winters.

PEOPLE & SOCIETY

A homogeneous and stable society, which is losing some of its conservative traditions. History of immigration from former colonies, and recently from eastern Europe. Urban areas and the south are more socially liberal. The north is more responsive to traditional Roman Catholic values. Family ties remain important.

INSIGHT: *Portugal is the world's leading producer of cork, which comes from the bark of the cork oak*

THE ECONOMY

Tourism. Vegetables, fruit, wine, cars, and clothing are exported, but agriculture and manufacturing are in decline. Resilient banking sector.

42°
Viana do Castelo
Vila Real
Douro
Porto
Vila Nova de Gaia
ATLANTIC OCEAN
Coimbra
40°
Santarém
SPAIN
Estoril
LISBON
Barreiro
Évora
Setúbal
38°
Beja
Algarve
Portimão
Faro
8°
0 100 km
0 100 miles
33°
Madeira
17°
Madeira Is.
0 50 km
0 50 miles
São Miguel
38°
30°
Azores
26°
0 200 km
0 200 miles
1000m/3281ft
500m/1640ft
200m/656ft
Sea Level

FACTFILE

OFFICIAL NAME: Republic of Portugal
DATE OF FORMATION: 1139
CAPITAL: Lisbon
POPULATION: 10.7 million
TOTAL AREA: 35,672 sq. miles (92,391 sq. km)
DENSITY: 302 people per sq. mile
LANGUAGES: Portuguese
RELIGIONS: Roman Catholic 97%, other 2%, Protestant 1%
ETHNIC MIX: Portuguese 98%, African and other 2%
GOVERNMENT: Parliamentary system
CURRENCY: Euro = 100 cents

Qatar

Projecting from the Arabian Peninsula into the Persian Gulf, Qatar was a founding member of OPEC. One of the region's wealthiest states due to oil and natural gas exports.

GEOGRAPHY

Flat, semiarid desert with dunes and salt pans. Vegetation is limited to small patches of scrub.

CLIMATE

Hot and humid. Temperatures in summer can soar to over 104°F (40°C). Rainfall is rare.

PEOPLE & SOCIETY

Only one in five residents is native-born; the rest are guest workers from across the Middle East, the Indian subcontinent, Southeast Asia and north Africa. Qataris were once nomadic Bedouins, but since the advent of oil wealth, most now live in Doha and its suburbs, leaving the north dotted with abandoned villages. Women enjoy relative freedom; most wear the veil.

INSIGHT: *There are twice as many men as women in Qatar*

THE ECONOMY

Steady supply of crude oil and huge natural gas reserves, plus related industries. All other raw materials and most foods are imported. Strong GDP growth. Economy is heavily dependent on foreign workforce.

Ar Ru'ays
51
Al Khuwayr
26
Gulf of Bahrain
Madīnat al Ka'bān
Al Khawr
Ash Shahaniyah
DOHA
Ar Rayyān
Umm Bāb
Al Wakrah
25
As Salwā
Persian Gulf
SAUDI ARABIA
UAE
0 30 km
0 30 miles
200m/656ft
Sea Level

FACTFILE

OFFICIAL NAME: State of Qatar
DATE OF FORMATION: 1971
CAPITAL: Doha
POPULATION: 1.41 million
TOTAL AREA: 4416 sq. miles (11,437 sq. km)
DENSITY: 332 people per sq. mile
LANGUAGES: Arabic
RELIGIONS: Muslim (mainly Sunni) 95%, other 5%
ETHNIC MIX: Qatari 20%, other Arab 20%, Indian 20%, Nepalese 13%, Filipino 10%, Pakistani 7%, other 10%
GOVERNMENT: Monarchy
CURRENCY: Qatar riyal = 100 dirhams

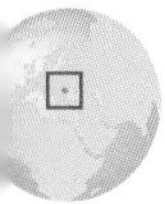

Romania

Once dominated by Poles, Hungarians, and Ottomans, Romania has been slowly converting to a market economy since the 1989 overthrow of its communist regime. It joined the EU in 2007.

GEOGRAPHY

Carpathian Mountains encircle the Transylvanian plateau. Wide plains to the south and east. Danube River forms southern border.

CLIMATE

Continental. Summers are hot and humid, winters are cold and snowy. Very heavy spring rains.

PEOPLE & SOCIETY

Romanians are ethnically distinct from their Slav and Hungarian (Magyar) neighbors. Hungarians are the largest minority, living mainly in Transylvania. They are protected by the influence of Hungary, unlike the Roma, who suffer from discrimination. The overall population is shrinking.

INSIGHT: *In 2001, Romania became the last country in Europe to lift its ban on homosexuality*

THE ECONOMY

Polluting, outdated heavy industries and unmechanized agricultural sector. Exports of textiles and metals have led growth in 2000s. Has plans to join euro currency zone in 2015. Privatization continues.

UKRAINE
Prut
48°
Satu Mare
Botoșani
HUNGARY
Baia Mare
Suceava
Oradea
Carpathian Mountains
Iași
Cluj-Napoca
Transylvania
Bacău
MOLD.
Arad
Târgu Mureș
46°
Timișoara
Sibiu
Brașov
Focșani
UKRAINE
Reșița
Galați
Carpații Meridionali
Buzău
Brăila
Drobeta-Turnu Severin
Pitești
Danube Delta
Ploiești
SERBIA
BUCHAREST
Constanța
Black Sea
44°
Craiova
Danube
22°
Mangalia
24°
26°
28°
BULGARIA
2000m/6562ft
1000m/3281ft
500m/1640ft
200m/656ft
Sea Level
0
100 km
0
100 miles

FACTFILE

OFFICIAL NAME: Romania
DATE OF FORMATION: 1878
CAPITAL: Bucharest
POPULATION: 21.3 million
TOTAL AREA: 91,699 sq. miles (237,500 sq. km)
DENSITY: 239 people per sq. mile
LANGUAGES: Romanian*, Hungarian
RELIGIONS: Romanian Orthodox 87%, Roman Catholic 5%, Protestant 4%, other 2%, Greek Orthodox 1%, Uniate 1%
ETHNIC MIX: Romanian 89%, Magyar 7%, Roma 2%, other 2%
GOVERNMENT: Presidential system
CURRENCY: Romanian leu

Russian Federation

The Russian Federation was the core of the old Soviet Union, which broke up in 1991. Russia is still the world's largest state. Its diversity is a source of both strength and problems.

GEOGRAPHY

The Ural Mountains divide the European steppes and forests from the tundra and forests of Siberia. South-central deserts and mountains.

CLIMATE

Continental in European Russia. Elsewhere climate ranges from sub-arctic to Mediterranean and hot desert.

PEOPLE & SOCIETY

Besides the ethnic Russian majority, there are 57 “nationalities” with territorial status, and a further 95 minorities without their own region. Most ethnic republics are in European Russia. The number of Muslims is rising, though the overall population is predicted to fall by 30% in 50 years. Nation-based separatism is brutally suppressed, as in Chechnya. HIV/AIDS is spreading. Healthcare and education are underfunded. Crime is a serious problem.

Murmansk
FINLAND
Kaliningrad
(Russ. Fed.)
Sankt Peterburg
(St Petersburg)
BELARUS
MOSCOW
Yaroslavl'
Tula
UKRAINE
Nizhniy Novgorod
Volga
Voronezh
Kazan'
Izhevsk
Ul'yanovsk
Rostov-na-Donu
Saratov
Chelny
Tol'yatti
Krasnodar
Volgograd
Samara
Yekaterinburg
Orenburg
Caucasus
GEORGIA
Astrakhan'
Groznyy
AZERBAIJAN

INSIGHT: *The Trans-Siberian Railroad, which runs 5578 miles (9297 km) from Moscow to Vladivostok, is the longest in the world, passing through eight time zones*

FACTFILE

OFFICIAL NAME: Russian Federation
DATE OF FORMATION: 1480
CAPITAL: Moscow
POPULATION: 141 million
TOTAL AREA: 6,592,735 sq. miles (17,075,200 sq. km)
DENSITY: 21 people per sq. mile
LANGUAGES: Russian*, other
RELIGIONS: Orthodox Christian 75%, Muslim 14%, other 11%
ETHNIC MIX: Russian 80%, other 13%, Tatar 4%, Ukrainian 2%, Chavash 1%
GOVERNMENT: Mixed presidential–parliamentary system
CURRENCY: Russian rouble = 100 kopeks

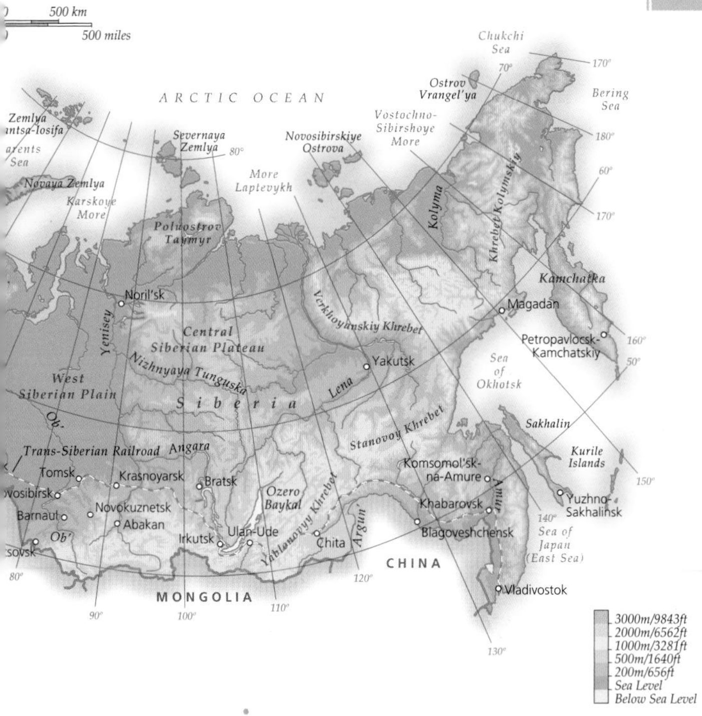
500 km
500 miles
Chukchi Sea
Ostrov Vrangel'ya
Bering Sea
ARCTIC OCEAN
Zemlya Frantsa-Iosifa
Barents Sea
Severnaya Zemlya
Novosibirskiye Ostrova
Vostochno-Sibirshoye More
More Laptevykh
Novaya Zemlya
Karskoye More
Poluostrov Taymyr
Kolyma
Khrebet Kolymskiy
Kamchatka
Noril'sk
Magadan
Verkhoyanskiy Khrebet
Yenisey
Central Siberian Plateau
Petropavlovsk-Kamchatskiy
Nizhnyaya Tunguska
Yakutsk
Sea of Okhotsk
West Siberian Plain
Lena
Siberia
Ob'
Sakhalin
Stanovoy Khrebet
Trans-Siberian Railroad
Angara
Kurile Islands
Komsomol'sk-na-Amure
Tomsk
Krasnoyarsk
Bratsk
Novosibirsk
Ozero Baykal
Barnaul
Novokuznetsk
Abakan
Khabarovsk
Amur
Yuzhno-Sakhalinsk
Yablonovyy Khrebet
Argun'
Irkutsk
Ulan-Ude
Chita
Blagoveshchensk
Sea of Japan (East Sea)
CHINA
MONGOLIA
Vladivostok
3000m/9843ft
2000m/6562ft
1000m/3281ft
500m/1640ft
200m/656ft
Sea Level
Below Sea Level

THE ECONOMY

Huge natural resources (oil and natural gas, precious metals, timber) account for 80% of exports. Important military, engineering, and scientific base. Wealth disparities and black-market activities have accompanied reforms. Organized crime syndicates own huge areas of the economy. Widespread tax evasion, corruption. Lingering inefficiencies in industry and agriculture. High oil prices brought strong GDP growth and budget surpluses in 2000s, allowing Russia to repay its Soviet-era debt. Stock market collapse, devaluation of rouble in 2008, then recession in 2009.

Rwanda

Rwanda lies just south of the equator in east central Africa, far from the nearest sea port. Since independence from France in 1962, ethnic tensions have dominated politics.

GEOGRAPHY

A series of plateaus descend from the ridge of volcanic peaks in the west to the Akagera River on the eastern border. The Great Rift Valley also passes through this region.

CLIMATE

Tropical, though tempered by the altitude. Two wet seasons are separated by a dry season, from June to August. Heaviest rain in the west.

PEOPLE & SOCIETY

For over 500 years the cattle-owning Tutsi minority were politically dominant over the land-owning Hutu. In 1959, violent revolt led to a reversal of the roles. Ethnic tensions are fierce; in the most recent violence, in 1994, over 800,000 people, mostly Tutsi, were massacred in an act of state-backed genocide; trials are ongoing. Most people live at subsistence level.

THE ECONOMY

Rwanda is reliant on aid, but (given stability) could become a big coffee and tea producer. Exports tin, coltan, and iron ore. Ecotourism is growing. Possible oil and gas reserves. Landlocked: high transportation costs.

INSIGHT: *Rwanda's parliament in 2008 was the first in the world to have more women members than men*

0 50 km
0 50 miles
UGANDA
TANZANIA
Akagera
DEM. REP. CONGO
Ruhengeri
Byumba
Gisenyi
Lake Kivu
KIGALI
2°
Kibuye
Gitarama
Kibungo
Cyangugu
Butare
30°
29°
BURUNDI
2000m/6562ft
1000m/3281ft
500m/1640ft

FACTFILE

OFFICIAL NAME: Republic of Rwanda
DATE OF FORMATION: 1962
CAPITAL: Kigali
POPULATION: 10 million
TOTAL AREA: 10,169 sq. miles (26,338 sq. km)
DENSITY: 1038 people per sq. mile
LANGUAGES: Kinyarwanda*, French*, Kiswahili, English*
RELIGIONS: Catholic 56%, traditional beliefs 25%, Muslim 10%, Protestant 9%
ETHNIC MIX: Hutu 90%, Tutsi 9%, other (including Twa) 1%
GOVERNMENT: Presidential system
CURRENCY: Rwanda franc = 100 centimes

St. Kitts & Nevis

A popular Caribbean tourist destination, St. Kitts and Nevis lies in the northern part of the Leeward Island chain. Nevis is the smaller and less developed of the two islands.

GEOGRAPHY

Volcanic in origin, with forested, mountainous interiors. Nevis has hot and cold springs.

CLIMATE

Tropical, tempered by trade winds. Little seasonal variation in temperature. Moderate rainfall.

PEOPLE & SOCIETY

The majority of the population are descended from former African slaves. There are small numbers of Europeans, and South Asians, and a community of Lebanese. Levels of emigration are high, and overseas remittances are an important source of national income. The government has pledged to retrain sugar workers. Native professionals and civil servants have largely replaced the former expatriate elite. The secessionist movement on Nevis remains an issue.

THE ECONOMY

Successful tourist industry is vulnerable to downturns in US market. Financial services. Once-key sugar industry closed down in 2005.

INSIGHT: *Nevis has been renowned as a spa since the 18th century, and is known as the "Queen of the Caribbean"*

0 5 km
0 5 miles
Dieppe Bay Town
St. Paul's
St Kitts
Cayon
ATLANTIC OCEAN
17°20′
Old Road Town
Golden Rock Airport
BASSETERRE
62°50′
62°45′
62°35′
17°15′
Caribbean Sea
The Narrows
Newcastle
62°40′
Nevis
17°10′
Charlestown
Zion
Bath
1000m/3281ft
500m/1640ft
200m/656ft
Sea Level

FACTFILE

OFFICIAL NAME: Federation of Saint Christopher and Nevis
DATE OF FORMATION: 1983
CAPITAL: Basseterre
POPULATION: 46,100
TOTAL AREA: 101 sq. miles (261 sq. km)
DENSITY: 332 people per sq. mile
LANGUAGES: English*, English Creole
RELIGIONS: Anglican 33%, Methodist 29%, other 22%, Moravian 9%, Roman Catholic 7%
ETHNIC MIX: Black 95%, Mixed race 3%, White 1%, other and Amerindian 1%
GOVERNMENT: Parliamentary system
CURRENCY: East Caribbean $ = 100 cents

St. Lucia

St. Lucia is one of the most beautiful of the Caribbean Windward Islands. Ruled by France and the UK at different times in its past, the island retains the character of both.

GEOGRAPHY

Volcanic and mountainous, with some broad fertile valleys. The Pitons, ancient lava cones, rise from the sea on the forested west coast.

CLIMATE

Tropical, moderated by trade winds. May–October wet season brings daily warm showers. Rainfall is highest in the mountains.

PEOPLE & SOCIETY

Population is a tension-free mixture of descendants of Africans, Caribs, and Europeans. Family life and the Roman Catholic Church are important to most St. Lucians. In rural areas, women often head the households and run much of the farming. Plantation and hotel owners are the richest group. There is growing local resistance to overdevelopment of the island for tourism.

THE ECONOMY

Bananas are still biggest export, but struggling to compete since loss of preferential access to EU market. Successful tourism. Offshore banking.

INSIGHT: *St. Lucia has two Nobel laureates, the most per capita in the world*

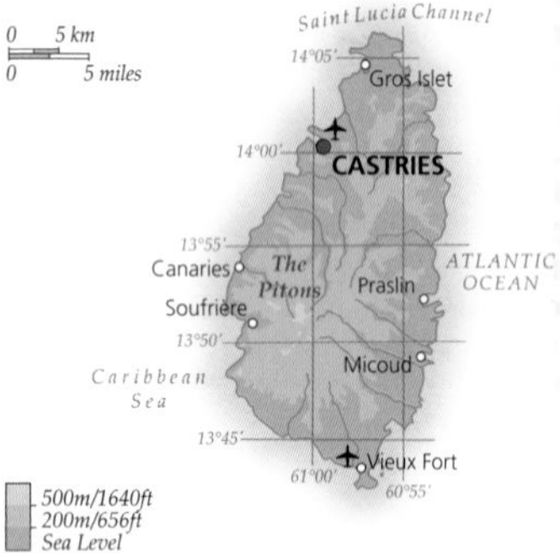
Saint Lucia Channel
0 5 km
0 5 miles
14°05'
Gros Islet
14°00'
CASTRIES
13°55'
Canaries
The Pitons
Praslin
ATLANTIC OCEAN
Soufrière
13°50'
Micoud
Caribbean Sea
13°45'
Vieux Fort
61°00'
60°55'
500m/1640ft
200m/656ft
Sea Level

FACTFILE

OFFICIAL NAME: Saint Lucia
DATE OF FORMATION: 1979
CAPITAL: Castries
POPULATION: 172,200
TOTAL AREA: 239 sq. miles (620 sq. km)
DENSITY: 730 people per sq. mile
LANGUAGES: English*, French Creole
RELIGIONS: Roman Catholic 90%, other 10%
ETHNIC MIX: Black 83%, Mixed race 13%, Asian 3%, White 1%
GOVERNMENT: Parliamentary system
CURRENCY: East Caribbean dollar = 100 cents

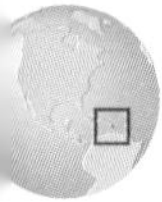

St. Vincent & the Grenadines

The islands of St. Vincent and the Grenadines form part of the Windward group in the Caribbean. St. Vincent is mostly volcanic, while the Grenadines are flat, mainly bare, coral reefs.

GEOGRAPHY

St. Vincent is mountainous and forested, with one of two active volcanoes in the Caribbean, La Soufrière. The Grenadines are 32 islands and cays, fringed by beaches

CLIMATE

Tropical, with constant trade winds. Hurricanes are likely during July–November wet season.

PEOPLE & SOCIETY

Population is racially diverse; intermarriage has reduced tensions. Society is informal and relaxed, but family life is strongly influenced by the Christian Church. Locals fear that their traditional lifestyle is being threatened by the expanding tourist industry.

INSIGHT: *The islands' precolonial inhabitants, the Carib, named them "Harioun" – home of the blessed*

THE ECONOMY

Dependent on agriculture and tourism. Bananas are the main cash crop. Tourism, targeted at the jet-set and cruise-ship markets, is concentrated on the Grenadines.

1000m/3281ft
500m/1640ft
200m/656ft
Sea Level
0 10 km
0 10 miles
La Soufrière
4078ft (1234m)
Chateaubelair
Georgetown
St Vincent
KINGSTOWN
Arnos Vale Airport
13°20'
13°10'
Bequia
13°00'
Caribbean Sea
Isle à Quatre
Baliceaux
Mustique
12°50'
The Grenadines
Canouan
Mayreau
Union I.
61°10'
12°40'
61°20'
ATLANTIC OCEAN

FACTFILE

OFFICIAL NAME: Saint Vincent and the Grenadines
DATE OF FORMATION: 1979
CAPITAL: Kingstown
POPULATION: 109,200
TOTAL AREA: 150 sq. miles (389 sq. km)
DENSITY: 834 people per sq. mile
LANGUAGES: English*, English Creole
RELIGIONS: Anglican 47%, Methodist 28%, Roman Catholic 13%, other 12%
ETHNIC MIX: Black 77%, Mixed race 16%, other 3%, Carib 3%, Asian 1%
GOVERNMENT: Parliamentary system
CURRENCY: East Caribbean dollar = 100 cents

Samoa

The Pacific islands of Samoa gained independence from New Zealand in 1962. Four of the nine volcanic islands are inhabited – Apolima, Manono, Savai'i, and Upolu.

GEOGRAPHY

Comprises two large islands and seven smaller ones. The two largest islands have rainforested, mountainous interiors surrounded by coastal lowlands and coral reefs.

CLIMATE

Tropical, with high humidity. Cooler in May–November. Cyclone season is December–March.

PEOPLE & SOCIETY

Ethnic Samoans are the world's second-largest Polynesian group, after the Maoris. Their way of life is communal and formalized. Extended family groups own 80% of the land. Each family has an elected chief, who looks after its political and social interests. Large-scale migration to the US and New Zealand reflects the country's lack of jobs and the attractions of a Western lifestyle.

THE ECONOMY

Exports fish, coconut products (oil, cream, copra), and nonu fruit. Growth of tourism, offshore banking, and light manufacturing (Japanese car parts). Dependent on aid and expatriate remittances. Rainforests are increasingly exploited for timber.

INSIGHT: *Samoa was named for the sacred (sa) chickens (moa) of Lu, son of Tagaloa, the god of creation*

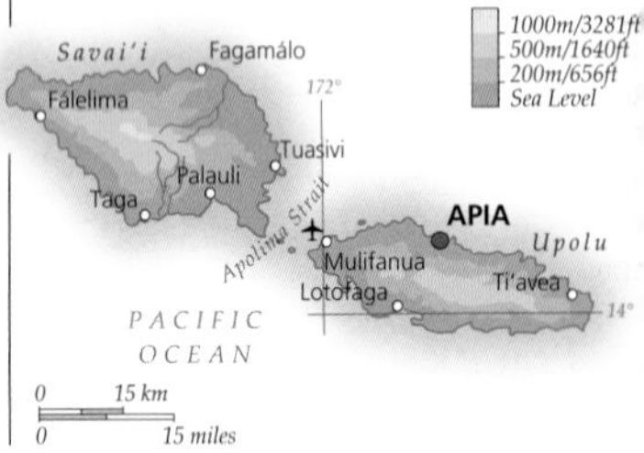
1000m/3281ft
500m/1640ft
200m/656ft
Sea Level
Savai'i
Fagamálo
Fálelima
172°
Tuasivi
Palauli
Taga
Apolima Strait
APIA
Upolu
Mulifanua
Lotofaga
Ti'avea
14°
PACIFIC OCEAN
0 15 km
0 15 miles

FACTFILE

OFFICIAL NAME: Independent State of Samoa

DATE OF FORMATION: 1962

CAPITAL: Apia

POPULATION: 178,800

TOTAL AREA: 1104 sq. miles (2860 sq. km)

DENSITY: 164 people per sq. mile

LANGUAGES: Samoan*, English*

RELIGIONS: Christian 99%, other 1%

ETHNIC MIX: Polynesian 90%, Euronesian (mixed European and Polynesian) 9%, other 1%

GOVERNMENT: Parliamentary system

CURRENCY: Tala = 100 sene

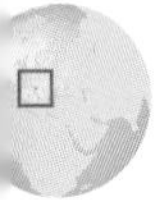

San Marino

Perched on the slopes of Monte Titano in the Italian Appennines, San Marino has maintained its independence since the 4th century CE, but Italy effectively controls most of its affairs.

GEOGRAPHY

Distinctive limestone outcrop of Monte Titano dominates wooded hills and pastures near Italy's Adriatic coast.

CLIMATE

High altitude and sea breezes moderate a Mediterranean climate. Hot summers and cool, wet winters.

PEOPLE & SOCIETY

Territory is divided into nine "castles," or districts. Tightly knit society, with 16 centuries of tradition. Strict immigration rules require 30-year residence before applying for citizenship. Living standards are similar to those in northern Italy. About 20,000 Sammarinesi live abroad, most in Italy.

INSIGHT: *Sales of postage stamps and coins contribute around 10% of the national income*

THE ECONOMY

Tourism provides over half of GDP. Banking: transparency has improved. Lower tax rates than Italy. Wine, cheese, olive oil, textiles, and ceramics are exported. Also relies on Italian subsidy and infrastructure.

44°
Dogana
Serravalle
Fiorina
Cailungo
Gualdicciolo
Borgo Maggiore
SAN MARINO
ITALY
Monte Titano
2424ft (739m)
Faetano
Murata
ITALY
Appennino
Chiesanuova
Montegiardino
12°30'
500m/1640ft
200m/656ft
Sea Level
0
4 km
0
4 miles

FACTFILE

OFFICIAL NAME: Republic of San Marino
DATE OF FORMATION: 1631
CAPITAL: San Marino
POPULATION: 31,400
TOTAL AREA: 23.6 sq. miles (61 sq. km)
DENSITY: 1308 people per sq. mile
LANGUAGES: Italian
RELIGIONS: Roman Catholic 93%, other and nonreligious 7%
ETHNIC MIX: Sammarinese 88%, Italian 10%, other 2%
GOVERNMENT: Parliamentary system
CURRENCY: Euro = 100 cents

São Tomé & Príncipe

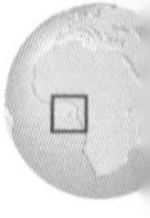

A former Portuguese colony, São Tomé and Príncipe comprises two main islands and surrounding islets, off the west coast of Africa. Elections in 1991 ended 15 years of Marxism.

GEOGRAPHY

Islands scattered across the equator. São Tomé and Príncipe are heavily forested and mountainous.

CLIMATE

Hot and humid, but cooled by the Benguela Current. Plentiful rainfall.

PEOPLE & SOCIETY

Population is mostly black, though Portuguese culture predominates. Blacks run the political parties. Society is well integrated and free of racial prejudice. Príncipe assumed autonomous status in 1995. There is a growing business class. Extended family offers main form of social security. One of Africa's highest aid-to-population ratios.

INSIGHT: *The population is entirely of immigrant descent: the islands were uninhabited when colonized in 1470*

THE ECONOMY

Cocoa provides 95% of export earnings. Coconuts, pepper, coffee also farmed. Tourism potential. Offshore oil may come onstream in 2012.

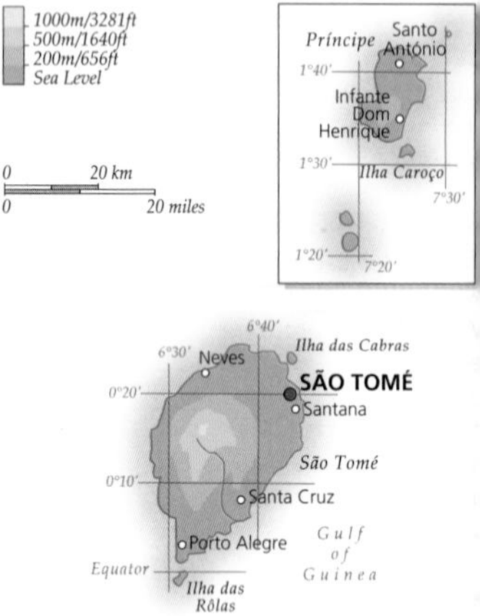
1000m/3281ft
500m/1640ft
200m/656ft
Sea Level
0
20 km
0
20 miles
Príncipe
Santo António
1°40'
Infante Dom Henrique
1°30'
Ilha Caroço
7°30'
1°20'
7°20'
6°40'
6°30'
Neves
Ilha das Cabras
SÃO TOMÉ
0°20'
Santana
São Tomé
0°10'
Santa Cruz
Porto Alegre
Gulf of Guinea
Equator
Ilha das Rôlas

FACTFILE

OFFICIAL NAME: Democratic Republic of São Tomé and Príncipe
DATE OF FORMATION: 1975
CAPITAL: São Tomé
POPULATION: 162,800
TOTAL AREA: 386 sq. miles (1001 sq. km)
DENSITY: 439 people per sq. mile
LANGUAGES: Portuguese Creole, Portuguese*
RELIGIONS: Roman Catholic 84%, other 16%
ETHNIC MIX: Black 90%, Portuguese and Creole 10%
GOVERNMENT: Presidential system
CURRENCY: Dobra = 100 céntimos

Saudi Arabia

Occupying most of the Arabian Peninsula, Saudi Arabia covers an area the size of western Europe. It is the world's largest oil producer and has a major petrochemicals industry.

GEOGRAPHY

Mostly desert or semidesert lateau. Mountain ranges in the west run arallel to the Red Sea and drop steeply o a coastal plain.

CLIMATE

In summer, temperatures often oar above 118°F (48°C), but in winter hey may fall below freezing. Rainfall s rare.

PEOPLE & SOCIETY

Most Saudis are Sunni Muslims vho follow the strictly orthodox Vahhabi interpretation of Islam and embrace sharia (Islamic law) in their laily lives. Women are obliged to wear he veil, cannot hold a driver's license, nd have no role in public life. The l-Sa'ud family has had absolute rule ince 1932. With the support of the eligious establishment, it controls ll political life.

THE ECONOMY

Vast oil and natural gas reserves. A third of workers are foreign. Attractive jobs for young Saudis are scarce, however.

INSIGHT: *Three million Muslims a year make the haj (pilgrimage) to the holy city of Mecca. Only practicing Muslims are allowed inside the city*

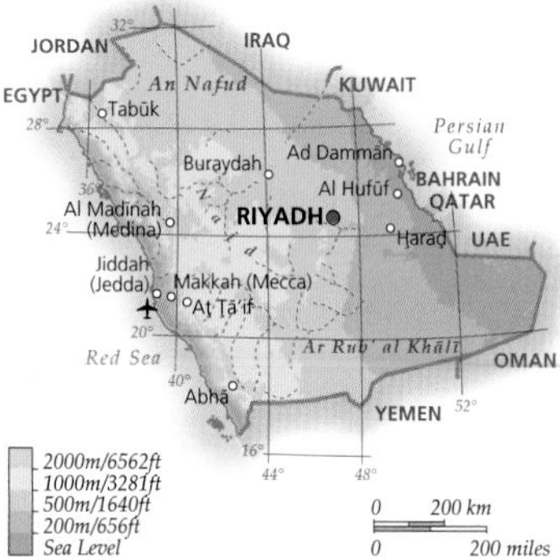
JORDAN
IRAQ
EGYPT
KUWAIT
An Nafud
Tabūk
Persian Gulf
Ad Dammān
Buraydah
BAHRAIN
Al Hufūf
QATAR
Al Madinah (Medina)
RIYADH
Harad
UAE
Jiddah (Jedda)
Makkah (Mecca)
At Tā'if
Ar Rub' al Khālī
Red Sea
OMAN
Abhā
YEMEN
32°
28°
24°
20°
16°
36°
40°
44°
48°
52°
2000m/6562ft
1000m/3281ft
500m/1640ft
200m/656ft
Sea Level
0 200 km
0 200 miles

FACTFILE

OFFICIAL NAME: Kingdom of Saudi Arabia
DATE OF FORMATION: 1932
CAPITALS: Riyadh
POPULATION: 25.7 million
TOTAL AREA: 756,981 sq. miles (1,960,582 sq. km)
DENSITY: 32 people per sq. mile
LANGUAGES: Arabic
RELIGIONS: (Native population) Sunni Muslim 85%, Shi'a Muslim 15%
ETHNIC MIX: Arab 72%, foreign (mostly S or SE Asian) 20%, Afro-Asian 8%
GOVERNMENT: Monarchy
CURRENCY: Saudi riyal = 100 halalat

Senegal

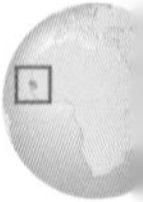

Senegal's capital, Dakar, stands on the westernmost cape of Africa. After independence from France, Senegal became a single-party state, but it has had multiparty elections since 1981.

GEOGRAPHY

Arid semidesert in the north. The south is mainly savanna bushland. Plains in the southeast.

CLIMATE

Tropical, with humid rainy conditions June–October, and a drier season December–May. The coast is cooled by northern trade winds.

PEOPLE & SOCIETY

Interethnic marriage has reduced ethnic tensions. Groups can be identified regionally. Dakar is a Wolof area, the Senegal River is dominated by the Toucouleur, and the Malinké mostly live in the east. The Diola (Jola) in Casamance have felt politically excluded, prompting a long-running secessionist struggle; a cease-fire has held since 2004. A large diaspora has raised global awareness of Senegalese culture and music.

THE ECONOMY

Good infrastructure, particularly port at Dakar. Fishing (though stocks diminishing). Remittances. Phosphate mining. Groundnuts. Development of tourism. Oil potential off Casamance.

INSIGHT: *Senegal's name derives from the Muslim Zenega Berbers who invaded in the 1300s*

Senegal
Saint-Louis
MAURITANIA
ATLANTIC OCEAN
Louga
Matam
Senegal
DAKAR
Thiès
Diourbel
Mbour
14°
Kaolack
Kaffrine
Tambacounda
MAL
GAMBIA
Casamance
Kolda
Gambia
Ziguinchor
GUINEA-BISSAU
GUINEA
16°
12°
200m/656ft
Sea Level
0 100 km
0 100 miles

FACTFILE

OFFICIAL NAME: Republic of Senegal
DATE OF FORMATION: 1960
CAPITAL: Dakar
POPULATION: 12.5 million
TOTAL AREA: 75,749 sq. miles (196,190 sq. km)
DENSITY: 169 people per sq. mile
LANGUAGES: Wolof, Serer, Pulaar, Diola, Mandinka, Malinké, Soninké, French*
RELIGIONS: Sunni Muslim 90%, traditional beliefs 5%, Christian 5%
ETHNIC MIX: Wolof 43%, Serer 15%, other 14%, Peul 14%, Toucouleur 9%, Diola 5%
GOVERNMENT: Presidential system
CURRENCY: CFA franc = 100 centimes

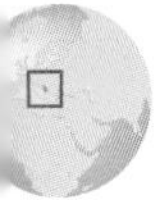

Serbia

The central and eastern region of what was once Yugoslavia, Serbia was a pariah state until Slobodan Milosevic was ousted in 2000. Montenegro broke away in 2006, and Kosovo in 2008.

GEOGRAPHY

Landlocked since secession of Montenegro. Fertile Danube plain in the north, rolling uplands in the center and southeast. Mountains in southwest.

CLIMATE

Continental in north, with wet springs and warm summers. Colder winters with heavy snow in south.

PEOPLE & SOCIETY

Serbs are Orthodox Christian, and their language uses Cyrillic script. The Catholic Magyars (Hungarians) live mainly in Vojvodina, which has been granted some autonomy. Society was severely shaken in the 1990s by interethnic conflict. EU integration is dependent on Serbia's cooperation in apprehending suspected war criminals.

INSIGHT: *The medieval Serbian Empire reached into northern Greece*

THE ECONOMY

Recovering from sanctions and 1999 NATO bombing: GDP is only just back to pre-1990 level. Reserves of coal, oil. Strong industrial base. Privatization ongoing. Foreign investment growing. Danube is a key transportation link.

HUNGARY
20°
0 50 km
0 50 miles
Subotica
46°
Vojvodina
Zrenjanin
Danube
CROATIA
Novi Sad
ROMANIA
Šabac
Pančevo
22°
BELGRADE
Smederevo
Danube
BOSNIA & HERZEGOVINA
Kragujevac
44°
Čačak
Kraljevo
Kruševac
Niš
Leskovac
MONTENEGRO
KOSOVO
(disputed)
BULG.
2000m/6562ft
1000m/3281ft
500m/1640ft
200m/656ft
Sea Level
MACEDONIA

FACTFILE

OFFICIAL NAME: Republic of Serbia
DATE OF FORMATION: 2006
CAPITAL: Belgrade
POPULATION: 7.75 million
TOTAL AREA: 34,116 sq. miles (88,361 sq. km)
DENSITY: 259 people per sq. mile
LANGUAGES: Serbian*, Hungarian
RELIGIONS: Orthodox Christian 85%, other 6%, Roman Catholic 6%, Muslim 3%
ETHNIC MIX: Serb 83%, other 10%, Magyar 4%, Bosniak 2%, Roma 1%
GOVERNMENT: Parliamentary system
CURRENCY: Dinar = 100 para

Seychelles

Formerly a UK colony, the Seychelles comprises 115 islands in the Indian Ocean. After 14 years as a one-party state, multiparty elections were introduced in 1993.

GEOGRAPHY

Mostly low-lying coral atolls, but 40, including the largest, Mahé, are mountainous and are the only granitic midocean islands in the world.

CLIMATE

Tropical oceanic climate. Hot and humid. Rainy season December–May.

PEOPLE & SOCIETY

The islands were uninhabited when French settlers arrived in the 18th century. Today, the population is homogeneous – a result of intermarriage between ethnic groups. Almost 90% of people live on Mahé. Living standards are among Africa's highest. Poverty is rare and the welfare system caters to all.

INSIGHT: *The Seychelles' unique species include the coco-de-mer palm, which produces the world's largest seeds*

THE ECONOMY

Tourism is main sector, based on appeal of beaches and exotic wildlife. Tuna is fished and canned for export. Re-export trade. Virtually no mineral resources. All domestic requirements are imported. High debt-servicing burden. Lack of foreign exchange.

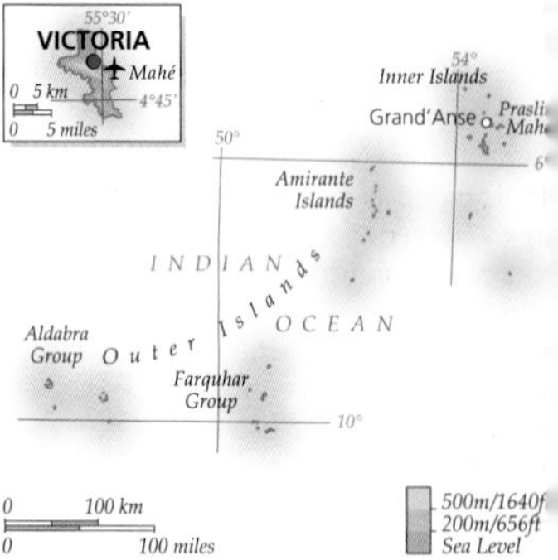
55°30'
VICTORIA
Mahé
0 5 km
0 5 miles
4°45'
Inner Islands
54°
Grand'Anse
50°
Amirante Islands
INDIAN OCEAN
Outer Islands
Aldabra Group
Farquhar Group
10°
0 100 km
0 100 miles
500m/1640ft
200m/656ft
Sea Level

FACTFILE

OFFICIAL NAME: Republic of Seychelles
DATE OF FORMATION: 1976
CAPITAL: Victoria
POPULATION: 84,600
TOTAL AREA: 176 sq. miles (455 sq. km)
DENSITY: 813 people per sq. mile
LANGUAGES: Creole*, English*, French*
RELIGIONS: Roman Catholic 90%, Anglican 8%, other (including Muslim) 2%
ETHNIC MIX: Creole 89%, Indian 5%, other 4%, Chinese 2%
GOVERNMENT: Presidential system
CURRENCY: Seychelles rupee = 100 cents

Sierra Leone

The west African state of Sierra Leone achieved ndependence from the UK in 1961. Today, trying to recover from ten ears of devastating civil war, it is one of the world's poorest nations.

GEOGRAPHY

Flat plain, running the length of the oast, stretches inland for 83 miles 33 km). Beyond, forests rise to highlands ear neighboring Guinea in the northeast.

CLIMATE

Hot tropical weather, with very igh rainfall and humidity. The dusty, ortheastern *harmattan* wind blows ovember–April.

PEOPLE & SOCIETY

Mende and Temne are the major thnic groups. Freetown's citizens are rgely descended from slaves freed om Britain and the US, resulting in strongly Anglicized Creole culture the capital. The countryside is less eveloped. A brutal civil war broke ut in 1991 and was not properly esolved until a 2001 peace greement. Two million people were isplaced during the conflict.

THE ECONOMY

Aid is vital: reconstruction will take years. Diamond exports, though smuggling is rife. Rutile and bauxite also mined. Coffee and cocoa are cash crops, but most farming is subsistence.

INSIGHT: *The British philanthropist Granville Sharp set up a settlement for freed slaves in Freetown in 1787*

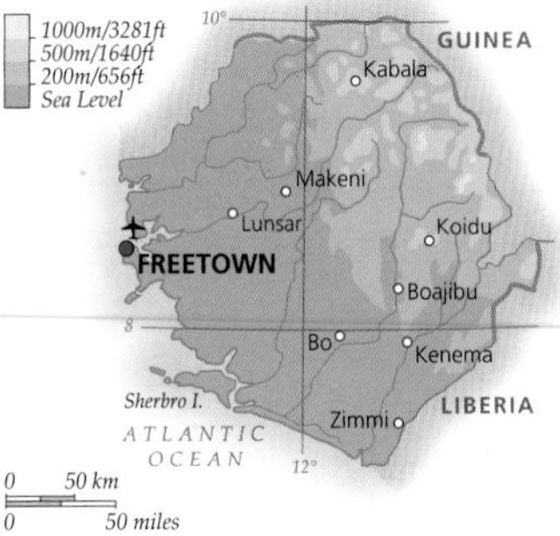
1000m/3281ft
500m/1640ft
200m/656ft
Sea Level
10°
GUINEA
Kabala
Makeni
Lunsar
Koidu
FREETOWN
Boajibu
8
Bo
Kenema
Sherbro I.
LIBERIA
Zimmi
ATLANTIC
OCEAN
12°
0 50 km
0 50 miles

FACTFILE

OFFICIAL NAME: Republic of Sierra Leone

DATE OF FORMATION: 1961

CAPITAL: Freetown

POPULATION: 5.7 million

TOTAL AREA: 27,698 sq. miles (71,740 sq. km)

DENSITY: 206 people per sq. mile

LANGUAGES: Mende, Temne, Krio, English*

RELIGIONS: Muslim 30%, traditional beliefs 30%, other 30%, Christian 10%

ETHNIC MIX: Mende 35%, Temne 32%, other 21%, Limba 8%, Kuranko 4%

GOVERNMENT: Presidential system

CURRENCY: Leone = 100 cents

Singapore

Linked to the southernmost tip of the Malay peninsula by a causeway, Singapore was established as a trading settlement in 1819. It is one of Asia's most important commercial centers.

GEOGRAPHY

Little remains of the original vegetation on Singapore Island. The other 54 much smaller islands are little more than swampy jungle.

CLIMATE

Equatorial. Hot and humid, with heavy rainfall all year round.

PEOPLE & SOCIETY

Dominated by the Chinese, who make up three-quarters of the community. The old English-speaking Straits Chinese and newer Mandarin-speakers are now well integrated. Malays are generally the poorest group. The population is skilled and industrious; there is a significant foreign workforce. Society is highly regulated; official campaigns aim to improve public behavior. Crime is limited and punishment can be severe.

THE ECONOMY

Wealth from success as entrepôt and center of high-tech industries, such as electronics and pharmaceuticals. Leads research in new biotechnologies. All food, energy, and water imported. Worst-ever recession in 2008–2009.

INSIGHT: *Chewing gum was banned outright from 1992 to 2004*

0 5 km
0 5 mi
MALAYSIA
Causeway
Pulau Ubin
Pulau Tekong
Lim Chu Kang
Choa Chu Kang
Bukit Panjang
Houngang New Town
Jurong
Bukit Timah
Changi International Airport
Jurong Industrial Estate
Queenstown
Bedok New Town
City
Telok Blangah
Sentosa
Pulau Brani
Sedat Pandan
South China Sea
1°20'
103°40'
103°50'
104°
Strait of Singapore
Urban areas
Open areas
Nature reserves

FACTFILE

OFFICIAL NAME: Republic of Singapore
DATE OF FORMATION: 1965
CAPITAL: Singapore
POPULATION: 4.74 million
TOTAL AREA: 250 sq. miles (648 sq. km)
DENSITY: 20,072 people per sq. mile
LANGUAGES: Mandarin*, Malay*, Tamil*, English*
RELIGIONS: Buddhist 55%, Taoist 22%, Muslim 16%, Hindu, Christian, Sikh 7%
ETHNIC MIX: Chinese 77%, Malay 14%, Indian 8%, other 1%
GOVERNMENT: Parliamentary system
CURRENCY: Singapore dollar = 100 cents

Slovakia

Landlocked in central Europe, Slovakia became a separate state in 1993, splitting ex-communist Czechoslovakia in two. It joined the EU in 2004 and the eurozone five years later.

GEOGRAPHY

The Tatra Mountains stretch along ıe northern border with Poland. outhern lowlands include the fertile anube plain.

CLIMATE

Continental. Moderately warm ımmers and steady rainfall. Cold winters ith heavy snowfalls.

PEOPLE & SOCIETY

The majority Slovaks are the ominant group. The Magyars Hungarians) seek protection of ıeir language and culture, backed y Hungary. Magyar parties exist the political mainstream, and n occasion form part of the ıling coalition. Ethnic Czechs ave dual citizenship. Roma are nrepresented and face significant scrimination. Rural eastern regions e least developed.

THE ECONOMY

Emphasis on heavy industry, especially cars. Inexpensive workforce. Rising foreign investment. Successful privatizations. Strong growth until 2009 recession. High unemployment.

INSIGHT: *From 1526 to 1784 Bratislava, then known as Pozsony, served as the capital of Hungary*

POLAND
20°
22°
18°
Carpathian Mts
Bardejov
Žilina
CZECH REPUBLIC
Martin
Prešov
Trenčín
Košice
UKRAINE
Banská Bystrica
AUS.
Trnava
Nitra
Lučenec
BRATISLAVA
48°
Danube
HUNGARY
0 50 km
0 50 miles
2000m/6562ft
1000m/3281ft
500m/1640ft
200m/656ft
Sea Level

FACTFILE

OFFICIAL NAME: Slovak Republic
DATE OF FORMATION: 1993
CAPITAL: Bratislava
POPULATION: 5.41 million
TOTAL AREA: 18,859 sq. miles (48,845 sq. km)
DENSITY: 286 people per sq. mile
LANGUAGES: Slovak*, Hungarian (Magyar), Czech
RELIGIONS: Roman Catholic 60%, other 22%, Atheist 10%, Protestant 8%
ETHNIC MIX: Slovak 86%, Magyar 10%, Roma 2%, Czech 1%, other 1%
GOVERNMENT: Parliamentary system
CURRENCY: Euro = 100 cents

Slovenia

Lying at the junction of central Europe and the Balkans, Slovenia seceded from socialist Yugoslavia in 1991. In 2004, it became the first former Yugoslav state to join the EU

GEOGRAPHY

Alpine terrain with hills and mountains. Forests cover almost half the country's area. There is a short coastline on the Adriatic Sea.

CLIMATE

Mediterranean climate on the small coastal strip. The alpine interior has continental extremes.

PEOPLE & SOCIETY

Long historical association with western Europe, accounts for the "Alpine" rather than "Balkan" outlook of Slovenia's people, despite close similarities to other former Yugoslavs. The absence of sizable Serb or Croat minorities made for a relatively peaceful secession from Yugoslavia. There are small communities of Italians and Magyars (Hungarians) in the southwest and east respectively.

THE ECONOMY

First new EU member to join eurozone (in 2007). Export-oriented, so vulnerable to global economic trends. Competitive manufacturing industry. Sizable state-owned sector remains.

INSIGHT: *A wheel found in a marsh in 2003 is claimed to be the world's oldest, pre-dating 3000 BCE*

1000m/3281ft
500m/1640ft
200m/656ft
Sea Level
AUSTRIA
HUNGA
Murska Sobota
Mura
Maribor
Drava
Ptuj
Jesenice
Kranj
Celje
LJUBLJANA
Sava
ITALY
16°
46°
Nova Gorica
Krško
Brežice
Postojna
Adriatic Sea
CROATIA
Kolpa
0 25 km
0 25 mi
14°

FACTFILE

OFFICIAL NAME: Republic of Slovenia
DATE OF FORMATION: 1991
CAPITAL: Ljubljana
POPULATION: 2.02 million
TOTAL AREA: 7820 sq. miles (20,253 sq. km)
DENSITY: 258 people per sq. mile
LANGUAGES: Slovenian*
RELIGIONS: Roman Catholic 96%, other 3%, Muslim 1%
ETHNIC MIX: Slovene 83%, other 12%, Serb 2%, Croat 2%, Bosniak 1%
GOVERNMENT: Parliamentary system
CURRENCY: Euro = 100 cents

Solomon Islands

The Solomons archipelago comprises several hundred coral reef islands scattered in the southwestern Pacific. Most of the population live on the six largest islands.

GEOGRAPHY

The six largest islands are volcanic, nountainous, and thickly forested. 'lat coastal plains provide the only :ultivable land.

CLIMATE

Northern islands are hot and humid ıll year round; farther south a cool eason develops. November–April wet eason brings cyclones.

PEOPLE & SOCIETY

Almost all Solomon Islanders are Aelanesian. Tensions are regional; Guadalcanal natives (Isatabu) fought gainst immigrant Malaitan workers in he 1998–2000 conflict, displacing housands and ruining the economy. ı 2003, Australian-led peacekeepers rrived to try to restore the rule of law.)utlying islands have pressed for utonomy. Animist beliefs exist longside Christianity.

THE ECONOMY

Subsistence farming and fishing sustain 75% of people. Cash crops are copra and cocoa. Gold deposits. Civil conflict bankrupted the government, closed the main gold mine, and cut trade links. Forests have been depleted.

INSIGHT: *The battle for Japanese-held Guadalcanal was the first major US offensive in the Pacific War during World War II*

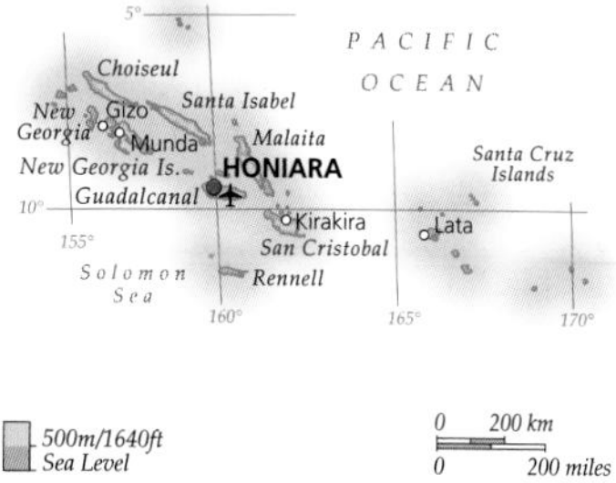
5°
PACIFIC OCEAN
Choiseul
New Georgia
Gizo
Santa Isabel
Munda
Malaita
New Georgia Is.
HONIARA
Santa Cruz Islands
Guadalcanal
10°
Kirakira
Lata
155°
San Cristobal
Solomon Sea
Rennell
160°
165°
170°
500m/1640ft
Sea Level
0 200 km
0 200 miles

FACTFILE

OFFICIAL NAME: Solomon Islands
DATE OF FORMATION: 1978
CAPITAL: Honiara
POPULATION: 523,200
TOTAL AREA: 10,985 sq. miles (28,450 sq. km)
DENSITY: 48 people per sq. mile
LANGUAGES: English*, Pidgin English, Melanesian Pidgin, c. 120 others
RELIGIONS: Anglican 34%, Catholic 19%, other Protestant 38%, other 9%
ETHNIC MIX: Melanesian 94%, Polynesian 4%, other 2%
GOVERNMENT: Parliamentary system
CURRENCY: Solomon Is. dollar = 100 cents

Somalia

A semiarid state occupying the Horn of Africa, Somalia was formed from the Italian and British colonies of Somaliland. Conflict has left it without effective government since 1991.

GEOGRAPHY

Highlands in the north, flatter scrub-covered land to the south. Coastal areas are more fertile.

CLIMATE

Very dry, except for the north coast, which is hot and humid. The interior has among the world's highest average annual temperatures.

PEOPLE & SOCIETY

The clan system forms the basis of all commercial, political, and social life. Most people are ethnic Somali. The minority Bantu are traditionally seen as socially inferior. Since the 1991 coup, Somalia has lacked a strong central authority. Somaliland has declared independence, while Puntland claims autonomy. Islamist militias now control most of the country: some have joined the latest attempt at a transitional government, but fighting continues.

THE ECONOMY

Ongoing war. Every commodity, except arms, is in short supply. Piracy and banditry. Few natural resources. Prone to drought. Somaliland region is more stable but its trade is hampered by lack of international recognition.

INSIGHT: *Until 1973, Somali was an unwritten language*

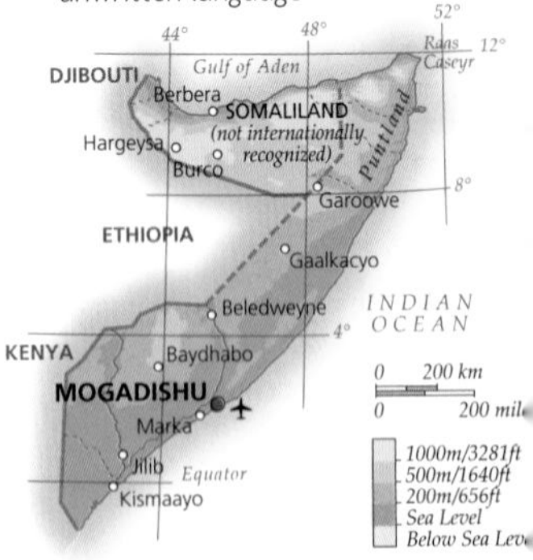

44°
48°
52°
12°
8°
4°
Raas Caseyr
Gulf of Aden
DJIBOUTI
Berbera
SOMALILAND
(not internationally recognized)
Hargeysa
Burco
Puntland
Garoowe
ETHIOPIA
Gaalkacyo
Beledweyne
INDIAN OCEAN
KENYA
Baydhabo
MOGADISHU
Marka
Jilib
Equator
Kismaayo
0 200 km
0 200 miles
1000m/3281ft
500m/1640ft
200m/656ft
Sea Level
Below Sea Level

FACTFILE

OFFICIAL NAME: Somalia
DATE OF FORMATION: 1960
CAPITAL: Mogadishu
POPULATION: 9.13 million
TOTAL AREA: 246,199 sq. miles (637,657 sq. km)
DENSITY: 38 people per sq. mile
LANGUAGES: Somali*, Arabic*, English, Italian
RELIGIONS: Sunni Muslim 98%, Christian 2%
ETHNIC MIX: Somali 85%, other 15%
GOVERNMENT: Transitional regime
CURRENCY: Somali shilin = 100 senti

South Africa

After 80 years of white minority rule, South Africa held its first multiracial, multiparty elections in 1994. Victory for the lacks marked the symbolic overturning of long years of apartheid.

GEOGRAPHY

Much of the interior is grassy veld. esert in the west and far north. ountains east, south, and west.

CLIMATE

Warm, temperate, and dry. ape Town has a Mediterranean climate. emiarid in the west.

PEOPLE & SOCIETY

The majority black population now ominates politically, but the minority hite community still controls the conomy. A small black middle class is rowing, but unemployment among lacks remains high. Over five million eople are HIV-positive, but the fight gainst AIDS is hampered by social ttitudes. Violent crime is a problem.

INSIGHT: *Over the last century, South Africa has produced over half f the world's gold*

THE ECONOMY

Africa's largest, most developed economy. Leading mineral producer, notably metals, diamonds, coal. Tourism is also key. Wealth gap has widened: jobs, housing, and better access to basic services are needed to fight poverty.

2000m/6562ft
1000m/3281ft
500m/1640ft
Sea Level
ZIMBABWE
BOTSWANA
MOZAMBIQUE
NAMIBIA
Limpopo
Kalahari Desert
TSHWANE/ PRETORIA
Middelburg
Johannesburg
Soweto
Vryburg
SWAZILAND
Vaal
Piet Retief
Upington
Kroonstad
Orange
Kimberley
BLOEMFONTEIN
Pietermaritzburg
LESOTHO
Northern Karoo
Durban
Middelburg
Drakensberg
INDIAN OCEAN
CAPE TOWN
Great Karoo
Beaufort West
East London
George
Port Elizabeth
Cape of Good Hope
0 400 km
0 400 miles

FACTFILE

OFFICIAL NAME: Republic of South Africa
DATE OF FORMATION: 1934
CAPITAL: Tshwane / Pretoria; Cape Town; Bloemfontein
POPULATION: 50.1 million
TOTAL AREA: 471,008 sq. miles (1,219,912 sq. km)
DENSITY: 106 people per sq. mile
LANGUAGES: English*, isiZulu*, isiXhosa*, Afrikaans*, 7 other official languages*
RELIGIONS: Christian 68%, animist and traditional beliefs 29%, other 3%
ETHNIC MIX: Black 79%, White 10%, Mixed race 9%, Asian 2%
GOVERNMENT: Presidential system
CURRENCY: Rand = 100 cents

Spain

Lodged between Europe, Africa, the North Atlantic, and the Mediterranean, Spain has occupied a pivotal global position since unification under Ferdinand and Isabella in 1492.

GEOGRAPHY

Mountain ranges in the north, center, and south, with a huge central plateau. Mediterranean lowlands. Verdant valleys in the northwest.

CLIMATE

Maritime in north. Hotter and drier in south. The central plateau has an extreme climate.

PEOPLE & SOCIETY

A vigorous ethnic regionalism, suppressed under Franco's fascist regime, now flourishes. There are 17 autonomous regions. People remain churchgoing, though Roman Catholic teachings on social issues are often flouted. Spanish women are increasingly emancipated, with strong political representation.

INSIGHT: *Over 3000 festivals and feasts take place each year in Spain*

THE ECONOMY

Decade of sustained growth, until construction boom ended in 2007, followed by global recession: unemployment soared. Large fishing fleet. Few natural resources. Proximity to Africa makes it a target for would-be economic migrants.

0 100 km
0 100 miles
Bay of Biscay
44°
A Coruña
Gijón
Santander
Bilbao
Donostia-San Sebastián
FRANCE
ANDORRA
Pyrenees
Vigo
42°
Ourense
León
Burgos
Logroño
Lleida
Valladolid
Soria
Zaragoza
Barcelona
Tarragona
8°
PORTUGAL
Ávila
Tagus
MADRID
Menorca
40°
Getafe
Mallorca
Palma
Valencia
Badajoz
Albacete
Ibiza
Islas Baleares
38°
Córdoba
Murcia
Alicante
2°
0°
Huelva
Sevilla
Granada
Cartagena
Málaga
Cádiz
Almería
36°
6°
4°
2°
Mediterranean Sea
2000m/6562ft
1000m/3281ft
500m/1640ft
200m/656ft
Sea Level

FACTFILE

OFFICIAL NAME: Kingdom of Spain
DATE OF FORMATION: 1492
CAPITAL: Madrid
POPULATION: 44.9 million
TOTAL AREA: 194,896 sq. miles (504,782 sq. km)
DENSITY: 233 people per sq. mile
LANGUAGES: Spanish*, Catalan*, Galician*, Basque*
RELIGIONS: Roman Catholic 96%, other 4%
ETHNIC MIX: Spanish 72%, Catalan 17%, Galician 6%, other 3%, Basque 2%
GOVERNMENT: Parliamentary system
CURRENCY: Euro = 100 cents

Sri Lanka

The teardrop-shaped island of Sri Lanka is separated from India by the Palk Strait. Ethnic Tamil rebels – the Tamil Tigers – were defeated in 2009, after a brutal 26-year civil war.

GEOGRAPHY

The main island is dominated by ugged central highlands. Fertile northern ›lains are dissected by rivers. Much of he land is tropical jungle.

CLIMATE

Tropical, with breezes on the coast nd cooler air in highlands. Northeast is riest and hottest.

PEOPLE & SOCIETY

The Sinhalese are mostly uddhist, while Tamils are mostly Hindu. Moors are the Muslim escendants of Arab traders. Tamils vere the minority group favored by ne British colonists. Majority-Sinhalese ower since independence in 1948 ueled tensions, erupting into civil var in 1983. The eventual government ictory in 2009 made this the nly rebel insurgency ever efeated in modern times.

THE ECONOMY

Garment industry. Remittances. Major tea exporter. Civil war drained government funds, deterred investors and tourists. Tsunami damage in 2004.

INSIGHT: *Sri Lanka elected the world's first woman prime minister, Sirimavo Bandaranaike, in 1960*

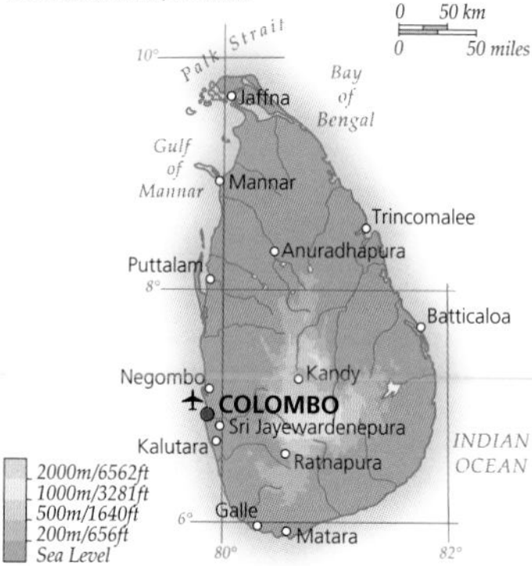
0 50 km
0 50 miles
10°
Palk Strait
Jaffna
Bay of Bengal
Gulf of Mannar
Mannar
Trincomalee
Anuradhapura
Puttalam
8°
Batticaloa
Negombo
Kandy
COLOMBO
Sri Jayewardenepura
Kalutara
Ratnapura
INDIAN OCEAN
2000m/6562ft
1000m/3281ft
500m/1640ft
200m/656ft
Sea Level
6°
Galle
Matara
80°
82°

FACTFILE

OFFICIAL NAME: Democratic Socialist Republic of Sri Lanka

DATE OF FORMATION: 1948

CAPITAL: Colombo

POPULATION: 20.2 million

TOTAL AREA: 25,332 sq. miles (65,610 sq. km)

DENSITY: 810 people per sq. mile

LANGUAGES: Sinhala*, Tamil*, English

RELIGIONS: Buddhist 69%, Hindu 15%, Muslim 8%, Christian 8%

ETHNIC MIX: Sinhalese 82%, Tamil 9%, Moor 8%, other 1%

GOVERNMENT: Parliamentary system

CURRENCY: Sri Lanka rupee = 100 cents

Sudan

The largest country in Africa, Sudan has undergone two civil wars between its Arab north and black African south. Darfur in the west now endures a terrible humanitarian crisis.

GEOGRAPHY

Lies within the upper Nile basin. Mostly arid plains, with marshes in the south. Highlands border the Red Sea in the northeast.

CLIMATE

North is hot, arid desert with constant dry winds. Rainy season ranging from two months in the center to eight in the south.

PEOPLE & SOCIETY

Two million people are nomads. Many ethnic groups. Key social divide is between Arabized Muslims in north, and mostly black African, largely Christian or animist peoples in south. Attempts to impose Arab and Islamic values were the root cause of civil war (1955–1972, 1983–2005). Ethnic violence by Arab militias in Darfur since 2003 has killed 300,000 people: huge refugee crisis. Women's rights are restricted.

THE ECONOMY

Oil exports. Cotton, sesame, gum arabic. Violence and drought hamper farming. Millions of people displaced.

INSIGHT: *Sudan's Sudd is the world's largest swamp*

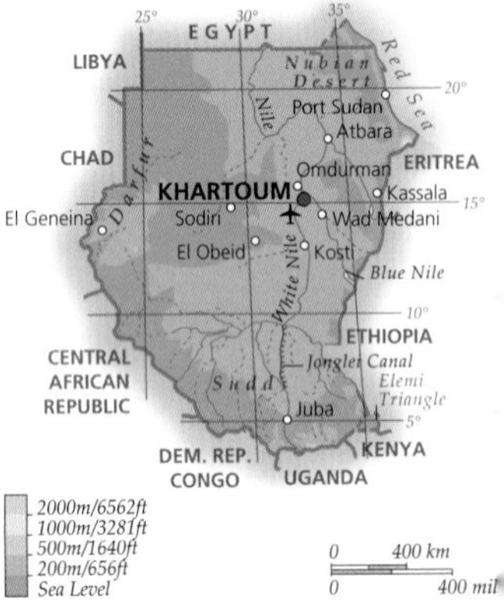
25°
30°
35°
EGYPT
LIBYA
Nubian Desert
Red Sea
20°
Nile
Port Sudan
Atbara
CHAD
Darfur
Omdurman
ERITREA
KHARTOUM
Kassala
15°
El Geneina
Sodiri
Wad Medani
El Obeid
Kosti
White Nile
Blue Nile
10°
ETHIOPIA
CENTRAL AFRICAN REPUBLIC
Jonglei Canal
Elemi Triangle
Sudd
Juba
5°
KENYA
DEM. REP. CONGO
UGANDA
2000m/6562ft
1000m/3281ft
500m/1640ft
200m/656ft
Sea Level
0 400 km
0 400 miles

FACTFILE

OFFICIAL NAME: Republic of the Sudan
DATE OF FORMATION: 1956
CAPITAL: Khartoum
POPULATION: 42.3 million
TOTAL AREA: 967,493 sq. miles (2,505,810 sq. km)
DENSITY: 44 people per sq. mile
LANGUAGES: Arabic*, African languages
RELIGIONS: Muslim 70%, traditional beliefs 20%, Christian 9%, other 1%
ETHNIC MIX: Black 59% (including Beja and Dinka 7%), Arab 40%, other 1%
GOVERNMENT: Presidential system
CURRENCY: Sudanese pound or dinar = 100 piastres

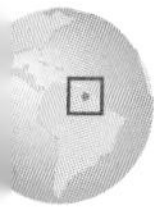

Suriname

Suriname is a former Dutch colony on the north coast of South America. Democracy was restored in 1991, after almost 11 years of military rule. The Netherlands is still the main supplier of aid.

GEOGRAPHY

Mostly covered by tropical ainforest. Coastal plain rises to central ›lateaus and the Guiana Highlands.

CLIMATE

Tropical. Hot and humid, but :ooled by trade winds. High rainfall, ›specially in the interior.

PEOPLE & SOCIETY

The Dutch brought laborers from ›outh Asia and Java. Independence saw nass emigration: over 300,000 urinamese live in the Netherlands. Of hose left, over 85% live near the coast, he rest in scattered rainforest ommunities. Indigenous Amerindians ›nly number a few thousand. *Bosnegers* – lescended from runaway African slaves – ›ought the military government in the ıte 1980s. Under civilian rule, each roup has had a political party epresenting its interests.

THE ECONOMY

Alumina and gold are the key exports. Rice and bananas are main cash crops. Oil production and tourism are growing. Excessive bureaucracy.

INSIGHT: *In a 1667 Anglo-Dutch deal, Holland gained Suriname but lost New Amsterdam (now New York)*

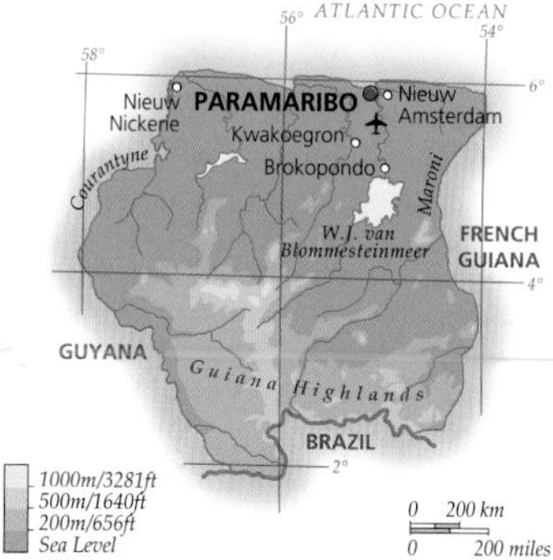
ATLANTIC OCEAN
56°
54°
58°
6°
4°
2°
Nieuw Nickerie
PARAMARIBO
Nieuw Amsterdam
Kwakoegron
Brokopondo
Courantyne
Maroni
W.J. van Blommesteinmeer
FRENCH GUIANA
GUYANA
Guiana Highlands
BRAZIL
1000m/3281ft
500m/1640ft
200m/656ft
Sea Level
0 200 km
0 200 miles

FACTFILE

OFFICIAL NAME: Republic of Suriname
DATE OF FORMATION: 1975
CAPITAL: Paramaribo
POPULATION: 519,700
TOTAL AREA: 63,039 sq. miles (163,270 sq. km)
DENSITY: 8 people per sq. mile
LANGUAGES: Sranan (Creole), Dutch*, Javanese, Sarnami, Hindi, other
RELIGIONS: Christian 48%, Hindu 27%, Muslim 20%, traditional beliefs 5%
ETHNIC MIX: South Asian 27%, other 25%, Creole 18%, Javanese 15%, Black 15%
GOVERNMENT: Parliamentary system
CURRENCY: Surinamese dollar = 100 cents

Swaziland

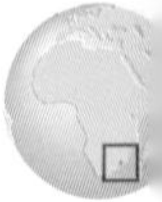

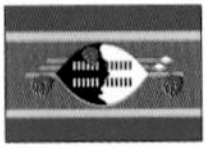

The tiny southern African kingdom of Swaziland is crippled with HIV/AIDS and economically dependent on South Africa. Vocal demands for multiparty democracy have been ignored

GEOGRAPHY

Mainly high plateaus and mountains. Rolling grasslands and low scrub plains to the east. Pine forests on western border.

CLIMATE

Temperatures rise and rainfall declines as the land descends eastward, from high to low grassy *veld*.

PEOPLE & SOCIETY

One of Africa's most conservative states, though there is pressure from urban-based modernizers. Political system promotes Swazi tradition and is dominated by powerful monarchy. Women face discrimination. Swaziland has world's highest prevalence of HIV/AIDS: chastity is urged to combat its spread.

INSIGHT: *Polygamy is practiced in Swaziland – when King Sobhuza died in 1982, he left 100 widows*

THE ECONOMY

Sugarcane is the main cash crop. Wood pulp and soft drink concentrates are also exported. Loss of workforce to HIV/AIDS, and high cost of health care.

0 25 km
0 25 mile
31°
32°
26°
27°
Piggs Peak
Tshaneni
SOUTH AFRICA
MBABANE
Siteki
Manzini
Bhunya
Sidvokodvo
Hlathikulu
MOZAMBIQU
Nhlangano
SOUTH AFRICA
1000m/3281ft
500m/1640ft
200m/656ft
Sea Level

FACTFILE

OFFICIAL NAME: Kingdom of Swaziland
DATE OF FORMATION: 1968
CAPITAL: Mbabane
POPULATION: 1.18 million
TOTAL AREA: 6704 sq. miles (17,363 sq. km)
DENSITY: 178 people per sq. mile
LANGUAGES: English*, siSwati*, isiZulu, Xitsonga
RELIGIONS: Christian 60%, traditional beliefs 40%
ETHNIC MIX: Swazi 97%, other 3%
GOVERNMENT: Monarchy
CURRENCY: Lilangeni = 100 cents

Sweden

The largest Scandinavian country by both population and area, Sweden has one of the world's most extensive welfare systems and is among the leading proponents of equal rights for women.

GEOGRAPHY

Heavily forested, with many lakes. Northern plateau extends beyond the Arctic Circle. Southern lowlands are widely cultivated.

CLIMATE

Southern coasts warmed by Gulf Stream. Northern areas have more extreme continental climate.

PEOPLE & SOCIETY

The nuclear family forms the basis of society, but the marriage rate is one of the lowest in the world, and cohabitation is now common. The model welfare system is paid for by a high tax burden. Women are well represented at all levels. A minority of 20,000 Sámi lives in the far north. Most industries and the bulk of population are based in and around the southern cities. An EU member since 1995, Sweden has voted not to join the euro.

THE ECONOMY

Companies of global importance, including Volvo, Saab, SFK, Ericsson. Highly developed infrastructure. Up-to-date technology. Skilled workforce.

INSIGHT: *Sweden has maintained a position of armed neutrality since 1815*

FINLAND
NORWAY
Arctic Circle
Lapland
Luleå
Umeå
Östersund
Gulf of Bothnia
Sundsvall
Uppsala
Västerås
Örebro
Vänern
STOCKHOLM
Norrköping
Vättern
Göteborg
Jönköping
Gotland
Öland
Kattegat
Helsingborg
Malmö
Baltic Sea
1000m/3281ft
500m/1640ft
200m/656ft
Sea Level
0 100 km
0 100 miles

FACTFILE

OFFICIAL NAME: Kingdom of Sweden
DATE OF FORMATION: 1523
CAPITAL: Stockholm
POPULATION: 9.25 million
TOTAL AREA: 173,731 sq. miles (449,964 sq. km)
DENSITY: 58 people per sq. mile
LANGUAGES: Swedish*, Finnish, Sámi
RELIGIONS: Evangelical Lutheran 82%, other 13%, Roman Catholic 2%, Muslim 2%, Orthodox Christian 1%
ETHNIC MIX: Swedish 86%, recent immigrant 12%, Finnish and Sámi 2%
GOVERNMENT: Parliamentary system
CURRENCY: Swedish krona = 100 öre

Switzerland

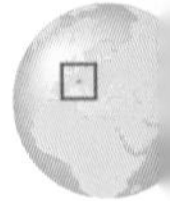

One of the world's most prosperous countries, Switzerland sits at the center of Europe. It has retained its neutral status through every major European conflict since 1815.

GEOGRAPHY
Mostly mountainous, with river valleys. The Alps cover 60% of its area; the Jura in the west cover 10%. Lowlands lie along the east–west axis.

CLIMATE
Most rain falls in the warm summer months. Winters are snowy, but milder and foggy away from the mountains. Avalanches are a problem.

PEOPLE & SOCIETY
Switzerland is composed of distinct German-Swiss, French-Swiss, and Italian-Swiss linguistic groups. In the east, a 35,000-strong minority speaks Romansch. The country is divided into 26 autonomous cantons (states), each with control over housing and economics. Public referenda are widely used to decide policy. Society is conservative; marriage is common but divorce is above the EU average rate.

THE ECONOMY
Diversified economy relies on services – the banking sector manages over a quarter of the world's offshore private wealth – and specialized industries (engineering, watches, etc).

INSIGHT: *Famed for its neutrality, Switzerland only joined the UN in 2002, and remains outside the EU*

GERMANY
Schaffhausen
Rhine
Lake Constance
Basel
Winterthur
Sankt Gallen
FRANCE
Jura
Zürich
AUSTRIA
Biel
Neuchâtel
Luzern
LIECHTENSTEIN
Lac de Neuchâtel
BERN
Chur
Rhine
Interlaken
Alps
Davos
Lausanne
Lake Geneva
Montreux
Rhône
Brig
Genève
Sion
Locarno
ITALY
6° FRANCE
ITALY 8°
Lake Maggiore
Lugano
10°
46°
3000m/9843
2000m/6562
1000m/3281
500m/1640ft
200m/656ft
0 50 km
0 50 miles

FACTFILE

OFFICIAL NAME: Swiss Confederation
DATE OF FORMATION: 1291
CAPITAL: Bern
POPULATION: 7.57 million
TOTAL AREA: 15,942 sq. miles (41,290 sq. km)
DENSITY: 493 people per sq. mile
LANGUAGES: German*, Swiss-German, French*, Italian*, Romansch*
RELIGIONS: Roman Catholic 42%, Protestant 35%, other 19%, Muslim 4%
ETHNIC MIX: German 64%, French 20%, other 9.5%, Italian 6%, Romansch 0.5%
GOVERNMENT: Parliamentary system
CURRENCY: Franc = 100 rappen/centimes

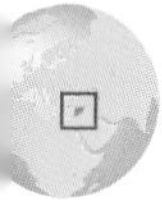

Syria

Stretching from the eastern Mediterranean to the Tigris River, Syria's borders are regarded as an artificial creation of French colonial rule by many Syrians. Foreign relations are turbulent.

GEOGRAPHY

A short stretch of coastal plain s backed by a low range of hills. The Euphrates River cuts through a vast nterior desert plateau.

CLIMATE

Mediterranean coastal climate. nland areas are arid. In winter, snow is common on the mountains.

PEOPLE & SOCIETY

Most Syrians live within 60 miles 100 km) of the coast. 90% are Muslim, ncluding the politically dominant Shi'a Alawis. In the north and west are groups of Kurds, Armenians, and Turkic-speaking peoples. Some 460,000 Palestinian refugees live in Syria, and over a million raqis have fled here since 2003. There s a growing gulf between rich and poor. Human rights are an issue, but women's rights are among the best n the Arab world.

THE ECONOMY

Oil, though production is falling. Natural gas. High defense spending. Large public sector. Agriculture: fruit, cotton, and grain. Under US sanctions.

INSIGHT: *Syria is an ancient land; there are at least 3500 as yet unexcavated archaeological sites*

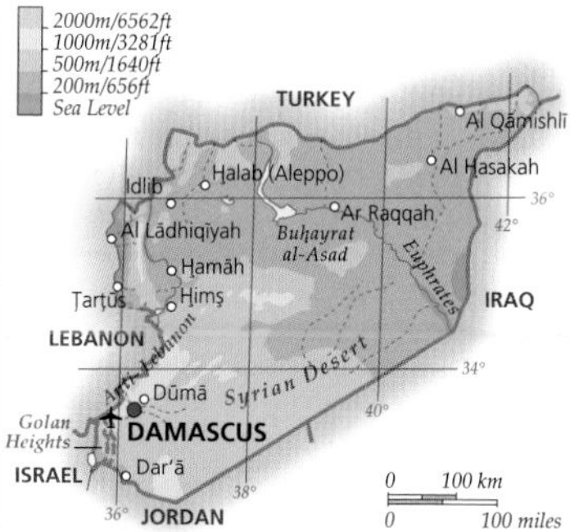
2000m/6562ft
1000m/3281ft
500m/1640ft
200m/656ft
Sea Level
TURKEY
Al Qāmishlī
Al Hasakah
Idlib
Halab (Aleppo)
Ar Raqqah
Al Lādhiqīyah
Buhayrat al-Asad
Euphrates
Hamāh
Ḩimş
Ţarţūs
IRAQ
LEBANON
Anti-Lebanon
Syrian Desert
Dūmā
DAMASCUS
Golan Heights
ISRAEL
Dar'ā
JORDAN
36°
34°
42°
40°
38°
0 100 km
0 100 miles

FACTFILE

OFFICIAL NAME: Syrian Arab Republic
DATE OF FORMATION: 1941
CAPITAL: Damascus
POPULATION: 21.9 million
TOTAL AREA: 71,498 sq. miles (184,180 sq. km)
DENSITY: 308 people per sq. mile
LANGUAGES: Arabic*, French, Kurdish, Armenian, Circassian, Assyrian, other
RELIGIONS: Sunni Muslim 74%, other Muslim 16%, Christian 10%
ETHNIC MIX: Arab 89%, Kurd 6%, other 3%, Armenian, Turkmen, Circassian 2%
GOVERNMENT: One-party state
CURRENCY: Syrian pound = 100 piastres

Taiwan

The republic of Taiwan (formerly Formosa) is on an island 80 miles (130 km) off the southeast coast of mainland China, which still considers it to be a renegade province.

GEOGRAPHY

Mountain region covers two-thirds of the island. Highly fertile lowlands and coastal plains.

CLIMATE

Tropical monsoon. Hot and humid. Typhoons July–September. Snow falls in mountains in winter.

PEOPLE & SOCIETY

Most Taiwanese are Han Chinese, descendants of the 1644 migration of the Ming dynasty from the mainland. The modern republic was created in 1949, when the nationalist Kuomintang was expelled from the mainland following Communist victory in the civil war. 100,000 emigrés established themselves as a ruling class. Initial resentment has subsided as a new Taiwan-born generation has taken over the reins of power. The aboriginal minority suffers discrimination.

THE ECONOMY

Successful economy of small, adaptable companies. High-tech goods: TVs, computers, and semiconductors. Rising trade, investment with China.

INSIGHT: *Taiwan lost its seat at the UN to Beijing in 1971: both claim to represent "China"*

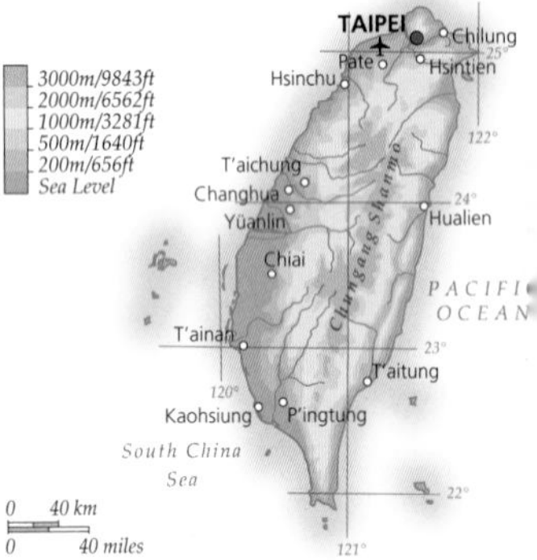
3000m/9843ft
2000m/6562ft
1000m/3281ft
500m/1640ft
200m/656ft
Sea Level
TAIPEI
Chilung
Pate
Hsintien
Hsinchu
T'aichung
Changhua
Yüanlin
Chiai
Hualien
Chungang Shanmo
PACIFIC OCEAN
T'ainan
T'aitung
Kaohsiung
P'ingtung
South China Sea
25°
24°
23°
22°
120°
121°
122°
0 40 km
0 40 miles

FACTFILE

OFFICIAL NAME: Republic of China (ROC)
DATE OF FORMATION: 1949
CAPITAL: Taipei
POPULATION: 23 million
TOTAL AREA: 13,892 sq. miles (35,980 sq. km)
DENSITY: 1844 people per sq. mile
LANGUAGES: Amoy Chinese, Mandarin Chinese*, Hakka Chinese
RELIGIONS: Buddhist, Confucianist, and Taoist 93%, Christian 5%, other 2%
ETHNIC MIX: Indigenous Chinese 84%, mainland Chinese 14%, aboriginal 2%
GOVERNMENT: Presidential system
CURRENCY: Taiwan dollar = 100 cents

Tajikistan

Tajikistan lies landlocked on the western slopes of the Pamirs in central Asia. Soon after the breakup of the USSR in 1991, civil war erupted between ruling communists and Islamists.

GEOGRAPHY

Mainly mountainous: bare slopes of the Pamir ranges, with fast-flowing rivers, cover most of the country. Small but fertile Fergana Valley in northwest.

CLIMATE

Continental extremes in the valleys. Bitterly cold winters in the mountains. Rainfall is low.

PEOPLE & SOCIETY

Unlike the other former Soviet republics of central Asia, Tajikistan is dominated by a people of Persian (Iranian) rather than Turkic origin. The main ethnic conflict is with the Turkic Uzbek minority. Russians are discriminated against; most fled in the 1992–1997 civil war, and standards of living fell dramatically. Islamist militants are active. Two million people work abroad, primarily in Russia.

THE ECONOMY

Mass poverty. Declining cotton revenue. Also exports aluminum. Uranium deposits. Transit route for Afghan opium. Corruption. Needs reforms to attract foreign investment.

INSIGHT: *Carpet-making, an ancient tradition learned from Persia, is still a major source of revenue*

0 100 km
0 100 miles
4000m/13124ft
3000m/9843ft
2000m/6562ft
1000m/3281ft
500m/1640ft
200m/656ft
70°
72°
68°
40°
74°
38°
UZBEKISTAN
Fergana Valley
Khujand
Isfara
Ŭroteppa
KYRGYZSTAN
CHINA
Panjakent
DUSHANBE
Norak
Pamirs
Qŭrghonteppa
Kŭlob
Farkhor
Khorugh
Amu Darya
AFGHANISTAN
PAKISTAN

FACTFILE

OFFICIAL NAME: Republic of Tajikistan
DATE OF FORMATION: 1991
CAPITAL: Dushanbe
POPULATION: 6.95 million
TOTAL AREA: 55,251 sq. miles (143,100 sq. km)
DENSITY: 126 people per sq. mile
LANGUAGES: Tajik*, Uzbek, Russian
RELIGIONS: Sunni Muslim 80%, other 15%, Shi'a Muslim 5%
ETHNIC MIX: Tajik 80%, Uzbek 15%, other 3%, Kyrgyz 1%, Russian 1%
GOVERNMENT: Presidential system
CURRENCY: Somoni = 100 diram

Tanzania

The east African state of Tanzania was formed in 1964 by the union of Tanganyika and the Zanzibar islands. A third of its area is game reserve or national park.

GEOGRAPHY

The mainland is mostly a high plateau lying to the east of the Great Rift Valley. Forested coastal plain. Highlands in the north and south.

CLIMATE

Tropical on the coast and Zanzibar. Semiarid on central plateau, semitemperate in the highlands. March–May rains.

PEOPLE & SOCIETY

99% of people belong to one of 120 small ethnic Bantu groups. Arabs, Asians, and Europeans make up the remaining population. Use of Kiswahili as the lingua franca has eliminated ethnic rivalries. The majority of Tanzanians are subsistence famers.

INSIGHT: *At 19,340 ft (5895 m), Kilimanjaro in northeast Tanzania is Africa's highest mountain*

THE ECONOMY

Heavily reliant on agriculture, including forestry and cattle. Coffee, cotton, tea, cashew nuts, sisal, and cloves are cash crops. Gold, diamonds, and gems are mined. Safari and beach tourism. Debt relief.

Equator
UGANDA
Lake Victoria
KENYA
Musoma
RWANDA
Mwanza
Kilimanjaro 19,340ft (5895m)
BURUNDI
Shinyanga
Serengeti Plain
Arusha
Moshi
4°
Masai Steppe
Kigoma
Tabora
Tanga
L. Tanganyika
Zanzibar
DODOMA
DEM. REP. CONGO
Morogoro
Dar es Salaam
Great Rift Valley
Iringa
8°
INDIAN OCEAN
Mbeya
ZAMBIA
Lindi
32°
Songea
Mtwara
MALAWI
L. Nyasa
Ruvuma
12°
MOZAMBIQUE
36°
40°
3000m/9843ft
2000m/6562ft
1000m/3281ft
500m/1640ft
200m/656ft
Sea Level
0 200 km
0 200 miles

FACTFILE

OFFICIAL NAME: United Republic of Tanzania
DATE OF FORMATION: 1964
CAPITAL: Dodoma
POPULATION: 43.7 million
TOTAL AREA: 364,898 sq. miles (945,087 sq. km)
DENSITY: 128 people per sq. mile
LANGUAGES: Kiswahili*, English*, other
RELIGIONS: Muslim 33%, Christian 33%, traditional beliefs 30%, other 4%
ETHNIC MIX: Native African (over 120 tribes) 99%, European, Asian, Arab 1%
GOVERNMENT: Presidential system
CURRENCY: Tanzanian shilling = 100 cents

Thailand

Thailand lies at the heart of mainland southeast Asia. Continuing rapid industrialization has resulted in massive congestion in the capital and a serious depletion of natural resources.

GEOGRAPHY

One-third is low plateau, drained by tributaries of the Mekong River. Central plain is the most fertile area.

CLIMATE

Tropical. Hot, humid March–May; monsoon rains May–October; cooler season November–March.

PEOPLE & SOCIETY

Buddhism is a national binding force. 600,000 hill tribes-people, with their own languages, live in the north and northeast. The Chinese minority is the most assimilated in the region. Malay Islamists in the undeveloped far south are fighting for secession. Politics has been unstable since the 2006 fall of pro-poor Prime Minister Thaksin.

INSIGHT: *Thailand, meaning "land of the free," is the only SE Asian nation never to have been colonized*

THE ECONOMY

Successful manufacturing. Natural gas reserves. Leading exporter of rice and rubber. Tourism, though sex industry harms image. 2004 tsunami damage.

0 200 km
0 200 miles
MYANMAR (BURMA)
LAOS
CAMBODIA
MALAYSIA
Mekong
Salween
Chiang Mai
Udon Thani
Khon Kaen
Phitsanulok
Nakhon Sawan
Ubon Ratchathani
Nakhon Ratchasima
BANGKOK
Ratchaburi
Pattaya
Gulf of Thailand
Chumphon
Isthmus of Kra
Nakhon Si Thammarat
Phuket
Songkhla
Hat Yai
Malay Peninsula
Andaman Sea
20°
16°
12°
8°
100°
104°
2000m/6562ft
1000m/3281ft
500m/1640ft
200m/656ft
Sea Level

FACTFILE

OFFICIAL NAME: Kingdom of Thailand
DATE OF FORMATION: 1238
CAPITAL: Bangkok
POPULATION: 67.8 million
TOTAL AREA: 198,455 sq. miles (514,000 sq. km)
DENSITY: 344 people per sq. mile
LANGUAGES: Thai*, Chinese, Malay, Khmer, Mon, Karen, Miao
RELIGIONS: Buddhist 95%, Muslim 4%, other (including Christian) 1%
ETHNIC MIX: Thai 83%, Chinese 12%, Malay 3%, Khmer and other 2%
GOVERNMENT: Parliamentary system
CURRENCY: Baht = 100 satang

Togo

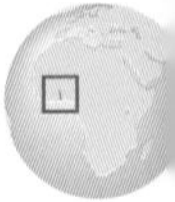

Togo lies sandwiched between Ghana and Benin in west Africa. General Eyadema ruled from 1967–2005; his son succeeded him. Lomé port is an important entrepôt for regional trade.

GEOGRAPHY

Central forested region bounded by savanna lands to the north and south. Mountain range stretches southwest to northeast.

CLIMATE

Coast hot and humid; drier inland. Rainy season March–July, with heaviest falls in the west.

PEOPLE & SOCIETY

Harsh resentment between Ewe in the south and Kabye in the north. Kabye control the military, but the north is less developed than the south. Extended family is important. Tribalism and nepotism are key factors in everyday life. Some ethnic groups, such as the Mina, have matriarchal societies.

INSIGHT: *The "Nana Benz," the entrepreneurial market-women of Lomé, control Togo's retail trade*

THE ECONOMY

Most people are farmers. Self-sufficient in staple foods. Togo's main cash crops are coffee and cocoa: cotton has declined. Its phosphate deposits are the most mineral-rich in the world, but easily extractable reserves are depleted and the sector needs investment.

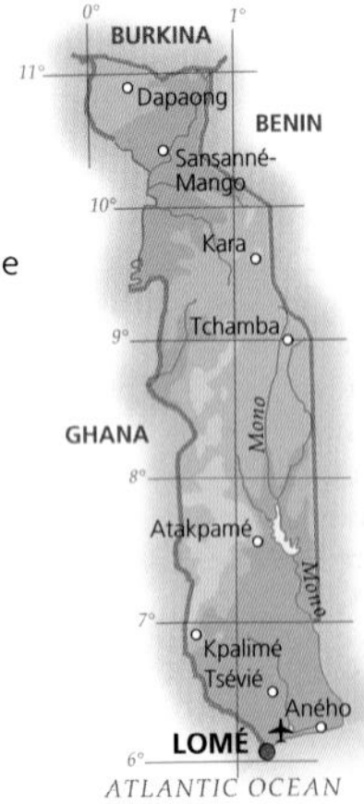
0°
1°
11°
10°
9°
8°
7°
6°
BURKINA
BENIN
GHANA
Dapaong
Sansanné-Mango
Kara
Tchamba
Mono
Atakpamé
Mono
Kpalimé
Tsévié
Aného
LOMÉ
ATLANTIC OCEAN

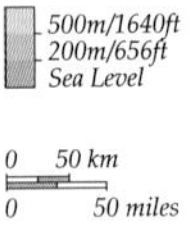
500m/1640ft
200m/656ft
Sea Level
0 50 km
0 50 miles

FACTFILE

OFFICIAL NAME: Republic of Togo
DATE OF FORMATION: 1960
CAPITAL: Lomé
POPULATION: 6.62 million
TOTAL AREA: 21,924 sq. miles (56,785 sq. km)
DENSITY: 315 people per sq. mile
LANGUAGES: Ewe, Kabye, Gurma, French*
RELIGIONS: Traditional beliefs 50%, Christian 35%, Muslim 15%
ETHNIC MIX: Ewe 46%, other African 41%, Kabye 12%, European 1%
GOVERNMENT: Presidential system
CURRENCY: CFA franc = 100 centimes

Tonga

Tonga is an archipelago of 170 islands in the South Pacific. Only 45 of these islands are inhabited. The king's powers have been challenged: democratic reforms are promised for 2010.

GEOGRAPHY

Easterly islands are generally low and fertile. Those in the west are higher and volcanic in origin.

CLIMATE

Tropical oceanic. Temperatures range between 68°F (20°C) and 86°F (30°C) all year round. Heavy rainfall, especially February–March.

PEOPLE & SOCIETY

Tonga is the last remaining Polynesian monarchy. All land belongs to the crown, but is administered by nobles who allot it to the common people. Respect for traditional values is high, though younger, Westernized Tongans are starting to question some attitudes. The first elected commoner became prime minister in 2006.

INSIGHT: *Unique in the Pacific, Tonga was never brought under foreign rule*

THE ECONOMY

Squashes and vanilla exported. Remittances. Potential for tourism and fisheries. Capital's business district destroyed in 2006 prodemocracy riots.

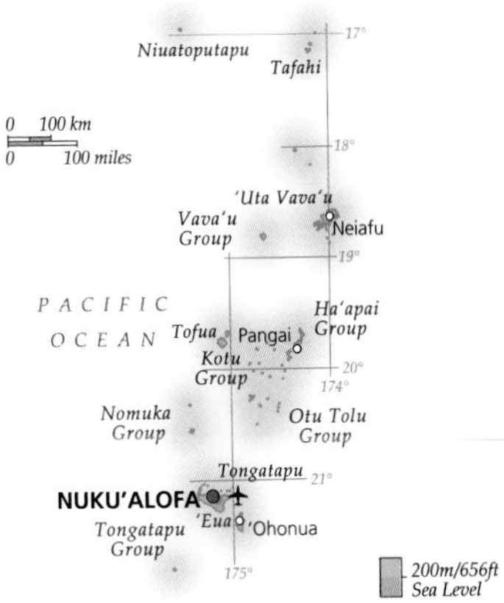
Niuatoputapu
Tafahi
17°
18°
0 100 km
0 100 miles
'Uta Vava'u
Vava'u Group
Neiafu
19°
PACIFIC OCEAN
Ha'apai Group
Tofua
Pangai
Kotu Group
20°
174°
Nomuka Group
Otu Tolu Group
Tongatapu
21°
NUKU'ALOFA
'Eua
'Ohonua
Tongatapu Group
175°
200m/656ft
Sea Level

FACTFILE

OFFICIAL NAME: Kingdom of Tonga
DATE OF FORMATION: 1970
CAPITAL: Nuku'alofa
POPULATION: 104,000
TOTAL AREA: 289 sq. miles (748 sq. km)
DENSITY: 374 people per sq. mile
LANGUAGES: English*, Tongan*
RELIGIONS: Free Wesleyan 41%, other 29%, Roman Catholic 16%, Church of Jesus Christ of Latter-Day Saints 14%
ETHNIC MIX: Tongan 98%, other 2%
GOVERNMENT: Monarchy
CURRENCY: Pa'anga (Tongan dollar) = 100 seniti

Trinidad & Tobago

The two islands of the former UK colony of Trinidad and Tobago are the most southerly of the Caribbean Windward Islands, lying just 9 miles (15 km) off the coast of Venezuela.

GEOGRAPHY

Both islands are hilly and wooded. Trinidad has a rugged mountain range in the north, and swamps on its east and west coasts.

CLIMATE

Tropical, with July–December wet season. Escapes the region's hurricanes, which pass to the north.

PEOPLE & SOCIETY

Trinidad's East Indian community is the Caribbean's largest and holds onto its Muslim and Hindu heritage. There are tensions with the mainly Christian blacks; political parties are divided along race lines. Blacks form the majority on Tobago. High rates of kidnapping and murder are an issue.

INSIGHT: *Trinidad and Tobago is the birthplace of steel bands and Calypso music*

THE ECONOMY

Oil and natural gas: it provides 75% of US imports of liquefied natural gas, but only 12 years of reserves left. Associated industries: second-largest producer of methanol. Tourism on wildlife-rich Tobago.

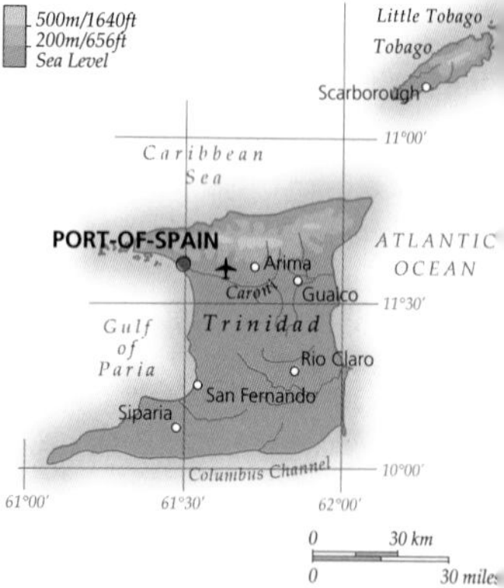
500m/1640ft
200m/656ft
Sea Level
Little Tobago
Tobago
Scarborough
11°00'
Caribbean Sea
PORT-OF-SPAIN
Arima
Caroni
Gualco
ATLANTIC OCEAN
11°30'
Gulf of Paria
Trinidad
Rio Claro
San Fernando
Siparia
Columbus Channel
10°00'
61°00'
61°30'
62°00'
0
30 km
0
30 miles

FACTFILE

OFFICIAL NAME: Republic of Trinidad and Tobago

DATE OF FORMATION: 1962

CAPITAL: Port-of-Spain

POPULATION: 1.34 million

TOTAL AREA: 1980 sq. miles (5128 sq. km)

DENSITY: 676 people per sq. mile

LANGUAGES: English Creole, English*, Hindi, French, Spanish

RELIGIONS: Catholic 32%, Hindu 24%, Protestant 28%, other 9%, Muslim 7%

ETHNIC MIX: East Indian 40%, Black 40%, Mixed race 18%, White, Chinese 1%, other 1%

GOVERNMENT: Parliamentary system

CURRENCY: Trin. & Tob. dollar = 100 cents

Tunisia

Tunisia has traditionally been one of the more liberal Arab states, moving toward a multiparty democracy, but its government is now facing a challenge from Islamic fundamentalists.

GEOGRAPHY

Mountains in the north are surrounded by plains. Vast, low-lying salt pans in the center. To the south lies the Sahara Desert.

CLIMATE

Summer temperatures are high. The north is often wet and windy in winter. Far south is arid.

PEOPLE & SOCIETY

The population is almost entirely of Arab-Berber descent, with Jewish and Christian minorities. Many still live in extended family groups, in which three or four generations are represented. Women have better rights than in most other Arab countries and make up over 30% of the workforce. Parliamentary and municipal quotas aim to increase their representation in politics. A low birth rate is a result of a long-standing family planning policy.

THE ECONOMY

Competitive and diversified. Expanding manufacturing. Exports olives, dates, citrus fruit, phosphates. Tourism. Free trade area with EU.

INSIGHT: *Tunisia was the center of trading empires from the 9th century BCE*

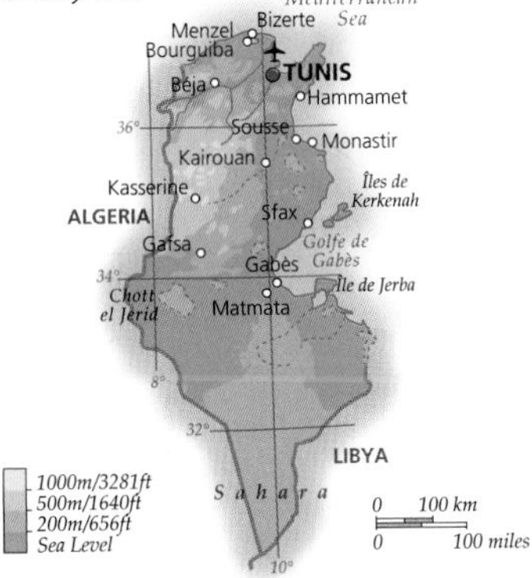
Mediterranean Sea
Bizerte
Menzel Bourguiba
TUNIS
Béja
Hammamet
36°
Sousse
Monastir
Kairouan
Kasserine
Îles de Kerkenah
ALGERIA
Sfax
Gafsa
Golfe de Gabès
Gabès
34°
Île de Jerba
Chott el Jerid
Matmata
8°
32°
LIBYA
1000m/3281ft
500m/1640ft
200m/656ft
Sea Level
Sahara
0 100 km
0 100 miles
10°

FACTFILE

OFFICIAL NAME: Republic of Tunisia
DATE OF FORMATION: 1956
CAPITAL: Tunis
POPULATION: 10.3 million
TOTAL AREA: 63,169 sq. miles (163,610 sq. km)
DENSITY: 171 people per sq. mile
LANGUAGES: Arabic*, French
RELIGIONS: Muslim (mainly Sunni) 98%, Christian 1%, Jewish 1%
ETHNIC MIX: Arab and Berber 98%, Jewish 1%, European 1%
GOVERNMENT: Presidential system
CURRENCY: Tunisian dinar = 1000 millimes

Turkey

Lying partly in the region of eastern Thrace in Europe, but mostly in Asia, Turkey's position gives it significant influence in the Mediterranean, the Black Sea, and the Middle East.

GEOGRAPHY

Asian Turkey (Anatolia) is dominated by two mountain ranges, separated by a high, semidesert plateau. Coastal regions are fertile.

CLIMATE

Coast has a Mediterranean climate. Interior has cold, snowy winters and hot, dry summers.

PEOPLE & SOCIETY

Despite racial diversity, Turkey has a strong sense of national identity, and close links with other Turkic states. Kurds, the largest minority, based in the southeast, have waged a violent campaign for greater autonomy intermittently since 1984. Islamist parties are challenging Turkey's cherished identity as a secular state. It has applied to join the EU, though progress will be slow.

THE ECONOMY

Liberalized economy, boosted by self-sufficient agriculture, and textiles, tourism, and manufacturing sectors. Route of Asian oil pipelines to Europe.

INSIGHT: *Turkey had two of the seven wonders of the ancient world: the tomb of King Mausolus at Halicarnassus (now Bodrum), and the temple of Artemis at Ephesus*

BULGARIA
GREECE
İstanbul
İstanbul Boğazi
Black Sea
Samsun
GEORGIA
Trabzon
ARMENIA
Dardanelles
Bursa
ANKARA
Eskişehir
Euphrates
Erzurum
Manisa
İzmir
Kayseri
Malatya
Van Gölü
Van
Aegean Sea
Konya
Diyarbakır
IRAN
Bodrum
Taurus Mts
Şanlıurfa
Tigris
Antalya
Adana
Gaziantep
IRAQ
İskenderun
Mediterranean Sea
SYRIA
40°
36°
28°
32°
36°
40°
44°
0 200 km
0 200 miles
3000m/9843ft
2000m/6562ft
1000m/3281ft
500m/1640ft
200m/656ft
Sea Level

FACTFILE

OFFICIAL NAME: Republic of Turkey
DATE OF FORMATION: 1923
CAPITAL: Ankara
POPULATION: 74.8 million
TOTAL AREA: 301,382 sq. miles (780,580 sq. km)
DENSITY: 252 people per sq. mile
LANGUAGES: Turkish*, Kurdish, Arabic, Circassian, Armenian, Greek, other
RELIGIONS: Muslim (mainly Sunni) 99%, other 1%
ETHNIC MIX: Turkish 70%, Kurdish 20%, other 8%, Arab 2%
GOVERNMENT: Parliamentary system
CURRENCY: New Turkish lira = 100 kurus

Turkmenistan

Stretching from the Caspian Sea into the central Asian desert, Turkmenistan has had less upheaval than most ex-Soviet states, but President Niyazov was a dictator.

GEOGRAPHY

Low Garagum Desert covers 80% of the country. Mountains on southern border with Iran. Fertile Amu Darya Valley in north.

CLIMATE

Arid desert climate with extreme summer heat, but sub-freezing winter temperatures.

PEOPLE & SOCIETY

Before Russia annexed the area in 1884, the Turkmen were a largely nomadic tribal people. Today, the tribal unit remains strong, with population clustered around desert oases. Relations with Uzbek and Russian minorities have become tense in recent years due to the "Turkmenization" of government, education, and religion. Political reform since Niyazov's sudden death in 2006 is slowly dismantling the old regime.

THE ECONOMY

State-controlled, though there is some private investment. Natural gas and oil are main resources. Overintensive farming of cotton. Black market.

INSIGHT: *President Niyazov created an elaborate personality cult, styling himself as Turkmenbashi – "head" of all Turkmen*

0 200 km
0 200 miles
KAZAKHSTAN
Garabogaz Aylagy
Köneürgenç
Daşoguz
UZBEKISTAN
Türkmenbaşy
Turan Lowland
Balkanabat
Amu Darya
Gumdag
Serdar
40°
Caspian Sea
Garagum
Türkmenabat
AŞGABAT
IRAN
Tejen
Atamyrat
Mary
55°
Garagum Kanaly
65°
60°
1000m/3281ft
500m/1640ft
200m/656ft
Sea Level
Below Sea Level
Serhetabat
AFGHANISTAN

FACTFILE

OFFICIAL NAME: Turkmenistan
DATE OF FORMATION: 1991
CAPITAL: Asgabat
POPULATION: 5.11 million
TOTAL AREA: 188,455 sq. miles (488,100 sq. km)
DENSITY: 27 people per sq. mile
LANGUAGES: Turkmen*, Uzbek, Russian, Kazakh, Tatar, other
RELIGIONS: Sunni Muslim 87%, Orthodox Christian 11%, other 2%
ETHNIC MIX: Turkmen 77%, Uzbek 9%, Russian 7%, other 5%, Kazakh 2%
GOVERNMENT: One-party state
CURRENCY: Manat = 100 tenge

Tuvalu

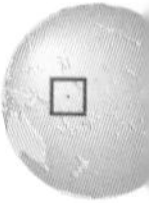

One of the world's smallest, most isolated states, Tuvalu lies in the central Pacific. The nine islands were linked to the Gilbert Islands (Kiribati) as a UK colony until independence.

GEOGRAPHY

A series of coral atolls, none more than 15 ft (4.6 m) above sea level. Poor soils restrict vegetation to bush, coconut palms, and breadfruit trees.

CLIMATE

Hot all year round. Heavy annual rainfall. Hurricane season brings many violent storms.

PEOPLE & SOCIETY

People are mostly Polynesian. Around half the population lives on Funafuti, where government jobs are based. Life is communal and traditional. Most people live by subsistence farming, digging pits out of the coral to grow crops. Fresh water is precious, due to frequent droughts.

INSIGHT: *Low-lying Tuvalu, like the Maldives, is set to disappear with rising sea levels*

THE ECONOMY

World's smallest economy. Remittances from Tuvaluan seafarers. Sale of fishing licenses. Copra, stamps, and coins exported. Income from trust fund and the lease of .tv Internet suffix.

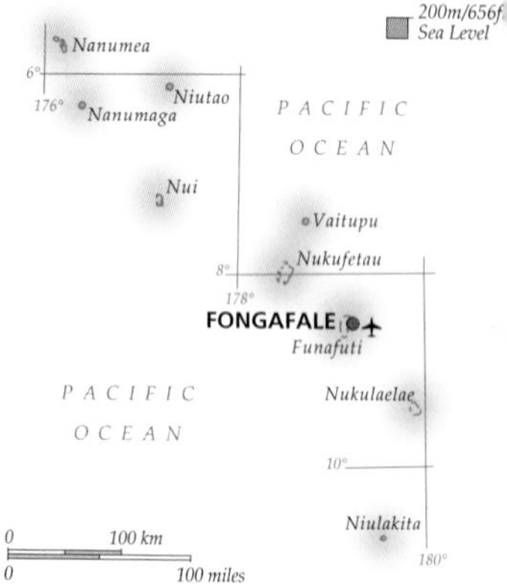
200m/656ft
Sea Level
Nanumea
6°
176°
Niutao
Nanumaga
PACIFIC
OCEAN
Nui
Vaitupu
Nukufetau
8°
178°
FONGAFALE
Funafuti
PACIFIC
OCEAN
Nukulaelae
10°
Niulakita
0
100 km
0
100 miles
180°

FACTFILE

OFFICIAL NAME: Tuvalu
DATE OF FORMATION: 1978
CAPITAL: Fongafale, on Funafuti Atoll
POPULATION: 11,100
TOTAL AREA: 10 sq. miles (26 sq. km)
DENSITY: 1110 people per sq. mile
LANGUAGES: Tuvaluan, Kiribati, English*
RELIGIONS: Church of Tuvalu 97%, Baha'i 1%, Seventh-day Adventist 1%, other 1%
ETHNIC MIX: Polynesian 92%, other 6%, Kiribati 2%
GOVERNMENT: Nonparty system
CURRENCY: Australian dollar and Tuvaluan dollar = 100 cents each

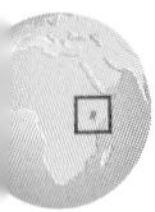

Uganda

Landlocked in east Africa, Uganda has a history of ethnic strife. Under President Museveni, steps have been taken to restore peace and to rebuild the economy and democracy.

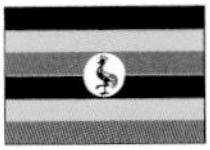

GEOGRAPHY

Predominantly a large plateau with the Ruwenzori mountain range and the Great Rift Valley in the west. Lake Victoria lies to the southeast. Vegetation is of savanna type.

CLIMATE

Altitude and the influence of the lakes modify the equatorial climate. Rain falls throughout the year; spring is the wettest period.

PEOPLE & SOCIETY

The mostly rural population comprises some 13 main ethnic groups. President Museveni has worked hard to break down ethnic animosities, but a noticeable north–south divide persists, with most development in the south. After two decades of brutal conflict with northern rebels, a final peace deal has been mediated but not yet signed; many refugees have returned home.

THE ECONOMY

Resource-rich, but undeveloped and poor. Exports coffee, fish, tea, and flowers. Oil exploration. Hydroelectric power is reducing oil imports. Great potential from mining. Debt relief.

INSIGHT: *Lake Victoria is the world's third-largest lake*

3000m/9843ft
2000m/6562ft
1000m/3281ft
500m/1640ft
SUDAN
KENYA
4°
2°
Arua
Gulu
Albert Nile
Lake Albert
Lake Kyoga
Victoria Nile
DEM. REP. CONGO
Great Rift Valley
Mbale
Tororo
Kabarole
Jinja
Mubende
Kasese
KAMPALA
Entebbe
Equator
Masaka
Sese Is.
Lake Edward
Mbarara
Lake Victoria
Kabale
TANZANIA
RWANDA
32°
34°
0 100 km
0 100 miles

FACTFILE

OFFICIAL NAME: Republic of Uganda
DATE OF FORMATION: 1962
CAPITAL: Kampala
POPULATION: 32.7 million
TOTAL AREA: 91,135 sq. miles (236,040 sq. km)
DENSITY: 425 people per sq. mile
LANGUAGES: Luganda, Nkole, Chiga, Lango, Acholi, Teso, Lugbara, English*
RELIGIONS: Catholic 38%, Protestant 33%, trad. beliefs 13%, Muslim 8%, other 8%
ETHNIC MIX: Baganda 17%, Banyakole 10%, Basoga 9%, Iteso 7%, other 57%
GOVERNMENT: Presidential system
CURRENCY: New Ug. shilling = 100 cents

Ukraine

The former "breadbasket of the Soviet Union," Ukraine lies on the north coast of the Black Sea. Politics is divided between pro-Russian sentiments and pro-European nationalism.

GEOGRAPHY

Mainly fertile steppes and forests. Carpathian Mountains in west, Crimean chain in south. Pripet Marshes in northwest.

CLIMATE

Mainly continental climate, with distinct seasons. Southern Crimea has Mediterranean climate.

PEOPLE & SOCIETY

Over 90% of people in the west are Ukrainian, but in cities in the east and south, and in Crimea, Russians form a majority. The government is wary of Crimean separatism. Tatars have been returning there since the Soviet Union's collapse and now comprise around 12% of the local population. Over five million people in Ukraine, Belarus, and Russia live in areas "contaminated" by the 1986 Chornobyl nuclear disaster.

THE ECONOMY

Minerals: 5% of global reserves. Slow reform of land laws, holding back agriculture. Oil/natural gas transit from Russia and the Caspian to Europe: natural gas price disputes with Russia. Political crisis.

INSIGHT: *Ukraine means "on the border," referring to its position on the edge of the old Russian Empire*

2000m/6562ft
1000m/3281ft
500m/1640ft
200m/656ft
Sea Level
BELARUS
Pripet Marshes
Chernihiv
Chornobyl'
Luts'k
KIEV
RUSS. FED.
POLAND
L'viv
Zhytomyr
Kremenchuts'ke Vdskh.
Kharkiv
Vinnytsya
Cherkasy
Dnipropetrovs'k
Luhans'k
Chernivtsi
HUNGARY
MOLDOVA
Zaporizhzhya
Donets'k
ROMANIA
Mykolayiv
Dnieper
Mariupol'
Odesa
Sea of Azov
Danube
Crimea
Sevastopol'
0 100 km
0 100 miles
Black Sea

FACTFILE

OFFICIAL NAME: Ukraine
DATE OF FORMATION: 1991
CAPITAL: Kiev
POPULATION: 45.7 million
TOTAL AREA: 223,089 sq. miles (603,700 sq. km)
DENSITY: 196 people per sq. mile
LANGUAGES: Ukrainian*, Russian, Tatar
RELIGIONS: Christian (mainly Orthodox) 95%, other 5%
ETHNIC MIX: Ukrainian 78%, Russian 17%, other 5%
GOVERNMENT: Presidential system
CURRENCY: Hryvna = 100 kopiykas

United Arab Emirates

Bordering the Gulf on the northern coast of the Arabian Peninsula, the seven states of the UAE are Abu Dhabi, Dubai, Sharjah, Ajman, Umm al Qaywayn, Ras al Khaymah, and Fujayrah.

GEOGRAPHY

Mostly flat, semiarid desert with dunes, salt pans, and occasional oases. Cities are watered by extensive irrigation systems.

CLIMATE

Summers are humid, despite minimal rainfall. Sand-laden *shamal* winds blow in winter and spring.

PEOPLE & SOCIETY

Emirians, who make up just a quarter of the population, are mostly Sunni Muslims of Bedouin descent, and largely city dwellers. In theory, women enjoy equal rights with men. Poverty is rare and there is no income tax. The 1970s oil boom encouraged the immigration of workers, mostly from Asia. Western expatriates are permitted a virtually unrestricted lifestyle. Islamism, however, is a growing force among the young.

THE ECONOMY

Major oil and natural gas exporter; plentiful reserves. Dynamic Dubai: free trade zone, financial center (but 2008 global downturn caught overextended banks). Water is scarce. Imports most food. Some emirates are less developed.

INSIGHT: *Mina Jabal Ali, in Dubai, is the largest man-made port in the world*

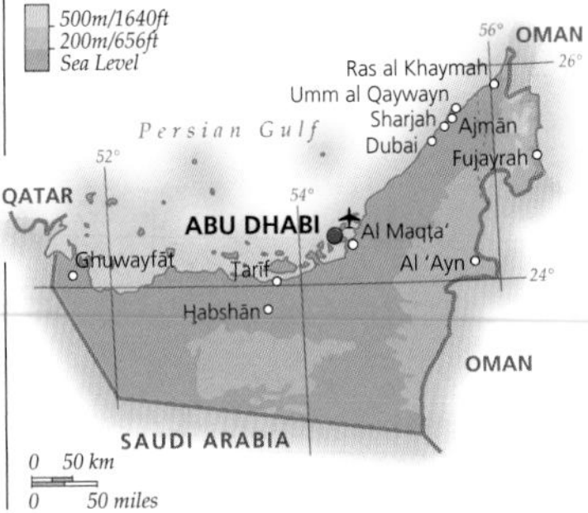
500m/1640ft
200m/656ft
Sea Level
56°
OMAN
26°
Ras al Khaymah
Umm al Qaywayn
Sharjah
Ajmān
Dubai
Fujayrah
Persian Gulf
52°
54°
QATAR
ABU DHABI
Al Maqta'
Ghuwayfāt
Tarif
Al 'Ayn
24°
Habshān
OMAN
SAUDI ARABIA
0 50 km
0 50 miles

FACTFILE

OFFICIAL NAME: United Arab Emirates
DATE OF FORMATION: 1971
CAPITAL: Abu Dhabi
POPULATION: 4.6 million
TOTAL AREA: 32,000 sq. miles (82,880 sq. km)
DENSITY: 142 people per sq. mile
LANGUAGES: Arabic*, Farsi, Indian and Pakistani languages, English
RELIGIONS: Muslim (mainly Sunni) 96%, Christian, Hindu, and other 4%
ETHNIC MIX: Asian 60%, Emirian 25%, other Arab 12%, European 3%
GOVERNMENT: Monarchy
CURRENCY: UAE dirham = 100 fils

United Kingdom

Separated from continental Europe by the English Channel, the UK consists of Great Britain (England, Wales, and Scotland), several smaller islands, and Northern Ireland.

GEOGRAPHY

Rugged uplands dominate the landscape of Scotland, Wales, and northern England. All of the peaks in the United Kingdom over 4000 ft (1219 m) are in highland Scotland. The Pennine mountains, known as the "backbone of England," run the length of northern England. Lowland England rises into several ranges of rolling hills, and there is an interconnected system of rivers and canals. Over 600 islands, many uninhabited, lie west and north of the Scottish mainland.

CLIMATE

Generally mild, temperate, and highly changeable. Rain is fairly well distributed throughout the year. The west is generally wetter than the east, and the south warmer than the north. Winter snow is common in upland areas.

PEOPLE & SOCIETY

The Scottish and Welsh nations remain recognizably distinct, and the creation of the Scottish Parliament and Welsh Assembly has given each country greater political autonomy. The future of devolved government in Northern Ireland remains problematic. People from other ethnic minorities account for 5% of the population; more than half of them were born in the UK. Asians and West Indians in most cities face deprivation and social stress; Asian women can be particularly isolated. In key areas such as policing, multiethnic recruitment has made little progress. Marriage is in decline. Over 40% of all births occur outside marriage, but most of them to cohabiting couples. Single-parent households account for just over a quarter of all families. Income inequality is greater now than in 1884, when records began.

FACTFILE

OFFICIAL NAME: United Kingdom of Great Britain and Northern Ireland
DATE OF FORMATION: 1707
CAPITAL: London
POPULATION: 61.6 million
TOTAL AREA: 94,525 sq. miles (244,820 sq. km)
DENSITY: 660 people per sq. mile
LANGUAGES: English*, Welsh*, other
RELIGIONS: Anglican 45%, other 39%, Catholic 9%, Presbyterian 4%, Muslim 3%
ETHNIC MIX: English 80%, Scottish 9%, other 5%, Welsh 3%, Northern Irish 3%
GOVERNMENT: Parliamentary system
CURRENCY: Pound sterling = 100 pence

THE ECONOMY

World leader in financial services, pharmaceuticals, and defense industries. Strong multinationals. Precision engineering and high-tech industries, including biotechnology and telecommunications. Energy sector based on declining North Sea oil and natural gas reserves. Innovative in computer software development. Flexible working practices. Long-term decline of manufacturing sector, particularly heavy industries and car manufacture, matched by rise in financial and other services. Nonparticipation in euro threatens former status as EU's largest recipient of inward investment, and has prompted some major investors to close UK factories. High levels of government, corporate, and consumer debt: institutional vulnerability to 2007–2008 global downturn. Bank bailouts and stimulus packages pushed the government's finances further into the red.

INSIGHT: *The UK has no formal written constitution, but a stable government system based on Parliament, which originated as a check on royal power in the 13th century*

Orkney Is.
Outer Hebrides
Shetlands Is.
Lerwick
60°
2°
Stornoway
58°
Inverness
Aberdeen
Scotland
Inner Hebrides
Oban
Dundee
56°
Glasgow
Edinburgh
Newcastle upon Tyne
Londonderry
Northern Ireland
Belfast
Carlisle
Isle of Man
North Sea
54°
Blackpool
Leeds
Liverpool
Blackburn
Manchester
Sheffield
IRELAND
England
Derby
Norwich
Birmingham
Leicester
Cambridge
52°
Wales
Swansea
Oxford
Thames
LONDON
Celtic Sea
Cardiff
Bristol
Reading
Dover
8°
Southampton
2°
ATLANTIC OCEAN
Exeter
Plymouth
0°
2°
50°
English Channel
6°
4°

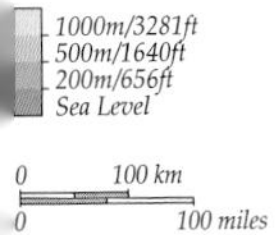
1000m/3281ft
500m/1640ft
200m/656ft
Sea Level
0 100 km
0 100 miles

United States of America

Stretching across the most temperate part of North America, and with many natural resources, the US is the world's leading economic power and third-largest country.

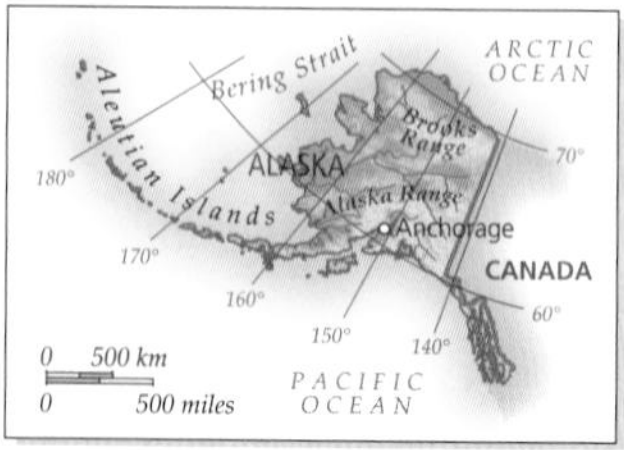
Bering Strait
ARCTIC OCEAN
Aleutian Islands
Brooks Range
ALASKA
Alaska Range
Anchorage
CANADA
180°
170°
160°
150°
140°
70°
60°
0 500 km
0 500 miles
PACIFIC OCEAN

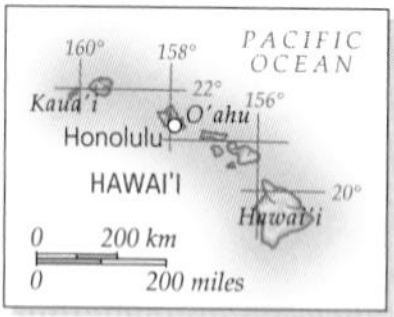
160°
158°
PACIFIC OCEAN
22°
156°
Kaua'i
O'ahu
Honolulu
HAWAI'I
Hawai'i
20°
0 200 km
0 200 miles

CANADA
Seattle
WASHINGTON
Spokane
Portland
PACIFIC
OCEAN
Coast Ranges
OREGON
IDAHO
Boise
Great Salt Lake
Great Basin
Reno
Sierra Nevada
Sacramento
Oakland
San Francisco
NEVADA
Salt Lake City
UTAH
Fresno
CALIFORNIA
Death Valley
Bakersfield
Las Vegas
Grand Canyon
Los Angeles
Colorado
ARIZONA
120°
San Diego
Phoenix
Tucson
MEXICO
110°

GEOGRAPHY

The US has a varied topography. Forested mountains stretch from New England in the far northeast, giving way to lowlands and swamps in the extreme south. The central plains are dominated by the Mississippi–Missouri River system and the Great Lakes on the Canadian border. The Rocky Mountains in the west contain active volcanoes and drop to the coast across the earthquake-prone San Andreas Fault. The southwest is arid desert. Mountainous Alaska is mostly Arctic tundra.

CLIMATE

There are four main climatic zones. The north and east are continental and temperate, with heavy rainfall, warm summers, and cold winters. Florida and the Deep South are tropical and prone to hurricanes. The southwest is arid desert, with searing summer heat and low rainfall. Southern California is Mediterranean, with hot summers and mild winters.

INSIGHT: *The United States of America has the world's oldest constitution. Drafted in 1787, it has operated continuously ever since, albeit with numerous amendments*

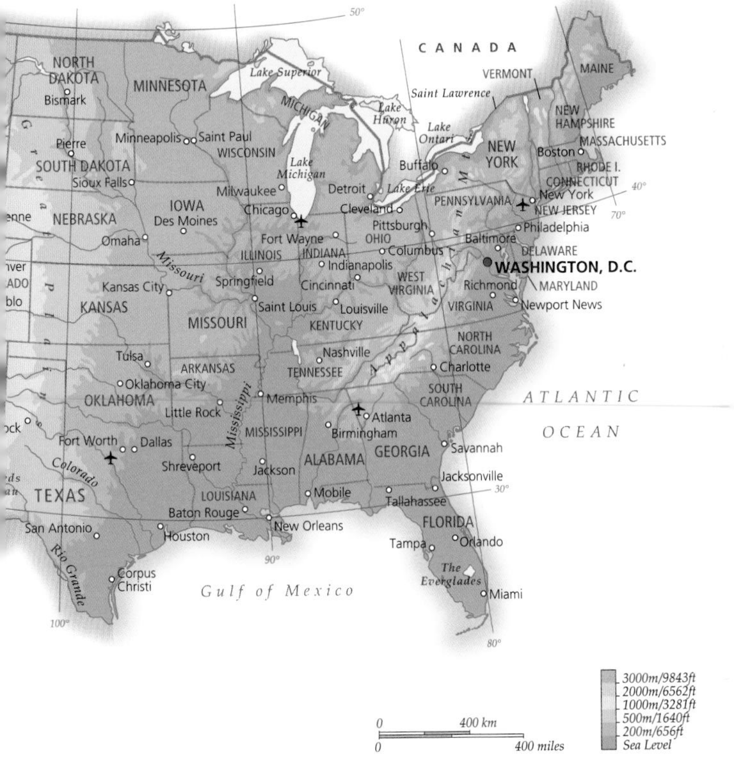
CANADA
NORTH DAKOTA
Bismark
MINNESOTA
Lake Superior
MICHIGAN
Lake Huron
Saint Lawrence
Lake Ontari
VERMONT
MAINE
NEW HAMPSHIRE
MASSACHUSETTS
Boston
RHODE I.
CONNECTICUT
New York
NEW JERSEY
Philadelphia
NEW YORK
Buffalo
Lake Erie
PENNSYLVANIA
Pierre
SOUTH DAKOTA
Sioux Falls
Minneapolis
Saint Paul
WISCONSIN
Lake Michigan
Milwaukee
Detroit
Chicago
Cleveland
Pittsburgh
IOWA
Des Moines
NEBRASKA
Omaha
Fort Wayne
OHIO
Baltimore
DELAWARE
WASHINGTON, D.C.
MARYLAND
ILLINOIS
INDIANA
Indianapolis
Columbus
Missouri
Springfield
Cincinnati
WEST VIRGINIA
Richmond
VIRGINIA
Newport News
Kansas City
KANSAS
Saint Louis
Louisville
MISSOURI
KENTUCKY
NORTH CAROLINA
Tulsa
ARKANSAS
Nashville
TENNESSEE
Charlotte
Oklahoma City
OKLAHOMA
Memphis
SOUTH CAROLINA
ATLANTIC
OCEAN
Little Rock
Mississippi
Atlanta
MISSISSIPPI
Birmingham
Fort Worth
Dallas
GEORGIA
Savannah
Colorado
Shreveport
Jackson
ALABAMA
Jacksonville
TEXAS
LOUISIANA
Mobile
Tallahassee
Baton Rouge
FLORIDA
San Antonio
Houston
New Orleans
Orlando
Tampa
Rio Grande
Corpus Christi
Gulf of Mexico
The Everglades
Miami
50°
40°
30°
70°
80°
90°
100°
0 400 km
0 400 miles
3000m/9843ft
2000m/6562ft
1000m/3281ft
500m/1640ft
200m/656ft
Sea Level

United States of America

INSIGHT: *By law, the actual records collected in a United States census must remain confidential for 72 years*

PEOPLE & SOCIETY

Although the demographic, economic, and cultural dominance of White Americans is firmly entrenched after over 400 years of settlement, the ethnic balance of the country is shifting. Barack Obama, whose father was African, became the first non-White US president in 2009. The African-American community, originally uprooted by the slave trade, has a strong consciousness. Less well organized socially but more numerous, and faster-growing, the Hispanic community is predicted to number over 25% of the population by 2050. Native Americans, dispossessed in the 19th century, are now among the poorest people. Constitutionally, state and religion are clearly separated. Conservative Christianity, however, is increasingly dominant politically. Living standards are high, but bad diet and insufficient exercise have left over a third of Americans obese.

THE ECONOMY

World's largest economy: well-established engineering and high-tech industries, huge resource base, global spread of US culture. Manufacturing is in decline as jobs are lost to low-wage economies. The combination of tax cuts, to boost consumer spending after the 2001 slowdown, and the rising defense budget for the "war on terror" drove the budget into a record deficit. Oil production was hit badly in 2005 by Hurricane Katrina, causing global price hikes. The "subprime" mortgage lending crisis of 2007 sent global stock markets plummeting. In 2008, Lehman Brothers bank crashed spectacularly, while other giants in the financial sector received huge bailouts. Further tax cuts and billion-dollar spending packages in 2009 attempted to lift the economy back out of recession, but the gaping budget deficit also needs to be brought under control.

FACTFILE

OFFICIAL NAME: United States of America
DATE OF FORMATION: 1776
CAPITAL: Washington, D.C.
POPULATION: 315 million
TOTAL AREA: 3,717,792 sq. miles (9,626,091 sq. km)
DENSITY: 89 people per sq. mile
LANGUAGES: English, Spanish, other
RELIGIONS: Protestant 52%, Catholic 25%, other 19%, Muslim 2%, Jewish 2%
ETHNIC MIX: White 62%, Hispanic 13%, African American 13%, other 7%, Asian 4%, Native American 1%
GOVERNMENT: Presidential system
CURRENCY: US dollar = 100 cents

Uruguay

Situated in southeastern South America, Uruguay returned to civilian government in 1985, after 12 years of military rule. Most land is used for farming: Uruguay is a major wool exporter.

GEOGRAPHY

Low, rolling grasslands cover 80% f the country. Narrow coastal plain. lluvial floodplain in southwest. Five vers flow westward and drain into ıe Uruguay River.

CLIMATE

Temperate throughout the ountry. Warm summers, mild winters, ıd moderate rainfall.

PEOPLE & SOCIETY

Uruguayans are largely second-or ıird-generation Italians or Spaniards. Vealth derived from cattle ranching ıabled the country to establish the rst welfare state in South America. espite economic decline since the 950s, a large, if less prosperous, ıiddle class remains. Though a Roman atholic country, Uruguay is liberal ı its attitude to religion and all forms re tolerated.

THE ECONOMY

Exports wool, meat, hides, rice, wood, soy. Rebounded from 1999–2002 economic crisis. Mineral potential.

INSIGHT: *Uruguay's rich pastures are ideal for raising livestock; animal products bring in over 40% of export earnings*

200m/656ft
Sea Level
0 100 km
0 100 miles
56°
30°
Uruguay
Rivera
BRAZIL
Salto
Tacuarembó
54°
ARGENTINA
32°
Embalse del Río Negro
Melo
Paysandú
Mirim Lagoon
Fray Bentos
Paso de los Toros
Mercedes
Treinta y Tres
Trinidad
Colonia del Sacramento
San José de Mayo
34°
River Plate
Las Piedras
Rocha
58°
Punta del Este
MONTEVIDEO
ATLANTIC OCEAN

FACTFILE

OFFICIAL NAME: Eastern Republic of Uruguay

DATE OF FORMATION: 1828

CAPITAL: Montevideo

POPULATION: 3.36 million

TOTAL AREA: 68,039 sq. miles (176,220 sq. km)

DENSITY: 50 people per sq. mile

LANGUAGES: Spanish*

RELIGIONS: Roman Catholic 66%, other 30%, Jewish 2%, Protestant 2%

ETHNIC MIX: White 90%, Mestizo 6%, Black 4%

GOVERNMENT: Presidential system

CURRENCY: Urug. peso = 100 centésimos

Uzbekistan

Sharing what is left of the Aral Sea with its neighbor, Kazakhstan, Uzbekistan lies on the ancient Silk Road between Asia and Europe. It is the most populous central Asian republic.

GEOGRAPHY

Arid and semiarid plains in much of the west. Fertile, irrigated farmland in the east lies below the peaks of the western Pamirs.

CLIMATE

Harsh continental climate. Summers can be extremely hot and dry; winters are cold.

PEOPLE & SOCIETY

Complex ethnic makeup. Ex-Communists are in firm control, but traditional social patterns based on clan, religion, and region have reemerged. Constitutional measures aim to control the influence of Islam: activities against Islamists have drawn international condemnation. Most people live in the fertile east. Birth rates are high, and the status of women continues to be low.

THE ECONOMY

Highly regulated. Reserves of natural gas, oil, coal, gold (has one of the world's largest gold mines), and other minerals. Cash crop is cotton: requires much irrigation. Grain imports necessary

INSIGHT: *The Aral Sea has shrunk to just a tenth of its former size, due to diversion of rivers for irrigation*

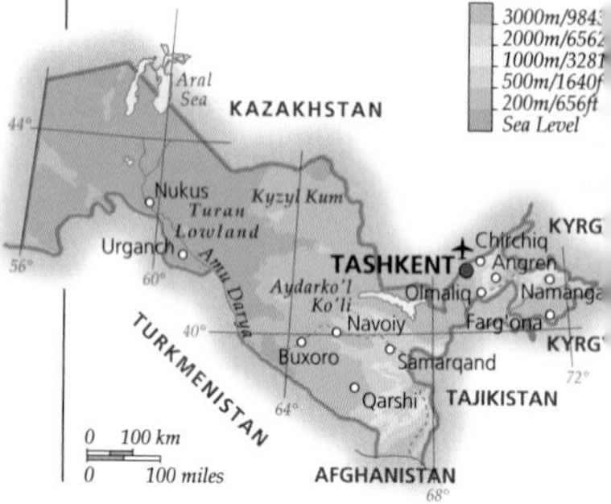

3000m/9843
2000m/6562
1000m/3281
500m/1640ft
200m/656ft
Sea Level
Aral Sea
KAZAKHSTAN
44°
Nukus
Kyzyl Kum
Turan Lowland
Urganch
Amu Darya
56°
60°
TASHKENT
Chirchiq
Angren
KYRG
Aydarko'l Ko'li
Olmaliq
Namanga
Navoiy
Farg'ona
40°
TURKMENISTAN
Buxoro
Samarqand
KYRG
72°
Qarshi
TAJIKISTAN
64°
0 100 km
0 100 miles
AFGHANISTAN
68°

FACTFILE

OFFICIAL NAME: Republic of Uzbekistan
DATE OF FORMATION: 1991
CAPITAL: Tashkent
POPULATION: 27.5 million
TOTAL AREA: 172,741 sq. miles (447,400 sq. km)
DENSITY: 159 people per sq. mile
LANGUAGES: Uzbek*, Russian, Tajik, Kazakh
RELIGIONS: Sunni Muslim 88%, Orthodox Christian 9%, other 3%
ETHNIC MIX: Uzbek 80%, other 6%, Russian 6%, Tajik 5%, Kazakh 3%
GOVERNMENT: Presidential system
CURRENCY: Som = 100 tiyin

Vanuatu

An archipelago of 82 islands and islets in the South acific, Vanuatu was ruled jointly by the UK and France from 1906 until independence in 1980. Politics is democratic but volatile.

GEOGRAPHY

Mountainous and volcanic, with oral beaches and dense rainforest. :ultivated land along the coasts.

CLIMATE

Tropical. Temperatures and rainfall ecline from north to south.

PEOPLE & SOCIETY

Indigenous Melanesians form a ıajority. Ni-Vanuatu culture is traditional; ocal social and religious customs are trong, despite centuries of missionary ıfluence. Subsistence farming and ishing are the main activities. 80% of the population lives on the 12 main slands. Women have lower social tatus than men and payment of ride-price is common.

INSIGHT: *With 105 indigenous tongues, Vanuatu has the world's highest per apita density of languages*

THE ECONOMY

Reliant on aid. Main export is copra; diversifying into beef, timber, kava. Tourism. Offshore banking: rules tightened after international pressure.

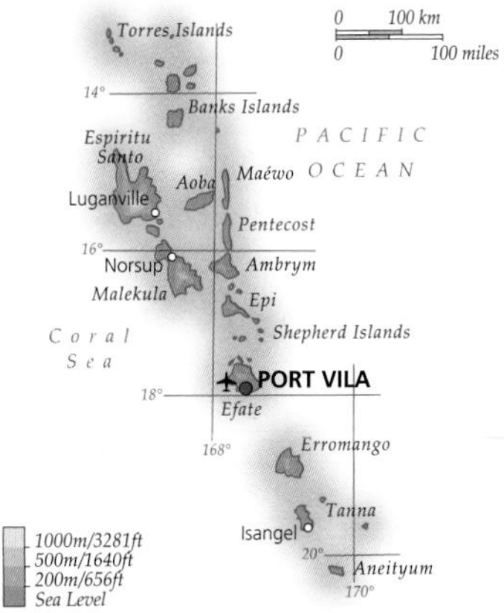
Torres Islands
0 100 km
0 100 miles
14°
Banks Islands
Espiritu Santo
PACIFIC OCEAN
Maéwo
Aoba
Luganville
Pentecost
16°
Norsup
Ambrym
Malekula
Epi
Coral Sea
Shepherd Islands
PORT VILA
18°
Efate
168°
Erromango
Tanna
Isangel
20°
Aneityum
170°
1000m/3281ft
500m/1640ft
200m/656ft
Sea Level

FACTFILE

OFFICIAL NAME: Republic of Vanuatu

DATE OF FORMATION: 1980

CAPITAL: Port Vila

POPULATION: 239,800

TOTAL AREA: 4710 sq. miles (12,200 sq. km)

DENSITY: 51 people per sq. mile

LANGUAGES: Bislama*, English*, French*

RELIGIONS: Presbyterian 37%, other 25%, Anglican 15%, Roman Catholic 15%, traditional beliefs 8%

ETHNIC MIX: Melanesian 98%, European 1%, other 1%

GOVERNMENT: Parliamentary system

CURRENCY: Vatu = 100 centimes

Vatican City

The Vatican City, or Holy See, the seat of the Roman Catholic Church, is a walled enclave in the Italian city of Rome. It is the world's smallest fully independent state.

GEOGRAPHY

The Vatican's territory includes 10 other buildings in Rome, plus the papal residence. The Vatican Gardens cover half the City's area.

CLIMATE

Mild winters with regular rainfall. Hot, dry summers with occasional thunderstorms.

PEOPLE & SOCIETY

The Vatican has about 800 permanent inhabitants, including over 100 lay persons. Thousands of lay staff are also employed. Citizenship can be acquired through long-term residence and holding a position within the City. The reigning pope has supreme legislative and judicial powers, and holds office for life. Though the Vatican City is officially neutral, papal opinion has a great influence on the world's 1.1 billion Roman Catholics.

THE ECONOMY

Investments and voluntary contributions made by Catholics worldwide (known as Peter's Pence) are backed up by tourist revenue and the issue of Vatican stamps and coins.

INSIGHT: *The Vatican City is the spiritual center for one in six of the world's population*

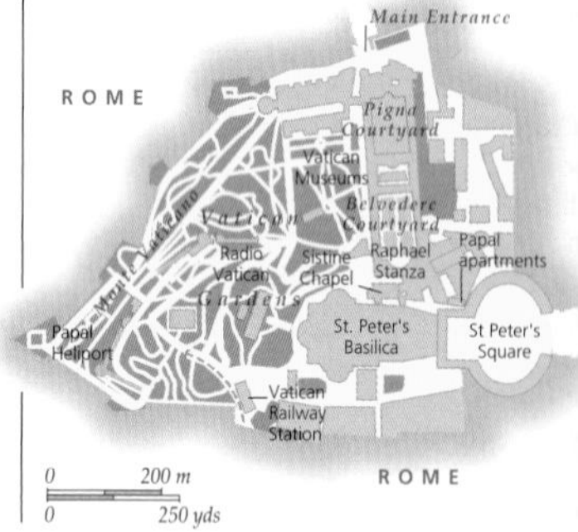
Main Entrance
ROME
Pigna Courtyard
Vatican Museums
Belvedere Courtyard
Vatican Gardens
Monte Vaticano
Radio Vatican
Sistine Chapel
Raphael Stanza
Papal apartments
Papal Heliport
St. Peter's Basilica
St Peter's Square
Vatican Railway Station
0
200 m
0
250 yds
ROME

FACTFILE

OFFICIAL NAME: State of the Vatican City
DATE OF FORMATION: 1929
CAPITAL: Vatican City
POPULATION: 800
TOTAL AREA: 0.17 sq. miles (0.44 sq. km)
DENSITY: 4706 people per sq. mile
LANGUAGES: Italian*, Latin*
RELIGIONS: Roman Catholic 100%
ETHNIC MIX: Cardinals are from many nationalities, but Italians form the largest group. The current pope is from Germany.
GOVERNMENT: Papal state
CURRENCY: Euro = 100 cents

Venezuela

Lying on the southern shores of the Caribbean, Venezuela was the first of Spain's colonies to seek independence. Despite large oil reserves, many Venezuelans still live in poverty.

GEOGRAPHY

Andes Mountains and the Maracaibo lowlands in the northwest. Central grassy plains are drained by the Orinoco River system. Forested Guiana Highlands in the southeast.

CLIMATE

Tropical. Hot and humid. Uplands are cooler. Orinoco plains are alternately parched or flooded.

PEOPLE & SOCIETY

Venezuela is historically a "melting pot," with immigrants from Europe and ll over Latin America. The few ndigenous Amerindians live in remote reas. Venezuela has one of the most urbanized societies in the region, with most of its population living in the northern cities. President Chávez's left-wing rhetoric raises opposition within Venezuela from urban society, and from the US.

THE ECONOMY

Oil accounts for 95% of exports. Reserves of coal, gold, other minerals. Nationalization program is enlarging the inefficient, corruption-prone state sector and deterring foreign investors.

INSIGHT: *Venezuela's Angel Falls is the world's tallest waterfall, with a total drop of 3210 ft (979 m)*

0 200 km
0 200 miles
Caribbean Sea
Maracay
Maracaibo
Valencia
CARACAS
Cabimas
Cumaná
Lago de Maracaibo
Barquisimeto
Barcelona
ATLANTIC OCEAN
Barinas
Llanos
Ciudad Guayana
San Cristóbal
Orinoco
Ciudad Bolívar
Meta
Angel Falls
GUYANA
COLOMBIA
Guiana Highlands
BRAZIL
2000m/6562ft
1000m/3281ft
500m/1640ft
200m/656ft
Sea Level
Equator
12°
8°
4°
72°
68°
64°
60°

FACTFILE

OFFICIAL NAME: Bolivarian Republic of Venezuela
DATE OF FORMATION: 1830
CAPITAL: Caracas
POPULATION: 28.6 million
TOTAL AREA: 352,143 sq. miles (912,050 sq. km)
DENSITY: 84 people per sq. mile
LANGUAGES: Spanish*, native languages
RELIGIONS: Roman Catholic 89%, Protestant and other 11%
ETHNIC MIX: *Mestizo* 69%, White 20%, Black 9%, Amerindian 2%
GOVERNMENT: Presidential system
CURRENCY: Bolívar fuerte = 100 céntimos

Vietnam

French rule of Vietnam ended in 1954. Divided at 17°N, the US-backed South fought the Communist North. Reunified after the North's 1975 victory, it is run as a single-party state.

GEOGRAPHY

A heavily forested mountain range separates the northern Red River delta lowlands from the Mekong Delta in the south.

CLIMATE

Cool winters in north; south is tropical, with even temperatures.

PEOPLE & SOCIETY

Ethnic Vietnamese dominate; the Chinese minority was viewed as a corrupt bourgeoisie by the victorious Communists after the war. Mountain-based minorities *(montagnards)* were also sidelined; tensions persist over the settling of highlands by lowlanders. Women play an active role in society. There is no political or press freedom.

INSIGHT: *Intense US bombing and defoliant spraying in the 1962–1975 Vietnam War has scarred the landscape*

THE ECONOMY

Liberal economic policy *(doi moi)* from 1986: now one of fastest-growing economies. Major rice exporter. Cheap labor. Strong manufacturing: textiles, electrical goods. Diverse resource base.

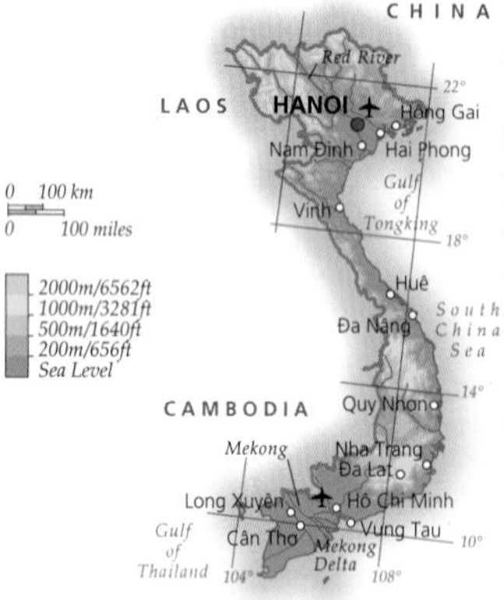
CHINA
Red River
22°
LAOS
HANOI
Hông Gai
Nam Đinh
Hai Phong
Gulf of Tongking
Vinh
18°
0 100 km
0 100 miles
2000m/6562ft
1000m/3281ft
500m/1640ft
200m/656ft
Sea Level
Huê
Đa Nẵng
South China Sea
14°
CAMBODIA
Quy Nhon
Mekong
Nha Trang
Đa Lat
Long Xuyên
Hô Chi Minh
Vung Tau
Gulf of Thailand
Cân Thơ
Mekong Delta
10°
104°
108°

FACTFILE

OFFICIAL NAME: Socialist Republic of Vietnam

DATE OF FORMATION: 1976

CAPITAL: Hanoi

POPULATION: 88.1 million

TOTAL AREA: 127,243 sq. miles (329,560 sq. km)

DENSITY: 701 people per sq. mile

LANGUAGES: Vietnamese*, Chinese, other

RELIGIONS: Nonreligious 81%, Buddhist 9%, Christian 7%, other 3%

ETHNIC MIX: Vietnamese 86%, other 10%, Tay 2%, Thai 2%

GOVERNMENT: One-party state

CURRENCY: Dông = 10 hao = 100 xu

Yemen

Located in southern Arabia, Yemen was formerly two countries: the People's Democratic Republic of Yemen (south and east) and the Yemen Arab Republic (northwest) were united in 1990.

GEOGRAPHY

Mountainous west with a fertile strip along the Red Sea. Arid desert and mountains elsewhere.

CLIMATE

Desert climate, modified by altitude, which affects temperatures by as much as 54°F (30°C).

PEOPLE & SOCIETY

Almost entirely of Arab and Bedouin descent, most Yemenis are Sunni Muslims, of the Shafi sect. In rural and northern areas, tribalism and Islamic orthodoxy are strong and most women wear the veil. Tension continues between the south, led by cosmopolitan Aden, and the more conservative north, though political opposition is now primarily from Islamists. Foreigners are subject to sporadic attacks and kidnappings.

THE ECONOMY

Instability deters investment. Considerable oil and natural gas reserves. Agriculture is the largest employer: qat (mild narcotic), coffee, and cotton.

INSIGHT: *Mokha, on the Red Sea, gave its name to the first coffee beans exported to Europe in the 1600s*

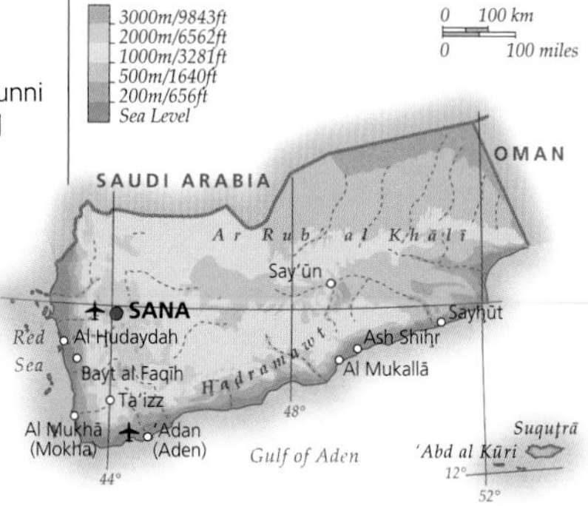
3000m/9843ft
2000m/6562ft
1000m/3281ft
500m/1640ft
200m/656ft
Sea Level
0 100 km
0 100 miles
SAUDI ARABIA
OMAN
Ar Rub' al Khali
Say'ūn
SANA
Sayhūt
Red Sea
Al Hudaydah
Ash Shihr
Al Mukallā
Bayt al Faqīh
Hadramawt
Ta'izz
Al Mukhā (Mokha)
'Adan (Aden)
Gulf of Aden
Suquṭrā
'Abd al Kūri
16°
12°
44°
48°
52°

FACTFILE

OFFICIAL NAME: Republic of Yemen
DATE OF FORMATION: 1990
CAPITAL: Sana
POPULATION: 23.6 million
TOTAL AREA: 203,849 sq. miles (527,970 sq. km)
DENSITY: 108 people per sq. mile
LANGUAGES: Arabic*
RELIGIONS: Sunni Muslim 55%, Shi'a Muslim 42%, Christian, Hindu, and Jewish 3%
ETHNIC MIX: Arab 99%, Afro-Arab, Indian, Somali, and European 1%
GOVERNMENT: Presidential system
CURRENCY: Yemeni rial = 100 fils

Zambia

Bordered to the south by the Zambezi River, Zambia lies at the heart of southern Africa. In 1991, it made a peaceful transition from single-party rule to multiparty democracy.

GEOGRAPHY

A high savanna plateau, broken by mountains in northeast. Vegetation mainly trees and scrub.

CLIMATE

Tropical, with three seasons: cool and dry, hot and dry, and wet. Southwest is prone to drought.

PEOPLE & SOCIETY

There are more than 70 different ethnic groups, but there are fewer tensions than in many African states. Major groups are the Bemba (in the northeast), Tonga (south), Nyanja (east), and Lozi (west). There are also thousands of refugees, mostly from the DRC and Angola. A National Gender Policy was issued in 2000 to redress inequalities between the sexes. The standard of living has fallen in real terms since independence. One in seven adults is infected with HIV/AIDS.

THE ECONOMY

Copper: output has risen since 2000, when decades of falling global prices ended. New agricultural exports, notably flowers. Debt relief.

INSIGHT: *Spray from Musi-o-Tunya (Victoria Falls) can be seen up to 20 miles (35 km) away*

1000m/3281ft
500m/1640ft
200m/656ft
L. Tanganyika
TANZANIA
32°
L. Mweru
DEM. REP. CONGO
24°
28°
Kasama
Mansa
12°
Mufulira
Chingola
Ndola
Kitwe
ANGOLA
Luanshya
Chipata
Kabwe
Mongu
LUSAKA
MOZAMBIQUE
16°
Zambezi
Monze
Choma
Lake Kariba
ZIMBABWE
Livingstone
NAMIBIA
BOTSWANA
Victoria Falls
0
200 km
0
200 mi

FACTFILE

OFFICIAL NAME: Republic of Zambia
DATE OF FORMATION: 1964
CAPITAL: Lusaka
POPULATION: 12.9 million
TOTAL AREA: 290,584 sq. miles (752,614 sq. km)
DENSITY: 45 people per sq. mile
LANGUAGES: Bemba, Tonga, Nyanja, Lozi, Lala-bisa, Nsenga, English*
RELIGIONS: Christian 63%, traditional beliefs 36%, Muslim and Hindu 1%
ETHNIC MIX: Bemba 34%, other 27%, Tonga 16%, Nyanja 14%, Lozi 9%
GOVERNMENT: Presidential system
CURRENCY: Zamb. kwacha = 100 ngwee

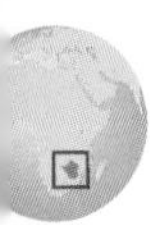

Zimbabwe

Situated in southern Africa, Zimbabwe achieved independence from the UK in 1980. President Robert Mugabe, in power since then, has become increasingly authoritarian.

GEOGRAPHY

High plateaus in center bordered by ambezi River in the north and Limpopo n the south. Rivers crisscross central area.

CLIMATE

Tropical, though moderated by the igh altitude. Wet season November–March. Drought is common in the astern highlands.

PEOPLE & SOCIETY

Two main ethnic groups: Shona n the north and east, and Ndebele in he south. Shona outnumber Ndebele y four to one. Whites are generally ar more affluent than Blacks. Official fforts to redress this imbalance such as land redistribution) have ecome increasingly aggressive. he political opposition to Mugabe ined him in a fractious unity overnment from 2009 in an ttempt to rebuild the country.

THE ECONOMY

Undermined by mismanagement, corruption, and international isolation. High unemployment. Hyperinflation. Stabilization could cost US$45 billion.

INSIGHT: *The ruins of the 1000-year-old city of Great Zimbabwe, after which the country is named, are near modern-day Masvingo*

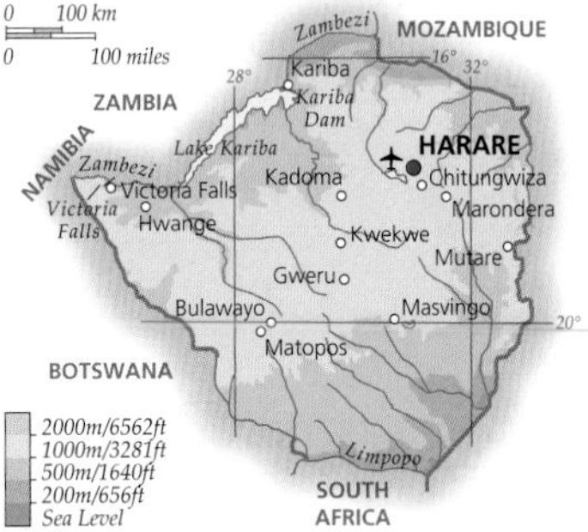
0 100 km
0 100 miles
Zambezi
MOZAMBIQUE
16°
32°
28°
Kariba
Kariba Dam
ZAMBIA
NAMIBIA
Lake Kariba
HARARE
Zambezi
Victoria Falls
Kadoma
Chitungwiza
Victoria Falls
Hwange
Marondera
Kwekwe
Mutare
Gweru
Bulawayo
Masvingo
20°
Matopos
BOTSWANA
2000m/6562ft
1000m/3281ft
500m/1640ft
200m/656ft
Sea Level
Limpopo
SOUTH AFRICA

FACTFILE

OFFICIAL NAME: Republic of Zimbabwe
DATE OF FORMATION: 1980
CAPITAL: Harare
POPULATION: 12.5 million
TOTAL AREA: 150,803 sq. miles (390,580 sq. km)
DENSITY: 84 people per sq. mile
LANGUAGES: Shona, isiNdebele, English*
RELIGIONS: Syncretic 50%, Christian 25%, traditional beliefs 24%, other 1%
ETHNIC MIX: Shona 71%, Ndebele 16%, other African 11%, White 1%, Asian 1%
GOVERNMENT: Presidential system
CURRENCY: Zimbabwe dollar suspended in 2009; US dollar and South African rand legal tender

Overseas territories

Despite the rapid process of global decolonization since World War II, around eight million people in more than 50 territories around the world continue to live under the protection of France, Australia, Denmark, the Netherlands, Norway, New Zealand, the UK, or the USA. These remnants of former colonial empires may have persisted for economic, strategic, or political reasons and are administered by the protecting country in a variety of ways.

AUSTRALIA

Australia's overseas territories have not been an issue since Papua New Guinea became independent in 1975. Consequently there is no overriding policy toward them. Norfolk Island is inhabited by descendants of the HMS *Bounty* mutineers and more recent Australian migrants. Phosphate is mined on Christmas Island.

Ashmore & Cartier Is. *Ref: 124 A3*

STATUS: External territory
CLAIMED: 1931
CAPITAL: Not applicable
POPULATION: None
AREA: 2 sq miles (5.2 sq km)

Christmas Island *Ref: 123 E5*

STATUS: External territory
CLAIMED: 1958
CAPITAL: The Settlement
POPULATION: 1400
AREA: 52 sq miles (135 sq km)

Cocos Islands *Ref: 123 D5*

STATUS: External territory
CLAIMED: 1955
CAPITAL: Not applicable
POPULATION: 574
AREA: 5.5 sq miles (14 sq km)

Coral Sea Islands *Ref: 126 B4*

STATUS: External territory
CLAIMED: 1969
CAPITAL: Not applicable
POPULATION: 8 (Meteorologists)
AREA: 1.2 sq miles (3 sq km)

Heard & McDonald Is. *Ref: 123 C7*

STATUS: External territory
CLAIMED: 1947
CAPITAL: Not applicable
POPULATION: None
AREA: 161 sq miles (417 sq km)

Norfolk Island *Ref: 124 D4*

STATUS: External territory
CLAIMED: 1774
CAPITAL: Kingston
POPULATION: 2100
AREA: 13 sq miles (34 sq km)

DENMARK

The Faeroe Islands have been under Danish administration since Queen Margreth I of Denmark inherited Norway in 1380. The Home Rule Act of 1948 gave the Faeroese control over all their internal affairs. Greenland first came under Danish rule in 1380. Denmark remains responsible for the island's foreign affairs.

Overseas territories

Faeroe Islands *Ref: 65 F5*

STATUS: External territory
CLAIMED: 1380
CAPITAL: Tórshavn
POPULATION: 49,000
AREA: 540 sq miles (1399 sq km)

Greenland *Ref: 64 D3*

STATUS: External territory
CLAIMED: 1380
CAPITAL: Nuuk
POPULATION: 57,500
AREA: 836,109 sq miles (2,166,086 sq km)

FRANCE

France has developed economic ties with its *Territoires d'Outre–Mer*, thereby stressing interdependence over independence. Overseas *départements*, officially part of France, have their own governments. Territorial *collectivités* and overseas *territoires* have varying degrees of autonomy.

Clipperton Island *Ref: 135 F3*
STATUS: Dependency of French Polynesia
CLAIMED: 1935
CAPITAL: Not applicable
POPULATION: None
AREA: 3.4 sq miles (9 sq km)

French Guiana *Ref: 41 H3*
STATUS: Overseas department
CLAIMED: 1817
CAPITAL: Cayenne
POPULATION: 221,500
AREA: 35,135 sq miles (91,000 sq km)

French Polynesia *Ref: 127 H4*
STATUS: Overseas country
CLAIMED: 1843
CAPITAL: Papeete
POPULATION: 264,000
AREA: 1608 sq miles (4165 sq km)

Guadeloupe *Ref: 37 G4*
STATUS: Overseas department
CLAIMED: 1635
CAPITAL: Basse-Terre
POPULATION: 441,000
AREA: 687 sq miles (1780 sq km)

Martinique *Ref: 37 G4*
STATUS: Overseas department
CLAIMED: 1635
CAPITAL: Fort-de-France
POPULATION: 402,000
AREA: 425 sq miles (1100 sq km)

Mayotte *Ref: 61 G2*
STATUS: Territorial collectivity
CLAIMED: 1843
CAPITAL: Mamoudzou
POPULATION: 194,000
AREA: 144 sq miles (374 sq km)

New Caledonia *Ref: 126 D5*
STATUS: Overseas territory
CLAIMED: 1853
CAPITAL: Nouméa
POPULATION: 249,000
AREA: 7347 sq miles (19,100 sq km)

Réunion *Ref: 61 H4*
STATUS: Overseas department
CLAIMED: 1638
CAPITAL: Saint-Denis
POPULATION: 827,000
AREA: 970 sq miles (2500 sq km)

Overseas territories

St Pierre & Miquelon *Ref: 21 G4*
STATUS: Territorial collectivity
CLAIMED: 1604
CAPITAL: Saint-Pierre
POPULATION: 6125
AREA: 93 sq miles (242 sq km)

Wallis & Futuna *Ref: 127 E4*
STATUS: Overseas territory
CLAIMED: 1842
CAPITAL: Mata'Utu
POPULATION: 13,484
AREA: 106 sq miles (274 sq km)

NETHERLANDS

The country's two remaining territories were formerly part of the Dutch West Indies. Both are now self-governing, but the Netherlands remains responsible for their defense.

Aruba *Ref: 37 E5*

STATUS: Autonomous part of the Netherlands
CLAIMED: 1634
CAPITAL: Oranjestad
POPULATION: 103,000
AREA: 75 sq miles (194 sq km)

Netherlands Antilles *Ref: 37 E5*

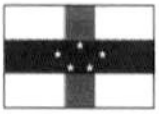

STATUS: Autonomous part of the Netherlands
CLAIMED: 1816
CAPITAL: Willemstad
POPULATION: 184,000
AREA: 371 sq miles (960 sq km)

NEW ZEALAND

New Zealand's government has no desire to retain any overseas territories. However, the economic weakness of Tokelau, Niue, and the Cook Islands has forced it to remain responsible for their foreign policy and defense.

Cook Islands *Ref: 127 G4*

STATUS: Associated territory
CLAIMED: 1901
CAPITAL: Avarua
POPULATION: 19,500
AREA: 91 sq miles (235 sq km)

Niue *Ref: 127 F5*
STATUS: Associated territory
CLAIMED: 1901
CAPITAL: Alofi
POPULATION: 1400
AREA: 102 sq miles (264 sq km)

Tokelau *Ref: 127 F3*
STATUS: Dependent territory
CLAIMED: 1926
CAPITAL: Not applicable
POPULATION: 1400
AREA: 4 sq miles (10 sq km)

NORWAY

In 1920, 41 nations signed the Spitsbergen treaty recognizing Norwegian sovereignty over Svalbard. There is a NATO base on Jan Mayen. Bouvet Island is a nature reserve.

Overseas territories

Bouvet Island *Ref: 49 D7*
STATUS: Dependency
CLAIMED: 1928
CAPITAL: Not applicable
POPULATION: None
AREA: 22 sq miles (58 sq km)

Jan Mayen *Ref: 65 F3*
STATUS: Dependency
CLAIMED: 1929
CAPITAL: Not applicable
POPULATION: 18 (Meteorologists)
AREA: 147 sq miles (381 sq km)

Peter I. Island *Ref: 136 A3*
STATUS: Dependency
CLAIMED: 1931
CAPITAL: Not applicable
POPULATION: None
AREA: 69 sq miles (180 sq km)

Svalbard *Ref: 65 F2*
STATUS: Dependency
CLAIMED: 1920
CAPITAL: Longyearbyen
POPULATION: 2100
AREA: 24,289 sq miles (62,906 sq km)

UNITED KINGDOM

The UK has the largest number of overseas territories. These are locally governed by a mixture of elected representatives and appointed officials.

Anguilla *Ref: 37 G3*

STATUS: Dependent territory
CLAIMED: 1650
CAPITAL: The Valley
POPULATION: 13,477
AREA: 37 sq miles (96 sq km)

Ascension Island *Ref: 49 C5*
STATUS: Dependency of St Helena
CLAIMED: 1673
CAPITAL: Georgetown
POPULATION: 940
AREA: 34 sq miles (88 sq km)

Bermuda *Ref: 17 E6*

STATUS: Crown colony
CLAIMED: 1612
CAPITAL: Hamilton
POPULATION: 67,800
AREA: 20 sq miles (53 sq km)

British Indian Ocean Territory
Ref: 122 C4

STATUS: Dependent territory
CLAIMED: 1814
CAPITAL: Diego Garcia
POPULATION: 4000
AREA: 23 sq miles (60 sq km)

British Virgin Is. *Ref: 37 F3*

STATUS: Dependent territory
CLAIMED: 1672
CAPITAL: Road Town
POPULATION: 22,000
AREA: 59 sq miles (153 sq km)

Cayman Islands *Ref: 36 B3*

STATUS: Dependent territory
CLAIMED: 1670
CAPITAL: George Town
POPULATION: 52,000
AREA: 100 sq miles (259 sq km)

Falkland Islands *Ref: 47 D7*

STATUS: Dependent territory
CLAIMED: 1832
CAPITAL: Stanley
POPULATION: 3100
AREA: 4699 sq miles (12,173 sq km)

Overseas territories

Gibraltar *Ref: 74 D5*

STATUS: Crown colony
CLAIMED: 1713
CAPITAL: Gibraltar
POPULATION: 28,800
AREA: 2.5 sq miles (6.5 sq km)

Guernsey *Ref: 71 D8*

STATUS: Crown dependency
CLAIMED: 1066
CAPITAL: St. Peter Port
POPULATION: 65,500
AREA: 25 sq miles (65 sq km)

Isle of Man *Ref: 71 C5*

STATUS: Crown dependency
CLAIMED: 1765
CAPITAL: Douglas
POPULATION: 76,500
AREA: 221 sq miles (572 sq km)

Jersey *Ref: 71 D8*

STATUS: Crown dependency
CLAIMED: 1066
CAPITAL: St. Helier
POPULATION: 91,600
AREA: 45 sq miles (116 sq km)

Montserrat *Ref: 37 G4*

STATUS: Dependent territory
CLAIMED: 1632
CAPITAL: Plymouth (uninhabitable)
POPULATION: 4500
AREA: 40 sq miles (102 sq km)

Pitcairn Islands *Ref: 125 G4*

STATUS: Dependent territory
CLAIMED: 1887
CAPITAL: Adamstown
POPULATION: 45
AREA: 18 sq miles (47 sq km)

Saint Helena *Ref: 49 D5*

STATUS: Dependent territor
CLAIMED: 1673
CAPITAL: Jamestown
POPULATION: 4299
AREA: 47 sq miles (122 sq km)

South Georgia & The Sandwich Islands *Ref: 49 C7*

STATUS: Dependent territory
CLAIMED: 1775
CAPITAL: Not applicable
POPULATION: None
AREA: 1387 sq miles (3592 sq km)

Tristan da Cunha *Ref: 49 D6*

STATUS: Dependency of St. Helena
CLAIMED: 1612
CAPITAL: Edinburgh
POPULATION: 270
AREA: 38 sq miles (98 sq km)

Turks & Caicos Islands *Ref: 37 E2*

STATUS: Dependent territor
CLAIMED: 1766
CAPITAL: Cockburn Town
POPULATION: 36,600
AREA: 166 sq miles (430 sq km)

UNITED STATES

US Commonwealth territories are self-governing incorporated territories that are an integral part of the US. Unincorporatec territories have varying degrees of autonomy

American Samoa *Ref: 127 F4*

STATUS: Unincorporated territory
CLAIMED: 1900
CAPITAL: Pago Pago
POPULATION: 65,600
AREA: 75 sq miles (195 sq km)

Overseas territories

Baker & Howland Islands *Ref: 127 E2*
STATUS: Unincorporated territory
CAPITAL: Not applicable
CLAIMED: 1856
POPULATION: None
AREA: 0.5 sq miles (1.4 sq km)

Guam *Ref: 126 B1*

STATUS: Unincorporated territory
CLAIMED: 1898
CAPITAL: Hagåtña
POPULATION: 178,000
AREA: 212 sq miles (549 sq km)

Jarvis Island *Ref: 127 G2*
STATUS: Unincorporated territory
CLAIMED: 1856
CAPITAL: Not applicable
POPULATION: None
AREA: 1.7 sq miles (4.5 sq km)

Johnston Atoll *Ref: 125 E1*
STATUS: Unincorporated territory
CLAIMED: 1858
CAPITAL: Not applicable
POPULATION: None
AREA: 1 sq mile (2.8 sq km)

Kingman Reef *Ref: 127 F2*
STATUS: Administered territory
CLAIMED: 1856
CAPITAL: Not applicable
POPULATION: None
AREA: 0.4 sq miles (1 sq km)

Midway Islands *Ref: 134 D2*
STATUS: Administered territory
CLAIMED: 1867
CAPITAL: Not applicable
POPULATION: None
AREA: 2 sq miles (5.2 sq km)

Navassa Island *Ref: 36 D3*
STATUS: Unincorporated territory
CLAIMED: 1856
CAPITAL: Not applicable
POPULATION: None
AREA: 2 sq miles (5.2 sq km)

Northern Mariana Islands *Ref: 124 C1*

STATUS: Commonwealth territory
CLAIMED: 1947
CAPITAL: Saipan
POPULATION: 86,600
AREA: 177 sq miles (457 sq km)

Palmyra Atoll *Ref: 127 G2*
STATUS: Unincorporated territory
CLAIMED: 1898
CAPITAL: Not applicable
POPULATION: None
AREA: 5 sq miles (12 sq km)

Puerto Rico *Ref: 37 F3*

STATUS: Commonwealth territory
CLAIMED: 1898
CAPITAL: San Juan
POPULATION: 4 million
AREA: 3515 sq miles (9104 sq km)

Virgin Islands *Ref: 37 F3*

V
I
STATUS: Unincorporated territory
CLAIMED: 1917
CAPITAL: Charlotte Amalie
POPULATION: 108,500
AREA: 137 sq miles (355 sq km)

Wake Island *Ref: 124 D1*
STATUS: Unincorporated territory
CLAIMED: 1898
CAPITAL: Not applicable
POPULATION: 200
AREA: 2.5 sq miles (6.5 sq km)

International organizations

This listing provides acronym definitions for the main international organizations concerned with worldwide economics, trade, and defense, plus an indication of membership.

ASEAN
Association of Southeast Asian Nations
ESTABLISHED: 1967
MEMBERS: Brunei, Cambodia, Indonesia, Laos, Malaysia, Myanmar, Philippines, Singapore, Thailand, Vietnam

CIS
Commonwealth of Independent States
ESTABLISHED: 1991
MEMBERS: Arm., Az., Belarus, Kaz., Kyrgy., Mold., Russia, Tajik., Turkmen.*, Ukraine*, Uzbek. **Unofficial members*

COMM *The Commonwealth of Nations*
ESTABLISHED: 1931; evolved out of the British Empire. Formerly known as the British Commonwealth of Nations.
MEMBERS: 53

EU *European Union*
ESTABLISHED: 1965; formerly known as EEC (European Economic Community) and EC (Economic Community)
MEMBERS: Austria, Belg., Bulg., Cyprus, Czech Rep., Denmark, Est., Fin., Fr., Ger., Greece, Hung., Ireland, Italy, Lat., Lith., Lux., Malta, Neth., Pol., Port., Rom., Slvka., Slvna., Spain, Swed., UK

G8 *Group of 8*
ESTABLISHED: 1994
MEMBERS: Canada, France, Germany, Italy, Japan, Russia, UK, US

IMF *International Monetary Fund* (UN agency)
ESTABLISHED: 1945
MEMBERS: 186

NAFTA
North American Free Trade Agreement
ESTABLISHED: 1994
MEMBERS: Canada, Mexico, US

NATO
North Atlantic Treaty Organization
ESTABLISHED: 1949
MEMBERS: Albania, Belg., Bulg., Canada, Croatia, Czech Rep., Denmark, Est., France, Ger., Greece, Hung., Iceland, Italy, Lat., Lith., Lux., Neth., Norway, Poland, Port., Rom., Slovakia, Slovenia, Spain, Turkey, UK, US

OPEC *Organization of Petroleum Exporting Countries*
ESTABLISHED: 1960
MEMBERS: Algeria, Angola, Ecuador, Iran, Iraq, Kuwait, Libya, Nigeria, Qatar, Saudi Arabia, United Arab Emirates, Venezuela

UN *United Nations*
ESTABLISHED: 1945
MEMBERS: 192; all nations are represented except Taiwan. The Vatican City has "observer status" only.

WTO *World Trade Organization*
ESTABLISHED: 1995
MEMBERS: 153

Abbreviations

This glossary provides a comprehensive guide to the abbreviations used in this atlas.

abbrev. abbreviation
Afgh. Afghanistan
Amh. Amharic
anc. ancient
Ar. Arabic
Arm. Armenia/Armenian
Aus. Austria
Aust. Australia
Az. Azerbaijan

Bas. Basque
Bel. Belorussian
Belg. Belgium/Belgian
Bos. & Herz. Bosnia & Herzegovina
Bul. Bulgarian
Bulg. Bulgaria
Bur. Burmese

C Central
C. Cape
Cam. Cambodian
Cast. Castilian
Chin. Chinese
Cord. Cordillera (Sp. mts.)
Cz. Czech
Czech Rep. Czech Republic

D.C. District of Columbia
Dan. Danish
Dominican Rep. Dominican Republic

E East
Emb. Embalse
Eng. English
Eq. Guinea Equatorial Guinea
Est. Estonia/Estonian

Faer. Faeroese
Fin. Finland/Finnish
Flem. Flemish
Fr. France/French

Geo. Georgia
Geor. Georgian
Ger. Germany/German
Gk. Greek

Heb. Hebrew
Hung. Hungary/Hungarian

I. Island
Ind. Indonesia, Indonesian
Is. Islands
It. Italian

Kaz. Kazakhstan/Kazakh
Kep. Kepulauan (Ind. island group)
Kir. Kirghiz
Kor. Korean
Kos. Kosovo
Kurd. Kurdish
Kyrgy. Kyrgyzstan

L. Lake, Lago
Lat. Latvia
Latv. Latvian
Leb. Lebanon
Liech. Liechtenstein
Lith. Lithuania/Lithuanian
Lux. Luxembourg

Mac. Macedonia
Med. Sea Mediterranean Sea
Mon. Montenegro
Mold. Moldova
Mt. Mount/Mountain
Mts. Mountains

N North
N. Korea North Korea
Neth. Netherlands
NW Northwest
NZ New Zealand

P. Pulau (Ind. island)
Peg. Pegunungan (Ind. mountain range)
Per. Persian
Pol. Poland/Polish
Port. Portugal, Portuguese
prev. previously

R. River, Rio, Río
Res. Reservoir
Rom. Romania/Romanian
Rus. Russian
Russ. Fed. Russian Federation

S South
S. Korea South Korea
SA South Africa
SCr. Serbian and Croatian
Serb. Serbia
Slvka. Slovakia
Slvna. Slovenia
Som. Somali
Sp. Spanish
St, St. Saint
Str. Strait
Swed. Swedish
Switz. Switzerland

Tajik. Tajikistan
Th. Thai
Turk. Turkish
Turkm. Turkmen
Turkmen. Turkmenistan

U.A.E. United Arab Emirates
UK United Kingdom
Ukr. Ukrainian
Urug. Uruguayan
US United States of America
Uzb. Uzbek
Uzbek. Uzbekistan

var. variant
Vdkhr. Vodokhranilishche (Rus. reservoir)
Vdskh. Vodoskhovyshche (Ukr. reservoir)
Ven. Venezuela

W West
W. Sahara Western Sahara
Wel. Welsh

Yugo. Yugoslavia

Zamb. Zambian

A

Aabenraa Denmark 67 A8
Aachen Germany 76 A4
Aalborg Denmark 67 B7
Aalst Belgium 69 B5
Aba Nigeria 57 G5
Ābādān Iran 102 C4
Abadan Turkmenistan *prev.* Bezmein, Büzmeýin 104 B3
Abashiri Japan 112 D2
Abéché Chad 58 D3
Aberdeen Scotland, UK 70 D3
Aberdeen South Dakota, USA 25 E2
Aberdeen Washington, USA 26 A2
Aberystwyth Wales, UK 71 C6
Abhā Saudi Arabia 103 B6
Abidjan Côte d'Ivoire 56 D5
Abilene Texas, USA 29 F3
Abomey Benin 57 F4
Abu Dhabi *capital of* United Arab Emirates *var.* Abū Ẓaby 103 D5
Abuja *capital of* Nigeria 57 G4
Abū Ẓaby *see* Abu Dhabi
Acapulco Mexico 33 E5
Acarai Mountains *mountain range* Brazil/Guyana 41 F3
Acarigua Venezuela 40 D1
Accra *capital of* Ghana 57 E5
Acklins Island *island* Bahamas 36 D2
Aconcagua, Cerro *peak* Argentina 46 B4
A Coruña Spain *Cast.* La Coruña 74 C1
ACT *see* Australian Capital Territory
Adalia *see* Antalya
Adalia, Gulf of *see* Antalya Körfezi
'Adan Yemen *Eng.* Aden 103 B7
Adana Turkey *var.* Seyhan 98 D4
Adapazarı Turkey *var.* Sakarya 98 B2
Ad Dahnā' *desert* Saudi Arabia *103 C5*
Ad Dakhla Western Sahara 52 A4
Ad Dawḩah *see* Doha
Addis Ababa *capital of* Ethiopia *Amh.* Ādīs Ābeba 55 C5
Adelaide Australia 131 B6
Adélie, Terre d' *territory* Antarctica 136 C4
Aden *see* 'Adan
Aden, Gulf of *sea feature* Indian Ocean 122 A3
Adige *river* Italy 78 C2
Ādīs Ābeba *see* Addis Ababa
Adıyaman Turkey 99 E4
Adriatic Sea Mediterranean Sea 78 D4
Aegean Sea Mediterranean Sea *Gk.* Aigaío Pélagos, *Turk.* Ege Denizi 87 D5
Aeolian Islands *see* Isole Eolie
Afghanistan *country* C Asia 104-105
Africa 50-51
Africa, Horn of *physical region* Ethiopia/Somalia 122 A3
Afyon Turkey *prev.* Afyonkarahisar 98 B3
Afyonkarahisar *see* Afyon
Agadez Niger 57 G3
Agadir Morocco 52 B2
Agassiz Fracture Zone *tectonic feature* Pacific Ocean 135 E4
Agen France 73 B6
Āgra India 116 D3
Agrigento Italy 79 C7
Agrínio Greece 87 B5
Aguarico *river* Ecuador/Peru 40 B4
Aguascalientes Mexico 32 D4
Ahaggar *mountains* Algeria *var.* Hoggar 53 E4
Ahmadābād India 116 C4
Ahvāz Iran 102 C4
Ahvenanmaa see Åland
Aigaío Pélagos *see* Aegean Sea
Aintab *see* Gaziantep
Aïr, Massif de l' *region* Niger 57 G2
Aix-en-Provence France 73 D6
Ajaccio Corse, France 73 E7
Ajdābiyā Libya 53 G2
Ajmer India 116 D3
Akaba *see* Al 'Aqabah
Akchâr *desert* Mauritania 56 C2
Akimiski Island *island* Canada 20 C3
Akita Japan 112 D3
Akjoujt Mauritania 56 C2
Akmola *see* Astana
Akmolinsk *see* Astana
Akpatok Island *island* Canada 21 E1
Akra Kanestron *see* Palioúri, Akrotírio
Akron Ohio, USA 22 D3
Aksai Chin *disputed region* China/India 108 B4
Aktau Kazakhstan *prev.* Shevchenko 96 A4
Akureyri Iceland 65 E4
Akyab *see* Sittwe
Alabama *state* USA 30 D3
Alacant *see* Alicante
Alajuela Costa Rica 34 D4
Alamogordo New Mexico, USA 28 D3
Åland *island group* Finland Fin Ahvenanmaa 67 D6
Al 'Aqabah Jordan *var.* Akaba 101 B7
Alaska *state* USA 18
Alaska, Gulf of *sea feature* Pacific Ocean 16 C3
Alaska Range *mountain range* Alaska, USA 18 C3
Albacete Spain 75 E3
Alba Iulia Romania 90 B4
Albania *country* SE Europe 83
Albany Australia 129 B7
Albany Georgia, USA 31 E3
Albany New York, USA 23 F3
Albany Oregon, USA 26 A3
Albany *river* Canada 20 B3

l Başrah Iraq *var.* Basra 102 C4
l Bayḑā' Libya 53 G2
lbert, Lake *lake* Uganda/Dem. Rep. Congo 59 E5
lberta *province* Canada 19 E4
lbi France 73 C6
lbuquerque New Mexico, USA 28 D2
lcácer do Sal Portugal 74 C4
ldabra Group *island group* Seychelles 61 G2
leg Mauritania 56 C3
leksandriya *see* Oleksandriya
leksandropol' *see* Gyumri
leksinac Serbia 82 E4
lençon France 72 B3
lessandria Italy 78 B2
lesund Norway 67 A5
leutian Basin *undersea feature* Bering Sea 134 D1
leutian Islands *islands* Alaska, USA 18 A3
leutian Trench *undersea feature* Pacific Ocean 134 D1
lexander Island *island* Antarctica 136 A3
lexandra New Zealand133 B7
lexandretta *see* İskenderun
lexandria *see* Al Iskandarīyah
lexandria Louisiana, USA 30 B3
lexandroúpoli Greece 86 D3
l Fāshir *see* El Fasher
lföld *see* Great Hungarian Plain
lgarve *region* Portugal 74 C4
lgeciras Spain 74 D5
lgeria *country* N Africa 52-53
lghero Italy 79 A5
lgiers *capital of* Algeria 52 D1
l Ḩasakah Syria 100 D2
l Ḩudaydah Yemen 103 B7
l Hufūf Saudi Arabia 103 C5
licante Spain *Cat.* Alacant 75 F4
ice Springs Australia 130 A4
Al Iskandarīyah Egypt *Eng.* Alexandria 54 B1
Al Ismā'īlīya Egypt *Eng.* Ismalia 54 B1
Al Jawf Saudi Arabia 102 B4
Al Jazīrah *region* Iraq/Syria 100 E2
Al Jīzah Egypt *var.* El Gîza 54 B1
Al Karak Jordan 101 B6
Al Khalīl *see* Hebron
Al Khārijah Egypt *var.* El Khârga 54 B2
Al Khums Libya 53 F2
Al Khurţūm *see* Khartoum
Alkmaar Netherlands 68 C2
Al Kufrah Libya 53 H4
Al Lādhiqīyah Syria *Eng.* Latakia 100 B3
Allahābād India 117 E4
Allenstein *see* Olsztyn
Allentown Pennsylvania, USA 23 F4
Alma-Ata *capital of* Kazakhstan *Rus./Kaz.* Almaty 96 C5
Al Madīnah Saudi Arabia *Eng.* Medina 102 A5
Al Mafraq Jordan 101 B5
Almalyk Uzbekistan *Uzb.* Olmaliq 105 E2
Al Manāmah *see* Manama
Al Marj Libya 53 G2
Almaty *see* Alma-Ata
Al Mawşil Iraq *Eng.* Mosul 102 B3
Almelo Netherlands 68 E3
Almería Spain 75 E5
Al Minyā Egypt 54 B2
Al Mukallā Yemen 103 C7
Alofi *capital of* Niue 127 F5
Alor, Kepulauan *island group* Indonesia 121 E5
Alps *mountain range* C Europe 62 D4
Al Qāhirah *see* Cairo
Al Qāmishlī Syria *var.* Kamishli 100 E1
Al Qunayţirah Syria 100 B4
Altai Mountains *mountain range* C Asia 108 C2
Altamura Italy 79 E5
Altar, Desierto de *Desert* Mexico/USA *var.* Sonoran Desert 32 A1
Altay China 108 C2
Altay Mongolia 108 D2
Altun Shan *mountain range* China 108 C3
Alturas California, USA 26 B4
Al Uqşur Egypt *Eng.* Luxor 54 B2
Alytus Lithuania *Pol.* Olita 89 B5
Amadeus, Lake *seasonal lake* Australia 129 E5
Amakusa-nada *island group* Japan 113 A6
Amami-Ō-shima *island* Japan 113 A8
Amarillo Texas, USA 29 E2
Amazon *river* South America 38 C3
Amazon Basin *region* C South America 42 D2
Ambanja Madagascar 61 G2
Ambarchik Russian Federation 97 G2
Ambato Ecuador 40 A4
Amboasary Madagascar 61 F4
Ambon Indonesia 121 F4
Ambositra Madagascar 61 G3
Ambriz Angola 60 B1
Amdo China 108 C4
Ameland *island* Netherlands 68 D1
American Falls Reservoir *Reservoir* Idaho, USA 26 E4
American Samoa *external territory* USA, Pacific Ocean 127 F4
Amersfoort Netherlands 68 D3
Amga *river* Russian Federation 95 F2
Amiens France 72 C3
Amīndīvi Islands *island group* India 114 C2
Amirante Islands *island group* Seychelles 61 H1
Amman *capital of* Jordan 101 B5
Ammassalik Greenland *var.* Angmagssalik 64 D4

Ammochostos *see* Gazimağusa
Āmol Iran 102 C3
Amorgós *island* Greece 87 D6
Amritsar India 116 D2
Amsterdam *capital of* Netherlands 68 C3
Amsterdam Island *island* French Southern and Antarctic Territories 123 C6
Am Timan Chad 58 C3
Amu Darya *river* C Asia 104 D3
Amundsen Gulf *sea feature* Canada 19 E2
Amundsen Plain *undersea feature* Pacific Ocean 136 B4
Amundsen Sea Antarctica 97 G4
Amur *river* E Asia 97 G4 107 E1
Anabar *river* Russian Federation 95 E2
Anadolu Dağları *see* Doğu Karadeniz Dağlarıı
Anadyr' Russian Federation 97 H1
Anápolis Brazil 43 F4
Anatolia *region* SE Europe 85 G3
Anchorage Alaska, USA 18 C3
Ancona Italy 78 C3
Andalucía *region* Spain 74 D4
Andaman Islands *island group* India 115 H2 119 A5
Andaman Sea Indian Ocean 122 D3
Andes *mountain range* South America 39 B6
Andijon Uzbekistan *Rus.* Andizhan 105 F2
Andhra Pradesh *state* India 115 E1
Andizhan *see* Andijon
Andorra *country* SW Europe 73 B6
Andorra la Vella *capital of* Andorra 73 B6
Ándros *island* Greece 87 D5
Andros Island *island* Bahamas 36 C1
Angara *river* C Asia 95 D3
Ángel de la Guarda, Isla *island* Mexico 32 B2
Angel Falls *see* Salto Ángel
Angeles Philippines 121 E1
Ángel, Salto *waterfall* Venezuela *Eng.* Angel Falls 41 F2
Ångermanälven *river* Sweden 66 C4
Angers France 72 B4
Anglesey *island* Wales, UK 71 C5
Angmagssalik *see* Ammassalik
Angola *country* C Africa 60
Angola Basin *undersea feature* Atlantic Ocean 49 D6
Angora *see* Ankara
Angoulême France 73 B5
Angren Uzbekistan 105 E2
Anguilla *external territory* UK, West Indies 37
Anhui *province* China *var.* Anhwei, Wan 111 C5
Anhwei *see* Anhui
Anjouan *island* Comoros 61 F2
Ankara *capital of* Turkey *prev.* Angora 98 C3
Annaba Algeria 53 E1
An Nafūd *desert region* Saudi Arabia 102 B4
An Najaf Iraq *var.* Najaf 102 B4
Annapolis Maryland, USA 23 F4
Ann Arbor Michigan, USA 22 C3
Annecy France 73 D5
Anshan China 110 D4
Ansongo Mali 57 E3
Antakya Turkey *var.* Hatay 98 D4
Antalaha Madagascar 61 G2
Antalya Turkey *prev.* Adalia 98 B4
Antalya, Gulf of *see* Antalya Körfezi
Antalya Körfezi *sea feature* Mediterranean Sea *Eng.* Gulf of Antalya, *var.* Gulf of Adalia 98 B4
Antananarivo *capital of* Madagascar *prev.* Tananarive 61 G3
Antarctica 136
Antarctic Peninsula *peninsula* Antarctica 136 A2
Antequera Spain 74 D5
Anticosti, Île d' *island* Canada 21 F3
Antigua *island* Antigua & Barbuda 37 G3
Antigua & Barbuda *country* West Indies 37
Anti-Lebanon *mountains* Lebanon/Syria 100 B4
Antipodes Islands *island grou* New Zealand124 D5
Antofagasta Chile 46 B2
Antsirañana Madagascar 61 G2
Antsohihy Madagascar 61 G2
Antwerp *see* Antwerpen
Antwerpen Belgium *Eng.* Antwerp 69 C5
Anyang China 110 C4
Aoga-shima *island* Japan 113 D6
Aomori Japan 112 D3
Aoraki *peak* New Zealand *var.* Cook, Mount 133 B6
Aosta Italy 78 A2
Aoukâr *Plateau* Mauritania 56 D3
Apeldoorn Netherlands 68 D3
Apennines *see* Appennino
Apia *capital of* Samoa 127 F4
Appalachian Mountains *mountain range* E USA 17 D
Appennino *mountain range* Italy *Eng.* Apennines 78 C4
Apure *river* Venezuela 40 D2
Aqaba *see* Al 'Aqabah
Aqaba, Gulf of *sea feature* Re Sea *Ar.* Khalīj al 'Aqabah 101 A8
'Aqabah, Khalīj al *see* Aqaba, Gulf of
Āqchah Afghanistan *var.* Āqcheh 104 D3
Āqcheh *see* Āqchah
Arabian Basin *undersea feature* Indian Ocean 122 B
Arabian Peninsula *peninsula* Asia 85 H5 94 B5 103 C5
Arabian Sea Indian Ocean 122 B3
Aracaju Brazil 43 H3
Arad Romania 90 B4

B

a‘labakk *see* Baalbek
alakovo Russian Federation 93 C6
ālā Morghāb Afghanistan 104 D4
alaton *lake* Hungary *var.* Lake Balaton, *Ger.* Plattensee 81 C7
alaton, Lake *see* Balaton
albina, Represa *Reservoir* Brazil 42 D2
aleares, Islas *island group* Spain *Eng.* Balearic Islands 75 H3
alearic Islands *see* Baleares, Islas
ali *island* Indonesia 120 D5
alıkesir Turkey 98 A3
alikpapan Indonesia 120 D4
alkanabat Turkmenistan *prev.* Nebitdag 104 B2
alkan Mountains *mountain range* Bulgaria *Bul.* Stara Planina 86 C2
alkhash Kazakhstan 96 C5
alkhash, Lake *see* Balkhash, Ozero
alkhash, Ozero *lake* Kazakhstan *Eng.* Lake Balkhash 94 C3
allarat Australia 131 C7
alsas *river* Mexico 33 E5
ălţi Moldova 90 D3
altic Port *see* Paldiski
altic Sea Atlantic Ocean 67 C7
altimore Maryland, USA 23 F4
altischport *see* Paldiski
altiski *see* Paldiski
amako *capital of* Mali 56 D3
ambari Central African Republic 58 D4
amenda Cameroon 58 B4
anaba *island* Kiribati *prev.* Ocean Island 127 E2
andaaceh Indonesia 120 A3
anda, Laut *see* Banda Sea
anda Sea *sea feature* Pacific Ocean *Ind.* Laut Banda 121 F4
andar-e ‘Abbās Iran 102 D4
andar-e Būshehr Iran 102 C4
Bandar Lampung Indonesia *prev.* Tanjungkarang 120 C4
Bandar Seri Begawan *capital of* Brunei 120 D3
Bandon Oregon, USA 26 A3
Bandundu Dem. Rep. Congo 59 C6
Bandung Indonesia 120 C5
Bangalore India 114 D2
Banggai, Kepulauan *island group* Indonesia 121 E4
Banghāzī Libya *Eng.* Benghazi 53 G2
Bangka, Palau *island* Indonesia 120 C4
Bangkok *capital of* Thailand *Th.* Krung Thep 119 C5
Bangladesh *country* S Asia 117
Bangor Northern Ireland, UK 71 B5
Bangor Maine, USA 23 G2
Bangui *capital of* Central African Republic 59 C5
Bani *river* Mali 56 D3
Banī Suwayf Egypt *var.* Beni Suef 54 B1
Banja Luka Bosnia & Herzegovina 82 B3
Banjarmasin Indonesia 120 D4
Banjul *capital of* Gambia 56 B3
Banks Island *island* Canada 19 E2
Banks Islands *island group* Vanuatu, Pacific Ocean 126 D4
Banks Peninsula *peninsula* New Zealand133 C6
Banks Strait *sea feature* Tasman Sea 131 C7
Banská Bystrica Slovakia *Ger.* Neusohl, *Hung.* Besztercebánya 81 C6
Bantry Bay *sea feature* Ireland 71 A6
Banyo Cameroon 58 B4
Banzare Seamounts *undersea feature* Indian Ocean 123 C7
Baotou China 109 F3
Baranavichy Belarus *Rus.* Baranovichi, *Pol.* Baranowicze 89 C6
Baranovichi *see* Baranavichy
Baranowicze *see* Baranavichy
Barbados *country* West Indies 37 H4
Barbuda *island* Antigua & Barbuda 37 G3
Barcaldine Australia 130 C4
Barcelona Spain 75 G2
Barcelona Venezuela 41 E1
Barcolod City Philippines 121 E2
Bareilly India 117 E3
Barentsburg Svalbard 65 F2
Barentsøya *island* Svalbard 65 G2
Barents Sea Arctic Ocean 137 H5
Bari Italy 79 E5
Barinas Venezuela 40 D2
Barisan, Pegunungan *mountains* Indonesia 120 B4
Barkly Tableland *plateau* Australia 130 B3
Barlavento, Ilhas de *island group* Cape Verde *var.* Windward Islands 56 A2
Bar-le-Duc France 72 D3
Barlee, Lake *lake* Australia 129 B 5
Barlee Range *mountain range* Australia 128 B4
Barnaul Russian Federation 96 D4
Barnstaple England, UK 71 C7
Barquisimeto Venezuela 40 D1
Barra *island* Scotland, UK 70 B3
Barranquilla Colombia 40 B1
Barrier Range *mountain range* Australia 131 C5
Barrow *river* Ireland 71 B6
Barstow California, USA 27 C7
Bartang *river* Tajikistan 105 F3
Bartica Guyana 41 G2
Baruun-Urt Mongolia 109 F2
Barwon River *river* Australia 131 D5
Barysaw Belarus *Rus.* Borisov 89 D5
Basarabeasca Moldova 90 D4
Basel Switzerland 77 B6
Basra *see* Al Başrah

Bonn Germany 76 B4
Boosaaso Somalia 54 E4
Borås Sweden 67 B7
Bordeaux France 73 B5
Borger Texas, USA 29 E2
Borisov *see* Barysaw
Borlänge Sweden 67 C6
Borneo *island* SE Asia 120-121
Bornholm *island* Denmark 67 C8
Bosanski Šamac Bosnia & Herzegovina 82 C3
Bosna *river* Bosnia & Herzegovina 82 C3
Bosna I Hercegovina, Federacija Admin. region *republic* Bosnia and Herzegovina 82 C4
Bosnia & Herzegovina *country* SE Europe 82-83
Bosporus *sea feature* Turkey *Turk.* İstanbul Boğazi 98 B2
Bossangoa Central African Republic 58 C4
Bosten Hu *Lake* China 108 C3
Boston Massachusetts, USA 23 G3
Bothnia, Gulf of *sea feature* Baltic Sea 67 C5
Botoşani Romania 90 C3
Botswana *country* southern Africa 60
Bouar Central African Republic 58 C4
Bougainville Island *island* Papua New Guinea 126 C3
Bougouni Mali 56 D4
Boulder Colorado, USA 24 C4
Boulogne-sur-Mer France 72 C2
Bourges France 72 C4
Bourgogne *region* France *Eng.* Burgundy 72 D4
Bourke Australia 131 C5
Bournemouth England, UK 71 D7
Bouvet Island *external territory* Norway, Atlantic Ocean 49 D7
Bowen Australia 130 D3
Bowling Green Kentucky, USA 22 C5
Bozeman Montana, USA 24 B2
Bozen *see* Bolzano
Brač *island* Croatia 82 B4
Bradford England, UK 71 D5
Braga Portugal 74 C2
Bragança Portugal 74 C2
Brahmaputra *river* Asia 117 G3
Brăila Romania 90 D4
Brainerd Minnesota, USA 25 F2
Brandon Canada 19 F5
Brasília *capital of* Brazil 43 F4
Braşov Romania 90 C4
Bratislava *capital of* Slovakia *Ger.* Pressburg, *Hung.* Pozsony 81 C6
Bratsk Russian Federation 97 E4
Braunau am Inn Austria 77 D6
Braunschweig Germany *Eng.* Brunswick 76 C4
Brazil *country* South America 42-43
Brazil Basin *undersea feature* Atlantic Ocean 49 C5
Brazilian Highlands *upland* Brazil 43 G4
Brazos *river* SW USA 29 G3
Brazzaville *capital of* Congo 59 B6
Brecon Beacons *hills* Wales, UK 71 C6
Breda Netherlands 68 C4
Bregenz Austria 77 B7
Bremen Germany 76 B3
Bremerhaven Germany 76 B3
Brescia Italy 78 B2
Breslau *see* Wrocław
Brest Belarus *Pol.* Brześć nad Bugiem, *prev.* Brześć Litewski, *Rus.* Brest-Litovsk 89 B6
Brest France 72 A3
Brest-Litovsk *see* Brest
Bretagne *region* France *Eng.* Brittany 72 A3
Brezhnev *see* Naberezhnyye Chelny
Bria Central African Republic 58 D4
Bridgetown *capital of* Barbados 37 H4
Brig Switzerland 77 B5
Brighton England, UK 71 E7
Brindisi Italy 79 E5
Brisbane Australia 131 E5
Bristol England, UK 71 D6
British Columbia *province* Canada 18-19
British Indian Ocean Territory *external territory* UK, Indian Ocean 122 C4
British Isles *islands* W Europe 70-71
British Virgin Islands *external territory* UK, West Indies 37
Brittany *see* Bretagne
Brno Czech Republic *Ger.* Brünn 81 B5
Broken Arrow Oklahoma, USA 29 G1
Broken Hill Australia 131 B6
Broken Ridge *undersea feature* Indian Ocean 123 D6
Bromberg *see* Bydgoszcz
Brooks Range *mountains* Alaska, USA 18 D2
Brookton Australia 129 B6
Broome Australia 128 C3
Brownfield Texas, USA 29 E2
Brownsville Texas, USA 29 G5
Bruges *see* Brugge
Brugge Belgium *Fr.* Bruges 69 A5
Brunei *country* E Asia 120 D3
Brünn *see* Brno
Brunswick Georgia, USA 31 E3
Brunswick *see* Braunschweig
Brusa *see* Bursa
Brussel *see* Brussels
Brussels *capital of* Belgium *Fr.* Bruxelles, *Flem.* Brussel 69 C
Brüx *see* Most
Bruxelles *see* Brussels
Bryan Texas, USA 29 G3
Bryansk Russian Federation 93 A5 96 A2
Brześć Litewski *see* Brest
Brześć nad Bugiem *see* Brest
Bucaramanga Colombia 40 C2
Buchanan Liberia 56 C5

ucharest *capital of* Romania 90 C5
udapest *capital of* Hungary 81 C6
udweis *see* České Budějovice
uenaventura Colombia 40 B3
uenos Aires *capital of* Argentina 46 D4
uenos Aires, Lago *lake* Argentina/Chile 47 B6
uffalo New York, USA 23 E3
ug *river* E Europe 90 C1
ujumbura *capital of* Burundi *prev.* Usumbura 55 B7
ukavu Dem. Rep. Congo 59 E6
ukhara *see* Buxoro
ulawayo Zimbabwe 60 D3
ulgan Mongolia 109 E2
ulgaria *country* E Europe 86
umba Dem. Rep. Congo 59 D5
unbury Australia 129 B6
undaberg Australia 130 E4
unia Dem. Rep. Congo 59 E5
uraydah Saudi Arabia 103 B5
urē Ethiopia 54 C4
urgas Bulgaria 86 E2
urgos Spain 75 E2
urgundy *see* Bourgogne
urketown Australia 130 B3
urkina *country* W Africa 57
urlington Iowa, USA 25 G4
urlington Vermont, USA 23 F2
urma *see* Myanmar
urnie Tasmania 131 C8
urns Oregon, USA 26 C3
ursa Turkey *prev.* Brusa 98 B3
ūrSa'īd Egypt *Eng.* Port Said 54 B1
urtnieku Ezers *lake* Latvia 88 C3
uru, Pulau *island* Indonesia 121 E4
urundi *country* C Africa 55
usselton Australia 129 B7
utembo Dem. Rep. Congo 59 E5
uton, Pulau *Island* Indonesia 121 E4
utte Montana, USA 24 B2
utuan Philippines 121 F2
Buxoro Uzbekistan *var.* Bokhara, *Rus.* Bukhara 104 D2
Büyükağrı Dağı *see* Ararat, Mount
Buzău Romania 90 C4
Büzmeýin *see* Abadan
Bydgoszcz Poland *Ger.* Bromberg 80 C3
Byerazino *river* Belarus *Rus.* Berezina 89 D6
Byzantium *see* İstanbul

C

Caazapá Paraguay 44 C3
Cabanatuan Philippines 121 E1
Cabimas Venezuela 40 C1
Cabinda *exclave* Angola 60 B1
Cabot Strait *sea feature* Atlantic Ocean 21 G4
Čačak Serbia 82 D4
Cáceres Spain 74 D3
Cachoeiro de Itapemirim Brazil 45 F1
Cadiz Philippines 121 E2
Cádiz Spain 74 D5
Caen France 72 B3
Cagayan de Oro Philippines 121 F2
Cagliari Italy 79 A5
Cahors France 73 B5
Cairns Australia 130 D3
Cairo *capital of* Egypt *Ar.* Al Qāhirah, *var.* El Qâhira 54 B1
Čakovec Croatia 82 B2
Calabar Nigeria 57 G5
Calabria *region* Italy 79 D6
Calafate *see* El Calafate
Calais France 72 C2
Calais Maine, USA 23 H1
Calama Chile 46 B2
Calbayog Philippines 121 F2
Calcutta *see* Kolkata
Caldas da Rainha Portugal 74 B3
Caldwell Idaho, USA 27 C3
Caleta Olivia Argentina 47 C6
Calgary Canada 19 E5
Cali Colombia 40 A3
Calicut India *see* Kozhikode 114 D2
California *state* USA 26-27
California, Golfo de *sea feature* Pacific Ocean *Eng.* California, Gulf of 32 B2 123 F2
Callabonna, Lake *lake* Australia131 B5
Callao Peru 42 A3
Caltanissetta Italy 79 C7
Camagüey Cuba 36 C2
Cambodia *country* SE Asia *Cam.* Kampuchea 119
Cambridge England, UK 71 E6
Cambridge New Zealand132 D2
Cameroon *country* W Africa 58-59
Campbell Plateau *undersea feature* Pacific Ocean 134 C5
Campeche Mexico 33 G4
Campeche, Bahía de *sea feature* Mexico *Eng.* Gulf of Campeche 33 G4
Campina Grande Brazil 43 H3
Campinas Brazil 45 E2
Campo Grande Brazil 44 C1
Campos Brazil 45 F2
Canada *country* North America 16-17
Canada Basin *undersea feature* Arctic Ocean *var.* Laurentian Basin 137 F2
Canadian River *river* SW USA 29 E2
Çanakkale Turkey 98 A3
Çanakkale Boğazı *see* Dardanelles
Canarias, Islas *islands* Spain *Eng.* Canary Islands 50 A2
Canary Basin *undersea feature* Atlantic Ocean 48 C4
Canary Islands *see* Canarias, Islas
Canaveral, Cape *coastal feature* Florida, USA 31 F4
Canberra *capital of* Australia 131 D6
Cancún Mexico 33 H3

Caniapiscau *river* Canada 21 E2
Caniapiscau, Réservoir *Reservoir* Canada 21 E3
Canik Dağları *mountains* Turkey 98 D2
Çankırı Turkey 98 C2
Cannes France 73 D6
Canoas Brazil 44 D4
Canterbury England, UK 71 E6
Canterbury Bight *sea feature* Pacific Ocean 133 C6
Canterbury Plains *plain* New Zealand 133 B6
Cân Thơ Vietnam 119 D6
Canton Ohio, USA 22 D4
Canton *see* Guangzhou
Cape Basin *undersea feature* Atlantic Ocean 49 D6
Cape Town South Africa 60 C5
Cape Verde *country* Atlantic Ocean 56 A2
Cape Verde Basin *undersea feature* Atlantic Ocean 48 C4
Cape York Peninsula *peninsula* Australia 124 B3
Cap-Haïtien Haiti 36 D3
Capri, Isola di *island* Italy 79 D5
Caquetá *river* Colombia 40 C4
CAR *see* Central African Republic
Caracas *capital of* Venezuela 40 D1
Carazinho Brazil 44 C3
Carbondale Illinois, USA 22 B5
Carcassonne France 73 C6
Cardiff Wales, UK 71 C6
Cardigan Bay *sea feature* Wales, UK 71 C6
Carey, Lake *lake* Australia 129 C5
Caribbean Sea Atlantic Ocean 36-37
Carlisle England, UK 70 D4
Carlsbad New Mexico, USA 28 D3
Carlsberg Ridge *undersea feature* Indian Ocean 122 B4
Carnavon Australia 128 A5
Carnegie, Lake *lake* Australia 129 C5
Carolina Brazil 43 F3
Caroline Island *see* Millennium Island
Caroline Islands *island group* Micronesia 126 B1
Caroní *river* Venezuela 41 F2
Carpathian Mountains *mountain range* E Europe *var.* Carpathians 63 E4
Carpathians *see* Carpathian Mountains
Carpaţii Meridionali *mountain range* Romania *Eng.* South Carpathians, Transylvanian Alps 90 B4
Carpentaria, Gulf of *sea feature* Australia 130 B2
Carson City Nevada, USA 27 B5
Cartagena Colombia 40 B1
Cartagena Spain 75 F4
Cartago Costa Rica 35 E4
Cartwright Canada 21 G2
Carúpano Venezuela 41 E1
Casablanca Morocco 52 C2
Casa Grande Arizona, USA 28 B3
Cascade Range *mountain range* Canada/USA 26 B2
Cascais Portugal 74 B3
Casper Wyoming, USA 24 C3
Caspian Sea *inland sea* Asia/Europe 94 B4
Castellón de la Plana Spain 75 F3
Castelo Branco Portugal 74 C3
Castries *capital of* St Lucia 37 G4
Castro Chile 47 B6
Cat Island *island* Bahamas 36 D1
Catania Italy 79 D7
Catanzaro Italy 79 D6
Cauca *river* Colombia 40 B2
Caucasus *mountains* Asia/Europe 93 A7
Caura *river* Venezuela 41 E2
Caviana, Ilha *island* Brazil 43 F1
Cawnpore *see* Kānpur
Caxias do Sul Brazil 44 D4
Cayenne *capital of* French Guiana 41 H3
Cayman Islands *external territory* UK, West Indies 36
Cebu Philippines 121 E2
Cedar Rapids Iowa, USA 25 G
Cedros, Isla *island* Mexico 32 A2
Ceduna Australia131 A6
Cefalù Italy 79 C6
Celebes *see* Sulawesi
Celebes Sea Pacific Ocean *Ind.* Laut Sulawesi 134 B3
Celje Slovenia 77 E7
Central African Republic *country* C Africa *abbrev.* CAR 58-59
Central, Cordillera *mountain range* Philippines 121 E1
Central Makrān Range *mountains* Pakistan 116 A3
Central Pacific Basin *undersea feature* Pacific Ocean 125 E1
Central Russian Upland *uplan* Russian Federation 94 B3
Central Siberian Plateau *see* Srednesibirskoye Ploskogor'ye
Central Siberian Uplands *see* Srednesibirskoye Ploskogor'ye
Central, Sistema *mountain range* Spain 74 D3
Cephalonia *see* Kefalloniá
Ceram Sea *Sea* Indonesia 121 F4
Cernăuţi *see* Chernivtsi
Cēsis Latvia *Ger.* Wenden 88 C
České Budějovice Czech Republic *Ger.* Budweis 81 B5
Ceuta *external territory* Spain, N Africa 52 C1
Cévennes *mountains* France 73 C6
Ceylon *see* Sri Lanka
Ceylon Plain *undersea feature* Indian Ocean 122 C4
Chad *country* C Africa 58
Chad, Lake *lake* C Africa 58 B3
Chāgai Hills *mountains* Pakistan 116 A2

hagos-Laccadive Plateau *undersea feature* Indian Ocean 122 C4
hagos Trench *undersea feature* Indian Ocean 122 C4
halkída Greece 87 C5
hallenger Deep *undersea feature* Pacific Ocean 134 B3
hâlons-en-Champagne France 72 D3
hambéry France 73 D5
hampaign Illinois, USA 22 B4
hañaral Chile 46 B2
handīgarh India 116 D2
hang, Ko *island* Thailand 119 C5
hangchun China 110 D3
hang Jiang *river* China *var.* Yangtze 111 B6
hangsha China 111 C6
haniá Greece 87 C7
hannel Islands *island group* California, USA 27 B8
hannel Islands *islands* UK 71 D8
hannel-Port-aux-Basques Canada 21 G4
hannel Tunnel France/UK 71 E7
hapala, Lago de *lake* Mexico 32 D4
hardzhev *see* Türkmenabat
hardzhou *see* Türkmenabat
hari *river* C Africa 58 C3
hārīkār Afghanistan 105 E4
härjew *see* Türkmenabat
harleroi Belgium 69 C6
harleston South Carolina, USA 31 F2
harleston West Virginia, USA 22 D5
harleville Australia 130 C4
harlotte North Carolina, USA 31 F1
harlotte Amalie *capital of* Virgin Islands 37 F3
harlottesville Virginia, USA 23 E5
harlottetown Canada 21 G4
harters Towers Australia 130 D3
hartres France 72 C3
Châteauroux France 72 C4
Chatham Islands *islands* New Zealand 134 D4
Chattanooga Tennessee, USA 30 D1
Chauk Myanmar 118 A3
Chaves Portugal 74 C2
Cheboksary Russian Federation 93 C5
Cheboygan Michigan, USA 22 C2
Chech, Erg *desert* Algeria/ Mali 56 D1
Che-chiang *see* Zhejiang
Cheju-do *island* South Korea 111 E5
Cheju Strait *sea feature* South Korea 111 E5
Chekiang *see* Zhejiang
Cheleken *see* Hazar
Chelyabinsk Russian Federation 96 C3
Chemnitz Germany *prev.* Karl-Marx-Stadt 76 D4
Chenāb *river* Pakistan 116 C2
Chengdu China 111 B5
Chennai India *prev.* Madras 115 E2
Cherbourg France 72 B3
Cherepovets Russian Federation 92 B4
Cherkasy Ukraine 91 E2
Cherkessk Russian Federation 93 A7
Chernigov see Chernihiv
Chernihiv Ukraine *Rus.* Chernigov 91 E1
Chernivtsi Ukraine *Rus.* Chernovtsy, *Rom.* Cernăuți 90 C3
Chernobyl' *see* Chornobyl'
Chernovtsy *see* Chernivtsi
Chernyakhovsk Kaliningrad, Russian Federation 88 B4
Chesapeake Bay *sea feature* USA 23 F5
Chester England, UK 71 D5
Cheyenne Wyoming, USA 24 D4
Chiang-hsi *see* Jiangxi
Chiang Mai Thailand 118 B4
Chiang-su *see* Jiangsu
Chiba Japan 113 D5
Chicago Illinois, USA 22 B3
Chiclayo Peru 42 A3
Chico California, USA 27 B5
Chicoutimi Canada 21 E4
Chifeng China *var.* Ulanhad 109 F2
Chihli *see* Hebei
Chihuahua Mexico 32 C2
Chile *country* S South America 46-47
Chile Basin *undersea feature* Pacific Ocean 135 G4
Chile Chico Chile 47 B6
Chile Rise *undersea feature* Pacific Ocean 135 G4
Chi-lin *see* Jilin
Chillán Chile 46 B4
Chiloé, Isla de *island* Chile 47 B6
Chimborazo *peak* Ecuador 38 A3
Chimbote Peru 42 A3
Chimkent *see* Shymkent
Chimoio Mozambique 61 E3
China *country* E Asia 108-109
Chinandega Nicaragua 34 C3
Chindwinn *river* Myanmar 118 A2
Chinghai *see* Qinghai
Chingola Zambia 60 D2
Chinook Trough *undersea feature* Pacific Ocean 134 D1
Chíos Greece 87 D5
Chíos *island* Greece *prev.* Khíos 87 D5
Chirchik Uzbekistan *Uzb.* Chirchiq 105 E2
Chirchiq *see* Chirchik
Chiriquí, Golfo de *sea feature* Panama 35 E5
Chişinău *capital of* Moldova, *var.* Kishinev 90 D3
Chita Russian Federation 97 F4
Chitré Panama 35 F5
Chittagong Bangladesh 117 G4
Chitungwiza Zimbabwe 60 D3
Choluteca Honduras 34 C3
Choma Zambia 60 D3

Chona *river* Russian Federation 95 E2
Chon Buri Thailand 119 C5
Ch'ŏngjin North Korea 110 E3
Chongqing *province* China *var.* Chungking 111 B5
Chonos, Archipiélago de los *island group* Chile 47 B6
Chornobyl' Ukraine *Rus.* Chernobyl' 91 E1
Choûm Mauritania 56 C2
Choybalsan Mongolia 109 F2
Christchurch New Zealand 133 C6
Christmas Island *external territory* Australia, Indian Ocean 122 D5
Christmas Island *see* Kiritimati
Christmas Ridge *undersea feature* Pacific Ocean 125 F1
Chuan *see* Sichuan
Chubut *river* Argentina 47 B6
Chudskoye Ozero *see* Peipus, Lake
Chuí *see* Chuy
Chukchi Plain *undersea feature* Arctic Ocean 137 G2
Chukchi Sea Arctic Ocean *Rus.* Chukotskoye More 137 F1
Chukotskoye More *see* Chukchi Sea
Chula Vista California, USA 27 C8
Chulym *river* Russian Federation 94 D3
Chumphon Thailand 119 C6
Chungking *see* Chongqing
Chuquicamata Chile 46 B2
Chur Switzerland 77 B7
Churchill Canada 19 G4
Chuuk Islands *island group* Micronesia 126 B1
Chuy Brazil *var.* Chuí 44 C5
Cienfuegos Cuba 36 B2
Cieza Spain 75 F4
Cilacap Indonesia 120 C5
Cincinnati Ohio, USA 22 C4
Ciudad Bolívar Venezuela 41 E2
Ciudad del Este Paraguay 44 C3
Ciudad de México *see* Mexico City
Ciudad Guayana Venezuela 41 E2
Ciudad Juárez Mexico 32 C1
Ciudad Obregón Mexico 32 B2
Ciudad Ojeda Venezuela 40 C1
Ciudad Real Spain 75 E3
Ciudad Valles Mexico 33 E3
Ciudad Victoria Mexico 33 E3
Clarence *river* New Zealand 133 C5
Clarion Fracture Zone *tectonic feature* Pacific Ocean 125 G1
Clarksville Tennessee, USA 30 D1
Clearwater Florida, USA 31 E4
Clermont Australia 130 D4
Clermont-Ferrand France 73 C5
Cleveland Ohio, USA 22 D3
Clipperton Fracture Zone *tectonic feature* Pacific Ocean 125 G2
Clipperton Island *external territory* France, Pacific Ocean 135 F3
Cloncurry Australia 130 C3
Clovis New Mexico, USA 29 E2
Cluj-Napoca Romania 90 B3
Clutha *river* New Zealand 133 B7
Coast Ranges *mountain range* W USA 26 A5
Coats Island *island* Canada 20 C1
Coats Land *physical region* Antarctica 136 B2
Coatzacoalcos Mexico 33 G4
Cobán Guatemala 34 B2
Cochabamba Bolivia 42 C4
Cochin India *see* Kochi 114 D3
Cochrane Canada 20 C4
Cochrane Chile 47 B6
Coco *river* Honduras/Nicaragua 34 D2
Cocos Basin *undersea feature* Indian Ocean 122 D4
Cocos Islands *external territor* Australia, Indian Ocean 122 D5
Cod, Cape *coastal feature* NE USA 23 G3
Coeur d'Alene Idaho, USA 26 C2
Coffs Harbour Australia 131 E6
Coihaique Chile 47 B6
Coimbatore India 114 D3
Coimbra Portugal 74 C3
Colchester England, UK 71 E6
Colmar France 72 E4
Cologne *see* Köln
Colombia *country* N South America 40-41
Colombo *capital of* Sri Lanka 115 E4
Colón Panama 35 F4
Colón, Archipiélago de *see* Galapagos Islands
Colorado *state* USA 24 C4
Colorado *river* USA 16 B5
Colorado *river* Argentina 47 C5
Colorado Plateau *upland region* S USA 28 B1
Colorado Springs Colorado, USA 24 D4
Columbia South Carolina, USA 31 F2
Columbia *river* NW USA 26 C1
Columbus Georgia, USA 30 D3
Columbus Mississippi, USA 30 C2
Columbus Nebraska, USA 25 E4
Columbus Ohio, USA 22 D4
Comayagua Honduras 34 C2
Comilla Bangladesh 117 G4
Communism Peak *peak* Tajikistan *Rus.* Pik Kommunizma, *prev.* Stalin Peak, Garmo Peak 105 F3
Como, Lago di *lake* Italy 78 B2
Comodoro Rivadavia Argentin 47 C6

Comoros *country* Indian Ocean 61
Conakry *capital of* Guinea 56 C4
Concepción Chile 47 B5
Concepción Paraguay 44 B2
Conchos *river* Mexico 32 C2
Concord New Hampshire, USA 22 G2
Concordia E Argentina 46 D3
Congo *country* C Africa 59
Congo *river* C Africa *var.* Zaire 51 C5
Congo Basin *drainage basin* C Africa 59 C5
Congo, Democratic Republic of *country* C Africa 59
Connecticut *state* USA 23 G3
Constance, Lake *river* C Europe 77 B6
Constantine Algeria 53 E1
Constantinople *see* İstanbul
Constanţa Romania 90 D5
Coober Pedy Australia 131 A5
Cook, Mount *see* Aoraki
Cook Islands *external territory* New Zealand, Pacific Ocean 127 G4
Cook Strait *sea feature* New Zealand 133 D5
Cooktown Australia 130 D2
Cooma Australia 131 D7
Coos Bay Oregon, USA 26 A3
Cootamundra Australia 131 D6
Copenhagen *capital of* Denmark 67 B7
Copiapó Chile 46 B3
Coppermine *see* Kuglukutuk
Coquimbo Chile 46 B3
Corabia Romania 90 B5
Coral Sea Pacific Ocean 130 E3
Coral Sea Islands *external territory* Australia, Coral Sea 130 E3
Corantijn *see* Courantyne
Cordillera Cantábrica *mountain range* Spain 74 D1
Córdoba Argentina 46 C3
Córdoba Spain 74 D4
Cordova Alaska, USA 18 D3
Corfu *see* Kérkyra
Corinth *see* Kórinthos
Corinth, Gulf of *see* Korinthiakós Kólpos
Corinto Nicaragua 34 C3
Cork Ireland 71 B6
Corner Brook Canada 21 G3
Coro Venezuela 40 D1
Coronel Oviedo Paraguay 44 C2
Corpus Christi Texas, USA 29 G5
Corrib, Lough *lake* Ireland 71 A5
Corrientes Argentina 46 D3
Corse *island* France *Eng.* Corsica 73 E7 84 D2
Corsica *see* Corse
Çorum Turkey 98 D2
Corvallis Oregon, USA 26 A3
Cosenza Italy 79 D6
Costa Blanca *coastal region* Spain 75 F4
Costa Brava *coastal region* Spain 75 H2
Costa Rica *country* Central America 34-35
Côte d'Ivoire *country* W Africa *Eng.* Ivory Coast 56 D4
Cottbus Germany 76 D4
Council Bluffs Iowa, USA 25 F4
Courantyne *river* Guyana / Suriname *var.* Corantijn 41 G3
Courland Lagoon *sea feature* Baltic Sea 88 B4
Coventry England, UK 71 D6
Covilhã Portugal 74 C3
Cowan, Lake *lake* Australia 129 C6
Cozumel, Isla de *island* Mexico 33 H3
Cracow *see* Kraków
Craiova Romania 90 B5
Cremona Italy 78 B2
Cres *island* Croatia 82 A3
Crescent City California, USA 26 A4
Crete *see* Kríti
Crete, Sea of Mediterranean Sea *Gk.* Kritikó Pélagos 87 D7
Crimea *see* Krym
Cristóbal Panama 48 A4
Croatia *country* SE Europe 82
Croker Island *island* Australia 128 E2
Crotone Italy 79 E6
Crozet Basin *undersea feature* Indian Ocean 123 B6
Crozet Islands *island group* Indian Ocean 123 B7
Crystal Brook Australia 131 B6
Cuanza *river* Angola 60 B2
Cuba *country* West Indies 36
Cubango *see* Okavango
Cúcuta Colombia 40 C2
Cuenca Ecuador 40 A5
Cuenca Spain 75 E3
Cuernavaca Mexico 33 E4
Cuiabá Brazil 43 E4
Culiacán Mexico 32 C3
Cumaná Venezuela 41 E1
Cumberland Maryland, USA 23 E4
Cunene *river* Angola/Namibia 60 B3
Cunnamulla Australia 131 C5
Curicó Chile 46 B4
Curitiba Brazil 44 D3
Cusco Peru *prev.* Cuzco 42 B4
Cuttack India 117 F5
Cuxhaven Germany 76 B3
Cuyuni *river* Guyana/Venezuela 41 F2
Cuzco *see* Cusco
Cyclades *see* Kykládes
Cymru *see* Wales
Cyprus *country* Mediterranean Sea 98 C5
Czechoslovakia *see* Czech Republic *or* Slovakia
Czech Republic *country* C Europe 80-81
Częstochowa Poland *Ger.* Tschenstochau 80 C4
Człuchów Poland 80 C3

D

Dacca *see* Dhaka
Dagden *see* Hiiumaa
Dagö *see* Hiiumaa
Dagupan Philippines 121 E1
Da Hinggan Ling *mountain range* China *Eng.* Great Khingan Range 109 G1
Dahomey *see* Benin
Dakar *capital of* Senegal 56 B3
Đakovo Croatia 82 C3
Dalain Hob China 108 D3
Dalaman Turkey 98 B4
Dalandzadgad Mongolia 109 E3
Đa Lat Vietnam 119 E5
Dalby Australia 131 D5
Dalian China 110 D4
Dallas Texas, USA 29 G3
Dalmacija *region* Croatia 82 B4
Daly Waters Australia 128 E3
Damān India 116 C5
Damas *see* Damascus
Damascus Syria *var.* Esh Sham, *Fr.* Damas, *Ar.* Dimashq 100 B4
Dampier Australia 128 B4
Damxung China 108 C5
Đa Nâng Vietnam 119 E4
Dandong China 110 D4
Daneborg Greenland 65 E3
Danghara Tajikistan 105 E3
Danmarksstraedet *see* Denmark Strait
Danube *river* C Europe 63 E4
Danville Virginia, USA 23 E5
Danzig *see* Gdańsk
Danzig, Gulf of *76 C2 Gulf* Poland 80 C2
Dar'ā Syria 101 B5
Dardanelles *sea feature* Turkey *Turk.* Çanakkale Boğazı 98 A2
Dar es Salaam Tanzania 55 C7
Darfur *Cultural region* Sudan 54 A4
Darhan Mongolia 109 E2
Darien, Gulf of *sea feature* Caribbean Sea 35 G5
Darling *river* Australia 131 C6
Darmstadt Germany 77 B5
Darnah Libya 53 H2
Dartmoor *region* England, UK 71 C7
Dartmouth Canada 21 F4
Darwin Australia 128 D2
Dashhowuz *see* Daşoguz
Daşoguz Turkmenistan *prev.* Tashauz, *Turkm.* Dashhowuz 104 C2
Datong China 110 C4
Daugava *see* Western Dvina
Daugavpils Latvia *Ger.* Dünaburg, *Rus.* Dvinsk 88 D4
Dāvangere India 114 D2
Davao Philippines 121 F3
Davao Gulf *gulf* Philippines 121 F3
Davenport Iowa, USA 25 G3
David Panama 35 E5
Davie Ridge *undersea feature* Indian Ocean 123 A5
Davis Sea Indian Ocean 136 D3
Davis Strait *sea feature* Atlantic Ocean 64 C3
Dawei Myanmar *prev.* Tavoy 119 B5
Dayr az Zawr Syria 100 D3
Dayton Ohio, USA 22 C4
Daytona Beach Florida, USA 31 F4
Dead Sea *salt lake* SW Asia *Ar.* Al Baḩr al Mayyit, Baḩrat Lūt, *Heb.* Yam HaMelaḩ 101 B5
Death Valley *valley* W USA 27 C6
Deatnu *river* Finland/Norway 66 D2
Debrecen Hungary *prev.* Debreczen, *Ger.* Debreczin 81 D6
Debreczen *see* Debrecen
Debreczin *see* Debrecen
Decatur Illinois, USA 22 B4
Deccan *plateau* India 106 B3 115 D1
Děčín Czech Republic *Ger.* Tetschen 80 B4
Dej Romania 90 B3
Delaware *state* USA 23 F4
Delémont Switzerland 77 A7
Delft Netherlands 68 C4
Delfzijl Netherlands 68 E1
Delhi India 116 D3
Del Rio Texas, USA 29 F4
Demchok *disputed region* China/India *var.* Dêmqog 108 B4
Demopolis Alabama, USA *30 C2*
Dêmqog *see* Demchok
Denali *see* Mount McKinley
Denham Australia 129 A5
Den Helder Netherlands 68 C2
Denizli Turkey 98 B4
Denmark *country* NW Europe 67
Denmark Strait *sea feature* Greenland/Iceland *var.* Danmarksstraedet 65 D4
Denpasar Indonesia 120 D5
Denton Texas, USA 29 G2
Denver Colorado, USA 24 D4
Dera Ghāzi Khān Pakistan 116 C2
Derby England, UK 71 D6
Derg, Lough *lake* Ireland 71 B6
Desē Ethiopia 54 C4
Deseado *river* Argentina 47 C6
Des Moines Iowa, USA 25 F3
Despoto Planina *see* Rhodope Mountains
Dessau Germany 76 D4
Detroit Michigan, USA 22 D3
Deutschendorf *see* Poprad
Deva Romania 90 B4
Deventer Netherlands 68 D3
Devollit, Lumi i *river* Albania 83 D6
Devon Island *island* Canada 19 F2
Devonport Tasmania, Australia 131 C8
Dezfūl Iran 102 C3
Dhaka *capital of* Bangladesh *var.* Dacca 117 G4

Durrës Albania 83 C5
Dushanbe *capital of* Tajikistan *var.* Dyushambe, *prev.* Stalinabad 105 E3
Düsseldorf Germany 76 A4
Dutch Harbor Alaska, USA 18 B3
Dutch West Indies *see* Netherland Antilles
Dvinsk *see* Daugavpils
Dyushambe *see* Dushanbe
Dzaudzhikau *see* Vladikavkaz
Dzhalal-Abad Kyrgyzstan *Kir.* Jalal-Abad 105 F2
Dzhambul *see* Taraz
Dzhezkazgan see Zhezkazgan
Dzvina *see* Western Dvina

E

Eagle Pass Texas, USA 29 F4
East Antarctica *region* Antarctica 136 C3
East Cape *coastal feature* New Zealand 132 E2
East China Sea Pacific Ocean 111 E5
Easter Fracture Zone *tectonic feature* Pacific Ocean 135 G4
Easter Island *island* Pacific Ocean 135 F4
Eastern Ghats *mountain range* India 117 B5
Eastern Sierra Madre *see* Sierra Madre Oriental
East Falkland *island* Falkland Islands 47 D7
East Indiaman Ridge *undersea feature* Indian Ocean 23 D5
East Indies *island group* Asia 122 E4
East London South Africa 60 D5
Eastmain *river* Canada 20 D3
East Pacific Rise *undersea feature* Pacific Ocean 135 F4
East Siberian Sea *see* Vostochno-Sibirskoye More
East St Louis Illinois, USA 22 B4
East Timor *country* SE Asia 121
East Novaya Zemlya Trench *var.* Novaya Zemlya Trench. *Undersea feature* Kara Sea 137 H4
Eau Claire Wisconsin, USA 22 A2
Ebolowa Cameroon 59 B5
Ebro *river* Spain 75 F2
Ecuador *country* NW South America 40
Ede Netherlands 68 D3
Ede Nigeria 57 F4
Edgeøya *island* Svalbard 65 G2
Edinburgh Scotland, UK 70 C4
Edirne Turkey 98 A2
Edmonton Canada 19 E5
Edward, Lake *lake* Uganda/ Dem. Rep. Congo 59 E6
Edwards Plateau *upland* S USA 29 F4
Efate *Island* Vanuatu *prev.* Sandwich Island 124 D4
Effingham Illinois, USA 22 B4
Eforie-Sud Romania 90 D5
Egadi, Isole *island group* Italy 79 B6
Ege Denizi *see* Aegean Sea
Eger *see* Ohře
Egypt *country* NE Africa 54
Eighty Mile Beach *beach* Australia 128 C3
Eindhoven Netherlands 69 D5
Eisenstadt Austria 77 E6
Eivissa *see* Ibiza
Elat Israel 101 A7
Elazig Turkey 99 E3
Elba, Isola d' *island* Italy 78 B4
Elbasan Albania 83 D6
Elbe *river* Czech Republic/ Germany 81 B5
Elbing *see* Elbląg
Elbląg Poland *Ger.* Elbing 80 D2
El'brus *peak* Russian Federation 93 A7
El Calafate Argentina *var.* Calafate 47 B7
Elche Spain *Cat.* Elx 75 F4
Elda Spain 75 F4
Eldoret Kenya 55 C6
Eleuthera *island* Bahamas 36 C1
El Fasher Sudan *var.* Al Fāshir 54 A4
El Geneina Sudan 54 A4
Elgin Scotland, UK 70 C3
El Gîza *see* Al Jízah
El Ḩank *cliff* Mauritania 56 D1
Elista Russian Federation 93 B6
El Khalīl *see* Hebron
El Khârga *see* Al Khārijah
Elko Nevada, USA 27 D5
Ellensburg Washington, USA 26 B2
Ellesmere Island *island* Canada 19 F1
Ellsworth Land *region* Antarctica 136 A3
Elmira New York, USA 23 E3
El Mreyyé *desert* Mauritania 56 D2
El Obeid Sudan 54 B4
El Paso Texas, USA 28 D3
El Puerto de Santa María Spain 74 D5
El Qâhira *see* Cairo
El Salvador *country* Central America 34
Eltanin Fracture Zone *tectonic feature* Pacific Ocean 135 E5
El Tigre Venezuela 41 E2
Elx *see* Elche
Ely Nevada USA 27 D5
Emden Germany 76 B3
Emerald Australia 130 D4
Emmen Netherlands 68 E2
Empty Quarter *see* Ar Rub' al Khali
Ems *river* Germany/Netherlands 76 B3
Encarnación Paraguay 44 C3
Enderbury Island *atoll* Kiribati 136 C2
Enderby Land *region* Antarctica 136 C2

Enderby Plain *undersea feature* Indian Ocean 123 B7
England *national region* UK 70-71
English Channel *sea feature* Atlantic Ocean 71 D7
Enguri *river* Georgia *Rus.* Inguri 99 F1
Enid Oklahoma, USA 29 F1
Ennedi *plateau* Chad 58 D2
Enns *river* Austria 77 D6
Enschede Netherlands 68 E3
Ensenada Mexico 32 A1
Entebbe Uganda 55 B6
Enugu Nigeria 57 G5
Eolie, Isole *island group* Italy *Eng.* Lipari Islands, *var.* Aeolian Islands 79 D6
Eperies *see* Prešov
Eperjes *see* Prešov
Épinal France 72 E4
Equatorial Guinea *country* W Africa 59
Erdenet Mongolia 109 E2
Erechim Brazil 44 D3
Erenhot China 109 F2
Erevan *see* Yerevan
Ereğli Turkey 98 C4
Erfurt Germany 76 C4
Erie Pennsylvania, USA 22 D3
Erie, Lake *lake* Canada/USA 17 D5
Eritrea *country* E Africa 54
Erivan *see* Yerevan
Erlangen Germany 77 C5
Ernākulam India 114 D3
Er Rachidia Morocco 52 C2
Erzerum *see* Erzurum
Erzgebirge *mountain range* Czech Republic/Germany *var* Krušné Hory 77 D5
Erzincan Turkey 99 E3
Erzurum Turkey *prev.* Erzerum 99 F3
Esbjerg Denmark 67 A7
Esch-sur-Alzette Luxembourg 69 D8
Escuintla Guatemala 34 B2
Eşfahān Iran 102 C3
Esh Sham *see* Damascus
Eskişehir Turkey 98 B3
Esmeraldas Ecuador 40 A4
Esperance Australia 129 C6
Espiritu Santo *Island* Vanuatu 124 D3
Espoo Finland 67 D6
Esquel Argentina 47 B6
Essaouira Morocco 52 B2
Essen Germany 76 A4
Essequibo *river* Guyana 41 G3
Estelí Nicaragua 34 D3
Estevan Canada 19 F5
Estonia *country* E Europe 88 D2
Ethiopia *country* E Africa 54-55
Ethiopian Highlands *upland* E Africa 50 D4
Etna, Mount *peak* Sicily, Italy 79 D7
Etosha Pan *salt basin* Namibia 60 C3
Eucla Australia 129 D6
Eugene Oregon, USA 26 A3
Eugene Washington, USA 26 B1
Euphrates *river* SW Asia 102 C4
Europe 62-63
Evansville Indiana, USA 22 B5
Everest, Mount *peak* China/ Nepal 108 B5
Everett Washington, USA 26 B1
Everglades, The *wetlands* Florida, USA 31 F5
Évvoia *island* Greece 87 C5
Exeter England, UK 71 C7
Exmoor *region* England, UK 71 C7
Exmouth Australia 128 A4
Exmouth Gulf *gulf* Australia 128 A4
Exmouth Plateau *undersea feature* Indian Ocean 123 E5
Eyre North, Lake *salt lake* Australia131 B5
Eyre Peninsula *peninsula* Australia131 A6
Eyre South, Lake *salt lake* Australia131 B5

F

Fada-N'gourma Burkina 57 E4
Faeroe Islands *external territory* Denmark, Atlantic Ocean *Faer.* Fóroyar, *Dan.* Færøerne 65 F5
Færøerne *see* Faeroe Islands
Faguibine, Lac *lake* Mali 57 E3
Fairbanks Alaska, USA 18 D3
Fairlie New Zealand 133 B6
Faisalābād Pakistan 116 C2
Faizabad *see* Feyzābād
Falkland Islands *external territory* UK, Atlantic Ocean 47 D7
Fallon Nevada, USA 27 C5
Falun Sweden 67 C6
Famagusta *see* Gazimağusa
Farafangana Madagascar 61 G4
Farāh Afghanistan 104 C5
Farasān, Jazā'ir *island group* Saudi Arabia 103 B6
Farewell, Cape *headland* New Zealand 132 C4
Farewell, Cape *see* Nunap Isua
Farghona *see* Farg'ona
Farg'ona Uzbekistan *prev.* Novyy Margilan, *Uzb.* Farghona 105 F2
Fargo North Dakota, USA 25 E2
Farkhor Tajikistan 105 E3
Farmington New Mexico, USA 28 C1
Faro Portugal 74 C4
Farquhar Group *island group* Seychelles 61 G2
Farvel, Cap *see* Nunap Isua
Faxaflói *bay* Iceland 64 D5
Faya Chad 58 C2
Fayetteville Arkansas, USA 30 A1
Fayetteville North Carolina, USA 31 F1
Fdérik Mauritania 56 C1
Fear, Cape *coastal feature* North Carolina, USA 31 G2
Fehmarn *island* Germany 76 C2
Fehmarn Belt *sea feature* Germany 76 C2

Feira de Santana Brazil 43 G3
Fellin *see* Viljandi
Fengtien *see* Liaoning
Fenoarivo *see* Fenoarivo Atsinanana
Fenoarivo Atsinanana Madagascar *prev.* Fenoarivo 61 G3
Fens, The *wetland* England, UK 71 E6
Fergana *see* Farg'ona
Ferizaj Kosovo *prev.* Uroševac 83 D5
Ferrara Italy 78 C3
Ferrol Spain 74 C1
Fès Morocco *Eng.* Fez 52 C2
Feyzābād Afghanistan *var.* Faizabad 105 E3
Fez *see* Fès
Fianarantsoa Madagascar 61 G3
Fier Albania 83 D6
Figueira da Foz Portugal 74 C3
Figueres Spain 75 G2
Figuig Morocco 52 D2
Fiji *country* Pacific Ocean 127
Finland *country* N Europe 66-67
Finland, Gulf of *sea feature* Baltic Sea 67 E6
Fiordland *physical region* New Zealand 133 A7
Firenze Italy *Eng.* Florence 78 C3
Fishguard Wales, UK 71 C6
Fitzroy *river* Australia 128 C3
Fitzroy Crossing Australia 128 D3
Fiume see Rijeka
Flagstaff Arizona, USA 28 B2
Flanders *region* Belgium 69 A5
Flensburg Germany 76 B2
Flinders Island *island* Australia 131 C7
Flinders Ranges *mountain range* Australia 131 B6
Flinders River *river* Australia 130 C3
Flin Flon Canada 19 F5
Flint Michigan, USA 22 C3
Flint Island *island* Kiribati 127 H4
Florence Alabama, USA 30 C2
Florence South Carolina, USA 31 F2
Florence *see* Firenze
Florencia Colombia 40 B3
Flores Guatemala 34 B1
Flores *island* Indonesia 121 E5
Flores, Laut *see* Flores Sea
Flores Sea Pacific Ocean *Ind.* Laut Flores 121 E5
Florianópolis Brazil 44 D3
Florida *state* USA 31 E4
Florida, Straits of *sea feature* Bahamas/USA 31 F5 36 B1
Florida Keys *island chain* Florida, USA 31 F5
Flórina Greece 86 B3
Flushing *see* Vlissingen
Foča Bosnia & Herzegovina 82 C4
Focşani Romania 90 C4
Foggia Italy 79 D5
Fogo *island* Cape Verde 56 A3
Foligno Italy 78 C4
Fongafale *capital of* Tuvalu 127 E3
Fonseca, Gulf of *sea feature* El Salvador/Honduras 34 C3
Forlì Italy 78 C3
Formentera *island* Spain 75 G4
Former Yugoslav Republic of Macedonia *see* Macedonia
Formosa Argentina 46 D2
Formosa *see* Taiwan
Formosa Strait *see* Taiwan Strait
Fóroyar *see* Faeroe Islands
Fortaleza Brazil 43 H2
Fortescue River *river* Australia 128 B4
Fort Collins Colorado, USA 24 D4
Fort-de-France *capital of* Martinique 37 G4
Forth *river* Scotland, UK 70 C4
Forth, Firth of *inlet* Scotland, UK 70 D4
Fort Lauderdale Florida, USA 31 F5
Fort McMurray Canada 19 F4
Fort Myers Florida, USA 31 E4
Fort Peck Lake *lake* Montana, USA 24 C1
Fort Saint John Canada 19 E4
Fort Smith Canada 19 E4
Fort Smith Arkansas, USA 30 A1
Fort Wayne Indiana, USA 22 C4
Fort William Scotland, UK 70 C3
Fort Worth Texas, USA 29 G3
Foveaux Strait *sea feature* New Zealand 133 A7
Fox Glacier New Zealand 133 B6
Franca Brazil 45 E1
France *country* W Europe 72-73
Francistown Botswana 60 D3
Frankfort Kentucky, USA 22 C5
Frankfurt *see* Frankfurt am Main
Frankfurt am Main Germany *Eng.* Frankfurt 77 B5
Frankfurt an der Oder Germany 76 D5
Fränkische Alb *mountains* Germany 77 C6
Frantsa-Iosifa, Zemlya *islands* Russian Federation *Eng.* Franz Josef Land 137 G4
Franz Josef Land *see* Frantsa-Iosifa, Zemlya
Fraser Island *island* Australia 130 E4
Frauenburg *see* Saldus
Fray Bentos Uruguay 44 B5
Fredericksburg Virginia, USA 23 E4
Fredericton Canada 21 F4
Frederikshavn Denmark 67 B7
Fredrikstad Norway 67 B6
Freeport Bahamas 36 C1
Freeport Texas, USA 29 G4
Freetown *capital of* Sierra Leone 56 C4
Freiburg im Breisgau Germany 77 B6

Fremantle Australia 129 B6
French Guiana *external territory* France, N South America 41
French Polynesia *external territory* France, Pacific Ocean 135 E3
French Southern and Antarctic Territories *French overseas territory* Indian Ocean *Fr.* Terres Australes et Antarctiques Françaises 123 C7
Fresnillo Mexico 32 D1
Fresno California, USA 27 B6
Fobisher Bay *see* Iqaluit
Frome, Lake *salt lake* Australia 131 B5
Frunze *see* Bishkek
Fu-chien *see* Fujian
Fuerte Olimpo Paraguay 44 B1
Fuerteventura *island* Spain 52 A3
Fuhkien *see* Fujian
Fujian *province* China *var.* Fu-chien, Fuhkien, Fukien, Min 111 D6
Fukien *see* Fujian
Fukui Japan 113 C5
Fukuoka Japan 113 A6
Fukushima Japan 112 D4
Fulda Germany 77 C5
Fünfkirchen *see* Pécs
Fushun China 110 D3
Furnas, Represa de *Reservoir* Brazil 45 E1
Fuxin China 110 D3
Fujian China *prev.* Linchuan 111 D6
FYR Macedonia *see* Macedonia

G

Gaalkacyo Somalia 55 E5
Gabès Tunisia 53 E2
Gabon *country* W Africa 59
Gaborone *capital of* Botswana 60 D4
Gabrovo Bulgaria 86 D2
Gadsden Alabama, USA 30 D2
Gaeta, Golfo di *sea feature* Italy 79 C5
Gafsa Tunisia 53 E2
Gagnoa Côte d'Ivoire 56 D5
Gagra Georgia 99 E1
Gairdner, Lake *lake* Australia 131 B6
Galapagos Fracture Zone *tectonic feature* Pacific Ocean 135 F3
Galapagos Islands *islands* Ecuador, Pacific Ocean *var.* Tortoise Islands, *Sp.* Archipiélago de Colón 135 G3
Galapagos Rise *undersea feature* Pacific Ocean 135 G3
Galaţi Romania 90 D4
Galesburg Illinois, USA 22 B4
Galicia *region* Spain 74 C1
Galilee, Sea of *see* Tiberias, Lake
Galle Sri Lanka 115 E4
Gallego Rise *undersea feature* Pacific Ocean 135 F3
Gallipoli Italy 79 E5
Gällivare Sweden 66 D3
Gallup New Mexico, USA 28 C2
Galveston Texas, USA 29 G4
Galway Ireland 71 A5
Gambia *country* W Africa 56
Gambia *River* Africa 56 C3
Gambier, Îles *island group* French Polynesia 135 E4
Gan *see* Gansu
Gan *see* Jiangxi
Gäncä Azerbaijan *Rus.* Gyandzha, *prev.* Kirovabad, Yelisavetpol 99 G2
Gand see Gent
Gander Canada 21 H3
Gandía Spain 75 F3
Ganges *river* S Asia 116 F4
Ganges Fan *Undersea feature* Bay of Bengal 122 D3
Ganges, Mouths of the *wetlands* Bangladesh/India 117 G4
Gangtok India 117 G3
Gansu *province* China *var.* Gan, Kansu 111 B5
Gao Mali 57 E3
Gaoual Guinea 56 C4
Gar China *var.* Shiquanhe 108 A4
Garagum Kanaly *canal* Turkmenistan *prev.* Karakumskiy Kanal 104 C3
Garagum *desert* Turkmenistan *var.* Kara Kum, Karakumy 104 C2
Garda, Lago di *lake* Italy 78 B2
Gardīz Afghanistan 105 E4
Garissa Kenya 55 C6
Garmo Peak *see* Communism Peak
Garonne *river* France 73 B5
Garoowe Somalia 55 E5
Garoua Cameroon 58 B4
Gary Indiana, USA 22 B3
Gaspé Canada 21 F4
Gastonia North Carolina, USA 31 E1
Gävle Sweden 67 C5
Gaya India 117 F4
Gaza Gaza Strip 101 A6
Gazandzhyk *see* Bereket
Gazanjyk *see* Bereket
Gaza Strip *disputed territory* SW Asia 101 A6
Gaziantep Turkey *prev.* Aintab 98 D4
Gazimağusa Cyprus *var.* Famagusta *Gk.* Ammochostos 98 C5
Gdańsk Poland *Ger.* Danzig 80 C2
Gdingen *see* Gdynia
Gdynia Poland *Ger.* Gdingen 80 C2
Gedaref Sudan 54 C4
Geelong Australia 131 C7
Gëkdepe *see* Gökdepe
Gemena Dem. Rep. Congo 59 C5
General Eugenio A. Garay Paraguay 44 A1
General Santos Philippines 121 F3

Geneva *see* Genève
Geneva, Lake *lake* France/ Switzerland *Fr.* Lac Léman, *var.* Le Léman, *Ger.* Genfer See 77 A7
Genève Switzerland *Eng.* Geneva 77 A7
Genfer See *see* Geneva, Lake
Genhe China 109 F1
Genk Belgium 69 D5
Genoa *see* Genova
Genova Italy *see* Genoa 78 B3
Genova, Golfo di *sea feature* Italy 78 B3
Gent Belgium *Fr.* Gand, *Eng.* Ghent 69 B5
Geok-Tepe *see* Gökdepe
George South Africa 60 D5
George V Land *physical region* Antarctica 136 C4
Georgenburg *see* Jurbarkas
George Town *capital of* Cayman Islands 36 B3
Georgetown *capital of* Guyana 41 G2
George Town Malaysia 120 B3
Georgia *country* SW Asia 99 F2
Georgia *state* USA 31 E3
Gera Germany 76 C4
Geraldton Australia 129 A5
Gereshk Afghanistan 104 D5
Germany *country* W Europe 76-77
Gerona *see* Girona
Getafe Spain 75 E3
Gettysburg Pennsylvania, USA 23 E4
Gevgelija Macedonia 83 E6
Ghana *country* W Africa 57
Ghanzi Botswana 60 C3
Ghardaïa Algeria 52 D2
Gharyān Libya 53 F2
Ghaznī Afghanistan 105 E4
Ghent *see* Gent
Gibraltar *external territory* UK, SW Europe 74 D5
Gibson Desert *desert region* Australia 128 C4
Gijón Spain *var.* Xixón 74 D1
Gilbert Islands *see* Tungaru
Gilbert River *river* Australia 130 C3
Gillette Wyoming, USA 24 C3
Gingin Australia 129 B6
Girin *see* Jilin
Girne Cyprus *var.* Kyrenia 98 C5
Girona Spain *var.* Gerona 75 G2
Gisborne New Zealand 132 E3
Giurgiu Romania 90 C5
Gjirokastër Albania 83 D6
Gjøvik Norway 67 B5
Glasgow Scotland, UK 70 C4
Gleiwitz *see* Gliwice
Glendale Arizona, USA 28 B2
Glendive Montana, USA 24 D2
Gliwice Poland *Ger.* Gleiwitz 81 C5
Gloucester England, UK 71 D6
Glubokoye *see* Hlybokaye
Gobi *desert* China/Mongolia 108 D3
Godāveri *river* India 106 B3 115 E1
Godoy Cruz Argentina 46 B4
Godthåb *see* Nuuk
Godwin Austin, Mount *see* K2
Goiânia Brazil 43 F4
Gökdepe Turkmenistan *prev.* Geok-Tepe, *prev.* Gëkdepe 104 B3
Golan Heights *disputed territory* SW Asia 100 B4
Gold Coast *coastal region* Australia 131 E5
Goldingen *see* Kuldīga
Golmud China 108 D4
Goma Dem. Rep. Congo 59 E6
Gomel' *see* Homyel'
Gómez Palacio Mexico 32 D2
Gonaïves Haiti 36 D3
Gonder Ethiopia 54 C4
Gongola *river* Nigeria 57 G4
Good Hope, Cape of *coastal feature* South Africa 60 C5
Goondiwindi Australia 131 D5
Goose Lake *lake* W USA 26 B4
Goré Chad 58 C4
Gorē Ethiopia 55 C5
Gore New Zealand 133 B7
Gorgān Iran 102 D3
Gorki *see* Horki
Gor'kiy *see* Nizhniy Novgorod
Gorlovka *see* Horlivka
Gorontalo Indonesia 121 E4
Gorzów Wielkopolski Poland *Ger.* Landsberg 80 B3
Gospić Croatia 82 B3
Gosford Australia 131 D6
Gostivar Macedonia 83 D5
Göteborg Sweden 67 B7
Gotel Mountains *mountain range* Nigeria 57 G4
Gotland *island* Sweden 67 C7
Gotō-rettō *island group* Japan 113 A6
Göttingen Germany 76 C4
Gouda Netherlands 68 C4
Gough Island *external territory* UK, Atlantic Ocean 49 D7
Gouin, Réservoir *Reservoir* Canada 20 D4
Gouré Niger 57 G3
Governador Valadares Brazil 43 G4 45 F1
Govĭ Altayn Nuruu *mountain range* Mongolia 109 E3
Gozo *island* Malta 79 C7
Grafton Australia 131 E5
Grampian Mountains *mountains* Scotland, UK 70 C3
Granada Nicaragua 34 D3
Granada Spain 75 E4
Gran Canaria *island* Spain 52 A3
Gran Chaco *region* C South America 38 C4 44 A2 46 D2
Grand Bahama *island* Bahamas 36 C1
Grand Banks *undersea feature* Atlantic Ocean 48 B3
Grand Canyon *valley* SW USA 28 B1
Grande, Rio *river* Brazil 45 E1
Grande, Rio *River* Mexico/ USA 17 B6
Grande Comore *island* Comoros 61 F2
Grande Prairie Canada 19 E4
Grand Erg Occidental *desert region* Algeria 52 D2

Grand Erg Oriental *desert region* Algeria/Tunisia 53 E3
Grand Falls Canada 21 G3
Grand Forks North Dakota, USA 25 E1
Grand Junction Colorado, USA 24 C4
Grand Rapids Michigan, USA 22 C3
Graudenz *see* Grudziądz
Graz Austria 77 E7
Great Abaco *island* Bahamas 36 C1
Great Ararat *see* Ararat, Mount
Great Australian Bight *sea feature* Australia 129 D6
Great Barrier Island *island* N NZ 132 D2
Great Barrier Reef *coral reef* Coral Sea 130 C4
Great Basin *region* USA 26 D4
Great Bear Lake *lake* Canada 19 E3
Great Dividing Range *mountain range* Australia 130-131
Great Exhibition Bay *inlet* New Zealand132 C1
Great Wall of China *ancient monument* China 110 C4
Greater Antilles *island group* West Indies 36 C3
Great Exuma Island *island* Bahamas 36 C2
Great Falls Montana, USA 24 B1
Great Hungarian Plain *plain* SE Europe *Hung.* Alföld 81 D7
Great Inagua *island* Bahamas 36 D2
Great Khingan Range *see* Da Hinggan Ling
Great Lakes, The *lakes* N America *see* Erie, Huron, Michigan, Ontario, Superior 17 C5
Great Nicobar *island* India 115 H3
Great Plain of China *region* China 106 E2
Great Plains *region* N America 16-17 C5
Great Rift Valley *valley* E Africa/SW Asia 55 C6
Great Salt Desert *see* Kavīr, Dasht-e
Great Salt Lake *salt lake* Utah, USA 24 B3
Great Sand Sea *desert region* Egypt/Libya 53 H3
Great Sandy Desert *desert* Australia 128 C4
Great Sandy Desert *see* Ar Rub' al Khali
Great Slave Lake *lake* Canada 19 E4
Great Victoria Desert *desert* Australia 129 C5
Greece *country* SE Europe 86-87
Green Bay Wisconsin, USA 22 B2
Greenland *external territory* Denmark, Atlantic Ocean *var.* Grønland 64
Greenland Sea Atlantic Ocean 65 F2
Greenock Scotland, UK 70 C4
Greensboro North Carolina, USA 31 F1
Greenville South Carolina, USA 31 E2
Greifswald Germany 76 D2
Gregory Range *mountain range* Australia 130 C3
Grenada *country* West Indies 37 G5
Grenoble France 73 D5
Greymouth New Zealand 133 B5
Grey Range *mountain range* Australia 124 B4
Grimsby England, UK 71 E5
Groningen Netherlands 68 E1
Grønland *see* Greenland
Groote Eylandt *island* Australia 130 B2
Grootfontein Namibia 60 C3
Grosseto Italy 78 B4
Grosskanizsa *see* Nagykanizsa
Groznyy Russian Federation 93 B7 96 A4
Grudziądz Poland *Ger.* Graudenz 80 C3
Grünberg in Schlesien *see* Zielona Góra
Guadalajara Mexico 32 D4
Guadalcanal *island* Solomon Islands 124 C3
Guadalquivir *river* Spain 74 D4
Guadeloupe *external territory* France, West Indies 37 G4
Guadiana *river* Portugal/Spain 74 C4
Gualeguaychú Argentina 46 D4
Guam *external territory* USA, Pacific Ocean 126 B1
Guanare Venezuela 40 D1
Guanare *river* Venezuela 40 D2
Guangdong *province* China *var.* Kuang-tung, Kwangtung, Yue 111 C6
Guangxi *autonomous region* China *var.* Kwangsi 111 B6
Guangzhou China *Eng.* Canton 111 C6
Guantánamo Cuba 36 D3
Guaporé *River* Bolivia/Brazil 32 D3
Guarapuava Brazil 44 D3
Guatemala *country* Central America 34
Guatemala Basin *undersea feature* Pacific Ocean 135 G3
Guatemala City *capital of* Guatemala 34 B2
Guaviare *river* Colombia 40 D3
Guayaquil Ecuador 40 A4
Guayaquil, Golfo do *sea feature* Ecuador/Peru 40 A5
Guernsey *island* Channel Islands 71 D8
Güney Dogu Toroslar *mountain range* SE Turkey 99 F3
Guiana Highlands *upland* N South America 38 C2
Guider Cameroon 58 B4
Guimarães Portugal 74 C2
Guinea *country* W Africa 56
Guinea, Gulf of *sea feature* Atlantic Ocean 49 D5
Guinea-Bissau *country* W Africa 56
Guiyang China 111 B6
Guizhou *province* China *var.* Kuei-chou, Kweichow, Qian 111 B6

Gujarāt *state* India 116 C4
Gujrānwāla Pakistan116 C2
Gujrāt Pakistan 116 C2
Gulf, The *sea feature* Arabian Sea *var.* Persian Gulf 122 B2
Gulfport Mississippi, USA 30 C3
Gulu Uganda 55 B6
Gumbinnen *see* Gusev
Gunnbjørn Fjeld *mountain* Greenland 64 D4
Guri, Embalse de *Reservoir* Venezuela 41 E2
Gusau Nigeria 57 F3
Gusev Kaliningrad, Russian Federation *prev.* Gumbinnen 88 B4
Gushgy *see* Serhetabat
Guwāhāti India 117 G3
Guyana *country* NE South America 41
Gwalior India 116 D3
Gyandzha *see* Gäncä
Gyangzê China 108 C5
Győr Hungary *Ger.* Raab 81 C6
Gyumri Armenia *Rus.* Kumayri, *prev.* Leninakan, Aleksandropol'99 F2
Gyzylarbat *see* Serdar

H

Ha'apai Group *islands* Tonga 127 F5
Haapsalu Estonia *Ger.* Hapsal 88 C2
Haarlem Netherlands 68 C3
Haast New Zealand 133 B6
Hachijō-jima *island* Japan 113 D5
Hachinohe Japan 112 D3
Hadejia *river* Nigeria 57 G3
Ḩaḑramawt *Mountain range* Yemen 103 C7
Hagåtña Guam 126 B1
Hague, The *see* 's-Gravenhage
Haibowan *see* Wuhai
Haicheng China 110 D4
Haifa *see* Hefa
Ḩā'il Saudi Arabia 102 B4
Hailar *see* Hulun Buir
Hainan *island* China *var.* Hainan Dao 106 D3 111 C8
Hainan *province* China *var.* Qiong 111 C7
Hainan Dao *see* Hainan Dao
Hai Phong Vietnam 118 D3
Haiti *country* West Indies 36
Hajdarken *see* Khaydarkan
Hakodate Japan 112 D3
Ḩalab Syria 100 B2
Ḩalānīyāt, Juzur al *Island group* Oman 103 D6
Halden Norway 67 B6
Halfmoon Bay New Zealand 133 A7
Halifax Canada 21 F4
Halle Germany 76 C4
Hallein Austria 77 D7
Halls Creek Australia 128 D3
Halmahera, Pulau *island* Indonesia 121 F3
Halmahera Sea *Sea* Indonesia 121 F4
Halmstad Sweden 67 B7
Hamada Japan 113 B5
Hamadān Iran 102 C3
Ḩamāh Syria 100 B3
Hamamatsu Japan 113 C5
Hamar Norway 67 B5
Hamburg Germany 76 C3
Hämeenlinna Finland 67 D5
HaMelaḩ, Yam *see* Dead Sea
Hamersley Range *mountain range* Australia 128 B4
Hamhŭng North Korea 110 E4
Hami China 108 C3
Hamilton Canada 20 D5
Hamilton New Zealand 132 D3
Hamm Germany 76 B4
Hammerfest Norway 66 D2
Handan China 110 C4
HaNegev *desert region* Israel *Eng.* Negev 101 A6
Hangayn Nuruu *mountain range* Mongolia 108 D2
Hangzhou China 111 D5
Hannover Germany *Eng.* Hanover 76 B4
Hanoi *capital of* Vietnam 118 D3
Hanover *see* Hannover
Hanzhong China 111 B5
Hapsal *see* Haapsalu
Ḩaraḑ Yemen 103 C5
Harare *capital of* Zimbabwe 61 E3
Harbin China 110 E3
Hargeysa Somalia 55 D5
Hari *river* Indonesia 120 B4
Harīrūd *river* C Asia 104 D4
Harper Liberia 56 D5
Harrisburg Pennsylvania, USA 23 E4
Harstad Norway 66 C2
Hartford Connecticut, USA 23 G3
Har Us Nuur *lake* Mongolia 108 C2
Hasselt Belgium 69 D5
Hastings New Zealand 132 E4
Hastings Nebraska, USA 24 E4
Hatay *see* Antakya
Hatteras, Cape *coastal feature* North Carolina, USA 31 G1
Hattiesburg Mississippi, USA 30 C3
Hat Yai Thailand 119 C7
Haugesund Norway 67 A6
Hauraki Gulf *gulf* New Zealand 132 D2
Havana *capital of* Cuba *Sp.* La Habana 36 B2
Havelock North Carolina, USA 31 G1
Havre Montana, USA 24 C1
Havre-Saint-Pierre Canada 21 F3
Hawaii *state* USA 135 E2
Hawaiian Islands *islands* USA 125 F1
Hawaiian Ridge *undersea feature* Pacific Ocean 134 D2
Hawera New Zealand 132 D4
Hawke Bay *bay* New Zealand 132 E4

Hawlēr *see* Arbīl
Hawthorne Nevada, USA 27 C6
Hay River Canada 19 E4
Hays Kansas, USA 25 E4
Hazar Turkmenistan *prev.* Cheleken 104 A2
Heard & McDonald Islands *islands* Indian Ocean 123 C7
Hebei *province* China *var.* Hopeh, Hopei, Ji; *prev.* Chihli 110 C4
Hebron West Bank *var.* Al Khalīl, El Khalil, *Heb.* Ḥevron 101 D7
Heerenveen Netherlands 68 D2
Heerlen Netherlands 69 D6
Hefa Israel *prev.* Haifa 101 A5
Hefei China 111 D5
Hei *see* Heilongjiang
Heidelberg Germany 77 B5
Heilbronn Germany 77 B5
Heilongjiang *province* China *var.* Hei, Hei-lung-chiang 110 E3
Hei-lung-chiang *see* Heilongjiang
Helena Montana, USA 24 B2
Hells Canyon *valley* Idaho/ Oregon USA 26 C3
Helmand *river* Afghanistan 104 C5
Helmond Netherlands 69 D5
Helsingborg Sweden 67 B7
Helsinki *capital of* Finland 67 D6
Henan *province* China *var.* Honan, Yu 111 C5
Hengduan Shan *mountain range* China 111 A6
Hengelo Netherlands 68 E3
Hengyang China 111 C6
Henzada *see* Hinthada
Herāt Afghanistan 104 C4
Hermansverk Norway 67 A5
Hermosillo Mexico 32 B2
Herning Denmark 67 A7
Heywood Islands *island group* Australia 128 C3
Hiiumaa *island* Estonia *Ger.* Dagden, *Swed.* Dagö 88 C2
Hildesheim Germany 76 C4
Hilversum Netherlands 68 C3
Himalayas *mountain range* S Asia 106 B2
Himora Ethiopia 54 C4
Ḥimş Syria 100 B3
Hinchinbrook Island *island* Australia 130 D3
Hindu Kush *mountain range* C Asia 105 E4
Hinthada Myanmar *prev.* Henzada 118 A4
Hiroshima Japan 113 B5
Hitachi Japan 112 D4
Hjørring Denmark 67 A7
Hlybokaye Belarus *Rus.* Glubokoye 89 D5
Hobart Tasmania 131 C8
Hobbs New Mexico, USA 29 E3
Hô Chi Minh Vietnam *var.* Ho Chi Minh City, *prev.* Saigon 119 E6
Ho Chi Minh City *see* Hô Chi Minh
Hodeida *see* Al Ḥudaydah
Hoek van Holland Netherlands 68 B4
Hoggar *see* Ahaggar
Hohe Tauern *mountain range* Austria 77 C7
Hohhot China 109 F3
Hokitika New Zealand 133 B5
Hokkaidō *island* Japan 112 D2
Holguín Cuba 36 C2
Holland *see* Netherlands
Hollabrunn Austria 77 E6
Holon Israel 101 A5
Holyhead Wales, UK 71 C5
Hombori Mopti, Mali 57 E3
Homyel' Belarus *Rus.* Gomel' 89 E7
Honan *see* Henan
Honduras *country* Central America 34-35
Honduras, Gulf of *sea feature* Caribbean Sea 34 C2
Hønefoss Norway 67 B6
Hông Gai Vietnam 118 E3
Hong Kong China *var* Xianggang 111 C6
Honiara *capital of* Solomon Islands 126 C3
Honshū *island* Japan 112 D3
Hoorn Netherlands 68 C2
Hopa Turkey 99 E2
Hopedale Canada 21 F2
Hopeh *see* Hebei
Hopei *see* Hebei
Hopkinsville Kentucky, USA 22 B5
Horki Belarus *Rus.* Gorki 89 E5
Horlivka Ukraine *Rus.* Gorlovka 90 G3
Horn, Cape *see* Hornos, Cabo
Hornos, Cabo *Eng* Cape Horn *coastal feature* Chile 47 C8
Horsham Australia 131 C7
Hospitalet *see* L'Hospitalet de Llobregat
Hot Springs Arkansas, USA 30 B2
Houston Texas, USA 29 G4
Hovd Mongolia 108 C2
Hövsgöl Nuur *lake* Mongolia 108 D1
Hradec Králové Czech Republic *Ger.* Königgrätz 81 B5
Hrodna Belarus *Rus.* Grodno 89 B5
Huacho Peru 42 A3
Huainan China 111 D5
Huambo Angola 60 B2
Huancayo Peru 42 B3
Huang He *river* China *Eng.* Yellow River 110 C4
Huánuco Peru 42 B3
Huaraz Peru 42 B3
Hubei *province* China 111 C5
Hubli India 114 C2
Hudson *river* NE USA 23 F3
Hudson Bay *sea feature* Canada 16 C4
Hudson Strait *sea feature* Canada 19 H3
Huê Vietnam 118 E4
Huehuetenango Guatemala 34 B2
Huelva Spain 74 C4
Huesca Spain 75 F2
Hughenden Australia 130 C4
Hull *see* Kingston upon Hull
Hulun Buir China *var.* Hailar 109 F1

Irkutsk Russian Federation 97 E4
Iron Mountain Michigan, USA 22 B2
Ironwood Michigan, USA 22 B1
Irrawaddy *river* Myanmar 118 B2
Irrawaddy, Mouths of the *wetlands* Myanmar 118 A4
Irtysh *River* Asia 94 C3
Iruña *see* Pamplona
Ishim *River* Kazakhstan/Russian Federation 94 C3
Isiro Dem. Rep. Congo 59 E5
İskenderun Turkey *Eng.* Alexandretta 98 D4
Iskŭr *river* Bulgaria 86 C1
Iskŭr, Yazovir *Reservoir* Bulgaria 86 C2
Islay *island* Scotland, UK 70 B4
Islāmābād *capital of* Pakistan 116 C1
Ismaila *see* Al Ismā'īlīya
Isnā Egypt 54 B2
İsparta Turkey 98 B4
Israel *country* SW Asia 100-101
Issyk-Kul, Ozero *lake* Kyrgyzstan 105 G2
İstanbul Turkey *var.* Stambul, *prev.* Constantinople, Byzantium, *Bul.* Tsarigrad 98 B2
İstanbul Boğazi *see* Bosporus
Itabuna Brazil 43 G4
Itagüí Colombia 40 B2
Italy *country* S Europe 78-79
Ittoqqortoormiit Greenland 65 E3
Iturup *island* Japan/Russian Federation (disputed) 112 E1
Ivanhoe Australia 131 C6
Ivano-Frankivs'k Ukraine 90 C2
Ivanovo Russian Federation 92 B4
Ivittuut Greenland 64 B4
Ivory Coast *see* Côte d'Ivoire
Ivujivik Canada 20 D1
Iwaki Japan 112 D4
Izabal, Lago de *lake* Guatemala 34 C2
Izhevsk Russian Federation 93 C5 96 B3
İzmir Turkey *prev.* Smyrna 98 A3
İzmit Turkey *var.* Kocaeli 98 B2
Izu-shotō *island group* Japan 113 D6

J

Jabal ash Shifā *desert* Saudi Arabia 102 A4
Jabalpur India 116 E4
Jackson Mississippi, USA 30 C2
Jacksonville Florida, USA 31 E3
Jacksonville Texas, USA 29 G3
Jacmel Haiti 36 D3
Jaén Spain 75 E4
Jaffna Sri Lanka 115 E3
Jagdaqi China 109 G1
Jiangxi *province* China 111 C6
Jaipur India 116 D3
Jajce Bosnia & Herzegovina 82 C4
Jakarta *capital of* Indonesia 120 C5
Jakobstad Finland 66 D4
Jakobstadt *see* Jēkabpils
Jalālābād Afghanistan 105 E4
Jalal-Abad *see* Dzhalal-Abad
Jalandhar India 116 D2
Jalapa *see* Xalapa
Jamaame Somalia 55 D6
Jamaica *country* West Indies 36
Jamālpur Bangladesh 117 G4
Jambi Indonesia 120 B4
James Bay *sea feature* Canada 20 C4
Jammu & Kashmir *disputed region* India/Pakistan 116 D2
Jāmnagar India 116 B4
Jan Mayen *external territory* Norway, Arctic Ocean 65 F3
Japan *country* E Asia 112-113
Japan, Sea of Pacific Ocean 112 B3
Jarvis Island *external territory* USA, Pacific Ocean 125 F2
Java *see* Jawa
Java Sea Pacific Ocean *var.* Laut Jawa 122 D4
Java Trench *undersea feature* Indian Ocean 122 D4
Jawa *island* Indonesia *var.* Java 120 C5
Jawa, Laut *see* Java Sea
Jayapura Indonesia 121 H4
Jaz Mūrīān, Hāmūn-e *lake* Iran 102 E4
Jedda *see* Jiddah
Jefferson City Missouri, USA 25 G4
Jēkabpils Latvia *Ger.* Jakobstadt 88 C4
Jelgava Latvia *Ger.* Mitau 88 C3
Jember Indonesia 120 D5
Jena Germany 76 C4
Jenīn *var.* Janīn, Jinīn; *anc.* Engannim. West Bank 101 D6
Jérémie Haiti 36 D3
Jerevan *see* Yerevan
Jericho West Bank 101 B5
Jerid, Chott el *salt lake* Africa 84 D4
Jersey *island* Channel Islands 71 D8
Jerusalem *capital of* Israel 101 B5
Jhelum Pakistan 116 C2
Ji *see* Hebei
Ji *see* Jilin
Jiangsu *province* China *var.* Chiang-su, Kiangsu, Su 111 D5
Jiangxi *province* China *var.* Chiang-hsi, Gan, Kiangsi 111 C6
Jiaxing Zhejiang, China 111 D5
Jibuti *see* Djibouti
Jiddah Saudi Arabia *Eng.* Jedda 103 A5
Jiftlik Post West Bank 101 D7
Jihlava Czech Republic *Ger.* Iglau 81 B5
Jilin *province* China *var.* Chi-lin, Girin, Ji, Kirin 110 E3
Jilin China 110 E3
Jīma Ethiopia 55 C5
Jin *see* Shanxi

Jinan China 111 C4
Jingdezhen China 111 D5
Jinhua China 111 D5
Jining *see* Ulan Qab
Jinotega Nicaragua 34 D3
Jinsha Jiang *river* China 108 D5
Jinzhou China 110 D4
Jīzān Saudi Arabia 103 B6
João Pessoa Brazil 43 H3
Jodhpur India 116 C3
Joensuu Finland 67 E5
Johannesburg South Africa 60 D4
Johnston Atoll *US unincorporated territory* Pacific Ocean 125 E1
Johor Bahru Malaysia 120 C3
Joinville Brazil 44 D3
Joliet Illinois, USA 22 B3
Jönköping Sweden 67 B7
Jonquière Canada 21 E4
Jordan *country* SW Asia 100-101
Jordan *river* SW Asia 101 B5
Joseph Bonaparte Gulf *gulf* Australia 128 D2
Jos Plateau *upland* Nigeria 57 G4
Juan Fernandez, Islas *islands* Chile 46 A4
Juàzeiro Brazil 43 G3
Juàzeiro do Norte Brazil 43 G3
Juba Sudan 55 B5
Júcar *river* Spain 75 E3
Judenburg Austria 77 D7
Juigalpa Nicaragua 34 D3
Juiz de Fora Brazil 43 G5 45 F2
Juneau Alaska, USA 18 D4
Junggar Pendi *desert* China 108 C2
Junín Argentina 46 D4
Jura *mountains* France/ Switzerland 77 A7
Jura *island* Scotland, UK 70 B4
Jurbarkas Lithuania *Ger.* Jurburg, *var.* Georgenburg 88 B4
Jurburg *see* Jurbarkas
Juruá *river* Brazil/Peru 42 C2
Juticalpa Honduras 34 D2
Jutland see Jylland
Juventud, Isla de la *island* Cuba 36 B2
Jylland *peninsula* Denmark *Eng.* Jutland 67 A7
Jyväskylä Finland 67 D5

K

K2 *peak* China/Pakistan *Eng.* Mount Godwin Austen 116 D1
Kaachka *see* Kaka
Kaakhka *see* Kaka
Kabale Uganda 55 B6
Kabinda Dem. Rep. Congo 59 D7
Kābol *see* Kabul
Kabul *capital of* Afghanistan *Per.* Kabol 105 E4
Kachch, Gulf of *sea feature* Arabian Sea 116 B4
Kachch, Rann of *wetland* India/ Pakistan *var.* Rann of Kutch 116 B4
Kadugli Sudan 54 B4
Kaduna Nigeria 57 G4
Kaédi Mauritania 56 C3
Kâgheț *Physical region* Mauritania 56 D1
Kagoshima Japan 113 A6
Kahramanmaraş Turkey *var.* Marash, Maraş 98 D4
Kai, Kepulauan *island group* Indonesia 121 G4
Kaifeng China 111 C5
Kaikohe New Zealand 132 C2
Kaikoura New Zealand 133 C5
Kainji Reservoir *Reservoir* Nigeria 57 F4
Kairouan Tunisia 53 E1
Kaiserslautern Germany 77 B5
Kaitaia New Zealand 132 C2
Kajaani Finland 66 E4
Kaka Turkmenistan *prev.* Kaakhka, *var.* Kaachka 104 C3
Kakhovka Ukraine 91 F4
Kakhovs'ka Vodoskhovyshche *Reservoir* Ukraine 91 F3
Kalahari Desert *desert* southern Africa 60 C4
Kalamariá Greece 86 C3
Kalámata Greece 87 B6
Kalāt Afghanistan 104 D5
Kalbarri Australia 129 A5
Kalemie Dem. Rep. Congo 59 E7
Kalgoorlie Australia 129 C6
Kalimantan *geopolitical region* Indonesia *Eng.* Indonesian Borneo 120 D4
Kaliningrad *external territory* Russian Federation 96 A2
Kaliningrad Kaliningrad, Russian Federation *prev.* Königsberg 88 A4
Kalinkavichy Belarus *Rus.* Kalinkovichi 89 D7
Kalinkovichi *see* Kalinkavichy
Kalisch *see* Kalisz
Kalispell Montana, USA 24 B1
Kalisz Poland *Ger.* Kalisch 80 C4
Kalmar Sweden 67 C7
Kalpeni Island *island* India 114 C3
Kama *river* Russian Federation 92 D4
Kamchatka *peninsula* Russian Federation 97 H3
Kamchiya *river* Bulgaria 86 E2
Kamina Dem. Rep. Congo 59 D7
Kamishli *see* Al Qāmishlī
Kamloops Canada 19 E5
Kampala *capital of* Uganda 55 B6
Kâmpóng Cham Cambodia 119 D6
Kâmpóng Chhnăng Cambodia 119 D5
Kâmpóng Saôm Cambodia 119 D6
Kâmpôt Cambodia 119 D6
Kampuchea *see* Cambodia
Kam"yanets'-Podil's'kyy Ukraine 90 C3
Kananga Dem. Rep. Congo 59 D7
Kanazawa Japan 112 C4

Kandahār Afghanistan *var.* Qandahār 104 D5
Kandi Benin 57 F4
Kanivs'ke Vodoskhovyshche *Reservoir* Ukraine 91 E2
Kandy Sri Lanka 115 E3
Kanestron, Ákra *see* Palioúri, Akrotírio
Kangaroo Island *island* Australia 131 B7
Kangertittivaq *region* Greenland 64 E3
Kangikajik *headland* Greenland 65 E4
Kanjiža Serbia 82 D2
Kankan Guinea 56 D4
Kano Nigeria 57 G4
Kānpur India *prev.* Cawnpore 117 E3
Kansas *state* USA 24-25
Kansas City Kansas, USA 25 F4
Kansas City Missouri, USA 25 F4
Kansk Russian Federation 97 E4
Kansu *see* Gansu
Kaohsiung Taiwan 111 D7
Kaolack Senegal 56 B3
Kapfenberg Austria 77 E7
Kaposvár Hungary 81 C7
Kapsukas *see* Marijampolė
Kapuas *river* Indonesia 120 D4
Kara-Balta Kyrgyzstan 105 F2
Karabük Turkey 98 C2
Karāchi Pakistan 116 B4
Karaganda Kazakhstan 96 C4
Karakol Kyrgyzstan *prev.* Przheval'sk 105 G2
Kara Kum *see* Garagum
Karakumskiy Kanal *see* Garagum Kanaly
Karakumy *see* Garagum
Karamay China 108 C2
Karamea Bight *gulf* New Zealand 133 C5
Karasburg Namibia 60 C4
Kara Sea *see* Karskoye More
Kardítsa Greece 86 B4
Kariba, Lake *lake* Zambia/ Zimbabwe 60 D3
Karimata, Selat *strait* Indonesia 120 C4
Karkinits'ka Zatoka *sea feature* Black Sea 91 E4
Karl-Marx-Stadt *see* Chemnitz
Karlovac Croatia 82 B3
Karlovy Vary Czech Republic *Ger.* Karlsbad 81 A5
Karlsbad *see* Karlovy Vary
Karlskrona Sweden 67 C7
Karlsruhe Germany 77 B5
Karlstad Sweden 67 B6
Karnātaka *state* India 114 D1
Kárpathos *island* Greece 87 E7
Kars Turkey 99 F2
Karshi Uzbekistan *prev.* Bek-Budi, *Uzb.* Qarshi 104 D3
Karskoye More Arctic Ocean *Eng.* Kara Sea 137 H3
Kasai *river* Dem. Rep. Congo 59 C6
Kasama Zambia 61 E2
Kaschau *see* Košice
Kāshān Iran 102 C3
Kashi China 108 A3
Kasongo Dem. Rep. Congo 59 E6
Kassa *see* Košice
Kassala Sudan 54 C4
Kassel Germany 76 B4
Kastamonu Turkey 98 C2
Katanning Australia 129 B6
Kateríni Greece 86 B4
Katha Myanmar 118 B2
Katherine Australia 128 E2
Kathmandu *capital of* Nepal 117 F3
Katsina Nigeria 57 G3
Katowice Poland 81 C5
Kauen *see* Kaunas
Kaunas Lithuania *Ger.* Kauen, *Pol.* Kowno, *Rus.* Kovno 88 B4
Kavadarci Macedonia 82 E5
Kavála Greece 86 C3
Kavaratti Island *island* India 114 C3
Kavīr, Dasht-e *Salt pan* Iran 102 D3
Kawasaki Japan 113 D5
Kayan *river* Indonesia 120 D3
Kayes Mali 56 C3
Kayseri Turkey 98 D3
Kazakhstan *country* C Asia 96
Kazan' Russian Federation 96 B3
Kazandzhik *see* Bereket
Kazanlŭk Bulgaria 86 D2
Kecskemét Hungary 81 D7
Kediri Indonesia 120 D5
Keetmanshoop Namibia 60 C4
Kefalloniá *island* Greece *Eng.* Cephalonia 87 A5
Keá *see* Tziá
Kelang *see* Klang
Kelmė Lithuania 88 B4
Kelowna Canada 19 E5
Kemerovo Russian Federation 96 D4
Kemi Finland 66 D4
Kemi *river* Finland 66 D3
Kemijärvi Finland 66 D3
Kendari Indonesia 121 E4
Këneurgench *see* Köneürgench
Kénitra Morocco 52 C2
Kennewick Washington, USA 26 C2
Kenora Canada 20 A3
Kentucky *state* USA 22 C5
Kenya *country* E Africa 55
Kerala *state* India 114 D3
Kerch Ukraine 91 G4
Kerguelen *island group* Indian Ocean 123 C7
Kerguelen Plateau *undersea feature* Indian Ocean 123 C7
Kerki *see* Atamyrat
Kérkira *see* Kérkyra
Kérkyra Greece 86 A4
Kérkyra *island* Greece *prev.* Kérkira, *Eng.* Corfu 86 A4
Kermadec Islands *island group* Pacific Ocean 125 E4
Kermadec Trench *undersea feature* Pacific Ocean 125 E4
Kermān Iran *var.* Kirman 102 D4
Kermānshāh Iran *prev.* Bākhtarān 102 C3
Kerulen *river* China/Mongolia 109 E2

Ketchikan Alaska, USA 18 D4
Key West Florida, USA 31 E5
Khabarovsk Russian Federation 97 G4
Khanka, Lake *lake* China/ Russian Federation 110 E3
Khankendy *see* Xankändi
Kharkiv Ukraine *Rus.* Khar'kov 91 G2
Khar'kov *see* Kharkiv
Khartoum *capital of* Sudan *var.* Al Khurţūm 54 B4
Khāsh Iran 102 E4
Khaskovo Bulgaria 86 D2
Khaydarkan Kyrgyzstan *var.* Khaydarken, Hajdarken 105 E2
Khaydarken *see* Khaydarkan
Kherson Ukraine 91 E4
Kheta *river* Russian Federation 94 D2
Khíos *see* Chíos
Khirbet el 'Aujā et Tahtā West Bank 101 D6
Khmel 'nyts'kyy Ukraine 90 D2
Khodzhent *see* Khŭjand
Khojend *see* Khŭjand
Khokand *see* Qo'qon
Kholm Afghanistan 105 E3
Khon Kaen Thailand 118 C4
Khorog *see* Khorugh
Khorugh Tajikistan *Rus.* Khorog 105 F3
Khouribga Morocco 52 C2
Khudzhand *see* Khŭjand
Khŭjand Tajikistan *var.* Khodzheut, Khojend, *Rus.* Khudzhand *prev.* Leninabad 105 E2
Khulna Bangladesh 117 G4
Khvoy Iran 102 B3
Kiangsi *see* Jiangxi
Kiangsu *see* Jiangsu
Kičevo Macedonia 83 D5
Kiel Germany 76 C2
Kielce Poland 80 D4
Kiev *capital of* Ukraine *Ukr.* Kyyiv 91 E2
Kiffa Mauritania 56 C3
Kigali *capital of* Rwanda 55 B6
Kigoma Tanzania 55 B7
Kikládhes *see* Kyklades
Kikwit Dem. Rep. Congo 59 C6
Kilimanjaro *peak* Tanzania 55 C7
Kilkís Greece 86 B3
Killarney Ireland 71 A6
Kimberley South Africa 60 D4
Kimberley Plateau *upland* Australia 128 D3
Kindia Guinea 56 C4
Kindu Dem. Rep. Congo 59 D6
King Island *island* Australia 131 C7
Kingissepp *see* Kuressaare
Kingman Reef *external territory* USA, Pacific Ocean 125 F2
King Sound *sound* Australia 128 C3
Kingsport Tennessee, USA 31 E1
Kingsville Texas, USA 29 G5
Kingston Canada 20 C5
Kingston *capital of* Jamaica 36 C3
Kingston upon Hull England, UK *var.* Hull 71 E5
Kingstown St Vincent & The Grenadines 36 G4
King William Island *island* Canada 19 F3
Kinneret, Yam *see* Tiberius, Lake
Kinshasa *capital of* Dem. Rep. Congo *prev.* Léopoldville 59 B6
Kirghizia *see* Kyrgyzstan
Kiribati *country* Pacific Ocean 127
Kirin *see* Jilin
Kiritimati *island* Kiribati *var.* Christmas Island 127 G2
Kirkenes Norway 66 E2
Kirklareli Turkey 98 A2
Kirksville Missouri, USA 25 F4
Kirkūk Iraq 102 B3
Kirkwall Scotland, UK 70 C2
Kirman *see* Kermān
Kirov Russian Federation 92 C4 96 B3
Kirovabad *see* Gäncä
Kirovakan *see* Vanadzor
Kirovohrad Ukraine 91 E3
Kiruna Sweden 66 C3
Kisangani Dem. Rep. Congo *prev.* Stanleyville 59 D5
Kishinev *see* Chişinău
Kismaayo Somalia 55 D6
Kisumu Kenya 55 C6
Kitakyūshū Japan 113 A5
Kitami Japan 112 D2
Kitchener Canada 20 C5
Kitwe Zambia 60 D2
Kivu, Lake *lake* Rwanda/Dem. Rep. Congo 55 B6 59 E6
Kızıl Irmak *river* Turkey 98 C2
Kizyl-Arvat *see* Serdar
Kladno Czech Republic 81 A5
Klagenfurt Austria 77 D7
Klaipėda Lithuania *Ger.* Memel 88 B4
Klamath Falls Oregon, USA 26 B4
Khang Malaysia *var.* Kelang 120 B2
Ključ Bosnia & Herzegovina 82 B3
Knin Croatia 82 B4
Knoxville Tennessee, USA 31 E1
Knud Rasmussen Land *region* Greenland 64 D1
Kōbe Japan 113 C5
Koblenz Germany 77 B5
Kobryn Belarus 89 B6
Kocaeli *see* İzmit
Kočani Macedonia 83 E5
Kōchi Japan 113 B6
Kochi India *see* Cochin 114 D3
Kodiak Alaska, USA 18 C3
Kodiak Island *island* Alaska, USA 18 C3
Koedoes *see* Kudus
Kohīma India 117 H3
Kohtla-Järve Estonia 88 D2
Kokand *see* Qo'qon
Kokchetav Kazakhstan 96 C4
Kokkola Finland 66 D4
Koko Nor *see* Qinghai
Koko Nor *see* Qinghai Hu

Kokshaal-Tau *mountain range* Kyrgyzstan 105 G2
Kola Peninsula *see* Kol'skiy Poluostrov
Kolguyev, Ostrov *island* Russian Federation 92 D2
Kolhumadulu Atoll *island* Maldives 114 C5
Kolka Latvia 88 C3
Kolkata India *var.* Calcutta 117 F4
Köln Germany *Eng.* Cologne 76 B4
Kol'skiy Poluostrov *peninsula* Russian Federation *Eng.* Kola Peninsula 63 F1 92 C2
Kolwezi Dem. Rep. Congo 59 D8
Kolyma *river* Russian Federation 95 G2
Kommunizma, Pik *see* Communism Peak
Komoé *river* Côte d'Ivoire 57 E4
Komotiní Greece 86 D3
Komsomol'sk-na-Amure Russian Federation 97 G4
Kondoz Afghanistan *var.* Kondūz, Kunduz, Qondūz 105 E3
Kondūz *see* Kondoz
Köneürgench Turkmenistan *prev.* Kunya-Urgench, *prev.* Këneurgench 104 C2
Kong Christian IX Land *region* Greenland 64 D4
Kong Christian X Land *region* Greenland 64 E3
Kong Frederik VI Kyst *region* Greenland 64 C4
Kong Frederik VIII Land *region* Greenland 64 E2
Kong Frederik IX Land *region* Greenland 64 C3
Kong Karls Land *island group* Svalbard 65 G2
Kong Oscar Fjord *fjord* Greenland 65 E3
Konia *see* Konya
Königgrätz *see* Hradec Králové
Königsberg *see* Kaliningrad
Konispol Albania 83 D7
Konjic Bosnia & Herzegovina 82 C4
Konya Turkey *prev.* Konia 98 C4
Kopaonik *mountains* Serbia 83 D4
Koper Slovenia 77 D8
Koprivnica Croatia 82 B2
Korçë Albania 83 D6
Korčula *island* Croatia 82 B4
Korea Bay *bay* China/North Korea 110 D4
Korea Strait *sea feature* Japan/ South Korea 110-111 E5
Korinthiakós Kólpos *sea feature* Greece *Eng.* Gulf of Corinth 87 B5
Kórinthos Greece *Eng.* Corinth 87 B5
Kōriyama Japan 113 D4
Korla China 108 C3
Korosten' Ukraine 90 D1
Kortrijk Belgium 69 A6
Kos *island* Greece 87 E6
Kosciusko, Mount *peak* Australia 131 D7
Košice Slovakia *Ger.* Kaschau, *Hung.* Kassa 81 D6
Köslin *see* Koszalin
Kosovo *country* SE Europe 83 D5
Kosovska Mitrovica *see* Mitrovicë
Kosrae *island* Micronesia 126 C2
Kossou, Lac de *lake* Côte d'Ivoire 56 D4
Kostanay Kazakhstan *var.* Kustanay 96 C4
Kostyantynivka Ukraine 91 G3
Koszalin Poland *Ger.* Köslin 80 B2
Kota India 116 D4
Kota Bharu Malaysia 120 B3
Kota Kinabalu Malaysia 120 D3
Kotka Finland 67 E5
Kotlas NW Russia 92 C4
Kotuy *river* Russian Federation 95 E2
Koudougou Burkina 57 E4
Kourou French Guiana 41 H2
Kousséri Cameroon 58 B3
Kouvola Finland 67 E5
Kovel' Ukraine 90 C1
Kovno *see* Kaunas
Kowno *see* Kaunas
Kozáni Greece 86 B4
Kozhikode India *see* Calicut 114 D2
Kra, Isthmus of *coastal feature* Myanmar/Thailand 119 B6
Kragujevac Serbia 82 D4
Krakau *see* Kraków
Kraków Poland *Eng.* Cracow, *Ger.* Krakau 81 D5
Kraljevo Serbia 82 D4
Kranj Slovenia 77 D7
Krasnodar Russian Federation 93 A6
Krasnovodsk *see* Türkmenbaşy
Krasnoyarsk Russian Federation 96 D4
Krasnyy Luch Ukraine 91 H3
Kremenchuk Ukraine 91 F2
Kremenchuts'ke Vodoskhovyshche *Reservoir* Ukraine 91 E2
Krems an der Donau Austria 77 E6
Kretinga Lithuania *Ger.* Krottingen 88 B3
Krichev *see* Krychaw
Krishna *river* India 114 C1
Kristiansand Norway 67 A6
Kristianstad Sweden 67 B7
Kríti *island* Greece *Eng.* Crete 87 C7
Kritikó Pélagos *see* Crete, Sea of
Krivoy Rog *see* Kryvyy Rih
Krk *island* Croatia 82 A3
Kroonstad South Africa 60 D4
Krottingen *see* Kretinga
Krung Thep *see* Bangkok
Kruševac Serbia 83 E4
Krušné Hory *see* Erzgebirge
Krychaw Belarus *Rus.* Krichev 89 E6
Kryms'kyy Pivostriv *peninsula* Ukraine *var.* Crimea 90 F4

Kryvyy Rih Ukraine *Rus.* Krivoy Rog 91 E3
Kuala Lumpur *capital of* Malaysia 120 B3
Kuala Terengganu Malaysia 120 B3
Kuang-tung *see* Guangdong
Kuantan Malaysia 120 C3
Kuba *see* Quba
Kuching Malaysia 120 C3
Kuçovë Albania *prev.* Qyteti Stalin 83 D6
Kudus Indonesia *prev.* Koedoes 120 D5
Kuei-chou *see* China Guizhou
Kugluktuk Canada *prev.* Coppermine 19 E3
Kuito Angola 60 C2
Kuldīga Latvia *Ger.* Goldingen 88 B3
Kullorsuaq Greenland 64 C2
Kŭlob Tajikistan *Rus.* Kulyab 105 E3
Kulyab *see* Kŭlob
Kum *see* Qom
Kuma *river* Russian Federation 93 B7
Kumamoto Japan 113 B6
Kumanovo Macedonia 83 E5
Kumasi Ghana 57 E5
Kumayri *see* Gyumri 99 F2
Kumo Nigeria 57 G4
Kumon Range *mountain range* Myanmar 118 B1
Kunashir *island* Japan/Russian Federation (disputed) 112 E1
Kunduz *see* Kondoz
Kunja-Urgenč *see* Köneürgench
Kunlun Mountains *see* Kunlun Shan
Kunlun Shan *mountain range* China *Eng.* Kunlun Mountains 106 B4
Kunming China 111 B6
Kununurra Australia 128 D3
Kupang Indonesia 120 E5
Kür *see* Kura
Kura *river* Azerbaijan/Georgia *Az.* Kür 99 G2
Kurashiki Japan 113 B5
Kurdistan *region* Turkey 99 F4
Küre Dağları *mountains* Turkey 98 C2
Kuressaare Estonia *prev.* Kingissepp, *Ger.* Arensburg 88 C2
Kurgan–Tyube *see* Qŭrghonteppa
Kurile Islands *islands* Pacific Ocean 112 E1
Kurile Trench *undersea feature* Pacific Ocean 134 C2
Kurnool India 114 D2
Kushiro Japan 112 E2
Kushka *see* Serhetabat
Kustanay *see* Kostanay
Kütahya Turkey *prev.* Kutaiah 98 B3
Kutaiah *see* Kütahya
K'ut'aisi Georgia 99 F2
Kutch, Rann of *see* Kachch, Rann of
Kuujjuaq Canada 21 E2
Kuujjuarapik Canada *prev.* Poste-de-la-Baleine 20 D2
Kuusamo Finland 66 E3
Kuwait *country* SW Asia 102 C4
Kuwait City *capital of* Kuwait 102 C4
Kuytun China 108 C2
Kvitøya *island* Svalbard 65 G1
Kwangju South Korea 111 E4
Kwango *river* Dem. Rep. Congo 59 C7
Kwangtung *see* Guangdong
Kweichow *see* Guizhou
Kykládes *island group* Greece *prev.* Kikládhes, *Eng.* Cyclades 87 D6
Kyrenia *see* Girne
Kyrgyzstan *country* C Asia *var.* Kirghizia 105
Kýthira *island* Greece 87 B6
Kyushu-Palau Ridge *undersea feature* Pacific Ocean 124 B1
Kyyiv *see* Kiev
Kyyivs'ke Vodoskhovyshche *Reservoir* Ukraine 91 E1
Kyōto Japan 113 C5
Kyūshū *island* Japan 113 B6
Kyzylorda Kazakhstan 96 B5

L

Laâyoune Western Sahara 52 B3
Labé Guinea 56 C4
Laborca *see* Laborec
Laborec *river* Slovakia *Hung.* Laborca 81 E5
Labrador *region* Canada 21 F2
Labrador Sea Atlantic Ocean 64 B5
Laccadive Islands *see* Lakshadweep
La Ceiba Honduras 34 D2
Lachlan River *river* Australia 131 C6
La Coruña *see* A Coruña
La Crosse Wisconsin, USA 22 A2
Ladoga, Lake *see* Ladozhskoye Ozero
Ladozhskoye Ozero *lake* Russian Federation *Eng.* Lake Ladoga 92 B3
Ladysmith Wisconsin, USA 22 A2
Lae Papua New Guinea 126 B3
La Esperanza Honduras 34 C2
Lafayette Louisiana, USA 30 B3
Laghouat Algeria 52 D2
Lagos Nigeria 57 F5
Lagos Portugal 74 C4
Lagouira Western Sahara 52 A4
La Grande Oregon, USA 26 C3
La Habana *see* Havana
Lahore Pakistan 116 C2
Laï Chad 58 C4
Laila *see* Laylá
Lajes Brazil 44 D3
Lake Charles Louisiana, USA 30 B3
Lake District *region* England, UK 71 C5
Lakewood Colorado, USA 24 D4
Lakshadweep *island group* India *Eng.* Laccadive Islands 114 B2
La Ligua Chile 46 B4
La Louvière Belgium 69 B6
Lambaré Paraguay 44 B3

Libreville *capital of* Gabon 59 A5
Libya *country* N Africa 53
Libyan Desert *desert* N Africa 50 C3
Lichuan China 111 B5
Liechtenstein *country* C Europe 77 B7
Liège Belgium 69 D6
Liegnitz *see* Legnica
Lienz Austria 77 D7
Linz Austria 77 D7
Liepāja Latvia *Ger.* Libau 88 B3
Liffey *river* Ireland 71 B5
Ligurian Sea Mediterranean Sea 78 A3
Likasi Dem. Rep. Congo 59 E8
Lille France 72 D2
Lillehammer Norway 67 B5
Lilongwe *capital of* Malawi 61 E2
Lima *capital of* Peru 42 B4
Limassol Cyprus *var.* Lemesos 98 C5
Limerick Ireland 71 A6
Límnos *island* Greece *var.* Lemnos 86 D4
Limoges France 72 C5
Limón Costa Rica 35 E4
Limpopo *river* southern Africa 60 D3
Linares Chile 46 B4
Linares Spain 75 E4
Linchuan *see* Fuzhou
Lincoln England, UK 71 D5
Lincoln Nebraska, USA 25 F4
Lincoln Sea Arctic Ocean 64 E1
Linden Guyana 41 G2
Lindi Tanzania 55 C8
Line Islands *island group* Kiribati 127 G2
Linköping Sweden 67 C6
Linz Austria 77 D6
Lion, Golfe du *sea feature* Mediterranean Sea 73 D6
Lipari, Isola *island* Italy 79 D6
Lipari Islands *see* Isole Eolie
Lira Uganda 55 B6
Lisbon *capital of* Portugal *Port.* Lisboa 74 B3
Litani *river* SW Asia 91 B4
Lithuania *country* E Europe 88-89
Little Andaman *island* India 115 G2
Little Minch *sea feature* Scotland, UK 70 B3
Little Rock Arkansas, USA 30 B2
Liuzhou China 111 C6
Liverpool England, UK 71 D5
Livingstone Zambia 60 D3
Livno Bosnia & Herzegovina 82 B4
Livorno Italy 78 B3
Ljubljana *capital of* Slovenia 77 D7
Ljusnan *river* Sweden 67 B5
Llanos *region* Colombia/ Venezuela 41 E2
Lleida Spain *Cast.* Lérida 75 F2
Lobatse Botswana 60 D4
Lobito Angola 60 B2
Locarno Switzerland 77 B7
Lodja Dem. Rep. Congo 59 D6
Łódź Poland *Rus.* Lodz 80 D4
Lofoten *island group* Norway 66 B3
Logroño Spain 75 E2
Loire *river* France 72 B4
Loja Ecuador 40 A5
Lokitaung Kenya 55 C5
Loksa Estonia *Ger.* Loxa 88 D2
Lombok, Pulau *island* Indonesia 120 D5
Lomé *capital of* Togo 57 E5
Lomond, Loch *lake* Scotland, UK 70 C4
London Canada 20 C5
London *capital of* UK 71 E6
Londonderry Northern Ireland, UK 70 B4
Londonderry, Cape *coastal feature* Australia 128 D2
Londrina Brazil 44 D2
Long Beach California, USA 27 C8
Long Island *island* Bahamas 34 D2
Long Island *island* NE USA 23 G3
Longreach Australia 130 C4
Long Strait *Strait* Russian Federation 95 H2
Longview Texas, USA 29 G3
Longview Washington, USA 26 B2
Longyearbyen Svalbard 65 F2
Lop Nur *lake* China 108 C3
Lorca Spain 75 E4
Lord Howe Island *island* Australia 124 C4
Lord Howe Rise *undersea feature* Pacific Ocean 124 D4
Lorient France 72 A4
Los Alamos New Mexico, USA 28 D1
Los Angeles California, USA 27 C7
Loslau *see* Wodzisław Śląski
Los Mochis Mexico 32 C3
Losonc *see* Lučenec
Losontz *see* Lučenec
Lot *river* France 73 B5
Louangphrabang Laos 118 C3
Loubomo Congo 59 B6
Louisiana *state* USA 30 B3
Louisville Kentucky, USA 22 C5
Louisville Ridge *undersea feature* Pacific Ocean 125 E4
Lovech Bulgaria 86 C2
Lower California *see* Baja California
Lower Hutt New Zealand
Loxa *see* Loksa
Loyauté, Îles *island group* New Caledonia 126 D5
Loznica Serbia 82 C3
Lu *see* Shandong
Luanda *capital of* Angola 60 B1
Luanshya Zambia 60 D2
Lubango Angola 60 B2
Lubbock Texas, USA 29 E2
Lübeck Germany 76 C3
Lublin Poland *Rus.* Lyublin 80 E4

Lubny Ukraine 91 F2
Lubumbashi Dem. Rep. Congo 59 E8
Lucapa Angola 60 C1
Lucena Philippines 120 E2
Lučenec Slovakia *Hung.* Losonc, *Ger.* Losontz 81 D6
Lucerne *see* Luzern
Lucknow India 117 E3
Lüderitz Namibia 60 C4
Ludhiāna India 116 D2
Lugano Switzerland 77 B7
Lugo Spain 74 C1
Luhans'k Ukraine 91 H3
Luleå Sweden 66 D4
Lumsden New Zealand 133 A7
Lüneburg Germany 76 C3
Luninyets Belarus 89 C6
Luoyang *var.* Honan, Lo-yang. China 110 C4
Lusaka *capital of* Zambia 60 D2
Lushnjë Albania 83 D6
Lūt, Baḩrat *see* Dead Sea
Luts'k Ukraine 90 C1
Luxembourg *country* W Europe 69 D8
Luxembourg *capital of* Luxembourg 69 D8
Luxor *see* Al Uqşur
Luzern Switzerland *Fr.* Lucerne 77 B7
Luzon *island* Philippines 121 E1
Luzon Strait *sea feature* Philippines/Taiwan 107 E3
L'viv Ukraine *Rus.* L'vov 90 C2
L'vov see L'viv
Lyepyel' Belarus *Rus.* Lepel' 89 D5
Lyon France 73 D5
Lyublin *see* Lublin

M

Ma'ān Jordan 101 B6
Maas *see* Meuse
Maastricht Netherlands 69 D6
Macao *external territory* Portugal, E Asia *var.* Macau 111 C7
Macapá Brazil 43 F1
Macau *see* Macao
Macdonnell Ranges *mountains* Australia 130 A4
Macedonia *country* SE Europe officially Former Yugoslav Republic of Macedonia, *abbrev.* FYR Macedonia 83
Maceió Brazil 43 H3
Machala Ecuador 40 A5
Mackay Australia 130 D4
Mackay, Lake *lake* Australia 128 D4
Mackenzie *river* Canada 19 E4
Mackenzie Bay *sea feature* Atlantic Ocean 136 D3
Macleod, Lake *lake* Australia128 A4
Mâcon France 72 D5
Macon Georgia, USA 31 E2
Madagascar *country* Indian Ocean 61
Madagascar Basin *undersea feature* Indian Ocean 123 B5
Madagascar Plateau *undersea feature* Indian Ocean 123 A6
Madang Papua New Guinea 126 B3
Madeira *river* Bolivia/Brazil 42 D2
Madeira *island group* Portugal 52 A2
Madhya Pradesh *state* India 117 E4
Madison Wisconsin, USA 22 B3
Madiun *prev.* Madioen. Indonesia 120 D5
Madona Latvia *Ger.* Modohn 88 D3
Madras *see* Chennai
Madre de Dios *river* Bolivia/ Peru 42 C3
Madrid *capital of* Spain 75 E3
Madurai India 114 D3
Magadan Russian Fed. 97 G3
Magallanes *see* Punta Arenas
Magallanes, Estrecho de *see* Magellan, Strait of
Magdalena *river* Colombia 40 B2
Magdeburg Germany 76 C4
Magelang Indonesia 120 C5
Magellan, Strait of *sea feature* S South America *Sp.* Estrecho de Magallanes 47 B8
Maggiore, Lake *lake* Italy/ Switzerland 78 B2
Mahajanga Madagascar 61 G3
Mahalapye Botswana 60 D4
Mahanādi *river* India 117 F5
Mahārashtra *state* India 116 D5
Mahé *island* Seychelles 61 H1
Mahilyow Belarus *Rus.* Mogilëv 89 E6
Mährisch-Ostrau *see* Ostrava
Maicao Colombia 40 C1
Maiduguri Nigeria 57 H4
Maimana *see* Meymaneh
Maine *state* USA 23 G1
Maine, Gulf of *gulf* USA 23 G2
Mainz Germany 77 B5
Maio *Island* Cape Verde 56 A3
Maíz, Islas del *islands* Nicaragua 35 E3
Majorca *see* Mallorca
Majuro *island* Marshall Islands 126 D1
Makarska Croatia 82 B4
Makarov Basin *undersea feature* Arctic Ocean 137 G3
Makassar Indonesia *prev.* Ujungpandang 121 E4
Makassar Strait *strait* Indonesia 120 D4
Makeyevka *see* Makiyivka
Makhachkala Russian Federation 93 B7 96 A4
Makiyivka Ukraine *Rus.* Makeyevka 91 G5
Makkah Saudi Arabia *Eng.* Mecca 103 A5
Makkovik Canada 21 F2
Malabo *capital of* Equatorial Guinea 59 A5
Malacca, Strait of *sea feature* Indonesia/ Malaysia 106 C4 119 C8 120 B3

Maladzyechna Belarus *Rus.* Molodechno, *Pol.* Molodeczno 89 C5
Málaga Spain 74 D5
Malakal Sudan 55 B5
Malang Indonesia 120 D5
Malanje Angola 60 C2
Malatya Turkey 99 E3
Malawi *country* southern Africa 61
Malay Peninsula *peninsula* Malaysia/Thailand 119 D8
Malaysia *country* Asia 120
Malden Island *atoll* Kiribati 125 F2
Maldives *country* Indian Ocean 114 C4
Male' *capital of* Maldives 114 C4
Malekula *island* Vanuatu 124 D3
Mali *country* W Africa 57
Malindi Kenya 55 C7
Mallorca *island* Spain *Eng.* Majorca 75 H3
Malmö Sweden 67 B7
Malta *country* Mediterranean Sea 79 C8
Malta Montana, USA 24 C1
Malta Channel *sea feature* Mediterranean Sea 79 C7
Maluku *island group* Indonesia *var.* Moluccas 107 E4 121 F4
Maluku, Laut Pacific Ocean *Eng.* Molucca Sea 121 F4
Mamberamo *river* Indonesia 121 H4
Mamoudzou *capital of* Mayotte 61 G2
Man, Isle of *island* UK 71 C5
Manado Indonesia 121 F3
Managua *capital of* Nicaragua 34 D3
Manama *capital of* Bahrain *Ar.* Al Manāmah 103 C5
Mananjary Madagascar 61 G3
Manaus Brazil 42 D2
Manchester England, UK 71 D5
Manchester New Hampshire, USA 23 G2
Manchurian Plain *plain* E Asia 107 E1
Mandalay Myanmar 118 B3
Mangalia Romania 90 D5
Mangalore India 114 C2
Manicouagan, Réservoir *Reservoir* Canada 21 E3
Manihiki *atoll* Cook Islands 125 F3
Maniitsoq Greenland 64 C3
Manila *capital of* Philippines 121 E1
Manisa Turkey *prev.* Saruhan 98 A3
Manitoba *province* Canada 19 G4
Manizales Colombia 40 B3
Manjimup Australia 129 B7
Mannar Sri Lanka 115 E3
Mannar, Gulf of *sea feature* Indian Ocean 114 D3
Mannheim Germany 77 B5
Manono Dem. Rep. Congo 59 E7
Mansel Island *island* Canada 20 C1
Mansfield Ohio, USA 22 D4
Manta Ecuador 40 A4
Mantes-la-Jolie France 72 C3
Mantova Italy *Eng.* Mantua 78 B2
Mantua *see* Mantova
Manurewa New Zealand 132 D3
Manzhouli China 109 F1
Mao Chad 58 B3
Maoke, Pegunungan *mountains* Indonesia 121 H4
Maputo *capital of* Mozambique 61 E4
Mar, Serra do *mountains* Brazil 38 D4
Maracaibo Venezuela 40 C1
Maracaibo, Lago de *inlet* Venezuela 40 C1
Maracay Venezuela 40 D1
Maradi Niger 57 F3
Marāgheh Iran 102 C3
Marajó, Ilha de *island* Brazil 43 F2
Marañón *river* Peru 42 B2
Maraş *see* Kahramanmaraş
Marash *see* Kahramanmaraş
Marbella Spain 74 D5
Marble Bar Australia 128 B4
Mar Chiquita, Laguna *salt lake* Argentina 46 C3
Mardān Pakistan 116 C1
Mar del Plata Argentina 47 D5
Mardin Turkey 99 E4
Margarita, Isla de *island* Venezuela 41 E1
Māragow, Dasht-e- *desert* Afghanistan 104 C5
Mariana Trench *undersea feature* Pacific Ocean 124 B1 126 B1
Marías, Islas *islands* Mexico 32 C4
Maribor Slovenia 77 E7
Marie Byrd Land *region* Antarctica 136 B4
Mariehamn Finland 67 D6
Marijampolė Lithuania *prev.* Kapsukas 88 B4
Marília Brazil 44 D2
Maringá Brazil 44 D2
Marion, Lake *lake* South Carolina, USA 31 F2
Mariscal Estigarribia Paraguay 44 B2
Maritsa *river* SE Europe 86 D3
Mariupol' Ukraine *prev.* Shdanov 91 G3
Marka Somalia 55 D6
Marmara, Sea of *see* Marmara Denizi
Marmara Denizi Turkey *Eng.* Sea of Marmara 98 B2
Marne *river* France 72 D3
Marotiri *Island group* French Polynesia 125 F4
Maroua Cameroon 58 B3
Marowijne *river* French Guiana/Suriname 41 H3
Marquesas Fracture Zone *tectonic feature* Pacific Ocean 125 G3
Marquesas Islands *island group* French Polynesia *Fr.* Îles Marquises 125 G3

Marquette Michigan, USA 22 B1
Marquisas, Îles *see* Marquesas Islands
Marrakech Morocco *Eng.* Marrakesh 52 C2
Marrawah Australia 131 C8
Marree Australia 131 B5
Marsala Italy 79 C6
Marseille France 73 D6
Marshall Islands *country* Pacific Ocean 126-127
Martin Slovakia *prev.* Turčianský Svätý Martin, *Ger.* Sankt Martin, *Hung.* Turócszentmárton 81 C5
Martinique *external territory* France, West Indies 37
Mary Turkmenistan *prev.* Merv 104 C3
Maryborough Australia 131 E5
Maryland *state* USA 23 F4
Masai Steppe *grassland* Tanzania 55 C7
Mascarene Basin *undersea feature* Indian Ocean 123 B5
Mascarene Islands *island group* Indian Ocean 61 H4
Mascarene Plain *undersea feature* Indian Ocean 123 B5
Mascarene Plateau *undersea feature* Indian Ocean 123 B5
Maseru *capital of* Lesotho 60 D4
Mas-ha Bank 101 D6
Mashhad Iran *var.* Meshed 100 E3
Masindi Uganda 55 B6
Maşīrah, Jazīrat *Island* Oman 103 E6
Maşīrah, Khalīj *bay* Oman 103 E6
Mason City Iowa, USA 25 F3
Masqaţ *see* Muscat
Massachusetts *state* USA 23 G3
Massawa *see* Mits'iwa
Massif Central *upland* France 73 C5
Massoukou Gabon 59 B6
Masterton New Zealand 133 D5
Matadi Dem. Rep. Congo 59 B7
Matagalpa Nicaragua 34 D3
Matamoros Mexico 33 E2
Matanzas Cuba 36 B2
Matara Sri Lanka 115 E4
Mataram Indonesia 120 D5
Mataró Spain 75 G2
Mato Grosso *upland* Brazil 43 E3
Matosinhos Portugal 74 C2
Matsue Japan 113 B5
Matsuyama Japan 113 B5
Matterhorn *peak* Italy/ Switzerland 77 B7
Maturín Venezuela 41 E1
Maun Botswana 60 D3
Mauritania *country* W Africa 56
Mauritius *country* Indian Ocean 61 H4 123 B5
Mawlamyine Myanmar *prev.* Moulmein 118 B4
Mayaguana *island* Bahamas 36 D2
Mayfield New Zealand 133 C6
Mayotte *external territory* France, Indian Ocean 61 G2
Mayyit, Al Baḩr al *see* Dead Sea
Mazār-e Sharīf Afghanistan 104 D3
Mazatlán Mexico 32 C3
Mažeikiai Lithuania 88 B3
Mazury *region* Poland 80 D3
Mazyr Belarus *Rus.* Mozyr' 89 D7
Mbabane *capital of* Swaziland 61 E4
Mbaké Senegal 56 B3
Mbala Zambia 61 E1
Mbale Uganda 55 C6
Mbandaka Dem. Rep. Congo 59 C5
Mbeya Tanzania 55 B8
Mbuji-Mayi Dem. Rep. Congo 59 D7
McKinley, Mount *peak* Alaska, USA *var.* Denali 18 C3
Mead, Lake *lake* SW USA 28 A1
Mecca *see* Makkah
Mechelen Belgium 69 C5
Mecklenburger Bucht *bay* Germany 76 C2
Medan Indonesia 120 B3
Medellín Colombia 40 B2
Médenine Tunisia 53 F2
Medford Oregon, USA 26 A4
Medina *see* Al Madīnah
Mediterranean Sea Atlantic Ocean 84-85
Meekatharra Australia 129 B5
Meerut India 116 D3
Megísti *island* Greece 98 B4
Mek'elē Ethiopia 54 C4
Mekong *river* SE Asia 106 D3
Mekong, Mouths of the *wetlands* Vietnam 119 D6
Melanesia *region* Pacific Ocean 126 C3
Melanesian Basin *undersea feature* Pacific Ocean 134 C3
Melbourne Australia 131 C7
Melbourne Florida, USA 31 F4
Melekeok *capital of* Palau 126 A1
Melghir, Chott *Salt lake* Algeria 53 E2
Melilla *external territory* Spain, N Africa 52 C1
Melitopol' Ukraine 91 F4
Melo Uruguay 44 C4
Melville Island *island* Australia 128 E2
Melville Island *island* Canada 19 E2
Memel *see* Klaipėda
Memel *see* Neman
Memphis Tennessee, USA 30 C1
Mendaña Fracture Zone *tectonic feature* Pacific Ocean 135 G3
Mende France 73 C6
Mendeleyev Ridge *undersea feature* Arctic Ocean 137 G2
Mendocino Fracture Zone *tectonic feature* Pacific Ocean 134 D2
Mendoza Argentina 46 B4
Menengiyn Tal *plain* Mongolia 109 F2
Menongue Angola 60 C2

Mitrovicë Kosovo *prev.* Kosovska Mitrovica 83 D5
Mits'iwa Eritrea *var.* Massawa 54 C4
Mitumba, Monts *Mountain range* Dem. Rep. Congo 59 E7
Miyazaki Japan 113 B6
Mjøsa *lake* Norway 67 B5
Mljet *island* Croatia 83 C5
Mmabatho South Africa 60 D4
Mo Norway 66 C3
Mobile Alabama, USA 30 C3
Moçambique Mozambique 61 F2
Mocímboa da Praia Mozambique 61 F2
Mocoa Colombia 40 B4
Mocuba Mozambique 61 E3
Modena Italy 78 B3
Modesto California, USA 27 B6
Modohn *see* Madona
Modriča Bosnia & Herzegovina 82 C3
Mogadiscio *see* Mogadishu
Mogadishu *capital of* Somalia *Som.* Muqdisho, *It.* Mogadiscio 55 D6
Mogilëv *see* Mahilyow
Mo i Rana Norway 66 C3
Mojave California, USA 27 C7
Mojave Desert *desert* W USA 27 C7
Moldavia *see* Moldova
Molde Norway 67 A5
Moldova *country* E Europe *var.* Moldavia 90
Molodechno *see* Maladzyechna
Molodeczno *see* Maladzyechna
Molotov *see* Perm'
Moluccas *see* Maluku
Molucca Sea *see* Maluku, Laut
Mombasa Kenya 55 C7
Monaco *country* W Europe 73 E6
Monclova Mexico 33 E2
Moncton Canada 21 F4
Mongo Chad 58 C3
Mongolia *country* NE Asia 108-109
Monroe Louisiana, USA 30 B2
Monrovia *capital of* Liberia 56 C5
Mons Belgium 69 B6
Montague Seamount *undersea feature* Atlantic Ocean 45 H1
Montana *state* USA 24 C2
Montauban France 73 C6
Mont Blanc *peak* France/Italy 62 D4
Mont-de-Marsan France 72 B6
Monte Cristi Dominican Republic 37 E3
Montego Bay Jamaica 36 C3
Montenegro *Country* SE Europe 83 D5
Monterey California, USA 27 B6
Montería Colombia 40 B2
Montero Bolivia 42 D4
Monterrey Mexico 33 E2
Montes Claros Brazil 43 G4
Montevideo *capital of* Uruguay 44 C5
Montgomery Alabama, USA 30 D2
Monthey Switzerland 77 A7
Montpelier Vermont, USA 23 F2
Montpellier France 73 C6
Montréal Canada 21 E4
Montserrat *external territory* UK, West Indies 37
Monywa Myanmar 118 A3
Monza Italy 78 B2
Moora Australia 129 B6
Moore, Lake *lake* Australia 129 B6
Moorhead Minnesota, USA 25 E2
Moosonee Canada 20 C3
Mopti Mali 57 E3
Morava *river* C Europe 82 E4
Moravská Ostrava *see* Ostrava
Moray Firth *inlet* Scotland, UK 70 C3
Moree Australia 131 D5
Morelia Mexico 33 E4
Morena, Sierra *mountain range* Spain 74 D4
Morghāb *river* Afghanistan/ Turkmenistan 104 D4
Morioka Japan 112 D3
Mornington Abyssal Plain *undersea feature* Pacific Ocean 135 G5
Morocco *country* N Africa 52
Morogoro Tanzania 55 C7
Mörön Mongolia 108 D2
Morondava Madagascar 61 F3
Moroni *capital of* Comoros 61 F2
Morotai, Pulau *island* Indonesia 121 F3
Morova *river* Poland 80 C6
Morris Jesup, Kap *headland* Greenland 65 E1
Moscow *capital of* Russian Federation *Rus.* Moskva 92 B4 96 B2
Mosel *river* W Europe *Fr.* Moselle 77 A5
Moselle *river* W Europe *Ger.* Mosel 72 E4
Mosgiel New Zealand 133 B7
Moshi Tanzania 55 C7
Moskva *see* Moscow
Mosquito Coast *coastal region* Nicaragua 35 E3
Moss Norway 67 B6
Mossendjo Congo 59 B6
Mossoró Brazil 43 H2
Most Czech Republic *Ger.* Brüx 80 A4
Mostaganem Algeria 52 D1
Mostar Bosnia & Herz. 82 C4
Mosul *see* Al Mawşil
Motril Spain 75 E5
Motueka New Zealand 133 C5
Moulins France 72 C4
Moulmein *see* Mawlamyine
Moundou Chad 58 C4
Mount Gambier Australia 131 B7
Mount Isa Australia 130 B4
Mount Magnet Australia 129 B5
Mount Vernon Illinois, USA 22 B5
Mouscron Belgium 69 A6
Moyobamba Peru 42 B2

Moyu China 108 B2
Mozambique *country* SE Africa 61
Mozambique Channel *sea feature* Indian Ocean 61 F3
Mozyr' *see* Mazyr
Mpika Zambia 61 E2
Mtwara Tanzania 55 C8
Muang Không Laos 119 D5
Muang Xaignabouri *see* Xaignabouri
Mudanjiang China 110 E3
Mufulira Zambia 60 D2
Muğla Turkey 98 A4
Mulhouse France 72 E4
Mull *island* Scotland, UK 70 B3
Muller, Pegunungan *mountains* Indonesia 120 C3
Multān Pakistan 116 C2
Mumbai India *var.* Bombay 117 C5
München Germany *Eng.* Munich 77 C6
Muncie Indiana, USA 22 C4
Munich *see* München
Münster Germany 76 B4
Muqdisho *see* Mogadishu
Mur *river* C Europe 77 E7
Murchison River *river* Australia 129 B5
Murcia Spain 75 F4
Mures *river* Hungary/Romania 81 D7
Murfreesboro Tennessee, USA 30 D1
Murgab Tajikistan 105 F3
Murgap *river* Turkmenistan *var.* Murghab 104 C3
Murghab *see* Murgap
Müritz *lake* Germany 76 D3
Murmansk Russian Federation 92 C2 96 C1
Murray *river* Australia 131 B6
Murray Fracture Zone *tectonic feature* Pacific Ocean 135 E2
Murray Ridge *Undersea feature* Arabian Sea 122 B3
Murwillumbah Australia 131 E5
Murzuq Libya 53 F3
Muş Turkey 99 F3
Muscat *capital of* Oman *Ar.* Masqaţ 103 E5
Musgrave Ranges *mountain range* Australia 129 D5
Musters, Lago *lake* Argentina 46 C6
Mu Us Shadi *Desert* China 109 E3
Mvonioälv *river* Finland/ Sweden 66 D3
Mwali *island* Comoros 61 F2
Mwanza Tanzania 55 B6
Mwene-Ditu Dem. Rep. Congo 59 D7
Mweru, Lake *lake* Dem. Rep. Congo/Zambia 59 D7
Myanmar *country* SE Asia *var.* Myanmar 118-119
Myeik Myanmar *prev.* Mergui 119 B5
Mykolayiv Ukraine *Rus.* Nikolayev 91 E4
Mykonos *island* Greece 87 D5
Mysore India 114 D2
Mzuzu Malawi 61 E2

N

Naberezhnyye Chelny Russian Federation *prev.* Brezhnev 93 C5
Nablus West Bank *var.* Nābulus, *Heb.* Shekhem 101 D6
Nābulus *see* Nablus
Nacala Mozambique 61 F2
Naga Philippines 120 E2
Nagano Japan 112 C4
Nagasaki Japan 113 A6
Nāgercoil India 114 D3
Nagorno-Karabakh *region* Azerbaijan 99 G2
Nagoya Japan 113 C5
Nāgpur India 116 D4
Nagqu China 108 C5
Nagykanizsa Hungary *Ger.* Grosskanizsa 81 C7
Nagyszombat *see* Trnava
Naha Japan 113 A8
Nain Canada 21 F2
Nairobi *capital of* Kenya 55 C6
Najaf *see* An Najaf
Najrān Saudi Arabia 103 B6
Nakamura Japan 113 B6
Nakhichevan' *see* Naxçıvan
Nakhon Ratchasima Thailand 119 C5
Nakhon Sawan Thailand 119 C
Nakhon Si Thammarat Thailand 119 C6
Nakuru Kenya 55 C6
Nal'chik Russian Federation 96 A4
Namangan Uzbekistan 105 E2
Nam Co *lake* China 108 C4
Nam Đinh Vietnam 118 D3
Namib Desert *desert* Namibia 60 B3
Namibe Angola 60 B2
Namibia *country* southern Africa 60
Nampa Idaho, USA 26 C3
Namp'o North Korea 110 E4
Nampula Mozambique 61 F2
Namur Belgium 69 C6
Nanchang China 111 C5
Nancy France 72 D3
Nānded India 116 D5 114 D1
Nanjing China 111 D5
Nanning China 111 B6
Nanortalik Greenland 64 C5
Nansen Basin *undersea featur* Arctic Ocean 137 G4
Nantes France 72 B4
Napier New Zealand 132 E4
Naples *see* Napoli
Napo *river* Ecuador/Peru 42 B2
Napoli Italy *Eng.* Naples 79 D5
Narbonne France 73 C6
Nares Strait *sea feature* Canada/Greenland 64 C1
Narew *river* Poland 80 E3
Narmada *river* India 116 D4
Narva Estonia 88 E2
Narva *river* Estonia/Russian Federation 88 E2
Narva Bay *sea feature* Gulf of Finland *Est.* Narva Laht, *Rus.* Narvskiy Zaliv 88 E2

Narva Laht *see* Narva Bay
Narvik Norway 66 C3
Narvskiy Zaliv *see* Narva Bay
Naryn Kyrgyzstan 105 G2
Nāshik India 116 C5
Nashville Tennessee, USA 30 D1
Nâșir, Buḥeiret *see* Nasser, Lake
Nassau *capital of* Bahamas 36 C1
Nasser, Lake *reservoir* Egypt *var.* Nâșir, Buḥeiret 54 B2
Natal Brazil 43 H3
Natal Basin *Undersea feature* Indian Ocean 123 A5
Natitingou Benin 57 E4
Naturaliste Plateau *undersea feature* Indian Ocean 123 E6
Natzrat Israel *Eng.* Nazareth 101 A5
Nauru *country* Pacific Ocean 126 D3
Navapolatsk Belarus *Rus.* Novopolotsk 89 D5
Navassa Island *external territory* USA, West Indies 36 D3
Navoiy Uzbekistan *Uzb.* Nawoly 104 D2
Nawābshāh Pakistan 116 B3
Nawoly *see* Navoiy
Naxçıvan Azerbaijan *Rus.* Nakhichevan' 99 G3
Náxos *island* Greece 87 D6
Nay Pyi Taw *capital of* Myanmar 118 B3
Nazareth *see* Natzrat
Nazca Peru 42 B4
Nazrēt Ethiopia 55 C5
Nazwá Oman 103 E5
N'Dalatando Angola 60 B2
Ndélé Central African Republic 58 C4
N'Djamena *capital of* Chad 58 B3
Ndola Zambia 60 D2
Nebitdag *see* Balkanabat
Nebraska *state* USA 24-25 E3
Neches *river* S USA 29 H3
Neckar *river* Germany 77 B5
Necochea Argentina 47 D5
Neftezavodsk *see* Seýdi
Negēlē Ethiopia 55 C5
Negev *see* HaNegev
Negro, Río *river* Argentina 47 C5
Negro, Rio *river* Brazil/Uruguay 44 C4
Negro, Rio *river* N South America 40 C1
Neiva Colombia 40 B3
Nellore India 115 E2
Neman *river* NE Europe *Bel.* Nyoman, *Lith.* Nemunas, *Ger.* Memel, *Pol.* Niemen 88 B4
Nemunas *see* Neman
Nemuro Japan 112 E2
Nepal *country* S Asia 117
Neris *river* Belarus/Lithuania *Bel.* Viliya, *Pol.* Wilja 88 C4
Ness, Loch *lake* Scotland, UK 70 C3
Netherlands *country* W Europe *var.* Holland 68-69
Netherlands Antilles *external territory* Netherlands, West Indies *prev.* Dutch West Indies 37 E5
Netze *see* Noteć
Neubrandenburg Germany 76 D3
Neuchâtel, Lac de *lake* Switzerland 77 A7
Neumünster Germany 76 C2
Neuquén Argentina 47 C5
Neusiedler See *lake* Austria/ Hungary 77 E6
Neusohl *see* Banská Bystrica
Neutra *see* Nitra
Nevada *state* USA 26-27
Nevers France 72 C4
Nevşehir Turkey 98 C3
New Amsterdam Guyana 41 G2
Newark New Jersey, USA 23 F3
New Britain *island* Papua New Guinea 126 B3
New Brunswick *province* Canada 21 F4
New Caledonia *external territory* France, Pacific Ocean 126 C5
New Caledonia *island* Pacific Ocean 124 D3
New Caledonia Basin *undersea feature* Pacific Ocean 124 D4
Newcastle Australia 131 D6
Newcastle upon Tyne England, UK 70 D4
New Delhi *capital of* India 116 D3
Newfoundland & Labrador *province* Canada 21 F2
Newfoundland *island* Canada 21 G3
Newfoundland Basin *undersea feature* Atlantic Ocean 48 B3
New Georgia Islands *island group* Solomon Is 126 C3
New Guinea *island* Pacific Ocean 126 B3
New Hampshire *state* USA 23 G2
New Haven Connecticut, USA 23 G3
New Ireland *island* Papua New Guinea 126 C3
New Jersey *state* USA 23 F4
Newman Australia 128 B4
New Mexico *state* USA 28-29
New Orleans Louisiana, USA 30 C3
New Plymouth New Zealand 132 D3
Newport Oregon, USA 26 A3
Newport News Virginia, USA 23 F5
New Providence *island* Bahamas 36 C1
Newry Northern Ireland, UK 71 B5
New Siberian Islands *see* Novosibirskiye Ostrova
New South Wales *state* Australia 131 C6
New York *state* USA 23 F3
New York New York, USA 23 F3
New Zealand *country* Pacific Ocean 132-133
Neyshābūr Iran 102 D3
Ngaoundéré Cameroon 58 B4
N'Giva Angola 60 C3

N'Guigmi Niger 57 H3
Nha Trang Vietnam 119 E5
Niagara Falls *waterfall* Canada/ USA 23 E3
Niamey *capital of* Niger 57 F3
Niangay, Lac *lake* Mali 56 E3
Nias, Pulau *island* Indonesia 120 B3
Nicaragua *country* Central America 34-35
Nicaragua, Lago de *lake* Nicaragua 34 D3
Nice France 73 E6
Nicobar Islands *island group* India 115 H3
Nicosia *capital of* Cyprus *var.* Lefkosia, *Turk.* Lefkoşa 98 C5
Nicoya, Península de *peninsula* Costa Rica 34 D4
Niemen *see* Neman
Nieuw Amsterdam Suriname 41 H2
Niğde Turkey 98 D4
Niger *country* W Africa 57
Niger *river* W Africa 56-57 D3
Niger, Mouths of the *delta* Nigeria 57 F5
Nigeria *country* W Africa 57
Niigata Japan 112 C4
Nijmegen Netherlands 68 D4
Nikolayev *see* Mykolayiv
Nikopol' Ukraine 91 F3
Nile *river* N Africa 54 B3
Nile Delta *wetlands* Egypt 54 B1
Nîmes France 73 D6
Ninetyeast Ridge *undersea feature* Indian Ocean 123 C5
Ningbo China 111 D5
Ningxia *autonomous region* China 110-111 B4
Nioro Mali 56 D3
Nipigon, Lake *lake* Canada 20 B4
Niš Serbia 82 E4
Nitra Slovakia *Ger.* Neutra, *Hung.* Nyitra 81 C6
Nitra *river* Slovakia *Ger.* Neutra, *Hung.* Nyitra 81 C6
Niue *external territory* New Zealand, Pacific Ocean 127 F4
Nizāmābād India 114 D1
Nizhnevartovsk Russian Federation 96 D3
Nizhniy Novgorod Russian Federation *prev.* Gor'kiy 93 C5 96 B3
Nkongsamba Cameroon 58 B4
Norak Tajikistan 105 E3
Nord Greenland 65 E2
Nordaustlandet *island* Svalbard 65 G1
Norfolk Virginia, USA 23 F5
Norfolk Island *external territory* Australia, Pacific Ocean 124 D4
Noril'sk Russian Federation 96 D3
Norfolk Ridge *undersea feature* Pacific Ocean 124 D4
Norman Oklahoma, USA 28 F2
Normandie *region* France *Eng.* Normandy 72 B3
Normandy *see* Normandie
Normanton Australia 130 C3
Norrköping Sweden 67 C6
Norseman Australia 129 C6
North Albanian Alps *mountains* Albania/ Montenegro 83 D5
North America 16-17
North Andaman *island* India 115 G2
North Atlantic Ocean 64-65
North Australian Basin *undersea feature* Indian Ocean 124 A2 128 A2
North Bay Canada 20 D4
North Cape *coastal feature* New Zealand 132 C1
North Cape *coastal feature* Norway 66 D2
North Carolina *state* USA 31 F1
North Dakota *state* USA 24-25 D2
North Fiji Basin *undersea feature* Coral Sea 124 D3
Northern Cook Islands *islands* Cook Islands 127 G4
Northern Cyprus, Turkish Republic of *disputed region* Cyprus 98 C5
Northern Dvina *river* Russian Federation *see* Severnaya Dvina 63 G2
Northern Ireland *province* UK 70-71
Northern Mariana Islands *external territory* USA, Pacific Ocean 124 C1
Northern Sporades *see* Vóreies Sporádes
Northern Territory *territory* Australia 130 A3
North European Plain *region* N Europe 62 E3
North Frisian Islands *islands* Denmark/Germany 76 B2
North Island *island* New Zealand 132 G2
North Korea *country* E Asia 110
North Little Rock Arkansas, USA 30 B1
North Platte Nebraska, USA 25 E4
North Platte *river* C USA 24 D3
North Pole *ice feature* Arctic Ocean 137 G3
North Sea Atlantic Ocean 70 E2
North Siberian Lowland *lowlands* Russian Federation 94-95
North Taranaki Bight *gulf* New Zealand 132 D3
North Uist *island* Scotland, UK 70 B3
Northwest Territories *territory* Canada 19 E3
Norway *country* N Europe 66-67
Norwegian Sea Arctic Ocean 137 G5
Norwich England, UK 71 E6
Noteć *river* Poland *Ger.* Netze 80 C3
Nottingham England, UK 71 D6
Nottingham Island *island* Hudson Strait 20 D1
Nouâdhibou Mauritania 56 B2
Nouakchott *capital of* Mauritania 56 B2

Nouméa *capital of* New Caledonia 126 D5
Nova Gradiška Croatia 82 C3
Nova Iguaçu Brazil 43 F5 45 F2
Novara Italy 78 B2
Nova Scotia *province* Canada 21 F4
Novaya Zemlya *islands* Russian Federation 137 H4
Novaya Zemlya Trench *see* East Novaya Zemlya Trench
Novi Sad Serbia 82 D3
Novokuznetsk Russian Federation *prev.* Stalinsk 96 D4
Novopolotsk *see* Navapolatsk
Novosibirsk Russian Federation 96 D4
Novosibirskiye Ostrova *islands* Russian Federation *Eng.* New Siberian Islands 95 F1
Novo Urgench *see* Urgench
Novyy Margilan *see* Farg'ona
Nsanje Malawi 61 E3
Nsawam Ghana 57 E5
Nubian Desert *desert* Sudan 54 B3
Nu'eima West Bank 101 D7
Nuevo Laredo Mexico 33 E2
Nuku'alofa *capital of* Tonga 127 F5
Nukus Uzbekistan 104 C2
Nullarbor Plain *region* Australia 129 D6
Nunap Isua Island *coastal region* Greenland *var.* Uummannaruaq *Dan.* Kap Farvel 64 C5
Nunavut *Territory* Canada 19 F3
Nunivak Island *island* Alaska, USA 18 B2
Nuoro Italy 79 A5
Nuremberg *see* Nürnberg
Nürnberg Germany *Eng.* Nuremberg 77 C5
Nusa Tenggara *islands* East Timor / Indonesia 120 E5
Nuuk Greenland *var.* Godthåb 64 C4
Nyainqêntanglha Shan *mountain range* China 108 D5
Nyala Sudan 54 A4
Nyasa, Lake *lake* E Africa 51 D5
Nyeri Kenya 55 C6
Nyima China 108 C4
Nyíregyháza Hungary 81 E6
Nyitra *see* Nitra
Nykøbing Denmark 67 B8
Nyköping Sweden 67 C6
Nyngan Australia 131 D6
Nyoman *see* Neman

O

Oakland California, USA 27 B6
Oakley Kansas, USA 25 E4
Oamaru New Zealand 133 B7
Oaxaca Mexico 33 F5
Ob' *river* Russian Federation 96 D4
Oban Scotland, UK 70 C4
Obihiro Japan 112 D2
Obo Central African Republic 58 D4
Oceania 124-125
Ocean Island *see* Banaba
Oceanside California, USA 27 C8
Ochamchira *see* Och'amch'ire
Och'amch'ire Georgia *Rus.* Ochamchira 99 E1
Ödenburg *see* Sopron
Odense Denmark 67 B7
Oder *river* C Europe 80 C4
Odesa Ukraine *Rus.* Odessa 91 E4
Odessa see Odesa
Odessa Texas, USA 29 E3
Odienné Côte d'Ivoire 56 D4
Oesel *see* Saaremaa
Ofanto *river* Italy 79 D5
Offenbach Germany 77 B5
Ogaden *plateau* Ethiopia 55 D5
Ogallala Nebraska, USA 24 D4
Ogbomosho Nigeria 57 F4
Ogden Utah, USA 24 B3
Ogdensburg New York, USA 23 F2
Oger *see* Ogre
Ogre Latvia *Ger.* Oger 88 C3
Ogulin Croatia 82 B3
Ohio *state* USA 22 D4
Ohio *river* N USA 22 B5
Ohrid Macedonia 83 D6
Ohrid, Lake *lake* Albania/ Macedonia 83 D6
Ohře *river* Czech Republic/ Germany *Ger.* Eger 81 A5
Ōita Japan 113 B6
Okavango *river var.* Cubango southern Africa 60 C3
Okavango Delta *wetland* Botswana 60 C3
Okayama Japan 113 B5
Okazaki Japan 113 C5
Okeechobee, Lake *lake* Florida, USA 31 F4
Okhotsk Russian Federation 97 G3
Okhotsk, Sea of Pacific Ocean 134 C1
Okinawa *island* Japan 113 A8
Oki-shotō *island group* Japan 113 B5
Oklahoma *state* USA 29 F1
Oklahoma City Oklahoma, USA 29 F2
Okushiri-tō *island* Japan 112 C2
Okāra Pakistan 116 C2
Öland *island* Sweden 67 C7
Olavarría Argentina 46 D4
Olbia Italy 79 B5
Oldenburg Germany 76 B3
Oleksandriya Ukraine *Rus.* Aleksandriya 91 E3
Olenëk Russian Federation 97 E3
Ölgiy Mongolia 108 C2
Olhão Portugal 74 C4
Olita *see* Alytus
Olmaliq *see* Almalyk
Olmütz *see* Olomouc
Olomouc Czech Republic *Ger.* Olmütz 81 C5
Olsztyn Poland *Ger.* Allenstein 80 D2
Olt *river* Romania 90 B5
Olympia Washington, USA 26 B2

Omaha Nebraska, USA 25 F4
Oman *country* SW Asia 103 D6
Oman, Gulf of *sea feature* Indian Ocean 103 E5, 122 B3
Omdurman Sudan 54 B4
Omsk Russian Federation 96 C4
Onega *river* Russian Federation 92 C4
Onega, Lake *see* Onezhskoye Ozero
Onezhskoye Ozero *lake* Russian Federation *Eng.* Lake Onega 92 B3
Ongole India 115 E2
Onitsha Nigeria 57 F5
Onslow Australia 128 A4
Ontario *province* Canada 18 B3
Ontario, Lake *lake* Canada/USA 17 D5
Oostende Belgium *Eng.* Ostend 69 A5
Opole Poland *Ger.* Oppeln 80 C4
Oporto *see* Porto
Oppeln *see* Opole
Oradea Romania 90 B3
Oran Algeria 52 D1
Orange River *river* southern Africa 60 C4
Oranjestad Netherlands Antilles 37 E5
Orantes *River* Asia 100 B3
Ordu Turkey 98 D2
Ordzhonikidze *see* Vladikavkaz
Örebro Sweden 67 C6
Oregon *state* USA 26
Orël Russian Federation 83 A5
Orem Utah, USA 24 B4
Orenburg Russian Federation 93 C6 96 B4
Orense *see* Ourense
Orestiáda Greece 86 D3
Orinoco *river* Colombia/ Venezuela 41 E3
Oristano Italy 79 A5
Orkney *islands* Scotland, UK 70 C2
Orlando Florida, USA 31 E4
Orléans France 72 C4
Örnsköldsvik Sweden 67 C5
Orantes *river* SW Asia 100 B3
Orosirá Rodópis *see* Rhodope Mountains
Orsha Belarus 89 E5
Orsk Russian Federation 93 D6 96 B4
Oruro Bolivia 42 C4
Ōsaka Japan 113 C5
Osborn Plateau *undersea feature* Indian Ocean 123 C5
Ösel *see* Saaremaa
Osh Kyrgyzstan 105 F2
Oshawa Canada 20 D5
Oshkosh Wisconsin, USA 22 B2
Osijek Croatia 82 C3
Oslo *capital of* Norway 67 B6
Osmaniye Turkey 98 D4
Osnabrück Germany 76 B3
Osorno Chile 47 B5
Oss Netherlands 68 D4
Ossora Russian Federation 97 H2
Ostend *see* Oostende
Östersund Sweden 67 C5
Ostrava Czech Republic *Ger.* Mährisch-Ostrau, *prev.* Moravská Ostrava 81 C5
Ostrołęka Poland 80 D3
Ostrowiec Świętokrzyski Poland 80 D4
Ōsumi-shotō *island group* Japan 113 A7
Otago Peninsula *peninsula* New Zealand 133 B7
Otaru Japan 112 D2
Oti *river* Africa 57 E4
Otranto, Strait of *sea feature* Albania/Italy 79 E5
Ottawa *capital of* Canada 20 D4
Ottawa *river* Canada 20 D4
Ou *river* Laos 118 C3
Ouachita *river* SE USA 30 B2
Ouagadougou *capital of* Burkina 57 E3
Ouarâne *desert* Mauritania 56 D2
Ouargla Algeria 53 E2
Ouessant, Île d' *island* France 72 A3
Ouésso Congo 59 C5
Oujda Morocco 52 D2
Oulu Finland 66 D4
Oulu *river* Finland 66 D4
Oulujärvi *lake* Finland 66 E4
Ounasjoki *river* Finland 66 D3
Our *river* W Europe 69 E7
Ourense Spain *Cast.* Orense 74 C2
Ourinhos Brazil 44 D2
Ourthe *river* Belgium 69 D6
Outer Hebrides *island group* UK *var.* Western Isles 70 B3
Outer Islands *island group* Seychelles 61 H2
Ouyen Australia 131 C6
Oviedo Spain 74 D1
Owando Congo 59 C6
Owen Fracture Zone *tectonic feature* Arabian Sea 122 B3
Owensboro Kentucky, USA 22 B5
Oxford England, UK 71 D6
Oxnard California, USA 29 C7
Oyem Gabon 59 B5
Oyo Nigeria 57 F4
Ozark Plateau *plain* Arkansas/ Missouri, USA 25 G5
Ózd Hungary 81 D6

P

Paamiut Greenland 64 B4
Pachuca Mexico 33 E4
Pacific-Antarctic Ridge *undersea feature* Pacific Ocean 136 B5
Pacific Ocean 134-135
Padang Indonesia 120 B4
Paderborn Germany 76 B4
Padova Italy *Eng.* Padua 78 C2
Padre Island *island* Texas, USA 29 G5
Padua *see* Padova
Paducah Kentucky, USA 22 B5
Paeroa Waikato, New Zealand 132 D3

Pafos *see* Paphos
Pag *island* Croatia 82 A3
Pago Pago *capital of* American Samoa 127 F4
Paide Estonia *Ger.* Weissenstein 88 D2
Paihia New Zealand 132 D2
Painted Desert *desert* SW USA 28 C1
País Valenciano *cultural region* Spain 75 F3
Pakistan *country* S Asia 116
Pakokku Myanmar 118 A3
Palagruza *island* Croatia 83 B5
Palau *country* Pacific Ocean *var.* Belau 124 B2 126
Palawan *island* Philippines 121 E2
Palawan Passage *passage* Philippines 121 E2
Paldiski Estonia *prev.* Baltiski, *Eng.* Baltic Port, *Ger.* Baltischport 88 C2
Palembang Indonesia 120 C4
Palencia Spain 74 D2
Palermo Italy 79 C6
Palikir *capital of* Micronesia 126 C2
Palioúri, Akrotírio *coastal feature* Greece *var.* Akra Kanestron 86 C4
Palk Strait *sea feature* India/Sri Lanka 115 E3
Palliser, Cape *headland* New Zealand 133 D5
Palm Springs California, USA 27 D8
Palma Spain 75 G3
Palmer Land *physical region* Antarctica 136 A3
Palmerston North New Zealand 132 D4
Palmyra *see* Tudmur
Palmyra Atoll *external territory* USA, Pacific Ocean 125 F2
Palu Indonesia 121 E4
Pamir *river* Afghanistan/ Tajikistan 105 F3
Pamirs *mountains* Tajikistan 105 F3
Pampa Texas, USA 29 E2
Pampas *region* South America 46 C4
Pamplona Spain *var.* Iruña 75 F1
Pānāji India 114 C2
Panama *country* Central America 35
Panamá, Golfo de *sea feature* Panama 35 F5
Panama Canal *canal* Panama 35 F4
Panama City *capital of* Panama 35 F5
Panama City Florida, USA 30 D3
Panćevo Serbia 82 D3
Panevėžys Lithuania 88 C4
Pantanal *region* Brazil 38 C4
Pantelleria *island* Italy 79 B7
Papeete *capital of* French Polynesia 127 H4
Paphos Cyprus *var.* Pafos 98 C5
Papua *province* Indonesia *prev.* Irian Jaya 121 H4
Papua New Guinea *country* Pacific Ocean 126
Paracel Islands *disputed territory* Asia 120 D1
Paragua *river* Venezuela 41 E3
Paraguay *country* South America 44
Paraguay *river* C South America 38 C4 44 B2
Parakou Benin 57 F4
Paramaribo *capital of* Suriname 41 G2
Paraná Argentina 46 D4
Paraná *river* C South America 46 D3
Paranaíba Brazil 43 G2
Paraparaumu New Zealand 132 D4
Pardubice Czech Republic *Ger.* Pardubitz 81 B5
Pardubitz *see* Pardubice
Parepare Indonesia 121 E4
Paris *capital of* France 72 C3
Paris Texas, USA 29 G2
Parma Italy 78 B3
Pärnu Estonia *Rus.* Pyarnu, *prev.* Pernov, *Ger.* Pernau 88 C2
Páros *island* Greece 87 D6
Pasadena California, USA 27 C7
Pasadena Texas, USA 29 G4
Passo Fundo Brazil 44 D3
Pasto Colombia 40 B4
Patagonia *region* S South America 47 C6
Pathein Myanmar *prev.* Bassein 118 A4
Patna India 117 F3
Patos, Lagoa dos *lagoon* Brazil 44 D4
Pátra Greece 87 B5
Pattani Thailand 119 C7
Pattaya Thailand 119 C5
Patuca *river* Honduras 34 D2
Pau France 73 B6
Pavlodar Kazakhstan 96 C4
Pavlograd *see* **Pavlohrad**
Pavlohrad Ukraine *Rus.* Pavlograd 91 G3
Paysandú Uruguay 44 B4
Pazardzhik Bulgaria *prev.* Tatar Pazardzhik 86 C2
Pearl *river* SE USA 30 C3
Peawanuck Canada 20 C2
Peć *see* Pejë
Pechora *river* Russian Federation 92 D3
Pecos Texas, USA 29 E3
Pecos *river* SW USA 28 D2
Pécs Hungary *Ger.* Fünfkirchen 81 C7
Pegasus Bay *bay* New Zealand 133 C5
Pegu *see* Bago
Peipsi Järv *see* Peipus, Lake
Peipus, Lake *lake* Estonia/ Russian Federation *Est.* Peipsi Järv, *Rus.* Chudskoye Ozero 88 D2
Peiraías Greece *var.* Piraiévs, *Eng.* Piraeus 87 C5
Pejë Kosovo *prev.* Peć 83 D5
Pekalongan Jawa, Indonesia 120 C4
Pekanbaru Indonesia 120 B3
Peking *see* Beijing
Pelagie, Isola *island* Italy 79 B8
Peloponnese *see* Pelopónnisos

Pelopónnisos *peninsula* Greece *Eng.* Peloponnese 87 B5
Pelotas Brazil 44 C4
Pelotas *river* Brazil 44 C3
Pematangsiantar Indonesia 120 B3
Pemba *island* Tanzania 51 E5
Pendleton Oregon, USA 26 C2
Pennines *hills* England, UK 70 D4
Pennsylvania *state* USA 23 E3
Penong Australia 131 A6
Penonomé Panama 35 F5
Penrhyn *atoll* Cook Islands 125 F3
Penrhyn Basin *undersea feature* Pacific Ocean 135 E2
Pensacola Florida, USA 30 D3
Penza Russian Federation 93 B5
Penzance England, UK 71 C7
Peoria Illinois, USA 22 B4
Percival Lakes *lakes* Australia 128 C4
Pereira Colombia 40 B3
Périgueux France 73 B5
Perm' Russian Federation *prev.* Molotov 93 D5 96 B3
Pernau *see* Pärnu
Pernik Bulgaria *prev.* Dimitrovo 86 C2
Pernov *see* Pärnu
Perpignan France 73 C6
Persian Gulf *sea feature* Arabian Sea *var.* The Gulf 122 B2
Perth Australia 129 B6
Perth Scotland, UK 70 C3
Perth Basin *undersea feature* Indian Ocean 123 E6
Peru C South America 42
Peru-Chile Trench *undersea feature* Pacific Ocean 135 G3
Perugia Italy 78 C4
Pescara Italy 78 D4
Peshāwar Pakistan 116 C1
Petah Tikva Israel 101 A5
Peterborough England, UK 71 E6
Peterborough Canada 20 D5
Peter the First Island *island* Antarctica 136 A4
Petra see Wādī Mūsā
Petrich Bulgaria 86 C3
Petroaleksandrovsk *see* To'rtko'l
Petrograd *see* St Petersburg
Petropavlovsk Russian Federation 96 C4
Petropavlovsk-Kamchatskiy Russian Federation 97 H3
Petrozavodsk Russian Federation 92 B3
Pevek Russian Federation 97 G1
Pforzheim Germany 77 B6
Phangan, Ko *island* Thailand 119 C6
Philadelphia Pennsylvania, USA 23 F4
Philippine Basin *undersea feature* Pacific Ocean 124 B1
Philippine Trench *undersea feature* Philippine Sea 124 A2
Philippines *country* Asia 121
Philippine Sea Pacific Ocean 121 F1 124 A1
Philippopolis *see* Plovdiv
Phnom Penh *capital of* Cambodia 119 D6
Phoenix Arizona, USA 28 B2
Phoenix Islands *island group* Kiribati 127 F3
Phôngsali Laos 118 C3
Phuket Thailand 119 B7
Phuket, Ko *island* Thailand 119 B7
Phumĭ Sâmraông Cambodia 119 D5
Piacenza Italy 78 B2
Piatra-Neamţ Romania 90 C3
Piave *river* Italy 78 C2
Picton New Zealand 133 C5
Pielinen *lake* Finland 66 E4
Pierre South Dakota, USA 25 E3
Piešťany Slovakia *Ger.* Pistyan, *Hung.* Pöstyén 81 C6
Pietermaritzburg South Africa 60 D4
Pihkva Järv *see* Pskov, Lake
Piła Poland *Ger.* Schneidemühl 80 C3
Pilar Paraguay 44 B3
Pilchilemu Chile 46 B4
Pilcomayo *river* C South America 44 B2 46 D2
Pilsen *see* Plzeň
Pinar del Río Cuba 36 A2
Píndos *mountain range* Greece *Eng.* Pindus Mountains 86 A4
Pindus Mountains *see* Píndos
Pine Bluff Arkansas, USA 30 B2
Pine Creek Australia 128 E2
Pinega *river* Russian Federation 92 C3
Pineiós *river* Greece 86 B4
Pínes, Akrotírio *coastal feature* Greece 86 C4
Ping, Mae Nam *river* Thailand 118 C4
Pinsk Belarus *Pol.* Pińsk 89 B4
Piraeus *see* Peiraías
Piraiévs *see* Peiraías
Pisa Italy 78 B3
Pisco Peru 42 B4
Pishpek *see* Bishkek
Pistyan *see* Piešťany
Pitcairn Islands *external territory* UK, Pacific Ocean 125 G4
Piteå Sweden 66 D4
Piteşti Romania 90 C4
Pittsburgh Pennsylvania, USA 23 E4
Piura Peru 42 A2
Pivdennyy Bug *river* Ukraine 91 E3
Plasencia Spain 74 D3
Plata, Rio de la *river* Argentina/ Uruguay *var.* River Plate 44 B5 46 D4
Plate, River *see* **Plata, Rio de la**
Platte *river* C USA 25 E4
Plattensee *see* Balaton
Plenty, Bay of *bay* New Zealand 132 E3
Pleven Bulgaria 86 C1
Płock Poland 80 D3
Ploieşti Romania 90 C4

Plovdiv Bulgaria *Gk.* Philippopolis 86 C2
Plungė Lithuania 88 B4
Plymouth *capital of* Montserrat 37 G3
Plymouth England, UK 71 C7
Plzeň Czech Republic *Ger.* Pilsen 81 A5
Po *river* Italy 78 B2
Pocatello Idaho, USA 26 E4
Po Delta *wetland* Italy 78 C3
Podgorica *capital of* Montenegro 83 C5
Pohnpei Island *island* Micronesia 126 C2
Pointe-Noire Congo 59 B6
Poitiers France 72 B4
Poland *country* E Europe 80-81
Polatsk Belarus 89 D5
Pol-e Khomrī Afghanistan 105 E4
Poltava Ukraine 91 F2
Poltoratsk *see* Aşgabat
Polynesia *region* Pacific Ocean 127
Pomeranian Bay *bay* Germany/ Poland 80 B2
Pompano Beach Florida, USA 31 F5
Ponca City Oklahoma, USA 29 G1
Pondicherry India 115 E2
Ponta Grossa Brazil 44 D2
Pontevedra Spain 74 C1
Pontianak Indonesia 120 C4
Poona *see* Pune
Poopó, Lake *lake* Bolivia 42 C5
Popayán Colombia 40 B3
Poprad Slovakia *Ger.* Deutschendorf 81 D5
Porbandar India 116 B4
Pori Finland 67 D5
Porsgrunn Norway 67 B6
Portalegre Portugal 74 C3
Port Angeles Washington, USA 26 A1
Port Arthur Texas, USA 29 H4
Port Augusta Australia 131 B6
Port-au-Prince *capital of* Haiti 36 D3
Port Blair India 115 G2
Port Douglas Australia 130 D3
Port Elizabeth South Africa 60 D5
Port-Gentil Gabon 59 A6
Port Harcourt Nigeria 57 F5
Port Hardy Canada 18 D5
Port Harrison *see* Inukjuak
Port Hedland Australia 128 B4
Portland Australia 131 B7
Portland Maine, USA 23 G2
Portland Oregon, USA 26 B2
Port Lincoln Australia 131 A6
Port Louis *capital of* Mauritius 61 H4
Port Macquarie Australia 131 E6
Port Moresby *capital of* Papua New Guinea 126 B3
Porto Portugal *Eng.* Oporto 74 C2
Porto Alegre Sao Tome and Principe 44 D4
Port-of-Spain *capital of* Trinidad & Tobago 37 G5
Porto-Novo *capital of* Benin 57 F5
Porto Velho Brazil 42 C3
Portoviejo Ecuador 40 A4
Port Said *see* Būr Saʻīd
Portsmouth England, UK 71 D7
Port Sudan Sudan 54 C3
Portugal *country* SW Europe 74
Port-Vila *capital of* Vanuatu 126 D5
Porvenir Chile 47 B7
Posadas Argentina 46 E3
Posen *see* Poznań
Poste-de-la-Baleine *see* Kuujjuarapik
Pöstyén *see* Piešťany
Potenza S Italy 79 D5
P'ot'i Georgia 99 E2
Potosí Bolivia 42 C5
Potsdam Germany 76 D4
Póvoa de Varzim Portugal 74 C2
Powder *river* N USA 24 C2
Powell, Lake *lake* SW USA 24 B5
Poza Rica Mexico 33 F4
Poznań Poland *Ger.* Posen 80 C3
Pozo Colorado Paraguay 44 B2
Pozsony *see* Bratislava
Prag *see* Prague
Prague *capital of* Czech Republic *Cz.* Praha, *Ger.* Prag 81 B5
Praha *see* Prague
Praia *capital of* Cape Verde 56 A3
Prato Italy 78 B3
Pratt Kansas, USA 25 E5
Preschau *see* Prešov
Prescott Arizona, USA 28 B2
Presidente Prudente Brazil 44 D2
Prešov Slovakia *Ger.* Eperies, *var.* Preschau, *Hung.* Eperjes 81 D5
Prespa, Lake *lake* SE Europe 83 D6 86 A3
Presque Isle Maine, USA 23 G1
Pressburg *see* Bratislava
Preston England, UK 71 D5
Pretoria *capital of* South Africa *see* Tshwane 60 D4
Préveza Greece 86 A4
Prijedor Bosnia & Herzegovina 82 B3
Prilep Macedonia 83 E5
Prince Albert Canada 19 F5
Prince Edward Island *province* Canada 21 F4
Prince Edward Islands *island group* South Africa 123 A7
Prince George Canada 19 E5
Prince of Wales Island *island* Canada 19 F2
Prince Rupert Canada 18 D4
Princess Charlotte Bay *bay* Australia 130 C2
Princess Elizabeth Land *region* Antarctica 136 C3
Príncipe *island* Sao Tome & Principe 59 A5

Pripet *river* Belarus/Ukraine 90 C1
Pripet Marshes *wetlands* Belarus/Ukraine 90 C1
Priština *capital of* Kosovo 83 D5
Prizren Kosovo 83 D5
Prome *see* Pyay
Prossnitz *see* Prostějov
Prostějov Czech Republic *Ger.* Prossnitz 81 C5
Provence *region* France 73 D6
Providence Rhode Island, USA 23 G3
Providencia, Isla de *island* Colombia 35 E3
Provo Utah, USA 24 B4
Prudhoe Bay Alaska, USA 18 D2
Przheval'sk *see* Karakol
Pskov Russian Federation 92 A4
Pskov, Lake *lake* Estonia/ Russian Federation *Est.* Pihkva Järv, *Rus.* Pskovskoye Ozero 88 D3
Pskovskoye Ozero *see* Pskov, Lake
Ptich' *see* Ptsich
Ptsich *river* Belarus *Rus.* Ptich' 89 D6
Pucallpa Peru 42 B3
Puebla Mexico 33 F4
Pueblo Colorado, USA 22 D4
Puerto Aisén Chile 47 B6
Puerto Barrios Guatemala 34 C2
Puerto Carreño Colombia 40 D2
Puerto Cortés Honduras 34 C2
Puerto Deseado Argentina 47 C6
Puerto Maldonado Peru 42 C4
Puerto Montt Chile 47 B5
Puerto Natales Chile 47 B7
Puerto Plata Dominican Republic 37 E3
Puerto Princesa Philippines 120 E2
Puerto Rico *external territory* USA, West Indies 37 F3
Puerto San Julián Argentina 47 C7
Puerto Suárez Bolivia 42 D4
Puerto Vallarta Mexico 32 D4
Pula Croatia 82 A3
Pune India *prev.* Poona 114 C1
Puno Peru 42 C4
Punta Arenas Chile *prev.* Magallanes 47 B7
Puntarenas Costa Rica 34 D4
Purmerend Netherlands 68 C3
Purus *river* Brazil/Peru 42 C3
Pusan South Korea 110 E4
Putrajaya *capital of* Malaysia 120 B3
Putumayo *river* NW South America 38 B3
Pyapon Myanmar 118 B4
Pyarnu *see* Pärnu
Pyay Myanmar *prev.* Prome 118 A4
Pyongyang *capital of* North Korea 110 E4
Pyramid Lake *lake* Nevada, USA 27 C5
Pyrenees *mountain range* SW Europe 62 C4

Q

Qaanaaq Greenland *var.* Thule 64 D1
Qābatiya West Bank 101 D7
Qaidam Pendi *basin* China 108 D4
Qalqīlya West Bank 101 D7
Qamdo China 108 D5
Qandahār *see* Kandahār
Qaqortoq Greenland 64 C4
Qara Qum *see* Karakumy
Qarshi *see* Karshi
Qasigiannguit Greenland 64 C3
Qatar *country* SW Asia 103 D5
Qattara Depression *see* Qaţţārah, Munkhafaḑ al
Qaţţārah, Munkhafaḑ al *desert basin* Egypt *Eng.* Qattara Depression 54 A1
Qeqertarsuaq Greenland 64 B3
Qeqertarsuaq *island* Greenland 64 B3
Qian *see* Guizhou
Qilian Shan *mountain range* China 108 A4
Qimusseriarsuaq *bay* Greenland 64 C2
Qinā Egypt 54 B2
Qingdao China 110 D4
Qinghai *province* China *var.* Chinghai, Koko Nor, Qing, Tsinghai 108 D4
Qinghai Hu *lake* China *var.* Koko Nor 108 D4
Qingzang Gaoyuan *plateau* China *Eng.* Plateau of Tibet 110 A4
Qiong *see* Hainan
Qiqihar China 110 D3
Qira China 108 B4
Qitai China 108 C3
Qom Iran *var.* Kum 102 C3
Qondūz *river* Afghanistan 105 E4
Qondūz *see* Kondoz
Qo'qon Uzbekistan prev. Kokand, *var.* Khokand, 105 E2
Quba Azerbaijan *Rus.* Kuba 99 H2
Québec Canada 21 E4
Québec *province* Canada 20 D3
Queen Charlotte Islands *islands* Canada 18 D4
Queen Charlotte Sound *sea feature* Canada 18 D5
Queen Elizabeth Islands *islands* Canada 19 F1
Queensland *state* Australia 130 C4
Queenstown New Zealand 133 B6
Quelimane Mozambique 61 E3
Querétaro Mexico 33 E4
Quetta Pakistan 116 B2
Quezaltenango Guatemala 34 B2

Quibdó Colombia 40 B2
Quimper France 72 A3
Quy Nhơn Vietnam 119 E5
Qing *see* Qinghai
Quito *capital of* Ecuador 40 A4
Qŭrghonteppa Tajikistan *Rus.* Kurgan–Tynbe 105 E3
Qyteti Stalin *see* Kuçovë

R

Raab *see* Győr
Raab *see* Rába
Rába *river* Austria/Hungary *Ger.* Raab 81 C7
Rabat *capital of* Morocco 52 C2
Race, Cape *coastal feature* Canada 21 H4
Rach Gia Vietnam 119 D6
Radom Poland 80 D4
Radviliškis Lithuania 88 C4
Ragusa Italy 79 D7
Rahīmyār Khān Pakistan 116 C3
Raipur India 117 E5
Rājahmundry India 115 E1
Rājasthān *state* India 116 C3
Rājkot India 116 C4
Rājshāhi Bangladesh 117 G4
Rakaia *river* New Zealand 133 C6
Rakvere Estonia *Ger.* Wesenberg 88 D2
Raleigh North Carolina, USA 31 F1
Ralik Chain *islands* Marshall Islands 126 D1
Râmnicu Vâlcea Romania *prev.* Rîmnicu Vîlcea 90 B4
Ramallah West Bank 101 D7
Ramree Island *island* Myanmar 118 A3
Rancagua Chile 46 B4
Rānchi India 117 F4
Randers Denmark 67 A7
Rangiora New Zealand 133 C6
Rangitikei *river* New Zealand 132 D4
Rangoon *see* Yangon
Rankin Inlet Canada 19 G3
Rapid City South Dakota, USA 24 D3
Rarotonga *island* Cook Islands 127 G5
Rasht Iran 102 C3
Ratak Chain *islands* Marshall Islands 126 D1
Ratchaburi Thailand 119 C5
Rat Islands *island group* Alaska, USA 18 A2
Raukumara Range *mountain range* New Zealand 132 E3
Rauma Finland 67 D5
Ravenna Italy 78 C3
Rāwalpindi Pakistan 116 C1
Rawson Argentina 47 C6
Razgrad Bulgaria 86 D1
Reading England, UK 71 D6
Rebecca, Lake *lake* Australia 129 C6
Rebun-tō *island* Japan 112 D1
Rechytsa Belarus 89 D7
Recife Brazil 43 H3
Recklinghausen Germany 76 G4
Red Deer Canada 19 E5
Redding California, USA 27 B5
Red River *river* S USA 30 B3
Red River *river* China/ Vietnam 118
Red Sea Indian Ocean 122 A3
Reefton New Zealand 133 C5
Regensburg Germany 77 C5
Reggane Algeria 52 D3
Reggio di Calabria Italy 79 D6
Reggio nell' Emilia Italy 78 B3
Regina Canada 19 F5
Rehoboth Namibia 60 C4
Reichenberg *see* Liberec
Reid Australia 129 D6
Reims France *Eng.* Rheims 72 D3
Reindeer Lake *lake* Canada 17 C4
Reni Ukraine 90 D4
Rennes France 72 B3
Reno Nevada, USA 27 B5
Resistencia Argentina 46 D3
Reşiţa Romania 90 B4
Resolute Canada 19 F2
Réunion *external territory* France, Indian Ocean 123 B5
Reus Spain 75 G2
Reutlingen Germany 77 B6
Reval *see* Tallinn
Revel *see* Tallinn
Revillagigedo, Islas *island* Mexico 32 B4
Rey, Isla del *island* Panama 35 F5
Reykjavík *capital of* Iceland 65 E5
Reynosa Mexico 33 E2
Rēzekne Latvia *Ger.* Rositten, *Rus.* Rezhitsa 88 D4
Rezhitsa *see* Rēzekne
Rheims *see* Reims
Rhine *river* W Europe 62 D3
Rhode Island *state* USA 23 G3
Rhodes *see* Ródos
Rhodope Mountains *mountain range* Bulgaria/Greece *Gk.* Orosirá Rodópis, *Bul.* Despoto Planina 86 C3
Rhône *river* France/Switzerland 62 C4
Ribeirão Preto Brazil 45 E1
Riberalta Bolivia 42 C3
Rîbniţa Moldova 90 D3
Richfield Utah, USA 24 B4
Richland Washington, USA 24 C2
Richmond Kentucky, USA 22 C5
Richmond New Zealand 133 C5
Richmond Virginia, USA 23 E5
Richmond Range *mountain range* New Zealand 133 C5
Ricobayo, Embalse de *reservoir* Spain 74 D2
Riga *capital of* Latvia *Latv.* Rīga 88 C3
Riga, Gulf of *sea feature* Baltic Sea 88 C3
Riihimäki Finland 67 D5
Rijeka Croatia *It.* Fiume 82 A3
Rimah, Wādī ar *dry watercourse* Saudi Arabia 103 B5

Rimini Italy 78 C3
Rîmnicu Vîlcea *see* Râmnicu Vâlcea
Riobamba Ecuador 40 A4
Rio Branco Brazil 42 C3
Río Cuarto Argentina 46 C4
Rio de Janeiro Brazil 45 F2
Río Gallegos Argentina 47 C7
Rio Grande Brazil 44 D4
Rio Grande *river* N America 16 B6
Rio Grande Rise *undersea feature* Atlantic Ocean 49 C6
Río Verde Mexico 33 E3
Rishiri-tō *island* Japan 112 D1
Rivas Nicaragua 34 D3
Rivera Uruguay 44 C4
Riverside California, USA 27 C8
Riverton New Zealand 133 A7
Rivne Ukraine *Rus.* Rovno 90 C2
Riyadh *capital of* Saudi Arabia *Ar.* Ar Riyāḍ 103 C5
Rize Turkey 99 E2
Rkîz Mauritania 56 C3
Road Town *capital of* British Virgin Islands 37 F3
Roanne France 73 D5
Roanoke Virginia, USA 23 E5
Roanoke *river* SE USA 31 G1
Robinson Range *mountain range* Australia 129 B5
Rochester Minnesota, USA 25 F3
Rochester New York, USA 23 E3
Rockford Illinois, USA 22 B3
Rockhampton Australia 130 D4
Rock Island Illinois, USA 22 B3
Rock Springs Wyoming, USA 24 C3
Rockstone Guyana 41 G2
Rocky Mountains *mountain range* Canada/USA 18-19 D4
Rodez France 73 C6
Ródhos *see* Ródos
Ródos *island* Greece *var.* Ródhos, *Eng.* Rhodes 87 E6
Ródos Greece *Eng.* Rhodes 87 E6
Rodosto *see* Tekirdağ
Roeselare Belgium 69 A5
Roma Australia 131 D5
Roma *see* Rome
Romania *country* SE Europe 90
Rome *capital of* Italy *It.* Roma 78 C4
Rome Georgia, USA 30 D2
Rønne Denmark 67 B8
Ronne Ice Shelf *ice feature* Antarctica 136 B3
Roosendaal Netherlands 68 C4
Rosario Argentina 46 D4
Roseau *capital of* Dominica 37 G4
Rosenau *see* Rožňava
Rositten *see* Rēzekne
Ross Ice Shelf *ice feature* Antarctica 136 B4
Ross Sea Antarctica 136 B4
Rostak *see* Ar Rustāq
Rostock Germany 76 C2
Rostov-na-Donu Russian Federation 96 A3
Roswell New Mexico, USA 28 D2
Rotorua New Zealand 132 D3
Rotorua, Lake *lake* New Zealand 132 D3
Rotterdam Netherlands 68 C4
Rouen France 72 C3
Rovaniemi Finland 66 D3
Rovno *see* Rivne
Rovuma *river* Mozambique/ Tanzania 61 F2
Roxas City Philippines 121 E2
Rožňava Slovakia *Ger.* Rosenau, *Hung.* Rozsnyó 81 D6
Rozsnyó *see* Rožňava
Ruatoria New Zealand 132 E3
Ruawai New Zealand 132 D2
Rudnyy Kazakhstan 96 C4
Rudolf, Lake *see* Lake Turkana
Rügen *headland* Germany 76 D2
Rukwa, Lake *lake* Tanzania 55 B7
Rumbek Sudan 55 B5
Rundu Namibia 60 C3
Ruoqiang China 108 C3
Ruse Bulgaria 86 D1
Russian Federation *country* Europe/Asia 92-93 96-97
Rust'avi Georgia 99 F2
Rutland Vermont, USA 23 F2
Rutog China 108 B4
Rwanda *country* C Africa 55
Ryazan' Russian Federation 93 B5 96 B3
Rybinskoye Vodokhranilishche *Reservoir* Russian Federation *Eng.* Rybinsk Reservoir 92 B4
Rybnik Poland 81 C5
Ryūkyū-rettō *island group* Japan 113 A8
Ryukyu Trench *Undersea feature* East China Sea 134 B2
Rzeszów Poland 81 E5**Saale** *river* Germany 76 C4

S

Saarbrücken Germany 77 A5
Saare *see* Saaremaa
Saaremaa *island* Estonia *var.* Saare, Sarema, *Ger.* Ösel, *var.* Oesel 88 C2
Šabac Serbia 82 C3
Sabadell Spain 75 G2
Sabah *cultural region* Borneo 120 D3
Sab'atayn, Ramlat as *desert* Yemen 103 C7
Sabhā Libya 53 F3
Sabzevār Iran 102 D3
Sacramento California, USA 27 B6
Ṣa'dah Yemen 103 B6
Sado *island* Japan 112 C4
Safi Morocco 52 B2
Saginaw Michigan, USA 22 C3
Sahara *desert* N Africa 50 B3
Sahel *region* W Africa 50 B3
Saïda Lebanon *anc.* Sidon 100 B4
Saidpur Bangladesh 117 G3
Saigon *see* Hô Chi Minh
Saimaa *lake* Finland 67 E5
Saint-Brieuc France 72 A3

Saint Catherines Canada 20 D5
Saint-Chamond France 73 D5
St Christopher & Nevis *see* St Kitts & Nevis
St Cloud Minnesota, USA 25 F2
St-Denis *capital of* Réunion 61 H4
Saintes France 72 B5
Saint-Étienne France 73 D5
Saint George Australia 131 D5
St. George's *capital of* Grenada 37 G5
St Helena *external territory* UK, Atlantic Ocean 49 D5
St Helier *capital* Jersey 71 D8
Saint-Jean, Lake *lake* Canada 21 E4
Saint John Canada 21 F4
St John's *country capital* Antigua and Barbuda 37 G3
Saint John's Canada 21 H3
St Joseph Missouri, USA 25 F4
St Kitts & Nevis *country* West Indies *var.* St Christopher & Nevis 37
St.-Laurent-du-Maroni French Guiana 41 H2
Saint Lawrence *river* Canada 21 E4
Saint Lawrence, Gulf of *sea feature* Canada 21 F3
St. Lawrence Island *island* Alaska, USA 18 C2
Saint-Lô France 73 B3
Saint Louis Senegal 56 B3
St Louis Missouri, USA 25 G4
St Lucia *country* West Indies 37
Saint-Malo France 72 B3
Saint-Nazaire France 72 B4
Saint Paul Minnesota, USA 25 F2
St-Paul, Île *island* French Southern and Antarctic Territories 123 C6
St Peter Port *capital of* Guernsey 71 D8
St Petersburg Russian Federation *Rus.* Sankt-Peterburg, *prev.* Leningrad, Petrograd 92 B3 96 B2
St Petersburg Florida, USA 31 E4
Saint Pierre & Miquelon *external territory* France, Atlantic Ocean 21 G4
St Vincent, Cape *see* São Vicente, Cabo de
St Vincent & The Grenadines *country* West Indies 37
Saipan *island country capital* Northern Mariana Islands 124 B1
Sakākah Saudi Arabia 102 B4
Sakakawea, Lake *lake* North Dakota, USA 24 D2
Sakarya *see* Adapazarı
Sakhalin *island* Russian Federation 97 H4
Sal *island* Cape Verde 56 A2
Salado *river* Argentina 46 C3
Şalālah Oman 103 D6
Salamanca Spain 74 D2
Sala y Gómez *island* Chile, Pacific Ocean 135 F4
Saldus Latvia *Ger.* Frauenburg 88 B3
Salekhard Russian Federation 96 D3
Salem India 114 D2
Salem Oregon, USA 26 A3
Salerno Italy 79 D5
Salerno, Golfo di *sea feature* Italy 79 D5
Salihorsk Belarus *Rus.* Soligorsk 89 C6
Salima Malawi 61 E2
Salinas California, USA 27 B6
Salisbury England, UK 71 D7
Salisbury Island *island* Canada 20 D1
Salonica *see* Thessaloníki
Salso *river* Italy 79 C7
Salt *see* As Salţ
Salta Argentina 46 C2
Saltillo Mexico 33 E2
Salt Lake City Utah, USA 24 B4
Salto Uruguay 44 B4
Salton Sea *lake* California, USA 27 D8
Salvador Brazil 43 G4
Salween *river* SE Asia 111 A6
Salzburg Austria 77 D6
Salzgitter Germany 76 C4
Samara Russian Federation 93 C6 96 B3
Samarinda Indonesia 121 E4
Samarkand Uzbekistan 104 D2
Sambre *river* Belgium 69 B7
Samoa *country* Pacific Ocean 127 F4
Samobor Croatia 82 B3
Sámos *island* Greece 87 D5
Samothrace *see* Samothráki
Samothráki *island* Greece *Eng.* Samothrace 86 D3
Samsun Turkey 98 D2
Samui, Ko *island group* Thailand 119 C6
San *river* Poland 81 E5
Saña Peru 42 A3
Sana *capital of* Yemen *var.* Şan'ā' 103 B7
Sanandaj Sinneh. Iran 102 C3
San Andrés, Isla de *island* Colombia 35 E3
San Angelo Texas, USA 29 F3
San Antonio Chile 46 B4
San Antonio Texas, USA 29 F4
San Antonio *river* S USA 29 G4
San Antonio Oeste Argentina 47 C5
Sanāw Yemen 103 C6
San Bernardino California, USA 27 C7
San Carlos Uruguay 44 C5
San Carlos de Bariloche Argentina 47 B5
San Clemente Island *island* W USA 27 C8
San Cristóbal Venezuela 40 C2
San Diego California, USA 27 C8
Sandwich Island *see* Efate
San Fernando Trinidad & Tobago 37 G5
San Fernando Venezuela 40 D2
San Fernando de Noronha *island* Brazil 43 H2
San Francisco California, USA 27 B6
Sangir, Kepulauan *island group* Indonesia 121 F3

Shikoku Basin *undersea feature* Philippine Sea 134 B2
Shikotan *island* Japan/Russian Federation (disputed) 112 E2
Shikārpur Pakistan 116 B3
Shimonoseki Japan 113 A5
Shinano-gawa *river* Japan 112 C4
Shingū Japan 113 C5
Shinyanga Tanzania 55 B7
Shiquanhe *see* Gar
Shīrāz Iran 102 D4
Shkodër Albania 83 D5
Shostka Ukraine 91 E1
Shreveport Louisiana, USA 30 A2
Shrewsbury England, UK 71 D6
Shumen Bulgaria 86 D2
Shymkent Kazakhstan *prev.* Chimkent 96 B5
Šiauliai Lithuania *Ger.* Schaulen 88 B4
Šibenik Croatia 82 B4
Siberia *region* Russian Federation 97 E3
Siberut, Pulau *island* Indonesia 120 B4
Sibiu Romania 90 B4
Sibolga Indonesia 120 B3
Sibu Malaysia 120 C3
Sibut Central African Republic 58 C4
Sibuyan Sea *sea* Philippines 121 E2
Sichuan *province* China *var.* Chuan, Ssu-ch'uan, Szechwan 111 B5
Sichuan Pendi *depression* China 111 B5
Sicilia *island* Italy *Eng.* Sicily 79 C7
Sicily, Strait of *sea feature* Mediterranean Sea 79 B7
Sicily *see* Sicilia
Sidi Bel Abbès Algeria 52 D1
Sidon *see* Saïda
Siednesibirskoye Ploskogor'ye *plateau* Russian Federation *Eng.* Central Siberian Plateau 97 E3
Siegen Germany 76 B4
Siena Italy 78 B3
Sierra Leone *country* W Africa 56
Sierra Madre del Sur *mountain range* Mexico 33 E5
Sierra Madre Occidental *mountain range* Mexico *var.* Western Sierra Madre 17 B6
Sierra Madre Oriental *mountain range* Mexico *var.* Eastern Sierra Madre 32 D2
Sierra Nevada *mountain range* Spain 75 E4
Sierra Nevada *mountain range* W USA 27 B6
Sighişoara Romania 90 C4
Siglufjördhur Iceland 65 E4
Siguiri Guinea 56 D4
Siirt Turkey 99 F3
Siling Co *lake* China 108 C5
Silkeborg Denmark 67 A7
Sillein *see* Žilina
Šilutė Lithuania 88 B4
Simeulue, Pulau *island* Indonesia 120 A3
Simferopol' Ukraine 91 F5
Simpson Desert *desert* Australia 130 C4
Sinai *desert* Egypt 54 B1
Sincelejo Colombia 40 B1
Sines Portugal 74 B4
Singapore *country* SE Asia 120
Singapore *capital of* Singapore 120 C3
Sinkiang *see* Xinjiang Uygur Zizhiqu
Sinnamary French Guiana 41 H2
Sinop Turkey 98 D2
Sint-Niklaas Belgium 69 B5
Sintra Portugal 74 B3
Sion Switzerland 77 B7
Sioux City Iowa, USA 25 F3
Sioux Falls South Dakota, USA 25 E3
Siracusa Italy *Eng.* Syracuse 79 D7
Siret *river* Romania/Ukraine 90 C4
Sirikit Reservoir *Reservoir* Thailand 118 C4
Sirte, Gulf of *see* Surt, Khalīj
Sisak Croatia 82 B3
Sisimiut Greenland 64 C3
Sittoung *river* Myanmar 118 B4
Sittwe Myanmar *prev.* Akyab 118 A3
Sivas Turkey 98 D3
Sjælland *island* Denmark 67 B7
Skagerrak *sea feature* Denmark/Norway 67 A6
Skellefteå Sweden 66 D4
Skopje *capital of* Macedonia 83 E5
Skövde Sweden 67 B6
Skovorodino Russian Federation 97 F4
Skye *island* Scotland, UK 70 B3
Slavonski Brod Croatia 82 C3
Sligo Ireland 71 B5
Sliven Bulgaria 86 D2
Slonim Belarus 89 C6
Slovakia *country* C Europe 81
Slovenia *country* SE Europe 77
Slov'yans'k Ukraine 91 G3
Słupsk Poland *Ger.* Stolp 78 C2
Slutsk Belarus 89 C6
Smallwood Reservoir *reservoir* Canada 21 E3
Smara Western Sahara *var.* Semara 52 B3
Smederevo Serbia 82 D3
Smolensk Russian Federation 92 A4
Smyrna *see* İzmir
Snake *river* NW USA 26 D4
Snowdonia *mountains* Wales, UK 71 C5
Sobradinho, Represa de *Reservoir* Brazil 43 G3
Sochi Russian Federation 93 A7 96 A3
Société, Îles de la *islands* French Polynesia *Eng.* Society Islands 127 H4
Society Islands *see* Société, Îles de la
Socotra *see* Suquţrá
Sodankylä Finland 66 D3

Sweden *country* N Europe 66-67
Sweetwater Texas, USA 29 F3
Swindon England, UK 71 D6
Switzerland *country* C Europe 77
Sydney Australia 131 D6
Sydney Canada 21 G4
Syeverodonets'k Ukraine 91 G1
Syktyvkar Russian Federation 92 D4 96 C3
Sylhet Bangladesh 117 G4
Syracuse *see* Siracusa
Syracuse New York, USA 23 E3
Syr Darya *river* C Asia 104 D1
Syria *country* SW Asia 100-101
Syrian Desert *desert* SW Asia *Ar.* Bādiyat ash Shām 101 C5
Szczecin Poland *Ger.* Stettin 80 B3
Szczeciński, Zalew *bay* Germany/Poland 80 A2
Szechwan *see* Sichuan
Szeged Hungary *Ger.* Szegedin 81 D7
Szegedin *see* Szeged
Székesfehérvár Hungary *Ger.* Stuhlweissenburg 81 C6
Szekszárd Hungary 81 C7
Szolnok Hungary 81 D6
Szombathely Hungary *Ger.* Steinamanger 81 B6

T

Tabariya, Bahrat *see* Tiberius, Lake
Tábor Czech Republic 81 B5
Tabora Tanzania 55 B7
Tabrīz Iran 102 C2
Tabuaeran *island* Kiribati 127 G2
Tabūk Saudi Arabia 102 A4
Tacloban Philippines 120 F2
Tacna Peru 42 C4
Tacoma Washington, USA 26 B2
Tacuarembó Uruguay 44 C4
Tadmur *see* Tudmur
Taegu South Korea 110 E4
Taejŏn South Korea 110 E4
Tafassâsset, Ténéré du *desert* Niger 57 G2
Taguatinga Brazil 43 F3
Tagus *river* Portugal/Spain *Port.* Tejo, *Sp.* Tajo 74 C3
Tahiti *island* French Polynesia 127 H5
Tahoe, Lake *lake* W USA 27 B5
Tahoua Niger 57 F3
T'aichung Taiwan 111D6
Taieri *129* New Zealand 133 B7
Taihape New Zealand 132 D4
T'ainan Taiwan 111 D6
Taipei *capital of* Taiwan 111 D6
Taiping Malaysia 120 B3
Taiwan *country* E Asia *prev.* Formosa 111
Taiwan Strait *sea feature* East China Sea/South China Sea *var.* Formosa Strait 111 D7
Taiyuan China 110 C4
Ta'izz Yemen 103 B7
Tajikistan *country* C Asia 105
Tajo *see* Tagus
Takapuna New Zealand 132 D2
Takla Makan *see* Taklimakan Shamo
Taklimakan Shamo *desert region* China *var.* Takla Makan 108 B3
Talamanca, Cordillera de *mountains* Costa Rica 35 E4
Talas Kyrgyzstan 105 F2
Talaud, Kepulauan *island group* Indonesia 121 F3
Talca Chile 46 B4
Talcahuano Chile 46 B4
Taldykoigan Kazakhstan 96 C5
Tallahassee Florida, USA 30 D3
Tallinn *capital of* Estonia *prev.* Revel, *Ger.* Reval, *Rus.* Tallin 88 D2
Talsen *see* Talsi
Talsi Latvia *Ger.* Talsen 88 B3
Tamale Ghana 57 E4
Tamanrasset Algeria 53 E4
Tambo Australia 130 C4
Tambov Russian Federation 93 B5
Tamil Nādu *state* India 114 D2
Tampa Florida, USA 31 E4
Tampere Finland 67 D5
Tampico Mexico 33 F3
Tamworth Australia 131 D6
Tanami Desert *desert* Australia 128 E3
Tananarive *see* Antananarivo
Tanega-shima *island* Japan 113 B7
Tanga Tanzania 55 C7
Tanganyika, Lake *lake* E Africa 51 D5
Tanger Morocco *var.* Tangiers 52 C1
Tanggula Shan *mountain range* China 108 C4
Tangiers *see* Tanger
Tangra Yumco *lake* China 108 B5
Tangshan China 110 D4
Tanimbar Islands *see* Tanimbar, Kepulauan
Tanimbar, Kepulauan *island group* Indonesia *Eng.* Tanimbar Islands 121 F5
Tanjungkarang *see* Bandar Lampung
Tan-Tan Morocco 52 B3
Tanzania *country* E Africa 55
Taoudenni Mali 57 E2
Tapa Estonia *Ger.* Taps 88 D2
Tapachula Mexico 33 G5
Tapajós *river* Brazil 43 E2
Taps *see* Tapa
Ţarābulus *see* Tripoli, Lebanon
Ţarābulus al-Gharb *see* Tripoli, Libya
Taranto Italy 79 E5
Taranto, Golfo di *sea feature* Mediterranean Sea 79 E5
Tarapoto Peru 42 B2
Tarawa *island* Kiribati 127 E2
Taraz Kazakhstan *prev.* Dzhambul, Zhambyl 96 C5
Tarbes France 73 B6

Tarcoola Australia 131 A5
Târgovişte Romania *prev.* Tîrgovişte 90 C4
Târgu Mureş Romania *prev.* Tîrgu Mureş 90 C4
Tarija Bolivia 42 C5
Tarim Basin *basin* China 108 B3
Tarim He *river* China 108 B3
Tarn *river* France 73 C6
Tarnów Poland 81 D5
Tarragona Spain 75 G2
Tarsus Turkey 98 D4
Tartu Estonia *prev.* Yur'yev, *var.* Yurev, *Ger.* Dorpat 88 D3
Ţarţus Syria 100 B3
Tashauz *see* Daşoguz
Tashkent *capital of* Uzbekistan *var.* Taškent, *Uzb.* Toshkent 105 E2
Taškent *see* Tashkent
Tasman Bay *inlet* New Zealand 132 C4
Tasmania *state* Australia 131 C8
Tasman Basin *undersea feature* Tasman Sea 124 D5
Tasman Plateau *undersea feature* Pacific Ocean 124 C5
Tasman Sea Pacific Ocean 134 C4
Tassili-n-Ajjer *desert plateau* Algeria 53 E4
Tatabánya Hungary 81 C6
Tatar Pazardzhik *see* Pazardzhik
Taubaté Brazil 43 F5 45 E2
Taumarunui New Zealand 132 D3
Taunggyi Myanmar 118 B3
Taunton England, UK 71 D7
Taupo New Zealand 132 D3
Taupo, Lake *lake* New Zealand 132 D3
Tauragė Lithuania 88 B4
Tauranga New Zealand 132 D3
Taurus Mountains *mountain range* Turkey *see* Toros Dağları 94 D4
Tavoy *see* Dawei
Tawau Malaysia 120 D3
Taymyr, Ozero *lake* Russian Federation 97 E2
Taymyr, Poluostrov *peninsula* Russian Federation *Eng.* Taymyr Peninsula 97 E2
Taymyr Peninsula *see* Taymyr, Poluostrov
Tbilisi *capital of* Georgia *Geor.* T'bilisi, *prev.* Tiflis 99 F2
Te Anau New Zealand 133 A7
Te Anau, Lake *lake* New Zealand 133 A7
Tedzhen *see* Tejen
Tegal Indonesia 120 C5
Tegucigalpa *capital of* Honduras 34 C2
Teheran *see* Tehrān
Tehrān *capital of* Iran *prev.* Teheran 102 C3
Tehuacán Mexico 33 F4
Tehuantepec, Golfo de *sea feature* Mexico 33 G5
Tejen Turkmenistan *prev.* Tedzhen 104 C3
Tejo *see* Tagus
Te Kao New Zealand131 C1
Tekirdağ Turkey *It.* Rodosto 98 A2
Te Kuiti Waikato, New Zealand 132 D3
Tel Aviv-Yafo Israel 101 A5
Teles Pires *river* Brazil 43 E3
Tell Atlas *plateau* Africa 84 C3
Telschen *see* Telšiai
Telšiai Lithuania *Ger.* Telschen 88 B4
Temuco Chile 47 B5
Ténéré *physical region* Niger 57 G2
Tenerife *island* Spain 52 A3
Tennant Creek Australia 130 A3
Tennessee *state* USA 30 D1
Tennessee *river* SE USA 31 C1
Tepelenë Albania 83 D6
Tepic Mexico 32 D4
Teplice Czech Republic *Ger.* Teplitz, *prev.* Teplice-Šanov, *Ger.* Teplitz-Schönau 80 A4
Teplice-Šanov *see* Teplice
Teplitz *see* Teplice
Teplitz-Schönau *see* Teplice
Teraina *island* Kiribati 127 G2
Teresina Brazil 43 G2
Termez Uzbekistan 105 E3
Terneuzen Netherlands 69 B5
Terni Italy 78 C4
Ternopil' Ukraine *Rus.* Ternopol' 90 C2
Ternopol' *see* Ternopil'
Terrassa Spain 75 G2
Terre Haute Indiana, USA 22 B4
Terres Australes et Antarctiques Françaises *see* French Southern and Antarctic Territories
Terschelling *island* Netherlands 68 C1
Teruel Spain 75 F3
Teseney Eritrea 54 C4
Tessalit Mali 57 E2
Tete Mozambique 61 E3
Tétouan Morocco 52 C1
Tetovo Macedonia 83 D5
Tetschen *see* Děčín
Tevere *river* Italy 78 C4
Texas *state* USA 28-29 F3
Texarkana Arkansas, USA 30 A2
Texas City Texas, USA 29 G4
Texel *island* Netherlands 68 C2
Thailand *country* SE Asia 118-119
Thailand, Gulf of *sea feature* South China Sea 119 C6
Thames *river* England, UK 71 D6
Thar Desert *desert* India/ Pakistan 116 C3
Tharthār, Buḩayrat ath *lake* Iraq 102 B3
Thásos *island* Greece 86 C3
Thaton Myanmar 118 B4
Theiss *see* Tisza
Thermaic Gulf *see* Thermaïkós Kólpos
Thermaïkós Kólpos *sea feature* Greece *Eng.* Thermaic Gulf 86 B4
Thessaloníki Greece *var.* Salonica 86 B3
The Valley *dependent territory capital* Anguilla 37 G5

V

W

Z